FRANK NORRIS

FRANK NORRIS A Life

Joseph R. McElrath Jr.

Jesse S. Crisler

University of Illinois Press

Urbana and Chicago

Frontispiece photo of Frank Norris courtesy of Joseph R. McElrath Jr.

Library of Congress Cataloging-in-Publication Data
McElrath, Joseph R.
Frank Norris : a life / Joseph R. McElrath, Jr.,
Jesse S. Crisler.
p. cm.
Includes bibliographical references and index.
ISBN-13: 978-0-252-03016-1 (cloth : alk. paper)
ISBN-10: 0-252-03016-8 (cloth : alk. paper)
1. Norris, Frank, 1870–1902.
2. Novelists, American—19th century—Biography.
I. Crisler, Jesse S. II. Title.
PS2473.M339   2005
813'.4—dc22   2005007105

To
Anthony Bliss,
Curator of Rare Books and Manuscripts,
the Bancroft Library

Contents

Illustrations

Preface

When Frank Norris (1870–1902) appeared on the literary scene in the late 1890s, he created a sensation. Some critics enthused over his vibrant style, imaginative verve, and piquant sense of humor. But other reactions were heated, recalling the hostile receptions given impressionist painters in the 1870s, realistic novelists such as William Dean Howells in the 1880s, and—more recently—authors of "dirty books" such as Henry Miller and J. D. Salinger. The "ultra-realism" of Norris's 1900 novel *A Man's Woman* offended squeamish book reviewers because of its graphic descriptions of keen physical suffering, a surgical procedure, two descents into mental illness, and—for good measure—the braining of a horse. Even the avant-garde Jack London, then just beginning to earn a name for himself, bridled before Norris's realistic technique in *The Octopus* (1901). But it was the novel published in early 1899, *McTeague,* that most outraged latter-day Victorians, earned Norris the sobriquet of "The American Zola," and secured for him his present place in American literary history.

Although influenced by writers such as Robert Louis Stevenson and Rudyard Kipling, Norris had chosen in his mid-twenties to follow in the footsteps of Emile Zola, the French "father" of a self-consciously post-Darwinian school of writing known as naturalism. The guiding principle of literary naturalism through the 1880s and into the 1890s was a radical fidelity to nature and thus the truthful depiction of the whole of the human condition in light of the most recent scientific findings and hypotheses. These included not only physical science but the budding fields of psychology and social science. Rejecting all metaphysical or supernatural explanations of natural phenomena—including those regarding human experience—Zola crafted prose fictions to illustrate the modern fruits of inductive reasoning. While not wholly denying free will, he attempted credible demonstrations of how human beings, viewed as phenomena, are largely governed like other creatures by "conditions." The environments in which his characters come to maturity, and which continue to influence them, mightily determine the nature of their personalities and behavior. Complementing such environmental determinisms are those of heredity, which account for certain fixed, rather than acquired, traits of individuals and their predispositions to particular forms of behavior as they react to ever-changing conditions. And, as in Darwin's account of natural selection, unforeseeable "chance" events take their toll in Zola's works as new developments suddenly benefit characters who readily adapt to them or render unfit those who previously fared well in a "survival-of-the-fittest" natural order.

Zola did not erase the line between humanity and the lower life forms from which it had evolved. But, as Norris also did in an aptly entitled manuscript that was published posthumously in 1914, *Vandover and the Brute,* Zola frankly pictured the ways in which *La Bête Humaine* (the title of one of his novels) is, indeed, "the human animal" or a "brute" not so far removed from its antecedents as we might prefer to imagine. *McTeague,* brought to press fifteen years earlier, hazarded an "animalistic" subject matter that Norris's more restrained American contemporaries treated much less explicitly. Hamlin Garland, Stephen Crane, Kate Chopin, and James Lane Allen ran risks when referring to human sexuality before an 1890s readership not used to open acknowledgments of this link between the beasts of the field and their own species. Norris, however, opted to address directly and at some length the sexual arousal of his hero: "The male virile desire in him tardily awakened, aroused itself, strong and brutal"; "The fury in him was as the fury of a young bull in the heat of high summer." Norris even attends to his heroine who, when McTeague first embraces her, "[gives] up in an instant." What "leap[s] to life in her" is "something that had hitherto lain dormant, something strong and overpowering . . . that shouted and clamored for recognition."

Sexuality was not the only instinct-driven or genetically programmed response to environmental stimuli that Norris repeatedly treated in this and six other novels, as well as in short stories and essays. His canon is replete with observations of the ways in which humans, like other mammals, are at least as much controlled by external and internal determinants as they are in control of the courses of their lives—the ratio varying according to the types of individuals he represents. In this respect, Norris was, like Zola, rejecting the simplistic notion advanced by idealists of previous generations, most memorably in America by Ralph Waldo Emerson through the 1840s, that we are the master of our own fate and able at every moment to shape the course of our lives by freely making rational choices.

Norris did feature characters who gain—or regain—control of their lives and thus experience positive outcomes. The last novel he completed, *The Pit*, ends on a relatively happy note, as the two principal characters finally prove adaptable to things as they are. It seems at the novel's conclusion that they will likely flourish in the future. But the course of this couple's past experiences, recorded in previous chapters, prompts one to wonder how they will fare over the long term, as new circumstances arise and possibly trigger ingrained predispositions to self-destructive behavior that could undermine their resolve to amend their ways. And the continuing relevance of the Norris canon, formed as American literature and culture in general made its transition from a Victorian to a modernist sensibility, depends largely upon such recognitions of the complexity of the human condition in an unpredictable natural order.

As if to illustrate the seeming cunning with which conditions in the present transmute over time in unexpected ways, Norris's generation viewed his 1903 best-seller *The Pit* as his masterpiece and claim to fame. The next generation, however, turned to *The Octopus*, his most commercially successful novel through 1902 and the one that by the 1960s was receiving attention as an American classic. Then, in the 1970s, came *McTeague*'s turn for magnum-opus status, despite the fact that it sold less well during Norris's lifetime than his now least-admired novel, *A Man's Woman*, and Norris's own opinion that *The Octopus* was a better work of art.

Norris died at the age of thirty-two, just as he was achieving international celebrity. This loss to American letters brought forward a plethora of eulogies at the same time that reviews of *The Pit* cascaded into periodicals. Never before was Norris's life and career so prominent a subject in the press, nor has it been since. His short but colorful life invited the production of a biography that was sure to have popular appeal, and Norris's widow informed his first biographer that two prominent cultural-history writers, Thomas Beer and Van Wyck Brooks, told her of their intentions to take up the project. But it was not until three decades after Norris's death that Franklin's Walker's Ph.D. dissertation, shorn of its documentation, was published by the mass-market firm of Doubleday as *Frank Norris: A Biography*. Even more striking is the fact that, since 1932, Walker's relatively brief and decidedly breezy book has remained the only one of its kind—until now.

Since 1971, when we began collaborating as graduate students at the University of South Carolina on a variety of books and articles concerning Norris, numerous scholars have declared their intent to write a new biography, each followed first by silence and then by withdrawal from the project because of the dearth of new biographical evidence within reach. Walker, in the early 1930s, could call upon Norris's relatives, friends, and professional associates for their recollections. Such sources have, of course, been unavailable for decades. All that remains is the relatively small body of interviews, notes, and correspondence that Walker deposited at the Bancroft Library of the University of California at Berkeley. These documents—fully exploited in the present volume—could not in themselves provide the wherewithal for a biography that would take the reader well beyond what Walker had already provided. The Frank Norris Collection of manuscripts, notes, clippings, and memorabilia later assembled by James D. Hart at the Bancroft complemented what was in the Franklin Dickerson Walker Collection. Even so, the critical mass requisite for the construction of a full-scale history of Norris's life was still lacking.

To create a new biography we had to go beyond these collections after taking our cues for research from the suggestive comments of Norris's contemporaries and the implications of data encountered in his surviving papers. Necessary as well was the recovery of the published testimonies of those who knew him. So too was the gathering of the facts concerning the various contexts in which Norris passed his life (familial, social, geographical, academic, and professional), from which we might infer the kinds and qualities of his experiences. This mandated travel to and research in England, France, and Italy. In the United States, we had to consult information sources in Boston, New York, the District of Columbia, Key West, St. Louis, Chicago, San Francisco, San Diego, Sacramento, and many less familiar cities and towns in between. The cues in the collections at the Bancroft also prompted protracted searches for pertinent information in the many turn-of-the-century periodicals that were not available in microform when Walker spent the two years of research that went into his book. In short, on our own and with the much-appreciated assistance of many generous colleagues, it has taken over three decades for us to accumulate, analyze, and correlate sufficient data to warrant the writing of this volume, which not only corrects erroneous claims made by Walker and the contemporaries of Norris with whom he conferred; more than four times the length of Walker's book, ours provides a fuller and more detailed account of Norris's personal life and professional career, often treating matters never addressed in *Frank Norris: A Biography*.

Walker began his book by sounding these keynotes: Norris was a boy who had barely become a man at the time of his death; and it was his "boyish" qualities that account for the greatness of his achievement as a writer. There followed the story of a world-class artist whose displays of "boyishness" Walker rather condescendingly describes in such a way as to suggest a personality characterized by arrested development and protracted immaturity. We begin differently, with a chapter providing an overview of Norris's writings, thought, and turn-of-the-century cultural situation. True, he could and did write in a lighthearted manner as a droll *littérateur,* recalling Bret Harte, Anthony Hope, Oscar Wilde, and even W. S. Gilbert. While his eclectic canon finds him in an antic mood on many occasions, he more often appears as the fin-de-siècle sophisticate than the juvenile prankster. When this post-Victorian author and thinker waxed serious—sometimes as ponderously as the more earnest Victorians did when plumbing Truth and distinguishing Right from Wrong—he was far from callow. Norris's was a quest for something better in life than was had by his bourgeois father, flighty mother, and less-than-serious contemporaries in the arts whom he satirized in his novels and short stories and denounced in his nonfiction writings.

There was nothing boyish about his determination to succeed as an author, his resilience in the face of numerous professional setbacks, and his dedication to the humanistic task of shedding new light on what it means to be *la bête humaine.* On the personal level, as will be seen in contemporaneous testimonies to a life well lived, his was a different but equally important accomplishment. Kind, considerate, loyal to his friends, and devoid of the egotism that some may associate with the personalities of artistes, Norris appears to have modeled human nature at its best. One never knows for certain, of course. All that is possible in any reconstruction of what was is an interpretation of the evidence that is before one. Should we err in our impression, revisionists will at least, we hope, take comfort in the fact that the empirical foundation for the study of Norris's life and works is now much broader and deeper than it has been heretofore.

Acknowledgments

We are indebted to the following scholars who assisted us at many stages of our research and writing: the late James D. Hart, who assembled the Frank Norris Collection at the Bancroft Library; Anthony Bliss of the Bancroft Library, to whom this volume is dedicated and from whom, since the 1980s, we have received unequaled assistance in gathering information about Norris's life and works; Richard Allan Davison; Donald Pizer; Donna Danielewski; Robert C. Leitz III; Allys Palladino-Craig; Douglas K. Burgess; Don L. Cook; James B. Stronks; Benjamin F. Fisher; Louis J. Budd; Helen Burke; Stanley Wertheim; Charles L. Crow; William B. Dillingham; Warren French; Don Graham; Barbara Hochman; Joseph Pais; Don Blume; Eric Carl Link; Charles Johanningsmeier; Glen Love; Christine Harvey; and David Teague. Their many generous contributions of new information and their kind counsel over three decades were essential to the completion of this project.

We thank Joel Myerson and Gary Scharnhorst for their careful readings of the manuscript and the suggestions for improvement they generously offered.

This biography would not have been possible without the support of the Florida State University; Brigham Young University; the National Endowment for the Humanities; the Bibliographical Society of America; the American Philosophical Society; the Frank Norris Society; Lou Ann Crisler; and Sharon M. McElrath.

Chronology

1867 Gertrude Glorvina Doggett and B. F. (Benjamin Franklin) Norris marry in Chicago.

1868 Birth of Grace Colton.

1869 Death of Grace.

1870 Birth of Frank (Benjamin Franklin Norris Jr.) and baptism at Trinity Episcopal church.

1871 Birth of Florence Colton.

1872 Death of Florence.

1876 Frank enters the Allen Academy.

1877 Birth of Albert Lester.

1878 Norrises sail to England in June, returning in September.

1881 Birth of Charles Gilman.

1882 Frank may have entered the Harvard School in the fall (enrollment date uncertain).

1883 B. F. visits San Francisco for the first time.

1884 B. F. purchases house at 1822 Sacramento Street in San Francisco.

1885 Norris family begins residence in San Francisco; Frank enters the Belmont School in September and withdraws before the end of the fall term.

1886 Frank is enrolled at San Francisco's Boys' High School for some months, is confirmed at St. Luke's Episcopal church, and begins art study at the California School of Design.

1887 Frank departs San Francisco with B. F. to continue art study at the South Kensington School of Art and Design in London; in Chicago they learn that Lester Norris has died; Gertrude, Charles, and niece Ida Carleton accompany B. F. and Frank to London and reside in Paris, where Frank studies under William Bouguereau at the Académie Julian; B. F. returns alone to the United States in September.

1888 Frank and Gertrude tour Italy; Charles returns to the United States with cousin Ida in April; Gertrude departs for San Francisco in August; Frank continues art studies with Bouguereau and writes a prose narrative set in the Middle Ages, which he sends to Charles in installments.

1889 Frank's first article, "Clothes of Steel," appears in the *San Francisco Chronicle;* he returns from Paris with the manuscript of a novel or novella entitled "Robert d'Artois"; he works on another prose fiction entitled "Vandover and the Brute" and prepares to take the University of California entrance examination.

1890 Frank composes *Yvernelle: A Legend of Feudal France;* he is a freshman at the University of California at Berkeley, where he starts writing and drawing for student publications.

1891 Frank becomes a member of the Phi Gamma Delta ("Fiji") fraternity; he begins to publish short stories in regional magazines (*Argonaut, The Wave,* and *Overland Monthly*); his poetical romance, *Yvernelle,* is available for sale in November.

1892 B. F., estranged from Gertrude, reestablishes his residence in Chicago.

1893 Gertrude initiates a divorce suit.

1894 Frank completes his senior year and withdraws from the University of California with an honorable dismissal; Gertrude and B. F. are divorced; Gertrude and Charles reside in Cambridge, Massachusetts, near Harvard, where Frank lives in Grays Hall during the academic year as a "special student"; he enrolls in English 22, which he approaches as a creative writing course, and he is most likely working on the manuscripts for *Vandover and the Brute* and *McTeague.*

1895 For English 22 Frank writes themes directly related to *Vandover* and *McTeague;* he prepares a collection of short stories that Houghton, Mifflin, and Co. declines to publish; Lovell, Coryell, and Co. accepts it or a similar collection (never published); Frank returns to San Francisco and contributes articles to *The Wave;* in October he departs for South Africa to write local-color articles for the *San Francisco Chronicle;* in Johannesburg he is witness to the Jameson Raid.

1896 Frank enlists in the Uitlanders' militia, joining its mounted troops; returns to San Francisco as his South African articles are appearing in the *Chronicle;* accepts a position with *The Wave* as staff writer and associate editor; becomes a member of the Bohemian Club; and meets Jeannette Black.

1897 Frank continues to write fiction and nonfiction for *The Wave;* assembles a collection of short stories with the title "Ways That Are Dark" (never published); completes the composition of *McTeague* in the fall; and begins writing *Moran of the Lady Letty.*

1898 *The Wave* serialization of *Moran* commences in January; Frank visits New York City and New Orleans prior to his arrival in St. Louis, where he spends time with Jeannette Black, a student at the Monticello Female Seminary in Godfrey, Illinois; he moves to New York City in February to work for S. S. McClure's newspaper syndicate, *McClure's* monthly magazine, and the Doubleday and McClure Company; serves as *McClure's* correspondent during the Spanish-American War; recuperates from malaria in San Francisco; sees the book publication of *Moran;* begins writing *Blix* and doing research for *A Man's Woman;* returns to New York City and the S. S. McClure firm in October; and prepares *McTeague* for publication.

1899 As *McTeague* is published, Frank completes *Blix* for serialization in the *Puritan Monthly,* continues work on *A Man's Woman;* conceives the "Trilogy of the Epic of the Wheat"; visits California to conduct research for *The Octopus;* becomes engaged to Jeannette Black; returns to New York City in August; and, in December, joins the newly formed firm of Doubleday, Page, and Co. as a manuscript reader. The *San Francisco Chronicle* begins serializing *A Man's Woman* in July, and Doubleday and McClure publish its third novel by Norris, *Blix,* in September. Publishers Grant Richards and William Heinemann decline the manuscript for *Vandover and the Brute* in November.

1900 Frank and Jeannette marry at St. George's Episcopal church in New York City on 12 February, a week after *A Man's Woman* is made available for sale. He continues the composition of *The Octopus;* becomes Theodore Dreiser's champion at Doubleday, Page, when he reads the manuscript of *Sister Carrie;* and he and Jeannette move from Washington Square in Manhattan to Roselle, New Jersey, where he completes *The Octopus* in December. B. F. Norris dies in Chicago in October.

1901 The Norrises go to Chicago to conduct research for the second volume in the wheat trilogy, *The Pit.* Jeannette becomes pregnant, and they visit San Francisco as *The Octopus* is published in early April. They return to New York City and depart shortly thereafter to spend two months at Greenwood Lake in New Jersey, with Frank continuing his manuscript-reading work. They return to Washington Square in July and then move to Manhattan's Upper West Side. In addition to writing

The Pit, Frank begins to produce a large number of short stories and articles for periodicals solicitous of work from the hand of the author of *The Octopus.*

1902 Birth of Jeannette Williamson Norris, nicknamed Billy, in January. Frank completes *The Pit* in June, arranging to begin serialization in the *Saturday Evening Post* magazine in September. While visiting friends on Long Island, the Norrises have Billy baptized at St. Andrew's Dune church in Southampton Township. In August they depart New York City to establish permanent residence in San Francisco. Frank purchases acreage near Gilroy for a country home; he and Jeannette make plans for a round-the-world trip, during which he will research the third volume of the wheat trilogy, *The Wolf.* Jeannette successfully undergoes an appendectomy. Shortly afterwards, Frank suffers appendicitis; his appendix bursts, and, on 25 October, he dies from peritonitis. Doubleday, Page, and Co. receives bound copies of *The Pit* in early November; when formally published two months later, it is one of the best-sellers of 1903.

FRANK NORRIS

1

FRANK NORRIS'S PLACE IN AMERICAN CULTURAL HISTORY: AN OVERVIEW

The American novelist Frank Norris was a universally well-liked person with an inextinguishable joie de vivre, a fine sense of humor, a gift for maintaining long-term friendships, and a degree of self-confidence that early career-related disappointments could not dampen. These are not, of course, warrants for the writing of a biography. They simply make pleasurable the task of telling the story of a man whose passing in 1902, at the age of thirty-two, prompted an outpouring by those who knew him of testimonials to a life well lived.[1] The fact that, three decades after Norris's death, Franklin Walker, his first biographer, could easily obtain positive recollections through correspondence and interviews is only further encouragement to complement and, when necessary, correct his portrait.[2] It is now clear that there was much more to the story of this personable individual than Walker was able to discern in 1932, or his successors have discerned in articles, parts of books, M.A. theses, and Ph.D. dissertations. However, our principal reasons for devoting extended attention now to Norris are of another kind.

His vital accomplishments as a still readable literary artist and insightful observer of American life account for his present high status in U.S. cultural history. He has long stood as a "touchstone" figure who, in two distinct ways, provides immediate access to what was transpiring in American thought and literary expression at the close of the nineteenth century and the beginning of the twentieth.

This eminently respectable man—baptized, confirmed, married, and given last rites by the Episcopal church—was in many of his works a distinctly conventional writer who understood and deliberately appealed to the dominant tastes of his contemporaries and many of their widely shared assumptions about life at the turn of the century. Norris's own interests matched those of various readerships, ranging from high- to middle- and, on occasion, lowbrow. His eclecticism manifests itself in his many informed allusions to classical authors such as Homer and Horace; to modern masters such as Sir Walter Scott and Honoré de Balzac; to popular contemporaries such as Bret Harte, Lew Wallace, and William Dean Howells; to turn-of-the-century celebrities such as Richard Harding Davis and David Belasco; and to the authors of the pulp fiction of his day. In Norris's writings, one character's quotation from a play by Shakespeare or Racine may stand cheek-by-jowl with another's reference to a now-forgotten potboiler novel of 1888, Archibald C. Gunter's *Mr. Potter of Texas*. Norris took into account and reflected the enthusiasms of the whole of the American reading public. Such multifarious literary influences are apparent even in his most original works, to the same degree as long-embraced doctrines such as Emersonian self-reliance and the Anglo-American's conceit of racial superiority.

Norris's third novel, *Blix*, is exemplary of how he worked within traditional boundaries. While it does display some traits of post-Victorian modernity—for example, it tests the limits of tolerance for the liberated New Woman represented by its heroine intent upon becoming a physician—in the main, this sprightly romance of 1899 treats courtship and the flowering of true love in a way that gratified the most Victorian of readers in Norris's and his parents' generations. In this scrupulously "clean-minded" work—dedicated to Norris's mother, no less—the narrator even informs the reader that sex has had nothing to do with the hero's realization that he has unwittingly fallen in love with the heroine. It is remarkable that Norris rendered such idealistic plots and characterizations, preferred by genteel readers of the late nineteenth century, in a manner that remains credible and enjoyable today.

To be described thus as a traditionalist whose virtue lay in gratifying the tastes of his readers and revalidating their ways of seeing things is not, of course, an advantage in one respect. The present reputations of *great* literary figures, painters, and composers since the early nineteenth century typically depend upon their being perceived as members of an avant-garde, bravely violating and innovatively transcending established criteria for artistic production. Edouard Manet and Paul Gaugin, for example, have long been heroicized for their bold departures from convention and their anticipation of and influence on modernist values in the visual arts. More traditional artists of the late nineteenth century, such as the men under whom Norris studied drawing and painting in the 1880s, have not fared so well. And yet, as with Norris's writings of the kind, the equally artful but more conventional paintings of Virgil Williams, Emil Carlsen, and William Bouguereau serve an important cultural function. They tell one what Cézanne's and Van Gogh's signature works cannot: how late Victorians typically saw and understood the world before them. That they do so in a compelling way accounts in part for the fact that their creators have not been wholly overshadowed by more experimental contemporaries, nor by their twentieth- and twenty-first-century successors who distanced themselves yet farther from late nineteenth-century artistic values.

Another case in point, like *Blix,* is Norris's final novel, *The Pit,* posthumously published in 1903. In no respect a work of art that foreshadows early twentieth-century modernist experiments in form by contemporaries such as Sherwood Anderson and Theodore Dreiser, it appealed strongly to the popular as well as the more sophisticated, "high-culture" readerships of its time. It embodied traditional convictions regarding the essentials of a successful marriage and the threat to a happy union posed by the egotistical self-absorption of either of the partners (a problem Norris also examined in *A Man's Woman* [1900]). *The Pit* is a profoundly "serious" work of fictive psychology fashioned in light of the events and probable cultural influences leading to the divorce of Norris's own parents in 1894. At the same time, he crafted the novel for the mass market; it became a best-seller viewed by many critics as his masterpiece. That it continued to speak engagingly to Norris's generation was evident as late as 1917: like three others of his works, *The Pit* was adapted as a silent film and distributed nationally to movie houses.

At the same time, Norris was indeed a touchstone figure as a member of the avant-garde. Book reviewers in his own time, like later literary historians, recognized him as a remarkably versatile writer whose most innovative works marked a radical departure from not only prevailing literary conventions but the preferred worldview of the vast majority of his contemporaries. In *McTeague,* the 1899 novel that is now seen as his masterpiece, he ignored the long-standing boundaries for "appropriate" subject matter in American art, treating types of characters, kinds of experience, and decidedly post-Victorian concepts that would become commonplace in more adventuresome novels and plays by the 1930s, particularly in John Steinbeck's early works. But in

1899, when Victorian standards were still in place, seven months before *Blix* typed the kind of novel privileged by the guardians of public morality, Norris was the author of a perverse, dirty book. The transgressiveness of *McTeague* is reflected by the fact that, as late as 1924, when Erich von Stroheim's almost literal cinematic adaptation of the novel was released as *Greed*, reviewers judged it a perverse, dirty film.[3]

When the novel appeared, no less respectable an authority on aesthetics than William Dean Howells celebrated what he saw as its many little miracles of observation. Willa Cather admired Norris's adaptation of the literary methods of the French novelist Emile Zola to create a truthful study of American life. But "vulgar," "gruesome," "gross," "sordid," "revolting," and "stomach-turning" are typical of the epithets that outraged American and English reviewers hurled at *McTeague*—reacting as they had for two decades to Zola's novelistic violations of Anglo-American taboos.[4] Their reasons are immediately apparent upon a first reading. To cite one of many possible examples, Norris includes something uniformly omitted in other American and English novels of the 1890s. The omission is a curious one, discoverable even in works representative of a progressive realist movement that was in place in the United States at the time. Unlike those reading about them, no characters in novels published by respectable firms felt the need to, or did, urinate. Urination is not, per se, an essential element of world-class literature—any more than is the heroine of *McTeague* being seized by a fit of vomiting, or her siblings' being victimized by an obsessive, abusive father governed by a need to maintain order in his life. A pants-wetting scene featuring her young brother may now seem a trivial enhancement of an already quite sensational novel—though this was not the case at the end of the nineteenth century, since Norris was obliged to rewrite the passage prior to the third 1899 printing. The English publisher Grant Richards informed the American firm Doubleday and McClure that he would not market the book for British readers unless the bowdlerization occurred. He was adamant about this, and it was not until 1941 that a publisher restored the text of *McTeague* to its original condition.[5]

There need be little debate, however, about the importance of another deliberate oversight common in contemporaneous prose fictions pretending to be true to human nature but declining to deal with aspects that polite Victorians saw as rankly animalistic. Acknowledgments of sexuality as a factor in courtship and marriage were rare; and, when authors did attend to instinct-rooted drives that linked human behavior to that of the barnyard, they acknowledged the "lower" or "brutal" dimension of human nature in an ultradiscreet manner. For example, *The Scarlet Letter* (1850) hardly encourages the reader to imagine what role sexual appetite plays in the conception of Hester Prynne's illegitimate daughter. Had Hawthorne prompted his reader to do so, he would have risked the charge of animalism in art—the very indictment later leveled at Zola and Norris. Just how distasteful human sexuality was for many as late as 1896 may be seen in Norris's withering review of a novel by a fellow San Franciscan, Mrs. J. R. Jarboe. Her *Robert Atterbury* dealt with, as Norris phrased it, "the 'ultimate physical relation of man and woman.' A dangerous subject truly." Jarboe advanced the thesis that marriage is nothing "but legalized prostitution"—to which Norris responded with a decidedly post-Victorian perspective on, and acceptance of, the indelible characteristics of the human animal, the *bête humaine* of Zola's canon. Is it not true, Norris asked in his review, that "humanity still is, and for countless generations will be, three-quarters animal, living and dying, eating and sleeping, mating and reproducing even as animals; passing the half of each day's life in the performance of animal functions?"[6] That such is indeed the case was for Norris the warrant to produce art that frankly acknowledged as natural the condition in which mankind finds itself.

Great American novels such as Howells's *The Rise of Silas Lapham* (1885) and merely noteworthy ones such as Charles W. Chesnutt's *The House behind the Cedars* (1900) did not reflect agreement with Norris. They featured lovers who are, so to speak, neutered. In 1893, even so irreverent and daring a writer as Stephen Crane proceeds by implication when describing his heroine's seduction, rejection by her lover, and descent into prostitution in *Maggie;* and reference to her surrender to the bartender Pete occurs euphemistically only after the event is history. Two years later, in *Rose of Dutcher's Coolly,* Hamlin Garland repeatedly alludes to the dangers of sexual experience his chaste heroine faces, illustrating his point only briefly in the harassment of this unchaperoned country girl by a conductor and equally ill-mannered brakeman during a train ride. She is not only unresponsive to their crude advances; she herself never knows randiness in any scene in this novel—not even when with the man who wins her heart and then her hand in marriage. Readers of Theodore Dreiser's 1900 novel *Sister Carrie* had to infer Carrie Meeber's means of becoming the "kept woman" of Drouet and Hurstwood. Further, is Carrie *ever* subject to erotic impulses? One cannot tell. In *McTeague,* however, male *and female* sexual arousal is treated frankly. And Norris goes well beyond the one American predecessor in this respect

of whom he was aware: James Lane Allen in 1896 belied his reputation as
a genteel romance writer in *Summer in Arcady* by confessing the truth of
the matter.[7] He was considerably more reticent than Norris, however, as he
dreamily rhapsodizes in the work originally entitled "Butterflies" about the
way in which Nature draws males and females together to accomplish procreation. That a mainstream commercial firm in New York City decided to
publish *McTeague* in 1899 is nothing less than startling. That Norris's more
candid study of sexuality in real life, *Vandover and the Brute,* could not appear in print until 1914 is less surprising.

Norris's penchant for exposing the "whole truth, and nothing but," as he saw
it, found a broader scope than this. To the best kind of modern literature, he
explained in 1901, "belongs the wide world for range, and the unplumbed
depths of the human heart, and the mystery of sex, and the problems of life,
and the black, unsearched penetralia of the soul of man."[8] Not only individuals but the aggregate that is society fell within his ken, as is seen in the full
title he gave *Vandover* in manuscript. When Charles G. Norris arranged for
the novel's posthumous publication in 1914, he ignored the subtitle; but his
brother composed *Vandover* as "A Study of Life and Manners in an American
City at the End of the Nineteenth Century."[9] Like Balzac and his successor in
this respect, Zola, Norris was sociologically oriented at a time when sociology
was only beginning to assume its present definition as a discipline. As had
Harold Frederic in *The Damnation of Theron Ware* (1896), he focused on
the manners and mores of representative Americans, observing the stresses
felt by those in the midst of an increasingly pluralistic society undergoing
rapid transformations that called into question the values, truths, and ultimate
certainties with which they had been reared.

Norris was born in March 1870, as Americans were attempting to put
the Civil War behind them and to restore the conditions of normalcy that
they knew prior to 1861. Many invested considerable energy in turning back
the clock, particularly in the South through the 1880s and 1890s, as may be
seen in the short stories and novels of Thomas Nelson Page and even after
the turn of the century in the works of Thomas Dixon Jr. Returning to the
good old days "befo' the wah," known by Norris's maternal grandmother in
Charleston, South Carolina, was not easy. The southern economy was in ruin.
Washington, D.C., dictated a forced modification of the political order—and,
in consequence, the social order—until shortly after Rutherford B. Hayes's

election to the U.S. presidency in 1876. The Reconstruction era was a period of confusion: *de*construction of the Old South was the plan of the congressmen known as Radical Republicans; what was being reconstructed other than the prewar union of states was therefore not clear; and if the intent was not merely to punish but to make the South conform to what was prevalent in the righteous North, that too was problematic. How was the South to mimic a region that was itself undergoing constant redefinition in the decades after the war? The protean character and inventive dynamism of the North invited a study in contrasts with the relative stasis observable across most of the South. Birmingham, Alabama, for all of its industrial development, was not the Pittsburgh of Andrew Carnegie and Henry Clay Frick. Atlanta diligently attempted to recover from General William Tecumseh Sherman's torch; but it was not the city of Norris's birth vigorously effacing all signs of Mrs. O'Leary's legendary cow's having kicked over a lantern.

Whatever the exact cause of the conflagration, Chicago emerged from the Great Fire of October 1871 with little of the antique remaining to conceal the modern forces that were transforming America into a global economic power that could, by 1898, with impunity wrest the Philippines, Puerto Rico, and Cuba from the Old World's control. This dynamic hub of commerce in the Midwest, where Norris lived until he was fifteen years old, epitomized urbanization, technological progress, industrial expansion, the inflow of venture capital at home and from abroad, and the irresistible drift toward grand amalgamations promising economies of once unimaginable scale and productivity. It was at the center of this national manufacturing and distribution nexus that Norris's father oversaw a wholesale jewelry and watch business growing by leaps and bounds and generating considerable wealth for him and his family. Opportunities abounded for the quick-witted and shrewd—not to mention the ruthless—who could seize the moment without hesitation. Benjamin Franklin Norris was most aptly named by his parents. As B. F.'s son Frank would illustrate in *McTeague,* with its hero's rise from lowly carboy in a mine to proprietorship of a dental practice on San Francisco's Polk Street, the American Dream was alive and well—even for those who are as slow-witted but diligent as that hero. At the same time, though, conditions had changed since Benjamin Franklin became the American avatar for success and Ralph Waldo Emerson advised all to have confidence in their ability to hitch their wagons to a star—as *McTeague* also illustrates in its nightmarish denouement.

Complexities of modern life that are not normally taken into account by simplistic purveyors of the Dream did not, it appears, hobble Norris's father. B. F. suffered from a "nervous" problem to which family correspondence alluded vaguely,[10] but it was obviously not an insuperable obstacle to the attainment of his goals. These complexities, however, overwhelm McTeague, at least as dramatically as they would George and Lennie in *Of Mice and Men* and Willy Loman in *Death of a Salesman*. Yes, the man to whom Norris introduces the reader in *McTeague* is known and deferred to on Polk Street as Dr. McTeague, and he demonstrates a level of competence commensurate with his degree of success. This self-made man is virtuous in his public and private lives. He is reliable and hardworking. He thus meets the criteria for success specified by the myth, Norris waggishly viewing late nineteenth-century dentistry as an occupation for which a man even so intellectually limited as his hero can become qualified. All's well—until "progress" reveals the negative consequences it inevitably leaves in its wake. What precipitates McTeague's descent into poverty and degeneration to violent alcoholism are changes that have occurred not within him but without in post–Civil War society. Moving from a frontierlike environment that evokes memories of the gold rush of 1849—the mine in the Sierra Nevadas where he was reared and began to learn the craft of dentistry—he enters the modern socioeconomic order, represented by San Francisco in the 1890s. Dr. McTeague fares well for years, but in urban California one of the new classes of credentialed specialists that had arisen since midcentury—graduates of schools of dentistry—holds sway and has successfully lobbied for governmental regulation of practitioners.

Born too late in a century that now stands as a Rubicon in many respects, McTeague faces a problem not known by the itinerant dentist of the previous generation with whom he apprenticed in the northern California hinterlands and became a journeyman in the traditional way of qualifying for an occupation. McTeague's informal training does not meet the standards for licensing by the state of California; and once the authorities discover him practicing dentistry without a diploma from a dental college, they notify him that he must immediately cease and desist. McTeague and his only slightly more sophisticated wife are overwhelmed by their loss of income and McTeague's inability to obtain gainful employment.

They are not the only figures in the Norris canon who find themselves discomfited by the distinctively modern forces reshaping American life as the century drew to a close. Chicago, like San Francisco by the 1880s, was also a locus for the rise of trusts and a proportionate decline in the opportunities for individuals as self-reliant as B. F. Norris. Luck was at least as important as pluck for those who hoped to prove upwardly mobile, as was becoming increasingly clear for the native born. Like the newly arrived immigrants for whom Chicago was a destination and for whom economic titans such as the grain broker and meatpacker Philip D. Armour were future employers, those less blessed by Dame Fortune came to resemble cogs in grand machines run by a select few celebrated by Social Darwinists as "the fittest." As Grover Cleveland observed in the final state of the union address of his first term in office, wealth and thus tremendous power had by 1889 become concentrated in the hands of fewer and fewer captains of industry and commerce who, with the protection of high import tariffs and virtually free from governmental restraints, wielded ever-expanding control over their fellow Americans.

Outside the city in the states to the east and west of Illinois, one could not escape to the old order wistfully recalled by many as bucolic. As in the South, so in the Midwest. Nostalgic keening for the past would account for the success of many a sentimental writer from the region, such as the elegaic poets James Whitcomb Riley and Paul Laurence Dunbar. Whether white or black, one longed for the life of pastoral simplicity allegedly once enjoyed by the noble yeoman who tilled the soil gladly; then refreshed himself at the local counterpart of *The Swimming Hole* idealized in oil on canvas by Thomas Eakins in 1883; and then passed the evening contentedly watching his well-scrubbed children resembling the two innocents pictured in Winslow Homer's *Boys in a Pasture* (1874) or the several sturdy rural youths playing *Snap-the-Whip* (1872). In 1901 in *The Octopus*, Norris would reveal his appreciation of such images. He acknowledged without irony and celebrated the occasions when the real measures up to such ideal conceptions of life in the United States. One cannot in this respect term Norris a cynic, like his older contemporary, Ambrose Bierce, or his younger, H. L. Mencken. The worst that one can say at such moments in his canon of over three hundred writings is that he was conventional as he imaged or articulated essentials of the rustic version of the American Dream.

To tell the whole truth, however, he also followed the progressive lead of Hamlin Garland who, in his 1891 collection of short stories, *Main-Travelled Roads*, exposed the fantasy—cherished by those who did not live in the country—of ever-idyllic agrarian contentment free from the taint of modern urban-industrial life. As with Norris's California growers of wheat and hops in *The Octopus*, so with Garland's midwesterners: the railroad barons who transport their produce, the bankers who hold their mortgages, and the companies that manufacture and sell farm machinery have the agriculturalists at their mercy. "Under the Lion's Paw," the title of one of Garland's stories, succinctly characterizes the agriculturalist's predicament as little different from that of those who labor at the pleasure of their employers in the burgeoning industrial centers.

As if it were not enough for agriculturalists to be subject to the whims of those parties, the vagaries of climate, and the tender mercies of the speculators at the Chicago Board of Trade who fixed the per-bushel prices they would receive, grain producers soon found themselves affected negatively from another direction. Thanks to improved transportation systems, the post–Civil War marketplace in which they competed with other growers was no longer national but international. No matter how hard or efficiently the wheat grower worked his land, a bumper crop in Argentina or Russia could lower the price of wheat at home and result in a foreclosed mortgage and emigration from the farm to the city. There the ruined agriculturalist would compete for wages depressed by the influx of cheap, immigrant labor.

Heeding Emerson's exhortation in his 1836 essay *Nature* to take charge of one's own life and fashion it as one desires it to be was becoming increasingly difficult for many, particularly those who were not as wealthy as the Sage of Concord. As the century waned, control seemed to reside more and more in the hands of someone else or, worse, to be exercised by some faceless thing or invisible force. Clarification was imperative. Writers of various kinds could at least attempt to provide it, and Frank Norris was one of them. He was particularly sensitive to this sense of loss of command over one's life and to a suspicion that had become a conviction for some of his contemporaries: that a puppet's movements, governed by the ways in which its strings are pulled from above, was the apt analogy for their own activities day in and day out. In the Norris canon, though, it is not only members of the working and middle class who register this. Some of those who pull the strings from above, represented in *The Octopus* and *The Pit,* confess their own sense of powerlessness, pointing to forces, conditions, and operating systems that function as *their* puppetmasters. In the former novel, a railroad magnate alleges that he is impotent vis-à-vis policy concerning how his corporation operates. Shelgrim proclaims that he does not govern his monopolistic "octopus" with a stranglehold on all who must use its facilities. Rather, iron laws of supply and demand that he cannot check determine that railroads have to function rapaciously in a laissez-faire capitalist environment.[11] In the latter novel, the hero—a bullish wheat speculator at the Chicago Board of Trade—"corners" the whole of the May harvest and is thus able to name its price. But Curtis Jadwin, even before he attempts to extend his control to the July harvest, discovers that market forces render him their thrall and dictate his every action.[12] The titans in both novels see themselves as subject to forces they cannot resist, just like the small-time farmers, the large-scale agribusinessmen, the middlemen who distribute the wheat, and those around the globe who must purchase it to sustain themselves.

The Octopus and *The Pit* are not wholly fictions but exposés: the real-life counterpart of the fictional railroad magnate, Shelgrim, was Collis P. Huntington, the head of the Southern Pacific Railroad, which was known as "the octopus" long before Norris began his research for his novel in the spring of 1899. The original for the hero of *The Pit*, Curtis Jadwin, was the millionaire Philip D. Armour's nemesis at the Chicago Board of Trade, the millionaire Joseph Leiter. Norris interviewed Huntington; Leiter's escapades were front-page news for years, until his defeat by Armour in 1898. Norris was dealing with fact, as his 1901 and 1903 readers well knew. Like subsequent writers associated with the "muckraking" tradition in American letters, he could demonize the men at the top of the economic feeding chain. See, for example, his 1902 short story "A Deal in Wheat," which can serve as fodder for any firebrand literary historian intent upon either demonstrating the inhumaneness sanctioned by capitalism or holding forth in neo-Marxist fashion about "commodification" in American life.[13] Unlike writers such as the socialist Jack London, however, Norris was prone to attempt what he saw as balanced, full-scope representations of the whole of the predicaments he treated in works such as *The Octopus* and *The Pit*. Hence, he objectively presents the view of those situations from the top, the middle, and the bottom of the economic pyramid. One will note that even in "Life in the Mining Region," a nonfiction piece reporting in September 1902 on the anthracite coal miners' strike in Wilkes-Barre, Pennsylvania, Norris gives as much attention to the mine owners' and consumers' perspectives as he does to the difficult position of the strikers agitating for better wages and working conditions.[14] Norris was never an ideologue, right- or left-wing. After the publication of *The Octopus*, when the journalist George H. Sargent asked him what was his unstated solution for the socioeconomic problem he had treated, Norris explained that he was merely a novelist. Having researched the historical situation in 1880s California, upon which the main plot was based, and having gathered more recent data pertaining to the operations of the state's agriculturalists and the Southern Pacific Railroad, he could shed light on human behavior in an economic context in a true-to-life and, he hoped, interesting way. But, he protested to Sargent, one should turn to a political economist and not a literary man for a comprehensive proposal for a solution of the "present discontents."[15] Norris was not a Henry George nor an Emma Goldman. He was as stumped as the majority of his contemporaries by the question of how one might rein in or redirect in a comprehensively ameliorative way the forces at work in the modern socioeconomic order that he pictured. The best that he could come up with was the suggestion implied by the tragic dimensions of these two volumes in his never-completed "Trilogy of the Epic of the Wheat": surely there must be some way to render more humane the operations of an economy that, while accomplishing benign purposes such as the production and distribution to the world of an essential foodstuff, wreaks so much havoc in the lives of so many individuals. This very point is enunciated interrogatively by the heroine of *The Pit* as that novel closes.

In the second half of the twentieth century, much was made in the media of the experience of "future shock"—a sense of disorientation in the face of the accelerated rate of change that technological progress had effected.[16] Particularly trying was the rapid and unceasing diffusion of information that defied processing before the arrival of the next set of data. The popular conceit was true in one respect: it certainly explained the harried condition of those inclined to embrace the notion in the 1970s. In another respect, though, this was a myopic, ahistorical theory. Washington Irving and James Kirke Paulding alluded to essentially the same phenomenon in the first half of the nineteenth century; Henry David Thoreau echoed them at midcentury in *Walden*. Indeed, one can go much farther back in time to detect signs of the same state of mind. The pastoral poetry popular in Renaissance courts and Virgil's eclogues and georgics, written in the first century B.C., stand as escapist reactions to the stresses of then "modern" life. One should not, therefore, make too much of what transpired after the Civil War. Not to diminish the trying complexities faced by Norris and his contemporaries, or the validity of Norris's depiction of them, there is no need for hyperbole of the "-shock" variety when characterizing the period, especially since some of its characteristics were unquestionably reassuring.

One should not overlook the obvious: dramatically improved communications and transportation capabilities; expanding educational opportunities; a skyrocketing increase in literacy spurring the proliferation of newspapers and magazines; a burgeoning economy despite periodic financial "panics"; advances in medical science; and progress especially in public health and sanitation that, had it been more rapid, might have prevented the early deaths of three of Norris's siblings from cholera, meningitis, and diphtheria. Another sign of progress testified to by *Blix* in 1899 was the fact that the New Woman of Henry James's *Daisy Miller* had been asserting herself more and more since that novella first saw print in 1878. The immediate prospects for another sizeable constituency, African Americans, were less promising. Norris never gave fictional treatment to what was then known as the "Negro Problem," but he was not alone in recognizing the portent represented by the advancement of the man whom he termed one of the greats of his age, his fellow Doubleday, Page, and Co. author Booker T. Washington.[17] Washington's 1901 autobiography *Up from Slavery*—like his many public addresses and articles—bristled with positive assessments of how far African Americans had come since 1865 and modeled the means of overcoming setbacks such as disfranchisement. Above all, though, Norris reveled in the advances of his age in applied science: unlike Thoreau and Hawthorne, who lamented the appearance of "the machine in the garden," Norris was never more enthusiastic than when describing the wonders wrought by mechanical engineers. To conclude, as some commentators have,[18] that the locomotive as it is imaged in *The Octopus* represents one of the menacing developments facing mankind in the modern era is to ignore Norris's unqualified admiration throughout his canon for such awe-inspiring creations as the battleship *Oregon,* the grand cargo vessel *City of Everett,* steam-driven harvesting machines that cut wheat at one end and pour the grain into sacks at the other, and even San Francisco's high-tech garbage disposal facility ("the largest in the world").[19]

Norris indeed had his share of problems with which to deal. But he wrote more than just "problem fiction," grimly highlighting the ill effects of radical transformations of American life. Many of his productions are not only light-hearted, whimsical, and fun to read but joyful and even celebratory in tone. Even his "serious" works that wax grim include interludes that are vibrantly affirmative of life. The first half of *McTeague,* unlike the second, is dominantly comical in tone. While there were personal setbacks this achievement-oriented fellow would happily have not faced, he undoubtedly understood that one could have fared worse than to have been born Frank Norris.

Despite the periodic depressions endemic to capitalist economies then and now, individuals such as B. F. and Frank's mother Gertrude flourished, reproduced, and—evolutionarily speaking—conferred remarkable adaptational advantages upon their offspring. Their second child and B. F.'s namesake entered life in an upper-middle-class family, enjoying the security inherent in that socioeconomic stratum. At a time when the completion of high school was not at all commonplace, Frank pursued a college-preparatory education into his fifteenth year. The young gentleman then began full-time study of drawing and painting at the California School of Design in San Francisco, followed by two years at the Académie Julian in Paris. When he turned to writing, funding his apprenticeship and journeyman work was not a problem. The panic of 1893, for example, made no difference to him as he spent his last year at the University of California preparing for the profession of authorship. In the autumn of 1894 he enrolled for a year as a special student at Harvard, where he developed two novels and fashioned a collection of short stories. So far as can be determined, Norris did not experience the rigors of a full-time job until he was twenty-six.

Given the consequences for his biography and the interpretation and evaluation of his works by academic critics through much of the twentieth century, Norris's admirers cannot help but wish that he had not so obviously been "born to the manner." The premise seen repeatedly in the writings of left-leaning academics is that such a gilded young man could not possibly have understood what was transpiring in the day-to-day life of "the people." Foreign to him, so this line of thought runs, were those outside "the better class" to which he belonged. He never produced a work such as Upton Sinclair's 1906 proletarian classic *The Jungle*. And it is indeed true that Norris did not singlemindedly side against the members of his own class and identify solely with the oppressed, although he had the opportunity in works such as *The Octopus*. He was, allegedly, too much the patrician. One major critic wrote in 1969 about Norris's attitude toward the lower-class characters in *McTeague*: "[They] must have seemed to [him] slightly ridiculous. They were not simply placed in class cages for study; they were also labeled and condescendingly described by their keeper, Norris, in terms that suggest his subconscious opinion of them." Especially in the treatment of the novel's hero, "the reader feels with a chill Norris's aloofness." Another influential study proclaimed in 1985 that Norris uniformly depicts characters who do not share his social standing or ethnicity as "the Other," a brutelike underclass threatening the bourgeois status quo.[20]

Three frequently reproduced and truly uncharacteristic images of Norris, created by a too-artful photographer, Arnold Genthe, at the turn of the century, encourage this perception of him. Although Genthe has been chastised for photographing the denizens of San Francisco's Chinatown in ways that reinforce unflattering, racist stereotypes, it appears not to have occurred to anyone that he could just as easily enhance an Anglo-American subject in formal portraits as deliberately as he allegedly demeaned a Chinese-American one. Many commentators have uncritically regarded his atypical representations of Norris as the ultimate Brahmin worthy of caricature by his contemporary, the political cartoonist Thomas Nast. Is it any wonder that, when *this* Norris employs a tone of objectivity as he describes the lowly and downtrodden, his behavior might suggest Olympian aloofness and condescension? Or, in his comic portrayals of denizens of the lower socioeconomic order, did not this snobbish Norris invite interpretation as one with a supercilious attitude toward, and heartless disdain for, those less sophisticated than he?

The irony is that no other photographer treated Norris as Genthe did. And none of Norris's contemporaries verbally described him as an ultra-elitist in the numerous eulogies and memoirs appearing at the time of his death, nor in interviews and correspondence with Franklin Walker in 1930–32. The opposite impression of Norris's personality was universally recorded. For example, after explaining that he had known him for no less than twelve years, Frank Morton Todd proclaimed in 1902 that Norris

> had no satellites. He was above it. It would have been no satisfaction to him to have somebody revolving around him. He would not have degraded a friend to that position, nor kept one that would have demeaned himself so far. He was thoroughly a part of his crowd, and never tried to be a larger part than the other fellow. His wit was always well-timed and happy—never studied or pretentious, but simple and natural. He must have been conscious of his difference from the rest [of us]. . . . Yet he was never guilty of an affectation, and he scorned . . . that contemptible masquerade of puffed-up self-indulgence, that wretched, cheating imposition on the artist's suffering friends, called the "eccentricity of genius."[21]

It certainly is no advantage in the academy today for an author to have been an upper-middle-class Anglo-Saxon male who never experienced race or gender bias, much less oppression of any sort. It would have been better for his image and credibility if Norris had been born out of wedlock like Jack London and had to struggle against nearly insuperable odds to become a world-class writer. Or if, like Stephen Crane in his pre–*Red Badge of Cour-*

Arnold Genthe's portrait of Frank Norris. (Courtesy of the California History Room, California State Library, Sacramento, California.)

age days, he had lived the down-at-the-heel bohemian life when he came to New York City to make a name for himself. Or if he had to transcend the effects of racism and a lack of higher educational opportunities as had Paul Laurence Dunbar and Charles W. Chesnutt.

Despite the disadvantages of wealth, this privileged individual's coign of vantage was not so removed from quotidian life that he was unable to see and understand what the less well-heeled London and Dreiser were registering at the turn of the century. Norris also brought into focus the national competitive arena in which laissez-faire capitalism encouraged, rewarded, and punished opponents in contests for which the rules of engagement were not fixed, save by generally describable "laws," such as that of supply and demand and "survival of the fittest." He repeatedly looked beyond the economic realm to the larger context in which Nature operated in similarly patterned ways, frequently proving as unpredictable as the economy, and revealed heartless "laws" that no one could transgress. Norris could see that individuals appeared intelligible in a like manner, as to some degree masters of their own fates but obviously governed by natural and manmade conditions. In fact, for decades Norris's reputation has been that of a fiction writer whose best-known works embody a deterministic view of the human condition like those of Crane, London, and Dreiser. He was no more condescending nor emotionally detached than they and his principal transatlantic mentor, Emile Zola, sometimes were when illustrating from a post-Darwinian perspective how the "less fit" reveal their tragic maladaptations in a survival-of-the-fittest world. Norris often wrote sympathetically about types of humanity both fit and unfit to survive, flourish, and reproduce. Consider, for example, the sensitive portrayal of the German immigrant victimized by the railroad, Hooven, and the lugubrious fate of his family in *The Octopus*. A comparison with depictions of the same sort in John Steinbeck's *In Dubious Battle* would be appropriate. Indeed, F. Scott Fitzgerald was convinced that Steinbeck's *Of Mice and Men* and *Grapes of Wrath* plagiarized *McTeague* and *The Octopus*.[22] Be that as it may, Norris was no more deficient in humane sentiment than was Steinbeck.

This biography deals with an author whose historical importance relates directly to how he fully reflected the more traditional and popular literary values and attitudes of his time. It also treats an avant-garde artist, even a cultural vandal, who on other occasions moved daringly beyond the conventional in his choices of subject matter and deliberately violated late-Victorian proprieties for the sake of fashioning a more comprehensive and true-to-life description of the modern era in the United States as he experienced and understood it. Related to this second signature trait of the Norris canon is an important reason for expanding and refining Franklin Walker's 1932 portrait of Norris. As Emile Zola established in France a new school of writing known as naturalistism in the 1880s, Norris did the same for a U.S. tradition still discernible not only in its formative influences on subsequent movements, such as Freudianism and existentialism, but also in the practice of recent writers, such as Don DeLillo, who stands at the end of a long line of major figures categorized the way Norris was in his time. These include Norman Mailer, William Kennedy, William Styron, Saul Bellow, John Dos Passos, John Steinbeck, James T. Farrell, Edith Wharton, Jack London, and Theodore Dreiser.[23]

The Norris canon is remarkably various, representative of many schools, sensibilities, and tendencies. Its tonality ranges from sang-froid seriousness to a droll insouciance worthy of Oscar Wilde, and even a whimsicality reminiscent of W. S. Gilbert's librettos. But, at the time of his death, his principal identity was as a naturalistic novelist. Or, as reviewers referred to him, he was the "American Zola": the first ardent, wholly committed disciple of Zola and practitioner of the Zolaesque literary methodology in America. He can be said to have imported the naturalistic novel with the 1899 publication of *McTeague,* if by "naturalistic" one means a work not merely influenced by Darwinism but specifically Zolaesque in the application of a post-Darwinian worldview. Stephen Crane, too, was Darwinian, especially in his short-story masterpiece "The Open Boat" (1897). But the author of *Maggie* and the *The Red Badge of Courage* never wrote a work that resembles a Zolaesque novel in length, breadth, depth, detail, and—one may say—poundage. Among Norris's American contemporaries at the turn of the century, one must turn to Theodore Dreiser to see the like in *Sister Carrie,* which Norris promoted for publication at the firm where he worked part-time as a manuscript reader. But Dreiser's novel was stillborn. It was effectively suppressed upon its publication in 1900 because of second thoughts at Doubleday, Page, and Company about being associated with a novel in which a morally lax young female "makes good." Another publisher marketed *Sister Carrie* in 1907, but it drew little attention. It was not until 1912—ten years after Norris's death—that a third effort met with success and initiated a long string of printings. At the turn of the century, Norris was the "father" of the American school, and—strange to say, perhaps—he was the only early American practitioner who theorized at length about naturalism and promoted it as the signature of the "modern" in literature.

Not, alas, until Norris reaches his twenty-fourth year will this biography address the impact of Zola upon his imagination and how it provided him with the means of moving beyond experiments in imitation to find his own voice as an interpreter of *la bête humaine*. But an overview of Norris's career and place in American cultural history would not accomplish its purpose without a brief description of the school of writing in question, especially since it has never stood in such high relief as the romantic (Hawthorne and Melville) or the modernist (Faulkner and Hemingway). It is even overshadowed today by the intervening movement of realism (Howells and Frederic).

Suffice it to say that the main similarity between a late nineteenth-century naturalist and the theorists of these other schools was that they all judged previous modes of representing and interpreting reality as inadequate. In the late eighteenth and early nineteenth century, romantics had derided the artificiality and abstractness of neoclassical art; in the second half of the nineteenth century, realists chided the romantics for their too imaginative or idealistic distortions of reality and flamboyant emotionality; and, as the realists continued their assault on the romantic literary establishment, it was the naturalists' turn to identify a better path. The complaint was that the whole of human experience had not yet been treated, and the portions selected for presentation and illumination by both romantics and realists had not been handled in a way appropriate for a positivistic, post-Darwinian age. The findings of scientists mandated a redefinition of humanity's place in the natural world and, by extension, the relationship between the individual and society. Put in more general terms by Zola, life had too long been falsely represented and perversely interpreted by moralists, philosophical and theological idealists, conventional religionists, genteel fabulists, and egotists of all stripes intent upon imaging reality as they self-servingly wanted it to be, rather than how it actually is. That is, Zola too would have been outraged upon reading the 1896 novel that provoked Norris, Jarboe's *Robert Atterbury*.

Zola—an art critic as well as a novelist—borrowed the term *naturalisme* from art historians as he propagandized for a new kind of literature that called a spade a spade. The term denoted a revolutionary development that occurred during the Renaissance, as practitioners in the visual arts turned away from nonrealistic, supernaturally focused modes of representation common to the Middle Ages in Christian Europe. Initiating a shift from a dominantly theocentric point of view to a more geo- and anthropocentric perspective in the

fifteenth century, they invented the means of creating images of life characterized by empirical fidelity to physical reality. Valued were three-dimensional
perspective; real-world proportionality, detail, and coloration; and—whether
the subject was contemporary, historical, or mythological—lifelikeness. Thus
did they also facilitate more accurate interpretations of their all-inclusive
subject—Nature, or reality at large.

Masaccio's and Raphael's natural world, however, was not Zola's and
Norris's. The revival of interest in the realism of classical Greco-Roman artists—the actual foundation for the *reinvention* of art in the Renaissance—accompanied a rebirth of scientific inquiry that, by the late nineteenth century,
had long since disclosed the inner workings of a physical reality ultimately
reducible to two components, neither of which was spiritual: matter and energy. An antireligionist and strident materialist who denied the very existence
of the supernatural, Zola rejected as well as ridiculed all art that proffered
a spiritualistic, or what he termed "metaphysical," representation of human
experience. Literature that served up supernatural explanations for natural
events was anathema to him. Any work that did not depict human beings as
wholly natural phenomena, and human experience as solely the manifestation
of the conditions of phenomena, originated in a prescientific, self-deluding
imagination.[24]

Charles Darwin, not so deliberately provocative an iconoclast, was a major influence on Zola's thought and aesthetic. Darwin had theorized credibly
about evolution in *On the Origin of Species by Means of Natural Selection*
(1859) and *The Descent of Man and Selection in Relation to Sex* (1871). Zola
saw Darwin's hypothesis that one can understand natural processes wholly in
terms of Nature's self-contained operations and without resort to supernatural
agencies for explanation as inarguably verified. Unlike Darwin, who avoided
stirring up religionists as deftly as he could, Zola went on to produce inflammatory novels, the premise of which was that human behavior in a godless
universe *must* be pictured and interpreted in only such terms. Norris, an
Episcopalian, was more temperate: he privately turned neither to Darwin's
agnosticism nor Zola's militant atheism, striking the traditional compromise
regarding the separate spheres of reason and faith. He privately abided by
his decision to make a Kierkegaardian leap into the irrational; and, when
he did assign characters religious beliefs that affected their attitudes and
behavior, he did not pillory those who had embraced non- or suprarational
tenets of Christianity. Norris does not, for example, lampoon Father Sarria
in *The Octopus* when he proclaims his faith in the Pauline doctrine of Res-

urrection. But, whatever Norris's private convictions about the relationship between the supernatural and the natural, standing publicly as a naturalistic author involved eschewing a theocentric worldview for one that was geo- and anthropocentric. Norris wrote positivistically and never produced fictions in which he advanced spiritualistic causes of natural phenomena.[25]

As with Zola, Norris in 1902 declared his admiration for *The Expression of the Emotions in Man and Animals*, the 1872 study in which "Darwin had taken the adult male and female human and tracked down their every emotion, impulse, quality and sentiment."[26] Although neither Zola nor Norris could allude to *gene pools* or other concepts and terms that are now commonplace, they were not far off the mark. That rational mankind descended from lower, nonrational life forms that were determined in their actions solely by instinct was a given for both novelists, as was the concomitant idea that, while the human being evolved as a rational creature, it did not—and could not—sever its ties with its ancestors, and many of the predispositions and traits its antecedent species genetically transmitted are not vestigial. They are either observably active or latent and can at any moment be activated to strongly influence or govern the behavior of the human animal. For example, what Norris termed a self-preservation instinct, and another that is female-gender-specific—the preservation of one's offspring at all costs—suddenly manifest themselves unmediated by thought and unmitigated by Victorian moral proscriptions in a group of characters in *Vandover and the Brute*. During a shipwreck, a man in the water threatens to overturn a lifeboat overfilled with men, women, and children. Nature asserts itself: the majority demands his death, and he is killed. In *McTeague,* the genetically programmed predisposition of males and females to become sexually active is similarly asserted. Norris offers the fury of a bull in rutting season as the analogue for the condition of his sexually aroused, unmarried hero—and not because of his previously described slow-wittedness and draught-horselike disposition. Instead, as with a bull or a cow, he is motivated by an instinct-driven need to reproduce rather than a desire to transgress Victorian ethics. The outcome of this Victorian's struggle with his libido is not sexual intercourse; he observes the proscription against premarital coitus. But, to the dismay of Victorian moralists, the procreative drive that ineluctably reveals itself in McTeague is indeed an "animalistic" inheritance of the human gene pool—one subsumed by a larger gene pool of mammals, which is, in turn, subsumed by the pool containing all creatures who do not reproduce asexually. It is what McTeague has in common with the canary he keeps and Vandover with his pet terrier.

As noteworthy are Norris's treatments of an acquisitive instinct and an ingrained predisposition to establish dominance over others. Both are offered as compelling behavioral motivations for characters in *McTeague* and *Vandover and the Brute,* but he relates them more broadly to the antisocial workings of a capitalist economy. In *The Octopus* and *The Pit,* the motivations originating in these instincts are traceable from their consequences in the socioeconomic order. The "iron law" of supply and demand is normally thought of as the principal determinant, or as the apologia for the suffering that many experience as supply exceeds demand or demand exhausts supply; in either case, someone's ox is gored. Norris certainly gives that attention. But greed and an irresistible drive to control situations for the sake of self-aggrandizement, not to mention the sweet taste of victory, also play central roles in the economic arena. From Norris's first published novel, *Moran of the Lady Letty* (1898), through his seventh, only one features neither marked acquisitiveness nor a rage for dominance as a motivation: the atypical *Blix.*

This is not to say that Norris as a naturalist saw human experience as the mere playing out of the consequences of genetic inheritance. Like Zola, he also dealt with the nature-versus-nurture question, and he dramatically emphasized environment as a determinant of human behavior: to be reared in a capitalistic milieu may also render one especially aggressive as an economic combatant, determined to prove him- or herself fit to survive and flourish rather than unfit and thus slated for failure or even extinction. Or, such an environment, in its shaping influence over decades, may mightily reinforce the promptings of the acquisitive instinct—with nature and nurture working hand-in-hand to cause someone to be the way he or she is or to do what he or she does.

This is also not to say that Norris denies free will. Although the concept appears largely irrelevant in *McTeague,* given the low intelligence of the principal characters and their unawareness of the degree to which they are susceptible to genetic and environmental determinants, Norris develops this novel in such a way that, when they make choices that prove critical to how their lives proceed, it is clear which inherited or acquired traits are, in effect, making their choices for them as they respond to the exigencies they encounter. Pavlov's dogs come to mind more frequently than during the reading of any of Norris's other novels. But elsewhere in the Norris canon one finds fictional situations and characterizations that prompt the reader to ask why his characters do not elect courses different from the ones that lead them to disaster. Neither Vandover nor, in *The Octopus,* Annixter appears to have inherited intellectual limitations so obvious as those of McTeague and his wife Trina. Norris does not negate the possibility that, with an appropriate exercise of reason and will, both Vandover and Annixter *might have* escaped their calamitous experience. Other of Norris's personages—most notably in *A Man's Woman* and *The Pit*—do rise above their seemingly fixed traits of character to strike out in new directions. It was essential for this naturalistic novelist, however, to show that free will does not preclude the complexities that attend the human animal—the complications that follow from having descended from "lower" life forms and being as subject to environmental influences and instinctive drives as they.

One other complexity, or essential, of naturalism as it manifests itself in Norris's writings requires attention in light of his 1901 description of the best kind of literature. Again, as Norris declared, to it "belongs the wide world for range, and the unplumbed depths of the human heart, and the mystery of sex, and the problems of life, and the black, unsearched penetralia of the soul of man."[27] Two key terms here are "unplumbed" and "unsearched," in light of a criticism that has been directed at not only Norris but the naturalistic school as a whole: What is there to plumb or search, since Norris has reduced human experience to a formula of X (genetic inheritance) + Y (environmental conditions) = Z (the outcome)? Do not his naturalistic writings stand as variations upon one and the same theme?

In reply, one may note what the conclusion of *The Pit* illustrates: the unanticipated exercise of even a modicum of free will may modify the outcome. The heroine chooses to terminate her drift into an adulterous relationship; what appears the likely outcome through the greater part of the penultimate chapter is not what happens in the novel's conclusion. Thus, the most important term Norris uses in the declaration above is "mystery." How X + Y plays out, though it may appear foreseeable, cannot be known until Z manifests itself; and Z may prove quite different from what the reader expected. In Norris's naturalistic writings, the outcome is often not what his characters anticipate. For example, in *Vandover* the hero has sexual intercourse with a "fast" young woman who, to his mind, displays less-than-virtuous characteristics and invites seduction. She is, however, not what she seems, and she commits suicide in consequence of her surrender. In *The Octopus*, the leader of a wheat ranchers' group, Magnus Derrick, manages a plan to defeat the railroad corporation that is gouging agriculturalists throughout the state. That they will fail is not wholly unpredictable, he realizes, but it was unimaginable that his actions would create a situation in which his son Harran is shot to death. Another character, Dyke, plants hops because the price for them has risen dramatically; it does not occur to him that the railroad will raise its shipping rate commensurately, and he is ruined when it does just that. Woe to the character in the Norris canon who, like Curtis Jadwin in *The Pit*, proclaims at a critical juncture in his tale, "'You can't tell me anything about it. I've got it all figured out.'"[28] As with Sophocles's Creon and Shakespeare's Othello, such certainty is a slippery slope, leading in Jadwin's case to financial ruination, a mental breakdown, and a protracted physical illness.

That life remains mysterious despite Norris's identification of post-Darwinian "laws" governing the biosphere may be obscured for some readers who do not give sufficient weight to the fact that he is ever writing in the past tense. As an omniscient narrator and informed commentator, he is situated so that what he describes and interprets is history; and in his retrospectives he is at leisure to illustrate the truism that hindsight is twenty-twenty. This is not true of his characters, whose perspectives are not his. They are dealing with new developments in the present and cannot depend upon prescience to avoid mistakes in judgment. What they see is blurred as the present rushes forward into the future.

Further complicating the situations Norris treats is what has been recognized as the third "force" at work in the triumvirate of determinisms featured by literary naturalists: to heredity and environment is added the rule of chance. The addition found its sanction not only in observations of the seeming cunning with which life can take the most unpredictable turns. Darwin's theory of natural selection is grounded in chance or accidental events at the genetic level: *random* mutations that may or may not confer adaptational advantages in the struggle for existence. Darwin's theory focuses upon what had already occurred—in his case, over a vast expanse of time. He wisely did not speculate about what is occurring in the unruly present and likely to take place in the future, save in the most general terms. For example, those species that were well-adapted to their environments, and thus had passed fitness-to-survive tests, are likely to persist—unless an unpredictable development such as a random mutation occurs. Even a slight change in the physical environment may suddenly render a fit species unfit. As to the individual member of the species, merely being in the wrong place at the wrong time, or the right place at the right time, can spell either extirpation or longevity and continued reproductive success. As pictured by Darwin rather than other thinkers of the nineteenth century, who provided a more comforting impression, evolution brings the gamester's dice to mind.

A constant in Norris's fictional works—whether they are naturalistic or related to other schools of writing—is the chance-event theme, articulated in the simplest terms in one of his nonfiction articles of 1897. As he interviewed the California painter Charles Rollo Peters at his cabin in Monterey, Norris admired a piece of his furniture that was "a marvel of carving" and "the rarest of curios." He ended the article by telling us, "I was wondering how large must have been the sum that Peters was obliged to pay for the wonder, when by one of those extraordinary coincidences that are all the time happening, he said: 'I gave the fellow twenty-five dollars for that bed.'"[29] Some coincidences are not so happy. In *McTeague*, Trina Sieppe falls from a swing and requires dental work; it just so happens that the best friend of her cousin, Marcus Schouler, is Dr. McTeague. And so, initiated by an accident, begins the course of events leading to Mrs. Trina McTeague being beaten to death. At the time of their engagement, Norris writes: "From the first they had not sought each other. Chance had brought them face to face, and mysterious instincts as ungovernable as the winds of heaven were at work knitting their lives together. Neither of them had asked that this thing should be—that their destinies, their very souls, should be the sport of chance."[30] The extraordinary is seen also in the freakish circumstance of Trina's one-time purchase of a lottery ticket and her winning today's equivalent of roughly seventy-five thousand dollars. It is a blessing for Trina until, much later, the mortal consequences of her good fortune prove like those of a fatal curse.

In short, Norris gives the reader with one hand a set of cogent explanations of human behavior and a formulaic interpretation of why the lives of his characters take the shape they do—or, more accurately, the way they *did* in the histories he reports with a tone suggestive of certainty. Little remains mysterious by the time a plot reaches its terminus and the outcome of hereditary influences, environmental developments, and chance events is neatly illustrated. From his other hand the reader receives something quite different, as Norris demonstrates that uncertainty prevails when a character is dealing with the present and future, neither of which is so easily interpreted as the past.

❧

Such an emphasis upon uncertainty when delineating the human condition may bring to mind treatments of the same theme by Ernest Hemingway,

Jean-Paul Sartre, or Albert Camus. But it would be a mistake to characterize Norris as a protomodernist or as prescient of distinctively twentieth-century ideas and attitudes. Although Norris was a progressive artist and thinker, the architectural icon with which one might best associate him is neither New York City's Guggenheim Museum nor the Empire State Building but rather the Fuller, or Flatiron, Building at the intersection of Fifth Avenue and Broadway. Its construction was completed the year Norris died, and it was then what is hardly evident now: a skyscraper proclaiming modernity. Viewed as it appeared from the vantage point of Madison Square in 1902, it anticipates what was to come architecturally in the following decades as it broke from convention in a radically daring way. The same is true of the Norris canon, literarily and intellectually. Upon closer examination, though, one cannot overlook the Flatiron Building's profuse Gilded Age ornamentation that harks back to the 1880s and 1890s—as does Norris's style of writing.

When Walker's biography was published in 1932, the year following the completion of the Empire State Building, Norris's works appeared as antiquated and quaint to those who delighted in art deco, as did nearby structures still sporting either Victorian gingerbread or art-nouveau architectural motifs. Walker wrote accordingly in a patronizing tone. Since then, Norris's importance in American cultural history has been consistently acknowledged, but the period characteristics of his writings so strenuously criticized by literary modernists and their appreciative interpreters through the 1960s have as consistently prevented a fair assessment of his works and unprejudiced description of their author. The ideological loyalties of these commentators have also taken their toll; like Norris's contemporaries Brander Matthews, Theodore Roosevelt, and Richard Harding Davis, he has never been accused of being "politically correct" in the present sense of that term.

Since the 1970s, when a new appreciation of Norris's most periodized novel, *McTeague,* began to develop, however, what was once considered melodramatically fustian, imagistically heavy-handed, and dismayingly pseudoscientific in his canon has ceased to elicit modernist condescension. That historical distance on the period Norris typed in so many ways has finally been achieved was recently suggested by Jean Strouse's fair-minded, revisionist portrait of the much-maligned J. Pierpont Morgan; and, like her *Morgan: American Financier,* Alyn Brodsky's *Grover Cleveland: A Study in Character* transcended considerable prejudice to present a balanced assessment of Cleveland's life and works in 2000.[31] Even Norris's art instructor in Paris in 1887–89, William Bouguereau, is now celebrated for what he accomplished

The Fuller building. (Courtesy of Joseph R. McElrath Jr.)

as an Academic painter, rather than ridiculed for what he did not accomplish as an artist who shied away from impressionism and postimpressionist styles of representation.

This biography presents much new information concerning Frank Norris's private life and career, as it traces the developments that led to his being acknowledged as the American Zola and one of the major novelists of his day. It examines Norris on his own terms and those of his era, rather than ours. It aims to take the reader into much wider realms of Norris's experience than were possible for Franklin Walker in the early 1930s and to present a more accurate record of the particulars of Norris's life than Walker's limited resources and his reliance upon the often erroneous recollections of Norris's brother Charles and other contemporaries permitted. But, above all, it attempts to communicate what it meant to be an individual who adventured upon life as energetically as Thoreau advised his Victorian readers of *Walden* to do in 1854, but who discovered in consequence that his world was like neither Thoreau's, Emerson's, nor Hawthorne's. A Rubicon had been crossed by 1870, and this biography deals with a remarkable individual who assumed the task of, and took pleasure in, mapping the turn-of-the-century landscape for his contemporaries—and for us.

2

ANTECEDENTS

Given Frank Norris's emphasis in his writings on the role of heredity and environment in shaping the lives of individuals, it is inconceivable that he did not reflect at length upon their effects on him as he passed from adolescence into adulthood. But he never wrote anything like an autobiography or even letters offering his take on the relationship between nature and nurture in his own makeup. To do so was unwarranted before 1898, when at twenty-seven he completed his literary apprenticeship as a staff writer for a San Francisco magazine, *The Wave.* He had done well as the prolific author of short stories and articles for this weekly. Still, who would care about his personal history until he accomplished something more substantial? Into the autumn of 1902, he could hardly spare the time for such an indulgence: in the four years before his death he was preoccupied with launching a career in New York City as a novelist. His pace now appears frenetic: the first novel appeared in late 1898, followed by two in 1899, one in 1900, and another, the enormous *Octopus,* in 1901. The publication of *The Octopus* was followed by an outpouring of short stories and literary essays at the same time that he was writing *The Pit.*

In his articles, two interviews, and the relatively small number of letters that have survived, Norris revealed much about what he had seen and done, what he thought, and what he had read. He was no stranger to the first-person singular in an age of impressionistic journalism. But his self-disclosures could not be called "intimate." This is especially the case with regard to his early years; Norris himself provides virtually no assistance to a biographer. For example, Charles F. Lummis of *Land of Sunshine* magazine wrote Norris's employer and publisher Doubleday and McClure Company for biographical information. Norris began his 9 April 1900 reply, "Born Chicago, 1870," and he immediately leaped to the late 1880s. When Isaac F. Marcosson of the *Louisville Times* had asked for the same in early December 1898, Norris prefaced his sketch with, "I find it difficult to write about myself," and for some reason he erased his birth in Chicago and residence there until his fifteenth year: "I was 'bawn 'n raise' in California," he declared. Then he hopped to June 1895 and his twenty-fifth year.[1] When Franklin Walker wrote his biography of 1932, he had to depend almost entirely on Frank's brother Charles for information about the early years, 1870–85. Charles was born in 1881, and much of what he may have learned from family members or possibly recalled from his toddler days through his teens had become garbled by 1930–32, when Walker interviewed and corresponded with him.

Although he did not leave behind any kind of memoir, in his fictional and nonfiction writings Norris repeatedly reveals a preoccupation with how he was "bawn 'n raise'," that is, as a member of a particular racial and ethnic community. Thus, any consideration of the effects of that ancestry and recent family history upon Norris's developing self-conception and identity must begin with his awareness of something that his brother did not emphasize: his Anglo-Saxon pedigree and the advantages it conferred upon him genetically and, given the upper-class WASP circles in which he moved, environmentally.

Norris repeatedly enunciated his belief in the racial superiority of the Anglo-Saxon, which over time had become the Anglo-Norman, the British, and the Anglo-American type. So keen was his admiration that he looked beyond the Anglo-Saxons to include in his encomia the antecedent Frieslanders across the North Sea from England: the Angles, Saxons, Jutes, and Frisians who in the fifth century migrated to and established Anglo-Saxon hegemony in England. Known to Norris and his contemporaries as the Great March, the impulsive westering of this aggressive and acquisitive people, with not a little Viking heredity later added to the mix, accounted for the conquest of North America and the subjugation of the American West. Norris would several times appropriate the gallant scenario, most expansively in his 1902 essay "The Frontier Gone at Last": "When we—we Anglo-Saxons—busked ourselves for the first stage of the march, we began from that little historic reach of ground in the midst of the Friesland swamps, and we set our faces Westward, feeling no doubt the push of the Slav behind us. Then the Frontier was Britain . . . the Wild West of the Frisians of that century." Many years later, the trek was resumed in the New World, and "promptly a hundred thousand of the more hardy rushed to the skirmish-line and went at the [American] wilderness as only an Anglo-Saxon can," all the way to the Pacific. There came a pause, after which there were new reasons for celebration of Anglo-Saxon vigor:

> [O]n the first of May, 1898, a gun was fired in the Bay of Manila, still farther Westward, and in response the skirmish line crossed the Pacific, still push-ing the Frontier before it. Then came a cry for help from Legation Street in Peking, and as the first boat bearing its contingent of American marines took ground on the Asian shore, the Frontier—at last after so many centu-ries, after so many marches, after so much fighting, so much spilled blood, so much spent treasure—dwindled down and vanished; for the Anglo-Saxon in his course of empire had circled the globe and brought new civilization to the old civilization, and reached the starting point of history, the place from which the migrations began.[2]

To his credit, Norris at other times qualified his praise by limning the negative characteristics of the Anglo-Saxon that came along with the positive. He fully discloses the inhumanely self-serving, predatory traits of the type in *Moran of the Lady Letty, Vandover and the Brute,* and *The Pit.* Moreover, he sometimes wittingly or unwittingly undercuts his generalizations about inferior peoples by writing positively about subgroups and individuals who did not fit the contemporary inferior-race stereotypes. Still, he was a racist, as were the vast majority of his contemporaries in the western world. Even victims of racist thinking such as the novelist Charles W. Chesnutt, a turn-of-the-century champion of the African American group of which he acknowl-edged his membership, accepted the premise that racial inheritance made a difference. While Chesnutt was publicly guarded in his comments about his own makeup, he was keenly aware of his black-white "blood" ratio of between $7/8$ and $15/16$ white, and this shows repeatedly in his fictional writings. To the dismay of many readers today, it was no accident that the most sophisticated and accomplished African American characters he created resembled him genetically. Whiteness need not count for much with regard to certain racial subgroups, however: in "Uncle Wellington's Wives," Chesnutt, like Thoreau in *Walden,* Howells in *An Imperative Duty,* and Norris in *McTeague,* did not hesitate to rehearse the shortcomings of the lowly Irish American.

At the turn of the century in segregated America, upper-middle-class individuals such as Chesnutt, on one side of the color line, and Norris, on the other, often reflected a pride in family history that today may be associated with snobbery at the top of the socioeconomic ladder. Chesnutt displays aristocratic airs when distinguishing between those who were "shot free" in the Civil War and his own ancestors, who were "born free"—an important distinction in postbellum America. That all of his antecedents of whom he was aware were free men and women of color he did not hesitate to emphasize in his correspondence. Norris did not write of such familial matters so far as we know, but some of his short stories treat an analogous source of pride.

How Norris thought about Anglo-American bloodlines is especially clear in an 1895 story in a series of five entitled "Outward and Visible Signs." The fifth, subtitled "Thoroughbred," defines that superior condition by way of contrasting its hero with another American character named Jack Brunt, who is also descended from English immigrants. Here Norris turned to fine distinctions within the same gene pool, positing heredity and awareness of the high standards for behavior modelled by one's ancestors as determinants of character. "Perhaps it made no difference between the two men that Wesley Shotover's ancestors were framing laws, commanding privateers and making history generally in the days of the *Constitution* and the *Bonhomme Richard,* when Brunt's were being leased out to labor contractors to grub and grapple under the whip with the reluctant colonial soil." They are both "Americans and American-born," but there is yet another family-history difference distinguishing this thoroughbred: "[A] certain document that a Shotover had helped to draw up told them both that all men were created free and equal." The difference tells later when Shotover faces down an angry mob threatening Barry Vance, the woman he loves, while his rival, Brunt, flees the scene. "Perhaps," Norris speculates, "Shotover got the courage . . . he did out of his love for Barry, or perhaps he underestimated the danger or was too imaginative to appreciate it, or perhaps he felt the old privateer blood of the Shotovers of 1812 stir in him and believed that it all was what was expected of him as their descendant. Ancestors are sometimes an inconvenience in this way. A man has to live up to them."

The same thoroughbred reappears later the same year in another short story, "A Defense of the Flag." It is St. Patrick's Day, and San Francisco's Irish have arranged to have their homeland's colors flown atop City Hall. Shotover is indignant. He bribes a porter to gain access to the flagpole, lowers the Irish and raises the American flag, refuses to cooperate with the Irishmen he has enraged, even when threatened with a revolver, and is beaten senseless and carried off to jail. Most pertinent is his ancestral motivation: "Shotover was American-bred and American-born, and his father and mother before him and their father and mother before them, and so on and back till one brought up in the hold of a ship called the *Mayflower,* further back than which it is not necessary to go."[3]

Shotover's family history is not exactly that of Frank Norris, whose patriotism will later be seen to have been almost as fervent. But Norris's lineage is traceable to 1620 when the Pilgrims arrived, back to England and Scotland, and then to Holland at the time that the Pilgrims resided in Leiden, and even "further back than which it is not necessary to go." When Norris in 1898 waxed chauvinistic during the Spanish-American War, displayed in 1896 the airs of an Anglophile as he demeaned South Africa's Boers, and throughout his writing career privileged certain types of Americans over others, he did so at least in part because of the identity conferred upon him by the confluence of two bloodlines resulting from the marriage of B. F. Norris and Gertrude Doggett.

As a Doggett, Gertrude could claim a much more illustrious past than her husband. The first of that name, Thomas Doggett, did not cut a fine figure in Massachusetts when he arrived. He was a virtually penniless yeoman who sailed from England in May 1637 on the *Marey Anne.* It was not until the death of his second of three wives, Elizabeth Humphrey, that he inherited the land accounting for his rise to prosperity. But Gertrude's lineage actually went further back, to 1620, thanks to Thomas Doggett's great-grandson and namesake. He married Joanna Fuller and thus gave Frank Norris a claim to fame like Shotover's. She was the great-granddaughter of Samuel Fuller, a passenger on the fabled *Mayflower.* Other notable forbears of Gertrude from the seventeenth century include: Nathaniel Wales, whom Richard Mather (father of Increase and grandfather of Cotton Mather) mentions in his journal as a shipmate on the *James,* which docked at Boston on 17 August 1635; Wales's father-in-law, Humphrey Atherton, a Massachusetts legislator; and, on the other side of the Atlantic Ocean, the Reverend John Forbes, a distinguished divine of the Church of Scotland, expelled by James I in 1606 because of his contributions to the growing influence of Scottish Presbyterianism. Forbes emigrated in 1611 to Middleburg, Holland, near the English Separatists—the *Mayflower* pilgrims—then living in Leiden. Not himself a Separatist, he was eventually elevated to a bishopric and did not join the Puritans of several varieties who were emigrating to the New World. However, his son John Fobes—who had dropped the r from his surname—did.[4]

Successive generations expanded the landholdings of Thomas Doggett. His grandson, also a Thomas Doggett, took the financial interests in the family in a new direction by becoming involved in shipping at the site on the North River in Marshfield, Massachusetts, where his grandfather had ultimately settled. But the next Thomas Doggett, who married Joanna Fuller, brought the family back to land-based investment and agriculture after his father's death in 1736. He sold the property in Marshfield and put the yield into real estate in Middleboro, thereby providing a healthy inheritance for his three sons—the youngest of whom, Simeon, was Gertrude's great-grandfather. He made the most of his share by learning carpentry and erecting a substantial home in Middleboro after marrying a devout Anglican, Abigail Pratt, from North Carolina. Although Simeon was a staunch Tory during the American Revolution, he managed to keep his property and died a respectable American at the age of eighty-seven in 1823.

With Simeon the Doggett family had attained a social and economic position that allowed the new generation to contemplate vocations other than farming and river transport. The youngest of his three sons, Simeon Jr., graduated Brown University in 1788. As his 1852 biographer noted, the elder Simeon, "though not rich, was in easy circumstance, and was able to . . . maintain him there."[5] At Brown, though, the younger Simeon took turns in his way of thinking not at all intended by his father. After diligent study of classical authors and prolonged reflection on religious doctrine, Simeon Jr. concluded that the Anglicanism of his parents did not square with his conception of Christianity, and he was ordained a Congregational minister in 1793. Given to further reflection and swayed by the rationalism of the Enlightenment, he made the leap to Unitarianism when serving in Rhode Island, delivering a subsequently published sermon that openly defended Unitarian doctrine. Since he taught as well as preached, 1796 found him in Taunton, Massachusetts, where he was the first preceptor of the Bristol Academy, a position he held until 1813, before moving to Mendon for a ministerial position. In 1831, it was on to Raynham for another until 1845. When he died there in 1852, he was the oldest Unitarian minister in the country. Simeon is thus a particularly important figure vis-à-vis the familial cultural influences on Norris's mother and her siblings two generations later; and his marriage certainly did not injure the reputation of the Doggetts. He was the husband of Anonima Warner "Nancy" Fobes, the daughter of one of the descendants of the seventeenth-century Bishop John Forbes of Scotland and Holland. Nancy's father was also a minister, the Reverend Perez Fobes, a Harvard graduate who was by turns Congregational and Unitarian and who became a professor and then an administrator at Brown. Nancy's mother, née Prudence Wales, was the daughter of the Reverend John Wales, another Harvard graduate.

Other distinguished New Englanders figure in the lines of descent leading to Gertrude Doggett Norris. Amidst a much greater tangle of names and occupations traceable through the American Doggetts, back to the English Fullers, and then through the Dutch Lees to the Hungerfords (a Wiltshire clan in the 1100s), suffice it to say that the Doggett, Fobes, and Wales families are the principal ones bearing upon what it meant to be Gertrude.[6]

Noteworthy in all three family lines is the strong tradition of clericalism that led Charles Norris to generalize about his mother's Unitarian background when interviewed by Franklin Walker. As significant is the valuing of education in these family circles. For example, of the five sons of Gertrude's paternal grandparents who lived to maturity, one became a territorial judge who cofounded Jacksonville, Florida. Another was a medical doctor. A third practiced for a brief period as an attorney, before his death at twenty-two. Not surprisingly, one of Gertrude's uncles served as a minister in Bridgewater, Massachusetts. Gertrude's father Samuel was politically active in Mendon, Massachusetts, and served in that state's General Court.

Samuel Wales Doggett was born in 1800. Like his older brother, Judge John Locke Doggett of Jacksonville, Florida, he read law and migrated to the South from Massachusetts. Practicing first in Abbeville, South Carolina, he moved on to Charleston, where in 1824 he married Harriet Wotton, who was born in that seaport in 1804 to James and Chloe Campbell Wotton. Like his father, Samuel became an educator. He founded and directed for fifteen years a female seminary; and, with his brother-in-law James A. Wotton, he instituted the first free public school in Charleston.

We at last come to Gertrude's brothers and sisters. Samuel's oldest son and namesake, born in 1824, accompanied his parents to Massachusetts in 1838 when a cholera epidemic struck. He returned to Charleston in 1844, after teaching in Raynham and Bridgewater, and in 1845 he opened a seminary in Jacksonville, Florida. Teaching next in New Orleans, he was drawn by late 1850 to the gold rush and California's El Dorado County. By 1858 he was in San Francisco, where he served as secretary to the Board of Education, practiced law, and became involved in real estate. The next son, Simeon Locke Doggett, born in 1829, was admitted to the Massachusetts bar in 1856. He moved to Dubuque, Iowa, where he opened a high school and taught German, French, Latin, and Greek.[7] William Alfred Doggett, born in 1839, differed from his brothers in that he went into business, selling clocks and jewelry in Chicago by 1858 and sewing machines in Lincoln, Nebraska, by 1880.[8] Theophilus Melancthon Doggett, born in 1833, was practicing law by 1857 in Chicago.[9] A soldier in the Union army, he did not survive the Battle of Shiloh in 1862. Lawrence Bryant Doggett, born in 1845, also died a Union soldier and prisoner of war at Andersonville, Georgia, in August 1864.[10] These latter two sons of Samuel were not forgotten in Gertrude's family. When reflecting upon the significance of the Spanish-American War, their nephew Frank listed the most memorable events in American military history, citing Shiloh but remembering as well the viciously inhumane treatment of Union soldiers at Andersonville.[11]

Gertrude also had three sisters: Julia Harriet Doggett Wheeler, Malvina Campbell Doggett Hale, and Narcissa Newton Doggett Carleton, born in 1827, 1831, and 1836, respectively. Despite the head of the family's having established a ladies' seminary in Charleston, their marriages did not suggest as great a concern for their education as for the Doggett sons: Julia married a farm laborer, Malvina a house painter, and Narcissa a boot-factory worker.[12] For all three it was a step down from the home environment maintained by a father who, in 1870, could estimate his personal and real estate value at fifty thousand dollars.[13] Gertrude was the exceptional daughter. Born on 20 May 1841 in Mendon, the youngest girl, she was either doted upon by a father and mother who gave her opportunities not enjoyed by her sisters, or she bridled before their lackluster lot, seizing opportunities for sophistication and personal advancement and not marrying until she was in her mid-twenties. Like her paternal grandfather, father, and two brothers, she qualified herself for teaching. As they were wont to change careers when greener pastures beckoned, she too leaped the fence, taking a much greater risk than they ever did. In the 1860s, acting was not a respectable profession for a woman, and it was a remarkable choice for one whose family history was chock-full of practicing and preaching Anglicans, Congregationalists, and Unitarians.

Gertrude's theatrical career was short-lived but highly profitable. Had she not left the classroom for the stage, she would not have attracted the eye of the increasingly wealthy Chicagoan whom she married in a ceremony presided over by a Unitarian minister.

Gertrude Doggett Norris. (Courtesy of the Bancroft Library, University of California at Berkeley.)

Of the Norris family there is much less to tell, especially about B. F.'s paternal line. Gertrude married "up" financially when she became B. F.'s wife, but she was less successful in terms of adding thereby to the formidable gallery of distinguished ancestors that her own children might point to with admiration and see as role-model figures. Unlike the Doggetts, Norris children were not given names evoking high intellectual or artistic achievement, such as Melancthon, Newton, Locke, and Bryant. That Frank Norris and his father were named after Benjamin Franklin was not quite the same thing, since Franklin was better known across the United States for his "practical" achievements as a poor boy made good and the clever common-sense aphorisms of his perennially popular *Poor Richard's Almanack* than for his flights into the realms of higher thought. B. F. and his father Josiah, born in New York in 1803, were not thinkers but doers—the latter scratching a living from the soil, and the former escaping from the farm to more profitable enterprises as soon as he could. B. F.'s mother, born Lydia Colton in 1805 at Longmeadow, Massachusetts, was fully occupied as a farmer's wife and mother of six.

Lydia Colton did have one thing in common with Gertrude Doggett: Her fourth great-grandfather, George Colton, antecedents unknown, also appeared in Massachusetts in the seventeenth century.[14] He settled in Longmeadow, where he and his offspring began to develop their landholdings. Family lands subdivided for inheritances did not, however, continue long to support Colton's descendants, and B. F.'s grandfather, Henry Colton, born in 1771, had to go out on his own to make his fortune with his wife, née Lydia Booth, in 1770 at Enfield, Connecticut. Trying his luck as a farmer in upstate New York and then eastern Michigan, he apparently met with modest success as an agriculturalist and spent the remainder of his days not far from the town of Pittsfield, near Ann Arbor.

In 1825, B. F.'s mother married Josiah Norris—antecedents undiscovered—near Rochester, New York, at Brighton.[15] Accompanying Lydia's parents to Pittsfield and living there until both had died, the Norrises moved farther west to Austerlitz, just east of Grand Rapids, with their five children.[16] Lydia had given birth to four sons and a daughter: David B. (1827), James Henry (1830), Sarah M. (1833), and Josiah B. (1839). B. F. was the second youngest, born on the farm at Pittsfield on 10 January 1836.[17]

The history of B. F.'s siblings is as plainspun as that of their grandparents and parents. David moved away early, and his occupation is unknown, since he was not listed in the 1850 census. He died in 1857, leaving a three-year-old daughter, Lydia Estelle, to be reared by his parents. James, who went by his middle name, Henry, inherited the family farm in 1865, sold it four years later, and moved to Grand Haven in Muskegon County, where he became an engineer in a sawmill owned by a relative of his wife. In 1900, working as a night watchman, he died from burns caused by an explosion at the Grand Rapids Vapor Steam Company.[18] When Sarah expired is not known: listed in the 1850 U.S. Census, she does not reappear in that of 1860. But if *The Pit* is true to the Norris family's oral history as Frank knew it, the testimony of the novel's hero to his departed sister Sadie indicates that she passed on early, well before her brother B. F. had made his fortune as a businessman.[19] His brother, Josiah B. Norris, left the farm for the Civil War, serving in the Sixth Michigan Cavalry as a wagoner from September 1862 to March 1863 and then reenlisting. He was honorably discharged in April 1864. By 1866 Josiah had moved to Chicago, where he was associated in business with B. F. until 1872. He described himself as a "traveling agent" in his military pension application in 1882, and the retired salesman remained in Chicago until his death in 1922.[20] B. F.'s was the single and grand success story in his generation's chapter of Norris family history.

Living at Pittsfield until after he turned fourteen, B. F. crossed the state with his parents to Austerlitz but did not remain long with them. As Charles related to Walker and others, B. F. early began to suffer from a lifelong hip ailment that caused a pronounced limp. He was thus not suited for manual labor on the eighty-acre farm his father purchased north of the Grand River; nor was he amenable to being placed at a boarding school in Grand Rapids. When his father brought him to town for that purpose, B. F. bolted. He entered a watch and jewelry store searching for employment, and he found it on the spot. No documentation is available indicating which store set him on the road to wealth, but Aaron Dikeman, the first jeweler in Michigan doing business west of Ann Arbor and by 1850 the most prosperous, is the one most likely to have had sufficient business to permit the hiring of an apprentice in his store on Monroe Street, just north of the Michigan Central railroad line.[21] Though Charles believed that his father apprenticed for two years and then became a salesman for a New York City firm, exactly what followed in the 1850s as B. F. initiated his career in the timepiece and jewelry trade remains unknown. However, that the seventeen-year-old considered Grand Rapids his home in 1853 is evident in his personal Bible.[22]

Four years later, on 9 May 1857, he married seventeen-year-old Ruth A.

Rossiter in Lockport, Illinois, southwest of Chicago. Their daughter Florence was born in the late spring of 1859, and in 1860 the three were still living in the same town on the Illinois and Michigan Canal. Listed by a census taker as a watchmaker with real property valued at eight hundred dollars and a personal estate of five hundred dollars, the onetime apprentice provided boarding for an apprentice of his own, eighteen-year-old Theodore B. Sterrin.[23] B. F. would maintain a residence in Lockport until 1867, though he was commuting on the Chicago and Alton Railroad to Chicago where, by 1865, he was doing business and listed in its city directory.[24] In the meantime, at some point after 1853, B. F. had opened the first brick-and-mortar establishment of his own farther south on the Chicago and Alton line: a jewelry store in Peoria, Illinois. So related a journalist for the *Peoria Transcript,* whose encomium was quoted in 1872 in the *Thirteenth Annual Price-List* of B. F. Norris and Co., by this point no longer a retail operation in Peoria but a wholesale one conducted on a national scale.[25] The journalist enthusiastically recalled a recent visit—circa 1870, it appears—to B. F.'s impressive showrooms at 197 Broadway in New York City and 123 Lake Street in Chicago. When B. F. opened and closed the Manhattan offices and decided to consolidate his business in Chicago cannot be determined; neither the New York branch office nor B. F.'s personal address, oddly enough, appeared in a directory. What is known, though, is that along the way to the successful establishment of a major midwestern wholesale jewelry house, B. F.—like his eighteenth-century namesake—was not inclined to tolerate associates who might retard his steady advancement toward membership in the upper middle class.

An in-law and a partner in the 1860s, Henry D. Rossiter, did not make the grade. In 1866, B. F.'s brother Josiah replaced him; and well before 1872, when he went off on his own, Josiah had to make way for a lean and hungry young Scottish immigrant named William M. Alister, who joined B. F. as a clerk and bookkeeper in 1865 and would become an in-law himself on 31 December 1873, when he married Narcissa Doggett Carleton's daughter, Gertrude's niece Ella.[26] By 1884, the two men were partners in the firm of B. F. Norris, Alister, and Company. B. F. had now risen well above middle-class standing. The 1870 U.S. Census cited his personal estate as twenty-thousand dollars, up from five hundred a decade earlier; and, since 1860, the value of his real estate holdings had risen from eight hundred to fifty thousand dollars. Two domestic servants were in his employ. In 1880 the census included three servants and a coachman in his household.[27]

The aggressive businessman who had found his stride as a traveling sales representative in the 1850s did not fare so well in his home life in the 1860s. Having accumulated capital sufficient to raise himself to the proprietorship of a store, he did not settle down in Peoria. The small but flourishing canal town of the mid-nineteenth century was only a step toward the next venture. Having amassed the capital, he cast his lot at the crossroads of midwestern commerce, Chicago, as well as in the heart of the national trade in jewelry, watches, and silverware, lower Manhattan. As he once commuted by rail and river between Lockport and Peoria, and then shuttled back and forth between Lockport and Chicago, his intrastate travel extended to interstate as he established a forward position in New York City, where the *Peoria Transcript* journalist found him. That is, the erstwhile traveling salesman became himself the employer of the sales representatives he dispatched from Chicago. But even after he closed his New York offices, he never ceased packing suitcases and trunks nor cutting short the time he spent at home as he again and again hit the rails for business, pleasure, and health-related reasons. The peripatetic, often absent father and husband whom Frank Norris came to know had well before 1870 established a dominant pattern of behavior that, as will later be seen, had much to do with his second divorce.

The first divorce occurred circa 1867 when, according to William M. Alister, B. F. ended his relationship with Ruth and their daughter. Alister could be no more specific about the date than to offer a rough approximation: "Must have been in 1867." One day B. F. left his home at Lockport for Chicago, never to return. Charles did not mention this sordid episode in Norris family history to Franklin Walker. But a city directory confirms Alister's testimony given when B. F.'s will was probated in 1900, for in 1867 B. F. was boarding at the Revere House in Chicago at the corner of Clark and Kinzie—and courting the twenty-five-year-old actress Gertrude Doggett, who had made her stage debut at McVicker's Theatre on Christmas Eve, 1866. What became of Ruth Rossiter Norris and her daughter Florence is not known, save that Alister testified to their deaths having occurred prior to 1900.[28]

As her brothers and sisters were one after another leaving the Mendon, Massachusetts, homestead, Gertrude Doggett found her own occasion for departure in the invitation of her brother Simeon to come to Dubuque, Iowa, and teach in his school.[29] She arrived there, it appears, in the late 1850s and, by 1861, had acquired sufficient experience to earn her a position in Chicago. The city directory does not reveal where she taught that year; it only cites her occupation as teacher.[30] Her position in 1862–63, however, was at the Kinzie School, at the corner of Ohio and LaSalle Streets, where she worked for four years. The records of this school, published each year in the annual report of the Chicago Department of Public Instruction, depict a young woman almost as upwardly mobile in her respective professional sphere as her husband-to-be. In her second year she earned somewhere between $300 and $425, the figure depending on how much her previous experience counted. The next year's report, however, indicates that her talents were much appreciated. If she earned the maximum indicated in the previous report, she had seen her salary rise by roughly 25 percent to $525. This was a higher salary than those of ten other faculty members; only the principal of the school made more, and the head assistant made twenty-five dollars less than she. Gertrude had been promoted to the rank of principal instructor, teaching approximately eighty students in the ninth and tenth grades. In her fourth year, two of her colleagues, who were assistants to the principal, passed her to earn seven hundred dollars each. Still, her salary rose again by nearly 20 percent to $625, as she taught some seventy-five eighth- and ninth-grade students,[31] whereupon she ended her association with the Kinzie School to pursue a stage career.

How much Gertrude had developed her talents as a thespian prior to the move to Iowa her son Charles did not know. Her nephew, Laurence Locke Doggett, Simeon's son, did recall, though, that his father "took a great deal of pains to train [Aunt Gertrude] in elocution and literature, especially the plays of Shakespeare."[32] Complementing this datum in Laurence's autobiography is another in the 24 December 1866 issue of the *Chicago Republican:* "Miss Gertrude Doggett . . . has for sometime been a faithful teacher in our public schools, pursuing her dramatic studies after a hard day's work in the school-room."[33] Her mentor was Anna Cruise Cowell, a leading actress of the era;[34] and, the same day that the *Republican* blurb appeared, Gertrude moved beyond invisibility as a bit player learning the fundamentals. She starred as Elvira in Richard Brinsley Sheridan's adaptation of August von Kotzebue's *The Spaniards in Peru,* a repertory standard known as *Pizarro.* In her first professional appearance in a major role at McVicker's Theatre, Gertrude impressed the *Republican* reviewer as an actress able "to inspire favorable feelings in all hearts." That was only the beginning of a warm appreciation noting the predictable signs of her inexperience but ranking her performance well above that of the typical neophyte. Very likely a male, the author was obviously charmed by the attractive Miss Doggett:

She is youthful, fine-looking, and graceful in her movements; absolute perfection in her part, and much more self-possessed before the footlights than
is often the case in "first appearances." Something too mechanical, perhaps,
in her gestures, but not more than was to be expected from a lady anxious
to perfect herself in the "business" of the stage. As she gains experience,
and learns to rely upon her own resources rather than the instruction of the
teacher, this mechanical action will become easy and natural, and, of course,
all the more perfect because of the long and careful drilling she has received
in the *minutia* of stage attitudes and expression. Miss Doggett certainly has
reason, and her friends also, to be satisfied with her first appearance. She has
many of the elements of success, and we have reason to know that they are
backed with a determination to rise in her profession that would win laurels
under far less favorable auspices.[35]

Other reviewers were even more positive. The *Evening Journal* predicted
that Gertrude "will assuredly attain a high position in the profession." The
Tribune dwelt upon her "form" as "singularly graceful and dignified" and her
countenance and tone of voice as "indicative of deep and fine sensibilities":
"[S]he has asserted herself an artiste of no ordinary talent."[36]

On 31 December and New Year's Day she went on to display her talent
as a comedienne in the role of the Duchess de Torrenueva in James Robinson Planché's *Faint Heart Never Won Fair Lady.* How much training she
had undergone was signalled by her next role, playing Emilia to Cowell's
Desdemona on 5 January 1867.[37] Not confirmed is Charles's testimony that
she joined a road company shortly thereafter; nor is it determinable, despite
searches conducted by several scholars, how much acting followed her successful Chicago debut.[38] What is clear is that B. F. Norris pursued her and
that the quintessential bourgeois appealed strongly to the budding artiste.

They were married under peculiar circumstances that spring, on 27 May
1867.[39] The ceremony did not take place in the church of the clergyman
who presided. Instead, likely because of the transdenominational proscription of marriage to a divorced person, they were privately joined in matrimony at 295 Chicago Avenue, the home of the Reverend Robert Collyer,
an English immigrant and Methodist minister who in 1859 transferred his
allegiance to Unitarianism and that year began his two decades of service
to the Unity Church at the corner of Chicago and Dearborn Streets.[40] The
marriage thus began under a cloud, and the narrative possibly related to it
would have brought to mind those of the "penny dreadfuls." Three decades

later, Theodore Dreiser recycled the basic elements in *Sister Carrie.* The wayward, financially well-off husband pursues the attractive young actress at a vulnerable moment in her life, when her career may not have been taking off as she thought it would. Confirming the contemporaneous mythology of morally loose women on the stage, the young actress perhaps lures the stage-door-Johnny away from his wife and child; but, whatever the exact circumstances leading to B. F.'s alienation from Ruth and Florence, the actress accepts his proffered wealth and the easy lifestyle of an upper-middle-class wife that it ensured. Less demeaning scenarios are possible. For example, the only scriptural warrant for divorce was marital infidelity—B. F.'s or Ruth's. If that was the case, one cannot now tell which one was more sinned against than sinning. But it may have been that B. F.'s absences from home and preoccupation with business accounted for waywardness on his first wife's part. Did Frank's novelist brother Charles hear something of his father's side of the story? It may be significant that the hero of his *Pig Iron* (1925), who resembles B. F. in several respects, falls in love with a prostitute, lives with her for a short while, is abandoned by her, and sends monthly checks to her for decades. This might approximate what Charles had been told by B. F. or his mother. His mother certainly did not dwell upon the challenge to her own respectability that was her marriage to a divorcé. What actually transpired in 1866–67, however, was effectively buried in the years that followed. It was not until over 120 years after the fact that James B. Stronks uncovered B. F.'s first marriage while searching for documents related to Norris family history in the Cook County Records Office.[41]

By 5 March 1870, when Frank was born, the Norrises had successfully donned the cloak of normalcy. Their histories had not been the subject of newspaper gossip, since Gertrude and B. F. did not assume a high profile in social life until they moved to San Francisco. To all appearances, they were just another married couple approaching middle age—plain old nouveau riche among hundreds of their kind in Gilded Age Chicago. They even joined the Episcopal church.

3

THE CHICAGO YEARS

Ironically, it is less difficult to trace Frank Norris's lineage through several lines back to and beyond the seventeenth century than it is to discover what it was like for him to reach adolescence in the home of his parents. When he died in 1900, B. F. left behind no documents descriptive of his son. His mother grieved Frank's early death until her passing in 1919, but only brief references to Gertrude's frequent comments about him occur in the correspondence of his brother, Charles G. Norris, and Charles's wife, Kathleen Thompson Norris. Unfortunately, they had to do with Frank as Gertrude remembered him in his late twenties and early thirties.[1] As to Charles as an information source, he was eleven years younger than Frank and only four when in 1885 the Norris family left Chicago for San Francisco. Franklin Walker wrote in his 1930 interview notes that Charles "doesn't remember much about Frank" before 1886. And yet, unfortunately, Charles exercised a profound influence on how his brother's life, through age sixteen, has been pictured and interpreted.

When Charles was overseeing the production of the Argonaut Manuscript Limited Edition of Frank's works published in late 1928, he served as the expert consultant for several of the distinguished authors who wrote introductions for the ten volumes. Among them was the California novelist and short-story writer Charles Caldwell Dobie, who produced a brief—but, as of then, the most detailed—description of the early history and home life of the family.[2] It offered the inspirational tale of young B. F. bidding farewell to his crusty, emotionally detached father, turning from Michigan farm life and the possibility of formal education to apprenticeship in the jewelry and timepiece trade. B. F.'s own propensity for crustiness is not at all touched upon in this rags-to-riches encomium.

Dobie traces in similar fashion the teaching career of the more sophisticated Gertrude Doggett with marked aesthetic interests and a decided flair for the histrionic. According to the regional mythology concerning New England and the South still current in the 1920s, hers was the "mixed blood of a Northern and Southern mother." Thus, reasons Dobie, the passionate and easily excited "southern" element in her temperament accounts for her rising above the dictates of a New England conscience with her daring trial in 1866–67 of the disreputable calling of actress. Invoking the seventeenth-century imagery of the worldly, far-from-pious cavaliers who served Charles I, as opposed to that English king's dour, Puritan adversaries, Dobie goes on admiringly: "In estimating [her] character one must always take into account the dashing Cavalier strain from [South Carolina] running like a shining thread through the somberness of the Puritan birthright." And again he indulges in fabulous rhetoric: "Determination from New England, dash and a sense of the dramatic from [South Carolina]—here was a combination that was hard to beat."[3] Dobie does not say so, but it was also hard to bear at times.

It was no accident that Dobie so positively portrayed this strong-willed extrovert, whom Kathleen Thompson Norris described as "a woman of great violence of emotion."[4] One would be hard put to imagine a more devoted son than his information source, Charles, was to the dominating yet emotionally needy, self-pitying mother pictured in the letters he exchanged with Kathleen during their 1908–9 courtship. What Gertrude had suffered in life was fully disclosed to the sympathetic and eager-to-please fiancée in San Francisco. Charles, employed in New York City and responding in his letters to Kathleen's discoveries in family history, could go on at great length in a compassionate way about the travails of being Gertrude Norris: her husband's adamant opposition to her ever returning to the stage, where she might after all have become a star; the early deaths of four children; and her divorce at a time when the stigma of the "grass widow" negatively affected her social standing in 1890s San Francisco.

That Gertrude expected and received the full measure of support and appreciation from her offspring is beyond question. How many young men would host their mothers during their honeymoons, as Charles did? For two weeks Kathleen and he spent the evenings following their 30 April 1909 wedding in New York City listening to a practiced elocutionist, famous in San Francisco for her public performances of Robert Browning's poetry. During the honeymoon, she gave readings of the late Frank Norris's works as well as others by writers such as Rudyard Kipling and Francis Thompson. They heard all of *McTeague* and *The Pit* and a goodly portion of Browning's *The Ring and the Book*.[5]

Frank was still living with his mother in 1898 when, at twenty-seven, he moved from San Francisco to New York City. One notes in *The Pit* that the heroine's literary-minded younger sister, Page Dearborn, was cut from the same cloth as Gertrude in one respect. Relating that her beau "wants to be more than a mere money-getting machine" and "to cultivate his mind and understand art and literature," Page announces, "I'm going to read to him. We're going to begin with the 'Ring and the Book.'"[6] The tweaking allusion to Gertrude that could be understood only by family members and close friends was, of course, not an unkind one. Simply put, Gertrude loved to perform.

Frank's letters to her have not survived,[7] and he refers to her in none of those addressed to others. By way of direct communication, all we have are the copies of *McTeague* and *The Octopus* that he inscribed to her and his formal dedication of *Blix* to "My Mother."[8] But in 1892, he was the twenty-two-year-old fair-haired son to whom Gertrude turned for emotional support when her marriage was in its death throes, and his role as comforter thereafter could not have been wholly different from that assumed by Charles after Frank's death.

For what it was like to be Gertrude's son before 1886, one cannot turn to Charles, who remembered nothing from his own experience with Frank until that year. Despite the absence of direct comments regarding his mother, it is to Frank, perforce, that one returns as the more reliable source of information of the kind seen in his characterization of Page Dearborn in *The Pit*. Thanks to this and his other fictional uses of his personal experiences in that Chicago-based novel, and even after allowing for exaggerations, we can infer a good deal in general about some of the maternal, and paternal, influences at work during Frank's youth. Unlike his brother, who never made artistic use of his experiences with his mother, Frank was capable of viewing her sympathetically and critically in the medium of prose fiction.

Charles informed Walker that Gertrude had indeed been the model for his brother's heroine in *The Pit*, Page's sister Laura. "There is no question that my brother had my mother in mind for the character of Laura Dearborn." Charles may well have told Dobie the same in 1928, but if so, Dobie did not register the full implications of his remark. Charles may have had in mind only Gertrude's resemblance to the novel's disarmingly attractive, talented, and dynamic heroine. In fact, the character Frank fashioned also displays many less-than-admirable, quite annoying traits. This markedly self-absorbed heroine, the prima donna of *The Pit* whose "grand manner" irritates even her devoted sister Page, also hopes for the theatrical career that Gertrude attempted to launch. Like Gertrude, Laura does not become the new Modjeska or Bernhardt but marries instead. When her marriage sours, as Gertrude's did, there is good reason to think that Laura might have become a star. Histrionic is not the word; she is positively operatic in her flamboyant reactions to the neglect of a restless, work-oriented, ever-absent husband—like B. F. Laura's bloodlines are also New Englandish and southern, and she repeatedly displays the trait in Gertrude noted by Kathleen Norris, "great violence of emotion." Indeed, the mood swings Gertrude's son assigned to Laura suggest manic-depression. Dobie, however, saw none of what *The Pit* suggested about life in the Norris household in later years and perhaps during Frank's childhood as well.

When celebrating the admirable traits of B. F.'s character, Dobie again missed the cues that *The Pit* offers. He did not observe anything of B. F. in Laura's husband Curtis, whose ardor when near-maniacally courting Laura has cooled dramatically after three years of marriage, resulting in their living essentially separate lives—precisely one of Gertrude's complaints when she took B. F. to court for alimony in 1894. *Not* relevant in the novel, of course, is the happy resolution of Laura's and Curtis's marital problems, save as an indication of one long-term consequence of Frank's having been a witness for years of the failure of his parents' marriage. This is not to say that he was psychologically scarred for life, but all of his novels and many of his short stories deal with the negative and positive dynamics of male-female relationships. *The Pit*, *A Man's Woman*, and *Blix* are especially significant in that they address the question of adjustments that might be made to ensure the likelihood of marital success.

That Dobie did not reflect upon these consequences of a troubled home when describing Frank's preoccupations as a writer was no fluke. Charles appears to have been so anxious to put a positive face upon the histories of his parents that Dobie could assign only one blemish to B. F. It was a trait over which he made much, since he did not care for the Presbyterian—or Calvinistic—personality type rapidly sketched for him by Charles. As to Gertrude, Dobie exercised the same license. Despite her "dashing" southern "sense of the dramatic," she too was a scion of the Puritans. Otherwise, though, Charles's and Frank's parents were just about perfect.

In fairness to Charles, it should be remembered that much of what he did learn about his parents' relationship had, after 1892, been filtered through the medium of a "scorned woman." Gertrude's fury over abandonment by B. F. caused her to list herself as "widow" in city directories years before B. F. died. But Charles did deliberately dissemble when communicating with Dobie. The paean to ideal parenthood into which Dobie launches, after announcing that Frank Norris lived a relatively untroubled life characterized by "romantic moments but no brutal ones," is preposterous. Nor "do we find," Dobie wrote, "a single red, raw instance in the lives of his parents. The early history of the elder Norrises is full of struggle against circumstances, but there are no sordid passages in it, not even what one would call a bare-knuckle encounter."[9] Dobie was kept in the dark about the divorce and the tawdry developments that precipitated it. He was similarly unaware of the "bare-knuckle" brawl over the financial settlement demanded by Gertrude, reported in sensational detail in Chicago and San Francisco newspapers.

Exactly when it became apparent in Chicago or San Francisco that B. F.'s and Gertrude's marriage was on the rocks is moot. *The Pit's* hero and heroine are not, of course, exact representations of Norris's parents; and, although it is tempting to do so, one cannot blithely assume that the termination of connubial bliss after three years, pictured in *The Pit,* directly correlates with Gertrude and B. F.'s relationship at the time that Frank was born (almost three years after their wedding ceremony). But, at the risk of engaging in cartoonlike simplicities, one can assume that their incompatibility was manifest by the time that Frank was in his early teens. On the one hand, B. F. was the quintessential bourgeois whose nightlife recreations eventuated in his luring an attractive young actress from a life of toil into one of leisure. This adventure reaching its finale, he returned to the one thing he knew well and enjoyed pursuing for the long term, his business interests, until another woman and adventure entered his life in the early 1890s. On the other hand, Gertrude was the retired artiste and former teacher with wide-ranging cultural interests not shared by the burgher husband who would, according to Charles, make light of her son Frank's aesthetic inclinations. Cartoonlike or not, it is far from coincidental that in *The Octopus* as well as *The Pit* we find the same kind of incompatibility illustrated: Magnus Derrick is the restless agribusinessman; his wife Annie is the onetime instructor at a seminary for young ladies whose passion for poetry her husband does not share.

Given the wealth that B. F. brought to the marriage and the luxuries it bestowed upon a young woman previously supporting herself in low-paying occupations, the only limitations upon Gertrude's free-and-easy lifestyle were biological. In Chicago she conceived and delivered five children: Grace Colton, 1869; Benjamin Franklin Jr., 1870; Florence Colton, 1871; Albert Lester, 1877; and Charles Gilman, 1881. (Lester, like Frank, would be known by his middle name.) But in the circles in which Gertrude moved, motherhood brought few onerous obligations. Domestic servants resided in her homes; nurses and governesses were affordable. The sole, memorable manifestation of maternal care Charles recalled for Walker was that his mother regularly performed readings—of romances, novels, poems, and dramatic selections— for her boys. And thus the seemliness of Gertrude's interactions with her son and his bride as audience during their honeymoon: it was her way of relating to others as teacher, actress, society dame, and even as mother. When travel interrupted the normal course of her children's education, tutors may have been employed, though there is no evidence that this was a concern of either parent. And, while the society columns of the *Chicago Tribune* do not confirm this, those of the *San Francisco Chronicle* indicate that Gertrude was remarkably ambitious socially and footloose—though not as often in transit as her husband was after the family had moved from Chicago to San Francisco in 1885.[10] His jewelry and watch business remained headquartered in Chicago, and he was often away from home for that reason as well as others having to do with his health problems and the need for recreation at fashionable resorts that he shared with Gertrude. Gertrude declared in 1894, when taking legal action against him to secure an appropriate alimony, that B. F. was a resident of San Francisco for nine years, during which he spent "fully one-half of that time in Chicago and in traveling about the world."[11]

The same social columns in both cities, chronicling the comings and goings of many other parents in the beau monde, indicate that Gertrude and B. F. were typical for their class. Biographies of prominent aristocrats of the Gilded Age abound in descriptions of similar arrangements in which parenting was far from a full-time occupation and marriages of convenience were hardly uncommon. Still, Gertrude and B. F. were, by modern standards, rather careless with the sacred charge that proper Victorians made much of when reflecting upon the noblest of institutions, the family. Norris's writings are not rich in depictions of happy homes and parents involved in their children's lives. Indeed, few children appear at all, and demonstratively affectionate parents like Dyke in *The Octopus* and Mrs. Sieppe in *McTeague* are exceptional.

In 1932, Walker—guided to his conclusions by Charles and Dobie—depicted the early years in Chicago and San Francisco in positive terms, with no references to negative developments. He was less laudatory toward B. F. and Gertrude than the fulsome Dobie; but, overall, he was considerably less negative in that, unlike Dobie, he did not have an axe to grind. Dobie's essay, instead of continuing to detail the family history in glowing terms as it had at its beginning, became an exposé on two fronts: it was designed to appeal to the subscribers of H. L. Mencken's monthly magazine, *American Mercury*, in which it was first printed.[12]

Mencken was famous for debunking and railing against bourgeois American life, and he did not discourage iconoclastic Dobie from overturning a popular misconception concerning the author of *McTeague*, which had recently been adapted for film by Erich von Stroheim. That this gritty 1899 portrait of life among the lowly was written from the bottom up, from the perspective of one who knew intimately the ways of an American underclass, was, Dobie announced as though uncovering a fraud deliberately perpetrated, a fantasy entertained by those who had been led to confuse Norris with Jack London and other authors with truly proletarian roots and ineradicable lower-class affinities. *McTeague*, Dobie delighted in trumpeting, was written from the top down by a patrician who, even as a boy, was living in the lap of luxury in Chicago, far from stockyards, slaughterhouses, and untidy neighborhoods like San Francisco's grubby Polk Street, where *McTeague* is set. From Charles he had learned that the Norrises, having returned to Chicago from an 1878 visit to Europe, were occupying

> an imposing house with marble steps on Michigan Avenue at Park Row; six horses are in the stable; the coachman wears varnished boots and a cockade. On wintry days, the family carriage is replaced by a gorgeous sleigh provided with a heavy lap robe, the letter N embroidered in its centre. A country home flourishes in Wisconsin—at Lake Geneva. . . . In the drawing room of the Michigan Avenue mansion is an original Raphael, picked up on a grand tour of the Continent, and in the boudoir a massive walnut set, with mirrors

towering almost to the ceiling. A set of four pieces costing $700—an amazing sum in those days.[13]

Given the dearth of information about Norris's life in Chicago, this sketch is priceless, despite Dobie's defamatory use of it in his exposé. That Charles was born three years after that European vacation does not call into question the scale on which the Norrises had become accustomed to living by 1881, when they moved to 10 Lake Park Place (Park Row).[14] Nor does the fact that he was only four when the family departed from the sumptuous residence in question preclude appreciation of the full measure of B. F.'s tireless dedication to his business affairs and grand success as a capitalist. Then again, none of the houses in which Frank previously lived as a boy—at 904 Michigan Avenue

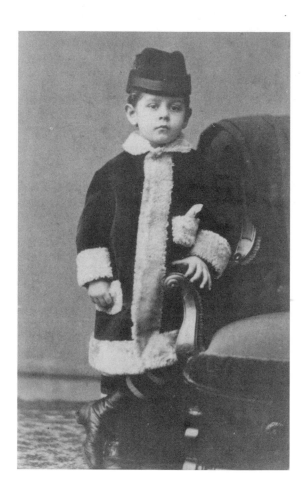

Young "Frankie" Norris. (Courtesy of the Bancroft Library, University of California at Berkeley.)

in 1870–75 and 722 Michigan Avenue in 1876–79 (renumbered 2023 during the family's continued residence there in 1880–81)—could be described as modest. And the family did indeed escape from the city to a local watering hole for the rich, Lake Geneva in Wisconsin, during the summers.[15]

Dobie's other exposé was even more damning. This revelation exercised a much greater influence on historians' and critics' interpretations of Norris's personality and his works—the end result being that he has been perceived by many as a most peculiar literary naturalist. Dobie was the first to allege that, unlike Emile Zola, Norris never transcended the conventional moral biases with which he was inculcated in his parents' home. Vis-à-vis sex and other matters traditionally associated with vice, that is, he remained eminently Victorian as he paradoxically allied himself with a blatantly anti-Victorian school of writing. And how could it be otherwise, wondered Dobie, given Frank's father's Calvinistic religiosity and "the somberness of [Gertrude's] Puritan birthright"? As it turns out, though, one learns more from Dobie about his own post- and anti-Victorian ethical perspective than the actual moral climate of the Norris household and how it affected Frank.

The context for Dobie's hostile behavior merits comment. As of the late 1920s, the post–World War I *génération perdue* revolt from small-town life, provincial values, and the pieties of the bourgeoisie (the "booboisie," as Mencken termed them) was showing no signs of fatigue, as may be seen in the essays of Mencken and the novels of Sinclair Lewis. One of the *bêtes noires* for those in the "smart set" was the Puritan. To this archetype and whipping boy Dobie linked a thoroughly Presbyterian B. F. Norris and a Gertrude who descended from the "Puritan Doggetts" of New England. According to Dobie, Norris's novel *Vandover and the Brute* confirmed their moralistic dominance over young Frank.[16] Dobie did not see the hero's hypermoralistic attitude toward human sexuality and his guilty struggle with his own libido as something proffered by Norris for the reader's interpretation and understanding. Instead, with Freudianism in vogue in the 1920s, Dobie read the novel as autobiographical, eliding the distinction between the truly Victorian hero troubled by his sexuality and the author who sensitively fashioned a character troubled by his sexuality. Although Charles did not enable him to point to any specific family connections with a church or churches in Chicago through 1885, Dobie characterized young Frank as victimized by severely religious parents with a wholly negative attitude toward sex and a punitive disposition toward a son registering the promptings of instinct as he entered puberty.

Charles did recall a church membership in San Francisco after 1885, though, and thus Dobie's apparent inference that a Puritan reign of terror in that city was an extension of what had been transpiring in Chicago. He depicted in detail the whole of the Norris family being associated with San Francisco's First Presbyterian church. Dobie even gave Ida Carleton, Gertrude's sister Narcissa's daughter—who for some unknown reason lived with them from 1886 or 1887 until her marriage in 1892—a role in his tale. He pictured her as a sunday-school teacher like B. F. at the church now known as the Old First. But there is no confirmation of either the uncle or the niece ever having taught—nor having done anything by way of service to the congregation—in the voluminous records of that still-vital church on the corner of Van Ness Avenue and Sacramento Street.[17] Although Gertrude was socially involved with the Old First through its Doctor's Daughters charitable organization,[18] B. F. was the only Norris ever to become a member.

To what extent was B. F. the stern Calvinist who induced a hysterical reaction to sexuality in his son? He may have attended one of the two Presbyterian churches in Grand Rapids, Michigan, where he lived in the 1850s. But neither the First nor Westminster church records there include his name among its members. That Robert Collyer, the minister who presided at the Norrises' wedding in 1867, was—of all things distant from Calvinism and late nineteenth-century Presbyterianism—a Unitarian hardly augurs well for the possibility that B. F. was preoccupied with sin, salvation, and predestination. Well before 1850, Unitarianism was waggishly (and unfairly, of course) characterized by fundamentalist Christians as the last step before atheism.

B. F. Norris's Presbyterianism is further called into question when one finds in the records of another Chicago church that Gertrude and he became communicants at Trinity Episcopal, where Gertrude was baptized on 18 October 1868, with B. F. as one of her sponsors. Grace Colton Norris was also baptized there on 4 April 1869, Frank on 15 May 1870, and Lester on 18 November 1877. Presumably Florence, for whom no record has been found, was also baptized as Episcopalian in 1871. On 22 April 1869, the day after her death from spinal meningitis, Grace was buried from the same Episcopal church, just as Florence, a victim of the cholera infantum from which Frank had narrowly escaped when a child, likely was in 1872. It is true that B. F. and Gertrude's mother, Harriet Doggett, joined Chicago's Second Presbyterian church in May 1876, almost a decade after she became his mother-in-law.

But the alleged Calvinist was still listed in the Trinity Episcopal records as a parishioner in 1882.

Whatever the degree to which B. F. can be described as a Puritan when he joined San Francisco's First Presbyterian on 11 November 1887, it is significant that he did not become a parishioner until more than three years after he purchased his house on Sacramento Street, a short walk away. He certainly was not a stickler regarding the discipline of that denomination. Years later, when on 13 January 1895 he was formally dismissed by request from the Old First's membership roll, he had been unchurched for the three years in which he deserted his family, reestablished residence in Chicago, obtained a divorce, and remarried. Then it was not a Presbyterian church to which he transferred but Chicago's Plymouth Congregational.

The last church to which he belonged had as its head a former Presbyterian minister, a renegade who resigned from the Fourth Presbyterian in Chicago because of creedal differences, the Reverend David Swing.[19] B. F. was dismissed from Plymouth Congregational on 14 February 1900, having become a member of the Central church of Chicago. Unaffiliated with any traditional Protestant denomination, he died later that year. His funeral service took place in the hotel at which he resided, the Lexington.[20]

It appears from B. F.'s sporadic alliances with Presbyterian churches, and his on-again, off-again involvements with other denominations and nondenominational groups, that he was the excitable kind of person who "got religion" on occasion, his enthusiasm waxing and waning and requiring special revivals before he found himself again paying pew rent. This squares with Charles's having told Walker that B. F. was an admirer of the world-famous, emotion-stirring evangelist Dwight L. Moody. Charles in this instance spoke from personal experience: the guest registry of the Hotel del Coronado near San Diego records the arrival on 20 March 1889 of B. F., Gertrude, Charles, and Ida Carleton; registering on the same day at that resort were Moody and one of his colleagues, the composer George C. Stebbins.[21] Moreover, Charles told Walker that Stebbins "spent a fortnight with us" during one of Moody's visits to San Francisco. That the effects of B. F.'s being periodically inspired to spiritual heights by men like Moody wore off tallies also with Frank's portrayal, early in *The Pit*, of Curtis Jadwin as a fervent, scripture-quoting Moodyite whose ardor for serving the Christ is fierce but relatively short-lived. Once he falls under the spell of Laura, she is his all-absorbing infatuation, and the born-again good-and-faithful servant is not resurrected in the remainder of the novel. That he next loses interest in Laura and becomes fixated on another source of titillation, speculation on wheat futures at the Chicago Board of Trade, spells a restless type-A personality ever searching for the next source of intense stimulation, whether sacred or secular. That, too, aligns with Charles's comments on his father's personality.

Dobie could have hardly developed honestly his thesis about the seamlessly Puritan home environment of the Norrises had Charles told him all of what he told his wife Kathleen. In an interview, Kathleen reflected in 1957 on the contradictions inherent in the notion that B. F. could be genuinely Christian and, at the same time, treat her mother-in-law the way he did:

> NORRIS: . . . my husband said it was Christmas day when his mother received the notice that her husband was suing for divorce. But meanwhile he was so pious that he travelled with Moody and [Ira D.] Sankey.
> DUNCAN: The revivalists.
> NORRIS: Yes. The evangelists. So it was a very queer background.[22]

Even in light of all that she had heard from Charles and Gertrude, Kathleen was puzzled. Apparently subject to radical mood swings, B. F. remains a puzzle; and one of the data not available for its solution, despite Dobie's imaginative reconstruction of B. F.'s personality, is his attitude toward sex. The final irony is that neither Charles nor Kathleen, Gertrude nor Frank, left behind a single comment on B. F.'s views concerning sexuality.

Such, happily, is not the case with Gertrude. Thanks to Charles, who as a novelist did not hesitate to write about sex in an uninhibited manner, we know something about her attitude, which was far from prudish. Although Walker, too, chose to characterize her as Puritan, he might have instead quoted what Charles also told him after confiding that Frank "always radiated sex and the women were very conscious of it." Charles continued, "This he inherited from his mother who was quite outspokenly interested in it."

For all of Dobie's prattle about the "Puritan Doggetts," Gertrude—like Laura, who displays a full knowledge of Episcopalian ritual and is married in Chicago's St. James's Cathedral—remained what she was when in 1868 she became a parishioner at Trinity Episcopal in Chicago: a participant in a measurably more liberal, worldly, and sophisticated religious community than either the Presbyterian or that represented by Moody. In San Francisco, it was at her church, St. Luke's Episcopal at the corner of Clay Street and Van Ness Avenue, that Frank received the requisite instruction in doctrine and was confirmed on Easter Sunday, 6 April 1886. He would be buried from the same church. On 20 September 1892, Gertrude's niece Ida was married there. Her granddaughter, Frank's child, would be baptized an Episcopalian and also attend St. Luke's. How religious was Gertrude? As with B. F. at the Old First, so with his wife at St. Luke's. In its archives, there is no record of her teaching sunday school or making any other special commitment. Frank was the only member of the family known to have participated in any educational program of a church—at the turn of the century in New York City at St. George's Episcopal on Stuyvesant Square.

Frank Norris demonstrates in his canon a remarkable familiarity with the Bible and the *Book of Common Prayer.* Echoes of the prayer book reverberate throughout his work; biblical incident, phraseology, and doctrine surface again and again. One reasonably suspects that it all began in boyhood with Gertrude reading from the prayer book and the Bible to her sons. But that the Norris home can be described as rigorously religious, whatever its denominational emphasis, is at least debatable. That it was "Puritan" in tonality—well, really, how much could Mrs. Grundy prevail in the home of a couple with a history like B. F.'s and Gertrude's? After all, their relationship was initiated behind the scenes in one of the ultimate sinks of iniquity for the Puritan imagination: the theatrical world. Frank was expert at articulating the points of view of characters who made classically Victorian responses to their own sexuality; he understood that state of mind fully. His own points of view—explicitly stated and implied—were, however, decidedly post-Victorian.

This is not to say that *Vandover* is wholly without autobiographical significance. There can be no doubt that the Episcopalian boy of 1885, approaching his sixteenth birthday when he moved from Chicago to San Francisco, knew the trials common to American adolescents of his time or of a century and more later. But that Frank could legitimately serve in 1928 as Dobie's Victorian-era poster boy conforms with neither the known facts of Norris family history nor what one finds in his canon.

Years before what Victorians moralistically referred to as the "brute within" manifested itself sexually in Norris's own experience, when he was ready to begin his formal education at the age of six, there was no question as to whether he would be attending one of Chicago's public schools. Nor would there be when he moved to San Francisco. It was to a prestigious private school that he went in September 1876. The Allen Academy, an "English, Classical, and Polytechnic School" at the corner of Michigan Avenue and Twenty-Second Street, was conducted according to Christian principles: thirteen of the twenty members of its board of visitors were ministers, as was common in schools of its caliber at the time. But it offered no formal religious instruction. That was the responsibility of parents and their churches. Secular, "classical" education to prepare for admission to elite institutions of higher learning was the school's primary mission. The other two tracks, which Norris's parents did not select for him, were preparation for a business career and a general course of study advertised as equivalent to a college education at a non–Ivy League school. The curriculum at the Allen Academy was rigorous, including the study of Latin and Greek (requisites for admission to Harvard, Yale, and the like), algebra and geometry, and their predictable complements in science, history, geography, writing, and speech. The president, Ira W. Allen, was LL.D.; five of the eleven instructors at the time of Norris's admission had earned the master's degree.[23]

The clientele was definitely upscale. The meatpacker and grainbroker Philip D. Armour's sons were in attendance as B. Frankie Norris Jr. of 722 Michigan Avenue became a student in the Primary and Preparatory Program. (In passing, one notes the first instance in which Norris either experiments with different renderings of his name or is misnamed or misinitialed.) The catalogue for the academic year 1876–77 describes well-ventilated, carpeted, and elegantly appointed classrooms. The pupils even left their shoes at the door and wore slippers during the day to ensure a healthful, dust-free atmosphere.

Frank—listed as B. Frank Norris in the 1877–78 catalogue published in June 1878—completed his second year without interruption. The catalogue for the following year is not extant, but there is no reason to echo Charles to the effect that Frank was yanked out of Chicago and put a year behind in his schooling. Walker took at face value Charles's testimony about a tour of Europe that the family began in the summer of 1878; and he erred in reporting that Frank, Lester, and their parents—Charles was not yet born—did not return until the next summer. In fact, they were gone for only three months, when school was not in session. They sailed from New York City on 5 June 1878 for Liverpool, England. Boarding the same Cunard steamer *Scythia* at Liverpool on 31 August 1878 for the return voyage, they debarked in New York City on 10 September—in time for Frank to return to Chicago and begin his third year at the Allen Academy a few days after the start of the fall term on 9 September.[24] Their itinerary in Europe, however, remains largely a mystery. Charles related that they returned from the continent to stay in Brighton, south of London on the English Channel; that they visited Paris is a given. Dobie did not report where they purchased the "original Raphael."

The Allen Academy catalogue for Norris's fourth year, too, is not extant. Thus we cannot be sure that he completed his three-year Primary and Preparatory program on schedule. But either in June 1879 or June 1880, he advanced to the academy's four-year Classical Course of Study. The catalogue for 1880–81 does survive, and Frank—now Frank B. Norris—had completed his first or second year. The catalogue does not specify what level he had attained by June 1881, and given how long his college-preparatory experience lasted, one has reason to wonder whether his advancement actually depended upon years or instead decisions made by the faculty as to when he moved to a higher level. The Allen Academy catalogues for the next two years are unavailable, further obscuring the situation, particularly how Norris was faring as a student.

The academic record recommences in the 1883–84 catalogue of another Chicago prep school to which Frank had transferred by September 1883, the Harvard School for Boys at 2101 Indiana Avenue at Twenty-First Street.[25] Again, the catalogue did not indicate his class ranking in its Higher Education Department; nor did it specify his course of study (Classical or Scientific). But, given that in the fall of 1885 he entered yet another college-preparatory school on the West Coast, it appears that he was again on the Classical track.

Once more, in this new school, he was among the children of Chicago society's elite: the sons of the tycoons George M. Pullman, Marshall Field, and Philip D. Armour were fellow students. Their five-year Higher Department program not only took a year longer to complete than Allen's but the curriculum was more demanding: one took French or German along with Greek and Latin; and to Allen's algebra and geometry requirements the Harvard School added trigonometry. Exactly how far Norris advanced in the two years he spent there cannot be determined. Even if the catalogue for 1884–85 were extant, one would be able to establish only whether he remained enrolled.

Possible evidence of Norris's standing when he entered the Harvard School in 1883 is the catalogue's description of a History of Greece and Rome course taken in the fourth year. Norris's copy of the required text survives; he signed it and under "Harvard School" gave the date of "Apr. 3rd/84."[26] However, this may mean only that he took that particular course but was otherwise in his third year. Or, the dating may mean nothing more than that he obtained the book that year, since another extant book used in the third year course of study at Harvard he had received as a Christmas present many years earlier, in 1878.[27]

There is good reason to give so much attention to such detail. Ideally, Norris would have concluded his preparation for higher education at the Harvard School by June 1885. Were he, as the dating of the book for the Greek and Roman history course suggests, a full-fledged fourth-year student in 1883–84, why would he be a student at yet another prep school in Belmont, California, in the autumn of 1885? Something may have gone awry while he was at the Harvard School, and what Charles had been told about events of 1883–85 may shed light on this.

Though he was too young to have "recollections of this at all," Charles informed Walker that B. F. "brought the family for the winter to Oakland [California] in '83 and we rented a house on the shore of Lake Merritt. The next year we came again and that time spent the winter at the Palace Hotel [in San Francisco]—some two or three months." That is, during the winters of 1883–84 and 1884–85, Frank was absent for some time before he returned to the Harvard School, in the company of one of his parents or, perhaps, a factotum who would care for him while Gertrude and B. F. remained in San Francisco with Lester and Charles. It has not proven possible to verify Charles's secondhand knowledge concerning either winter; but it is conceivable, given what happened after Frank was brought to San Francisco, that his parents did what they forbore to do in 1878 when they returned from Europe in time for Frank to begin his third year at the Allen Academy: interrupt his progress as a student. Certainly, their attitude toward the importance of a classical education had changed by late 1885, after Frank had bid Chicago farewell. That fall, his college-preparatory schooling was not only interrupted but terminated, and neither Charles nor any other source suggests that B. F. and Gertrude were troubled by that.

In short, we will never know how academically adept Norris was by the age of fifteen. All that can be inferred from the sophistication he displayed much later is that his interests in history, western thought, and the arts originated to some degree in the kind of liberal-studies intellectual orientation he had been introduced to as a child and exposed to for a decade. What he thought about immersion in such an Ivy League–plotted regimen is also unrecorded. He did characterize his later educational experiences, but not those of his prep school years. As an adult, when his thoughts turned to childhood and adolescence there was something else of much greater interest to him. He focused repeatedly on the personality traits that had spontaneously emerged in his youth and how they—rather than academic experience—determined the course of his life.

When Walker interviewed her in 1930, Norris's widow Jeannette claimed that the disastrous life experience known by the hero of *Vandover and the Brute* was, in part, Norris's imaginative construction of how his life might have turned out. *Vandover* is not straight autobiography, but it does incorporate in its first chapter experiences like those Norris had in Chicago and then San Francisco. The first chapter is especially important in that its portrait of a shy, somewhat introverted young Vandover suggests what was taking place in Norris's life when he was *not* at school.

    That Vandover was eight when he arrived in San Francisco and Norris was fifteen is one indication of how he distanced himself from the character he created. Another is the death of Van's mother: she expires on the platform after they have just detrained. At the same time, certain traits assigned to the young hero correspond to Norris's own as they are revealed in his personal experience–based nonfiction writings about children who manifest artistic predispositions at an early age and rather fully by the time they are fifteen:

> [Vandover] seemed to be a born artist. At first he only showed bent for all general art. He drew well, he made curious little modellings in clayey mud; he had a capital ear for music and managed in some unknown way of his own to pick out certain tunes on the piano. At one time he gave evidence of a genuine talent for the stage. For days he would pretend to be some dreadful sort of character . . . he would dress himself in an old smoking-cap, a red table-cloth and one of his father's discarded Templar swords, and pose before the long mirrors ranting and scowling. At another time he would devote his attention to literature, making up endless stories with which he terrified himself, telling them to himself in a low voice for hours after he had got into bed. Sometimes he would write out these stories and read them to his father after supper. . . . Once he even wrote a little poem which seriously disturbed the Old Gentleman, filling him with formless ideas and vague hopes for the future.[28]

The Old Gentleman is, as B. F. became in San Francisco, an entrepreneur invested in real estate who, again like B. F., has little aesthetic experience and does not quite know how to relate to a son with interests so different from his own. He nevertheless provides, as did B. F., the funding for his son to receive formal instruction in drawing and painting. Another autobiographically significant reflection having to do with the artistically inclined young person is seen in an 1896 sketch, "Western Types: An Art Student": "He starts early [in life] at his work. Even at the High School he covers the flyleaves of all his books with pictures, and carves the head of the principal in chalk. At home he has made fearful copies of the sentimental pictures in the *Home Book of Art.*" What follows in this sketch is immediately pertinent to Norris's own experience in 1885–86, when his formal academic experience ended and he began to study art. "His parents are astonished, become vaguely ambitious and send him to the Art School before he has hardly begun his education."[29]

Six years later, Norris returned to the same subject and to personal recollections in his 1902 essay "Story-Tellers vs. Novelists," which includes a lengthy scenario featuring the "born" storyteller's irrepressible penchant for imaginatively transforming all within his or her ken into the stuff of narrative art.[30]

Thus did Norris, when an adult, make sense of how and why he was so different from his own "Old Gentleman." So did he register why he, after trying his hand at drawing and painting and then taking stock of his resources when he was nineteen or twenty, chose authorship as his profession. To his mind, he was "born" to find a career in one of the arts. But there is another pertinent dimension of such remembrances in *Vandover* and these other pieces: the experiences of the representative youth described in them are those of a solitary figure whose relationships are with parents. There are no references to a youth's peer group, to interactions with similarly talented youths, or to friends. Charles did not comment on this. Dobie therefore could not discern Norris's stressful, perhaps traumatic, experience when he moved to San Francisco. It was not sexual but social.

The move to San Francisco took place at a particularly crucial stage in the personality development of an adolescent who soon had more to deal with than the persistent skin problems recalled by his brother. Uprooted from the midwestern urban environment he knew as home, Norris was undoubtedly not loath to put more distance between himself and the Bournique Dancing Academy. Everyone who was anyone socially, as will be seen in the Chicago newspaper society columns, sent their children there, where they learned how to participate in a cotillion, especially the German cotillion popularly referred to through the end of the century as a "german." Charles told Walker that Frank especially detested the black velvet suit he wore when it was time for the students to perform for their parents. Norris refers to germans several times in his writings, derisively on each occasion.

More to the point, the relocation to the West Coast abruptly broke friendships of long standing. Summarily terminated by his parents were all the group affiliations he had achieved. Furthermore, shortly after being yanked across the continent to 1822 Sacramento Street, he learned that he would not be living with his parents and brothers in San Francisco.

As the summer of 1885 drew to a close, Frank bid farewell to Lester and Charles and boarded a train that would take him southward down the peninsula to the countryside outside of Belmont in San Mateo County. A mile and a quarter away from the Southern Pacific railroad station, on what was only the year before the secluded country estate of the financier William C. Ralston's widow, the city boy entered a boarding school newly opened by the former president of the University of California, William T. Reid. As with the Allen Academy and the Harvard School, the Belmont School's first promotional catalogue proclaimed dedication to the noble end of placing its first group of twenty-five boys at an Ivy League college—specifically Reid's alma mater, Harvard.[31]

It was perhaps at this time that Gertrude's brother, William A. Doggett, encountered the "melancholy boy" he recalled when interviewed by a journalist shortly after his nephew's death.[32] Frank's situation at the time may well have resembled that of his father, who had a similar experience described by Kathleen Norris. The pathetic version of the poor-boy-made-good story she heard from Charles differs significantly from the upbeat one about B. F. that Dobie rendered: "I know that my father-in-law was a Michigan man. And he left home to go to school. And on the way with his father, he was so heartbroken at the idea of going to school that he ran away from his father and . . . into this jewelry shop and asked the man if he wanted a boy. The man did want a boy. And for quite a little while Mr. Norris, as a little boy, slept under the counter. And then he wrote his father and the father consented, that if he had a job and was on his own feet, he could stay."[33] With B. F., one speculates that the acorn did not fall far from the tree. Perhaps he reasoned, as his own father did, that parental indifference builds character. Why Gertrude also thought it wise to add another disruption to the one Frank so recently experienced challenges one's imagination.

Charles, too, resided at the Belmont School, and his memories of the place were not happy. When stationed at Fort Dix during World War I, he wrote to his wife about how terribly he missed her when they parted: "I shall never forget the sensation of my boyhood on Sunday nights when I had to go back to Belmont School after spending the weekend at home. It was the same when you went away."[34]

It is telling that Frank's writings include no reference whatsoever to his experiences at Belmont, his previous visits to the West Coast, nor his parents' absences from Chicago in 1883–85 as they made preparations in San Francisco for the relocation of their children.

4

THE CITY BY THE BAY

That Frank Norris became a novelist associated with San Francisco, rather than Chicago or New York City, was one of those accidental developments of the kind emphasized by literary naturalists as a determinant of the course of individual lives. It was not a simple choice made by him but a consequence of either his father's heredity or an acquired characteristic resulting from one or more physical ailments from which his father suffered. Variously referred to as hip-joint disease, neuralgia, and nervous problems in family correspondence and by Charles when talking with Franklin Walker, B. F.'s condition from youth—what made him unsuited for farm work with his father—was a painful one exacerbated by exposure to the cold. That his business offices and showroom were in downtown Chicago, a city renowned for its mordantly frigid temperatures and cutting winds in winter, prevented for years a seasonal removal from the western shore of Lake Michigan. But his condition had worsened in 1882. He could certainly afford to seek relief, and in 1883 he did so with the aid of his mother-in-law.

By 1870, Gertrude's aging parents had come to Chicago to live with the Norrises. Her father Samuel died in 1872, and his widow remained with them until 1885, when she went to live with her son William in Nebraska. On 1 February 1883, Mrs. Doggett wrote for B. F. a letter of introduction to Gertrude's eldest brother Samuel in San Francisco, an attorney and real estate agent who lived at either 631 Sacramento or 180 Perry Street. (The city directory discloses that Samuel moved frequently, apparently purchasing homes that he occupied only until he could profit from their sale.) Wrote Mrs. Doggett, "This letter will be given you by Mr. Norris who is visiting California hoping to improve his health, which has for the past year been considerably impaired." She went on to testify to B. F.'s high character in light of her having resided with the Norrises for the past thirteen years. "Your own father who lived with Mr. Norris for the three years preceding his death," she added, "both loved and respected him."[1]

Samuel was agreeable. So too, B. F. found, was the California weather and the sojourn at Lake Merritt in Oakland. In addition, spas featuring therapeutic hot springs dotted the landscape from Calistoga to the north down to Gilroy to the south, all within easy distance by rail. As Charles related to Walker, B. F. "was so captivated by the climate that he returned home and nothing could persuade him to live longer in Chicago." B. F. worked out an arrangement whereby his business associate, his niece Ella's husband William M. Alister, would oversee the establishment on State Street in Chicago when B. F. wintered on the West Coast.

The earliest confirmation in print of the Norrises' presence in San Francisco following the appearance of B. F. at Samuel's front door is a 2 June 1884 listing in one of the San Francisco newspapers of an unclaimed letter at the post office, addressed not to B. F. but to "Norris Frank Mrs." and indicating that she did more than just pass the winter at the Palace Hotel. Gertrude too had found good reason to prolong her stay in San Francisco. That autumn her husband closed the first of his many real estate deals there, buying a home in the city. Aware, as might well be expected of a seasoned entrepreneur, that his personal property might be subject to liens should market for the luxury goods he sold take a turn for the worse, he immediately transferred to his wife the ownership of the house on Sacramento between Van Ness and Franklin. Two days later, on 21 October 1884, the society columnist of the *San Francisco Chronicle* announced that the elegantly appointed home of Henry T. Scott—proprietor with Irving M. Scott and George W. Prescott of the Union Iron Works—had changed hands: "B. F. Norris, a capitalist of Chicago, has purchased the residence 1822 Sacramento street, where he and Mrs. Norris will reside this winter."[2]

It was not until several months later that Gertrude made her formal debut in the social columns as one of the local noteworthies. It was reported on 9 June 1885 that she and B. F. had visited one of the fashionable watering holes for the rich down the California coast: the fabulously ornate Hotel del Monte at Monterey, built by the Southern Pacific Railroad in 1880, where

Frank would later situate several short stories and articles. The *San Francisco Chronicle* announced that by 12 June they had returned to the city to attend a progressive euchre party on Van Ness Avenue, where Gertrude won one of the two first prizes. Meanwhile, Frank was in Chicago under someone else's care: it was not until two weeks later, 26 June, that the academic year at the Harvard School ended. He may have remained there for nearly two months more with his father who, according to the same 16 June 1885 social column, departed San Francisco for Chicago that very day, "to return here in August." This would not be inconsistent with Gertrude's next visit to a resort in July: "Mrs. B. F. Norris will return from Santa Cruz this week" was the announcement in the 4 August 1885 issue of the *Chronicle*. There was no mention of any other family member—Frank, Lester, or Charles—being with her.[3]

As the nation grieved the passing of President Ulysses S. Grant in early August, Frank had his own losses to mourn upon his departure from the Windy City in the company of his well-traveled father. As he drew nearer to the socially ambitious mother he had not seen for months, perhaps he already knew that they would be reunited for only a short while. Or perhaps it would not be an entire surprise to learn shortly after detraining that he would soon find himself in a dormitory at the Belmont School.

He did not remain at this third prep school for very long, though. In 1952, the San Francisco attorney M. C. Sloss, who was also a student there that first year of the academy's operation, still remembered vividly the accident that brought Gertrude's and B. F.'s son back to San Francisco from Belmont before the end of the fall term (though he was wrong about Norris's age and class ranking). He wrote to James D. Hart, who was assembling the Frank Norris Collection of the Bancroft Library at the time:

> In addition to those who, like myself, were in the senior class, preparing for college, there was a number of younger boys. One of these was Frank Norris who, as I recall, was about twelve years old. He was a quiet, unaggressive boy who, at that time, gave no indication of the great talent which he displayed later. I recall one incident of no great significance. The boys in the school were playing football one afternoon. Frank Norris was running with the ball and was tackled and thrown. When he arose his left arm was broken above the wrist in both bones. He left the school for the necessary treatment and I think did not return during the school year. Whether he came back in the following year I do not know as I was no longer there.[4]

Norris did not return to Belmont that academic year nor the next. His college-prep days simply ended in late 1885, before he had reached his sixteenth year. Thus concluded the Classical Course grind intended to fit him for admission to Harvard, Princeton, or Yale. He was home to stay with his brothers and—when they were in town—his parents for the next year and a half. He was enrolled for some months at Boys' High School (renamed Lowell in 1894) on Sutter Street between Gough and Octavia in San Francisco, after which his formal academic experience ended without his having earned a diploma.[5]

∽

As of May 1887, B. F. Norris had been listed twice in the city directory as a "capitalist" and a third time as a "jeweller." His son Frank made his first appearance in 1887, as an art student residing at 1822 Sacramento. It was not an unusual development for a teenager such as Frank to follow in his father's footsteps by turning aside from academics to prepare himself for a paying profession. For example, James "Jimmy" Swinnerton, who became a cartoonist for the *San Francisco Examiner*, did the same three years later when he was fourteen. Providing the opportunity for young people to learn the craft of drawing and painting from experienced instructors was the raison d'être of the school Frank had entered: the California School of Design, founded in 1873 by the two-year-old San Francisco Art Association. Ability and promise, rather than a command of trigonometry or a diploma, were the requisites for Norris's admission. He was no different in this respect from other San Franciscans of his generation who attended the school and rose well above cartoon work. These included Ernest Peixotto, Guy Rose, Eric Pape, Charles Rollo Peters, and Francesca Del Mar.

In 1886 the director of the school on Pine Street was Virgil Williams. He was known as a dedicated educator and an accomplished—but not first-rank—landscape artist. Norris would study under other instructors. But until 18 December 1886, when he died at fifty-six from "neuralgia of the heart" at his Mount St. Helena ranch in the Napa Valley, Williams was his mentor. At the funeral service in the rooms of the Art Association, where the distinguished Unitarian minister and art lover Horatio Stebbens eulogized Williams, Norris was present and honored as one of the deceased's "favorite pupils and ex-pupils." Along with three men beginning successful careers at the time—Amadée Joullin, John A. Stanton, and Christian Jorgensen—Norris joined six others who bore Williams's casket to the hearse for burial at the Laurel Hill Cemetery.[6]

Renamed the Mark Hopkins Institute of Art and relocated in the Mark Hopkins mansion on Nob Hill in 1893, the present San Francisco Art Institute

Frank Norris, art student. (Courtesy of Joseph R. McElrath Jr.)

on Chestnut Street descends directly from the well-funded and sophisticated school at which Norris—like his contemporaries in New York, Chicago, London, and Paris—learned to draw from the antique. An extraordinarily large collection of plaster casts donated by the French government was delivered to the school for this purpose in 1873, including the *Apollo Belvedere, Germanicus, Discobuus, Faun with Child, Venus de Milo,* bas-reliefs selected from the frieze of the Parthenon, twenty-five busts, thirty-six statuettes, and twenty-four casts from life. The students made constant use of them. As Norris complained in 1897, in the old school of the Art Association the "students used to be drilled and drilled and drilled in drawing from the antique."[7]

Mastering the techniques requisite for the credible rendering of color, shading, texture, and three-dimensionality also involved the representation of dully reflective brass pots, half-filled glass goblets, fruit glistening with moisture, and other *nature morte* staples. In his 1896 sketch "Western Types: An Art Student," Norris gently satirized the young artist who chooses to devote himself to the mastery of the genre: "On week days he works—and he works hard—at the School of Design—the Art Institute. For the past five years he has been working away here desperately, painting carrots, dead fish, bunches of onions, and, above all, stone jugs. He toils at these jugs with infinite pains. If he can manage to reproduce truthfully the little film of dust that gathers upon them, he is happy. A dusty stone jug is his ideal in life." Years later, continued Norris, one meets this now-seasoned artist "on his way home in the evening and he takes you to supper and shows you his latest 'piece.' It is a study of turnips and onions, grouped about a dusty stone jug."[8]

The school did not neglect the composition of landscape paintings, of course, given Virgil Williams's modest triumphs with the genre. And no matter how pious and morally scrupulous B. F. may have been when periodically under the spell of Dwight L. Moody, his son studied at a school in which—as in Europe—drawing from the nude was an essential feature of the curriculum. Well before Norris moved to California, the School of Design advertised its Life Class in the newspapers, with Virgil Williams instructing the male students and Ernst Narjot teaching the ladies separately.[9]

Only one memoir, written by a fellow San Franciscan, commemorates Norris's primary interest as an artist as of early 1887. Ernest Peixotto, with whom Frank would maintain a lifelong friendship, related in 1933 that he was one of the shy young man's "few intimate friends," and "his life at that time and again a very few years later, was quite closely interwoven with my own." He went on,

When first I knew him, Frank Norris was a tall, good looking lad of seventeen, studying art, as I was, in the Art School in San Francisco. For . . . it is not generally known that, before he began to write, he set out seriously to become a painter. During these early student days, his particular interest seemed to center in the study of animals, and . . . [he] had already mastered a fairly good pen and ink technique and knew his animals well. We often met together, he and I, out to the Presidio Reservation, and there, in the cavalry barracks, we used to sit by the hour, and sketch the heads and rumps, the knee joints, and flexible fetlocks of the restless horses.[10]

Despite Peixotto's appreciation of his skill, the San Francisco Art Association selected none of Norris's works for display in the exhibitions it staged into 1887, as Benoni Irwin, Thomas Hill, and Amadée Joullin succeeded the late Virgil Williams as the interim directors of the school, with the able assistance of the Art Association's treasurer, whose name merits mention in passing. Colonel George W. Grannis would be immortalized by Norris as the proprietor of a dog hospital and employer of Marcus Schouler in *McTeague*.

Then, one of the true masters of "stone jugs," whose now widely recognized genius in the production of still-life paintings was the equal of that of any number of Dutch and Belgian artists of the seventeenth and eighteenth centuries—and comparable to those of the nineteenth-century French impressionist Henri Fantin-Latour—arrived on the scene. The Danish-American painter Emil Carlsen assumed the directorship of the School of Design in late April 1887; his move from the East Coast delayed the opening of the spring term from 2 to 16 May. Carlsen, unfortunately, did not remember Norris when Franklin Walker contacted him in 1930—for very good reasons. He was not only just settling in but dealing with an unprecedented enrollment. From fifty-one in the previous term the number had leapt to seventy-three.[11] And only a month after the start of the spring term, Norris departed from San Francisco, not to see Peixotto again until the next year nor to visit the Presidio and the studios of the School of Design until 1889, when Arthur F. Mathews, who also studied under Virgil Williams, assumed the directorship.

In the meantime, as her son initiated his formal apprenticeship as a painter, Gertrude was proving well advanced as an adept in the social arts. The evening of 30 January 1886 she hosted "a small reception . . . to Miss Florence Godley and her affianced, Lieutenant Cantwell, and their bridesmaids, groomsmen and the 'best man.' . . . The evening was delightfully passed by the young people with music and dancing. At 11 o'clock supper was served, the guests soon taking their departure. The toilets of the guests and the hostess were unusually beautiful." The bride-to-be was the daughter of a neighbor living at 1818 Sacramento, and three nights later Gertrude treated the same group to a playgoing party at the Baldwin Theater, followed by a supper. Frank, standing in for his father, joined her for the wedding at Trinity church on 11 February, and Gertrude's striking toilet caught the attention of the social columnist: "Black lace over pink satin, caught up with pink feathers." Two evenings earlier—without her husband—she was garbed even more splendidly at a "fancy-dress surprise party tendered to Mrs. James de la Montanya by her daughter Jennie": "Mrs. B. F. Norris, as the Queen of Hearts, wore a long black velvet robe, adorned with red velvet cut in heart shapes, which trimmed the dress from the neck down; high collar and hair powdered." By 1 March, however, B. F. had returned to town. Despite his troubles with his hip, he was in Gertrude's company at a musical and dance entertainment—a "soirée musicale et dansante"—that Dr. and Mrs. Boyson hosted at the Palace Hotel.[12]

Then it was Gertrude's turn to take flight in mid-March 1886, with or without Lester and Charles, and over a week before the former's Easter vacation school recess would commence. "Mrs. B. F. Norris has gone East. She will be absent several weeks visiting Chicago and other Eastern cities." She returned the first week of April. With the advent of June, she was again packing her bags to join her friends in the summer exodus from the city to one of the fashionable seaside resorts: "Mrs. B. F. Norris and family go to Santa Cruz for a portion of this summer."[13]

Gertrude Norris, in short, had formed her social network, and the parties named in the news notes about her were prominent social personages whose movements the press regularly reported long before her arrival in the Bay Area. Navy personnel were frequently present at the gatherings she attended, which thus provided entrée to that sector of San Francisco life that her son enjoyed: Frank would in the 1890s prove one of the ardent fans of the "Great White Fleet" and demonstrate in his writings that he knew by sight and name the warships stationed on the West Coast. Included also in Gertrude's network, and thus Frank's in the years to come, was one or more members of the staff of the *San Francisco Chronicle*, for its coverage of her and other family members was uniformly more comprehensive than that of its chief rival, the *Examiner*. Frank's first publication of any kind appeared in the *Chronicle;* his first formal writing arrangement with a periodical was with that daily; and when foul play or an accident at sea in 1895–96 was suspected as the cause for Frank's disappearance during an ocean voyage, it was the *Chronicle* that was privy to new developments in the search for him.

Gertrude's establishment of connections within the beau monde would facilitate Frank's membership in the Bohemian Club and gain him access to the mansion of the railroad magnate Collis P. Huntington, which Gertrude identified in her copy of *The Octopus* as the setting for the extravagant Gerard dinner attended by the character Presley.[14] Her industrious cultivation of acquaintances even made possible the months-long stay on Santa Anita ranch in San Benito County, where Norris did his on-the-ground research concerning wheat growing for that novel over a decade later. Tracing the links along the chain to that end provides an interesting study in how the "right connections" are formed and serve their purposes.

Gertrude was present ("Pale blue satin en traine, covered with draperies of white lace; diamonds") on 7 September 1886 when the Episcopal bishop William I. Kip—who had administered the sacrament of confirmation to Frank the previous April at St. Luke's—presided over the wedding of Miss Ellen Bonsal Torbert and Valentine Perry Snyder. Present too was Mrs. Joaquin Bolado, née Julia Abrego, who owned Santa Anita ranch at the time. Three years later, on 19 December 1889, Gertrude's niece Ida attended a reception given within the same large social circle by Mrs. Henry Williams, at which Mrs. Bolado's daughter Julia, or "Dulce," was among the guests. Dulce was also present with Frank and Ida on 26 December at a reception hosted by Dr. and Mrs. A. H. Vorhees.[15] Dulce, who married Gaston Ashe (also at the Vorhees's reception) in December 1891, had inherited the Santa Anita ranch by the time Norris was their guest in 1899. When *The Octopus* was published in 1901, Norris sent her and his fellow Bohemian Club member Gaston an inscribed copy acknowledging their facilitation of his research: "In grateful remembrance of certain days passed in the Santa Anita Country where the scene of the following story has been laid."[16]

Yes, it pays to know the "right" people. Gertrude did, and—thanks to her—so did Ida and Frank.

The right people who played a role in Norris's life also included B. F.'s acquaintances. It might as easily have been Dwight L. Moody or Ira D. Sankey, but Charles Norris informed Franklin Walker that it was Moody's other colleague, George C. Stebbins, who suggested what should be done to advance the chosen career of B. F.'s talented son: He really should be sent abroad if he was serious about becoming a professional artist. Shortly thereafter, again according to Charles, an English visitor to the Norris home echoed Stebbins and opined that the best destination was neither Paris nor Rome. London, he advised, was just the thing for a young man like Frank.

The notion of going abroad for this purpose was hardly radical. Virtually everyone who was serious about a career as a painter made the transatlantic voyage. Prominent San Franciscans such as Alexander Harrison and Toby Rosenthal had perfected their techniques in Europe. In 1887, Charles Rollo Peters and Arthur F. Mathews were already in Paris working under the direction of Gustave Boulanger and Jules-Joseph Lefebvre. Indeed, the California School of Design had become a feeder school for the Académie Julian in Paris, which was flooded with ambitious Americans from across the country into the 1930s. The suggestion upon which B. F. acted was peculiar in one respect. In late 1880s San Francisco newspaper articles on the art scene in England, one does not normally encounter reports of anyone leaving San Francisco to study there. This 12 June 1887 bit of news was therefore exceptional: "Frank Norris and Miss Francesca Del Mar, two students of the School of Design, will leave for Europe shortly to continue their art studies. Mr. Norris will go to London and Miss Del Mar to Paris."[17] Hers was the standard plan, and she became a student at the Académie Julian in the ateliers of two men under whom many another San Franciscan worked, Tony Robert-Fleury and William Bouguereau.

In one respect, it made sense for Frank Norris to go to London. The English were, of course, dotty about animal portraiture; and over the next two years, the painting by Norris that garnered the most praise, Charles told Walker, was a portrait of his mother's cat. Moreover, the teenager who spent hours with Ernest Peixotto at the stables of the Presidio military reservation in San Francisco retained his infatuation with horses, leading him in 1896 to declare in all seriousness, "I take it that a well conducted Horse Show is the finest sight the *grand monde* has to offer."[18] The next year, his celebration of the art of Frederic Remington concluded thus: "Remington's horses should be accorded a place in the world's art, beyond the mere transitory popularity of magazine illustration. Perhaps no artist who ever lived understands horse action so well as this American illustrator of ours; and, as for character, one has only to compare them with the stuffed melodramatic lay figures of Rosa Bonheur to note how absolutely true they are, how thoroughly faithful to nature, how indisputably equine."[19] And so, for perhaps another reason than his father's preference for London, he was scheduled to depart for an immersion in the culture that nurtured the great English animal portraitists George Stubbs, Edwin Landseer, Thomas S. Cooper, and Herbert T. Bricksee. His destination was the South Kensington School of Art and Design, housed at the present Victoria and Albert Museum.

His departure two days earlier was announced in the *San Francisco Chronicle* on 13 June 1887: "B. F. Norris and his son Frank left for Europe last Saturday." Disclosed as well was another datum relevant to the character of Norris family life and the state of B. F.'s relationship with Gertrude: Lester, Charles, and she were not in the party. Ida Carleton, too, would remain in San Francisco to attend the wedding of May Adele Fargo and George Taylor Stewart, M.D., on 15 June.[20] But traveling with no company other than his son cannot now be construed as a hardship for B. F. In June 1887 it became clear for the first time that Norris's restless father traveled alone to Chicago and other destinations not only for business reasons but because he preferred to be away from home on his own at least periodically. Still, the announcement in the 13 June 1887 issue of the *Chronicle* that B. F. would be adventuring upon Europe for many weeks without *any* familial baggage remains somewhat startling: "Mr. Norris expects to travel considerably on the Continent, and will leave his son in London to study art." Foreshadowed thus were the nearly exact conditions under which he would desert his wife and children in 1892—to take an around-the-world tour.

Had B. F. and Frank proceeded directly to London, and had B. F. been inclined to dally a bit there before venturing upon the Continent, father and son might have joined the San Francisco Anglophiles who were arriving there *en masse* to celebrate Queen Victoria's Jubilee. A death in the family, however, precluded the possibility of their witnessing any of the proceedings.

5

FROM OUT OF THE BLUE

Diphtheria had long been a significant menace, especially to children, in all regions of the United States. With some frequency through 1885 and into 1887, San Francisco newspaper editorials had been calling for relief, demanding thorough flushings of the city's sewers. The conventional wisdom was that "miasmas" emanating from putrid matter therein were the cause of not only diphtheria but malaria and a host of other virulent diseases. Journalists reacted each time the number of new cases of diphtheria reported to the local public-health authorities spiked. Alarm was warranted; no dependable means for controlling the often fatal infection were available. The discovery of the bacillus responsible for the disease had occurred only a few years before in Germany: Edwin Klebs identified it in 1883 and, independently, so did Friedrich Löffler in 1884. It was not until 1890, however, that Emil von Behring and Kitasato Shibasaburo developed an antitoxin. Still, there was no noteworthy decline in the number of cases per year worldwide before Behring made available a toxin-antitoxin mixture in 1913 and Gaston Ramon introduced refinements that yielded a highly effective vaccine in 1923. Sad to say, mass immunizations of children in the United States and Canada did not begin until the next decade.

The disease is transmitted not by sewer fumes but by person-to-person droplet infection and was easily contracted by children in crowded areas in which poor personal-hygiene habits prevailed. Those mortally infected typically experienced the initial lesion in the membranes of the nasal cavity; from there it would spread downward to the tonsillar region and beyond. Or, if first located in the latter area, the lesion spread upward. In both sequences, it began to cause toxemia—blood poisoning—which would ultimately damage the heart (toxic myocarditis) and nervous system (paralysis).

The disease could be cruelly deceptive. A victim of toxemia might recover from the inflammation of the heart muscle and appear to have regained his or her health. But it was only a matter of time before the effects of the toxin still being produced began wreaking havoc on the nervous system. Paralysis of the palate and some eye muscles might at first suggest only a temporary setback, transient and not severe. One could appear on the road to wellness, and it might be as late as the eighth week that paralysis recurred and advanced to the point at which it critically affected swallowing and breathing, with death following shortly thereafter. Death might occur by another means first, though, and much more quickly: as the lesion spread to the larynx and caused it to swell, asphyxiation was often the result. What Gertrude, Charles, and Ida witnessed at 1822 Sacramento Street was no picturesque demise of the kind seen in theatrical melodramas, Academic paintings, and prose romances of the mid-nineteenth century. But the spectacle of Lester's death on 18 June 1887 was certainly pathetic.[1] B. F. and Frank, in Chicago at the time, could do no more than try to imagine what it was like after they received word that the boy had not only fallen ill but had already passed on. So reported the trade magazine, *Jewelers' Weekly,* published in New York City. It had learned from a Chicago source that "B. F. Norris, of B. F. Norris, Alister & Co . . . left his wife and son, Albert Dustin [*sic*] Norris, in San Francisco on June 11 in perfect health, but on the 20th received a telegram from his wife stating that his son had been stricken with diphtheria and suddenly died."[2] Given his alacritous decline, Lester's appears to have been one of the three cases of diphtheria reported to the Board of Health on 16 June.[3] If so—and the timing would square with the death-by-asphyxiation scenario—it is noteworthy that Gertrude did not contact B. F. until four days later. Yet more worthy of note with regard to her personality, however, is the lamentable way in which she privileged her own grief and disregarded the bereavement felt by her husband and elder surviving son. When Charles told Walker what followed, he did not refer to the self-centeredness typed later by the Gertrude-like heroine of *The Pit*. But he did relate that, per Gertrude's instructions, B. F. and Frank were totally excluded from firsthand experience of Lester's death. She told them not to return to San Francisco for the funeral and interment at Mountain

View Cemetery in Oakland. They did not have time to do so, since Gertrude
fled the scene three days after she informed B. F. of what had happened. So
reads a 27 June 1887 newspaper account: "Mrs. B. F. Norris, accompanied
by her son and niece . . . left on Thursday [23 June] for Chicago, where she
will join her husband and proceed to Europe for an indefinite time."[4] The
diminished family reunited by 27 June and proceeded to New York on 2 July,
all but Frank now planning to return to the United States in the fall.[5]

❧

The four Norrises and Ida sailed from New York City on 9 July 1887 on the
Cunard Line's steamship *Umbria,* passing the recently dedicated Statue of
Liberty at the start of the week-long transatlantic voyage. They stopped at
Queenstown (now Cobh) on the southeast coast of Ireland at 5:00 A.M. on
16 July, arriving at Liverpool the same day.[6] B. F.'s itinerary had changed. He
would remain with his wife rather than travel extensively in Europe on his
own as he had planned in June. They spent no more than a week in England
at the Morley Hotel on Trafalgar Square, according to Charles. Late July
found them in Paris on the Right Bank of the Seine. The Norrises had taken
rooms at the Hôtel du Louvre, a decidedly upscale hotel at which the head
of the Southern Pacific Railroad, Collis P. Huntington, was staying. The *San
Francisco Chronicle* duly noted this, as well as their revised plan for a return
to San Francisco in January 1888, rather than in the fall.[7] Before the end of
the month, they had moved into an apartment at 35 Boulevard Haussmann,
by which time B. F. had decided to return, alone, to San Francisco well before
January. From that address, on 31 July 1887, Gertrude wrote to her brother
Samuel in San Francisco, bringing him up to date:

> It is a lovely Sabbath afternoon. The chimes of the cathedral bells for ves-
> pers [sound] through the open casement—Narcisse, the concierge, is singing
> a merrie roulade in the court below—and the sun is shining and the sweet
> air is blowing gently from the green heights of Montmartre as I look from
> my chamber window!
> But all these glad surroundings of joyous life only deepen the gloom for
> those who are in the valley of the Shadow of Death! My Boy! My Darling! He
> is gone and all the bright hope that centred in him are buried for ever!
> And I still live on!
> God gave him to me for ten sweet years—and but little more than one short
> month ago, his sweet brown eyes beamed with love for me—his little heart was
> beating warm within his breast—his little form bounding with life and hope,
> and his little brain teeming with budding thoughts and comprehensions.—

And now, it is all over! Why? Why? Ah! Who can tell me? God, only, some day will make it plain.

Dear brother, you too have seen the grave close over your loved and cherished. And so I can write to you for, ah, only those who have sorrowed like me can *know*.[8]

Gertrude had other news to impart, but she soon returned to keening for Lester after a cryptic but certainly foreboding reference to her relationship with B. F.:

And my husband is still with me, but for me here-after the world is changed! Life, so far as life is a matter of personal desire and satisfaction, has ceased and stopped for me. I have duties to the living which I cannot abandon.

> *But the tender grace of a day that has gone*
> *Can never come back to me.*

Mr. Norris will return about the last of September but I cannot face the thought of returning to that desolated home! We will probably remain here until January when we will plan an excursion into Italy but as we will keep these apartments until spring our address will be the same. How I wish I might hear from you! Because you knew him and loved him you are dearer to me now,—

Ever truly, Gertrude

The two lines she paraphrased were from Alfred Lord Tennyson's "Break, Break, Break," a poem lamenting the loss of a loved one:

And the stately ships go on
    To their haven under the hill;
But O for the touch of a vanished hand,
    And the sound of a voice that is still!

Break, break, break,
    At the foot of thy crags, O Sea!
But the tender grace of a day that is dead
    Will never come back to me.

Her son Frank's original itinerary, too, had changed. He did not begin art studies at the South Kensington School of Art and Design but departed from London with his family, to reside in Paris with his mother, brother, and cousin long after the *San Francisco Chronicle* announced, on 29 August 1887, his father's intention to abide his grieving wife's company for only two months rather than three: "B. F. Norris of this city will sail from Liverpool on September 3rd, coming direct to San Francisco. Mrs. Norris and her sons will remain in Paris until spring."[9]

Her husband's departure did not constitute a great loss. Gertrude found herself in the situation of a single parent much of the time because of B. F.'s inability or unwillingness to cultivate an appreciation of, or greater tolerance for, the arts. It was rough going, she informed Samuel, as she passed her days with minimal spousal companionship: "I go about with the children through the galleries and museums and cathedrals, simulating an interest I do not feel." In the months ahead, seventeen-year-old Frank would first develop his special bond with his mother. He was to become the fair-haired son compensating for her husband's shortcomings as comforter.

B. F.'s not being able to take even three months of grieving and a month and a half of residence amidst the temples of culture in Paris was not forgotten by Frank when composing *The Pit* in 1902. Curtis and Laura Jadwin do not have children and suffer no great loss during the first three years of their marriage. But the B. F.–Gertrude relationship was the source of one similar development in their history: "Once in the period of these three years Laura and her husband had gone abroad. But her experience in England—they did not get to the Continent—had been a disappointment to her. The museums, art galleries, and cathedrals were not of the least interest to Jadwin, and though he followed her from one to another with uncomplaining stoicism, she felt his distress, and had contrived to return home three months ahead of time."[10] Gertrude was not so accommodating as Laura. As B. F. sailed to England and then home, and the autumn advanced, she maintained her plan, or most of it. The *San Francisco Chronicle* reported in October: "Mrs. B. F. Norris, with her two sons and niece . . . will go to Italy during the winter months."[11]

According to Charles, the train ride across France into Italy in early 1888 did not include Ida. It was also taken without him. Gertrude placed his cousin and him with a family named Quatremain on the Left Bank's Rue de Lille when Frank and his mother headed south. That Gertrude's grief was assuaged during the trip as her interest in aesthetic experience was rekindled is clear in Walker's interview notes. But the boy who had been left behind apparently still felt resentment over forty years later. Charles pettishly recalled Gertrude's and Frank's return to Paris thus: "They enjoyed the trip to Italy as if it were a honeymoon—brought back many things."

One can rough out their itinerary from Frank's subsequent references to Italian locales in his writings: Milan, Turin, Florence, Sienna, Rome, and Naples. An allusion to "a painted background of a hill city, like those of

Perugino's pictures," in his 1897 article "Latin Quarter Christmas" suggests a visit to Perugia; and most memorable were a ballet at La Scala in Milan, the scenes of grape cultivation and wine making in Tuscany, St. Paul's basilica outside of Rome, the ceiling of the Sistine Chapel, the singing of the "Miserere" by a choir therein, and the sight of Mount Vesuvius.[12]

References to such experiences are paltry in number, however, in comparison to those having to do with opera in Norris's writings, and it is safe to assume that he also enjoyed a performance at La Scala. It was in Paris that Norris discovered opera. Charles recounts that he was "quite mad" about it, returning again and again to hear the same pieces at l'Opéra, such as Giacomo Meyerbeer's *Les Hugenots* and *Le Prophète*. Charles remembered going to a matinée with Frank that was conducted by no less a personage than the composer of *Faust*, Charles Gounod. Norris would later make more extensive literary use of this perennial favorite than of any other opera to which he referred or from which he appropriated characterization and plot elements for his prose fictions. (This is the opera featured in the first chapter of *The Pit* and the fourteenth of *Vandover and the Brute*.) His familiarity with the standard repertoire of the grand opera companies of his time soon became remarkably extensive; no other novelist of his generation, Edith Wharton included, displayed a fuller knowledge or more profound influence upon his or her writing style.

How could it be otherwise, given years of his mother's cultivating a taste for the extravagant by reading to him the works of romancers such as Walter Scott and Edward Bulwer-Lytton? He received James Baldwin's *The Story of Roland*, inscribed "from Mamma," in his Christmas stocking in 1883. He had early on made acquaintance with the chivalric splendors of Jean Froissart's *Chroniques*, dealing in the grand manner with the Hundred Years' War of the fourteenth century. This was complemented by what he learned of Greek and Roman military history in his Classical Course studies at the Allen Academy and Harvard School. Treatments of classical Greek and Roman subjects by Jacques Louis David and other Academic painters only heightened his taste for the dramatic moment—not to mention fortifying an appreciation of the melodramatic. One should not be surprised by Frank's quite literary performance when Charles and he left the Paris opera house one day to find forty colorfully dressed cuirassiers controlling traffic. On hearing a cab horn sound, one of the mounts reared. Frank, as though quoting a caption for a book illustration, declared: "He hears the call to battle!" Nature was imitating art before his very eyes.

That Scott's *Ivanhoe* and *Quentin Durward,* like the *Chroniques* and the *Chanson de Roland,* had suffused Norris's imagination with colorful war-related scenes from the Middle Ages was apparent in another way and accounted in part for the affection in which Charles held his memory. Frank, the "born storyteller," was a good friend to the much younger sibling, who recalled for Walker their relationship in 1886–88: "Before they had gone to Paris Frank had begun to be interested in . . . lead soldiers and would spend a great deal of his time telling stories about them. . . . He became so engrossed in these stories that he forgot that it was only a game. After they went to Paris the games continued," and Charles would buy "lead soldiers packed in fig tins," spending "all day long in setting them up for the time when Frank came home."

But all was not sweetness and light in Paris. Charles also characterized his brother then as absent-minded, unkempt, and possessed of a terrible complexion that daily doses of cod-liver oil were supposed to remedy. His mother was distressed by the "rotten French" he had begun to learn at the Harvard School; along with the cod-liver oil she dosed him daily with oral renderings of the eminently correct and graceful prose of François Fénelon's *Les Aventures de Télémaque.*

Norris would have been independent much sooner had the simple plan of B. F. delivering his son to London not changed. Instead, he spent almost two months in Paris with a father who was always up by 8:00 A.M., "had no use for laziness," and—as Charles delicately phrased it—"thought a man, to amount to anything, should have a fire-cracker up his ass." When B. F. returned to the United States in September 1887, his son's situation was only slightly modified. The mother whom Charles recalled as "intensely ambitious for Frank" and "always a driving force" remained with him as he passed into his eighteenth year in March 1888. Finally, at the end of that month, she, along with Charles and Ida, crossed the channel and departed from Liverpool on the *Etruria,* arriving in New York on 8 April. Ida, presumably with Charles in her care, resumed residence in California.[13] But Gertrude was not ready to return to the scene of the disaster that occurred in June 1887. She sailed back to France, and did not bid farewell to Frank until 18 August 1888, sailing on *La Bretagne* from Le Havre, reaching New York a week later and entraining for San Francisco to devote herself to the creation of an enduring testimony to the fond memory of the lost son.[14] The Lester Norris Memorial Kindergarten opened on 12 December 1888 at 1231 Pacific Street, and Gertrude funded its operation until fire destroyed it in 1906. A portrait of Lester hung in the school was described thus in an annual report of the Golden Gate Kindergarten Association: "Underneath the handsomely framed portrait is the illuminated text: 'Their angels do always behold the face of my Father.' This is in a carved frame of white, blue, and gold, exquisitely beautiful in design and finish." The quality of this work of art was such that, as with Frank's first book *Yvernelle,* it was exhibited in Chicago at the Columbian Exposition of 1893.[15]

Frank, alone at last, settled in at 1 Rue de Lille with the Quatremain family and returned to the work he had come to Paris to do. Over a year earlier, as Gertrude informed her brother Samuel when she wrote her otherwise tearful letter of late July 1887, there was one bit of good news to report: "Frank has been fortunate in entering the *atelier* of Bouguereau, the great painter."

6

THE ACADÉMIE JULIAN

Why was Gertrude Norris so enthusiastic about her son finding a place in Bouguereau's studio? More important, what did Frank think, then and later, of the man under whom he studied?

Born in 1825, William Bouguereau was, by the 1870s, one of the great Academic painters of nineteenth-century France. Working under his direction in Paris was equivalent to being the student of Lawrence Alma-Tadema in England. Both men, along with their remarkable contemporary Jean Léon Gérôme, stood squarely in the great tradition descended from Raphael, to Jacques Louis David, and to Jean Auguste Ingres. Their work represents the technical values privileged by the artistic establishment of their time, and especially France's influential, government-supported Academy of Fine Arts. "Academic" is the term used now to differentiate their grand treatments of traditional "high culture" subject matter—mythological, historical, religious, and generally "classical" events and personages—from what today draws crowds to most major exhibitions of nineteenth-century art. For those whose interest in painting commences chronologically with the 1870s and French impressionism, Bouguereau's formal portraits of Madonnas and Alma-Tadema's of gracefully posed Grecian maidens have a special historical significance: they represent the kind of painting from which Claude Monet turned away to treat water lilies, haystacks, and more commonplace human figures with a very different aim and technique. Practitioners and champions of impressionism long reveled in the notion of such a valiant avant-garde having liberated art from the "tyranny" of the Academic.

By the time Norris arrived in Paris, even traditionalists not particularly sympathetic to the avant-garde were having second thoughts about painters like Bouguereau and Alma-Tadema. In an 1887 article appearing in the *San Francisco Chronicle,* a critic made clear his distaste for Bouguereau's *Cupid Victorious* (or *Eros Triumphant*), hung at the Paris Salon: "It is a companion picture to his 'Cupid Disarmed' [or *Eros Disarmed*] that was so much admired in last year's Salon. It is faultless in conception and execution, but like all that artist's works classic and cold as an iceberg. The 'Cupid Victorious' holds a bow in his right hand and arrow in the left. . . . A little girl with butterflies' wings buries her pretty little head behind cupid's neck. Both are of course in the midst of a blue sky surrounded by fleecy white clouds." Alma-Tadema was given similar treatment a month later, when his painting at the Royal Academy exhibition in London was reviewed as an exquisite piece of make-believe. *The Women of Amphissa,* featuring "a picture of a Greek marketplace with a dozen sleeping or just waking priestesses," wrote the *San Francisco Examiner* reviewer, displays "all of Tadema's familiar characteristics, extraordinary details, and brilliant coloring, but also shows, like all his pictures, only the Greece of fairyland."[1]

Academicians, and especially the representatives of the artistic establishment who decided what kinds of paintings would be exhibited at the Salon, could be just as critical of their more innovative contemporaries, caustically commenting upon impressionist works as unfinished and resembling preliminary studies rather than final products. Typical was the observation that a cluster of red daubs intended to suggest a clutch of poppies was nothing less than the admission of incompetence in drawing and painting. "Finish" was the hallmark of Academic works featuring near-photographic exactitude at any viewing distance; meticulous drawing, careful brushwork, and fidelity to natural coloration and surface textures were prized. The final touch was the application of a "licked surface" of multiple layers of clear lacquer that virtually erased all signs of brush strokes. A chief goal was to eliminate so far as possible the very suggestion of the artist's hand and to maximize the illusion of life itself—even when the subject was mythological or allegorical, the historical event pictured was melodramatically exaggerated, or the human figures imaged had been enhanced to the level of the preternatural. Ironically, one might term a work of the kind preposterous and at the same time have to admit that it was lifelike—for example, that cupids seen leaning on clouds were indisputable triumphs of child portraiture.

This is not to say that one *had to* choose sides between the Academic establishment and the impressionist renegades by the late 1880s. One might, without getting into a high dither, appreciate the strengths and acknowledge the limitations of both traditions and modes of representation, as was the habit of Frank Norris. When later engaging in art criticism, he made qualitative judgments. But his far-from-doctrinaire attitude toward the various kinds of art being exhibited in his time brings to mind the positive principle he wittily enunciated in 1895 when reveling in the horsemanship and athletic prowess he witnessed during a polo match. Although an experienced horseman himself, he announced that he could not understand how the players were able to perform certain remarkable feats. No matter, though, for the point of being there at the match was enjoyment of the spectacle. Striking developments in the polo match, however they were accomplished, were pleasurable; and the sensible person "takes them as a whole without asking questions, as one would shrimps."[2]

When focusing on art, he *did* understand how the performers engineered their effects, but he typically opened himself to the possibility of appreciating them without regard to school-related loyalties and animosities. What's good is good. Some cupids delight; others cloy.

In 1895 he applied this principle when writing about literature representative of the schools of romanticism, realism, and naturalism, advising readers not to "higgle with your terms; don't belong to any 'school.' If you read books instead of writing them, read with a view to the *general effect produced*. If the book is good, it is good whether it is [Sir Walter Scott's romantic] *Ivanhoe,* [William Dean Howells's realistic] *The Rise of Silas Lapham,* or *La Bête Humaine* of M. Zola."[3] While he did become a champion of literary naturalism, that did not preclude his enjoyment of and respect for the accomplishments of writers who were unlike Zola.

Likewise, Norris did not feel compelled to declare exclusive allegiance to one camp or another when, in *The Pit,* Laura Jadwin articulates the conventional wisdom regarding Bouguereau's preemimience in his field of endeavor. He also allowed to pass without authorial comment the contrary opinion of her dinner guest, Sheldon Corthell:

> "We will have our coffee in the art gallery," Laura said, "and please smoke."
> He lit a cigarette, and the two passed into the great glass-domed rotunda.
> "Here is the one I like best," said Laura, standing before the Bouguereau.

"Yes?" he queried, observing the picture thoughtfully. "I suppose," he remarked, "it is because it demands less of you than some others. I see what you mean. It pleases you because it satisfies you so easily. You can grasp it without any effort."

"Oh, I don't know," she ventured.

"Bouguereau 'fills a place.' I know it," he answered. "But I cannot persuade myself to admire his art."

"But," she faltered, "I thought Bouguereau was considered the greatest—one of the greatest—his wonderful flesh tints, the drawing, and colouring—"

"But I think you will see," he told her, "if you think about it, that for all there is *in* his picture—back of it—a fine hanging, a beautiful vase would have exactly the same value upon your wall." He indicated a small canvas to the right of the bathing nymphs, representing a twilight landscape.

Drawing Laura's attention away from the Bouguereau to the landscape piece, Corthell privileges this more somber work that he finds expressive of the melancholy "felt at the moment" by an unnamed western American artist. "'Oh, yes,'" he declares emphatically, "'I prefer it to the nymphs.'"[4]

Given that Bouguereau's oeuvre is not so familiar today as Manet's or Renoir's or Van Gogh's, explanation as to what Laura admires and Corthell finds superficial and emotionally inexpressive is in order. Another character, Sam Gretry, responds in yet another way to his first sight of the same "large Bouguereau that represented a group of nymphs bathing in a woodland pool." He tells Laura's husband, "'This is what the boys down on the Board [of Trade] would call a bar-room picture.'"[5] Norris does not name the painting, but the one in question is *The Nymphaeum*. This canvas was completed in 1878; it is now at the Haggin Museum in Stockton, California. It is populated by a bevy of delicious nudes, porcelainlike in their blemish-free appearance and yet far from "cold" or static in their vigorous physicality. The female figures are rendered as both erotic and innocent, as unaware of onlookers as they seem to be of the modern bias in favor of young ladies being clothed even at poolside. They are, as Laura notes, both expertly drawn and colored with "wonderful flesh tints." At the same time, even as one appreciates Bouguereau's skill, one might acknowledge that the fantasy given such rich embodiment is just that—a fantasy. To opine, as Corthell does, that a fine vase would have served as well for interior decoration does, however, take one too far down this path and reflects a dismissive point of view never expressed by Norris.

Even in the 1896 satirical portrait of "An Art Student," where the type of painter described for our amusement is assigned a loyalty to Bouguereau,

Norris does not sound a negative note: "Art with him is *paint*. He condescends to no other medium than oil and colored earths. Bouguereau is his enthusiasm; he can rise no higher than that, and he looks down with an amused smile upon the illustrators, the pen-and-ink men, Gibson, Smedley, Remington, and the rest. 'Good in their way, oh, yes, but Gibson is very superficial, you know.'"[6] Norris's own point of view is positive with regard to both types of artists. His catholicity is seen in his ranking those three men working as illustrators in a different medium as worthy of admiration alongside an accomplished Academician working with oil and colored earths. One need not look down upon the drawings of Charles Dana Gibson, W. T. Smedley, and Frederic Remington simply because one appreciates Bouguereau.

His admiration extended also to the impressionists, who were so unlike Bouguereau and the pen-and-ink men. He was far from hostile to the San Franciscan Charles Rollo Peters, who produced many twilight landscapes of the kind that appeals to Sheldon Corthell. Almost a decade after he and Peters had been students together at the Julian, Norris interviewed him for an article in which he appreciatively described him as working in the impressionist manner, specializing in late evening and night scenes, or "nocturnes."[7]

In short, Norris carried no discernible prejudices with him when he left Paris, and he did not become a partisan of any particular school, or kind, of art thereafter. Nor did this relatively inexperienced aspirant bring any biases to Paris in 1887, save the preference for realistic animal portraiture noted by Ernest Peixotto and a dislike of drill work having to do with drawing from the antique. After all, Norris arrived at the Julian with less than two years of formal training in drawing and painting; and while he may have been precocious, he was not a prodigy. That no works by him had been shown at the art exhibitions of the California School of Design testifies to the fact that he was still the tyro who had much to learn and whose good fortune it was to be guided in his progress by a man whose drawing and painting skills could be questioned by no one.

Norris's entry into the *atelier de gauche*, Bouguereau's studio at the Académie Julian, in July 1887 was not only fitting but, in light of his later work as a writer, prophetic. For all of his realistic technique, and especially his mastery of human physiology, Bouguereau was no more a painterly realist than his pupil-become-writer, who later distanced himself deliberately from the confines of literary realism. Bouguereau never took Gustave Courbet's turn toward light-of-common-day realism in the mid-nineteenth century; nor did he plumb character in the manner of two psychological realists of the seventeenth century, Rembrandt van Rijn and Diego Velásquez, or Henri Fantin-Latour of the nineteenth. Bouguereau's was more a romantic than realist sensibility. The same is true of Norris-the-writer who, in his 1901 essay "A Plea for Romantic Fiction," would defend romance writers in the face of attacks by advocates of realism. Norris never gave such free rein to fancy as Bouguereau, with his immaculately dressed shepherdesses, well-scrubbed bourgeois maidens sensitive to the appeal of a well-scrubbed natural order, madonnas and saints, and Greco-Roman mythological figures. And no one is observed in a glamorously or provocatively naked state in any of Norris's writings. But the composite portrait of the milkmaid Hilma Tree in *The Octopus* is an idealization of the feminine worthy of Bouguereau. Western American womanhood at its best, by Norris's lights, she is pictured as a veritable earth-mother figure, a Ceres when she does not recall Persephone. Noteworthy, too, in this respect is the heroine of *Blix*, Travis Bessemer. She is the subject of several cameos in which her wholesomeness of mind and body, sprightliness, and empathetic concern for the man in her life nearly approach perfection of this sort in the Norris canon. Moreover and more lugubriously, we find in *The Octopus* the homeless widow Hooven begging on the streets of San Francisco to provide food for her young daughter. Bouguereau, too, was no stranger to the melodramatic use of the maudlin, for example, in his portrait of an *Indigent Family,* or in one of Eve grieving the death of her son Abel, *First Mourning,* which Norris had the opportunity to see at the Salon of 1888 and the Exposition Universelle of 1889.

As to Zola's naturalism, less can be said. Bouguereau did not deal with the sordid and noisome seen in the works of Courbet, Edgar Dégas, and Henri de Toulouse-Lautrec. He was never typed as Zola was by 1888, when an American journalist could with impunity refer to him as "the novelist of filth."[8] And yet, given Norris's professional—and undoubtedly personal—interest in the sex drive, Bouguereau's treatments of sex are pertinent. Bouguereau was rather daring in this regard, focusing on the female in tasteful but unmistakably explicit ways. His *Spring,* for example, depicts a naked young woman about whom cupids are swarming like bees drawn to a honey pot. This easily uncoded mythological representation of her sexual arousal was so disturbing—the female pictured is strikingly true to life—that it was physically attacked when publicly exhibited in Omaha, Nebraska, in 1891: a man named Carey J. Warbington threw a chair at the canvas, and it had to be returned to Bouguereau for repair. As to the male figure, Bouguereau was more reticent, resorting in one of his most familiar, often reproduced paintings to the mythological figure of a Satyr, whose primary trait is lechery: "satyriasis" is the term for a condition of excessive or uncontrollable sexual desire in a male. His *Nymphs and Satyr* depicts the male figure, with the Satyrs' ears, legs, and horns of a goat, being dragged by nymphs toward a pool while more naked and sumptuously drawn sisters across the pool are beckoned to assist in his immersion. The narrative content is intended as comical. The theme suggested from a decidedly male perspective is "too much of a good thing."

In the United States, this painting became Bouguereau's most widely known work, for in 1882 it literally became a "barroom picture" and tourist attraction. Edward S. Stokes, one of the owners of the Hoffman House at Broadway and Twenty-fifth Street in New York City, purchased it and had it

William Bouguereau, *The Nymphaeum.* (Reprinted by permission of the Haggin Collection, the Haggin Museum, Stockton, Calif.)

William Bouguereau, *Nymphs and Satyr.* (Reprinted with permission. © Sterling and Francine Clark Art Institute, Williamstown, Mass.)

hung in the hotel's bar beneath a red velvet canopy, where it was illuminated by a crystal chandelier. It also made a second appearance behind the bar in a mirror commensurate with the painting's size, roughly ten by eight feet. Norris is likely to have seen this grand "Salon machine," as such oversized works were termed. The Fifth Avenue Hotel at which he stayed when visiting New York from the late 1880s through the mid 1890s was only two blocks away.

Subjects having to do with human sexuality had long been treated in Academic art and were no rarity in other kinds from the 1870s onward. The visual arts were well in advance of literature in this respect, and at both the California School of Design and the Académie Julian Norris was finding warrant for the contributions he would one day make to closing the gap.

Established in 1868 by Rodolphe Julian, the academy Norris attended quickly became a great success. As the California School of Design prepared one for the Julian, so the Julian prepared one for the premier institution in Paris, the Ecole des Beaux-Arts. At the Julian one readied oneself for the rigorous examination that was the narrow gate for admission to the Beaux-Arts, but there was none required for entrance to the Julian itself. One paid one's fees in advance and commenced preparation for passing those tests, or one entered with the more limited ambition of qualifying more immediately for a career as a painter, sculptor, engraver, interior decorator, illustrator, or draughtsman.

Many of the instructors were Academic artists of the first rank, but no obstacles were put in the way of the student who wished to take a path different from theirs. An encouragement of experimentation not equalled at the Beaux-Arts prevailed and accounted in part for the popularity of this school that drew students with diverse interests from across Europe and North America. It was at the Julian that Pierre Bonnard, Maurice Denis, Ker Xavier Roussel, Edouard Vuillard, and Paul Ranson—the principal members of a post-Academic and postimpressionist group—formed the "brotherhood" of the Nabis (or self-styled "prophets") at the same time that Norris was pursuing his more traditional course of study. Even more illustrative of what was possible at the Julian is the fact that Alphonse Mucha, that touchstone of art nouveau, was Norris's fellow student in 1887–88.

Norris never expressed disappointment with the Julian. But in his 1900 article on "Student Life in Paris" for *Collier's Weekly*, he did relate his surprise when he arrived in the summer of 1887 and found that the men's studios were not in the romantic environment about which he had read, the exotic bohemian Latin Quarter on the Left Bank. Rather, they were in a similarly run-down but markedly less colorful part of the city on the other side of the Seine, blocks beyond and to the northeast of the Opéra. The Julian had since been relocated several times, so he made it clear that he meant "the original Julian, the old place over the smelly feather-cleaning establishment in the smelly court off the smelly Rue de Faubourg Saint-Denis"—number forty-eight on that street leading to the Gare du Nord.[9] Mondays began with the students in the eight studios choosing their models for the week. As each of the forty or so posed in the nude to win the favor of the men present, related Norris, it was "easy to imagine a white-slave market." Then came the seating of the students, "a veritable *affaire*. Everybody wants to sit on the front row of low tabourets, because from this position one looks upward at the model; and the articulation of joints and the attachment of muscles—the whole anatomical scheme—seen thus foreshortened, is particularly interesting, and at the same time easy to draw." These stools, however, were already spoken for as the week began.

On Saturdays, the master of a studio decided on the basis of merit which ten men's projects should be "'classed' first." One might occupy the front row for a while but, if one were not among these ten, the place would have to be surrendered when the chosen arrived. "This complication always gives rise to scenes," announced Norris; and it also gave rise later to anecdotes that could be developed in full in the manner of Norris's 1897 "'This Animal of a Buldy Jones.'" In this broadly humorous piece, an altercation at the Julian results in insistence upon a duel by a fellow named Camme, who is expert in the use of pistol and sword. The Chicagoan, Yale graduate, and accomplished athlete he challenges, Buldy Jones, has the choice of weapons: he opts for baseballs and knocks unconscious his inept French adversary.

This account has long been read as a short story, in part because Norris—who was in San Francisco when he composed it—has his narrator refer to being at the "'Dead Rat' the other day."[10] The narrator is indeed a fictional one, since this was a well-known establishment in Paris once frequented by Arthur Rimbaud. It would also serve as the setting for a work by Tolouse-Lautrec, *Private Room at the Rat Mort*. Thus, when the narrator relates that he recently heard the story of the baseball duel retold by Roubault and learned that Choubersky had sent a written version to a friend in Morocco, one does not take that any more as fact than the reference to "Adler, who is now on the *Century* staff" and "who says that it's an old story among the illustrators."

But "Student Life in Paris," "'This Animal,'" and another Julian-related piece entitled "Buldy Jones, *Chef de Claque*,"[11] are all rooted in fact: they repeatedly refer by name to Norris's fellow students at the Julian between 1887 and 1889. None of these professional artists became as famous as Robert Henri, who also studied under Bouguereau in 1888, or Henri Matisse, who entered the Julian in 1891. Among Norris's companions were Jules O. Triquet, Italico Brass, Jean A. Marioton, George M. Haushaulter, Numa-François Gillet, James Wilson Morrice ("Horse" Wilson), Emile Bayard, Emile Bertrand, Jean R. Bazaine, and André V. E. Devembez. The artist who lost the baseball duel to Buldy Jones was Jean Baptiste Camme.[12]

Like Norris, these students enjoyed the attention of not only the heads of their studios but other masters as well. As Norris wrote in "Student Life," at Julian "there are two masters for each *atelier*, who give their services free, and who come Wednesdays and Saturdays to 'correct.' Some are not so regular, so conscientious as others; but Bouguereau, Tony Robert-Fleury, and [Jules] Lefebvre are always to be counted upon."

Having earned tribute thus, Norris executed commemorative cameos of each:

> Lefebvre, débonair, familiar, approachable, goes the rounds of his *atelier* as though holding a reception, often taking the *fusain* [charcoal for drawing] himself and "blocking in the figure" for the student.
> Fleury is a large, handsome, blue-serge gentleman [i.e., dressed as a businessman] with brown whiskers, who wears his red button of the Legion [of Honor] in his lapel, and who smells of cologne.
> Bouguereau looks more like a well-to-do butcher than like the painter of Aphrodites and Cupids. He is very fat, very red as to the face, very loud as to the breath, very wheezy as to the voice; his hands as well kept as a physician's, and he invariably prefaces his criticism with, "*Eh, eh, pas trop mal*" [Ah, well, not too bad].

One Saturday Bouguereau went beyond such encouragement. Whether Charles was still in Paris then or only heard later of his brother's achievement of distinction is not clear, but Walker did record in his notes that Frank's portrait of Gertrude's cat "was 'hung on the line' to his surprise and gratification." That is, his work had been "'classed' first," and the following Monday he was one of the ten upon whom Bouguereau had bestowed a front-row seat from which to observe the model.

None of the paintings Norris produced in Paris has survived, and thus one cannot tell how proficient he became. But the sojourn in France was not merely a lark. To have one's creation acknowledged as superior by a world-class artist such as Bouguereau spelled more than a dilettantish dabbling on the part of a *flâneur.*

⌒

One would hardly know this, however, from the three pieces of writing Norris devoted to the Julian experience. Never producing a formal memoir, he exploited the situation for the entertainment of his readership. Opting to sound the antic note, he developed the theme of fun-fun-fun in gay Par-ee and recorded his operagoing high jinks as one of the *claqueurs,* the young men paid to initiate applause at particular points in the performances. The zany dimensions of student social life displaced the less saleable subject of what he learned as an art student—boyish zest being much more marketable to the periodicals than, let us say, an explanation of the difference between an *esquisse* and an *étude,* or how Norris and his fellow students labored over both kinds of preliminary representations prior to beginning their paintings. In the novel he never saw published, *Vandover and the Brute,* Norris wrote for a popular readership; but he tucks in a development that verges upon requiring from its reader technical knowledge of the painterly craft. Rather than write an article on how one prepares through several steps for the execution of a painting, he used his experience to picture a fatal mistake that his artist-hero makes as he proceeds with a major project.

Vandover begins well with a painting to be entitled *The Last Enemy,* a Gérôme-like, Academic work featuring a lion stalking a man on his last legs in the desert. He confidently "blocks in" the figures with charcoal on his canvas, and he is pleased with the way in which they have been roughly outlined. But when he proceeds to the next step prior to the use of paint—three-dimensional definition of the figures in true-to-life spatial relationships to each other—the results are disastrous. "Grotesque and meaningless shapes" appear on the canvas; they are "mocking caricatures of those he saw in his fancy." At this turning point in the novel, Vandover concludes that he has wholly lost his artistic ability because of his excessive, immoral way of living, and he abandons all hope of recovering it. There is, however, a more technical, less moralistic explanation to be inferred from Norris's description of the situation.

Vandover succeeds at first because he had, according to the procedure Norris himself learned, begun his preparation for the painting with a series of *esquisses*—largely undetailed sketches of the individual entities he would later draw on his canvas. He transfers and modifies the roughly outlined figures, with the *esquisses* serving the function of models. At this point, he should have been ready to turn to a like number of *études*—three-dimensionally detailed studies of the same figures in the *esquisses,* normally derived from the observation of real-world models. But he has no such referents to guide his hand; he created no *études.* Nor does he have before him models of any kind. He is instead trying to draw the figures "he saw in his fancy [or imagination]."[13] While this might work for artists unconcerned with real-world perspective or fidelity to nature, this is not how representational art of the kind attempted by Academic painters was produced. Moreover, even Monet worked *en plein air* with real haystacks and water lilies as models.

The reader may be as surprised as Vandover by his incompetence. Vandover has previously enjoyed great success as an artist, and when explaining how that was so Norris provides a remarkably detailed picture of how he himself spent his days when working in the *atelier gauche* rather than playing in Paris. A nude female model before him on this earlier occasion, Vandover holds out his stick of charcoal, measuring the space that her body will occupy and marking his canvas accordingly. "After this, by aid of his mirror, he studied the general character of the pose for nearly half an hour." As did Leonardo da Vinci and the generations that followed his practice, Vandover consults the three-dimensional image reflected by the mirror to determine how he will position the three-dimensional image he will create on the single plane that is his canvas. That decided, he acts: "[W]ith a few strokes of his charcoal he laid off his larger construction lines with a freedom and a precision that were excellent." Continuing to observe the object-entity to be pictured, he proceeds past the *esquisse* stage to give definition to the outlined form as one would in an *étude:* "Upon these lines he made a second drawing a little more detailed, though as yet everything was [only] blocked in, angularly and roughly. Then, putting a thin flat edge upon his charcoal, he started the careful and finished outline." This, however, only marks the beginning of his work. At the end of an hour, he "had drawn and redrawn the articulation of the model's left shoulder" four times. "As she stood, turned sideways to him, one hand on her hip, the deltoid muscle was at once contracted and foreshortened. It was a difficult bit of anatomy to draw." Following the correct procedure according to Academic practice and continuing to use his mirror at the previously selected angle, Vandover earns Norris's praise: the drawing "was astonishingly good, vigorous and solid; better than all, it had that feeling for form that makes just the difference between the amateur and the genuine artist." And in a final revelation of his understanding of such matters,

Norris comments on Vandover's talent in terms that directly applied to the acknowledged strengths and limitations of Bouguereau: "[H]e drew these nude women better than any one in the school, perhaps better than any one in the city. Portrait work and the power to catch subtle intellectual distinctions in a face were sometimes beyond him, but his feeling for the flesh, and for the movement and character of a pose, was admirable."[14]

When Vandover later fails, it is not because of shortcomings in his character; it is not a moral but an intellectual failure. Somehow, he neglected to recall what he, like Norris, had learned from his "life study" training: To depict real-world entities such as men and lions credibly, one must observe them carefully, understand them in the sense of seeing them as they actually are, and draw them as they are—from life. Even the most fanciful imagined scene or narrative decided upon *before* the drawing begins requires the use of models if the product is to appear lifelike. For example, Bouguereau's response to the deaths of his wife and son within two months, *A Soul Brought to Heaven,* is anatomically precise in its representation of a deceased young woman, and it is as credible a representation of two angels bearing her to heaven as could be drawn from the models who posed for him.

It is a telling moment in the Norris canon not only in terms of what it reveals about his grasp of the discipline in which he was schooled. One of the legacies of his painterly experience was a fictional aesthetic that similarly downplayed the role of imaginative license and emphasized the Academic values of close observation of life and technical ability in its representation. This is not to say that Norris never exercised that license; several of his earliest works, such as "The Jongleur of Taillebois" (1891) and "Lauth" (1893), are patently fantastic and extravagantly test the limits of the romance genre as they entertain. In his serious-minded 1897 essay "Fiction Is Selection," however, he does not tout a Vandover-like resort to fancy or imagination. The only way that he can make positive use of the word "imagination" in relation to the production of art that is not merely imaginary or fantasylike in content is to redefine the term in a manner that will now appear familiar. The onetime student at the Julian who kept his eye on his model goes so far as to make the initially puzzling declaration that what is called imagination "is only observation after all."[15] In art that is true to life, rather than merely fantastic, one observes and interprets what one sees, specifically in human experience. As does the painter when deciding upon his or her subject and how he or she will treat it, one selects those aspects of human experience that will be used in characterization and the development of plot; combination and arrangement of what one has observed and selected for use *are,* in a nutshell, the exercise of imagination. One invents nothing save the way in which the entities selected for inclusion will be presented in relationship to each other.

The aesthetic is, obviously, an especially rationalistic one reminiscent of those enjoying popularity in the neoclassical era, or the Age of Reason. Indeed, Norris sounds decidedly pre-romantic in this instance and was possibly echoing Samuel Taylor Coleridge's definition of "secondary imagination," as was William Dean Howells when, in 1899, he expressed a point of view with which Norris was in perfect harmony: "It is a well ascertained fact concerning the imagination that it can work only with the stuff of experience. It can absolutely create nothing; it can only compose."[16] What is most noteworthy about the influence of the Julian years is that, psychologically, Norris as a writer appears to have rarely absented himself from the stool upon which he sat in Bouguereau's studio and from which he looked beyond his canvas to observe the life forms whose likeness he attempted to render with fidelity to nature. The artist worth his salt is perhaps not a slave to reality, but, in Norris's conception of himself, he had to be a dedicated observer who took his cues from without even when he was writing in an undeniably romantic way. In theory at least, real life was the "model" from which he could not turn away if he was to render human experience credibly.

Other legacies of the two years at the Julian, seen in a propensity for what may be termed shop- or studio-talk, surface throughout Norris's canon and indicate that his interests ranged well beyond the Academic. For example, in *The Pit,* Sam Gretry turns from Bouguereau's "bar-room picture" to another in the Jadwin mansion that manifests a very different technique associated with the impressionists, though Edouard Détaille was a much more conventional painter whose representative works are dominantly realist in style.

> "I like this one pretty well," continued Jadwin, moving to a canvas by Détaille. It was one of the inevitable studies of a cuirassier; in this case a trumpeter, one arm high in the air, the hand clutching the trumpet, the horse, foam-flecked, at a furious gallop. In the rear, through clouds of dust, the rest of the squadron was indicated by a few points of color.
> "Yes, that's pretty neat," concurred Gretry. "He's sure got a gait on. . . . Queer way these artists work," he went on peering close to the canvas. "Look at it close up and it's just a lot of little daubs, but you get off a distance"—he drew back cocking his head to one side—"and you see now. Hey—see how the whole thing bunches up. Pretty neat, isn't it?"[17]

Gretry's is a layman's discovery and only implies mildly what Norris understood: the careful planning necessary for all of the differently colored "daubs" in the background to cohere with the precisely drawn figures in the foreground at a particular viewing distance. Explicit, however, is Norris's understanding of a related technique, productive of the sensational effects achieved early in the century by Eugène Delacroix by means of the juxtaposition or superimposition of complementary colors, resulting in more brilliant coloration than is possible with the mixing of the two before they are applied to the canvas. Norris treats the matter in his 1901 essay "A Problem in Fiction": "Consider the study of a French cuirassier by Détaille; where the sunlight strikes the brown coat of the horse; you will see, if you look close, a mere smear of blue—light blue. . . . Stand at the proper distance and the blue smear resolves itself into the glossy reflection of the sun, and the effect is true."[18]

Going further into the question of how Norris ranged beyond the Academic, one may recall that, while he was still a student in San Francisco, Georges Seurat had already completed his masterpiece *Sunday Afternoon on the Island of the Grande Jatte,* first exhibited in Paris in 1886. Like Peixotto, who employed the same technique popularized by Seurat and Paul Signac, Norris was no stranger to pointillism. When in 1896 he reviewed recently completed works by Peixotto's wife-to-be, Mary "Mollie" G. Hutchinson, he revealed that her kind of work was not his cup of tea, though he was far from censorious when evaluating her *A Marshland in Brittany* as an

> admirable study in the impressionist style. . . . Miss Hutchinson is evidently a partisan of the vibration theory of color; seen close up her pictures show hundreds of little color dabs of green and vermillion and yellow—sometimes the crude, unmixed color. At a distance these dabs run together and produce a brilliant atmospheric effect that is at times very effective. From a personal point of view I have little sympathy for this method; it seems to savor too much of trickery. However, it has many supporters, and with these Miss Hutchinson's work is sure to be successful.[19]

The scope of Norris's interests appears to have been wide. But in 1888, when he commenced a major project of his own, he had no intention of doing anything other than meeting the Academic criteria for exhibition at the Paris Salon.

$\sim$

When it came time for Norris to prove himself as a promising young artist capable of producing an Academic work that might qualify for Salon exhibition in 1889 or 1890, he turned to a subject that was typical neither of Bouguereau nor Alma-Tadema. Nor was Vandover's inspiration, Gérôme, his guide. He felt the pull of another current in nineteenth-century cultural life. It had originated in the gothic revival of the late 1700s and then more broadly in the medievalism of the romantic movement—especially in the historical romances of the writer for whom Norris never diminished his admiration, Sir Walter Scott.

In painting, those who were as enamored of the Middle Ages as Norris need not necessarily have rejected the governing conventions for high art established during the Renaissance by Raphael, his contemporaries, and their loyal successors. While some artists did decide that treatments of medieval subjects invited the adoption of pre-Raphaelite styles of representation, the majority simply applied the Academic methods, for example, the American painter Julian R. Story. The son of the distinguished sculptor and poet William Wetmore Story, he studied at the Académie Julian in 1879–82 under Lefebvre and Gustave Boulanger, and in 1888 he won a medal at the Salon. In 1889 he won a second at the Exposition Universelle in Paris for the same grand "Salon machine" constructed on Academic principles and now displayed at the Telfair Museum in Savannah, Georgia. Measuring eleven by seventeen feet, *The Black Prince at Crécy* depicts a scene described in Froissart's *Chroniques* and other early histories dealing with the fourteenth century. Featured at its center is Edward of Woodstock, Prince of Wales and the eldest son of England's King Edward III, after the Battle of Crécy on 26 August 1346—a major turning point in the Hundred Years' War with France. This Black Prince—so named because of the color of his armor—stands to the left of and thoughtfully observes his slain enemy, King John of Bohemia, who lies among the four thousand others killed in the conflict. In short, it is the kind of painting that most visitors to the Telfair Museum cannot miss seeing but move past quickly to enjoy two much later works by artists who appeal to modern taste: Robert Henri's *La Madrileñita* and Frederick Carl Frieseke's *The Hammock*. But, in the late 1880s, Norris had undertaken a project of exactly this kind by the time Peixotto joined him at the Académie Julian.

Peixotto found Norris living in "a large, rather bourgeois apartment house" at the southern corner of the Rue de Lille as it ends at the Rue de Saints-Pères, close by the Gare D'Orsay (now the Musée D'Orsay). He reported

Julian Story, *The Black Prince at the Battle of Crécy*. (Reprinted by permission of the Telfair Museum of Art, Savannah, Ga.)

that Norris had become "violently interested in medieval armor and we used to go together to the Artillery Museum in the Hôtel des Invalides and gloat over the glorious coats-of-mail there displayed. We studied the beautifully chased arms and armor; we hefted the jousting helmets to test their weight; we sketched the lances and bucklers and corselets and the Italian suits-of-mail, as well as the rich trappings of the horses." Registering the enormity of the conception that seized Norris, Peixotto recalled that he "became so interested in all this, that he started to paint a huge historical picture of the 'Battle of Crécy'! The preliminary sketches were made and he even 'drew in' the large canvas that took up one entire end of his *pension* room."[20]

Peixotto did not specify how much time and energy Norris spent as he continued his work on the canvas. Nor did he comment upon how much research Norris performed to select a scene from the battle and to ensure historical accuracy. He did not recall, or perhaps did not know, that Norris traveled south from Paris to see the terrain at some of the locales where major developments in the Hundred Years' War occurred. This included Poitiers where, ten years after the victory at Crécy, the Black Prince again played a major role in the defeat of the French (a development Eugène Delacroix treated dramatically in his *Bataille de Poitiers*). At Poitiers, Norris wrote an octosyllabic poem simply entitled "Poitiers." Instead of a scene suggestive of violent conflict in the fourteenth century, he found a landscape reminiscent of somnolent Provence in summertime:

> *The land in lazy quiet lies*
> *Beneath [the sun's] rays, and basks and dreams.*
> *It is a long September's day,*
> *A peaceful Indian-summer noon,*
> *Nor does a single zephyr play*
> *To cool the heat or break the calm.*[21]

Peixotto did, however, shed light on a less positive moment in Norris's stay in France. One evening Guy Rose and he called upon Norris and learned that "he was thoroughly discouraged and had definitely decided to give up the picture, and to prove it he offered us the big canvas and stretcher, a precious quarry indeed for a couple of impecunious young Latin Quarter students." The canvas was so large that they could not take it down the stairs and had to lower it from the window to the courtyard below. "And that was the end of the 'Battle of Crécy'!" Peixotto claimed that the abandonment of the project was "symptomatic of Norris's general attitude toward his work" at this time, "and, soon after, he decided to go home."[22]

However, one has reason to wonder whether Norris made that decision on his own. Charles G. Norris offered a different account of what led to his brother's departure from Paris, the origins of this development taking one back years earlier to when the five- and six-year-old's big brother was ineffaceably linked in his memory to lead soldiers and the oral spinning of yarns about them. After Charles departed for San Francisco in late March of 1888, his kindly brother continued to play the role of raconteur through the mail. According to Charles, that act of fraternal kindness, rather than his frustration with painting, precipitated a command from B. F. to come home immediately.

Given the amount of time and energy Charles fondly recalled his brother giving to him in these six- to seven-thousand-word, illustrated installments of a picaresque narrative featuring Charles himself as the chivalric hero, one need not wonder why B. F. became exasperated about the way in which the return on his investment in art study manifested itself. Franklin Walker recorded in suggestive detail Charles's description of Frank's other project dealing with the Hundred Years' War—a bizarre story in which Charles was cast as a nephew of the Duke of Burgundy who becomes inebriated one day and kills someone. For this he is banished to Saxony by a Gaston le Fox (Gaston III, Comte de Foix [1331–91]), whence he has to escape within sixty days (for reasons we do not know, since these installments do not survive). Wedged at some point into the protracted tale was the plot of Frank Stockton's 1882 short-story sensation, "The Lady or the Tiger?" Charles finds himself in an asylum for the mentally ill, somehow extricating himself from a rooftop situation in which a "big insane man" orders him to jump off. Next locked in a signal tower, he sees the heroine of the tale fastened to a railroad yard switch, Frank here appropriating the grand rescue scene that concludes the fourth act of Augustin Daly's 1867 melodrama *Under the Gaslight*—at which point B. F. intervened, calling a halt to the yarn spinning.

This was not the only literary product of the Paris years. Charles also remembered that Frank brought home with him a no-longer-extant novelistic manuscript entitled "Robert d'Artois": "It was all about the figures in the Chronicles of Froissart" and, opined Charles, even a boy of eight had to judge it a "rotten novel." The example of its rottenness he offered was possibly more significant than he realized. Charles, himself an accomplished novelist by 1930, complained that Frank wrote a whole chapter in the unsatisfying way he did just so that he could make use of a concluding bit of dialogue that Walker recorded thus in his interview notes: "I ask for bread and you give me a stone; I ask for [blank] and you give me a scorpion." Perhaps a coincidence, it remains striking that the last datum concerning the Paris experience that Charles remembered echoes rather closely two sentences in scripture dealing with the relationship between a loving father, God, who cares deeply about and acts kindly toward his children when they ask a favor of Him—sentences that hardly enhance B. F.'s image as loving parent in the summer of 1889. The son who had been peremptorily ordered to cease whatever it was he was doing in Paris had shaped an entire chapter of his manuscript to the end of either quoting or paraphrasing the rhetorical questions posed by Jesus in Luke 11:11–12: "If a son shall ask bread of any of you that is a father, will he give him a stone? . . . Or if he shall ask an egg, will he offer him a scorpion?" Perhaps, for a young man who preferred to remain in Paris, neither of these questions was rhetorical, nor were the kindly answers implied so assured. If Frank Norris appealed for the boon of continued residence abroad, he was most definitely disappointed by a father who would not relent. His was the stone or scorpion, not the bread or egg. Home he came, never to return to Paris.

Norris's resentment at this juncture may also have been disclosed in *Vandover and the Brute,* where a similar development takes place. Like B. F., Vandover's father proposes that his son continue his art studies abroad. The two begin the journey to Europe, and then the "Old Gentleman" changes his mind as they reach Boston. "Vandover took his father's decision hardly," that is, with great difficulty or painfully. The "Old Gentleman" had "no college education himself, but in some vague way he felt convinced that Vandover would be a better artist for a four years' course at Harvard," after which he could go to Paris.[23] It is a great disappointment for Van as he complies with his father's wish, even though it makes little sense to him. The notion of a college degree being requisite for launching a professional career of any kind is not likely to prove a matter for argument today; but in 1889, it was at least debatable whether it was either necessary or advantageous for young men and women intent upon pursuing a painterly or literary career. Indeed, the "Old Gentleman" himself is rather vague on this point, as B. F.—for whom there is no record of formal education—undoubtedly was. Still, B. F.'s son, in part because of parental pressure, would be enrolled at a university in September 1890.

By 25 August 1889, Charles Rollo Peters had arrived in New York City en route from the Académie Julian to San Francisco, ready to pursue painting as his career. Peixotto, Guy Rose, and Eric Pape, like Arthur F. Mathews, remained in Paris. They were to do the same as Peters upon their returns. Frank Norris was less certain about his future when, on 24 August, he boarded at Le Havre the same ship that had carried his mother back to the United States a year earlier and identified himself in the passenger registry as a writer rather than an artist. *La Bretagne* arrived late in the night of 1 September at Pier 42 on the Hudson River, at the foot of Morton Street. Norris went directly to the Fifth Avenue Hotel across the street from Madison Square at the Twenty-third Street intersection of Broadway and Fifth, where his father had signed the guest register by 17 August.[24] On the one hand, he had accumulated a good deal of experience as an artist. On the other hand, as Charles related to Walker, the mother who also crossed the continent to meet him in the lobby of that hotel had, in effect, already served as his first literary agent, placing an illustrated essay on the armor he had studied and drawn with Peixotto in Paris: "Clothes of Steel" had appeared in the *San Francisco Chronicle* four months earlier.[25] And—for better or worse—he had begun a novel, or something like one, in "Robert d'Artois."

As it turned out, however, Norris pursued neither writing nor painting as an immediate means of making a living after unpacking at 1822 Sacramento Street. By personal choice, parental fiat, or mutual agreement after some possibly heated discussion, the nineteen-year-old continued to be financially dependent upon his father and found himself picking up where he left off in the autumn of 1885 when he departed from the classical course of study intended to prepare him for admission to Harvard, Princeton, or Yale. After almost four years of vocational training and over a year of living as an adult on his own, he found himself in the position of a high-school student ready to complete the work requisite for graduation and admission to the University of California in the fall of 1890.

7

STARTING OVER

That Frank Norris returned from Paris "an intelligent, sophisticated illiterate" was the rather severe judgment of one commentator in 1969.[1] In fact, his formal educational experience was not remarkably different from those of prominent authors such as William Dean Howells, Joel Chandler Harris, and Mark Twain when they were nineteen. Bret Harte and Charles W. Chesnutt were even employed as educators early in their lives, yet they too did not attend a college. Members of Norris's own generation such as Jack London, Stephen Crane, Theodore Dreiser, and Richard Harding Davis did enjoy some higher education, but all four left their respective alma maters without a degree. Norris and these other far-from-illiterate men were, however, ferocious readers with wide-ranging interests; and all were autodidacts, as they had to be in the mid- to late nineteenth century if they were to become professional authors.

Beginning in 1896, with his diatribe in *The Wave* against "The 'English Courses' of the University of California," Norris complained repeatedly that training for professions such as business, law, medicine, and even dentistry was available to the young man of his generation. But at which school could one obtain thorough preparation for a career in the writing of literature?[2] Howells had apprenticed in journalism, that is, *doing* journalism rather than "majoring" in it at a college. There was no such major offered at any American school in the nineteenth century. Chesnutt made trials in private, imitating those who had "arrived" until he happened upon a style and subject matter that he could make his own. Norris would have both kinds of experience, though he initially took a different route than they.

It is not known when in 1889 or 1890 he concluded—wrongly, as it turned out—that he could obtain at the University of California in Berkeley the hands-on vocational experience requisite for a fiction writer. The earliest surviving documentation of his intent dates from November 1891, by which time he was a sophomore and had discovered that the university was not at all focused on professional training like the California School of Design and the Académie Julian. Then petitioning the College of Letters to waive course requirements he did not deem pertinent to his career goals, he explained that the work required for Latin and mathematics might be more profitably devoted to other, more pertinent subjects: "I entered college with the view of preparing myself for the profession of a writer of fiction."[3] The College of Letters did not see things his way.

There was yet another reason, in addition to parental pressure and his desire to be a fiction writer, that Norris became a freshman in 1890. As with his departures from the Allen Academy, the Harvard School, the Belmont School, the California School of Design, and the Académie Julian, he had again broken the social ties he had formed. Once more, he "belonged" nowhere. As his classmate Harry M. Wright put it in a eulogy written in 1902 for the *University of California Chronicle,* when "Norris entered college I doubt if he had any friends here at all—the years of art study had broken off the friendships of the preparatory school. . . . He was slow in making friends at this time, strangely enough, for he was one of the most attractive men I ever met."[4] But it was only a matter of time before he would fully immerse himself in campus—and especially fraternity—life. As with his Paris adventure, about which he wrote almost exclusively in terms of how enjoyably boisterous *la vie Parisienne* was for the art student, much more is known about his extracurricular activities than his studies and initial trials in literature. The majority of fellow Berkeley students interviewed by Walker were Norris's fraternity brothers and not interested in careers related to the arts. These chums—with most of whom he maintained relationships to the time of his death—were Walker's primary information sources about the Berkeley years, since Norris himself had little to say about them other than that the university failed to meet the needs of an aspiring author.

As he proceeded with his new career plan, Norris did not wholly turn away from the visual arts. Like William Makepeace Thackeray before him

and much more so than James Thurber afterwards, he was qualified to illustrate works from his hand that might find a publisher. One need not have
mastered technique at the level of a Bouguereau or Alma-Tadema to meet
the requirements of most periodicals then published in the United States,
and Norris did not stop drawing and painting over the next several years as he
experimented with various literary genres. One of his roommates at the Phi
Gamma Delta—or "Fiji"—fraternity house near the Berkeley campus, Albert
J. Houston, remembered him in precisely the way Norris later would picture
his artist-hero at work in *Vandover and the Brute:* "Frank was always working
on his drawing, with a board and mirror for perspective." Leon J. Richardson, the cousin and 1891–92 assistant of Norris's Latin professor, George M.
Richardson, related to Walker that the sophomore sporting sideburns and
a mustache—"an average student . . . doing about C work"—would "always
sit in the front row and spend the time during class drawing pictures in his
Horace. Each ode he illustrated, having sometimes 3 or 4 pictures to the
page. The pictures were well drawn and illustrative of the text." Richardson
regretted in 1930 that he "did not offer him $10 for it as it would have been
an invaluable [memento]." In a 1914 pamphlet intended to boost sales of
Vandover and the Brute, Charles claimed that Norris used him as the model
for illustrations of short stories that he hoped would be published in book
form: "I remember how earnestly he worked on some of the illustrations for
this book, . . . keeping me posing for hours."[5]

There was another legacy of the vocational training in the visual arts
that he had received in lieu of traditional academic preparation for higher
education. It was attitudinal. Despite his rebuff from the College of Letters
in late 1891, Norris persisted as far as he could in his Montessori-like view
of the university as a locus for discovery—a smorgasbord at which he would
give his attention to what struck him as the appropriate fare. In the 1891
petition he announced, "I am willing to forego the diploma so thoroughly
am I persuaded that the course which leads up to it . . . would be more det-
rimental to me than otherwise."[6] The university would be a studio in which
he would pursue his own interests and, along the way, dumbfound those
with conventional expectations of what he *should have been doing* with the
educational opportunities he enjoyed. Charles testified that Frank was lazy
in Paris; and that he was lackadaisical as a student at Berkeley is the refrain
heard in the interviews of several fellow students. But, as will be seen, Norris's
rather healthy publication record in 1890–94 belies any suggestion of leth-
argy. Before he entered Berkeley, he had already begun writing a version of

Vandover and the Brute, the title page of which he dated 1889.[7] The same interviewees, moreover, described Norris as quite animated when engaged in extracurricular activities. They even noted that there were some professors and courses—or parts of courses—he actually enjoyed.

The fact of the matter regarding Norris's alleged lack of motivation and such displays of energetic engagement appears to have been disclosed in full by Leon J. Richardson, who observed that Norris could prove intellectually keen: "Horace seemed to be his favorite Latin writer and his ideas he assimilated quickly with real critical ability." At the same time, Norris balked when projects did not appeal to him. He was, added Richardson, "not so quick with the language work and displayed an individuality in his attitude towards study which marked him at the time." His instructor in the 1890s equivalent of a freshman English course, William Dallam Armes, was less kind. In 1902 he was still irritated by the young man who was "self-sufficient and impatient of criticism." A decade after Norris had been his student and little more than a month after his death, Armes—who knew how to hold a grudge—wrote a eulogy that reluctantly praised and forcefully criticized the nonconforming lad of yore who had, he vividly recalled, persisted in turning in expository prose essays that *never* succeeded in "forming an adequate treatment of the topic[s]" on which he wrote.[8] In other words, to paraphrase Giovanelli's verdict on the motivations of the heroine of Henry James's *Daisy Miller,* Norris did what he liked.

He would proceed at his own pace toward his goal at Berkeley, albeit the clip at which he moved could not be as rapid as he might have wished. That was the downside of the arrangement. Over the next four years the would-be author-illustrator who entered the Bachelor of Letters degree track had to do what was necessary to remain a formally enrolled student, and this involved the unthinkable: mastering basic mathematics. Also, as his essay on "The 'English Courses' of the University of California" makes clear, most of the literary-studies classes tried his patience. He did not care for the way in which they were taught by literary historians and critics with professional interests distinctly different from his own. But if his instructors were often less than vibrant, certain courses did feature *content* that was immediately pertinent and stimulating for this creative writer, for example, those dealing with French literature from the medieval period through the early 1890s— but not Emile Zola's novels. Ernest Peixotto's sister Jessica informed Walker that Zola was absent from the course on modern, realistic French writers taught by the associate professor of French and Spanish, Félicien V. Paget:

"He didn't mention Zola. At that time people did not tolerate Zola." Norris discovered Zola's novels on his own by, at the latest, 1894. His course work in English literature surveys treating the pre- and post-Restoration periods, a more specialized course on English poets of the fourteenth and fifteenth centuries, and others devoted to individual figures such as John Milton, Victor Hugo, and Alphonse de Lamartine would be reflected fully in Norris's highly allusive canon. That he had gravitated toward the study of medieval armor in Paris and had researched the Hundred Years' War in preparation for a grand painting of a scene from the Battle of Crécy complemented what he would learn in his required military science courses. Likeable or not, they too contributed to a canon disclosing Norris's unwavering interest in war and his penchant for employing martial imagery. See, for example, the description of the "day's campaign" at the Chicago Board of Trade in the third chapter of *The Pit*.[9] At the time of his death he was even projecting a trilogy dealing with the Civil War battle at Gettysburg, Pennsylvania.[10] But, again, Norris also had to meet requirements that had nothing to do with the career he envisioned, and he was certainly not prepared to distinguish himself in arithmetic, algebra, and geometry. For the first two he was "conditioned" and, for the third, given a failing grade during his freshman year.[11]

But in the late summer of 1889, passing grades, conditions and failures, and doing what was needful for the subsequent cancellations of those conditions and failures were in the future. Applicants to the university were required to take an entrance examination, and Norris had not been tested in this way for years. As Norris explained in his 1891 petition, before "entering college I was five years out of school and until within a few months never so much as looked into a geometry [book]."[12] It was actually less than five years, and it is unlikely that he had had no experience in geometry. Still, his situation upon his return from Paris was a daunting one.

Norris did not sequester himself totally in the months following his arrival in San Francisco in late August. On 26 December 1889, for example, he joined his cousin Ida Carleton and other socially prominent San Franciscans such as Dulce Bolado and her future husband, Gaston Ashe, at the reception for two hundred given at the home of Dr. and Mrs. A. H. Vorhees, one block below Sacramento on California Street.[13] In June 1890 he visited San Jose with his mother, Ida, and her closest friend Gertrude Goewey, going on with them to Lake Tahoe in early July.[14] Putting the "Robert d'Artois" and *Vandover* manuscripts aside, he also initiated work on a new book-length project: *Yvernelle* would be published two years later. At the same time, though, as Norris in the summer of 1889 began his herculean labors in preparation for taking the Berkeley entrance examination, the sentence marking the major turning point in the plot of *McTeague* was apropos: "Then the grind began."[15]

He had at least one tutor, remembered by Charles. Joachim H. Senger was an undistinguished philologist and professor of Greek and German whose fame now rests upon a nonacademic foundation: he was one of the 1892 founders of the Sierra Club, and Mount Senger in the Sierra Nevadas was named after him in 1894. What Norris thought of him and of the assistance he provided while he was enrolled at San Francisco's Urban Academy is not a matter of record.[16] Like another, much more distinguished faculty member under whom Norris studied geology and zoology during his junior year—the scientist, evolutionary idealist, Presbyterian religionist, and charter member of the Sierra Club Joseph LeConte—Norris never referred to Senger in writing. In fact, unlike Jack London, who studied for a short while at Berkeley and touted LeConte as a genius in his 1909 novel *Martin Eden,* Norris did not publicly acknowledge a debt of any kind to a professor at Berkeley—certainly not the curmudgeonly Armes, but not even the instructor of mathematics and his junior-year professor of astronomy, Armin O. Leuschner, to whom he was mightily beholden. Leuschner's initials "A.L." appear on Norris's transcript below his 1890 classification as a student with "limited" status; his was the authorization of admission to Berkeley despite Norris's deficiencies in mathematics.

The tutor-pupil match with Senger was an odd one, insofar as Norris did not later take courses in either Greek or German. Senger coached him instead in history, Latin, English, and—poor Senger!—mathematics. Lucy Senger wrote to Walker that Norris was "a genial young man, very polite and a good student." Her late husband "was always proud [of] his interest in his studies." But in one respect the professor had little reason to have become so sanguine. Norris's transcript confirms Jessica Peixotto's recollection that he "did not graduate because he could not do trigonometry." Albert J. Houston explained that the only reason Norris was able to satisfy the math requirements he did was that "all of the boys helped him crib it"; and, according to Benjamin Weed in 1930, Harry M. Wright—a fellow Fiji—was Norris's primary coach. Wright stated more bluntly than Leon J. Richardson the problem rooted in Norris's temperament: He "would have liked to graduate but did not wish to apply himself to things he did not like, especially mathematics."

Wright "would see him trying to learn the formulae" and "tried to show that it could be done by reasoning" instead. But Norris "did not feel that way about it," and that was the end of the matter. Mathematics was the principal reason for Norris's withdrawing from school on 23 May 1894, shortly before the graduation ceremony for his class. Rather than a diploma, he obtained on 20 September 1894 the "honorable dismissal" he requested,[17] by which time he was enjoying as a "special student" at Harvard University an academic environment more compatible with his interest in learning the one thing that drew him on: the craft of writing prose fiction.

What he did *not* enjoy at Harvard in 1894–95 was the experience of loneliness he first encountered when he began his tenure at Berkeley. Again, these uprootings and transitions were stressful. Norris's widow related that he was quite "lonesome" during the year in Cambridge; and, two or three years older than his fellow freshmen in the late summer of 1890, the twenty-year-old with a sallow complexion marked by past bouts with acne had the same experience when he entered Berkeley. Wallace W. Everett's account of how Ralph Hathorn, a sophomore in 1890, met Norris for the first time is revealing.

> Some time in December of 1890, a heavy storm had driven a large vessel ashore below the Cliff House in San Francisco. Thousands of spectators journeyed out to the beach to view the wreck, braving the racing wind and driving rain to witness the heavy seas and great combing breakers pound the ship to pieces on the shore before them. Ralph Hathorn, late that afternoon, saw a young fellow standing near him in the chill of this winter's afternoon without overcoat . . . and invited him to share his umbrella.[18]

The degree to which this francophone, dressed in the continental style, carried himself in the manner of a Parisian *boulevardier* worked against him on this campus. Ariana Moore remembered him as "different" throughout their years together at Berkeley. That he was clearly an "outsider" at the beginning of his freshman year was most dramatically measured by his close association with two male friends similarly situated by virtue of their ethnic identity: like Ernest and Jessica Peixotto, whose Portuguese ancestry was that of sephardic Jews, Myron Wolf and Maurice V. Samuels were representatives of the group that San Francisco society columnists referred to as Hebrews. As these columns in the *Chronicle, Examiner,* and *Wave* more often illustrated without comment, the social segregation of Jews and gentiles in the Bay Area was plainly a given—revealed by the names suggestive of ethnic origins that predictably appeared in clusters. Norris, Wolf, and Samuels dubbed themselves the "Three Musketeers" and related to each other on an equal footing in September 1890. According to Samuels, Norris even visited Coronado Beach near San Diego with him in the spring of 1891; and, as to his long-term relationship with Norris, Samuels had nothing but the most positive memories when he sent a memoir to Walker in 1930. But only one of the trio, the gentile, could have then become a candidate for membership in a fraternity such as Phi Gamma Delta. And yet, despite the Anglo-American pedigree blatantly suggested by the name Norris, anti-Semitism was so prevalent that Ralph Hathorn met resistance when sponsoring him. Some of the Fijis, explained Wright, thought that Norris "was a Jew" because of the company he kept on campus. Once that misunderstanding was cleared up, however, Norris "was as pleased as a child to join" the Delta Xi chapter.

Through the Berkeley years, Norris's address in the San Francisco directory was the familial home on Sacramento Street. Houston visited regularly there and often spent the night as Frank's guest. Norris never severed his ties with home life during the Berkeley years. But Charles noted that his brother lived at Professor Senger's home as he began his first semester; and Wallace W. Everett, after relating how Hathorn met Norris, reported that prior to being inducted into Phi Gamma Delta in June 1891 he "lived in a house on the north side of Bancroft Way, just east of Dana Street." Once Norris became a Fiji, though, he promptly moved into the stylish two-story fraternity house on Dana Street. It was hardly a step down from 1822 Sacramento, occupied as it was by twenty or more young men of Norris's social class. "It is a spacious house," wrote a local journalist in 1893, "with many large rooms and is admirably planned for the many entertainments and elaborate luncheons for which this fraternity is famous. Phi Gamma Delta Hall is conceded to be the most artistically furnished clubhouse in Berkeley."[19] Two years earlier, in an upstairs room, Norris installed some of the collectibles he had garnered in Paris, among them—remembered Harry M. Wright—a medieval casque, a skeleton hand, and a female bust. Frank M. Todd recalled tapestry, linked mail, and foils; and that skeleton hand, "the pride of his collection," was "hanging in a manacle" on the wall.[20] Such bric-a-brac was telling and went straight to the heart of another, extracurricular problem with which Norris dealt as he negotiated the closely related personal and professional identities by which he would be known when he obtained national visibility at the turn of the century.

The image problem Norris encountered remains a familiar one for not only adolescent American males but even those in their early twenties whose inclinations are artistic. It may not now be so exacerbated by John Ruskin's notion, articulated at midcentury in *Sesame and Lilies* and embodied dramatically in the Norris family itself, that "culture," like morality, is the province of the feminine, whereas the sphere of truly masculine interests in which men like B. F. Norris flourished has a distinctly different focus and tonality precluding any suggestion of the "sissy." Norris's response to the specter of unmanliness was not as exaggerated as Theodore Roosevelt's. But, in 1890–91, as he made his transition from the realm of the artiste, in which he had been a denizen since 1886, to the mainstream culture, in which males his age were preparing for decidedly masculine careers in business, medicine, and law, the heroes of the hour were the campus athletes and not those who had mastered the mandolin or, in Norris's case, the five-string banjo his mother had recently given him. Charles related that the present was intended as a means of keeping Frank at home; but, as has been noted, being a "townie" who commuted to and from the campus across the bay ran contrary to Norris's plan for seizing the opportunity to integrate himself with his male peer group. He did become a proficient performer with the banjo, but the call of the fraternity house and traditional masculine fellowship prevailed. That the banjo is now on display at the national offices of Phi Gamma Delta in Louisville, Kentucky, is thus symbolically fitting. For Norris's task was to reconcile, somehow, his dedication to the arts with his desire to be perceived and accepted as a "regular guy" and full-blooded Fiji.

He succeeded, but doing so could not have been a snap. He was far from physically imposing and would not put on weight until the turn of the century. Wright, having seen the "not overly strong" Norris "in black tights in the gym," likened him to "a great spider." He excelled at neither football nor baseball but the more androgynous sport of fencing. Frank M. Todd, who was Norris's familiar at Berkeley and Harvard, echoed Wright, observing that he "had no tendency to take part in athletics of any sort. Just didn't appeal to him. He was very individual in his interests and did what he pleased." When asked by Walker about Norris's months-long stay at Dulce Ashe's Santa Anita ranch in 1899, Todd opined that the Norris he knew at Berkeley would have been wholly out of place among wheat growers and their burly employees. That there was some truth to this Norris himself reflected in the less-than-flattering autobiographical characterization of the poet Presley in *The Octopus:* He is "different" from all of the other males in that novel. Further, as the peculiar curios in his room on Dana Street make obvious, Norris did not—and could not—wholly efface the signs of his artistic orientation. Even after becoming a Fiji, recounted Harry W. Rhodes, he "was rather sensitive about his art and writing and was continually joshed about it. The boys of the frat . . . would try to razz it out of him. Especially his drawing. As a result he kept very quiet about his work."

But work he did. Far from indolent in this respect, Norris edited, drew, and wrote for student publications, including the *Berkeleyan, Occident, Smiles,* and the university's *Blue and Gold* yearbook.[21] His short stories appeared off campus in regional periodicals such as *The Wave* and *The Argonaut.* In the more prestigious *Overland Monthly,* his illustrations accompanied his tales. A founding member of the Skull and Keys dramatic club, he not only acted in plays and skits on and off campus but authored the Junior Day farce *Two Pair,* performed in 1892, and at the same time another that never saw the stage, *The President's Address.*[22] In 1893 he wrote the lyrics for a "farce comedy" entitled *Minstrels;*[23] fashioned a parody of *Romeo and Juliet* the next year;[24] and, with his classmate Maida Castlehun and former Berkeley instructor Gelett Burgess, collaborated on the writing of a play entitled *Vehmegericht,* in which he performed in 1894.[25] According to Charles, a production of Sophocles's *Oedipus Rex* for which he had rehearsed did not make it to the boards. But J. R. Planché's *The Jenkinses* was produced in 1891,[26] as was Henry J. Byron's *Our Boys* in 1893[27] and W. S. Gilbert's *Engaged* in 1894.[28] Of all things peculiar, the Berkeley freshman had as early as November 1890 finished writing his first book and was trying to place it with a publisher.[29] The following year the sophomore saw its publication for the Christmas giftbook market by a prominent East Coast publisher, J. B. Lippincott of Philadelphia.

Bearing the formal publication date of 1892, *Yvernelle* appeared in November 1891. It was not a novel but a much less "masculine" kind of work constituting the only known product from Norris's hand that patently invited the "razzing" of fraternity brothers. A lengthy poetic narrative of the kind that had been required reading for students of his generation in college-preparatory programs, it brought to mind medieval romances and ballads as well as modern revivals of these genres by Scott and Tennyson. The medium and the subject matter of this volume, subtitled *A Legend of Feudal France,* could not fail to suggest effeteness and preciosity to the "boys of the frat." Its octosyllabic couplets tell of the unrequited love of the fair-haired maiden Yvernelle for Sir Caverlaye, who has been captivated by a less virtuous, dark-

Norris's artwork for a Berkeley student publication. (Courtesy of the Bancroft Library, University of California at Berkeley.)

haired, and more sensual siren named Guhaldrada. Having had his amorous adventure with her, the knight returns to his homeland, but not before his scorned lover pronounces a curse upon him: the next woman he kisses will suffer ruin. Caverlaye is thus reluctant to kiss the woman he really loves, Yvernelle—who misinterprets his reserve as indifference and brokenheart-edly decides to enter a convent and become a nun. Meanwhile, Caverlaye hits upon the solution for his problem: he kisses Guhaldrada, and her curse lights upon her own head. The obstacle to the flowering of true love is thus eliminated, and *Yvernelle* concludes with Caverlaye's furious ride across the countryside and his last-minute rescue of Yvernelle, who is on the verge of pronouncing the nun's vows of chastity, poverty, and obedience. The narra-tive ends happily. Although Guhaldrada seems rather unfairly burdened with all of the wages of sin and her brother is slain by the man who dishonored her, virtue more or less triumphs in Caverlaye's self-reformation, and chaste Yvernelle enjoys the fruits of devotion to her no-longer-inconstant swain.

The several reviews of the work were positive,[30] and it fared well locally. In October 1892, an "all requests" program of readings that a practiced elocu-tionist, George Riddle, delivered featured a lengthy reading from *Yvernelle*.[31] But no reviewer or auditor was so enthusiastic as Gertrude Norris, whose high-culture, Victorian tastes were embodied in her son's trial of a genre prized by her generation's admirers of Scott's *Marmion* and *The Lay of the Last Minstrel*. *Yvernelle*, reading as though it had been published at the be-ginning rather than the end of the nineteenth century, was the fulfillment of the former teacher's fondest dreams for the filial surrogate who might real-ize her abandoned artistic ambitions.[32] Gertrude had not only underwritten a portion of the cost of its production. Charles did not tell Walker that, in early 1893, the doting mother and impresario found another opportunity to put the limelight upon her fair-haired boy. She had become a member of the committee making arrangements for the exhibit of Californian literary accomplishments at the Columbian Exposition in Chicago. *Yvernelle* was one of the volumes in the display of works by the state's prominent authors.[33]

What B. F. thought of *Yvernelle* is not known but easily inferred. Accord-ing to Charles Norris, his characteristic assessment of his son's artistic orienta-tion and attainments was the scoffing expression "thimble-headed bobbism." What the author himself came to think, however, is a matter of record. He soon viewed *Yvernelle* as an embarrassment, and he attempted to collect and burn as many copies as he could of the oversized volume elegantly bound in both gold-stamped cloth and morocco. Seymour Waterhouse, a Fiji who preserved his own copy from the holocaust, stated that Norris destroyed "a good many." Still chagrined years later, he never mentioned *Yvernelle* when, as a novelist, he answered requests for biographical information from book reviewers and literary columnists.

But in late November or early December 1890, as the freshman was initially circulating the manuscript of *Yvernelle* among potential publishers and setting himself up for chaffings, he was also beginning to project a counterimage. By the time the bantering began, he had long since established himself as a masculine fellow. At the end of the spring semester of his freshman year, he was elected by his peers to be one of the principal figures in the long-standing campus event known as the "Bourdon Burial," named after the mathematical textbooks author Louis Pierre Marie Bourdon and originally based upon the annual ritualistic desecration of Euclid's *Elements* at Yale University. Each year since 1875 the Berkeley freshmen placed the most despised textbooks in a coffin and cremated them following a funereal procession through the city streets: consigned to the flames on 5 June 1891, accordingly, were Charles Davies's *Elements of Algebra on the Basis of M. Bourdon*, derived from Bourdon's *Eléments d'Algèbra*, and a textbook used in the expository writing course taught by William Dallam Armes, William Minto's *Manual of English Prose Literature, Biographical and Critical, Designed Mainly to Show Characteristics of Style*. Also a long-standing part of the tradition, the sophomores did all they could to disrupt the freshman ritual; violent encounters between the males of the two classes were de rigueur. Those unwilling to give or take a beating need not have considered participating.

That Norris qualified for the role of master of ceremonies is not surprising, given what he had done in that spring's issues of the student magazine *Occident*. There was no more prominent a critic than Norris of Minto's *Manual*, which proffered models of artful English prose to be imitated by Armes's students. In three pieces entitled "Stepterfetchit," Norris had parodied the styles of Thomas DeQuincey, Thomas Carlyle, and Thomas Babington Macaulay, signing himself "Dick Wincey," "Karl Aisle," and "'Mick' Aulay"—showing his hand in the last by adding "Norris, '94." For the 1891 Bourdon he served as the Pontifex Maximus—pope or high priest—whose duty it was to preside over that Friday evening's events in an outlandish outfit resembling a wizard's costume: the Pontifex led the procession, opened the "burial" ceremony, and then introduced three speakers dubbed the Damnator, the Maledictor, and the Laudator (whose charge was to lampoon the students who enjoyed the study of algebra). But Norris could not fulfill the requirements of his high office and instead became a legendary figure when a full account of the event entitled "Bourdon Buried: Berkeley Freshmen on the Rampage" appeared in the Saturday issue of the *San Francisco Chronicle:* "War was openly declared on Thursday evening. The sophomores decided upon a bold attempt at capturing and spiriting away Norris, the freshman Bourdon orator. To steal the orator was as good sport as capturing a dozen ordinary freshmen. At about 9 o'clock six intrepid sophomores entered the house of the Pontifex Maximus of the freshman class, seized poor Norris and, carrying him bodily to a carriage, drove away to a place of security with their unhappy victim."[34] According to Wright, they locked Norris in a barn miles away in Oakland. He escaped the next evening, too late to perform his duties and hold forth on how much he had suffered at the hands of Bourdon and, in his composition course, Minto. Although he was not able to add his own jeremiad to the other denunciations, two things were clear for those who now knew him by name: By the end of his freshman year he was much less the foreign-looking outsider whose ethnicity was dubious because of his association with two Jewish classmates; and he was neither a delicate poetaster nor foppish aesthete of the sort represented by Sheldon Corthell in *The Pit.* He would be ribbed for *Yvernelle,* but those fraternity brothers who teased him could do so only after acknowledging that he had proven himself a bona fide rowdy who could be counted upon for colorful high jinks in the years to come.

According to Wright, "He always entered into pranks with full zest." A case in point featured Seymour Waterhouse, who angrily learned of Norris's capacity for deviltry as he slipped into bed one night at the fraternity house. Norris fictionally reworked the event several years later in *The Octopus,* in a scene at Magnus Derrick's ranch when Annixter declines to eat a pudding that has been served with a sauce he detests. The irascible Annixter complains at unreasonable length that this "thick, gruel-like, colourless mixture, made from plain water and sugar," turns his stomach. He makes such a scene over his having been served this "sloop" that, before he turns in for the night, another wheat rancher at the table pours the gooey concoction between Annixter's bedsheets as a practical joke.[35] As with Annixter, who storms out into the night to return to his own ranch, Waterhouse did not find amusing the experience of sliding into the viscous mess put there by Norris, and he furiously stomped out of the fraternity house.

This was not the only time that Norris went too far. Harry W. Rhodes told Walker that Norris was always "inclined to be dramatic," echoing Houston, whose first sight of Norris found him dressed "in a long coat and two-peaked Sherlock Holmes cap which he had picked up abroad. He was always an actor, as was his mother." But Rhodes's much more striking recollection was of the first time the fraternities parked stage coaches on the sidelines at a campus football game and of Norris, beside himself with frustration as the Berkeley team performed poorly, yelling in the manner of a hod-carrier rather than a Victorian gent: "Why don't they catch that son of a bitch?" Football would again bring out the worst—by Victorian standards—in Norris's personality when, in the fall of 1896, he reported on the Bay Area games for *The Wave*, hectoring the players, second-guessing the coaches, and producing the most intemperate series of articles in all of his nonfiction. A similar trait is reflected in Norris's enthusiastic hazing of pledges and recently inducted Fijis. Rhodes related that he "would frequently startle the freshmen by bombastic question- ing and accusations at the dinner table." He thus documented the earliest instance in which Norris appears to have manifested the bullying disposition that, in the contemporary mythology of Anglo-Saxon supremacy, typed the race's genetically ingrained aggressiveness and culturally sanctioned appetite for dominance.

And yet Norris did not descend wholly into boorishness as he waxed macho. As Walt Whitman projected the image of being both "the poet" and one of the "roughs," counterpointing candid revelations of his sensitivities against his more "barbaric yawps," Norris strove for balance in the personality he was fashioning. Like his mother, he continued to participate in the social gatherings frequented by polite San Franciscans, and he even manifested hypersensitivity with regard to "proper" behavior. This yielded a cameo of a Norris so "scrupulously polite with the ladies" that it now appears the stuff of a scene designed for the comic stage. Walker recorded Jessica Peixotto's account of meeting him one day while crossing the campus. She came upon Norris as he was smoking his pipe, and he immediately put it in his pocket. Within a short while, as they stood there conversing, she could smell the cloth of his jacket burning. A gentleman need not be a prig. Jessica also recalled that Norris "liked independent women and," despite the outrage of the fac- ulty, "admired her when she led a movement to shorten skirts to shoe tops." But one simply did not smoke in the presence of the gentler sex, nor did one cut up in the way Norris did when, in the spring semester of his junior year, he attended with Harry M. Wright a series of lectures on reproduction that Joseph LeConte initiated on 22 April 1893.[36]

Amused by LeConte's description of a male spider inseminating a female

by transferring seminal fluid to her with his "feelers," Norris mimicked a solicitous male proffering his gift. In a falsetto voice, he made his appeal to her
sense of evolutionary altruism: "Madam, it is for the good of the race." Such
a performance would not have been appropriate in the presence of a young
lady, but it was perfectly suitable for a male context and for a performer intent
upon reinforcing the image of his masculinity that he had been developing
since his freshman year.

It remains debatable whether Norris suffered what may be legitimately
termed a "masculinity crisis." If he did, it was of brief duration; he had
proven remarkably adaptive, earning not only acceptance but popularity.
Yet he came to maturity in a culture in which eyebrows were raised at the
mere suggestion of a lack of virility in a young male, and Norris himself did
not rise above such prejudice in the years that followed. In his writings he
derided or lampooned effeminacy as he saw it manifested by males in social
life and the arts. He exalted manliness as it was traditionally defined, and he
self-consciously exercised the "masculine" voice and literary methods that
he admired in the writings of Robert Louis Stevenson, Rudyard Kipling,
and—as he termed him in 1896—the "Man of the Iron Pen," Emile Zola.[37]
He became, in short, one of the late nineteenth-century American literary
artists whose program it was to rescue literature from the feminine realm.
By the time he left Berkeley, the composition of another work like *Yvernelle*
was inconceivable.

Before turning to the literary evidence of Norris's reorientation and the
changes in the persona he projected by mid-1894, two other dimensions of
his experience during the Berkeley years demand attention.

It is not uncommon for students of his canon to assign Norris a significant
role in the unfolding of American intellectual history. Some have seen him as
a scion of the American transcendentalists, finding in his works suggestions
of a reemergence of early to mid-nineteenth-century philosophical points
of view like those of Emerson, Thoreau, and Whitman.[38] More typical are
those who see his work as directly related to developments in post-Darwinian
thought; and Norris—like Zola, Dreiser, and Crane—certainly merits such
consideration, given the overtly evolutionary context in which he set the majority of his novels and a goodly number of short stories. While never dubbed
a philosopher per se, Norris has consequently been scrutinized in terms of
how the themes of his works relate to the theses advanced by philosophic

contemporaries of Darwin such as Herbert Spencer and John Fiske, as well as the less well-known Berkeley faculty member, Joseph LeConte. In 1932, Walker only lightly touched upon Norris's relationship with LeConte, his geology and zoology professor. But since the mid-1960s, Norris's discipleship to this Christian religionist and philosophical idealist—so different from the agnostic Charles Darwin and that relentless foe of metaphysicians of all types, Emile Zola—has been a veritable *idée fixe* among all but a few interpreters of Norris's life and works.[39]

It perhaps goes without saying that Norris, like his schoolboy contemporaries, did not study philosophy when preparing for admission to Harvard, Princeton, and Yale. But in light of his alleged conversion to LeContean idealism, one may find it surprising that his Berkeley transcript records his having taken no course in philosophy. Nor did he enroll in one at Harvard. While the 1895 *Blue and Gold* yearbook identified him as a member of the Society for the Study of Ethics and Religion in his senior year,[40] no evidence of his active participation in this society has been unearthed. He does refer to Immanuel Kant's *Critique of Pure Reason* in one of the literary essays he published in 1901,[41] but the brief reference is only to a work suggestive of the far-reaching powers of the intellect. As to the extent of Norris's exposure to LeConte's thought outside of the geology and zoology courses he took in his junior year, he did voluntarily attend at least some of LeConte's lectures on reproduction. Whether he was present for the Bible studies conducted by LeConte on campus, attended LeConte's straightforward philosophical lectures and the colloquies in which he participated, or read any of his publications is not known. Again, Norris never directly referred to LeConte in his writings.[42]

What Norris understood of LeConte's philosophical and theological perspective was likely limited to the professor's departures from his formal lecture notes, when he shared his thoughts about the way in which geological history and the workings of natural selection relate to a divine will manifesting its intentions for the material world through evolutionary processes. Otherwise, Norris's philosophical and theological grounding at Berkeley was essentially the same as that of most English majors today: schools of thought represented by figures such as Plato and Kant received attention, as did writings such as Aristotle's *Poetics* that directly related to comprehension of the authors, works, and cultures being studied. Or, more accurately with regard to this student who "did what he liked," his studies were limited to those that dealt with subjects that caught his interest and might be of use to him as a professional author.

Joseph LeConte was himself an object of high interest. According to Norris's fellow students, he appears to have caught everyone's attention. And LeConte was a charmer in the lecture hall. In the "Things and People" column of *The Wave*, an unidentified contributor took his measure as a charismatic figure in 1896: "Professor Joe has one favorite lecture on glaciers that comes early in the Geology course. It is a masterpiece of scientific analysis, exquisitely blended with veritable eloquence. At its termination the class invariably bursts into enthusiastic applause."[43] He was also a celebrity beyond the campus. His movements in local society and about the United States were persistently charted by Bay Area social columnists. Still, although one learns from Seymour Waterhouse that Norris "liked LeConte greatly" and from Harry W. Rhodes that he "was interested in Uncle Joe's [geology] class," one is disappointed to find that, in addition to Norris's comical performance of spiderly insemination foreplay, the sole surviving, inarguably demonstrative consequence of LeConte's tutelage in 1892–93 was a limerick penned by Norris that Rhodes recited for Walker:

> *There once was an ichthyosaurus,*
> *Who lived when the earth was all porous.*
> *When he first heard his name,*
> *He fainted from shame,*
> *And departed a long time before us.*

One may assume that the courses conducted by LeConte introduced Norris to the essentials of evolutionary theory accounting for the extinction of species and the rise of new ones. Or, just as likely, he was reintroduced, since, in Wright's opinion, the theory was "a fairly fixed thing with the undergrads at [the] time." It was widely understood and generally accepted as verified. But what Norris thought of LeConte's attempts to reconcile Darwinism with Christian doctrine and, in particular, natural selection with the biblical concept of not only a compassionate but a just deity cannot be determined. Nor do we know what he thought of LeConte's extravagant idealism, which held that the material world enjoys no existence independent of the spiritual, since God is immanent, "resident in Nature, at all times and in all places directing every event and determining every phenomenon." In *Evolution: Its Nature, Its Evidences, and Its Relation to Religious Thought*, first published in 1888 and revised in 1891, LeConte proclaimed even more blatantly that physical reality is nothing other than the expression of the mind and will of God, that matter is spirit materialized: "[T]he phenomena of Nature are naught else than objectified modes of divine thought, the forces of Nature naught else than different forms of one omnipresent divine energy or will, the laws of Nature naught else than the regular modes of operation of that divine will, invariable because He is unchangeable." Thus, LeConte continues, more than faintly echoing Baruch Spinoza's monism, "the law of gravitation is naught else than the mode of operation of the divine energy in sustaining the cosmos."[44] So too, amidst humanity, are divine intention and action manifested directly in the operations of natural selection, the struggle for existence, the survival of the fittest, and the extirpation of the maladapted.

What did the Berkeley junior think of LeConte's optimistic belief that God, though his ways may be rough and even fatal for the members of a species, inexorably effects amelioration of the natural order over vast expanses of time? And what did he think in 1892–93 of LeConte's echoing of Ralph Waldo Emerson when explaining away "evil"—for example, the unmerited sufferings and deaths of his young siblings Grace, Florence, and Lester Norris—by terming it "only *seeming* evil"? Such dreadful developments LeConte refers to as the necessary means to a noble end, to the generation of "*real* good" in the form of nature's and mankind's improvement. "May we not say," asked LeConte in the face of all that mankind has endured through the ages, "that all physical evil is good in its general effect—that every law of Nature is beneficent in its general operation, and if sometimes evil in its specific operation, is so only through our ignorance" of what God is up to at that moment as he proceeds with his plan for the perfection of Nature?[45]

Norris's grasp of LeConte's unshakable ameliorism is reflected in his parodical use of the spider intent upon procreation "for the good of the race." For LeConte, Alexander Pope's article of faith held true: whatever is is right since it is originated by God. Thus, whatever occurs in the biosphere, "*seeming* evil" or immediately apparent "*actual* good," is "for the good of the race" as well as the species and varieties thereof. Philosophical adept he was not, but Norris did get the main point proffered by LeConte. And he did make use of it—satirically—in later years, in three instances assigning to his characters a LeContean point of view.

In *The Octopus*, a psychologically unhinged Presley echoes LeConte vis-à-vis the unruly and painful consequences of a tooth-and-claw struggle for dominance and then existence itself in California's San Joaquin Valley: escaping depression by choosing to take a positive view of the debacle he has witnessed, Presley finds comfort in the notion that "the individual suffers, but the race goes on . . . and all things, surely, inevitably, resistlessly work together for the good." Presley's mentor in this respect, Vanamee, is an even less mentally stable seer. Referring not only to the same bloody, inhumane, greed-motivated events in the San Joaquin but to the rape and death of his fiancée years earlier, he sounds the same *sursum corda* note: "Men perish, men are corrupted, hearts are rent asunder, but what remains untouched, unassailable, undefiled?" He declares to Presley, "'[Y]ou will find, if your view be large enough, that it is *not* evil, but good, that in the end remains.'" These are ironic moments in a novel that ends contrapuntally, with these two optimistic assertions ringing dissonantly in a grim, pessimistic tale. Norris devotes over six hundred pages of this large novel not to the representation of "*seeming evil*" that can be explained away à la LeConte but disturbing actualities, or real evil, rooted in historical events of 1880s and 1890s California.

The third use of what Norris understood of LeConte's gospel was more whimsical and is illustrative of the naïveté rather than the looniness of the heroine of *The Pit*. Sheldon Corthell prompts Laura to reflect upon how things just keep getting better and better as evolutionary time goes by. Unused to cosmic ruminations but doing the best she can to keep up her end of the conversation, she concludes that the "'individual—I, Laura Jadwin—counts for nothing. It is the type to which I belong that's important. . . . Then, let's see, the individual may deteriorate, but the type always grows better.'" How so? "'Something keeps [the type] from going below a certain point. . . . And that something is God.'"[46] Thank you, Joseph LeConte! Unfortunately for Laura, this grand insight proves of no use whatsoever as she struggles with many personal problems in the pages ahead. In one sense, the droll scene is a gratuitous embellishment meant to entertain the reader; in another, however, it quite meaningfully measures how irrelevant a LeContean revery is to life as pictured in *The Pit* and in *The Octopus*.

Given what was transpiring in the Norris family in the early 1890s, Gertrude and her elder son were not likely to have taken comfort in the LeContean notion that the vicissitudes they faced were part of a divine plan or necessary for "the good of the race."

That Gertrude and B. F. went their separate ways as occasion or whim dictated was the pattern suggested again and again in social columns through 1891. Gertrude was most frequently on her own as a vacationer and participant in various society events. B. F., commuting regularly between San Francisco and Chicago, was no stranger to solo flights, especially when it was reported that he planned to travel alone in Europe after delivering his son Frank to London in 1887. Despite the recent death of their son Lester, he sailed home alone from Paris a year before the boy's mother was psychologically ready to return to San Francisco. That this particular marriage may not have been made in heaven was the theme Bertha Rickoff sounded when Walker interviewed her. Recently arrived on the West Coast from New York City, where her father was a prodigious author of textbooks for D. Appleton and Company, this bluestocking became a close friend of Gertrude in late 1895 or early 1896 because of her lectures on literary matters before local groups to which Gertrude belonged, such as the Century Club. But despite their late acquaintance, only Charles among those Walker contacted appears to have known more about the private history of the Norris family. Rickoff, for example, was the only interviewee to mention that B. F. was not Gertrude's first choice for husband in the late 1860s. Not reported by Walker in his biography of Norris was her disclosure that "Mrs. Norris had married while on the stage after being disappointed over another man." The marriage was, or became, one of convenience in that Gertrude "never cared an awful lot for Mr. N[orris] and was inclined to neglect him for the children and her nieces, whom she was putting into society on his money." The marriage at last foundered while their son was a sophomore.

As B. F., Gertrude, and Ida registered at the Hotel del Coronado on 9 June 1891,[47] the final act of the melodrama upon which *The Pit* would in part be based had already commenced. According to the *San Francisco Chronicle*, the three did not return to the city until 29 July. But further on in the same social column, the reader is told that Frank and Charles had joined the party that returned to San Francisco a day later, on 30 July, without B. F. However long he actually stayed with his family at the Coronado during those seven weeks cannot be told, but he was now off on his own, arriving at the Hotel del Monte at Monterey by 17 August and then to the northeast at Saratoga by 28 September. Coming home some time between then and early January 1892, he was again *en famille*, according to the *Chronicle*, at the Hotel del Coronado, with Gertrude, Ida, and her friend and future bridesmaid Miss Goewey.[48] It is noteworthy, however, that his name did not appear in the guest registry book. "B. F. Norris and wife" was the entry for the two previous visits. The entry for 5 January 1892 instead reads "Mrs. B. F. Norris."[49] Whatever the exact circumstances, the 25 January *Chronicle* announcement of the return of the four marked the end of a lengthy chapter in B. F.'s life as sketched by the San Francisco press. This was the last time the *Chronicle* reported his having been in the company of his wife.

On 27 January 1892 his absence was especially conspicuous. Then began a series of social events hosted by Gertrude that had to do with Ida's engagement to Chaplain Frank Thompson of the U.S. navy.[50] B. F. was present at none of these, and, as Gertrude signed in at the Hotel del Coronado on 19 February 1892, sharing a room with a Mrs. Waters, he was in Chicago. Later that year, on 20 September, cousin Frank, rather than the uncle whose ward Ida had been for years, gave away the bride at St. Luke's Episcopal. The *Examiner* reported that it was at "the home of Mrs. B. F. Norris" that the reception was held. Further, Ida received callers at her aunt's—not her uncle's—home on Sacramento Street after her honeymoon.[51]

In one respect, little had changed publicly. For readers of the social columns there was nothing alarming or even remarkable about Gertrude, on 23 January 1893, beginning a tour of southern California with her niece and without B. F. On 24 January they arrived at the Hotel del Coronado. The absence of a reference to her husband is similarly not noteworthy when, on 3 June, Gertrude accompanied Frank to Chicago for the Columbian Exposition, visiting old friends while her son participated in activities arranged by Phi Gamma Delta for brothers from campuses across the nation.[52] According to Ralph Hathorn, Charles and Mrs. Ida Thompson were also in the party that remained in Chicago through the month and then "went off up into the Wisconsin lakes somewhere." Abounding in the columns were reports on women of Gertrude's social class enjoying the leisure that their husbands' businesses or their inheritances made possible. But few of Gertrude's acquaintances were as yet aware of the fact that her husband had bolted by May 1892—almost four months before Ida's wedding and a year and a half before his desertion of his family became a sensational story in the daily press.

At the time of Ida's wedding in September 1892, announced *The Wave*, B. F. was in New York City "under a physician's care."[53] He may or may not have been ill, given that Gertrude, Frank, or Ida was the West Coast information—or disinformation—source. But there was more to the story than either a medical problem or B. F.'s having decided to put distance between himself and his family.

No family member ever spelled out what happened between B. F. and the niece from whose wedding he was absent. But Charles's wife—then his fiancée, Kathleen Thompson—appears to have been referring to an unspeakably sordid development in a letter to Charles dated 26 November 1908: "And do you know, your mother told me all about your father,—the beginning of his nervous trouble—and your coming out here [to San Francisco], and Ida, and his trip, and all—A terrible, terrible story. It made me *sick* to look at her, stately and handsome in her silk, and think of her husband, after 27 dignified, confident years—suddenly *daring* to hurt her that way. And so *irretrievably.*"[54] One of Frank's personal friends whom he met at Berkeley, Eleanor M. Davenport, was quite specific—though wide of the mark—when she wrote to Walker in 1930: "I have always heard that Mr. Norris wanted [his wife] to go to Europe with him, which she refused to do because her children were young and that he then eloped with her niece." Whatever the nature of the "elopement" about which she had heard, and whatever B. F. did to—or with—Ida by 1892, *something* had happened. But the exact nature of the event remains veiled.

B. F.'s desertion of Gertrude was hurtful. Worse, in October 1892, he embarked on a trip around the world, and he was not alone. He traveled in the company of a woman named Belle—Belle Bovée, her will seems to indicate. She subsequently became the third Mrs. Norris.[55]

In mid-December 1893 Gertrude initiated divorce proceedings in Chicago, charging desertion.[56] Two weeks later, as the second semester of Frank Norris's senior year at Berkeley was about to commence, the story broke in the *San Francisco Chronicle:*

> The local Superior Court has been asked to adjust serious differences between Gertrude G. Norris and her husband. . . . The wife brought suit yesterday for separate maintenance and support. Her complaint is a voluminous document and arraigns Norris in an unpleasant manner for neglect and mistreatment of his family.
>
> According to the plaintiff's story, she became the wife of Norris in Chicago on May 27, 1867. . . . Mrs. Norris complains that her husband deserted her on May 25, 1892. She has since lived with her two children in this city, where, she says, her husband made his residence for the past nine years.
>
> From the complaint it appears that Norris owns a one-half interest in the wholesale jewelry firm of B. F. Norris, Alister & Co. . . . said to be worth $150,000 and to return an income of not less than $50,000 a year.

What triggered Gertrude's complaint resulting in an injunction against B. F.'s selling his San Francisco property was his having "given his agents, Madison & Burke, full power to sell . . . real estate," twelve pieces of property Gertrude thought were worth seventy-five thousand dollars and a net income of six hundred dollars per month. He did so, claimed Gertrude, to "prevent her securing alimony." This was not all that was charged, though. The *Chronicle* article continued:

It appears that Norris, although a resident of this city for nine years, has spent fully one-half of that time in Chicago and in traveling about the world. During his absence he allowed his wife for the support of herself and her children $175 a week. This amount was regularly paid by checks on the First National Bank until last October, when he reduced the allowance to $75 a week. Subsequently he stopped payment on three checks of $75 each, since which time he has made the plaintiff no allowance at all.

Mrs. Norris made a number of serious charges to explain her husband's conduct. She avers that ever since their separation he has been seeking to gain her consent that he should secure a divorce without opposition on the ground of desertion. She refused to assent to this arrangement, as she says, because she had not deserted her husband and no ground for divorce existed. . . . Norris is said to have told his wife that if she did not consent . . . he would not pay her a cent for maintenance and support. Failing to accomplish his purpose in this way he is said to have further threatened to cut off all support from his eldest son, who is a student in the State University pursuing his studies, the complaint says, in accordance with the particular and expressed wishes of his father.[57]

The *Morning Call* phrased this last threat in even more striking terms: Gertrude alleged that B. F. would "disinherit" Frank "unless he did his best to induce his mother to consent to a divorce without opposition."[58]

In Chicago, too, the fracas made news, B. F. proclaiming in the *Daily News*, "'There is not a word of truth in my wife's allegations as telegraphed from San Francisco.'" He was as livid as Gertrude as he continued to countercharge desertion for her refusal to accompany him on a round-the-world trip:

"I don't care to go into details in the matter, but my wife deserted me and, wishing a quiet and peaceable separation, I offered to give her all my property in San Francisco, which is worth over $100,000. I received a telegram yesterday saying that Mrs. Norris had obtained an injunction restraining me from disposing of my property in San Francisco. That is all I know of the present status of the case, except what has been published in the papers.

"Mrs. Norris had better have accepted my offer, for she will hardly secure as much through the courts. My attorney, Mr. Hardy, is now in California, looking after the case."[59]

On 22 June 1894 in San Francisco, the Superior Court finally settled the matter. Norris's parents were "absolutely released from the bonds of matrimony and all the obligations thereof." B. F. had correctly judged the likely outcome: The settlement was all of the San Francisco property. No alimony payments were to follow.[60]

Gertrude fared rather well financially. The residence at 1822 Sacramento had been in her name since 1884; but she had obtained from B. F. the present-day equivalent of more than a million dollars in real estate.

⌒

The divorce was finalized and the spring 1894 semester at Berkeley concluded in the same month. Frank Norris was perhaps wondering how what "*seemed* evil" in recent events could possibly prove "*actual* good," according to the logic of Joseph LeConte. Mother and son had much to mull when, in mid-July, they signed in at the Hotel Vendome in San Jose.[61] She had failed at her only marriage. He had just concluded four years at the university without receiving a degree. Now financially independent, Gertrude returned from San Jose to pack her trunks. She needed a more dramatic change of scene. So, too, did her son.

Norris, as Frank M. Todd informed Walker, had flirted with the notion that Harvard College might have more liberal graduation requirements than Berkeley. On 11 May 1894, he turned his attention to the application form to be read by its Committee on Admissions from Other Colleges. He requested senior class status, despite his listing of the course requirements he had not met at Berkeley: "Higher Algebra, Trigonometry, Conic Sections, [and] Astronomy unsatisfied." Also, for some reason, he did not provide the detailed information concerning his work on eleven subjects of study for which the committee asked; nor did he return the application "with certificates of scholarship and character from instructors." In the Harvard University Archives there is no evidence that Norris received a notice of acceptance. Still, Gertrude, Charles, and he made the transcontinental trip to Cambridge, taking rooms at the Brunswick Hotel in Boston. He learned that he was not to enjoy senior nor any other regular class standing. Instead, on 22 September he had to reapply for admission by filling out a new form for the Committee of the Faculty of Arts and Sciences on Special Students at Harvard College.

On 24 September 1894, Norris obtained provisional acceptance. A final decision awaited the arrival of "certificates of scholarship and character from instructors." Professor Senger wrote on Norris's behalf on 30 September. James Sutton, the recorder at the University of California, also testified to his character and academic standing in "every department except that of Mathematics." On 9 October Norris formally became a Special Student. No longer setting his sights on a degree, he explained in his second application that he was not sure which courses he meant to take: "I cannot state specific courses, but would like to take a general course [of study] in literature." His "object in taking these courses"? It remained the same as that with which he began his four years at Berkeley: "To be thoroughly prepared for a literary profession."[62]

8

THE SHORT-STORY WRITER
IN THE MAKING AT BERKELEY

At Harvard College in the late summer of 1894, Frank Norris again stood out as "different." Now twenty-four years of age and situated in 47 Grays Hall, he was easily the oldest student in the dormitory and could be mistaken as one of the younger instructors when going to and from class across College Yard, the grassy square upon which his window looked. There was another difference as well. Although his widow remembered him as lonely while at Harvard, he was not alone like the others in the hall who had just bid farewell to their parents. Situated a few blocks to the southeast on Main Street—renamed Massachusetts Avenue before his year in Cambridge ended—were his mother and brother Charles. Frank was putting the Berkeley experience behind him, and, as when she fled San Francisco shortly after Lester's death, Gertrude was distancing herself from the scene of another personal disaster reported fully in the daily press. All three did not return to San Francisco until after the close of the academic year.

Charles told Walker nothing of how he felt about being pulled out of school at age thirteen and taken across the continent the way Frank had been at fifteen. But Charles did remember the "boarding house" where his mother and he resided. This was Bernard C. Welch's Hotel Harvard at 221 Main Street. Charles recalled little else other than that Frank and he attended the first American performance of Paul M. Potter's four-act dramatic adaptation of George DuMaurier's best-selling novel of 1894, *Trilby.* It was staged at the

Boston Theatre in the spring of 1895, when "Trilby-mania" was at its height.[1] Also, and more important for admirers of *McTeague,* Charles identified a Miss Bates, who lived next-door at the Hotel Harvard. The spinster was the model for one of the characters in that novel, Miss Baker. She was a timely discovery insofar as the literary remains of the Harvard experience indicate that Norris had begun in earnest the composition of *McTeague.* That winter he was for the first time executing undeniably Zolaesque, sketchlike drafts dealing with characters and scenes intended for use in that naturalistic novel, which would be published four years later. Many of these sketches survive,[2] and it was in Cambridge that Frank Norris, as most readers today know him, first displayed his signature traits as an author.

Much less familiar are those characteristics that defined him as a University of California undergraduate trying to find his stride as an author in 1890–94.

Just how radical a turn he took as a writer while at Harvard is apparent when one turns back to his first book. It hardly seems possible that the poet preoccupied with medievalism who initiated the writing of *Yvernelle: A Legend of Feudal France* in late 1889 or 1890 would give the world *McTeague,* or a second novel for which he was also developing a portfolio of sketches while at Harvard, *Vandover and the Brute.* But there are other early publications, penned at the same time as *Yvernelle,* that even more dramatically prompt one to wonder how Norris could make the leap to avant-garde status after displaying at Berkeley a loyalty to aesthetic values that were beyond old-fashioned, as rechauffé as they were recherché.

To understand his orientation as he became a freshman, one must consider once again Norris's experience as an art student at the California School of Design and the Académie Julian. Its influence will be seen even more clearly than in *Yvernelle* in three shorter poetical works he published in October, November, and December of 1890 in the Berkeley student magazine *Occident.* These works, entitled "At Damietta, A.D. 1250," "Brunhilde," and "Les Enervés de Jumièges," like many an Academic painting, assume that the reader is familiar with what happened at Damietta, who Brunhilde was, and why an interment took place at Jumièges. Norris made few concessions to those who have not read about the events he describes. How he wrote these poems dramatically reflects the bookish study that ineluctably accompanied the learning of technique in drawing and painting. Academic painting—so often dealing with scenes derived from classical literature, history, and mythology—demanded much more from its originators and its consumers than a pastel portrait of a young girl by Renoir or an oil painting of flowers in a vase by Fantin-Latour. To paint or comprehend as an onlooker a picture featuring Achilles and Hector, Cincinnatus or Julius Caesar, or Halcyon and Ceyx, one must know the narratives concerning them. Little wonder that critics of impressionist works complained that, intellectually, they were empty, while salon machines such as Julian R. Story's *The Black Prince at Crécy* pictured a moment suggestive of multiple, complex historical developments and their psychological consequences for the central figure of that painting—*if* the person viewing it knew as much about the Hundred Years' War as Story and Norris did. In short, Academic paintings most often are elitist in their appeal—addressed to a liberally educated upper class and not to a mass spectatorship. In Norris's time, they undemocratically bespoke high culture, as distinguished from popular culture. And so did Norris's earliest Berkeley publications, signed with gothic panache, "Norrys, '94."

"At Damietta," for example, begins in medias res with

> *"Who can he be that rides so swift*
> *In from the desert's trackless drift,*
> *Who strikes his poignard in his steed*
> *To drive him to more furious speed?*
> *Ah, now I tremble lest he bring*
> *Ill tidings of my lord and king,*
> *So let us straightway to the hall*
> *Admit this horseman, and know all."*
> *Thus high-born Margeret made complaint,*
> *Wife of King Louis,—called the saint.*

The queen thus learns that King Louis is "prisoner in the soldan's hands." Soon thereafter, "The hordes of Saracen and Moor / On Damietta downward bore"; and it is only a matter of time before "[t]he crescent rises o'er the cross" at Damietta. That is to say, the implied, *ideal* readership for the poem has also read the *Memoir* of Jean de Joinville that in Paris had introduced Norris to the thirteenth-century historical figure about whom he had constructed a novel-length narrative, Robert d'Artois. Or the poem assumes that a reader is familiar with another text derived from the *Memoir* and that he or she can provide the historical context for Norris's description of what is transpiring. Such a reader—when he or she can be found—will recognize from the references to the captured king and to the queen residing at Damietta, Egypt, that the century is the thirteenth, that the first crusade of King Louis IX is in process, and that Damietta will soon be wrenched from the hands of the invading Europeans intent upon seizing control of the Holy Lands.

The climax is the scene in which the queen asks her seneschal to vow to slay her with his sword upon her command, should the enemy take the city. The sensational twist and chilling complication of the reading experience then occurs: he tells her that he had already resolved to do her the kindness of ending her life well before she made her request. But one has to wonder how many of Norris's fellow students persisted so far in their reading. The problem with the poem is again illustrated as soon as the seneschal delivers the reply in Joinville's *Memoir* that Norris found so memorable; for Norris then accelerates his movement toward the conclusion of his 132 lines by introducing the condensed account of subsequent events thus, "In history you know the rest."[3] That, of course, is the rub—most readers will not "know the rest." Nor will they have previously known the location of Damietta, that King Louis's forces conquered it and then lost it, and so forth. In 1890 on the Berkeley campus, Norris was assuming too much with regard to his readership.

One sees the same situation in "Brunhilde." It commences in the erudite manner with an epigraph in French from Geoffroi Rudel that, according to the elaborately detailed subtitle, Norris derived from his "*Chronique de Clotayre*, Lib. vii., Chap. ccxiii. (MS. of the XIII century)."[4] Norris's poem is an expansion upon the epigraph's description of the unpleasant death of the Frankish Queen Brunhilde at the hands of Clotaire II in 613 A.D. Tied to a spirited horse, she is dragged across the countryside—and through Norris's poem—to her death. Why, however, the poem does not make clear. It offers only generalizations that allude to details presumed to be already known by the reader. One is not told, for example, who Clotaire and his vengeful mother Fredegonde are, nor is it apparent why their animus toward Brunhilde is so homicidally extreme. And the reader faces a like predicament in the third poem, "Les Enervés de Jumièges." The speaker in the first section is the Frankish King Clovis of the fifth and sixth centuries who is setting adrift on the Seine a barge containing the half-dead bodies of his two sons. Their crime? They "revolted against my reign." But Norris does not name the speaker, and he does not tell the reader the nature of the revolt that occurred. Further, one *must* know beforehand that "Les Enervés" are the king's enfeebled sons whose corpses were finally brought ashore and interred by monks at Jumièges, or one cannot enjoy in this poem what is of genuine poetic merit.[5] And that, undoubtedly, was the experience of virtually all at Berkeley who were not as fascinated—indeed, infatuated—with French history as Norris had become while living in France.

The extent of Norris's focus on antiquity is again made clear in the subjects of the essays he produced as he met the requirements of his expository writing courses. None of the pieces he wrote is extant, but "Quentin Durward" was the title of the one he submitted in October 1890. The subject was the historical romance by Sir Walter Scott, set in the fifteenth century and dealing with the conflict between Louis XI of France and Charles the Bold of Burgundy. Quentin is a knight, and the romance is suffused with things chivalric in the manner of *Yvernelle*. The next essay, for November, was "Harold"—the king of the Saxons who met his death in 1066 when William the Conqueror invaded England. Norris's main information source was, presumably, Edward Bulwer-Lytton's historical romance, *Harold: The Last of the Saxon Kings*. December saw "Thomas à Becket"; January 1891, "European Civilization at the Outbreak of the Hundred Years' War"; February, "Joan of Arc"; March, "Heroes of the Iliad"; April, "Jongleurs and Trouvères of Mediæval France"; May, "Alfred the Great"; and, as he completed his writing requirements in his sophomore year, he chose to describe "A Young Englishman at an English University in the Early Part of the Sixteenth Century" in November and "The French Dwelling House of the Middle Ages" in February 1892. Surprising, thus, were the last two submissions: in April Norris vaulted toward modernity with "Constitution of 1791," that is, the *French* Constitution. Then in June he somehow managed to have accepted a fictional piece for his finale, a manuscript entitled "A Story."[6]

Given the dominantly medieval orientation seen in these essays, his earliest poetical publications, and the "Clothes of Steel" article for the *San Francisco Chronicle* that initiated his publishing history in March 1889, one rightly wonders whether "A Story" was "Lauth," published not in a student magazine but the prestigious *Overland Monthly* in March 1893. Or perhaps he pulled a fast one by recycling the manuscript of another short story set in the Middle Ages, "The Jongleur of Taillebois," which had appeared in the Christmas 1891 issue of *The Wave*.

These two short stories are biographically significant in a much more important way, though, for both mark Norris's realization that the obscurantism characteristic of works like "Les Enervés de Jumièges" would not do for one determined to earn his living by his pen someday. Like the poetical narrative *Yvernelle*, the two gothic romances in prose are decidedly old-fashioned pieces of storytelling, but they wisely make formal concessions suitable for a popular readership. They are rife with terminology appropriate for histori-cally accurate descriptions of the medieval world, but it does not get in the way any more than Edgar Allan Poe's elevated vocabulary and recondite al-lusions do in similar terror tales.

"Jongleur" is a straightforward account of the fantastic consequences of a cold-blooded murder and the burial of the corpse beneath a great pine tree. Many years later, the murderer Amelot has withdrawn from employment as a knight and become a *jongleur*, or troubadour, accompanying himself on his stringed instrument, a *vielle*, which—unbeknownst to him—was made from the tree that fed upon his long-deceased victim. One day he finds that he cannot control this instrument. It plays a weird melody by itself, casting a spell upon him, during which he unwittingly confesses his crime. Condemned to death, he enters a fortress where he will be hanged. He escapes from the warder in charge of him. The portcullis, or grate suspended in the gateway of the fortress, descends to block his escape, but it appears that Amelot can make his exit before it reaches the ground. Alas, it makes the same eerie sounds as the *vielle* as it descends. Amelot, astounded, pauses, and the port-cullis pins him to the ground with its pointed teeth. At the gibbet, his final thought is the realization that it too was manufactured from that same pine. Thus, the sounds made by the framework as he meets his death seemed "to thrill with ring of triumph and final exultation": "It was the last sound he ever heard."[7]

Summary does not do justice to the better qualities of this example of gothic romance writing. Suffice it to say that it is what it is; that similar tales updated to more modern settings were then enhancing Ambrose Bierce's reputation in San Francisco; and that works of the sort still find a market. Moreover, it is likely that those with a taste for romances will today prefer the rapidly paced, crisp sensationalism of "Jongleur" to the comparatively prolix and decidedly more sentimental *Yvernelle*.

Norris was adjusting his voice and refashioning his persona in an even more important way as he also distanced himself from "At Damietta" and "Brun-hilde" by trying his hand at short stories set in the present and the recent past. Well before *Yvernelle* finally made it through the press and emerged from the bindery in late 1891, he began experimenting with the produc-tion of a more democratic, up-to-date kind of storytelling with mass appeal, turning for assistance to the methods of a hugely successful writer, a contemporary who managed to have his cake and eat it too. Displaying literary sophistication while also engaging the keen interest of the so-called average reader, Rudyard Kipling had recently become a household name in the Anglo-American reading community, and Norris was falling under his sway by the end of his first semester at Berkeley. Neither of the two short stories that appeared in the *Occident* in December 1890 and March 1891—immediately after the publication of "Les Enervés de Jumièges" ended Norris's high-culture binge—rises to the level of Kipling. Still, both the subject matters and narrative techniques of "The Coverfield Sweepstakes" and "The Finding of Lieutenant Outhwaite" are testimonies to Norris's admiration, imitation being the sincerest form of flattery. They are also congruent with another alteration being made in the image that Norris was attempting to project: Kipling was the polar opposite of an aesthete; his voice and subject matter were blatantly, even aggressively masculine.

"The Coverfield Sweepstakes" is a colorful, animated monologue describing a horse race, replete with jargon (a pronounced signature trait of Kipling's realist renderings of speech) and delivered in a dialect that is an American analogue of the cockney and Irish brogue of the principal characters in Kipling's *Soldiers Three and Other Stories* (1890). The story-within-a-story monologue in "The Finding of Lieutenant Outhwaite" will likewise ring a bell for fans of Kipling, whose style proved far from inimitable for Norris. The story begins thus:

> "Who is that fat woman?" I asked.
> "You mean the one that just sang?" said Vandover.
> "No. The one in red on the sofa talking to Henkle. There—that one that just dropped her fan."
> "Oh that one; come up stairs and I'll tell you about her." So we went up stairs into the half-silence of the gentlemen's smoking and dressing rooms. . . . And Vandover told me all about it.
> "You remember Outhwaite," said he, "who killed Casimir Pouchkine in the duel at Monaco, ten years ago, and who died last February; well, when Outhwaite was yet a very little fellow at St. Cyr, his family had contracted him for a marriage with his cousin Denise Ennemond. Ever since Outhwaite could remember, he had looked upon this marriage as one of the events of the natural order of things and had come to regard it, without much emotion, as a matter of course. When he was sixteen he left St. Cyr, I don't know why, and went to Algiers with some relative—uncle I believe. In the course of time he entered the *chasseurs d'Afrique*, grew up with the army, saw some service, and got himself the grade of *sous-lieutenant*. At the time of receiving

his commission he had long cut loose from his uncle and was making shift for himself. He drank more absinthe than was good for him, lost money at roulette, did not win it back at the *courses,* and otherwise wasted his substance in riotous living. He got very wild and finally wound up by doing Pouchkine to death in his Monaco 'meeting.' (I don't know who the woman was.)"[8]

Vandover is the type of voluble yarn spinner who makes frequent appearances in Kipling's writings; he meets a friend who has not yet heard the tale that is forthwith told. As in many of Kipling's stories, this narrator's rapid-fire exposition of background information on the rakish Outhwaite appears excessive in detail and digressive. Indeed, it proves so later, since Pouchkine's death has nothing to do with the finding of Lieutenant Outhwaite by Denise Ennemond after a decade's separation; their not recognizing each other when they meet; their falling in love without knowing each other's true identity; and the revelation by Vandover that the fat woman in red downstairs is Outhwaite's wife, Denise. Actually, the whole story is a witty digression, since all that Vandover needed to say in answer to the question posed to him at the start was, "That fat woman is Outhwaite's wife." Both the style and the sense of humor closely resemble Kipling's.

Two months later, in the June 1891 issue of *Argonaut,* Norris made his first appearance in a nationally distributed monthly, this time mimicking even more overtly the already well-known champion of English imperialism by fashioning a colonial setting like the East African one in Kipling's 1890 novel *The Light That Failed.* As with Kipling's Brits, who repeatedly subdue uncooperative native populations in the name of progress and enlightened rule, so in "The Son of the Sheik" are Norris's French soldiers in North Africa intent upon suppressing Arab uprisings. The voice heard is the animated and digressive one of Vandover in the earlier story; and, as with the hero of *The Light That Failed,* the narrator is an artist with a keen eye for detail. Like Kipling, one of whose signature idiosyncrasies was the constant inclusion—without translation—of words and phrases of Indian origin, Norris peppers his text with unglossed references to the *bournous, haiks, douars,* and *yataghans* of the Kabyles—that is, the Arabs.

Norris's infatuation with Kipling would prove of long standing. His widow recalled many enthusiastic readings of Kipling's short stories and poems during their courtship years, 1897 through 1899. In 1897 Norris made it clear that few could demonstrate so thorough a familiarity with the Kipling canon as he did when, in the Christmas issue of *The Wave,* his "Perverted Tales" masterfully parodied the typical Kipling tale set in India. He displayed a preternaturally full recall of five of Kipling's collections of short stories published between 1889 and 1891.[9] But by the time Norris was a member of the senior class at Berkeley, the full impact of Kipling's tutelage was apparent in no less than eight short stories that in varying degrees paid homage to him. Between September 1893 and February 1895, when the last one saw print, Norris's stories in *The Wave, Overland Monthly,* and *Argonaut* displayed the unmistakable impress of Kipling's influence: all focus on modern conditions, and none on those of the remote past; the language of the characters as well as the narrator is smartly contemporary rather than fustian; and, as with "The Son of the Sheik," Norris continued to "borrow" from Kipling's large stock of quirky mannerisms.

For example, 1894's "After Strange Gods," in the "Outward and Visible Signs" series of five pieces he contributed to the *Overland Monthly,* appropriates a vintage Kiplingesque narrative situation featuring the retelling of an outlandish tale, the responsibility for which rests not with the skeptical narrator but the man from whom he first heard it. Added to the mix is the inclusion of shudder-inducing detail—another Kiplingesque trait that resulted in his reputation among genteel Anglo-American book reviewers for offensive descents into the gruesome and, by pre-Zola standards, the sordid. "After Strange Gods" begins,

> This is not my story. It is the story of my friend Kew Wen Lung, the *gong-toi,* who has his little green and yellow barber shop in Sacramento Street, and who will shave you for one bit, while you hold the shaving bowl under your chin. This price, however, includes the cleaning of the inside of your eyelids with a long sliver of tortoise shell held ever so steadily between his long-nailed finger tips. Kew Wen told me all about it over three pipes in his little room back of the shop.

The unnerving imagery having to do with the possibility of one's eye being cut by either a sliver of shell or the barber's long, curled finger nails is not a wholly gratuitous attention getter. The tale concerns a young Chinese woman who blinds her French lover so he will not see the way in which smallpox has ravaged her face—and she thus saves their relationship. Once the retelling of the bizarre love story with a "happy ending" is concluded, Norris avails himself of another hallmark device from the Kipling canon. The narrator, who seems to have labored mightily to render his account credible, undercuts what he has achieved by reminding the reader that "this is the story as my friend Kew Wen Lung, the *gong-toi,* told it to me. Personally, I do not believe very much of it; however, you may have it for what it is worth."[10] And one notes in passing that, as with Kipling's frequent use of foreign terms, Norris never defines *gong-toi*.

The other short stories produced during Norris's senior year are much less bizarre. "Travis Hallett's Half-Back" and the other four "Outward and Visible Signs" tales recall Kipling's preoccupation with virile young males in challenging situations: winning the love of a woman, manfully demonstrating their mettle in the face of intimidating circumstances, and, in the paired short stories entitled "Unequally Yoked" and "A Caged Lion," suffering the rueful consequences of a male-female mismatch like that of Norris's parents. In these latter two stories, published in 1893 and 1894, the hero is a world-renowned explorer who deliberately becomes a "nobody" because that is the price of winning the hand of the woman with whom he is infatuated. A majestic lion of a man becomes the heroine's lap dog. Unlike Kipling, Norris does not warrant the charge of misogyny in these two works. Like Kipling, though, he bridles here and later in his writings when the feminine sphere intrudes too much upon the masculine and emasculation is, or may prove, the consequence.

Another influence simultaneously at work in Norris's early short stories was that of an American author less familiar to present-day readers than Kipling. From the beginning of the 1890s through the next quarter century, Richard Harding Davis was as grand a literary figure, known not only for his ingratiatingly pleasant short stories but his widely admired impressionistic journalism. As he did with Kipling in "Perverted Tales," Norris would also write in 1897 an expert parody of the typical Davis tale, entitling the sendup "'Van Bubble's Story.'"[11] Like Kipling, Davis featured adventuresome, manly youths. But "Van Bubble" is a reference to Davis's best-known character in the early nineties, Courtlandt Van Bibber, a young New York City social swell who typed all that was noble and silly in life among the old-moneyed on Park Avenue and Long Island estates, in Boston's Back Bay, and at Newport, Rhode Island's watering hole for the wealthy. Davis collected the droll stories featuring the adventures of this somewhat obtuse but good-hearted and morally upright clubman in *Gallegher and Other Stories*, *Stories for Boys*, and *Van Bibber and Others* in 1891–92. They were so popular that a canny marketer brought out a Van Bibber brand of cigarettes. Norris dubbed his Van Bibberish young gent Desfield in 1894's "She and the Other Fellow" in his "Outward and Visible Signs" series, and he had him perform the sort of good deed for which Van Bibber was affectionately known nationwide. Desfield artfully separates the heroine from her new beau, going to extraordinary and finally comical lengths to provide a better man, his friend, with the opportunity to regain the affectionate regard in which she previously held him. All's well as the story ends, as is typically the case in Davis's tales of the kind.

All's not so well, though, in the earliest instance in which Davis's influence can be detected, Norris's "The Way of the World," published in *The Wave* in July 1892. As in Davis's Van Bibber stories, Norris's tone is one of kindly but Olympian detachment when describing an adventure of his hero; his voice echoes Davis's when Van Bibber again and again unexpectedly finds himself in a scrape. The embarrassing predicament in "The Way of the World" is, however, a bit more racy than those faced by Van Bibber and more like those later known by Vandover. It involves a young man's attachment to a less-than-virtuous showgirl. He is the model of the inexperienced, starry-eyed stage-door Johnny, naïvely having his first great romantic experience with a woman of the calculating and self-serving sort he does not at all understand. Never expecting that she would confer her favors upon another gent with the same largesse she has shown him, he is cruelly disappointed one evening to discover her entertaining someone else in her dressing room. He is then devastated to see that it is none other than his own father! Davis *never* descended to the sordid. But Norris had good reason to rise above, or delve below, the ever proper Davis at this time in his life. Two months earlier, his father had deserted Gertrude Norris to take a trip around the world in the company of another woman. Well before that excursion, though, it appears that B. F. Norris had given his son reason to think in terms of philandering fathers and to fashion a short story accordingly.

Not so unorthodox a tribute to Davis is one other short story worthy of special note. "The Most Noble Conquest of Man" is the closest that the Berkeley undergraduate ever came to plagiarism. This May 1894 piece, another in his "Outward and Visible Signs" series, is distinctively Norrisean in certain respects. The French epigraph declares that the horse is the most noble conquest of man, and Norris was never happier than when he could indulge his pleasure in horseflesh. The student at the California School of Design who drew horses hour after hour with Peixotto at the Presidio stables gives as much attention in "Brunhilde" to the exhausted horse that drags the queen to her death as he does to her expiration. Sir Caverlaye's ride across the countryside to rescue Yvernelle from a convent is protracted in part because

Norris judged the sterling performance of the knight's steed worthy of rapt attention. Norris was at the very top of his game when, in "The Coverfield Sweepstakes," he excitedly describes the mare Hecate pulling ahead of her competitors: "[H]er ears flat, her head stretched out, and her neck low, her four great hoofs pounding in alternate pairs, now on this side now on that with the regularity of a trip-hammer, rocking from side to side with that peculiar motion of a pacer."[12] Davis manifests no such infatuation in "Mr. Travers's First Hunt," from *Van Bibber and Others.* Nor does he display Norris's easy familiarity with paddock jargon and typical equine behavior. But Davis's and Norris's comical stories deal with an identical situation in one respect, and Davis's tale was inarguably Norris's inspiration.

Both stories present the reader with a young man who knows nothing about riding but must demonstrate that he is an expert if he is to obtain the hand of a young woman. He succeeds in his amorous quest despite his ignorance and ineptitude.

Davis's young Travers must impress the girl's father, Old Paddock, who will give his daughter only to a man who can ride. Forewarned by Miss Paddock, Travers pretends to be an equestrian, and her father immediately puts him upon a mount ominously named Satan. Carried across the countryside at breakneck speed, Travers somehow manages to stay in the saddle. Old Paddock misinterprets his luck as skill beyond anything he ever hoped for in a son-in-law, and Davis's brief story ends happily. What caught Norris's attention, however, is essentially an anecdote. Davis provides not even a glimpse at Travers's wife-to-be; and Travers himself is a rapidly executed sketch, a caricature rather than a character.

Norris's expansive variation upon what Davis wrought does not permit such a dismissive response from the reader. In his full-length short story, for example, the heroine rather than her father is the horse fancier to be impressed by Dick Taggart, and Norris makes it abundantly clear why Taggart would be willing to risk life and limb, if necessary, to earn the regard of this paragon of beauty and to win her away from the practiced horseman who is his rival. The narrator evokes images of Sir Walter Scott's Lady Rowena and Henry Fielding's Sophia Western, with a painter's eye:

> I remember that the first time I ever saw Virginia Forsythe I said she looked as if she might have canted right out of the pages of Scott, or from the frame of some old family portrait of the days of fox-hunting and Squire Western.
> She was in the saddle, riding down a country road at a very free hand gallop. The horse she was riding was her own,—a clean-barreled English thorough-

bred named "Conspirator," such as Leach used to draw, with an open gait, small pasterns, and closely docked tail. She rode wishbone style, with not too flowing divided skirts, finished off at the shoulders with a kind of postilion cape; . . . and her manner of riding her mount was as though the twain had become one flesh; and the picture she made on her fine horse cantering so freely through a country lane against a blue haze of a California landscape, with a bit of green hedge running into the background and a strip of yellow rye in the middle distance, was very fetching and very pretty.

Also possessed of a pleasant personality that is the polar opposite of the femme fatales in "Unequally Yoked" and "The Caged Lion," Virginia is a prize truly worthy of unstinted effort, and even a modicum of dissembling. Taggart pretends understanding each time she holds forth in remote technical language on matters equine. He even poses as a connoisseur, attempting to undercut his rival. Says Taggart, "'He's a good boy, but,'—he shook his head and smiled—'he don't know horse a little bit.'" He is in fact describing himself, and Taggart is shortly thereafter oblivious as to the meaning of the advice given him by the stablemen from whom he rents a horse. His plan is to stage an accidental meeting with Virginia. And so he sallies forth where angels would fear to trot.

The mare he has mounted—Norris gives her a personality as distinctive as the hero's and heroine's—"knew that Taggart did not know how to ride" and takes advantage of the situation. She begins to cut up, pivoting on her hind legs and going down streets sideways. A streetcar, however, spooks her, and, when the moment in which Taggart plans to impress Virginia occurs, she and his rival see the panicked horse streaking by, with Taggart holding on with both hands to the saddlehorn. Virginia must deftly save him. Humiliated, Taggart is unable to divert attention from the fact of his ineptitude, even with a witty quotation given him by a writer with often astonishing recall of scripture: "The horse is a vain thing for safety" (Psalms 33:17). Nursing his bruises at home, he is certain that his rival for Virginia's heart has prevailed.

Frank Norris is not remembered today for prose fictions with happy outcomes. For most readers, the gruesome death of Trina McTeague at the hands of her husband sounds the keynote in his canon. And although order has come out of chaos in the concluding chapter of *The Pit,* it ends with a somber chord suggestive of uncertainty and menace. But even after the Berkeley years, a surprising number of his less well-known works offer the consolation that things sometimes *do* go right. Some may find the twist in the plot that ends "The Most Noble Conquest" cloying and prefer the lighthearted, matter-of-fact way in which Richard Harding Davis's hero passes muster with his fiancée's father. Others, however, may be more receptive to the manner, intended as charming, in which Norris's heroine reveals that she is not as obsessed with life among the horsey set as Taggart assumed.

> That evening as Taggart lay poulticed and swathed on the sofa in his smoking room at home, wondering how soon he was going to die, and when Virginia and the Hated Rival were going to be married, the bell rang, . . . and he heard a voice that brought him up to a sitting posture immediately.
>
> He pulled off his bandages and limped into the parlor, and saw Virginia standing on the hearth-rug there.
>
> "Oh!" she cried, "I came to see your sister."
>
> "No," said Taggart, with sudden and monstrous egotism, "no, that is not so; you came to see *me*,—to see if I was hurt this afternoon," which made Virginia flush hotly and become very angry, because it was the exact truth.
>
> "But you didn't seem to be much concerned about me this afternoon when the brute threw me," said Taggart some hours later.
>
> "Dick," said Virginia reflectively (she was sitting on the arm of his chair), "Dick, you are a nice man, but,"—she shook her head at him hopelessly,—"you don't know about horses a little bit."[13]

As may be all too obvious now, Norris fully succeeded by the end of his sojourn at the University of California in taking the measure of what it meant to write as an approachable, popular author. With some guidance from Davis and Kipling he could produce pleasant, light fare—what was then thought of as summer reading suitable for the hammock. He had also found that more serious topics such as the emasculation of the "man's man" dictated a resort to neither gothic romance conventions nor elitist modes of versification. By 1894, the pretentious signature "Norrys" had become "Norris," and he had taken a turn that promised, someday, the development of a following.

One other major development during Norris's college years is worthy of note. Before Joseph LeConte came within his ken during his junior year and while Zola was not yet a discernible influence on his writings, Norris began dealing in fictional form with evolutionary theory. Thus, another influential literary figure in Norris's career was Robert Louis Stevenson. *The Strange Case of Dr. Jekyll and Mr. Hyde* appeared in 1886 and illustrated that one need not be Zolaesque nor intimately familiar with Darwin's writings to appropriate evolution-related ideas that had been "in the air" for decades. While Stevenson does not directly address evolution per se in *Dr. Jekyll and Mr. Hyde,* he does deal with a notion closely related to mankind's having descended from lower life forms: the concept of a more primitive, uncivilized, and anarchic self that, like the animalistic physical traits transmitted from prehuman antecedents to modern man, survives to some extent within each person. Given the right conditions, the theory went, this latent "second self," inherited from barbaric ancestors (the "brute within"), can become active and dominate the Victorian gent who houses it. Because of a potion concocted by the experimentally in-clined Dr. Jekyll, we have the strange case of a genteel and humane physician who periodically becomes, so to speak, his evil, murderous twin.

Whether Norris was directly influenced by Stevenson at this point in his life cannot be shown. His direct references to the Scotsman begin to appear in print much later than the Berkeley years, and comments made by Norris's contemporaries on his enthusiasm for Stevensonian adventure-romances such as *The Wrecker,* published in 1892, do not date his reading of them. But the "atavistic lapse" pictured by Norris in "The Son of the Sheik" at the end of his freshman year is closely related to the scenario in which the brute within is released.

"The Son of the Sheik" treated *Argonaut* subscribers not only to a Kip-lingesque adventure but the tale of—so the subtitle reads—"How a Pari-sianized Arab Found That Blood Is Thicker Than Water." The thoroughly Europeanized Arab in question is among the Frenchmen in General Pawrot's division of the African Service who have little to do and are killing time as best they can: "As the long, flat, black scow of the commissariat went crawling upon the torpid river with the advance-guard straggling along upon the right [bank]," they "lay upon the deck under the shadow of the scow's awning and talked and drank *kouscoussow.*" Someone offers the opinion that Arabs are patriotic. Bab Azzoun, a "Kabyle" transplanted to France at the age of ten, counters with colonialist condescension, derogating the race from which he sprang: "The Arabs are not sufficiently educated to be true patriots." This highly articulate savant, the author of several books, goes on to theorize at length about the nature of patriotism. Despite his North African origin, he personifies French rationalism at its smuggest. Arab horsemen suddenly ap-pear and attack the Frenchmen.

The narrator Thévenot cannot help but be impressed by the figure the Kabyles cut, "with their fierce red horses, their dazzling white *bournous,* their long, thin, murderous rifle-barrels, thundering and splashing past, while . . . from every black-bearded lip, was rolling their war cry: '*Allah, Allah-il-Allah!*'" The stressful situation triggers the emergence of a self that Thévenot and

Bab Azzoun himself thought long extirpated, and the atavistic lapse occurs. "[Bab Azzoun] was no longer the Parisian, the 'product of civilization.' . . . In an instant . . . all the long years of culture and education were stripped away. . . . [H]is long-forgotten native speech came rushing to his tongue, and in a long, shrill cry, he answered his countrymen in his own language." Crying, "*Allah-il-Allah, Mohammed ressoul Allah*," he leaps from the scow upon the back of a riderless horse and, now one with his people, speeds across the North African landscape and out of sight. "And that was the last I ever saw of Bab Azzoun."[14] Genes and the persisting influence of the environment in which he spent his first ten years account for what may be termed his degeneration to the "less civilized" state from which all thought he had evolved.

It makes little sense, of course, to think of evolution in terms of a single lifetime or portion thereof. Evolution requires vast expanses of time for measurable changes. The protracted process does not immediately lend itself to promising fictional possibilities, save as a general frame of reference for treatment of individuals within a radically more compressed period of time. Thus the value of the atavistic lapse scenario appropriated by Norris: while Bab Azzoun's development to a superior European condition mimics evolution in a "fast-forward" manner, genetic and environmental determinants that prove dominant over acquired characteristics reverse his "ascent" even more rapidly. Or, viewed with a cultural bias different from Norris's and more like Jack London's over a decade later in *The Call of the Wild*, Bab Azzoun does not degenerate but, under stress, lapses to his natural condition—which may ensure his survival over the long term in that he is better adapted to the North African environment then so hostile to true Europeans like Thévenot.

Two years later, in March 1893 when "Lauth" was published, Norris experimented again with the fictional possibilities of evolutionary theory, depicting another atavistic lapse but going on to test the limits of credibility and his readers' tolerance of the truly fantastic. By then he had been exposed in the lecture hall for over a semester to Joseph LeConte, whose influence may have been registered in this much zanier tale.

Spirituality is not a relevant consideration in "The Son of the Sheik." "Lauth" differs in that the Christian concept of the soul is now in the mix, and this invites speculation on the Presbyterian LeConte's possible intellectual contribution to the work. As Donald Pizer succinctly explains in *The Novels of Frank Norris*, LeConte's take on the ongoing evolution of the individual to a "higher" condition—rising farther and farther above and beyond his brute characteristics inherited from lower life forms—involves the nurturing of the soul throughout life. Doing this requires, according to LeConte, the ethical harnessing of the energy of the animalistic side of one's nature in the service of the spiritual. Not doing so spells stasis or possible degeneration to a more animalistic state.[15] This is not, in fact, Norris's theme in "Lauth," but the relationship between body and soul was the broader subject broached by LeConte and focused upon by his student in his short story.

Qualification regarding the extent of LeConte's influence is fully warranted, however. One need not have studied under LeConte to encounter for the first time this dualistic definition of human nature. The paradigm of the "lower" self versus the "higher" self, familiar to readers of Emerson's essays and especially the "Higher Laws" chapter of Thoreau's *Walden,* was no more a novelty in the 1890s than it had been when LeConte was born in 1823 into a slaveholding family on a Georgia plantation. The concept had been drilled into generations of Christian churchgoers for centuries. When focusing on mankind as an amalgam of "flesh" and "spirit," LeConte merely reiterated what Norris had heard from the pulpits of Trinity Episcopal church in Chicago and St. Luke's in San Francisco—not to mention during his preparation for confirmation. Norris could assume that virtually all of his readership was familiar with the concept of mankind's twofold nature. Indeed, what he brought to the table as a gothic novelty in this tale was something very much outside LeConte's range of interests: the bizarre consequences of a man no longer possessed of something that distinguishes him from lower life forms, a soul.

Lauth, participating in a civil revolt in medieval Paris, is no stranger to atavistic experience like Bab Azzoun's. The bolt he shoots from his arbalest—a crossbow-like device—buries itself in a man's neck. He has killed for the first time, and, as would happen to the hero of *Moran of the Lady Letty* in 1898, his excited reaction precipitates a rapid descent to a primitive state of being.

> In an instant a mighty flame of blood-lust thrilled up. . . . At the sight of blood shed by his own hands all the animal savagery latent in every human being woke within him,—no more merciful scruples now. *He could kill.* In the twinkling of an eye the pale, highly cultivated scholar, whose life had been passed in the study of science and abstruse questions of philosophy, sank back to the level of his savage Celtic ancestors. His eyes glittered, he moistened his lips with the tip of his tongue, and his whole frame quivered with the eagerness and craving of a panther in sight of his prey.

The long short story has only begun, however, when Lauth himself receives his death wound and a much more sensational treatment of a lapse from his former condition commences. Two days after Lauth's death, a fellow scientist, Chavannes, observes the corpse and wonders, "What was this mysterious, dreadful force that had brought [Lauth] to this state?" But the real question is, What is life? "Did he, Chavannes, or anybody *know* what it was?" Does life consist, as some believe, in God breathing a soul into man, and once the soul has left the body, that is death? It turns out that, well before the nineteenth century, Chavannes is something of a Darwinist, a smug materialist who quickly moves past the superstitious folderol of souls. "All forms of life," he avers, "were but the same; the vivifying spark that had once fired the body of Lauth was, *in nature,* no way different from that which flashed in the eye of a spirited horse, which gleamed in all the lower forms of animal life, which smouldered in the trees and vines, and slumbered, sluggish and all but extinguished, in the mollusk and sponge. . . . Soul? There was no soul. What mankind called soul was but life." And so Chavannes experiments in restoring the "spark" of life in Lauth with a transfusion of blood from live sheep.

The operation is a success in that Lauth is restored to life, but he is not quite the same fellow. Indeed, his "decline" from a human condition soon begins. "One evening, as Chavannes brought him his accustomed meal . . . Lauth of a sudden snarled out, and snapped at his hand with thorough apish savagery." From this time on, "the process of decay became rapidly more apparent; . . . the expression of the face lost all semblance to humanity; the hair grew out long and coarse, and fell matted over the eyes. The nails became claws, the teeth fangs." Readers of *Vandover and the Brute* will recognize the scene in which, one morning, Chavannes discovers Lauth "quite stripped, groveling on all fours in one corner of the room, making a low, monotonous growling sound, his teeth rattling and snapping together." In *Vandover* the cause for such behavior on the part of its hero is psychological; in "Lauth" the hero's self-conception has nothing to do with his literal *devolution* to a wholly brute condition—from a "he" to an "it." As this slide down the evolutionary scale continues, all likeness to the human form disappears. When Lauth arrives at the nadir of his experience, Norris's evolutionary flight of fancy reaches its zenith: "By some unspeakable process the limbs, arms, and features, slowly resolved themselves into one another. A horrible, shapeless mass lay upon the floor. . . . It lived, but lived not as do the animals or the trees, but as the protozoa, the jelly-fish, and those strangest lowest forms of existence wherein the line between vegetable and animal cannot be drawn." Finally, decomposition "had commenced; the thing was dead."[16]

Obviously, Chavannes was wrong about the soul. Once death has occurred and the soul has left the body—so the logic of the romance suggests—one plummets down the great chain of being from a position just below the angels and above all other mammals down to the initial life forms from which mankind ascended over eons.

Norris certainly pulled out all the stops for this performance. In this instance, Kipling does not and cannot come to mind. Hawthorne's moral fables may, given the emphasis on the human soul—though neither in "The Jongleur of Taillebois" nor "Lauth" does Norris appear to invite serious consideration as a moralist reflecting upon the relationship between the natural and supernatural. Indeed, one suspects that, as he proceeded with his composition, Norris was writing with tongue in cheek as he reveled in the extravagant. Some of Poe's tales instead appear the most appropriate American antecedents for this story. One thinks of Poe's equally detailed literary hoaxes; and the narrator of "Lauth," as he unblinkingly records as unvarnished fact the outcome of Chavannes's experiment, brings to mind the earnest and ingenuous storytelling of Poe's intellectually impaired narrators. At the same time, though, and as preposterous as "Lauth" may be for those inclined not to suspend disbelief for the sake of a quirky experience of the weird, it does make clear for a second time that, while at Berkeley, Norris was already focused on the possibilities for fiction writing that evolutionary theory had made available and that he was positioned to make more serious use of the same in the years that followed.

Norris, it should be added, was not the only San Francisco writer who recognized the grand melodramatic possibilities of evolution and devolution. Nor was he the only one to indulge in such an over-the-top *fantaisie.* Nine months later, in the Christmas 1894 issue of *The Wave,* John S. Partridge—not a student of LeConte—topped Norris's "Lauth" with an even more peculiar short story entitled "The Pineal Eye: A Record of Atavism." It concludes with the physician-narrator's announcement that he will soon be married to the "poor lizard-girl" for whom his pity has transmuted into love and the expectation of connubial bliss. Lizard-girl? Yes, indeed. Lovable as she is, this human being does have the physical characteristics of a lizard and, dragging her tail, behaves as such on all fours. She too is the victim of an experiment like Chavannes's, initiated when she was but a wee babe and designed to trigger devolution to a reptilian state. Partridge is no less whimsical and exuberant than Norris when his kindhearted narrator confronts Dr. Day, the mad scientist who vaunts his success in experimenting upon the poor girl. Called upon to explain himself, Dr. Day proudly proclaims his triumph:

"'I have proved the theory of evolution.'" That is, Dr. Day explains, "'by the exercise of a little will power and a little surgery, I have carried the highest mammal back to the reptilia. What are your Darwins and Huxleys compared to me?'"[17]

Thus did sophisticated scientific theories that had been popularized enter the realm of entertainment under the hands of writers like Norris and Partridge, who took these theories seriously but could not resist their potential for startling applications.

Turning from the Berkeley years to Norris's stay in Grays Hall at Harvard, one thus takes into account the influences of Kipling, Davis, probably Stevenson, and other much earlier writers. Given the character of many of his manuscripts produced in Cambridge in 1894–95, only one question remains: When did Norris become the thrall of Emile Zola?

Walker saw "Lauth" as the reflection of Norris's having begun reading the novels of Zola by early 1893. "Suggestions of Zola appear in some of the [early] short stories," he wrote, "particularly in *Lauth*." Donald Pizer was less certain about this three decades later. For good reason, he goes only so far as to note the resemblances between the short story and Stevenson's *Dr. Jekyll and Mr. Hyde* and Oscar Wilde's 1891 tale of physical and spiritual degeneration, *The Picture of Dorian Gray.* He then posits Norris's interest in the animalistic aspects of human nature as indicative of why he would later manifest Zola's influence in his writings. So strong was this shared interest of the two authors, Pizer opines, that it is no "wonder that Norris was seldom without his paperback Zola novel during his last years at Berkeley." He offers a variant interpretation of what Walker had learned in 1930–32: "[M]any of [Norris's] friends testify that while he was at Berkeley he was frequently seen about the campus with a French paper edition of Zola under his arm and was always ready to stop and defend the novelist, who to him embodied strength and truth but to most of them was of interest chiefly because of his obscenity." How long had Norris been doing this? The unfortunate fact of the matter behind Walker's generalized portrait of Zola's defender was stated by Walker himself: "It is almost impossible to determine just when Norris discovered Zola."[18]

Charles Norris told Walker that Frank was reading Zola when he returned from Europe in 1889. But one has to wonder how much credence should be given to Charles's recollection; he was only eight in 1889. Frank's wife told

Walker that she was sure he did not begin that early but instead at Berkeley. Jessica Peixotto related that in his senior year, "or later," Frank became enthusiastic about Zola. But Harry M. Wright was sure that Norris had developed his interest in Zola before his senior year when, along with Jessica, he took the two-semester French 15 course dealing with the "Realistic School" of writers. As has already been noted, however, Zola was not taught in that course. Frank M. Todd pushed the date back to 1891–92, when he first met Norris as a sophomore and they immediately began disagreeing about the merits of Zola's novels. But Todd, like Charles Norris, also was under the impression that Norris had already begun to read him when he was in Europe. And so one comes full circle: two witnesses claim that Norris discovered Zola in France, the others countering that it was *at some time* in 1890–94.

The question is an important one, given Norris's rise to celebrity as the "American Zola." But the thirty-year-old memories tapped by Walker leave us now where he found himself in 1932, concluding that it is not possible to determine when Norris discovered the ever-expanding Zola canon, especially since Norris published nothing that was truly Zolaesque in 1890–94. Had the public wished to give him a sobriquet before February 1895, when the last of his Berkeley compositions saw print, it might have been the "American Kipling"—though reviewers and literary columnists had already bestowed this title upon the other strong influence on Norris in the early 1890s, Richard Harding Davis.

Whatever was, exactly, the record of his reading, one can date from surviving evidence the time at which he turned from student of Zola to Zolaesque practitioner. This was at the beginning of the spring 1895 semester in the two-term English 22 course conducted by the Harvard instructor Lewis E. Gates.

9

THE NASCENT ZOLAIST AT
HARVARD COLLEGE

On 22 February 1899 in New York City, a few days before its formal publication, Frank Norris inscribed a copy of *McTeague: A Story of San Francisco* to the Harvard professor whom he hoped would remember the "embryonic form" in which he had read it. "But though you may have forgotten, . . . I have not forgotten [English 22], and your very good encouragement & criticism during the short time I was with you. I doubt very much if *McTeague* would ever have been expanded to its present . . . dimensions—if it had not been for your approval of the story in its first form. In a way you must share with me in the responsibility for its production now, as you certainly [were] its Godfather and Sponsor. At any rate it has given me great pleasure to dedicate the finished volume to you." The dedication was to L. E. Gates, under whose direction Norris had studied in the two-semester writing course and earned the grade of A.[1]

It was not the only course he took before he bid a final farewell to academia. He also studied French language and literature, earning a C for one full course and a B for two others that ran for only one semester. The internationally prominent Shakespeare scholar George Lyman Kittredge was his instructor in a third two-semester course offered by the Department of English; and oddly enough, given the frequency with which he would quote, paraphrase, and allude to the plays of Shakespeare,[2] Norris did not receive a final letter grade. His "Special Student" transcript reads "abs," indicating an "incomplete" for the course.[3] Once again, that is, Norris did what he liked. What he very much liked, as he made clear in his 1896 denunciation of Berkeley's Department of English, was what he found in Gates's English 22.

After he had completed his tirade in "The 'English Courses' of the University of California," Norris modulated to enthusiasm in a paean to Harvard. In fact, the majority of courses offered there were taught in the same manner as at Berkeley. But, no matter; all he recalled in 1896 was the writing course that delighted him.

> They order this matter better at Harvard. The literary student at Cambridge has but little to do with lectures, almost nothing at all with text books. He is sent away from the lecture room and told to look about him and think a little. Each day he writes a theme, a page if necessary, a single line of a dozen words if he likes; anything, so it is original, something he has seen or thought, not read of, not picked up at second hand. He may choose any subject under the blue heavens from a pun to a philosophical reflection, only let it be his own. Once every two weeks he writes a longer theme, and during the last six weeks of the year, a still longer one, in six weekly installments. Not a single suggestion is offered as to subject. The result of this system is a keenness of interest that draws three hundred men to the course and that fills the benches at every session of the class. The class room work consists merely in the reading by the instructor of the best work done, together with his few critical comments upon it by the instructor in charge. The character of the themes produced under this system is of such high order that it is not rare to come across one of them in the pages of the first-class magazines of the day. There is no sufficient reason to suppose that the California collegians are intellectually inferior to those of the Eastern States. It is only a question of the means adopted to develop the material.[4]

In other words, Norris found himself on 27 September 1894, when classes commenced, in a workshop situation like those now conducted in creative writing programs of colleges and universities across the United States. More immediately to the point, Norris was again in a learning environment like that of the Académie Julian, wherein one pursued one's own interests and was constructively criticized and counseled by a master. At Bouguereau's *atelier*, the great man identified and displayed the best drawings and paintings completed during the previous week; in Gates's course the "best work done" was read aloud to the students.

Gates himself was not a practicing prose fictionalist. At thirty-four years of age in September 1894, he was only beginning to demonstrate in print his skills as a literary critic, cultural historian, and impressionistic aesthetician.

But he had much to say about how fine literature *should* read. So did one of
the two men who assisted him in the teaching of English 22.

William Vaughn Moody, only a year older than Norris and soon to prove
himself as a poet and playwright, was one of Gates's assistants. The curt remarks that appear on the forty-five short "themes" by Norris that have survived were, however, made by Herbert Vaughan Abbott—five years Norris's
senior and just arrived at Harvard. Unfortunately, the longer pieces of writing Norris submitted biweekly in the fall are not extant, nor is the six-part
manuscript of the spring. But Gates's comments, one has to assume in light
of *McTeague's* dedication, had to be more positive than Abbott's normally
were when evaluating the "dailies." Given the warm inscription citing Gates's
"very good encouragement," one can also reasonably assume that he was a
kindly critic in person. He was a decidedly private man but not a spectral
figure who showed up on campus only when his classes met.[5] The bachelor
lived at 40 Matthews Hall. It was immediately next to Grays, a minute's stroll
from Norris's room.

Abbott did appreciate some of Norris's better qualities—commending
his work with brief comments such as "Concise," "Well planned," "A good
figure," and "Observant." Yet he as tersely chided his work: "Lacks unity,"
"Too loose," and "Prolix." A stickler for proper sentence structure, he advised
Norris, "Avoid the trailing participial clause."[6] The real problem with Abbott
surfaced as, in January 1895, the short compositions related to *McTeague*
began to reach his desk. His comments read: "A melodramatic subject matter not relieved by any felicity of treatment" (McTeague suffering an attack
of delirium tremens); "Not a toothsome subject" (Trina McTeague's death
and the discovery of her corpse by some young girls); and "Gruesome" (plot
summary for an early version of *McTeague*).[7] By 22 April 1895, after the one-
week spring recess, Abbott appears to have become somewhat reconciled to
Norris's flair for unsettling subject matter: a portrait of a drunk lying "face
downwards, blowing his fetid breath into the mud and filth of the alley,"
elicited only an ambivalent "Specific," and Norris's 30 April treatment of a
man having been run over by a train brought forth a noncommittal "Vivid"
as it ended with the image of the man's foot and ankle—this portion of the
severed limb only—buttoned into a shoe.

Even in light of his more positive reactions, though, Abbott was essentially
the pedantic William Dallam Armes of Berkeley reincarnated. He would go
on to become a professor of English at Smith College, and his publications
would be in the fields of eighteenth-century English literature and—no trail-

ing participial clauses, please!—English composition. He was not unfamiliar with newly crafted literature. In 1890–91 he had been a literary critic for a New York newspaper, the *Commercial Advertiser*. But more telling of the differences between Norris's and his temperament was the fact that he had grown up in the family of a nationally prominent Congregationalist minister who had succeeded no less a celebrity than Henry Ward Beecher at the Plymouth Church in Brooklyn. His father, Lyman Abbott, was the prolific author of theologically focused books and articles and had served as the associate editor of *The Christian Union*. In 1894 he was the editor-in-chief of an even more vigorous, social-reform-minded Christian periodical, *The Outlook*. One of his publications, which he coedited with his son in 1893, was *The Plymouth Hymnal*. In short, Herbert Vaughan Abbott was not the ideal mentor for a budding Zolaist, as was apparent in his reaction to the theme dated 7 January 1895, in which Norris described the inebriated McTeague beating and then raping his wife. Abbott wrote, in his longest comment on a Norris theme, "Morbid and repulsive in subject matter. Your manner is strong and effective but ask yourself why you present us with this subject. To force upon our unwilling attention a repulsive, painful and debasing image has in itself something akin to the brutal." There was no dedication of a book to Abbott and no inscription or even a letter to him when *McTeague* came off the press and emerged from the bindery in 1899. He joined LeConte and all of the other professors Norris never mentioned in print.

Thus the exceptional status of the professor to whom Norris dedicated *McTeague*.

Lewis Edwards Gates had religious familial roots as well. His mother was a great-granddaughter of Jonathan Edwards of "Sinners in the Hands of an Angry God" fame. Gates, however, did not write sermons. His *Three Studies in Literature* (1899) and *Studies and Appreciations* (1900) appropriate the imagery of redemption and bespeak a fervor like the Puritan divine's; but, though he was almost as hostile as Zola to writers whose focus was on the transcendental, his humanistic exhortations were tonally similar to Ralph Waldo Emerson's and Matthew Arnold's when defining the proper function of literature and the means by which it can achieve the noblest of ends. The goals he had in mind were the true representation and illumination of life as it actually is in the here and now, and thereby the sensitization of the reader to the wonder that is reality at large. He hoped to see the redemption of a

literary culture that had turned away from these high aims that he associated with the romantic movement in its prime. What Norris thought of such
theorizing is not known, since the notes he may have taken as Gates lectured
and made extemporaneous remarks have gone the way of virtually all such
records accumulated by 1902 and thereafter lost. One can only infer from
Norris's writings Gates's immediate and long-term influence. Three effects of
his thought are discernible, and each has to do with Gates's attitude toward
romanticism and its relationship to realism.

By the mid-1890s, when Norris came to Harvard, the cultural politics of
the literary establishment were those of zealous partisans "at war" with each
other in the literary columns of periodicals. The proponents of romanticism
and realism were as polarized as the theorists who sided with either the "an-
cients" or "moderns" in the era of Alexander Pope and Jonathan Swift; and
Norris's canon, which does not respect the hard-and-fast boundary between
the two schools of writing, is thus disturbing to some readers.

Such a neat distinction between the one camp that prized imaginative
invention and the other that championed representational art was, in fact,
problematic throughout the second half of the nineteenth century. Norris
was not the only writer of his day who blurred the distinction. For example,
critics touted Hamlin Garland's 1891 book of short stories, *Main-Travelled
Roads,* because of its radical realism, and yet the best-known piece in the
collection, "Under the Lion's Paw," concludes in a melodramatic manner
worthy of Alexander Dumas or Victor Hugo. Stephen Crane's *Maggie* is realistic in that, in 1893, it treated convincingly the steps by which an innocent
young girl with a good heart finds herself swept into prostitution. But, for
want of a better term, the poetical style of writing in this novella resembles
nothing from the hands of the authors William Dean Howells celebrated as
realists when propagandizing for the school. The story of Maggie Johnson,
whom Crane pictured with some preciosity as a flower that blossomed in the
mud puddle of a Manhattan slum, often reads as a surreal, nightmarish fairy
tale—more an imaginative creation than the transcription from real life that
one generally associates with the mimetic essential championed by proponents of realism.

Such elisions of the theoretically clear line between realism and romanticism were commonplace. Even *The Rise of Silas Lapham* found its author
in 1885 taking the imaginative liberty Nathaniel Hawthorne claimed for the
romancer over three decades earlier in his preface to *The House of the Seven
Gables:* Howells's scheduling of the disastrous loss to fire of the hero's new

house under construction warrants at least the raising of an eyebrow in that the conflagration occurs at just the right time to situate the principal personage for an heroic testing of his integrity and to complicate the plot with maximum dramatic effect. Norris would be chided by book reviewers as not merely a realist but an ultra-realist when *A Man's Woman* appeared in early 1900; yet he would energetically defend realism's adversaries in his 1901 essay "A Plea for Romantic Fiction." And thus the definitional compromise that Norris requires: holding the term naturalism in abeyance for the present, since the word is not used by Gates in *Studies and Appreciations* nor by Norris in print until he reviewed Zola's *Rome* in 1896, one resorts to romantic realist, or realist romantic, as the proper descriptor and arrives at the sanction Lewis E. Gates provided for an authorial self-conception of the kind in 1894–95.

Gates held in common with Howells this article of faith: romanticism began well at the end of the previous century. This is the shared assertion heard in Howells's *Criticism and Fiction* in 1891 and Gates's *Studies and Appreciations* in 1900. They agreed that the movement's original impetus was a praiseworthy fidelity to nature and thus to truth as it is known from actual—or what both men termed commonplace—experience. Gates is quite specific when focusing on romanticism at its best, seeing Wordsworth as its chief prophet and lauding *Lyrical Ballads*, first published in 1798, as the harbinger of a new era in civilized discourse. For Gates, romanticism in its purest manifestations achieved an appreciative understanding of everyday realities overlooked or deliberately neglected by pre-1798 artists. Gates dismisses the bulk of eighteenth-century literature with a word, "shallowness," as he praises Wordsworth's preface to *Lyrical Ballads* for specifying or suggesting "nearly all the aspects of the complete renovation of literature which the new age was to accomplish" by 1824.[8]

As to what went wrong as the nineteenth century advanced, Howells and Gates were very much in harmony again. Howells declared that the school had fallen into imaginative and emotional extravagance, and that it remained for realism to fulfill the mission that was romanticism's before it betrayed its original values and degenerated into meretriciousness.[9] One of Howells's characters complains about the unlifelike stuff served up by popular novelists in the mid- to late nineteenth century: the "commonplace is just that light, impalpable, aërial essence which they've never got into their confounded books yet." The character proposes that what is sorely needed is "the novelist who [can] interpret the common feelings of commonplace people."[10] Gates similarly lamented the pattern of decay seen in a turning away from everyday actualities by authors who "lived inside their own individual heads, in the circle of their own eccentric personalities—in fantastic air-spun worlds of their own devising." But he took hope in the fact that some romantics remained on the track that Wordsworth had laid, noting that at midcentury Elizabeth Barrett Browning modelled a standard for excellence in *Aurora Leigh* because she was able to find even in the most vulgar aspects of life, and among sordid characters, events and conditions that elevated what other artists saw as dull fact to high humanistic significance. Charlotte Brontë he also associated with romanticism and its great capabilities. Although she deals with exceptional circumstances, treating "passionate . . . primitive and elemental" conditions of experience, her works still ring true because "the life she puts before us is the actual world."[11] And so Gates, as the proponent of a renewed or rehabilitated romanticism, and Howells, on the other side of the fence as the chief advocate of realism, cherished the same end—a turn or return to the "actual," toward which they hoped their contemporaries would gravitate.

How, exactly, was romanticism to be refreshed and fortified at the end of the nineteenth century? As it turned out, either in the lecture hall or in his more direct involvements with Norris, Gates answered this question in a way that provided his student with the rationale for the loyalty he would display to both the romantic and realist camps. Or one can infer at least encouragement of the same sort from *Studies and Appreciations.* Chastising those latter-day romantics who declined to deal with "the routine of ordinary life" and the quotidian concerns of the "work-day world," Gates complained that they were not "passionately enough in love with the Actual to follow out its facts and their laws with patient fidelity through all their complications and variations." The more accomplished writers "saw life and they loved life in its large contours, in its pageantry, under its more moving and more typical aspects." Still, they often did not focus as much as they might have on the truths that are to be found in commonplace detail. "It remained for the scientific spirit with its fine loyalty to fact, and for realism with its delicate sense of the passing moment" to provide the missing element in their portraits of life and to facilitate a "return to the regions of the Actual."[12] In short, for Gates and *contra* Howells on this point, realism would not accomplish what romanticism had failed to achieve; rather, romanticism would be reinvigorated and correctly reoriented by an infusion of realism.

Norris was no Elizabeth Barrett Browning, and the "embryonic" version of *McTeague* that Gates read was hardly akin to the blank verse of *Aurora Leigh*.

But, *la voilà*, here was an apologia for the truthful treatment in *McTeague* of the extraordinary and the ordinary, the exercise of imagination tempered by "fine loyalty to fact." Here also was an environment at Harvard in which Norris might find encouragement to work on a novel as romantic as it was realistic.

The second possible influence of Gates may be seen in Norris's nonfiction. Again, all regular readers of literary columns in the 1890s were aware of the polarization of the romantic and the realistic, and the matter certainly came up in the course on modern French novelists taught by Félicien V. Paget at Berkeley in 1893–94. Thus, when Norris later served as a book reviewer and literary essayist, and he repeatedly employed the relationship between two schools as a frame of reference, he was not necessarily manifesting Gates's tutelage. But his bias was indeed Gates's in that he fully appreciated the value of realism but privileged romanticism, particularly the value-added form that an infusion of realistic detail and accuracy generated.

Third, when assailing romantics such as Byron for their shortcomings, and particularly a "craving egotism" that precluded a true perspective on things as they are in the whole of life, Gates happened to enunciate a point of view that would inform three of Norris's novels focusing on the ill effects of a degraded romantic culture encouraging self-centeredness: *A Man's Woman, The Octopus,* and his full assault on "the cruel cult of self," *The Pit.*[13]

General commentaries on Norris's life sometimes note that he "wrote" *Mc-Teague* and *Vandover and the Brute* while at Harvard. This was not the case. As has been noted, the character Vandover made his first appearance in the 1891 short story "The Finding of Lieutenant Outhwaite," and Norris revised from 1889 to 1895 his dating of the manuscript title page reading "Vandover and the Brute: A Story of Life and Manners in an American City at the End of the Nineteenth Century." Though he may not have begun in 1889 the *Vandover* we now know, he had already conceptualized to some degree such a work by the time he came to Harvard. And when he returned to San Francisco, as the 1895 redating of the title page indicates, he had at least made considerable progress with his manuscript, perhaps considering it finished. But it was not until the end of the decade that he brought this novel to anything like completion and, for the first time he is known to have done so, submitted it to a publisher. And *McTeague,* as Norris testified in his inscription to Gates, was in only "embryonic" form by the close of the spring 1895 semester.

How far did he advance each manuscript? In *A Novelist in the Making*, James D. Hart sedulously documents the relationships of the forty-four surviving daily themes of which he knew in 1970 to passages in the two novels as published and to those in a third, *Blix*. He valiantly advances the hypothesis that Norris's progress with *McTeague* and *Vandover* in 1894–95 could be chronologically gauged, the pertinent, dated themes indicating how much further Norris had taken each novel.[14] But the detailed calendar Hart constructs is finally only a speculative exercise, given that no documents of any kind external to the "dailies" afford verification.

Norris may have been producing any number of sketches and drafts of chapters for these novels *before* he came to Harvard, and any number of the themes submitted in the fall could have been extracted from a work or works he initiated during the Berkeley years. For example, Norris informed Charles F. Lummis of *Land of Sunshine* magazine on 9 April 1900 that *McTeague* was begun in 1895,[15] but the novel is based in part on the murder of a janitress by her McTeague-like Irish husband, reported in the San Francisco newspapers in October 1893. Norris did publish a good deal while at the University of California, but not enough to preclude the possibility that he was also moving forward with two—or more—novelistic projects.

But the situation in 1894–95 is even murkier. Any number of the "dailies" may have been newly fashioned for inclusion in one of his grander projects. Or, it cannot be determined how many were freshly composed but not conceived as related to a specific novelistic project. Not to try anyone's patience here, suffice it to say that in the fall 1894 semester, at least, one cannot be even relatively sure of the history or intended use of any of his dailies, except one. As though to test Abbott's taste and discernment with a piece of descriptive writing judged by the editors of *Argonaut* worthy of publication in 1891, Norris's "A Desert River" theme of 10 December 1894 minimally reworked a passage in "The Son of the Sheik." Abbott almost passed the test, since he admired Norris's vivid word choices, but Norris could not have been surprised when this stickler found something about which to cavil that the editors of *Argonaut* had not: Abbott complained that the sketch he read was "[u]nmassed and so not a clear unit of impression."

More to the point regarding the uncertain status of the fall themes in relation to larger manuscripts being developed is the two-paragraph description of a San Francisco locale that Norris turned in on 19 November. "An Uptown Avenue" begins, "Van Ness Avenue was very still. It was about 7 o'clock. Curtains were down in all the houses. Here and there a servant could be seen washing down front steps. In the doorways of some of the smaller houses were loaves of French bread and glass jars of milk, while near them lay the damp twisted roll of the morning paper." With "doorways" and "milk" changed to "vestibules" and "cream," and two paragraphs reduced to one, the text will be seen again in *Vandover*—though it might as easily have been inserted in, or extracted from, an early manuscript version of *McTeague* or *Blix*.[16] Similarly, the 17 December 1894 "A Cheap Parlor" may have been the Ur-text for passages in both *Vandover* and *Blix*: Ida Wade's parlor in the former novel is the same room decorated in kitsch manner at Travis Bessemer's home in the latter.[17] But Norris named neither young woman in the theme, and so once again one cannot say with certainty what his intention was in December or how the sketch related then to a more expansive piece of writing.

As to how these themes should be viewed now, Norris's experience at the California School of Design and the Académie Julian once more becomes relevant. One sketches gratuitously for the sake of capturing the appearance of a subject or for a particular project that will be based upon the sketch. One adds it to one's portfolio if there is not an immediate use for it; good work should not be wasted, as it may someday serve a worthwhile purpose. If one envisions production of a larger, complex work, one produces multiple sketches—to be transferred later to different sections of the canvas and then refined in their definitions and spatially correlated with each other. Sometimes one employs the same sketch for similar but ultimately quite different paintings.

Such was Norris's practice as a writer. He was not only the persistent notebook keeper his brother remembered, jotting down new words he wanted to use, figures of speech, story ideas, and piquant names for characters.[18] As the Harvard themes and the remains of a collection of short stories that he worked on from 1895 through late 1897 indicate, he maintained portfolios of holographs and printed works from which he could pull what he needed when opportunities for their use arose.[19] For example, the 23 November 1894 theme "The End of the Act" was a base-text for the piece with the same title that appeared in the *Harvard Advocate* on 3 April 1895; then for a portion of the setting of chapter 14 of the *Vandover* manuscript; and, as that manuscript continued to gather dust through 1902, for a similar setting in chapter 1 of *The Pit*.[20] The "A Merry Christmas" theme of 3 January 1895, picturing an inebriated woman just completing her Christmas shopping for toys and falling at full length upon the sidewalk, went into no novel but appeared as a seasonally discordant vignette in the Christmas 1897 issue of *The Wave*. "Tug

Wilson" of 5 March 1895 was set on *McTeague's* Polk Street in San Francisco; it saw print not in that novel but as "Types of Western Men: II, The Plumber's Apprentice" in *The Wave* on 2 May 1896. Unlike Charles, who had a genius for losing materials of the kind produced by his brother, Frank was a veritable pack rat, ever adding to his stash and not at all reluctant to "recycle" what he had in hand. In 1897's "Execution without Judgment," Norris updated the plot of 1891's "The Jongleur of Taillebois" from the Middle Ages to the nineteenth century; imposed Kings County, California, as its new setting; and replaced the murderer Amelot with a Mexican named Estorijo. Similarly, he relocated *Yvernelle's* plot near Pacheco Pass and Hollister, California, and retyped its cast of characters as "Spanish Mexican" in the 1901 short story "The Riding of Felipe."

In short, when Norris originally drafted a passage or gave initial development to a story situation may have little to do with the date on which he incorporated it in one or more versions of a subsequently published work. The obverse is also true. That Vandover does not make his first appearance in the surviving Harvard themes until 4 January 1895, in a scene destined for chapter 9 of the published novel, establishes as fact neither that Norris had already brought the novel to its midpoint nor that he extracted the theme from a half-completed manuscript of *Vandover and the Brute.* As moot is the significance of his not returning to the subject matter of *Vandover* for two months when, on 11 March, he completed a piece related to chapter 11 and then turned in three others: one on 14 March to be seen again in chapter 8 of the published novel, and two on 19 and 27 March that would read almost verbatim in chapter 4.[21]

What is most remarkable about the *Vandover*-related themes is not that the work was, in some way, "in progress," but that none of these compositions presages the arrival on the scene of an "American Zola." Such is not the case, though, with the *McTeague* studies, the first of which so upset Abbott because of its morbid, brutal, and powerfully repulsive character. Despite the brevity of this 7 January 1895 theme, readers of *Nana* and *La Bête Humaine* will immediately see Zola's influence in Norris's bold treatment of a form of abnormal, criminal behavior that would not receive widespread public attention in the United States until almost a century later. In the 1800s spousal physical abuse per se was not neglected. But the now openly discussed notion of violence against women having something to do in some cases with male sexual arousal was not standard conversational fare in Victorian America, and treatments of such matters earned Zola his notoriety—and Norris's attention.

At this early stage in *McTeague's* composition, 7 January 1895—Bessie McTeague was not renamed Trina until 19 February—Norris went where Kipling, Stevenson, and Richard Harding Davis never dared:

> The other teachers at the kindergarten often noticed that Bessie's fingertips were swollen and the nails purple as though they had been shut in a door. This was in fact the explanation that she offered. But she lied to them. McTeague her husband used to bite her finger-tips when he came home after drinking whiskey, crunching them between his strong large teeth, always ingenious enough to remember which were the sorest. If she resisted he brought her down with a blow of his immense bony fist between the eyes.
>
> Often these brutalities inflamed his sensual passions and he threw her, bleeding and stupid from his fists across the bed and then it was abominable, bestial, unspeakable.

It is not surprising that the rape did not make it into print when *McTeague* was first published. If not its 1899 publisher, then Norris himself may have conceded that Abbott's response in 1895 made sense: he had gone too far.

A few days later, on 11 January, Zola's example again suggested itself. Like the alcoholic Coupeau in *L'Assommoir,* Norris's hero suffers hallucinatory episodes of delirium tremens.

> He went out into the kitchen and crouched over the stove. Instead of trembling now, he was shivering. The fire was low and he picked up the poker to arouse it. The poker moved in his hand and grew cold. He looked at it and saw that it was a snake, a thick, black, wet snake, writhing slowly in his fist, its head and neck bent up sharply towards him, its tongue flickering in an out of its mouth. He flung it from him and saw it shrink into a coil as it struck the floor. Then he sprang back stretching out his hands and screaming until the effort brought the blood specks to his eyes. It was not because he knew the coiled horror upon the floor was a snake that he was afraid, a real snake would not have frightened him. It was because he knew that it was *not* a snake that he was afraid, horribly, frantically, unspeakably afraid.

What Norris was up to is obvious. And yet, after one attends to the 19 February description of Trina McTeague dying "with a rapid series of hiccoughs, that stirred the great pool of blood in which she lay," one is again disappointed by what the dailies reveal, or because of what they may conceal. In the eight *McTeague* pieces produced during the spring 1895 semester, it is clear that the new allegiance to Zola was guiding his hand with respect to what Abbott

<u>McTeague.</u>

The other teachers at the kindergarten often noticed that Bessie's fingertips were swolen and the nails purple as though they had been shut in a door. This was in fact the explanation she offered. But she lied to them. McTeague her husband used to bite her finger tips when he came home after drinking whiskey, crunching them between his strong large teeth, always ingenious enough to remember which were the sorest. If she resisted he brought her down with a blow of his immense, bony fist between the eyes.

Often these brutalities inflamed his sensual passions and he threw her, ~~across the~~ stupid ~~and~~ bleeding and stupid from his fists across the bed and then it was ~~best~~ abominable, bestial, unspeakable.

Norris's 7 January 1895 theme for English 22, corrections by William Vaughn Abbott. (Courtesy of the Bancroft Library, University of California at Berkeley.)

termed "gruesome" subject matter. But none indicates to what degree Norris had, as yet, embraced the dominant theme of Zola's works: his emphasis on the twin forces of heredity and environment as determinants governing characters such as Trina and McTeague.

Surely Norris was intent on writing more than a shockingly sordid "cautionary tale" about male alcoholism and the abuse of women in the print tradition of T. S. Arthur's *Ten Nights in a Barroom* (1858) and W. D. Howells's *The Lady of the Aroostook* (1879), the theatrical tradition of W. H. Smith's *The Drunkard* (1844), and the oral tradition of the Women's Christian Temperance Union speeches. Only a year after he left Harvard he presented himself to the readers of *The Wave* as an expert witness to the Zola canon, offering interpretive commentary on no less than eight of his novels.[22] But while Bessie (whose name suggests British ancestry) became Trina (or the more Germanic Katrina) on 19 February, "race" or heredity appears to have nothing to do with the rechristening. Further, none of the dailies refers to her immigrant parents in the novel and their European origin. In the Harvard themes it appears that Norris had not yet conceptualized Trina's all-important German-Swiss ancestry. Nor is there any suggestion that her Swiss genetic inheritance—her now-famous predisposition to hoarding—was to loom so large in her characterization by 1899. An emphasis on the shaping power of environment is as absent from the themes as the characters Zerkow, Maria Miranda Macapa, Old Grannis, and Miss Baker.

Again, one cannot know what Gates encountered in the six-part "fortnightly," where quintessential naturalistic themes may have stood forth. The closest one can come by way of empirical documentation of Norris's plan for the novel is the plot summary that Abbott received on 8 March 1895, the last daily, entitled "McTeague." It is a scenario with no mention of theme, Zolaesque or otherwise.

> McTeague who is a third class dentist on an up-town street marries Trina, a kindergarten teacher. Their misfortunes begin after a few years. McTeague, having no diploma, is forbidden to practice and begins to drink heavily. For a long time Trina supports the two, until she finally loses her place and in a short while the household falls into great poverty and misery. McTeague goes from bad to worse and finally ends by killing his wife. He manages to escape and goes back to the mines where the first part of his life had been spent. The facts concerning him come to light here and he is obliged to run for it. His way is across an arm of an Arizona desert, here he is ridden down by a deputy sheriff. The two are sixty miles from the nearest human being

and McTeague determines to fight, he kills the sheriff and is about to go on when he discovers that even in the fight the sheriff has managed to hand-cuff their wrists together. He is chained to the body sixty miles from help.

Bret Harte or any other romantic realist with a flair for the sensational, rather than a Zolaist, might have written this summary.

One may speculate, however, that in the dailies Norris wisely withheld from the unsympathetic Abbott the fuller conception of a naturalistic novel disclosed in the fortnightly submissions read by the more open-minded, less squeamish Gates, who understood the potential value of the "vulgar" and "sordid" in a work intended to be true to the "actual." While none of the professor's comments in 1895 are known, his copy of *McTeague* documents a wholly positive response in 1899. At the back of the volume in his own hand Gates acknowledged the novel's "Humor," "Charm," and Norris's "Humanizing of Mac."[23] No wonder Norris remembered Gates in 1895 as *McTeague's* godfather and sponsor.

The outcome of the *Vandover* and *McTeague* projects would not be known for years. However, such is not the case with another book launched at Harvard, the ungratifying result of which Houghton, Mifflin, and Company of Boston recorded in its letterbooks. While Norris was still in Cambridge, Massachusetts, the publishing firm wrote him this letter dated 21 June 1895.

> Dear Sir:
>
> We have read with interest your little collection of sketches and tales. Permit us to say that we find the work much in advance of what we saw before from your hand. We are however very conservative in the matter of volumes of short stories, for we rarely find them commercially successful and we cannot persuade ourselves that we should find it wise for us or for you, in our hands, to undertake this volume.
>
> As we are in doubt if you will be in Cambridge tomorrow we send this by mail and will hold the package subject to your order.
>
> > Truly yours
> > Houghton, Mifflin Co.

This is the first known submission by Norris of a collection of his short fiction. The manuscript "we saw before from your hand" refers not to another clutch of tales but to *Yvernelle,* which Houghton, Mifflin had declined in 1890.[24] The "sketches" to be returned were not literary ones but the drawings intended as illustrations, for which Charles remembered "posing for hours."[25]

The table of contents for this collection can be no more authoritatively described than the *Vandover* and *McTeague* manuscripts as of the summer of 1895. But the remains of this project provide a relatively reliable indication of which previously published pieces Norris had brought together as early as February 1895, when the five-part "Outward and Visible Signs" series completed its run with the piece subtitled "Thoroughbred." What survives in the Frank Norris Collection at the Bancroft Library are mounted tearsheets of the five stories, plus "A Caged Lion." As to others that Norris may have included, two qualify if Norris's organizing principle and title for the collection were, or resembled, the name of the series.

Strongly suggesting that "Outward and Visible Signs" was the collection's title is how Norris, the following year, named another series of thematically linked short stories for *The Wave.* Norris dubbed this second group of five stories dealing with how young men become engaged to marry "'Man Proposes,'" thus inviting the sophisticated reader to complete Thomas à Kempis's observation in his *Imitatio Christi:* man proposes, but God disposes. "Outward and Visible Signs" was a similarly clever choice for his book in the spring of 1895. It likewise prompts one to extrapolate from the part to the whole. Those who, like Norris, had to study the catechism in the *Book of Common Prayer* to qualify for their confirmation as Episcopalians will know the traditional definition of a sacrament: an outward and visible sign of an inward and spiritual grace. The outward "signs" he treated in the five linked stories and another, "A Caged Lion," are those of inward character, noble and ignoble. Revealed by the ends of these stories are grace and gracelessness, in the nonreligious senses of those terms, as displayed by young men and women when passing through stressful situations. If Norris retained the title for his book, it would have qualified two other short stories for inclusion: "Travis Hallett's Half-Back" and the companion piece of "A Caged Lion," "Unequally Yoked."

Returned by Houghton, Mifflin, all five—or from six to eight—short stories joined the other manuscripts in Norris's trunk as he prepared to leave Cambridge.

In the summer of 1895 Norris returned to San Francisco to reside for several months at the Hotel Pleasanton, where Bertha Rickoff recalled Gertrude living when she made her acquaintance. Only later would the Norrises return to the house on Sacramento Street that Gertrude made available for rent when they came east. Undaunted, Norris put the collection of short stories into the mail once more. In the fall, Lovell, Coryell, and Company of New York accepted it for publication,[26] as Norris continued work on the *Vandover* and *McTeague* manuscripts and began doing freelance work for *The Wave*.

10

ADVENTURING UPON LIFE

At twenty-five years of age, with his days as a student behind him, Frank Norris returned from Cambridge to San Francisco. Looking wholly to the future, he had obtained, so far as was possible, the only thing that he ever wanted from higher education: preparation for a literary profession. Once settled into the Hotel Pleasanton with his mother and brother, he entrained for Monterey, going down the coast to the Hotel del Monte where San Francisco's "Four Hundred" was turning out in full force to fill that grand hotel and enjoy polo matches, horse racing, and a pigeon shoot. Swimming was never a great attraction there, given the uncomfortable temperature of the Pacific that far north; but boating, coaching, dancing, dining, bowling, and being seen in one's best apparel with the right people were strong attractions for San Franciscans of Norris's class and the next rungs up the ladder. The influx began on Sunday, 25 August 1895. Norris arrived the following Tuesday evening, in time for the formal beginning of the gala the next day and ready to write about the festivities.

He had not sought employment as a reporter for a San Francisco newspaper. Norris would never in his life be identifiable thus, nor would he adopt a compressed prose style as a result of his work with dailies, as did many writers of his and the next generation. Never did he have to write in the terse, fact-focused manner demanded by blue-pencil-wielding editors. In his first postcollegiate trial as a literary man, he simply offered his services to *The*

Wave, descended upon Monterey, wrote as he pleased about "The Country Club at Del Monte," and subtitled the piece appropriately: "Impressions of an Observer." As appropriately, the onetime student who did as he liked signed himself "Dilettante." This was fitting in another way as well. For, after five years' preparation for fiction writing, he published only one short story in the three months he remained on the West Coast. "A Defense of the Flag" appeared in *Argonaut* in late October 1895, when he was on his way back to the East Coast, and it was not until 26 April 1896 that another fictional work of his saw print. He had decided instead to try his hand at the kind of first-person journalism written by Richard Harding Davis and other international celebrities.

His decision to do so in August 1895 was wise as well as fortuitous for those interested in having an initial benchmark for what was typical of his best descriptive writing as a professional. "The Country Club at Del Monte," published in two parts in *The Wave* on 31 August and 7 September, is one of his finest, most lively pieces of nonfiction and a touchstone in regard to essentials of his prose thenceforth.

As we have noted, Norris took every opportunity to express his enthusiasm for horses. But when describing the steeplechase competition at Del Monte, he transcended all previous accomplishments of this kind and, more important, rose to an unprecedented level of sophistication in the practice of literary impressionism. Bombarding the reader with sensory stimuli, Norris neglects only the sense of taste as he describes the competitors returning from the far end of the course to the hurdle near which he stood:

> All at once through the stillness you catch a subdued humming noise; as it comes nearer it breaks up into a series of rapidly succeeding shocks, a jarring rumble; suddenly it rises to a roar; it is like the fluttering and rippling of a gigantic flag blown by a tornado. It is the noise of hoofs at a furious gallop, the *"sonitu quattit ungula campum,"* and just when it is loudest, just when your ears are ringing with the great sound, just when the earth is beginning to tremble, you see the cap of the first rider suddenly flash up from over the hurdle; you can't see the horse as yet, he is running with his head low, and even yet the jockey is far from the hurdle; you catch sight of his face next, rising and falling with the motion of the invisible horse. . . . For a moment this head comes and goes, . . . and then on a sudden, long before you are expecting it, the whole body of the horse heaves itself above the jump; there is a smell of sweat and leather in the air, and a great whirl of dust; up above you there, almost over your head, you catch a glimpse of the soles of the "jock's" riding boots, the glint of shining horseshoes and the round belly

of the horse himself, the veins swelling, the flanks rigid, with the one long breath that the brute seems to hold as he goes over; then he strikes ground with a great shock.[1]

Norris had begun to develop a specialty of his, one that does not bring to mind any of his American contemporaries, even the master imagist of his generation, Stephen Crane. Norris's talent for rendering powerful olfactory effects has long been recognized, most memorably by Zelda Fitzgerald, who wrote to her fiancé Scott, a fan of *McTeague*, "I love you so terribly that I'm going to read 'McTeague'—but you may have to marry a corpse when I finish. . . . All authors who want to make things true to life make them smell bad—like McTeague's room—and that's my most sensitive sense. I do hope you'll never be a realist."[2] But critics have given virtually no attention to Norris's gift for fashioning aural imagery, prominent in the above passage from "The Country Club" and even more so in another one:

> As one approached the bowling alley one became aware of an increasing humming noise, a vague uninterrupted murmur, which, upon opening the doors of the alley, instantly resolved itself into three very distinct strains or chords.
> Lowest of all, and as if it were underneath the others, was the prolonged roll of balls—the bass, the heavy diapason. From time to time this broke up sharply into a multitude of clear treble notes, high-keyed and shrill, the noise made by the pins as the balls struck them. But highest of all, and dominating every other sound, was the staccato chatter of conversation from the great crowd of women on the benches at the lower end of the alley. The other noises were irregular, interrupted, this one never paused for an instant.[3]

Work of this peculiar kind would be one of his signatures in the years ahead.

The tongue-in-cheek auditor-narrator tweaking loquacious womankind immediately proves an equal-opportunity satirist. Norris next catches sight of one of the male luminaries of San Francisco's high society and fashions a vignette foreshadowing the characterization he would assign to *McTeague's* Mr. Sieppe, that comically fashioned embodiment of a Teutonic rage for order who is ever exasperated by a disorderly world resisting his control. Doing comical sendups of Germanic types, with their broken English, was ever a pleasure for Norris, and this one, published on 31 August 1895, provides the opportunity to note another salient trait of his. Norris's keen sense of the ridiculous, displayed repeatedly in the first half of *McTeague*, for example, was commented upon by book reviewers at the turn of the century but has been almost wholly neglected for the past century by critics preoccupied with the grimmer aspects of his canon. It was not until 1975 that two interpreters broke with tradition to emphasize the novel's comic dimensions.[4] Likewise, attention to the pathetic and tragic events of *The Octopus* and *The Pit* appears to have precluded enjoyment of those risible moments that Norris deliberately built into both.

In the first installment of "The Country Club," however, one cannot miss Norris's broad sense of humor as he focuses on the medical doctor in question—"a *Herr Doktor,* for he was German, very tall, almost abnormally straight"—who takes himself *very* seriously. Earlier in the evening, when introduced to a group of girls, "he would draw himself up very quick, clap his hands to his sides, palms inward, 'the little finger touching the seam of his trousers,' and, his shoulders rigid, allow his head to fall forward, as though he were decapitated." As to the bowling of this avatar of Prussian officiousness, it "was impressive, there was drama about it; one craned one's neck to watch it." Continued Norris,

> The Herr Doktor feeling himself the object of attention, began to display himself; he assumed attitudes, making great gestures, posing for the gallery, even going so far as to look all about him at the audience to watch the effect. He chose the largest, heaviest balls, poised them very accurately, and after sighting keenly down the alley, launched them forth with tremendous force; they spun out from his hands like solid shot, rumbled halfway along the raised track, and then fell off into the trough at one side. It was exasperating, never a one of them touched a pin. The Herr Doktor was annoyed, he frowned and shook his head, looking about him from one face to another. He tried to make it appear that his ill-success was due to the fact that he attempted that particular style of bowling, to bowl *that* way was immensely difficult. Of course, if he wanted to bowl as other people did, that was another thing; any one could bowl in the ordinary style.

Less pleasant but as noteworthy are other events at the hotel, upon which Norris reflects in a more serious manner. Like many other San Franciscans who protested pigeon-shooting competitions, Norris humanely laments a "sport" in which shotguns bring down the birds released from cages. Many of the downed pigeons are only wounded, he notes in the 7 September installment, and they either bleed to death or are dispatched by dogs and by boys using air rifles. As unpleasing for Norris is what he observes at the grand ball closing the Del Monte festivities. Today's readers are less likely to share his sentiments as he focuses on and then denounces the men present, whom he sees as unmanly and simpering. He terms the type "Brownies" (fairies or sprites), following other writers in *The Wave*. Anticipating a similar explosion of virility on the part of Ross Wilbur, the hero of 1898's *Moran of the Lady Letty,* a testosterone-suffused Norris turns away from this androgynous cluster wondering, "Where are the *men* in all this?" The author who had to prove himself a *real man* at Berkeley expostulates at some length about this. His essential theme can be found in this excerpt from the near tirade into which he has launched: "[O]ne cannot respect a man whose only fatigue comes from dancing too much, whose excitements are those of the ballroom and tea table, whose chief skill is that which he shows in handling a girl in a crowded dance room. . . . Let us have men who are masculine, men who have other things to think of besides fooling away their time in ballrooms. After all, *think* of a man who smells of perfume and sachet—one's gorge rises at it! I would rather a man smell of horse sweat, the nasty salt rime, the bitter, pungent lather that gathers where the girths gall and the check strap chafes."

The "softer side" of Norris did, however, manifest itself as well on 31 August in a way that stands as a caution for those who may take him at his word when holding forth on the subject of Anglo-Saxon supremacy and the ineluctable fate of the lesser races. Norris had already used negative stereotypical images of the residents of San Francisco's Chinatown in the "Outward and Visible Signs" story of early 1895 subtitled "Thoroughbred." Therein one Anglo-Saxon, with a Great Dane as purebred as he at his side, faces down a lawless, unsavory crowd of tong members intent upon mayhem. Readers of this piece and others featuring "the heathen Chinee" that he subsequently produced may be surprised to find Norris in this instance looking past racial difference to recognize a person like himself, the occasion for which occurs after he watches two Chinese pinsetters in the hotel's bowling alley risking life and limb to do their job.

> One should have seen the Chinamen—they were never at rest for a moment—without an instant stop they jumped about here and there, throwing back the heavy balls with one hand, setting up the pins with the other, toiling, perspiring, gamboling about like monkeys, going through all manner of antics, dodging a ball at one instant, and at another flattening their bodies against the wall, to avoid the flying pins, then back again with the quickness of cats, setting out the pins, rolling back the heavy balls. But even then they were not quick enough. One must be pretty quick to dodge nine balls and twenty-seven nine-pins, flying about in all directions at the same time. For all their twistings and turnings the balls or the pins hit them from time to time; a little move and a leg might have been broken; but the coolies hardly had the time to think of that; they could not even indulge in the poor satisfaction

of rubbing the place. If they should pause to consider one bruise, they were likely to get a dozen more.

"It made you tired to just to watch them," concludes Norris as he turns from them "to find other amusement." His apparent indifference to the "coolies" who gamboled about "like monkeys" and moved with "the quickness of cats" is, however, a pretense. For he has set up a conventional "white" perception of the "Chinaman" so that his readers can shortly thereafter reconsider its appropriateness. Hours later that night, Norris sees one of the bruised and exhausted pinsetters leaving the bowling alley, "going down the path toward the stables," returning to his sleeping quarters on the property. Norris is now empathetic as he notes how the man "shivered as he walked and once one almost fancied that he staggered a little." It is an individual and not a cartoon Mongolian who "passed behind the shadow of a great palm-tree and then came out again into the faint light further down the road. The soft rustle of his padded soles upon the gravel was the only sound that could be heard. He disappeared." Racism is sometimes a difficult master to serve and, for Norris on occasion, an impossible one.

After returning to San Francisco from Monterey, Norris contributed two other articles to *The Wave*. The first, published on 5 October 1895, reports that he had recently toured the bookstores of the city to see what novels and collections of short stories are popular. He was astonished to find that the question of the hour is, "Where are our American story tellers?" All that was selling were books by English authors! The prominent American writers William Dean Howells, Francis Marion Crawford, Harold Frederic, Thomas Nelson Page, Lew Wallace, and Richard Harding Davis are known by all, Norris reflects. And yet their books, he is chagrined to announce, "are *rari in a gurgito vasto*. Look at the stream, look at the flood, look at the very tidal wave of English fiction that overflows the shelves, that pours itself out upon the long tables, that is diked up in the show windows, that overwhelms the city, the whole country, in fact." He then begins to list the titles, indicating an English conquest of the American marketplace. It is not a particularly interesting essay, except in one respect: what is taking place stylistically in the just-quoted, long, repeatedly qualified, single sentence piling up more and more extravagant images of the deluge of English books that finally overwhelms not only San Francisco but the nation. Here is another, briefer example in the next paragraph: "It is like an invasion, a reconquest, a literary *revanche;* it is an army with banners flying."[5]

Encountered here in full for the first time is deliberately fashioned hyperbole of the reiterative kind that Norris would regularly employ through the rest of his literary career, for example, in *Vandover,* when the hero listens to the sounds emanating from San Francisco at night and offers a rather grim interpretation: "It was Life, the murmur of the great, mysterious force that spun the wheels of Nature and that sent it onward like some enormous engine, resistless, relentless. . . ." With the double adjectival description of that resistless and relentless force, Norris has only begun this sentence dealing with an engine of life, "driving before it the infinite herd of humanity, driving it on at breathless speed through all eternity, driving it no one knew whither. . . ." As the sentence continues, the participle "driving" gives way to others: "crushing out inexorably all those who lagged behind," "grinding them to dust," and then "riding over them. . . ." For the conclusion, Norris returns to "driving": "still driving on the herd that yet remained, driving it recklessly, blindly on and on toward some far-distant goal, some vague unknown end, some mysterious, fearful bourne forever hidden in the thick darkness."[6] What Vandover hears—identified in three words, "It was Life"—Norris qualifies with repeated rhythmic force and an extravagant collection of images in a sentence of no fewer than 112 words.

Stylistically, Norris had come a long way since the composition of his 18 December 1894 Harvard student theme in which he contented himself with a modest little clarification of the kind at the end of this sentence: "She came up the aisle slowly, pausing at the steps with little hesitating movements of the head and neck like a hen going into a strange barn." And when writing "Our Unpopular Novelists" and *Vandover,* he had obviously decided to ignore Herbert Vaughan Abbott's directive that he "[a]void trailing participial clauses." He enjoyed such constructions, including those with "trailing" adjectives, as seen in his 7 January 1895 student theme: "[H]e threw her, bleeding and stupid from his fists across the bed and then it was abominable, bestial, unspeakable."[7] Norris would commit worse crimes against the standard usages preached by Abbott, even dallying with that bane of the fastidious—mixed metaphors—as he constructed big bow-wow sentences such as this one in *The Octopus,* when Presley interprets a locomotive as a symbol of "vast power, huge, terrible": He sees it as "the leviathan, with tentacles of steel clutching into the soil, the soulless Force, the iron-hearted Power, the monster, the Colossus, the Octopus."[8]

Then again, there was precedent. Zola did the same in *La Débâcle* (1892) when picturing Kaiser Wilhelm during the Franco-Prussian War, "awaiting the outcome of the battle, his eyes on the giant chessboard, busily manoeuvering this dust-storm of men, the furious attack of these few black dots in the midst of eternal, smiling nature." His soldiers are metaphorical chess pieces, then dust blown across the countryside, and then dots on a map. When Zola is not mixing metaphors, he too indulges in reiteration and the generous massing of multiple complementary images, as in a sentence from *La Bête Humaine* picturing a railroad yard and describing the sounds emanating from a scene that is "immense, dreary, drenched with rain, pierced here and there by a blood-red light, vaguely peopled by opaque masses, isolated engines or carriages, bits of trains slumbering on side lines; and out of the depths of this sea of darkness came noises, the breathing of giants [i.e., locomotives] feverishly gasping, whistle-blasts like piercing shrieks of women being violated, distant horns sounding dismally amid the roar of the neighboring streets."[9]

Overwritten by modernist standards in place by 1920, such passages from Zola's and Norris's works illustrate exactly what Gertrude Stein and Ernest Hemingway's generation rejected in favor of minimalism. The scene treated in two lines in Ezra Pound's "In a Station of the Metro" would have required a full paragraph or more from Norris. It is not necessarily the case that Norris was violating the principle of *le mot juste* that Gustave Flaubert articulated and modernists treasured; rather than employing several words because he could not determine which was the singularly *juste* one, Norris makes unstinting use of *les mots justes—driving, crushing, grinding, riding*—to ensure full exactitude and a compelling experience of Vandover's aurally induced perception of life as a juggernaut. Moreover, Flaubert himself, a nineteenth-century novelist and hardly a modernist, was not innocent of prolixity, and Zola's flamboyant verbosity was the template for Norris's.

What enthralled Norris was Zola's overwhelming power as a descriptive writer, or such was his testimony when in June 1896 he first held forth on the subject. Reviewing the recently published *Rome*, Norris gave some attention to Zola's handling of the hereditary component of the "Gospel of Naturalism" but much more to a writer who was the master of producing the grand effects of art categorizable as sublime. When characterizing Zola's achievement in *Rome*, Norris describes the literary equivalent of a western American landscape painting by Albert Bierstadt:

> While, of necessity, lacking in the magnificent action of some of the *Rougon-Macquart* series [of novels], *Rome* is, nevertheless, crammed with tremendous and terrible *pictures,* hurled off, as it were, upon the canvas, by giant

hands wielding enormous brushes. As is the rule with this author's works, *Rome* leaves one with an impression of immensity, of vast illimitable forces, of a breadth of view and an enormity of imagination almost too great to be realized. You lay the book down, breathless; for the moment all other books, even all other *things*, seem small and trivial.[10]

That, in late 1895, Norris already felt this way about Zola is clear in the last essay contributed to *The Wave* prior to his return to the East Coast. Harvest and crushing time had come upon California's vineyards, and Norris again headed south, to the foot of San Francisco Bay. His subject was "A California Vintage: Wine-Making by Machinery on a Santa Clara Valley Ranch."[11]

Fiction is selection, as Norris declared in the title of one of his 1897 articles for *The Wave*, and so is artful nonfictional writing. Amidst all the possible focal points the scene before him offered, he selected nothing of the puny at the Casa Delmas winery in Mountain View for treatment. What riveted his attention was "the means whereby five hundred acres of grapes are turned into three hundred and fifty thousand gallons of wine"; what excited his imagination was "these enormous machines, these mountains of grapes, these seas of wine." And so he was off and running, following the wagonloads of green grapes he saw weighed and then pitchforked onto a conveyor belt carrying them upward to the crusher, "as though they had been caught up by a current, a great, perverse current, running up a hill. A vast, green river streamed upward incessantly, disappearing, whisking out of sight, through the narrow slit under the roof of the building." The grapes then tumbled into the crusher and thence to the fermentation vat, about which is heard "the noise of the machinery, the coughing of pumps, the clattering of pistons and eccentrics, and the prolonged purring of dynamos. It was night; the light from the incandescent bulbs flashed back at you from vats of wine like the convivial winking of an eye, bloodshot with drunkenness." Fermentation of red grapes in an already filled tank is given full literary treatment as the "must"—juice, pulp, and grapeskins—becomes an "immense, sticky, smoking mass; a little later it is boiling, bubbling, with a sullen, muttering sound, a thick, pink froth, like the spume of a hard-bitted horse, creaming up slowly from the center, dripping over the lip of the tank. . . . It is like a miniature Vesuvius." To paraphrase Norris when praising Zola's accomplishments in *Rome,* one can be relatively sure that, when Norris is done, the last word on the subject of wine making in the Santa Clara Valley has been said—though oenophiles may find so sensuous his rich, animated description of the wine-making process that they regret the relative brevity of his article. Those instead more interested in just how Zolaesque Norris had become by October 1895 will, however, discover their stimulant in the way in which Norris ends his essay.

Unlike Henry Adams when encountering the new face of reality uncovered by scientists by the end of the nineteenth century and symbolized for him by an impersonal "dynamo," Zola regularly personified and invested vitalistic characteristics in machines of all kinds: trains in *La Bête Humaine,* the distilling apparatus behind old Colombe's bar in *L'Assommoir,* and the Voreux mine of *Germinal* that "seemed evil-looking, a hungry beast couched and ready to devour the world." Even a pump at the mine has a personality of sorts, its "long, heavy respiration" continuing "without stop . . . like the congested breathing of a monster."[12] Zola's fanciful demonstrations of the pathetic fallacy were nothing short of an inspiration for Norris, and thus his return to the crusher for the grand finale of his essay.

> But, after all, the first operation seems to be the most fascinating, the process by which the grapes are pressed, the work that the crusher does. Straddled there at the top of the building, its mouth forever open, the clatter of its machinery incessantly calling for *more, more,* the crusher seems to be some kind of gigantic beast, some insatiable monster, gnashing the grapes to pulp with its iron jaws, vomiting them out again in thick and sticky streams of *must.* Its enormous maw, fed night and day by the heaped-up carloads of fruit, gorges itself with grapes, and spits out the wine, devouring a whole harvest, glutted with the produce of five hundred acres, and growling over its endless meal like some savage brute, some legendary mammoth, some fabulous beast, symbol of inordinate and monstrous gluttony.

Such passages abound in Norris's later writing. Readers of *The Octopus* and *The Pit* may remember any number of them. Such recall is not common with regard to Norris's early writings, however; and these "minor" works of 1895 indicate just how long Norris had been writing in this way before being dubbed Zola's American disciple by book reviewers.

On 12 October 1895, in the same issue of *The Wave* in which "A California Vintage" appeared, the editor John O'Hara Cosgrave—signing himself "The Witness" in the "Personalities and Politics" column—announced the good news about the book manuscript that Houghton, Mifflin, and Company had turned down in June: "Frank Norris, one of the most promising of our [San Francisco] writers, has had a volume of short stories accepted by Lovell, Coryell, and, I venture to believe, will have a reputation with the appearance of

his book."[13] The next bit of attention the Bay Area press gave Norris appeared in a publication of the Berkeley student body with which he maintained ties through the Phi Gamma Delta fraternity. It did not repeat the glad tidings about the forthcoming book. Instead, the *Berkeleyan* made a blink-inducing announcement as unanticipatable then as it is now for those not familiar with just how peripatetic Norris would be over the next three years: "Frank Norris '94 departed for Africa last Monday."[14] As with *The Wave*, when Norris went to Monterey and Mountain View, he had made an arrangement as a freelancer with the *San Francisco Chronicle*. His mission, the *Berkeleyan* declared, was to "write a series of articles on 'The Picturesque Side of African Life.'"

Why South Africa, of all places? John O'Hara Cosgrave provided a partial explanation in *The Wave* on 2 November 1895:

> Not for the mines alone has South Africa potent attractions. C. P. Huntington asserts that, were he young again, he would adventure to the country of Cecil Rhodes and repeat there again his triumphs; our best [mining] engineers are flocking to Johannesburg, and there is announcement yet of but one return, that of Mr. Wiltsee, [whom] fortunate investment has converted to a half-millionaire. The latest to leave California for that Southern clime is Frank Norris, who goes to the Transvaal for purposes of literary observation. He is to send letters to the *Chronicle,* and from them it may be possible to obtain a fair impression of that region.[15]

Johannesburg was effectively a "sister city" with San Francisco because of their similar gold-mining histories and cultures; a good many northern Californians with technical expertise worked in the Transvaal, and the same issue of *The Wave* reported that Alice Merry had gone there to wed Hal Tighlman of San Rafael. Also, thanks to his mother's social connections, Frank not only had an "in" with the *Chronicle* but with socially prominent figures such as the mining engineer John Hays Hammond, whom he would visit at his offices in Johannesburg and his home outside the city, at New Doornfontein, that winter. He would visit the Tighlmans as well.[16] In short, there was strong local interest in and a readership for articles about life in South Africa, and Cosgrave more than wished Norris well for his venture as he continued his 2 November write-up of his departure.

> Mr. Norris, I have long believed, is one of the men destined to win a reputation. He writes in a manner essentially literary. He has an excellent style and a trained faculty of observation. For this paper he described the recent shooting function at Del Monte in the manner of an artist—the proper blending

of reflection and description such as a writer should present. He has written several stories, some of which the *Overland* has published; a volume of his manuscripts has recently been accepted by Lovell, Coryell & Co. He is to be in South Africa two months or more, and I am sure that his descriptions will make excellent reading.

The Wave would not always be so sanguine, though. Another regular contributor to its pages, John Bonner, was not an Anglophile like Norris, nor did he see South Africa as "the country of Cecil Rhodes," as Cosgrave did. It was a nation governed by the Boers, the descendants of the Dutch colonists long since settled there who were energetically resisting the imperialistic designs of the English and the confederate outsiders of other nations whom the Boers termed "Uitlanders." Having read by 15 February 1896 Norris's unflattering descriptions of the Boers and sympathetic portrayals of an English minority denied full civil rights by the country's legitimate rulers, this Anglophobe who regularly descanted on England as the bully of the world complained that "so far as [Norris's] opinions are concerned, he was evidently absorbed, swallowed, and assimilated by the Englishmen among whom he fell. He sees with their eyes, hears with their ears, speaks with their tongue. His indignant rebuke of the impudence of the Boers' attempt to prevent their country being gobbled up by the English, recalls Thackeray's cockney on the Rhine, who called the Germans he met 'a lot of nasty foreigners, who don't even speak English.'" And yet, Bonner—who was quite correct about Norris's unqualified partisanship—could not refrain from praising his "graphic" style: "We see the country with the naked eye" in Norris's articles.[17]

In the seven pieces Norris wrote for early 1896 publication in the *Chronicle* and another that appeared in a weekly with national distribution, *Harper's Weekly*, much more than "the country" was his subject. His good fortune lay in not only placing his collection of short stories but in finding himself positioned to write about a major international crisis that erupted in the Transvaal a few weeks after his arrival.

Had Norris extracted a book from his African experiences, it might have resembled Richard Harding Davis's *The West from a Car Window* (1892) or three other volumes of travel literature that by 1895 had mightily enhanced Davis's reputation: *The Rulers of the Mediterranean, Our English Cousins,* and *About Paris.* According to his brother Charles, Norris planned "to start at Cape Town, go northeast to Johannesburg, trek north through Matabeleland [in southern Zimbabwe, formerly Rhodesia], then onward to the Nile, and down the river to Cairo."[18] The route was essentially that of the Cape Town–to-Cairo railroad, then the grand ambition of Cecil Rhodes, the autocratic prime minister of England's Cape Colony who not only wanted to see the railroad built but to bring under English control all of the territory in between.

Leaving San Francisco on 28 October for the four-and-a-half-day transcontinental railroad trip, Norris reached New York City with time to spare before the departure of the steamship taking him to Southampton, England. Personally and professionally, it was a serendipitous development that the American Line's *Berlin* did not sail from Manhattan until the morning of 6 November. In 1898, when Norris wrote the version of *Moran of the Lady Letty* serialized in *The Wave*, he would weave into its plot what he saw at the confluence of the East River and the Hudson on 5 November. Keen remained Norris's recollection of the patriotic fervor—and affection—he felt that day as a new U.S. navy armored cruiser left the New York Navy Yard and made its way past the Statue of Liberty, through the Verrazano Strait, and to the Atlantic on its way to Gardiner Bay, Long Island, where it would test its recently installed guns before proceeding to Newport, Rhode Island. Formally commissioned on 17 September 1895, the *Maine* was at last ready for duty, and on 5 November it began its fateful journey toward its fiery destruction on 15 February 1898 in the harbor of Havana, Cuba.[19]

The *Berlin* left its dock at 11:00 A.M. and a little over ten days later arrived at Southampton. Norris had twelve hours to spare before the departure of the Castle Line ship *Norham Castle*. On 17 November at the ungodly hour of 1:05 A.M., he was aboard and on his way southward to Cape Town via Madeira, leaving that port on 20 November and reaching his destination at 10 P.M. on 4 December.[20] He kept a journal during the voyage, referred to by Charles in 1914 and subsequently lost to posterity.[21] But Norris documented the second leg of his trip in his first *Chronicle* article, datelined Cape Town, 9 December 1895, and published in the *Chronicle* as "A Californian in the City of Cape Town" on 19 January.[22] (He cabled none of his sizeable essays to San Francisco; all made the weeks-long journey to the *Chronicle* by ship and rail.) As John Bonner noted, Norris's prose was vivid: "Upon the equator, [the *Norham Castle*] had slid through still, oily waters, blue as indigo, level as a cathedral floor, broken only by the quick flash and flight of hundreds of flying fish, flocks of them flushed by the great hull." Finally, they reached the "great 'Dark Continent,' dark enough under that moonless sky, stretching out there behind the horizon for so many miles of pathless forest and nameless desert." What he found was a bit disappointing. Cape Town was more provincial—or backward—than he expected. Yet to be built was a power plant making possible the use of electric lights.

As in the other locales he would describe, Norris gave his full attention to the national and ethnic diversity of the population, the topography, and the "feel" of Cape Town. Regional history was also his interest, as seen when he attends a circus and finds himself seated with Major Hamilton Goold-Adams. "It is very probable that this name means nothing to you," he told his San Francisco readers. But in "the history of South Africa it sounds as the names of Washington and Grant and Sheridan sound to us." And so Norris first demonstrates his imperialistic English view of what constitutes the history of South Africa at the time at which Botswana, to the north of South Africa, was Bechuanaland: "It was Goold-Adams, who as commander of the Bechuanaland border police, together with Major Forbes and Captain Wilson, defeated and subjugated Lobengula and his 5,000 Matabeles in the Matabele War of 1893–94." He is referring to the situation that developed to the east of Matabeleland in Mashonaland, where Cecil Rhodes had installed his lieutenant Dr. Leander Starr Jameson as governor in 1890. Repeated Matabele raids on the English settlers there had finally provoked retaliatory action directed by Jameson and successfully executed at great cost of English lives by men such as Goold-Adams, who survived the conflict. Wilson, along with thirty-four other men from Forbes's column, did not. Recalling lugubriously the fate of Wilson at the Shangani River debacle, Norris neither here nor elsewhere questions the righteousness of the English territorial expansionism that provoked indigenous populations to violence. He assumes in all of his South African essays the manifest destiny of the Anglo-Saxon to seize control of this portion of the globe.

Meanwhile, well before the manuscript of "A Californian in the City of Cape Town" reached San Francisco, a decidedly more sensational tale than the ones dealing with Norris's travel across the country was appearing in installments in the *San Francisco Chronicle*. Norris was supposed to cable his mother in early December when he arrived at Cape Town, but she received no word from him. A week later she started making inquiries and could not track him down. Over the next week she became more and more frantic. Was she now to lose the fourth of her five children?[23] Beginning on Christmas day, the *Chronicle* headlines read, "Friends of Frank Norris Anxious," then "Norris Reached Cape Town. . . . There His Trail Is Lost," and then "A Cable from Cape Town. Norris Is Now Believed to Be Safe." As late as 9 February 1896, he was still the subject of scareheads: "Norris Could Not Cable." The disappearance even made news in New York City, where the *Tribune* gave it attention on 29 December.[24]

The *Tribune* derived its report from the 25 December *Chronicle* article. It described Gertrude as "almost prostrated with grief and anxiety, and her friends fear for her health unless the present strain of uncertainty is relieved." She had received from Frank two letters posted in Chicago, two from New York, "a long one, in journal form, written on the *Berlin*" and mailed from England, a cablegram from Southampton, and another from Madeira—and then nothing after 20 November. Why she did not hear from him in December remains a mystery. When she finally did on 8 February, it was in a letter he wrote from Long's Hotel in Johannesburg on 6 January 1896, after he had learned of the well-publicized search she was conducting.

In one sense that was the end of the matter; in another it was not. As though he had taken to heart Henry James's advice in his 1884 "The Art of Fiction" about the importance of writing from personal experience, Norris often proved to be one of those *littérateurs* on whom nothing was lost. In *Moran* he gave his experience of having vanished from the face of the earth to that novel's hero: the shanghaied Ross Wilbur disappears from San Francisco for months and, like Norris, his fate is the subject of protracted speculation in the newspapers. This appears to be what Charles Norris had in mind when, in 1920, he directed the designer of the dust jacket for a reprinting of *Moran* to proclaim that the novel was "Based on Fact."[25] Apart from references to the explosion of the *Maine,* the only fact that Charles could have meant was an autobiographical one.

Norris left Cape Town on 10 December 1895 after posting his first article. His next, "From Cape Town to Kimberley Mine," found him traveling northeast by train over the karoo, "the vast table lying between Cape Town and Kimberley," a "baked and sun-cracked desert" featuring mirages, sand spouts, ostriches, and sheep that were feeding on "heaven knows what." It was as desolate as the high desert in western Utah through which he had passed on his way to New York in October. The town of Kimberley offered little relief. It was hideous in appearance, every building constructed from tin sheets and "never so much as a geranium growing in a tomato can to hide the staring ugliness." What he had come to see, however, was that for which an old Boer trader on the *Norham Castle* had whetted his appetite. Here we again see Norris's delight in recording "Dutch" or German English: "'Ven you shall see die olt Kimberley (he pronounced it Camerlay) mine, den shall you see die grossest hole ever in the ground ge-dug.'" Here also we also find the author of "A California Vintage" with another opportunity to focus on an immensity of the sort for which he had developed a taste under Zola's influence. At the center of an enormous *kopje*, or hill, in a mining compound was truly "die grossest hole ever in the ground ge-dug." It is only with great difficulty that Norris's eyes can adjust to the depth of the excavation, wherein it is almost impossible to make out the machinery and men he sees below.

> It is better than Niagara, better than the Coliseum, one of the biggest things imaginable. Conceive of a pit, a gulf, with sides perpendicular as those of a house, suddenly yawning at the end of a street, deep as an ocean. . . . Even the very sight of it, big as it appears, is deceptive; one-half way down the sides of this gulf, this extinct crater (for it is abandoned now), is the shaft-house of the De Beers mine, and while I stood leaning over the rail . . . I was watching what I thought to be the head of a Kaffir moving to and fro about the machinery of the hoisting gear, but as I watched the head divide itself, as it were, in two . . . I realized that what I thought was the head of one man [was] the bodies of two; and this was only half the way down the pit.[26]

A second essay on Kimberley, "In the Compound of a Diamond Mine," describes the work performed in the mine by the Kaffirs—the generic term for the members of the various nonwhite native groups employed by De Beers Consolidated Mines. Before long, however, Norris is drawn back to the immensity of the hole in the ground. This gargantuan pit is as fascinating to him as the mouth of the Voreux mine is to Zola in *Germinal:* "The entrance to the shaft is half way down the tremendous Kopje that I spoke of in my last letter. You are let down over the edge of the enormous pit in a flat car running on an inclined (horribly inclined) railway with wire cable for tracks, and you try to talk of something else on the way down and endeavor to seem interested in the machinery, while all the time you are looking out for soft spots on which you can jump if the cable should part."

This piece, datelined 16 December 1895, closes in a manner that contrasts sharply with what follows in the next article, set to the northeast of the Cape Colony, across the Orange Free State in the Transvaal. In his finale Norris abruptly turns from the mine and mining to a more intimately human subject as he reports on an accident suffered by one of the Kaffirs. As in "The Country Club at Del Monte" when the "Chinaman" who worked in the bowling alley emerges from a racial stereotype to stand forth as a fellow human being worthy of sympathy, so with the Kaffir upon whom a rock has fallen.

> His head was bruised, and the skin of his back scraped to the raw. The worst wound, however, was in his arm. Some jagged corner of the rock had dug through the biceps, gouging a fearful hole, laying bare the bone. Did you ever notice how a shot bird or rabbit will be, as it were, struck dumb by the wound, will suddenly become passive, inert, stupefied? So it was with the Kaffir: he made no sound, he hardly moved, merely turning his head from side to side, rolling his eyes about vaguely, now staring at the bandaged arm, now looking stupidly into the circle of faces about him. No one spoke. We could hear him drawing long breaths through his nose.

The man is brought out of the mine and carried away on a stretcher, and Norris ends his essay upon a pathetic note: "Just as I lost sight of him I saw him turn over upon his face and put his head down in the crook of his arm."[27]

Given Norris's reputation for racism, the moment is an ironic one. His sympathetic treatment of a person of color here does not extend to members of a lily-white South African group in his next essay: the Boer descendants of the Dutch, who contributed to Norris's own gene pool as part of the Anglo-Saxon "Great March." No flattering references to progenitors of the English who emigrated from the northern European coast come to mind when Norris focuses on the citizens of the South African Republic (the Transvaal) and the Orange Free State. Like Washington Irving and James Kirke Paulding when drawing sharp contrasts between the Dutch and English or Anglo-American inhabitants of New York State, Norris pictures the Boers at a decided disadvantage. But he never does so with the comic *ésprit* of these earlier authors.

"In the Veldt of the Transvaal" introduces the reader to an uncultivated countryside radically different from the desertlike karoo to the south, which immediately positions Norris to declare that the lazy, inefficient "Boers are responsible" for the veldt's fallowness. "In any country but South Africa, any country not inhabited by the Boer, one would see all this land covered with seas of grain or broken up into pasture lands or farms or fruit ranches. But all this infinite stretch of country, nearly as fertile as [California's San Joaquin Valley], is abandoned, desolate, unkempt, roamed over by a few herds of long-eared sheep." The Boers are "sluggish, unambitious, unenergetic, unspeakably stupid"; they are like their bullocks, "slow, placid, content, stupid." Their president is Paul Kruger: "Poor old, purblind, stupid, obstinate 'Oom Paul.'" His police, the Zarps, are "hardly able to read a newspaper." Further, the "ox-like, placid, country Boers" who engage in little more than subsistence agriculture are no different from their compatriots who make their living otherwise. They are all as different from the vigorous, quick-witted, and shrewdly entrepreneurial English as night is to day.

Norris goes on to describe the thriving city of Johannesburg where the English are ensconced. Approaching it from the south, he sees the Witwatersrand gold fields, naming the mines and explaining how they operate in a manner very different from that typical in California. He would later write another article featuring such an apolitical "local color" subject, "A Zulu War Dance." But the remainder produced while he was in Africa had a distinctly political focus. By the time he datelined "In the Veldt" 29 December 1895, a revolution was in the making in Johannesburg.

Terming the Boers "small fry"—recently hatched fish, that is—he speculated that they are "almost within the jaws of the big fish already. The big fish is never seen, and is but little talked of; he lives down yonder in Cape Town and his name is Cecil Rhodes. What part he is to play in the coming struggle is not yet discernible, but it would not be at all surprising if within the course of the next ten years a United States of South Africa, embracing everything between the Cape of Good Hope and the Zambesi river, should spring into existence with the Honorable Cecil as its first President." Norris opines to *Chronicle* subscribers that it "is not at all improbable that at the time this letter is read in San Francisco Johannesburg will be in a state of siege." He has heard that fifteen thousand rifles have been offloaded as baking powder at Mafeking, and six thousand horses are on their way from Swasiland and Basutaland. The Englishmen have sent their families out of town; they have stored six months' provisions; caches of rifles are ready for their use; and a call has gone out for the able-bodied to enlist for military service. Johannesburg, English as it is, is ruled by the Boers. But, suggests Norris at the end of "In the Veldt of the Transvaal," that is not likely to remain the case for long.[28]

Frank Norris's widow recalled for Walker that her husband used to like to quote the French novelist and short-story writer Alphonse Daudet, that life is not a romance. But at two points Norris's life reads very much like the adventure romances for which Robert Louis Stevenson was already well known and Richard Harding Davis would become famous in 1897–98 with the publication of *Soldiers of Fortune* and *The King's Jackal*. The second grand adventure and the greatest of Norris's life took place in the spring and summer of 1898, when he served as a correspondent during the Spanish-American War. The first began the very day that he posted "In the Veldt of the Transvaal" to San Francisco.

11

THE JAMESON RAID

What began on 29 December 1895, after Frank Norris sent off the manuscript of "In the Veldt of the Transvaal" from Johannesburg, is succinctly summarized by his brother Charles in his 1926 novel *Pig Iron*. He assigned to the character Vin Morrisey the adventure his brother had as the Boers suppressed an attempt to trigger an uprising of the Johannesburgers: "Vin had been having the most extraordinary experiences. He'd happened to be in Johannesburg at the time of Jameson's raid, had enlisted in the British army for the defense of the city, and upon the collapse of the column and suppression of the insurrection, had been jailed by the Boers, and the State Department at Washington had had its hands full keeping him from being hanged. He had been finally released and ordered out of the country."[1]

In fact, though, Charles exaggerated when, thirty years after his brother's return to the United States, he used him as his model for Vin Morrisey. The diplomatic dispatches of the State Department preserved at the Library of Congress repeatedly refer to John Hays Hammond and other key figures in the abortive coup, but they do not mention Norris once. He was not in danger of hanging; the Boers put no one to death after they restored order. They did not even jail Frank. Still, he was there when all hell broke loose, and this was inarguably an extraordinary experience wholly unanticipated when he left San Francisco. He did enlist in the service of the Uitlanders and wore one of their khaki uniforms. Mounted and carrying a rifle, he was even shot at by the Boers and shortly thereafter heeded the order to leave the Transvaal immediately.

The Uitlanders' justification for their long-planned uprising, which Norris echoed accurately, was not an apologia for imperialism. The English saw themselves as victims of harsh rule under the boorish, backward Boers. After all, as Norris complained in "In the Veldt," Johannesburg was not actually a "Dutch" city: "The language is English, most of the money in circulation is English, the stores are English, the population is almost entirely English—in fact Johannesburg is an English town, run by English capital" and surcharged with what the Boers so pathetically lacked, "English enterprise."[2] The English, in short, had established a domain in the very heart of a Boer republic; and, for some perverse reason, the Boers did not rejoice over the ongoing Anglicization of the Transvaal.

The situation in 1895 was as simple as it was historically complex. Because of English aggressiveness and "enterprise," the Boers had for a quarter of a century scurried to contain the Uitlanders, who were constantly attempting to expand their sphere of influence. To this end, the Boers did not share governance with any foreign nationals. Today, this appears quite understandable and reasonable; what nation would allow its guests with a reputation for sticky fingers to plant their flag in its midst? But in 1895 the exercise of Boer sovereignty was a cause for outrage in Johannesburg, as Norris explained: "The great trouble is that the English are not allowed to vote. This restriction is, of course, applied to all the Uitlanders, but it is especially hard upon the English, because the ratio of the English to the Dutch is as three to one." Writing to an American readership and confident that he could enlist San Franciscans in support of the English cause, Norris next invokes the memory of the Stamp Act and Boston Tea Party to elicit sympathy: "The taxes are very heavy and the money thus raised is wasted with absurd extravagance." Norris thus projects the "Spirit of '76" upon the Johannesburgers, despite the fact that in the 1770s the American spirit in question was as Anglophobic as the Boers' in the 1890s: "It is very curious to see the old, indomitable Anglo-Saxon spirit rousing up again in this far away corner of the world as it roused itself in the Puritan colonies in the days of 1776 over the identical question of taxation without representation." Norris is certain that this spirit will eventually prevail: "Of course, the English will get the franchise in time and not only the franchise, but probably the whole Transvaal as well. They have a good deal more than the proverbial inch already. It will not be the English if they do not get the entire ell to boot."

His confidence, as it turned out, was misplaced. The Boer War of 1899–1902 would not be a snap for the English, but they did finally prevail on the battlefield. Still, Norris would live to see England *not* getting the ell or even wanting it in 1902. The problem was that, by the end of the conflict, in which Boer civilians were widely known to have been brutalized by the English, pro-Boer sympathy had burgeoned in England, and this precluded implementation of the grand design entertained by Norris. The reason for not getting the ell in 1895–96 was, to Norris's dismay, also traceable to England. He was astounded to discover that the English government chose not to commit itself to the Uitlanders' cause when Dr. Leander Starr Jameson and his associates took the first steps toward "liberating" Johannesburg.

"The Uprising in the Transvaal," which Norris datelined Johannesburg, 5 January 1896, records his perceptions of how the insurrection began gallantly but then was allowed to fizzle into a humiliating defeat. He recalls his enthusiasm upon the arrival on 30 December of the great news about the "Jameson Raid": the day before, "Dr. Jameson had crossed the border with 600 men and eight Maxims [machine guns]. Then the insurrection leaped into life all in an instant."[3] On 31 December, Johannesburg was abuzz with excitement over the long-expected call to arms: the "same red-faced Englishmen in whipcord breeches" who were wont to trot up and down Commissioner Street on their Basuto polo ponies "were now on the gallop . . . carrying rifles instead of crops. . . . Around the [Consolidated Gold Fields of Africa] office surged a vast throng of men crowding in, one at a time, through the door over which was written 'Enroll here.' Each as he came out after signing his name and taking the oath, bore in his hands a clean, new Lee & Metford, the gun that kills at 1,000 yards." Norris, unaware of what was actually transpiring behind the scenes, felt he had reason to celebrate the farsighted leaders of a Reform Committee in Johannesburg who had, he was given to understand, thoroughly prepared for months for the "spontaneous" uprising that Jameson's incursion into the Transvaal would trigger. He lauded, too, the mastermind behind it all, Cecil Rhodes. The hero of the hour for Norris, though, was the Scottish physician who had emigrated to South Africa in 1878 and was as dedicated as Rhodes to the concept of a "united" South Africa in which the English ruled.

On 29 December 1895, Dr. Jameson and his soldiers had entered Boer territory from Pitsani in the British protectorate of Bechuanaland, continuing southeastward to Mafeking and on toward Johannesburg the next day. "From that time until he reached Doornkop, twelve miles from Johannesburg," the man whom Norris viewed as a liberator of the Uitlanders "had been marching steadily, halting only for about six hours' sleep, sustaining his own courage and that of his men by the assurances of aid from Johannesburg."

Jameson was then betrayed by his own people.

What Norris did not know then, or—if he learned of it later—chose not to make public, was that Jameson was a loose cannon. The intemperate Scotsman had acted on his own despite six telegrams between 26 and 28 December telling him not to initiate the insurrection: Johannesburg was not ready.[4] Cecil Rhodes tried to stop Jameson, only to find that Jameson's men had cut the telegraph wire to Mafeking. Moreover, England's High Commissioner Sir Hercules Robinson, once apprised of the public-relations disaster in the making, had on 31 December forbade all British subjects from assisting Jameson in any way.[5] Jameson never made it to Johannesburg, and, as Norris hotly observes, for some reason unknown to him the column of "exhausted, starving men" was cruelly "left to face 1,500 Boers within twelve miles of the town from which 12,000 men could have been sent" to relieve him. On "the 2nd of January, Jameson was attacked. He held out for five hours . . . then surrendered his entire command, Maxims, reserve horses, Nordenfeldts and all. The dash for Johannesburg ended in a fizzle." It was another "Charge of the Light Brigade," thought Norris: "'Someone had blundered.'" For Norris, Tennyson's six hundred who rode into the Valley of Death were now Jameson's at Krugersdorp and Doornkop. The Boers lost only two men, with two others wounded; they killed or wounded twenty-seven of Jameson's. Moreover, a dismayed Norris went on, when Robinson worked out an armistice with President Paul Kruger at Pretoria, he did not include Jameson and his gallants in its terms.

In the days and weeks following the debacle, England backpedaled as quickly as it could from Jameson's rash action. The man ultimately responsible for his behavior, Cecil Rhodes, had mightily embarrassed the crown and had to resign his position as the Cape Colony's prime minister. Further attempting damage control, England's Secretary for the Colonies Joseph Chamberlain made only a perfunctory objection to the Boers' trial in Pretoria of four of the Reform Committee leaders: Rhodes's brother Francis, Lionel Phillips, George Farrar, and the American John Hays Hammond. The crown accepted with what grace it could muster the death sentences handed down to them; only after it was clear that England had been brought to heel did President

Kruger commute the sentences to fifteen years' imprisonment. Kruger looked more civilized than the freebooting English when, in June 1896, he released the four from prison after the payment of twenty-five thousand pounds each, on the condition that they refrain from further interference in the Transvaal's internal affairs. Kruger also came off better in the press when he forbore punishing the man whom even the English had branded a criminal; he turned over Jameson to an English court, where he was tried and sentenced in late July to a fifteen-month prison term, without hard labor.[6]

The leopards—England and Jameson—had not actually changed their spots, however. Because of poor health, Jameson regained his freedom in fewer than six months. He returned to the Cape Colony to serve in its parliament from 1900 to 1902 and to become premier in 1904. Rhodes would return to Africa as well, to engage in the development of Rhodesia. Once face had been saved as much at it could be and a decent interval of public repentance had been observed, England and its imperialists went back to business as usual. Norris, too, never changed his pro-Uitlander, anti-Boer stance—even after the facts concerning Jameson became public knowledge. Indeed, he responded to the outbreak of the Boer War in 1899 with a *San Francisco Examiner* article defaming the lazy, thick-witted Boers in exactly the same way he had in 1895–96.[7]

Before an armistice restored a modicum of normalcy to Johannesburg, Norris awoke on 31 December 1896 to witness "The Frantic Rush from Johannesburg," as he titled the 11 March 1896 *Chronicle* article that he composed on his way back to the United States. Panic had struck the city, "which every one believed would soon echo with the rattle of Maxims instead of the wonted thunder of the [gold mines'] stamp mills."[8] One carriage on its way to catch a train at the Park Station carried a gaggle of actresses, and it echoed with "incessant little peals of laughter and cries of gaiety and enjoyment." But that was the exception, as those not slated to serve as combatants attempted to debouch from the city by rail. The streets leading to the station were choked with people who were "not so gay" and "to whom war was not the merry war of legend, the war *opéra comique.*" As the flood of terrified humanity passed before him, Norris waxed Zolaesque; Zola was famous for his masterful treatments of crowd scenes and the fury of mobs. Norris wrote: "The procession streamed by incessantly, over the sidewalks and out upon the streets; men and women, jaded horses, weeping children, terrified dogs dragged about by leashes of rope, Kaffirs with wide, rolling eyes, overworked porters, even occasional Hindoos, in turbans and yellow blouses, their precious rolls of silk and gold embroidery balanced on their heads." Shifting from visual to aural imagery as "the throng increased," Norris records "a great distressful murmur, a mingled and confused sound of the thousands of shuffling feet, the hum of voices, broken by shouts and cries, the creaking of overladen carts, the weeping of children and the lowing of excited oxen tethered to the tails of carts and cabs." Having already visualized the piles of trunks, boxes, furniture, and heaps of like items that parted the onrushing crowd "to right and left as a stranded snag would part a current," he recalls the "sounds rising into the air above the confusion of marching thousands mingled together in a vast, confused clamor. The plaint of an entire people, the lamentation of a tribal migration." All of this is prelude to the scene at the station itself, where a "dreadful struggle began":

> Men and women at grapple on the platforms, on the steps of the carriages, and even in the carriages themselves; lost children, frantic with terror, screaming in the press, officials powerless, caught in the jam and carried about like useless timber . . . a woman was struck on the temple by a Cornish miner and was seized with hysteria, hiccoughing and shouting, waving her arms, her hair about her eyes and her bonnet all awry; a window glass in a carriage was smashed all at once, and one could see a man's bloody hand and wrist agitated wildly above the heads of the crowd. The report spread that he had fought with a Kaffir on the floor of the carriage and that his throat was cut.

Yet more confusion manifests itself, as those arriving from the countryside to find safety in the city prove as "lashed on by fear" as those trying to board the same train to escape the city. Both groups reflected "the unreasoning, brute terror of mobs and herds of cattle; the terror that shuts its eyes and ears." The *tableau vivant* is that of survival of the fittest; self-preservation is the great first law driving the Uitlanders to and from the city and affording Norris the opportunity to write in the appropriate way, naturalistically.

With the departure of the passenger cars hitched hastily to those used to transport livestock to accommodate the hundreds of fleeing refugees, Norris ends his account of the day with a striking datum. In one of the open cattle cars speeding south toward the Vaal River, a "poor Swedish woman, the keeper of the little news stand in Rissek Street, gave birth to a child. What a birthday to remember!"

On New Year's Day, Norris next related in "The Frantic Rush," he enlisted in a mounted corps and—to his great disappointment—immediately found himself at a desk. The chief of police gave two Englishmen and him the job of marking out on a city map a thousand "beats" for police officers. One of the three stuck to his task, but Norris and the other, named Solz, bolted. They requested and obtained horses the next morning. With the hunting rifles Solz had brought with him from Kimberley, they joined mounted squads whose mission was to close down the canteens of the mines in the area. Solz and Norris also served as dispatch riders, though Norris lamented that only once did he perform this duty. Then, finally, he saw action. Riding back to town on the evening of 4 January, his squad of canteen closers approached the Wemmer Mine close to the city and spotted a group of Boers at a distance of fifteen hundred yards. It was a tense moment straight from the pages of Kipling.

> Both parties pulled up, and we sat for a moment in our saddles in the pelting rain, watching to see what the Boers would do, for at this time the armistice—the famous armistice that sacrificed Jameson—had been signed . . . and until now the Boers had never ventured so near the town. Before we could realize what had happened the Boers had fired on us, a thin wreath of gray smoke blotting them out of sight for an instant. On our side there was a moment of bewilderment, I think, and then, with great good sense, the officer in charge of the little party gave us word to withdraw and push on quietly to the town.

The next morning Norris came down with "South African fever," most likely malaria or dengue. According to his widow, he was nursed back to health at John Hays Hammond's home at New Doornfontein.

A week later he was on his feet again, though wobbly. Johannesburg was by then fully under the control of the Boers—or, as Norris phrased it, "in a state of siege." Communication with the outside world was impossible; one could not leave by train without an approved passport. Only Boer loyalists were free to travel without restriction. And so Norris's stay in Johannesburg ended as military law prevailed and the authorities rounded up those they would prosecute or deport.

> On the 10th of January, as near as I can remember it, at a time when I had just entered upon convalescence, Solz and I were called before one of the Landdrosts at the Government offices. We found several others there before us, young men for the most part—the canteen closers and dispatch riders whom we had seen about the streets during the early days of the rising. The Landdrost was monosyllabic and impolite, and handled our passports

as though he wished they had been death warrants. From his manner it was evident that we were not to be included in the general amnesty recently proclaimed to all those who should surrender their arms. He answered no questions, he offered no explanation, but called our names, handed us our passports, inflated himself at us as we cowered about the far side of the room, and then bellowed: "The Government gives you twenty-four hours to leave the Transvaal." And he mulcted each of us £5 for the passports.

And so he entrained for Cape Town and thence sailed home.

Norris's return voyage began the evening of 15 January 1896, when the Union Line ship *Moor* left its dock for England. As with his voyage to Cape Town in 1895, there was again a scheduled stop at Madeira, and on 31 January the *Moor* left that port for Plymouth, arriving at 6:30 A.M. on 4 February and going on the same day to Southampton, where Norris debarked.[9]

As he explained in "Rhodes and the Reporters," published in *The Wave* rather than the *San Francisco Chronicle,* it was an eventful trip. Among the fourteen first-cabin passengers was the Honorable Cecil Rhodes, "the Colossus of Rhodes, as South Africa calls him."[10] Norris, an unregenerate Anglophile, still held in high esteem the man whose grand scheme for seizing control of the Transvaal Jameson had ruined—in spite of the fact that Rhodes rather rudely ignored the very existence of his fellow passengers during the journey northward. Related Norris, the Honorable Cecil "boarded us after the *Moor* had left the docks at Cape Town and had anchored in the stream, and he left us at Plymouth early in the morning in a very gay little steam-yacht, all white paint and nickel railings. Between the two ends of the voyage he walked up and down the decks, or leaned over the side, or read a very great deal in a red book . . . [Marie Corelli's] *The Sorrows of Satan.* But he kept his own counsel and never talked or laughed or descended to anything like familiarity." He was no more forthcoming with the reporters who swarmed aboard at Madeira. Rhodes was, after all, returning to England to answer for the geopolitical "blunder" at Johannesburg, and his decision to keep his own counsel lest he further incriminate himself by a careless comment or risk misquotation by the press is understandable.

Rhodes made for good copy twice more. On 18 April 1896, a week after the publication of "Rhodes and the Reporters," Norris contributed to *The Wave* this anecdote illustrating that even so grand a Colossus was capable of the peccadilloes to which common humanity is subject:

Speaking of South African affairs puts us in mind of a rather good story on Cecil Rhodes, the multi-millionaire and ex-Premier of the Colony. On his return journey to England recently, Mr. Rhodes was detained by the break down of his steamer, the *Moor,* which was obliged to put into Dakar, on the Senegal coast. Mr. Rhodes went ashore with a boat load of passengers, and while strolling through one street of the town was offered a beautiful rug—or it might have been a bed quilt—made of bird skins by a native who asked twelve shillings in return. Mr. Rhodes was delighted with the skins, but was unwilling to pay more than ten shillings. For fully ten minutes he chaffered and haggled over the matter, and finally went his way without making the purchase. He was many times a millionaire, and controlled the output of the De Beers diamond mine, but would not pay two shillings more than he thought the rug to be worth.[11]

But the finest cameo of the Colossus Norris fashioned appeared in the *San Francisco Chronicle* the next day. In "A Steamship Voyage with Cecil Rhodes," he reported that when the *Moor* had broken down almost exactly on the equator, Rhodes did not fret and fume like the other passengers. Again, Norris was full of admiration.

As for Rhodes, who probably had more at stake than any of us could imagine, and about whom the fortunes of an empire were centered, who had more to lose than the whole Union Steamship Company was worth, as for him he went a-fishing. The ship hadn't stopped for more than an hour before we saw the great dorsal fin of a shark riding slowly above the water. . . . Ten minutes after that Cecil Rhodes had a shark hook out over the stern and was as intent upon the game as if there never had been any Reform Committee nor any insurrections or battles at Krugersdorp.

One should have seen him when the first shark struck and the barb went home, and the water under the stern of the ship was churned and lathered as though the screw had at length made up its mind to revolve. The honorable Cecil's hat was off, and his eyes were alight with the excitement of the thing, and the hands that guided empires were gripped over the taut, singing rope till the knuckles whitened, while his big, muscular body swayed and twitched and jerked with every struggle of the enormous maneater that fought him for the life he loved and measured his strength against that of the ex-Premier of South Africa.

It was a fine thing to see, and I would always like to remember Rhodes as he appeared at that time.

He had to qualify his portrait of the heroic Anglo-Saxon on the side of the angels by including the "rather good story on Cecil Rhodes" that had appeared in *The Wave* the previous week. "A strange man surely!" was the note on which he concluded his vignette illustrating the startling display of parsimony by this multimillionaire.[12]

The twenty-one-day voyage from Cape Town to England gave Norris plenty of time in which to compose his sixth and seventh articles for the *San Francisco Chronicle,* "The Frantic Rush from Johannesburg" and his description of "A Zulu War Dance." Coming ashore at Southampton on 4 February 1896, he enjoyed a layover, departing for New York City four days later on the *St. Louis,* a sister ship of the American Line steamer *Berlin* on which he had crossed the Atlantic in November. As with the voyage from Cape Town on the *Moor,* Norris's return to the United States from England was more complicated than his outbound one three months earlier, and he did not enjoy conditions conducive to writing. The *St. Louis* reached New York just before midnight on 15 February with 207 cabin and 171 steerage passengers desperately longing to set their feet upon terra firma once again. The *New York Tribune* reported, "Throughout the voyage the liner encountered heavy head seas and gales, which greatly delayed her."[13] As he had in August 1889 when he returned from his two-year stay in Paris, Norris took a cab to the Fifth Avenue Hotel, where he slept through what remained of the night.[14]

Before entraining for San Francisco, Norris mixed business with pleasure for several days, in Manhattan and during a brief visit to Cambridge, where he called upon an old friend who graduated from Berkeley in 1893 and with whom he had regularly socialized at Harvard. This was Harry Hull McClaughry, who was still attending law school in 1896, and who used to take meals with Norris at the same table in Memorial Hall in 1894–95. After supper they would often smoke their pipes together in McClaughry's dormitory room where, McClaughry recalled in 1931, many of the incidents recorded in *Vandover and the Brute* took place. There they enjoyed the Crème Violette consumed in chapter 16 of the novel. "We 'discovered' this liqueur in Boston one night and thereafter always kept a bottle of it in my room for an 'after dinner.'" In Norris's room was "'the famous tiled stove with flamboyant ornaments'" in which Vandover delights. Norris had purchased it for "exactly six dollars," and—like Vandover in chapter 12—he "never tired of extolling the virtues of this stove." Over six months had passed before the two renewed their acquaintance: "One cold winter night, snow on the ground, a tap on my door, a curt 'Come in,' and there stood Frank, back against the door, a soft 'Hello, Mister Man!' He was dressed in a long feather-weight cape overcoat and a straw hat. True, he had been with Jameson, but 'the damned scoundrels,'" McClaughry related in 1931, "had made a COOK out of him."[15]

While in Manhattan, Norris appears to have visited the editorial offices of *Harper's Weekly* to introduce himself as a witness to a major international event in South Africa and thus situate himself for a promising professional development. Writing for a San Francisco daily was a step toward establishing himself as a professional author, as was the occasional publication of his short stories in regional magazines. But success in a literary career in the 1890s ultimately involved two achievements: visibility in periodicals with national circulation such as *Harper's Weekly;* and, for a would-be novelist, not only the formation of relationships with firms located in New York City (the Harper's firm was also a book publisher) but migration from the hinterlands to that mecca in the realm of the American publishing industry. That a journalist in the employ of the *Chronicle* was present in Johannesburg when the Jameson Raid took place was the card he was able to play. The first article signed by him that was read across the country three weeks after he arrived in New York, "Street Scenes in Johannesburg during the Insurrection of January, 1896," appeared in the *Weekly* on 7 March.

Another, less toothsome development appears to have occurred while Norris was in New York. Located there as well were the editorial offices of Lovell, Coryell, and Company—the soon-to-dissolve firm that, according to the announcements in *The Wave* in November 1895, was to publish his collection of short stories.[16] As the Union Pacific carried him back to San Francisco, however, whatever confidence about the future Norris felt because of the arrangement with *Harper's Weekly* was offset by his having learned that the book would not see print. He never mentioned that collection again, in *The Wave* or elsewhere.

This setback was prelude to another in the months that followed. The *Harper's Weekly* article did not result in a demand from the East Coast for more work from his hand. It would not be for two years that the call from New York City came and he ended his association with the San Francisco weekly magazine that employed him in the spring of 1896.

12

THE *WAVE* JOURNALIST

Frank Norris's mother was relieved to find her son returned to her at last. Then, as her daughter-in-law Jeannette told Franklin Walker, she was "horrified" to see that he was not quite the same young man. The degenerative effects wrought by "African fever" were disturbing. (His Berkeley classmate Benjamin Weed related to Walker that Norris's hair, prematurely gray before he left for Cape Town, "had become white.") Even more upsetting for Gertrude was the Phi Gamma Delta insignia that "a Chinaman in South Africa" had tattooed on his arm, and worse was the snake figure that encircled his wrist. Less surprising a development, given the footlooseness of both mother and son, was their departure from San Francisco a few days after Frank's arrival. They sailed to San Diego with the Pacific Steamship Company and once again went on to sign the guest register at the Hotel del Coronado, on 25 February 1896.[1]

Returned to San Francisco, Norris was still not fully convalesced. Now he headed northeast to Placer County and the Sierra Nevadas, passing through Colfax to the mining town of Iowa Hill, and thence to the Big Dipper gold mine, where he was the guest of his onetime fraternity-house roommate Seymour Waterhouse. This was likely not his first trip to this mine. Somehow, Waterhouse had been in charge of operations there through the whole of his four years at Berkeley—a feat for which, he informed Walker with some pride, Norris greatly admired him. It was something of a Fiji reunion, for

Ralph Hathorn and George D. Blood were there as well. Frank regaled them with accounts of his South African adventures, and Waterhouse remembered Frank speaking of his having a letter of introduction to the Hammonds, dining at their home in New Doornfontein, and Hammond wearing a business suit at table. Frank had not brought formal clothing with him, and his considerate host wanted to put him at his ease. Also—no surprise here—Frank made it clear that he "had no use for Boers." The last bit Waterhouse could remember—or, understandably, could not forget—was that Norris wore his Uitlander uniform while at the mine.

Then, at twenty-six years of age, Norris came home and became a salaried employee for the first time.

The Wave was a well-established weekly magazine begun in 1890. It was originally the means by which the editor, Ben C. Truman, promoted the interests of the Southern Pacific Railroad, then headed by Collis P. Huntington. Truman was also this patently monopolistic corporation's press agent, and his aim was to use his magazine to make as attractive as possible travel on the lines of the railroad already known pejoratively as "The Octopus." More particularly, his assignment was to do what he could to encourage Californians to travel by rail to and enjoy the amenities of the elegant Hotel del Monte near Monterey—built in 1880 by the Southern Pacific's previous president, Charles Crocker, and rebuilt in 1887 after the original structure was destroyed by fire.

By 1896, however, no one could point to *The Wave* as a "railroad organ." Southern Pacific advertisements did appear in its pages, and until the demise of the weekly in 1901 it routinely derived revenue from sizeable ads for the hotel. But other railroads also made their pitches to *Wave* subscribers, as did many another resort without a history of close relationship to the Southern Pacific. Its articles featuring picturesque locales across the state spelled railroad passes for *Wave* writers, yet that was hardly an exceptional circumstance for representatives of the press at large who might consequently be inclined to give the much-maligned Southern Pacific positive treatment.

True, this magazine addressed to the well-to-do, once wittily subtitled "A Journal for Those in the Swim," did not excoriate "The Octopus" in the manner of that corporation's journalistic nemesis, the *San Francisco Examiner;* and the man who succeeded Truman, John O'Hara Cosgrave, disclosed that he knew Huntington personally when he wrote two highly appreciative eulogies upon his death in August 1900.[2] Further, *The Wave* was undeniably conservative in many respects. It never lionized the labor organizer, foe to railroad trusts, and socialist Eugene V. Debs. Still, one would be hard-pressed to demonstrate a toadying attitude toward the Southern Pacific in its editorial pages or elsewhere during Norris's tenure. More important, Norris himself showed no interest whatsoever in railroad politics in California until after he left *The Wave* and, over a year later, began his research for *The Octopus.*

Printed on calendered paper, *The Wave's* glossy leaves were attractively illustrated with drawings by local artists and high-quality halftone reproductions of photographs. It did not neglect international and national developments. Yet, while one might purchase issues in several other American cities and even at Brentano's bookstore in Paris, *The Wave* was ever a West Coast, regional publication, and, in 1896–98, its dominant focus in issues normally running to sixteen pages was the Bay Area. Cosgrave not only edited but wrote a good deal of the copy dealing with local events and personalities. He had to because of a fact that his magazine consistently concealed: *The Wave* was a shoestring operation in terms of the size of its staff. It enjoyed a healthy circulation of which it frequently boasted, until Cosgrave resigned in 1900 to edit *Everybody's Magazine* and, the next year, *The Wave* folded. But the high caliber of the writing it featured was fully dependent upon local authors willing to contribute their wares or submit them as piecework for a fee. Ambrose Bierce, for example, was in the employ of William Randolph Hearst's *Examiner* and never worked for Cosgrave. He chose to contribute short stories occasionally for the good reason that *The Wave* was clearly a cut above the daily newspaper in which everything he wrote might appear. Placing a story in *The Wave* was an attractive alternative in that it conferred a higher artistic status. Illustrators and painters whose works Cosgrave reproduced could likewise display their artistry to good advantage before subscribers able to purchase their wares. That is to say, despite advertising revenue and subscriptions, Cosgrave could not afford much hired help. The man or woman he could pay a salary had to make substantial and tonally sophisticated contributions to the issues; and he offered Norris the position of writer and associate editor on the basis of the high merit he had demonstrated as one of the volunteer authors whose work Cosgrave had been glad to receive.

Cosgrave puffed Norris in October and November 1895. In January 1896, as Norris was on his way back to the United States, Cosgrave was again impressed, having recently read "A Californian in the City of Cape Town." The editor reviewed not only books on a regular basis but periodicals as well, and on 25 January 1896 he noted that the *San Francisco Chronicle*

> had two interesting features last week—a short story by Stephen Crane and the first of Frank Norris's letters from Cape Town. Mr. Norris has written a great deal for The Wave, and is, without question, the most promising of the California *littérateurs*. There is a veritable literary quality in his style, and I am sure his letters from the Cape will prove interesting apart from the excitement incident to the Transvaal trouble. By the way, it is alleged that Norris was with Dr. Jameson in the raid on the Rand. That was the opportunity he always sought.[3]

From that last sentence it is also clear that personal acquaintance bolstered Cosgrave's admiration. *The Wave's* society columns, like those of the San Francisco dailies, had for years situated his sister Millicent and him in the same social swim as the Norrises.

The advisability of bringing Norris aboard was not at all called into question by another development, in March 1896. It was a special event when a work that appeared in *The Wave* drew the attention of other magazine editors. Cosgrave crowed on 7 March 1896 that Norris's "A California Vintage" was not merely the subject of comment but had been reprinted in the monthly magazine *Current Literature*.[4] And so, with Cosgrave's expectations running high, Norris began working for him full-time in mid-April 1896.

One cannot be more exact about when he began to receive the salary of twenty dollars per week recalled by Charles. Cosgrave—ever careful to mask the size of his operation—never announced the appointment of Norris to his staff. Indeed, as late as 19 December 1896 he referred to Norris only as a "frequent contributor," never identifying him as an employee. It was far preferable for a high-toned periodical to suggest that male writers for *The Wave* were men of letters of the old school whose observations and reflections bespoke leisure, education, and good breeding rather than work for pay. Not until 27 August 1898, six months after Norris resigned from his staff position, did Cosgrave first cite him, rather amorphously, as someone "long connected with the editorial department of *The Wave*."[5]

As his publicly cloaked tenure as a salaried employee extended to February 1898, Norris was serving what has traditionally been seen as his formal literary apprenticeship. Strictly speaking, it actually extended back to his departure from Harvard and included his earlier work for Cosgrave as well as for the *San Francisco Chronicle*. But so did Norris himself choose to de-

fine his 1896–98 *Wave* experience after he made the breakthrough to the
status of professional novelist, writing from New York City on 9 April 1900
to Charles F. Lummis that in 1896 he took the position of "associate editor
S.F. *Wave*,—wrote on an average of 30,000 words a week—including one
short story [per week]—for this paper for two years, best and only literary
experience [I] ever had." He could "think of nothing better for [a] young
man with 'literary aspirations' than [a] grind of this kind on *this kind of paper*
(*not* a daily, but a weekly)."[6] That Norris produced thirty thousand words per
week—the equivalent of over a hundred typed pages in double-space—does
not square with the more than 150 signed, pseudonymously signed, and unsigned *Wave* pieces known to be his. Nor can one reach thirty thousand even
by generously factoring in unattributable articles or paragraphs that he *may*
have written, his composition of "whitemail" (writeups of *Wave* advertisers
as "news"), and last-minute additions in proof of "filler" to eliminate blank
space in columns of text.

The "grind" that made Norris feel as though he was laboring so prodi-
giously did include editorial work—which was not at all his cup of tea. Charles
told Walker that Cosgrave once fired Frank because he could not write. But a
more likely cause of some sort of temporary falling out between the two men
was Cosgrave's discovery that his new employee was neither qualified to edit
copy for *The Wave* in 1896 nor then inclined to learn the essentials thereof.
Norris never manifested the shortcomings of Theodore Dreiser and Thomas
Wolfe: he did know how to shape commercially viable pieces of prose fiction
and essays on his own. There is no evidence that his editors ever had to slash
and burn, rearrange, and rewrite his manuscripts or serve as coauthors of his
works. But his surviving manuscripts and especially his letters make it clear
that, like Charlotte Brontë and William Makepeace Thackeray before him,
Norris never mastered conventional, grammar-based punctuation. Like F.
Scott Fitzgerald after him, he commanded a splendiferous vocabulary; yet,
again like Fitzgerald, spelling was altogether another matter. Thus, as with
Professor Senger, who tutored Norris in mathematics in 1890, so with the
man who hired Norris as associate editor of *The Wave*. Poor Cosgrave! Then
again, this writer could do what the editor Cosgrave could not.

If Cosgrave wanted a utility player on his small team, he could not have
fared better. Certainly contributing many more than the 150–plus pieces
known to be his, Norris wrote short stories, sketches, dialogues, closet dramas, and even the serialized novel *Moran of the Lady Letty* for Cosgrave.
When fictional copy of his own was not yet ready, he translated French short

stories. His nonfiction included literary essays and reviews of books, plays, and art exhibitions. He interviewed actors and actresses, playwrights, journalists, police officers, firefighters, prison guards and prisoners at San Quentin, a virtuoso pianist, the painter Charles Rollo Peters, a professional strong woman, and a man whose trained cats and dogs performed at the Orpheum Theater. His articles dealt with football games, tennis and polo matches, how nurses are trained, local oyster production, the process of producing bronze sculptures, what's wrong with the English Department at Berkeley, how a message sent from San Francisco reaches South Africa, San Francisco as a racial and ethnic melting pot, and—repeatedly—the U.S. navy ships on the West Coast. When Cosgrave asked for local-color articles of regional interest, Norris packed his bags, riding the rails northward through the Sonoma Valley to celebrate the food and wine that the Italian Swiss Colony in Asti served to visitors, eastward to observe the wheat harvest on Roberts Island near Stockton, and southward down the coast to write up Santa Cruz, Monterey, and the area inland from the coast triangularly defined by Hecker Pass, Gilroy, and Hollister. In his short stories, his geographical range was even wider. He set them farther east in the Sierra Nevadas and as far south as San Diego. The only additional function that Norris might have performed was that of an illustrator. Having completed the drawings that accompanied his South African articles for the *San Francisco Chronicle*, Norris ceased work of that kind. He is known to have drawn only once for Cosgrave, before he joined the staff. This was the cover art for a thirty-two-page pamphlet published in 1895, *American Labor and Its Foreign Leaders: Editorials from the San Francisco Wave*.[7]

The versatility Norris could energetically display, however, was not the reason that Cosgrave engaged his services. Cosgrave's point of view in the spring of 1896 was not Norris's retrospective in 1900 when he described for Charles F. Lummis how his *Wave* apprenticeship prepared him for success as a novelist. Nor was it Will Irwin's in 1909, when he introduced a collection of Norris's early short stories, *The Third Circle*, and focused on how those written for *The Wave* comprised the record of a "novelist in the making," quoting a like-minded Gelett Burgess, who viewed the same as the "studio sketches of a great novelist."[8] Cosgrave was aware of Norris's relatively modest accomplishments as a storyteller through October 1895 when his most recent fictional publication, "A Defense of the Flag," appeared in the *Argonaut*. But he needed someone who could do what Norris had as an essayist: strike the right balance, as Cosgrave had said in early November, between engaging description and thought-provoking reflection. It was an accomplished impressionistic journalist rather than the disheartened author of an unpublished collection of short stories whom Cosgrave turned loose upon San Francisco and its environs with an assignment as generous as that appreciated by Norris when he was Lewis E. Gates's student. It was the perfect arrangement for a man who did what he liked: as in English 22 at Harvard, Norris could choose any subject for treatment that promised the right balance between description and reflection. Will Irwin, who succeeded Norris at *The Wave,* had short stories mainly in mind when he said that Cosgrave gave Norris "a free hand." But he also referred to the camera-toting journalist thus: "Whatever his thought of that day, whatever he had seen with the eye of his flash [camera] or the eye of his imagination, he might write and print."[9] That such was the case is apparent in his first *Wave* contribution of 11 April, "Rhodes and the Reporters," in which he continued to write about his recent experiences in the same first-person manner he had in 1895's "The Country Club at Del Monte" and the South African articles that appeared in the *San Francisco Chronicle.* It was as though the directive from Cosgrave was, "Change nothing. You're doing just fine."

What would enhance the pages of *The Wave* were more "Impressions of an Observer," especially when they were like the last installment of the series of articles committed to the *San Francisco Chronicle,* "A Steamship Voyage with Cecil Rhodes." When it appeared on 19 April in that daily rather than his weekly, Cosgrave had good reason to rage against fate in that, qualitatively, he would not see its like in *The Wave* until 27 June 1896, when Norris again found his stride with "The Santa Cruz Venetian Carnival" and initiated a string of similarly engaging articles. The best of these include July's "A California Jubilee," treating the festivities in Monterey in observance of the U.S. acquisition of California during the Mexican War; October's "The Bivalve at Home," Norris's lyrical account of his visit to the oyster-cultivation beds at Belmont; and, later in October, "Italy in California," which purred about the idyllic afternoon Norris spent amidst the Tuscan-like vineyards in Asti. Surpassed nowhere in the Norris canon, however, is this passage from "A Steamship Voyage" brilliantly manifesting the descriptive-reflective skills that Cosgrave prized so highly:

> When you hear people exclaim over the splendors of the tropic ocean or see them written about either in Robert Louis Stevenson's novels or in the guide books of the Peninsular and Oriental or Castle steamship companies,

believe all that you hear and see and try to believe a great deal more. If you do this you will get an approximate idea of what can be done in the way of scenic effect south of the equator. But it is hard to imagine these waters without having passed through them.

You have heard of an ocean as smooth as glass, for instance, but have you any idea what such a sight really is? I remember having seen one thing that could approach it, and that was the floor of a certain basilica outside the walls of Rome (a certain San Paolo, if I remember right), a mosaic floor, polished and repolished till the great rose windows flashed from it as though from a mirror. We were given felt shoes that we might step out upon this floor, and we did so with trepidation and with reverence, while underneath us grew out myriads of very strange flowers, and arabesques and curious tracings that were as the weavings of many spiders. You must imagine a floor such as this stretching out from you on all sides forever and forever reflecting a sky filled at noon with the light of a vertical sun, and at morning and evening with all manner of red and pink and purple clouds. And very often the light of the sun in the sky and the flashing of his reflection in this wonderful sea would shimmer together at the star line and mingle and be as one, and the rim of the horizon would disappear and there would be no more sea nor any more sky, just a vast illimitable space, a vague, empty shimmer of light and air, a sort of glittering nirvana, through which you were floating, sustained by nothing and going nowhere. Everything else slipped from you. There was no longer sense of motion, or stability or anything that was of the earth. Nothing but yourself alone and looking out into this vast empty space full of light and air and glittering mist.

As we drew toward the equator the weather became warmer and the ship was covered with awnings from end to end. The officers wore white duck and the nine of us in the first cabin who were men took to tennis flannels and lemon squashes. At last sleeping below was out of the question. At night the cabin stewards would bring our beds upon the deck and make them up on the gratings of the hatchways, and here we would pass the nights, the long dark blue nights of the tropics, sometimes sleeping as the throbbing of the engines and the ripple of the water under the ship's fore-foot made us drowsy, but as often talking for hours over coffee and cigarettes until the sky began to whiten and the crew came to sluice down the decks, making it known that the day was breaking and that it was time for baths and breakfast.

These were days and nights to be remembered. It is just possible that I have exaggerated, or that I have remembered only their most perfect moments or that, just from Johannesburg stewing in the dust and smoke of abortive insurrection, ringing with the clamor of angry men, with memories of fever and bad food and drenching rains fresh in mind, they may have gained by contrast and appeared as it were in the glamour of a reflected light. At any rate they seemed very beautiful and it would be unfair to speak of them except from the point of view of a personal impression.[10]

The "personal impression" ever central to his South African articles was the
norm not only in his *Wave* nonfiction but in the essays written for other periodicals thereafter.

In his *Wave* short stories, though, another aesthetic prevailed. Writing
in the third-person singular, he maximized the appearance—or illusion—of
authorial objectivity. But authorial self-effacement in his articles was neither
Norris's practice nor Cosgrave's preference. The subjects Norris chose to
treat varied widely, from the peculiar artistic opportunities enjoyed by San
Franciscan authors in "An Opening for Novelists" to how San Francisco disposes of five hundred tons of garbage per day in another 1897 piece entitled
"Sanitary Reduction." What did not vary was Norris's presence—at center
stage—as observer and commentator. So subjective is his narrative voice that
the inferable subtitle of virtually all of his nonfiction that appeared in *The
Wave* may rightly be seen in the title he gave to his December 1896 essay
on San Francisco's annual horse show: "How It Strikes an Observer." Put in
fictional terms, Norris is the principal "character" in his accounts of what he
experienced in South Africa in 1895–96, northern California through early
1898, and then Cuba later in 1898. The same holds true even in 1901–2, when
he was writing for periodicals about what was transpiring in the publishing
world as he knew it from personal experience.

Had Norris gathered for a book and found a publisher for his South African essays, the structure would have naturally been a chronological arrangement. The unifying element in its "plot," though, would have been the same
as that of similar collections by Richard Harding Davis: Norris's personality,
through which he filtered all that he had seen.

Paradigmatic in this respect, and in others less subjective, is "The Santa Cruz
Venetian Carnival." That Norris himself and his experience are the point of
reference and the subject, respectively, of this *Wave* article is apparent at
once as he detrains on 18 June 1896 to make his way to the Sea Beach Hotel
and to write about that coastal city's carnival in its fifth day.[11]

> You got off the train feeling vaguely intrusive. The ride from [San Francisco]
> had, of course, been long and hot and very dusty. Perhaps you had been asleep
> for the last third of the way, and had awakened too suddenly to the conscious-
> ness of an indefinable sensation of grit and fine cinders, and the suspicion that
> your collar was limp and dirty. Then, before you were prepared for it, you were
> hustled from the train and out upon the platform of the station.

There was a glare of sunshine, and the air had a different taste that suggested the sea immediately. The platform was crowded, mostly with people from the hotels, come down to meet the train, girls in cool, white skirts and straw sailors, and young men in ducks and flannels, some of them carrying tennis rackets. It was quite a different world at once, and you felt as if things had been happening in it, and certain phases of life lived out, in which you had neither part nor lot. You in your overcoat and gritty business suit and black hat, were out of your element; as yet you were not of that world where so many people knew each other and dressed in white clothes, and you bundled yourself hurriedly into the corner of the hotel 'bus before you should see anybody you knew.

The town is fully decked out in the yellow and white carnival colors, inviting attention from one inclined to see things with a painterly eye. As he had a month earlier in "Van Alstyn Sees Polo at Burlingame" and would in July with "The Tennis Tournament" and in December 1896 with "How It Strikes an Observer," Norris composes a verbal painting redolent with sensationally colorful detail:

> The main street seen in perspective was as a weaver's loom, the warp white and yellow, the woof all manner of slow moving colors—a web of them, a maze of them, intricate, changeful, very delicate. Overhead, from side to side, from balcony to balcony, and from housetop to housetop, stretched arches and festoons and garlands all of white and of yellow, one behind another, reaching further and further into the vista like the reflections of many mirrors, bewildering, almost dazzling. Below them, up and down through the streets, came and went and came again a vast throng of people weaving their way in two directions, detaching against the background of the carnival colors a dancing, irregular mass of tints and shades. Here and there was the momentary flash of a white skirt, again the lacquered flanks of a smart trap turned gleaming to the sun like a bit of metal, a feather of bright green shrubbery overhanging a gate stirred for a moment in the breeze very brave and gay, or a brilliant red parasol suddenly flashed into view, a violent, emphatic spot of color, disappearing again amidst the crowd like the quick extinguishing of a live coal.

The aurally acute author of "The Country Club at Del Monte" next registers how "from all this gaiety of shifting colors, rose a confused sound, a vast murmur of innumerable voices blending overhead into a strange hum, that certain unintelligible chord, prolonged, sustained, which is always thrown off from a concourse of people." A strain of laughter, the rattle of stiffly starched shirts, bits of conversation, the shuffle of many feet, the band playing in the distance—the melange gives rise to a grand reflection not encountered in

"The Country Club," a celebratory metadescription or allegorization of the noisy revelers assembled for the day: "It is the voice of an entire city speaking as something individual, having a life by itself, vast, vague, and not to be interpreted; while over this mysterious diapason, this bourdon of an unseen organ, played and rippled an infinite multitude of tiny staccato notes, every one joyous, the gay treble of a whole community amusing itself."

The organizers and local participants in the carnival are inexperienced in staging a sophisticated fête but are earnestly doing the best they can with the humble materials with which they have to work. They are the rural counterparts of the plebeian, big-city characters of Polk Street whose Dickensian personalities and quirky behavior entertain the reader in the early chapters of *McTeague*. Norris finds their naïveté both charming and droll, not unkindly displaying another of his signature traits as a writer—his keen sense of the ridiculous—when the carnival's queen makes her entry that night into the pavilion where she is to preside over a ball.

> The procession moved up the floor of the pavilion toward the throne (which looked less like a throne than like a photographer's settee). It advanced slowly, headed by a very little girl in a red dress, resolutely holding a tiny dummy trumpet of pasteboard to her lips. Then in two files came the ushers, Louis Quatorze style. They were all in white—white lace, white silk, white cotton stockings—and they moved deliberately over the white canvas that covered the floor against the background of white hangings with which the hall was decorated. However, their shoes were black—violently so; and nothing could have been more amusing than these scores of inky black objects moving back and forth amidst all this shimmer of white. The shoes seemed enormous, distorted, grotesque. They attracted and fascinated the eye, and suggested the appearance of a migratory tribe of Brobdingnag black beetles crawling methodically over a wilderness of white sand.

Norris records several other risible developments of the same kind that night and the next day, risking the charge of condescension but terminating his drift in this direction in a timely manner. No longer arch, he confesses that he was quite won over by the spectacle on his second evening in Santa Cruz as darkness descended and a barge transported the queen to the pavilion, followed by a multitude of illuminated floats, barges, and gondolas. "At last here under the night the carnival was in its proper element":

> The incongruities, the little cheap makeshifts, so bare and bald in an afternoon's sun, disappeared, or took on a new significance; the tinsel was not tinsel any longer; the cambric and paper and paint grew rich and real; the

Queen's canopy, the necklaces of electric bulbs, the thousands of heaving lights, the slow-moving [barge of the queen] all seemed part of a beautiful, illusive picture, impossible, fanciful, very charming, like a painting of Watteau, the *Pèlerinage à Cythère*, seen by night. More lights and lanterns came crowding in, a wheel of red fireworks covered the surface of the water with a myriad of red, writhing snakes. The illusion became perfect, the sense of reality, of solidity, dwindled.

Whereupon, fully immersed in his experience of the fabulous, Norris performs a variation upon one of the more memorable imagistic flourishes in "A Steamship Voyage with Cecil Rhodes," his description of the shimmering ocean's surface becoming indistinguishable from the sky and suggestive of "vast illimitable space." Establishing a more distant view of the carnival scene and reframing it in a spatially larger context, he pictures an even more dreamlike spectacle that appears to have been projected against the night sky:

The black water, the black land, and the black sky merged into one vast, intangible shadow, hollow, infinitely deep. There was no longer the water there, nor the banks beyond, nor even the reach of sky, but you looked out into an infinite, empty space, sown with thousands of trembling lights, across which moved dim, beautiful shapes, shallops and curved prows and gondolas, and in the midst of which floated a fairy palace, glittering, fragile, airy, a thing of crystal and of gold, created miraculously, like the passing whim of some compelling genie.

One last observation of what is truly Norrisean in this piece of fine, polished writing is warranted. The essay concludes with a nocturnal reflection that reminds us once again why Cosgrave hired Norris and illustrates what was characteristic of his descriptive essays in which he repeatedly strove to take his readers beyond graphically rendered fact to considerations of a more global nature.

Norris tells us that Friday night has become Saturday. Santa Cruz, seen from a hill above the town at one o'clock in the morning, is deserted. But, as when he arrived on Thursday, Norris again hears a humming sound emanating from the city below him, this time prompting him to a very different, much more somber line of thought. All signs of human strivings of the previous two days having disappeared, Norris is left alone to reflect on the human condition in the face of an insentient Nature utterly unaware of the revelers' existence. The allegory now suggesting itself concerns the human condition as carnival-like in a wholly negative sense. It is ephemeral, full of sound and fury, and, in the larger scheme of things, signifying—what?

And then, in that immense silence, when all the shrill, staccato, trivial
noises of the day were dumb, you heard again the prolonged long hum that
rose from the city, even in its sleep, the voice of something individual, living
a huge, strange life apart, raising a virile diapason of protest against shams
and tinsels and things transient in that other strange carnival, that revel of
masks and painted faces, the huge grim joke that runs its fourscore years and
ten. But that was not all.

There was another voice, that of the sea; mysterious, insistent, and there
through the night, under the low, red moon, the two voices of the sea and of
the city talked to each other in that unknown language of their own; and the
two voices mingling together filled all the night with an immense and prolonged wave of sound, the bourdon of an unseen organ—the vast and minor
note of Life.

This melancholic philosophical perspective, dwarfing the significance of
not only the participants in the carnival but Norris himself, alerts one to the
fact that there was another side to the personality of the reflective essayist
for *The Wave* who fashioned vividly imagistic, even poetical and near-pre-
cious prose. "A Steamship Voyage with Cecil Rhodes" does not bring Zola to
mind. "The Santa Cruz Venetian Carnival," especially its conclusion, does. It
reminds one that Norris had already fallen under the sway of this sometimes
grimly pessimistic materialist. For it is not only Norris's but Zola's Nature
expressing itself in a lugubrious minor key in the "voices" that mingle in the
night. It lives a "huge, strange life" apart from that of mankind and all things
as "transient" as the individual's hopes, ambitions, and achievements. It is
Nature as Norris would later image it in *McTeague,* when its hero flees San
Francisco to the Sierras: "As far as one could look, uncounted multitudes of
trees and manzanita bushes were quietly and motionlessly growing, growing,
growing. A tremendous, immeasurable Life pushed steadily heavenward without a sound, without a motion. . . . The entire region was untamed. In some
places east of the Mississippi nature is cosey, intimate, small, and homelike,
like a good-natured housewife. In Placer County, California, she is a vast,
unconquered brute of the Pliocene epoch, savage, sullen, and magnificently
indifferent to man."[12]

Norris and his fictional characters, when they think of Nature, often employ the traditional romantic personification of a "she" with a "voice." But
Norris is only using a conventional figure of speech: no matter how aesthetically pleasing *it* sometimes is, Zola's and his Nature is finally the impersonal,
unconscious realm of matter manifesting energy and its effects through vast
expanses of time. If personified, she is "mysterious" in her ends, ruthlessly

"insistent" in her dictates, and neither a friend nor enemy of mankind. In short, it appears no coincidence that, in the same issue of *The Wave* in which "Santa Cruz" appeared, Norris for the second time proclaimed his allegiance to Zola in his essay "Zola as a Romantic Writer."

That piece of literary criticism, however, relates more directly to Norris's orientation as a fiction writer than as an essayist. More immediately pertinent regarding Zola's influence on his nonfictional prose for *The Wave* is the less well-known review of Zola's *Rome* published three weeks earlier, on 6 June 1896. Here the Zolaesque author of 1895's "A California Vintage" enthuses over how Zola's novel is "crammed with tremendous and terrible *pictures*, hurled off, as it were, upon the canvas, by giant hands wielding enormous brushes." Aiming to achieve the same effects, Norris continued in 1896 his attempts at fashioning prose that "leaves one with an impression of immensity, of vast illimitable forces, of a breadth of view and an enormity of imagination almost too great to be realized."[13] And he remained willing to accept the risk of being tagged as hyperbolic, or derided as bombastic, when he did so.

As to immensity and almost illimitable forces, in November 1896 Norris found an ideal opportunity to test his abilities: the process of "Moving a Fifty-Ton Gun" from the Union Iron Works to its emplacement site at the Lime Point Military Reservation on the northern shore of the Golden Gate. "I can imagine nothing more unwieldy of handling and transporting than this vast, inert mass of metal, a mighty dead weight, hanging back stubbornly like a balky mastodon." On that note, he attempts to render his experience of the awesome for his readers, taking them through the process of moving a seemingly immoveable object as he had observed it a few days before. He is amazed as an enormous crane deposits the hundred-thousand-pound weapon on a railroad flatcar. Next he sees it transferred to a specially rein-forced, eighty-five-foot barge for towing to Lime Point, where the gun is pulled ashore on greased skids and dragged up the steep hillside by an engine mounted approximately five hundred feet above. The engine, to hold to the earth while doing its punishing work, requires anchors placed twelve feet in the earth. Think of it! Soon, concludes Norris, the procedure will recommence after mounting of the engine another five hundred feet up the hill: "[W]hat an expenditure of energy" is his theme, "what straining of cables, what groaning of cranes and capstans, what panting and hiccoughing of over-taxed engines!" And yet there is in store an even greater marvel than this impending triumph of the mechanical over the force of gravity and the inertia of this "monster" gun:

And so foot by foot the leviathan is dragged up the hillside, and one of these days, some time next month, no doubt, it will be lodged on its carriage in the midst of cranks and little wheels and levers. Then what a change of front. The sulky leviathan that dragged sullenly back on those groaning wire cables that set the eight horse-power engine hiccoughing and sweating with exertion, that taxed the ingenuity and energy of a little army of toilers—behold, it comes to hand with sudden and marvelous docility; it has been bridled and bitted; it is obedient, gentle, even. The lifting crane of the Union Iron Works quivered as it grappled with it. Now a woman's wrist may deflect its muzzle, raise it and lower it at will, may guide it about subject to her flimsiest caprice.[14]

This was not, of course, Norris's first attempt to bowl the reader over with grand images ensconced in vigorously rhythmical prose. Two others find him experimenting similarly with the larger-than-life and thereby justifying expansive descriptions commensurate with their subjects. Six months earlier, in June 1896, he had happened across a similar opportunity across the bay at the Presidio where he used to draw with Ernest Peixotto. There the artillerymen practice their marksmanship with the twelve-inch breechloading mortars and fifteen-inch smoothbore cannons. Norris's aim is to convey the extraordinary, nearly unimaginable force with which these menacing implements of destruction propel their shells, though this is not apparent at first. "With the Peacemakers" instead begins in a manner different from "Moving a Fifty-Ton Gun." Norris goes into a good deal of technical detail about the ordnance, which would be of interest only to military enthusiasts like himself. He recovers lost ground by appealing to a broader readership with sensational detail about the devastation that will befall any enemy warship daring to approach with hostile intent. The mortars on the southern shore of San Francisco Bay can throw an eight-hundred-pound shell from three to five miles. "The man-of-war is not yet built that can withstand the shock of such a projectile. In falling it would crash through everything, would perforate the ship from deck to keelson." Likewise, the 450–pound balls of the cannons "will 'rack' a ship from end to end, loosening beams and supports, starting bolts, wrenching and jarring everything." Still, Norris's essay proves relatively slow going until, to save it from possible failure, he resorts to the device of personification—or vitalization of the inanimate—that Zola so often employed to enliven his novels. Suddenly, Norris waxes metaphorical in the most baroque manner, even hazarding a gratuitous bit of sexual imagery that would certainly not be out of place in one of Zola's works. Zola, too, could be zany in his flights of fancy. But Norris inarguably tests the limits of credibility and good taste in *The Wave* when he describes a new gun being initiated to service and focuses upon its "loins."

> The gunners at the Fort have an admirable expression, they speak of the "Life of a gun." Now this is fine and suggestive. It implies a certain individuality, a certain human or inhuman character to the guns that appeals to one. The "Life of a gun." You can fancy its birth in the forge in the midst of fire and molten ore; then its first shot and the certain grim quiver of joy running through its brazen loins with the recoil, when the savage, huge life is unleashed in a roar and a red flame.

Turning from this representation grotesquely suggesting adolescent-male sexual initiation and leaping to a new metaphor, Norris opts for an equally flamboyant experiment in characterization: "I never tire of looking at such a monster. You see it in the bastion, gripped solidly upon the stone work, its chin salient and resting upon the parapet, silent, very watchful; its muzzle is, as it were, its only feature, combining alike the expression of an eye and a mouth. The gun is some enormous animal, sphinx-like, nursing mysterious thoughts, fed with powder, speaking one terrible word."[15]

It was not Norris's finest hour, though what he was hoping to accomplish is certainly evident. He was much more successful four months later when dealing with the pride of the West Coast naval fleet and San Francisco's Union Iron Works, the battleship *Oregon*. It, too, intimidates because of its size and the power it conceals while at rest dockside, giving "an impression as of some tremendous brute . . . like a monster of a legend—living a life apart, lonesome, formidable and, if needs be, very terrible." Its guns? The problem once more, the less engaged reader may say, is to make something out of nothing. Put more kindly, it is to make these cannons and their overwhelming power as interesting for his readers as they are to Norris. To that end, they also must be given personalities, and he handles this much more artfully than he did with those at the Presidio. They are "huge, honest beasts of simple, candid character, docile under management . . . but so terrible, so resistless, that steel armor a foot in thickness is perforated by the shell they throw as if it were so much paper." Mounted in turrets, "they crane their long gray necks from the ports of these barbettes . . . on the watch always, occasionally moving from side to side with very slow, majestic motions, just as some enormous snake might stretch its neck and balance its head when aroused and ready to strike." As though to make up for the shortcomings of "With the Peacemakers," he ends this essay with a modified reprise of the previous image: "They live in pairs, two to each barbette, grim companions, brothers born in the forge, living their lives together fighting side by side, impassive and silent save at long intervals, when—their flanks all quivering—they speak one savage, terrible word."[16]

Norris's nonfictional writings for the *San Francisco Chronicle* and *The Wave* may not immediately bring to mind a "novelist in the making"—though the experience he gained while working as a journalist did indeed have much to do with the style of writing one encounters in his novels. These essays illustrate a series of trials with two major modes of description, the first of which is the fine writing and brilliant descriptive touches in "The Santa Cruz Venetian Carnival." But lest one think that Norris carefully crafted his more polished imagistic passages only when responding to the presence of the pretty, the author of *McTeague* could also harness his talents in the service of portraits of the ugly and repulsive, as in "Sanitary Reduction" of December 1897. Compare the pleasant vista of the gaily decorated main street in Santa Cruz with the impressions of the observer of this equally detailed portrait of the noisome features of San Francisco:

> Far off beyond the railroad tracks, where Eighth street widens out into hideous vacant lots, blotted and spotted with soap factories and tallow chandleries, are what is known as the Sanitary Reduction Works. On your way down to your office in the morning, at almost every other block, you go wide round a dripping grisly cart, with an Italian driver on the seat, and you try not to breathe too hard through your nose until you get well away. Scavengers' carts these are. . . . There are some three or four hundred of these carts that go the rounds of the street day after day, gathering offal, ashes, rags, bottles, sacks, dead cats and dogs, debris, cinders, tin cans, every imaginable and unimaginable description of castaway things, and carting them down the length of Eighth street, past the place where the football games are played and on across the railroad tracks and into those vague, hideous regions where [the garbage incinerator is located and] the tallest chimney west of the Rocky Mountains grows out of the soil like a gigantic pine.[17]

This, too, is fine writing, anticipating the unpleasant but visually and olfactorily powerful descriptions of sordid environments in *McTeague* and *Vandover and the Brute*. To return to a concern Norris had while a student at Berkeley, and which he continued to deal with during his *Wave* years, such indelicate treatments did not suggest the "feminine" or the hand of an aesthete as the more refined imagistic work in "A Steamship Voyage" and "Santa Cruz" may have.

The appeal of a "masculine" voice also motivated Norris's experiments with the second descriptive mode: the much more forceful, unruly, and undeniably exaggerative Zolaesque style first seen in "A California Vintage" and especially in his extravagant portrayal of the colossal crusher consuming league after league of grapes ascending to its maw on a conveyor belt. The long-term results for the Norris canon of such trials are numerous. For example, the grape crusher of 1895 reappears in altered guise in 1899 as the stamp-mill of *McTeague's* Big Dipper Mine, where its "enormous maw, fed night and day with carboys' loads, gorged itself with gravel, and spat out the gold, grinding the rocks between its jaws . . . like some savage animal, some legendary dragon, some fabulous beast." Exactly like the grape crusher, it is a "symbol of inordinate and monstrous gluttony." And, on the same page in that novel, gold miners in the mountains of the Sierras, dwarfed by the landscape as in "Santa Cruz," seem "like lice on mammoth's hides."[18] So is Norris himself "like some insignificant parasite upon the back of a mastodon" when on the deck of the *Oregon* in 1896. The "sphinx-like" guns in "With the Peacemakers" that seem to be "nursing mysterious thoughts" find their own kind years later at the end of *The Pit* in the image of Chicago's Board of Trade building "crouching on its foundations like a monstrous sphinx with blind eyes, silent, grave."[19]

There is thus good reason to recall not only Norris's concerns about the image he was projecting as a writer when at Berkeley but one of the long-term effects of the regimen to which he became accustomed as an art student. One begins his work on a hoped-for masterpiece by executing a series of *equisses* and then *études*, comparatively minor achievements in themselves but essential to the subsequent production of the work of art that may prove a major accomplishment. One has reason to recall as well Gelett Burgess's characterization of Norris's *Wave* writings as "studio sketches" made in preparation for more ambitious undertakings. But, in addition, such experiments deal not only with technique or style but choices of subject. For example, Norris's description in *The Wave* of the "Fast Girl" type in San Francisco became his characterization of Ida Wade in *Vandover and the Brute*.[20] *The Octopus* offers numerous cases in point. Norris's *Wave* article on the mountains of California's central coast as a refuge for criminals anticipates the story of Dyke's flight from the law. One on a steamer that will carry a shipment of wheat in relief of a famine in India looks forward to Presley's voyage aboard a similar vessel as *The Octopus* ends. Another article treats mechanical wheat harvesting, and yet another features the Mission San Juan Bautista where, with a change of its name, Angéle Varian is raped and Father Sarria serves as the priest in residence.[21]

That Norris would complete for publication no less than six novels between September 1898 and his death in October 1902, in addition to a considerable number of post-*Wave* short stories and articles, need not surprise one. His journalistic experiences during his apprenticeship years not only honed his skills as a writer capable of rapid composition. With month after month covering northern California life as his assignment, he was stockpiling the stuff from which he would draw for his longer prose fictions. One of those novels, for example, features a young man who writes nonfiction for a weekly in San Francisco until his efforts as a fiction writer earn him a berth with a publishing company in New York City. In its general outline and in many of its specifics, *Blix* follows Norris's own story as a *Wave* essayist. In one important respect, though, Norris was different from his hero, Condy Rivers. By the time that S. S. McClure hired him away from *The Wave,* Norris had published many more fictional works than Condy. He was very much the seasoned storyteller. Indeed, the other half of the record regarding his performance during his literary apprenticeship rightly continues to overshadow his journalistic achievements. No matter how accomplished Norris became as an essayist, it was his development as a fiction writer in 1896–98 that made possible his rise from regional writer to nationally famous author.

13

WRITING PROSE FICTION
FOR *THE WAVE*

Samuel S. McClure was the founder of a newspaper syndicate and proprietor of *McClure's Magazine*. He was also the co-owner of the book-publishing firm Doubleday and McClure Company, which would usher Frank Norris's first four novels into print. While Norris was working for *The Wave*, McClure was one of several New York powerbrokers to whom he was sending tearsheets of his publications with the hope of being rescued from the associate editorship of a weekly in the American publishing world's hinterland. When he finally succeeded with McClure and left *The Wave*, Norris was not the first of his generation in San Francisco to take flight, as John O'Hara Cosgrave noted in March 1898. When he announced Norris's departure, he also offered a short list of *Wave* writers who had also made the eastward trek that spelled success.

> Mr. Frank Norris having gone on to New York, there has occurred a delay in forwarding the MSS. of "Moran of the Lady Letty," the continuation of which did not arrive in time for insertion in this issue.
>
> [He] is the last of the band of California writers to shake off the San Francisco sand from his sabots. Gelett Burgess and Juliet Wilbor Tompkins, both of whom served in an editorial capacity on The Wave, are in New York—the former contributing to periodicals in general and the latter editing *The Puritan*. Geraldine Bonner is writing for several of the weeklies and monthlies in New York, and Bruce Porter is in Europe. It behooves us now to raise a new crop of *littérateurs* to take the places of those who have gone on.[1]

Cosgrave and Norris remained on good terms. Had Cosgrave initially resent-
ed the loss of the essayist who had become better known locally as a fiction
writer by early 1898, he could console himself with the notion that he was
complicit in Norris's success.

Ever searching periodicals for authors who might write for his syndicate,
McClure and his associates routinely scanned publications like *The Wave*.
When Norris followed Burgess to the East Coast, Cosgrave could reasonably
assume that he had played at least a small part in his subordinate's having
secured a more promising position. On 6 November 1897, three months before Norris received his job offer, Cosgrave had drawn attention to himself,
as well as to Norris, by offering McClure advice on how to run his magazine:
"The short stories in *McClure's* are out of place and should have appeared
in *Munsey's*. Save for the Kipling stories and the William Allen White contributions, the fiction in this magazine is generally inferior." The distinction
between what is "feminine" and "masculine" in literature then came into
play, Cosgrave complaining that the *McClure's* "yarns read as though they
were selected by the president of a feminine press club for publication in the
Young Ladies' Journal." He suggested that McClure turn to writers who produce stories with "the strong masculine flavor that his publication requires,"
naming Norris along with several others, including Arthur Conan Doyle and
Owen Wister.[2]

Norris's fictional creations for *The Wave*, however, were much more various than Cosgrave averred. "Masculine" is not the epithet that necessarily
comes to mind for any number of his short stories of 1896–98. Still, when
late 1897 is viewed in retrospect, one notes that Norris did provide confirmation of Cosgrave's characterization of him. As he neared the end of his
association with *The Wave*, he was on three parallel trajectories. One was
aimed at the production of a series of "dark" short stories that focused on
abnormal human experience, to be collected for a book that would strike no
one as intended for the fainthearted: it was to be be entitled *Ways That Are
Dark*. Another would take Norris through the completion of the Zolaesque
McTeague manuscript by the winter of 1897 when, according to his brother
Charles, he began circulating it among publishers. The third, given direction
by two "masculine" writers, Rudyard Kipling and Robert Louis Stevenson,
positioned Norris to begin writing the muscular adventure-romance *Moran
of the Lady Letty* before the end of 1897.

At the beginning of 1898, Norris's course as a professional storyteller
was set. In April 1896, however, he was far distant from these goals, work-

ing primarily as a journalist and only secondarily as someone who might occasionally contribute short stories if his editorial duties and nonfiction work permitted him time for their composition. It is striking that, of the sixty-five *Wave* publications of 1896 known to be his, only ten were short stories. It may surprise anyone familiar with Norris's declared professional goal that he did not come into his own as a fiction writer until his second year with *The Wave*. In addition, it was not until May 1897 that he clearly signaled, in "An Opening for Novelists," his decision to redefine his relationship with *The Wave*, making short stories his paramount concern.

Before Norris's book review celebrating naturalistic fiction, "A Summer in Arcady," appeared on 25 July 1896 and he left San Francisco to pay a visit to Seymour Waterhouse at the Big Dipper Mine,[3] eight of his ten short stories for the year had seen print. It appeared an energetic beginning, though it is possible that he composed several of them before April 1896. While he may have revised it in 1896, his first was certainly not a wholly new one. He pulled "Bandy Callaghan's Girl" from his portfolio for the 18 April issue; and it is unique in the Norris canon since, for some reason, he dated this 1896 publication 30 May 1894 at its end. It was of a piece with his "Outward and Visible Signs" stories that he wrote at Berkeley in 1894, save for its working-class cast of characters and, in its plot, a precipitous descent into the sordid that may have precluded acceptance by *Argonaut* in 1894 or 1895. The Irish-American hero the *Wave* reader encounters is vulgar, of the type that receives so much attention in *McTeague*. He is a none-too-quick-witted streetcar conductor and kin to the plumber's apprentice featured on 16 May 1896 in "The Heroism of Jonesee," another *Wave* publication recalling Norris's productions of 1894.

Such "literary slumming" need not be credited to Zola's influence. Charles Dickens did the same, and one can trace uses of "low" characters back to Shakespeare and beyond. In Norris's time, even Richard Harding Davis set romances on the other side of the tracks; and the journalist Edward W. Townsend, with whom Norris would later socialize in New York, had found success in 1895 with his amusing tales about a tough from the Bowery collected in *Chimmie Fadden*. Norris, however, was more adventuresome and explicit with his San Francisco hero, Bandy, who pursues a Chinese man to recover the five dollars out of which he has been cheated. From the start Norris tests the tolerance of his genteel readership; in a gratuitous touch, the thief displays the visible marks of leprosy on his face. Bandy chases him into the lurid nether regions of Chinatown, stumbles into an opium den, discovers and frees a "white slave," and soon dedicates himself to her reform. A love story appears to be in the making. But she cannot break her addiction and commits suicide.

"Bandy" and "The Heroism" are noteworthy not only as immediate instances of Norris's exercising the free hand granted him by Cosgrave and gravitating toward subjects sure to alarm the more conventional *Wave* subscriber. Unexpected tonal modulations of the sort that today continue to discomfit some readers of *McTeague* are evident, as when Norris narrates in a far-from-straightfaced manner plot developments they perceive as quite serious. Bandy's characterization is in part comical. Norris's voice is that of an amused observer, and the story ends with a lighthearted twist. Yet, at the tale's center are Bandy's loss of a young woman for whom he has come to feel affection, her pathetic situation as one whose addiction leads her to prostitution in Chinatown, and the discovery of her corpse. "The Heroism of Jonesee" affords a similar but less extreme experience as, through a series of comically rendered developments, the plumber's apprentice saves the virtue of a young lady. The situation with which this klutz deals is, however, far from amusing: a male sexual predator almost succeeds with his plan to violate the weeping maiden he has ensnared.

In between the publications of these short stories, Norris, on 25 April 1896, truly played the part of the enfant terrible of *The Wave* for the first time. Not until 26 June the next year, with "Little Dramas of the Curbstone," would he again turn to matters so unsettling, nor until 14 August 1897 in "A Reversion to Type" to so violent a plot. This was in the strange yarn he had spun from his South African experiences, and one has good reason to speculate that Cosgrave received complaints, since *The Wave* published nothing like "A Salvation Boom in Matabeleland" for almost a year.

As with Bandy Callaghan and Jonesee, the hero of "Salvation Boom" is from the lower socioeconomic order and no bright bulb. Traveling from Bechuanaland to Rhodesia, Otto Marks is a zealous servant of the Lord on an evangelical mission; and this Salvation Army sergeant suffers martyrdom at the hands of Matabele tribesmen. Once more, the situation is not a pleasant one inviting amusement. Yet, it was Norris's opportunity to parody for the first time the narrative style of the typical Rudyard Kipling colonial tale; to render ludicrous the religiosity of the earnest fundamentalist hero who, to pacify the warriors threatening him, unpacks and plays the organ he is transporting, singing the Moody and Sankey hymns so familiar to B. F. Norris; and to startle a *Wave* readership not accustomed to ultragraphic descriptions of violence. Otto's singing does not soothe the savage breasts of the natives who have surrounded him; and, when struck squarely in the face with a spear, he "spun about twice gripping at the air and then went over side-ways upon the key-board of the organ, his blood splashing the dazzling white of the celluloid keys."[4] The Matabele stab to death the Zulu boy who has tended to Otto's span of oxen. To avoid torture, the transport rider accompanying Otto tries to kill himself, bungling the attempt and only shooting off his chin. He is left to a slow death by the Matabele, crucified upon a telegraph pole.

As at Harvard when he upset Herbert Vaughan Abbott, Norris's evident intention in this gothic comedy was that of the fat boy in Dickens's *Pickwick Papers:* "I wants to make your flesh creep."[5] From the very start, Norris was fashioning for *The Wave* short stories that went to sensational extremes and often featured content describable as "dark."

What one *Wave* reader, Gertrude Norris, thought of these tales involving a leprous villain, opium addicts, prostitution, mayhem in Matabeleland, and mashers bent upon seduction can only be imagined. First the tattoos, and now this, from her boy who returned from the office in the evening to her tastefully appointed rooms at the Hotel Pleasanton.

Her son could and did make amends throughout his tenure with *The Wave,* counterpointing his studies of "Ways That Are Dark" with pieces that embodied "sweetness and light." He was on his best behavior when he initiated the five-installment series of courtship stories entitled "'Man Proposes'" on 23 May 1896. The first charmed the reader with a wholesome young woman of Norris's class who is staying with her family at a coastal resort like the Hotel del Monte. A gentlemanly naval officer whose ship is anchored offshore is courting her. Fine writing and salubrious sentiment adorn the scene when darkness descends and the two look out to the Pacific:

> It was pretty. The cruiser built itself up from the water as a huge, flat shad-ow, indistinct and strange against the gray blur of the sea and sky, looking less like a ship of war than like an island-built fortress, turreted and curious. The lights from her ports glowed like a row of tiny footlights, while the faint clamor of the marine band, playing a Sousa quickstep, came to their ears across the water, small and delicately distinct, as if heard through a telephone.
> All about them, seemingly coming from all quarters of the horizon at once, glowed the blue-white moonlight.

As delicately, Norris recounts their experiences that lead to a first kiss after he escorts her to her family's rooms. "This was how he proposed to her. Not a word of what was greatest in their minds passed between them. But for all that they were no less sure of each other."[6]

Writing of this sort, which would find its apotheosis in *Blix*, reappeared three weeks later in the third installment, a comical piece in which the hero, without making a formal marriage proposal, good-naturedly teases the heroine into setting a date for their wedding. The last of the series, completed on 4 July 1896, lacks such a happy conclusion, but—melodramatic as it is—it does not risk offense, as it ends with a young woman finding herself effectively engaged to a man she does not love. Historically important in that the story anticipates a major plot development in 1900's *A Man's Woman*, it cleverly situates the heroine on a sinking ship, certain that she and her infatuated companion will drown shortly. She nobly gladdens his last minutes with the falsehood he longs to hear. She tells him that she *does* care for him. Suddenly, they sight a ship on the horizon, their rescue is at hand, and she now has another problem with which to wrestle: How to reverse the effects of her kind but false declaration of her love?

The other two tales in the series, though, find Norris dealing with less innocuous situations. "'Man Proposes': No. 4" of 26 June 1896 presents another unintended self-entrapment, experienced this time by a polite but disingenuous young gent who has repeatedly protested his affection for a young woman but never intended anything more than a fling during his summer vacation at a resort. She has taken him at his word; moreover, another motivation is at work in that her parents and she are clearly lower-class, and marriage to him means upward mobility. As in 1892's "The Way of the World," the female-male imagery is that of the crafty spider and the unsuspecting fly caught in her web. Although he loves another, the hero's values are those of a gentleman; and, given the liberties he has taken during his summer romance—about which the rather crass young lady forcefully reminds him—he feels obliged to accede to her claim upon him. In short, human nature does not shine at its finest. He is the libertine who must now pay the price for the summer's recreation; she is the manipulative gold digger who has struck the main vein and, with her parents cheering her on, will mine it for all that it is worth.

The most significant of the five thematically linked stories is the second in the series, as it is keyed to the ongoing process of conceptualizing and fleshing out the bare-bones scenario for *McTeague* last seen in the themes Norris wrote at Harvard for English 22. On 30 May 1896, in "'Man Proposes': No. 2," McTeague's doppelgänger made his appearance:

He was a coal-heaver, and all that day he had been toiling at the dockyards with his fellows, carrying sacks of coal into a steamer's hold. The fatigue of work had been fearful; for full eight hours he had labored, wrestling with the inert, crushing weight of the sacks, fighting with the immense, stolid blocks of coal, smashing them with sledge-hammers, sweating at his work, grimed like a Negro with the coal-dust.

He was an enormous man, strong as a dray-horse, big-boned, heavily mus-cled, slow in his movements. His feet and hands were huge and knotted and twisted, and misshapen by hard usage. Through the grime of the coal-dust one could but indistinctly make out his face. The eyes were small, the nose flat, and the lower jaw immense, protruding like the jaws of the carnivora, and thrusting the thick lower lip out beyond the upper. His father had been a coal-heaver before him, and had worked at that trade until he had been killed in a strike. His mother had drunk herself into an asylum, and had died long ago.

Reaching his home, the coal heaver finds that a friend of his indisposed sister has prepared supper for him. The commonplace woman continues washing clothing in a tub as he eats, "his huge jaws working deliberately, incessantly." Sated at last, he watches her at her work, eying the curly wisps of hair on the nape of her neck. He turns his attention to how the "tips of her elbows were red," and he next notes that, as she scrubs the clothing against a washboard, "the little red flush came and went as her arms bent and straightened." Her rapid breathing leads to his observation of how "her big white throat alter-nately swelled and contracted." Sexually aroused, he ends the long silence. "'Say,' he exclaimed at length, with the brutal abruptness of crude, simple natures, 'listen here. I like you better'n any one else. What's the matter with us two gett'n married, huh?'"

As in chapter 2 of *McTeague*, when the dentist makes his virtually identical proposal to Trina Sieppe, the object of the coal heaver's desire is momentarily hysterical. Like Trina, she is "suddenly seized with the intuitive feminine fear of the male." The coal heaver persists and, his randiness peaking, embraces her. Roughly two months before his review lauded the popular American novelist James Lane Allen for bravely acknowledging in *Summer in Arcady* that even Victorian females experience sexual excitation, Norris has his hero-ine match the coal heaver's passion. Their "courtship" concludes with the two decidedly unattractive figures in a Zolaesque tableau like that featuring Trina's surrender to her husband-to-be in *McTeague's* fifth chapter:

She was warm from her exertions at the tub and as he stood over her she seemed to him to exhale a delicious feminine odor, that appeared to come alike from her hair, her mouth, the nape of her neck. Suddenly he took her in his enormous arms, crushing down her struggle with his immense brute strength. Then she gave up all at once, glad to yield to him and to his superior force, willing to be conquered. She turned her head to him and they kissed each other full on the mouth, brutally, grossly.[7]

Returned to San Francisco from the Big Dipper Mine by late September 1896, after two months' absence from *The Wave's* pages, the journalist—rather than short-story writer—was again very much in evidence. He celebrated the briny savor of oysters just tonged from their beds at Belmont as well as the Tuscan character of the bread and wine served at the Italian Swiss Colony in Asti. He wrote up his visit to the battleship *Oregon* and his observation of how the fifty-ton gun was transported to Lime Point. He interviewed performing artists visiting San Francisco. And Norris had penned no less than twelve articles dealing with local football games by the time he ended the hiatus in fiction writing that began on 5 July 1896.

After almost five months without a short story to his credit, "His Sister" found Norris on 28 November 1896 again dabbling with an off-color set of circumstances. It tells of a fellow who just misses meeting his sister, who has long since run away from home and become, if not a prostitute, at least a "fast girl" who knows how to show the boys a good time. The story also focuses on a less lurid but similarly serious matter. The protagonist is a young writer who, like Norris, still lives with his mother, and he complains to her that he has absolutely run out of ideas for short stories. The tale appears to be autobiographical in this respect; indeed, "His Sister" was not followed by another short story from Norris's hand for seven months, until the 26 June 1897 appearance of "Little Dramas of the Curbstone." The Christmas 1896 issue did contain a fictional work, "In the Heat of Battle." This was, however, not a short story but a closet drama dealing with an "eternal triangle" situation: to which of two men will she give her heart? Apart from this amateurish piece that Norris may have added to his portfolio while at Berkeley, the only other fictional productions were "Suggestions" of 13 March 1897 (a clutch of four minuscule sketches) and two more closet dramas: "The Puppets and the Puppy" of 22 May and "Through a Glass Darkly" of 12 June.

However fallow this season was for the short-story writer, "Suggestions" provides a glimpse of Norris continuing to give attention to the *McTeague* project. Its third part, entitled "Brute," is a comical reworking of the coal-heaver figure seen in the "'Man Proposes'" series—so much more dimwitted that he is dumbfounded as to how he should respond to the beauty of a violet: "He looked at it stupidly, perplexed, not knowing what to do; then instinctively his hand carried it to his mouth; he ground it between his huge teeth and slowly ate it. It was the only way he knew." The fourth of the "Suggestions," subtitled "Dental Parlors," however, made it clear that Norris was more advanced than this with his *McTeague* project. The sketch is virtually identical to the description of the hero's work environment appearing in the novel's first chapter. It reads in toto:

> His office, or, as he called it, his Dental Parlors, was on the second floor over the butcher shop and faced the street. He made it do for a bedroom as well; there was a washstand behind the screen in the corner, where he made his moulds, and he slept on a big carpet lounge against the wall opposite the window. In the window itself, which was bay, was his operating chair, his dental engine, and his movable rack, where he laid out his instruments, burrs, extractors, pluggers, his spirit lamp and his pellets of sponge gold. Three chairs, a bargain at the second-hand store, were ranged against one wall with military precision, under a steel engraving of the court of Lorenzo de Medici, which he had bought because there were a great many figures in it for the price. Over the sofa hung a rifle manufacturer's advertisement-calendar, which he never used. The other ornaments were a small marble-top center table, covered with back numbers of the *Dentist's Monthly Manual*, a stone pug dog sitting before the little stove, and a thermometer. There was a stand of shelves in one corner filled with Allen's *Practical Dentist*. On the top shelf McTeague kept his concertina and the bag of bird seed for the canary. The whole place exhaled a mingled odor of bedding, creosote and ether.[8]

With *McTeague* and perhaps *Vandover and the Brute* continuing to receive attention, the publication of forty-six articles and two translations of French fiction, and a desultory record of short-story production behind him by March 1897, the approach of spring marked the beginning of a season of discontent for Norris. It was a time for self-evaluation and readjustment of his professional life. He disappeared from the pages of *The Wave* in mid-March, not to end his leave of absence until mid-May.

As will be seen in his subsequently published writings and in the testimony of his friend Bruce Porter, the signs of a personal crisis showed forth clearly, and through the summer it was increasingly evident that Norris had resolved his personal crisis by making a firm decision: if not yet as a novelist, he would establish himself as the preeminent short-story writer on the West

Coast, and he would do so in the naturalistic manner by going to Zolaesque extremes, repeatedly playing the enfant terrible in earnest.

This was not apparent immediately upon Norris's return to the *Wave's* offices, signaled by the publication of the single article by him in the 15 May 1897 issue. In fact, the brio displayed in this work, "Among Cliff-Dwellers," suggests that nothing was amiss. The article bespeaks a general sense of well-being that is the natural consequence of the conviction that one has a full command of the subject he is treating. No sign of private turmoil is evident.

Radiating exuberance, Norris invites his readers to accompany him up the precipitous slopes of Telegraph Hill, where he will play the role of an amiable docent, explaining how evolution may be seen at work in a San Francisco neighborhood. Atop the hill is a self-contained, essentially isolated community so far removed from the city below that it is, as he says, a world apart. A racially and ethnically various population lives there, and its offspring meld the disparate physical and psychological traits of the Italian, Spaniard, and Native American or, in another instance, the Asian American and the African American. The spectacle to which Norris treats the reader also includes "a child who was half Jew, half Chinese, and its hair was red." Norris echoes Darwin's account of how new varieties of a species arise over time in situations in which members of parent stocks depart from their original environments and, under different conditions, evolve along separate lines. Accelerating variation on the hilltop, of course, is continuous interbreeding among already various members of the human species living there: "They are a queer, extraordinary mingling of peoples, these Cliff Dwellers, for they are isolated enough to have begun already to lose their national characteristics and to develop into a new race." The emphatically positive tone of this essay is noteworthy. While evolution is the topic, Norris gives no attention to the negative dimensions of the natural-selection process. Norris's tone echoes the vigorous, healthy fascination of Darwin in *On the Origin of Species* with what is transpiring in the "tangled bank" of Nature. Norris is keenly interested in these "race formers" on a peak that is "swarming and boiling with the life of them": "Here on this wart-like protuberance above the city's roof, a great milling is going on, and a fusing of peoples, and in a few more generations the Celt and the Italian, the Mexican and the Chinaman, the Negro and the Portuguese . . . will be merged into one type. And a curious type it will be."[9]

Such bonhomie as Norris here displays may be seen again and again through the winter of 1897–98 and the end of his tenure with *The Wave*. In the weeks and months that followed his choice of subjects was as eclectic as ever. In "Fencing for Women" and "Training of Firemen," for example, he uses his exaggerative skills to transform subjects with little innate appeal for a wide-spectrum readership into engaging articles. In the majority of cases, he succeeded at making his own curiosity about such matters contagious. With "A Bicycle Gymkhana" on 10 July 1897, he initiated a witty series of dialogues concerning San Francisco folkways and mores featuring a stylishly droll Justin Sturgis and an ingratiatingly naïve Leander. He fashioned short stories that are sensational, even luridly mysterious in the case of "The House with the Blinds"; but Norris *could* in such stories be inoffensive and no more "dark" in sensibility than he was in the pleasantly humorous "'This Animal of a Buldy Jones.'" Moreover, one finds that not all of the crises he could imagine were life-and-death ones. In the farcical "Shorty Stack, Pugilist," the climax involves the hero losing a boxing match—and his girlfriend. The cause is neither his genetic inheritance nor the environment in which he was reared. The unhappy outcome of the match has nothing to do with the forces at work in the universe but is the result of a silly mistake that Shorty made: he should not have consumed potato salad along with beer shortly before entering the ring. Even into the final phase of his relationship with *The Wave,* Norris continued to embody a mellowness suggesting contentment with his lot in life. In the 1 January 1898 issue appeared a masterful sketch that will be familiar to readers of *Vandover.* "At Home from Eight to Twelve" describes a social occasion in a way that brings to mind William Dean Howells and Richard Harding Davis rather than Kipling and Zola. Parents and educators might have recommended this wholesome piece as a model for imitation to children with literary ambitions.

Reading the post–March 1897 portion of the Norris canon selectively, one might conclude that little had changed in his life and writing career when his work again began to appear in *The Wave* in May. In fact, the continued publication of upbeat, lighthearted, and even exuberant creations took place as, in other works, Norris was hardly the congenial author with an engaging smile and a twinkle in his eye.

Just before Norris dropped out of sight in March 1897, one would not have erred by forming the opinion that, over the years, he had cut the figure of a dilettante. The painter had chosen to try writing instead, the Berkeley student did what he liked, and the fiction writer studying at Harvard departed Cambridge to become a journalist. The journalist, who also wrote short stories but lately appeared to have become a slacker in this regard, also had an interest in acting. In May 1896, as a member of the Bohemian Club, he took the part of a Welshman named Rarebit in its Christmas Low Jinks theatrical entitled "A Miracle Play: The Christmas Nightmare."[10] In 1897 he again made time for rehearsals with other prominent members of San Francisco society, who were staging a charity production of Thomas Robertson's comedy of manners, *Caste,* at the California Theater on 1 March. According to Cosgrave, Norris's performance as a plumber named Sam Gerridge "astonished his friends a good deal. His makeup was so accurate that he might have stepped out of a south-of-Market-street plumber's establishment and been taken for one of the journeymen."[11]

Other opportunities to turn away from his proclaimed vocation and fritter away his time abounded. Miss Cricket's "Debutante's Diary" column in the 13 March 1897 issue of *The Wave* reminds one of what it meant to be the gregarious Gertrude Norris's son. It prattled on at some length about the birthday celebration Mrs. B. F. Norris hosted in honor of Frank.

> We had ever so much fun. Fourteen were invited. You know it was a progressive dinner, and we changed partners at each course. I never expected to find enjoyment at a dinner party. They are usually so horribly stiff and one either gets a man who simply eats and eats and won't talk or else a bore, and then I never can find topics of conversation that last through eight or nine courses. But when one has a partner for [one] course [only] the attractiveness of each is doubled. Between times little trays bearing quaint cuttings from advertisements, tied up with ribbons, were passed around and later on read aloud by each recipient to the merriment of others.[12]

As *Moran of the Lady Letty* and *Blix* would make obvious, Norris became tired of the Miss Crickets, their chirping, and the endless round of social events over which they presided. Also, as the 22 May 1897 issue of *The Wave* illustrated vividly, Norris returned to work more than fed up with an inner circle of the San Francisco artistic community to which he had given too much of his time. With some of its members he had developed close personal relationships, but that counted for little when he turned on these bohemians, raging against their aestheticism and dilettantish behavior in "An Opening for Novelists."

These men included the muralist, stained-glass artist, and Swedenborgian visionary Bruce Porter; the architect Willis Polk; Porter Garnett, a master of fine printing, calligraphy, and wood carving; and Norris's longtime friend, the painter and illustrator Ernest Peixotto. The principal figure of this group of aesthetes known as Les Jeunes was another close friend, Gelett Burgess. He was the editor of the group's whimsical and self-consciously decadent little magazine published from 1895 to 1897, *The Lark*. Burgess's distinguishing trait was his inability or deliberate refusal to take anything seriously; self-consciously typing the decadent artist, he unabashedly reveled in the silly. His measure, positive and negative, was taken a year earlier when *The Wave* reported on a Les Jeunes dinner at Martinelli's restaurant in the North Beach neighborhood: "Toward the middle course a huge *pâté de volaille* was served. Mr. Burgess cut it open, and, lo! a flock of tiny larks flew out, and filled the room with their singing. The effect was pretty in the extreme."[13]

That Norris had decided to swear off insouciance during his March–May hiatus from *Wave* work is seen in his declaration of independence and new-found dedication to "serious" writing as he lambasts those in the Bay Area who had raised playfulness of this sort to a high art. In "An Opening for Novelists," as he called for the appearance of a short-story writer who truly and forcefully captures the dynamic character of life in San Francisco, Norris turned his derisive gaze on these local artists from whom he had divorced himself: "*Les Jeunes.* Yes, there are *Les Jeunes,* and *The Lark* was delightful—delightful fooling, but there's a graver note and a more virile to be sounded. *Les Jeunes* can do better than *The Lark*." He focused on the ring leader, whose claim to fame remains his nonsense quatrain, "The Purple Cow": "I never saw a purple cow, / I never hope to see one; / But I can tell you, anyhow, / I'd rather see than be one."[14] Rather than Burgess's cow, however, Norris targeted two of the insubstantial, fantastic characters about which Burgess wrote fiction, Vivette and Perilla, and the boneless cartoon figures named Goops, for which he was also famous.[15] What we need instead, thundered Norris, are vital, three-dimensional characters fully immersed in the flow of real-world experience—characters "who move and have their being, people who love and hate, something better now than Vivettes and Perillas and Goops." Further, he continued, it is "Life that we want" in literature, "the vigorous, real thing, not the curious weaving of words and the polish of literary finish." Effectively indicting himself not only for his own playfulness but for the fine writing he had labored to weave and polish since 1895, Norris barked: "Damn the 'style' of a story, so long as we get the swing and rush and trample of things that live. . . . We don't want literature, we want life. We don't want fine writing, we want short stories. Kipling saw it here and Stevenson as they passed through—read the unwritten tales of us as they ran."

It is thus clear why, six months later, Cosgrave recommended his colleague to McClure as a writer with a "masculine voice." Norris closes his tirade by advising young would-be writers to strike "but the right note, and strike it with all your might, strike it with iron instead of velvet, and the clang of it shall go round of the nations." He might have then alluded to Zola, the novelist of the "Iron Pen." Instead, he asks, which manly short-story writer will arise to claim the honor of being San Francisco's Kipling?[16]

Norris himself, of course, was the contender he had in mind.

This jeremiad, surprisingly, did not terminate his relationships with Peixotto, Porter, or even Burgess. Peixotto's diary records in May 1897 and thereafter ongoing meetings with Frank and social engagements with Gertrude Norris.[17] Frank later enjoyed the friendship of Burgess and Porter when he resided in New York City, as though "An Opening for Novelists" had never been written. Burgess and Peixotto perhaps knew that there were mitigating circumstances and that Norris was passing through a personal crisis when he became so volcanic. Bruce Porter certainly did, explaining that Norris was then "intensively 'worn out,' tired out; 'written out,' according to his own declaration." That was far from the worst development Porter recalled, though.

Burgess published the last issue of *The Lark* in April 1897. After filling in for Norris at *The Wave* from mid-March to mid-May, he departed San Francisco for Boston, where Copeland and Day published his first book, *Vivette; or, The Memoirs of the Romance Association.* Then he settled in New York City, while Norris, stuck in San Francisco, could do no more than resume his position with Cosgrave. Porter wrote about Norris's reaction to this, "when we had killed 'The Lark' and Burgess had gone on to New York to harvest a surprised [*sic*] reputation, I read a letter of his success to Frank at luncheon. To my amazement that vivid face went ash-grey, and beating the table with clenched fists [he shouted]—'Damn him! Damn him! He's got it and it belongs to me!'"[18]

This and "An Opening" were not the only indications that something was wrong at this point in Norris's life. Another article by Norris that appeared along with "An Opening" in the 22 May issue, "Metropolitan Noises: The Gamut of Sounds which Harass the Ears of San Franciscans," is pertinent. Given Norris's strong aural orientation, the noises of a city—like those of Santa Cruz—were not a peculiar subject choice for him. But what is peculiar in this essay is how his treatment of sound differed from previous ones. Complaining that San Francisco is "one of the noisiest cities between the oceans," he separates aural sensations into two registers, as he had in "The Santa Cruz Venetian Carnival": a low bass, the droning hum of which is constant; and a treble comprising "multifarious staccato notes, brief, incisive, a world of little sharp, high-keyed ear-jars." The former is "a vast, huge, soothing murmur, rather agreeable than otherwise." The ear-jarring latter, he observed in a manner telling of his emotional condition, "is the one that harries you. Listen to it long enough and it will 'get on your nerves.' A physician told me once, that in all the range of science there was nothing more irritating to a nervous patient than noise." One may initially be inclined to take Norris at his word that he is merely the objective analyst who disinterestedly recalls the physician's words and is not the "nervous patient" to whom he refers. However, in light of Porter's recollections, the dearth of new short stories from his hand, the recent hiatus in his work for *The Wave,* and the "Opening for Novelists" outburst, the conclusion of the essay prompts one to wonder how recently—and why—Norris consulted with that physician.

As it turns out, the physician was Norris's own. His next disclosure is revealing: "Perhaps you will never quite appreciate the importance of the noises of the city's streets until you shall fall ill—especially of a nervous complaint. Then you will realize the weight of my physician's words when he said that nothing could be more harrowing and more hurtful to a nervous patient than noise. In some highly organized subjects it will produce hysteria, mild insanity, becoming, in fact, a positive torture."[19]

The standard diagnosis of such a "nervous complaint" in 1897 was neurasthenia, a condition characterized by fatigue, loss of memory, feelings of inadequacy, lowered mood or unresponsiveness, and—contrarily—hyperreactivity to stimuli of various sorts.

Exactly what took place between March and May 1897 may never be known. Nor may we measure the precise degree to which Norris's own experience that winter and spring informed the depictions of the mental and emotional "breakdowns" of the hero of *Vandover,* Lloyd and Ward in *A Man's Woman,* Presley and Vanamee in *The Octopus,* and Laura and Curtis in *The Pit.* It is clear from Porter's memoir that Norris's frustration was keen. He had good reason to think that failure loomed large and to fear that, professionally, he would never advance farther than his position with *The Wave.* Physiologically, there was also something awry. That all was not well with Norris is suggested in a third piece of writing in the 22 May issue, though a qualification is immediately in order: this issue was not the first in which Norris displayed his pessimism. Recall, for example, the grim, Schopenhauerian reflection on the "carnival" of human strivings in 1896's "The Santa Cruz Venetian Carnival."

From the same cloth is the third piece in the 22 May issue, "The Puppets and the Puppy," an allegorical closet drama featuring a boy's toys in its cast of characters. It is the night after Christmas; the boy has long since gone to bed. Now at their leisure, the toys begin to discuss their ontological status! At the very beginning, a lead soldier strikes the dour keynote of this fantastic debate: "Well, here we are put into this Room, for something, we don't know what; for a certain time, we don't know how long; by somebody, we don't know who. It's awful." One is not reading *Waiting for Godot,* but the existential dilemma implied in these questions is their focus as the toys ponder the ultimate cause of and reason for their existence. They fail to generate a mutually agreeable theory concerning a purposeful design that an originating intelligence has given to life. Yet, even had they reached consensus, their labors would have been for naught. The discussion ends abruptly as the boy's fox terrier puppy rushes into the room and, behaving naturally, chews up some of the toys and knocks others down the heating register in the floor. The queen's bishop from a chess set, as he plummets down to the furnace, has the last, naturalistic word, "muttering, vaguely, something about the 'vast, resistless forces of nature.'"[20] No meaningful answer to the question of the toys' raison d'être is forthcoming.

One may reasonably assume that "The Puppets and the Puppy" relates to Norris's desire to produce a more intellectually sophisticated, serious kind of literature than he had previously. That the point of view is a naturalistic one that would manifest itself more frequently and fully in the months ahead also gives one reason to distance the piece from the more obviously malaise-ridden "An Opening for Novelists" and "Metropolitan Noises." The allegory need not have originated in clinical depression. But as Norris continued writing in the naturalistic vein through the fall, when he assembled the collection of new short stories entitled "Ways That Are Dark," there are at least two instances in which his nervous condition in March through May 1897 seems to be at least as influential as his decision to write more naturalistically.

About the first one can be less sure. For, while ostensibly an article, it reads as a short story, that is, more like an invention than an account of actual events. In "Little Dramas of the Curbstone," published on 26 June 1897, the unnamed narrator witnesses three extraordinary scenes on the streets of San

Francisco: a mother with a son who is blind and intellectually incapacitated; a paralytic little girl whose elderly mother cannot carry her when she refuses to try to walk any farther; and a boy in trouble with the law who—for some undiscovered reason—opts to be taken to jail rather than return home with his mother. The conclusion complements the grim procession of *les misérables* in an autobiographical way. Norris—the son of a reckless, now permanently absent father—has his narrator reflect on what all three families have in common: "[A]s I went along I wondered where was the father of that young fellow who was to spend his first night in jail, and the father of the little paralytic girl, and the father of the blind idiot, and it seemed to me that the chief actors in these three Little Dramas of the Curbstone had been somehow left out of the program." This suggestion of Norris's own unresolved issues concerning his irresponsible father is not what is most noteworthy, and disturbing, in "Little Dramas," however.

What raises the question of Norris's mental and emotional condition is a particularly chilling moment in the narration that prods one to ask, Is this autobiographical art? Or is it more dispassionately modelled upon Zola's example in *L'Assommoir* or *La Bête Humaine,* or perhaps the graphic scene in which Mr. Hyde physically attacks a young woman for no apparent reason in *The Strange Case of Dr. Jekyll and Mr. Hyde?*

When the kindly narrator encounters the first mother, she tells him that her son's affliction is twofold: he is "'blind and . . . an idiot—born that way— blind and an idiot.'" Suddenly, revulsion displaces the narrator's sympathy as he registers the full implications of such a condition and their visible manifestation before him. His voice abruptly modulates to resemble one of Poe's unhinged narrators:

> When I looked at the face of him I know not what insane desire, born of an unconquerable disgust, came up in me to rush upon him and club him down to the pavement with my stick and batter in that face . . . and blot it out from the sight of the sun for good and all. It was impossible to feel pity for the wretch. . . . His eyes were filmy, like those of a fish, and he never blinked them. His mouth was wide open.
>
> Blind and an idiot; absolute stagnation; life as unconscious as that of the jelly-fish; an excrescence; a parasitic fungus in the form of a man; a creature far below the brute. The last horror . . . was that he never moved; he sat there just as his mother had placed him, his motionless, filmy eyes fixed, his jaw dropped, his hands opened at the sides, his hat on the wrong side foremost. He would sit like that, I knew, for hours—for days, perhaps—would, if left to himself, die of starvation without raising a finger.[21]

One rightly dismisses the "facts" of this proffered piece of impressionistic journalism, which includes three such observations of abject misery in less than twenty-four hours. What are the odds that one could round up such a cast of characters during a stroll through the city? Yet even when one views "Little Dramas" as a fiction, the narrator's response to this imagined situation—in a work signed "Frank Norris"—is alarming.

Then again, shocking the reader was a defining effect of naturalistic literature in 1897.

Norris himself may not have been identical with his narrator in "Little Dramas," but his capacity for waxing wroth—as in "An Opening for Novelists"—cannot be denied. "The Sailing of the 'Excelsior'" is not "Little Dramas of the Curbstone." Wisely, one may think, Norris would not repeat that performance. But "The Sailing," too, invites consideration of Norris's emotional and mental instability. In this article, signed by him and published on 31 July 1897, he is exuberant once more as he celebrates the "Argonauts" departing San Francisco Bay for the Klondike following the discovery of gold there. He is not the only one excited. All of those on the dock bidding farewell to the intrepid gold seekers felt the drama of the moment, declares Norris. But then he recalls a single exception, a supine alcoholic dozing on the dock who triggered his anger:

> Did I say there was no one in that crowd who was indifferent? I was wrong. . . . He was reclining against a pile of boards, and the crowd had grown up around him, and he lay there oblivious to everything that was going forward. . . . Think of it! The city thrilling from end to end . . . the thousands of people rushing in to say farewell to their argonauts, and this man lay there under foot, so close to the ship that he could have laid his hand upon her hull, and cared not whether she swam or sank. . . . Never has a drunken man seemed so loathly to me. One fairly quivered with a desire to kick him from the stringpiece of the wharf and allow to perish in the water a man so utterly out of the race as this one.[22]

The quivering narrator's overreaction—openly identified by Norris as his own—is so extreme that one may entertain again an alternative explanation and speculate generously in Norris's favor that a desire to shock the reader once again is his primary motivation. One hopes that his "nervous complaint" did not prompt homicidal fantasies. Then again, viewed apart from "Little Dramas of the Curbstone," "The Sailing" is only a much more extreme expression of Norris's intolerance for a certain type of male, the underachiever.

The type made its appearance in 1895 in "The Country Club at Del

Monte," when Norris sneered at the simpering young men who devoted themselves to no greater challenge in life than dancing. Looking ahead to 1898,
one notes that the once effeminate—but since become ultramanly—hero of
Moran of the Lady Letty publicly berates his male contemporaries whose
energies have been channeled into attendance at tea parties and cotillions. As
one recalls Norris's own dilettantish behavior when reading his attack on the
dilettantism of Les Jeunes, so does one think of Norris himself when noting
his criticisms of underachievers, particularly those who spent as much time
as he had on social activities.

Again, one finds Norris at a turning point in his life, seeming to project on
those around him not only his own perceived shortcomings but fears about
how he might not realize his potential for remarkable achievements as a
writer and otherwise. And so it came to pass in the spring of 1897 that Norris embraced a certain course of action to preclude failure and did what was
necessary to establish himself as a professional writer of more than regional
reputation. By November he had written and assembled the new collection
of short stories. That he had completed the project was the testimony of a
friend whose acquaintance he had made during their undergraduate years
at Berkeley, Eleanor M. Davenport. In a *University of California Magazine*
article, she related that month that "Mr. Norris's readers are looking forward
to the appearance of 'Ways That Are Dark,' . . . illustrated by the author,
which is now in press."[23]

Davenport did not name the publisher with which the collection of short
stories was "now in press." Sad to say, like the previous collection of 1895, the
new one was not published in late 1897, nor in 1898, nor thereafter. Unfortunately, Davenport did not name any of the stories included by Norris; it is
impossible to identify them with certainty in the remains of the multiple collections Norris attempted in 1895–97 and possibly thereafter.[24] But included
in these remains are five he published in *The Wave* between 11 September
and 13 November 1897, each indicating rather clearly—or, more appropriately, *darkly*—why Norris opted for the book title he did.

"A Case for Lombroso" tells the story of the degenerations of a highborn
female and an upper-class male whose infatuation with each other results in
an abusive, sadomasochistic relationship from which neither can withdraw.
(Caesar Lombroso was a criminologist whose theory of the "born criminal"
was heredity-based, and genetic inheritance accounts in part for the degen-

eration Norris depicted in the short story.) "His Single Blessedness" introduces a hero who once wanted to draw attention to himself as an interesting character by inventing and repeatedly announcing the fiction that he hates children and cannot even tolerate their presence. It becomes his mantra and gradually a fact. The *idée fixe* produces an unintended consequence when he marries and his wife gives birth. She presents the infant daughter to him as he is lying on a sofa, putting the child on his chest; he pushes the baby off of him and jumps up. As he tells the narrator, he had recoiled from his own flesh and blood as though a snake had touched him. He *has to* tell his wife that he loathes the baby and will always feel that way. He does overcome his obsession at last—after his wife is committed to a doctor's care in a sanitarium. While he has recovered completely, she lapses into hysteria every time she sees him; and his daughter, as he tells the narrator, takes after her mother. "His Dead Mother's Portrait" is even more gruesome. It deals with the obsessive regard of a young man for his departed mother of sainted memory—as with the hero of *Vandover and the Brute* during his prepubescent years. Unlike Vandover, however, he has achieved his maturity without abandoning his childlike attitude of veneration and, again unlike Vandover, has dedicated his life to living up to the standards of behavior that he believes his angelic mother represents. He is the most morally pure, innocent male imaginable. At the story's end, his aged and mentally impaired mother is discovered to be a dancer in a San Francisco dive. At the Bella Union, she is the grotesque source of amusement and the butt of the jokes of the shameless young men who frequent the place.

Two of the five tales provide comic relief—of sorts. In "Fantasie Printanière," *McTeague's* Ryer makes his first appearance along with Mr. and Mrs. McTeague, Trina being named in print for the first time, and McTeague shorn of his identity as dentist. Mrs. Ryer plays a part like that of Maria Miranda Macapa in the published novel. This is a sprightly, tongue-in-cheek story of wife beaters, wife beating, and beaten wives—all of which is the stuff of burlesque entertainment as the markedly competitive wives come to fisticuffs at the end of a protracted, heated argument over which of their husbands is the more artful brutalizer of womankind. Related to *McTeague* as well is "Judy's Service of Gold Plate," featuring the Guatemalan Judy and the miserly Knubel, a.k.a Mexican Maria Miranda Macapa and Zerkow in *McTeague.* The fantastic story of a service of gold plate once owned by her family that Maria repeatedly tells Zerkow is Judy's told to Knubel; Zerkow's maniacal obsession with anything gold is Knubel's. As in the novel featuring the same *folie à deux,* Knubel marries Judy to enjoy the vicarious experience of the imaginary gold service. Also, as in the novel, Judy loses the recollection of the service and cannot retell the story about its beauty, and Knubel becomes convinced that Judy is hiding an actual set of gold pieces from him. As with Zerkow and Maria, Knubel cuts her throat. Knubel does not drown in San Francisco Bay like Zerkow, however; he is hanged for murder at the San Quentin penitentiary. Again—a reminder may here be necessary—all of this is related in a comical manner, with delusional and fatally violent behavior put in the service of the risible.

Other possible inclusions in the grim but sometimes amusing collection were these short stories published in July through October 1897: "The Strangest Thing," dealing with a violent alcoholic grave digger in Cape Town and giving in its plot a role to a dead baby in a coffin; "The Third Circle," a treatment of white slavery and opium addiction in Chinatown; "'Boom,'" another tale of obsession like "His Single Blessedness"; "A Reversion to Type," treating an atavistic lapse, its hero reverting to the genetically inherited traits of his criminal grandfather and degenerating to the point at which he can shoot another man in the face with a shotgun without giving it a second thought; and "The Associated Un-Charities," a particularly unnerving comedy recounting how Leander, from the earlier Justin Sturgis–Leander dialogues, played a joke on three blind professional beggars that sets them to fighting with each other and causes their arrest.

Although the volume was not published, its composition limns a self-defining choice that Norris had made. Not just pluck on the part of an author but luck was required for any one of the hundreds of books published each year to draw national attention. If he was to be one of the fortunate few to meet with success, Norris would make his debut as an author bearing no resemblance to the young man named on the title page of *Yvernelle: A Legend of Feudal France.* With the book's publication, his sense of humor would be seen as decadent, if not "sick." His preoccupation with the degenerate and with diseased individuals unable to control their bizarre and sometimes criminal behavior would bring down upon him the chastisements generously showered upon Zola. His preference for inducing blushes and administering shocks to the Victorian reader would result in his receiving the attention given to Kipling in the 1890s, when Kipling too was perceived as a writer who went "too far" and did so much more frequently than Stevenson. In short, Norris opted for stories that would result in startled responses like that made by Davenport to the 1897 works she had read in *The Wave:* "Mr. Norris has made such a specialty of horrors, that one wonders whether he is capable of anything else, whether he is going to confine himself to scare heads, or cultivate a broader field with some space in it for the pleasant side of life."[25]

As has been seen, Norris did produce for *The Wave* fictions that warmed the heart and perhaps strengthened the soul. But he had a decided talent for, and saw the "main chance" lying in, the kind of writing he did when exploring the shudder-inducing possibilities inherent in the *McTeague*-related pieces he wrote at Harvard. As his *Wave* apprenticeship ended, he had opted for the sensational as his trump card. At twenty-seven years of age he went down ways that were dark to extricate himself from what was, inarguably, a dead-end job. Though it was unthinkable that he had only five more years to live, he was fully aware that time was fleeting, and once he was confident that the publication of his book of short stories was a sure thing, he rushed down the path that led to the completion of *McTeague*.

In the fall of 1897 he was finally ready to complete the novelistic project on which he had been working under Lewis E. Gates's direction two years earlier at Harvard.

14

THE NOVELIST AT LAST AT WORK

McTeague differs from all of Frank Norris's previous writings in this respect: it is the first work about which it can be confidently assumed that anyone interested in the life of this author has read at least once and can recall with considerable specificity.

Memorable moments abound, including vaudevillian comic performances assigned to McTeague and the almost-as-cloddish Marcus Schouler in a novel in which, for approximately half its length, its narrator invites the reader to guffaw along with him. The dentist-hero gets a cue ball stuck in his mouth. He clownishly bungles the simple task of buying four tickets at the Orpheum Theater. An ultrascrupulous Victorian in this respect, he "does the right thing" by proposing marriage to the young woman in his operating chair from whom he stole a kiss while she was under the effects of ether. The Heises, Ryers, Mrs. Sieppe, and her niece Selina are far from peculiar. But, in the early chapters, one must turn to Charles Dickens to find so quirky and amusing a group as Old Grannis, Miss Baker, Maria Miranda Macapa, Zerkow, Mr. Sieppe, and Trina's Uncle Oelbermann. Even after events take a more serious turn, and when in retrospect one views an early pivotal event of the plot with dire long-term consequences, one is hard-pressed to keep a straight face as Marcus gives permission to his pal Mac to court Trina, the cousin Marcus has long thought of as his own "girl." The scene in which he sacrifices his interests for the sake of his only friend, complete with mock-heroic authorial allusions to the paradigmatic friendships of David and Jonathan and Damon and Pythias, is a masterful drollery that might have delighted the readership of *The Wave*—particularly when Norris notes that the transfer takes place without either man consulting Trina about the matter.

That Trina is years later seen expiring in a pool of her own blood after being beaten by the husband who has become a violent, sadistic alcoholic; that Marcus too dies at Mac's hands; and that other similarly gruesome events loom in the future—none of this appears in the cards as the main story and two subplots develop through ten jolly chapters. That it all makes sense, logically and dramatically, by the novel's end is the triumph for which Norris hoped, and which he achieved in roughly three months during the autumn of 1897.

Given the novel's complex structure, consistently developed characterizations, thematic richness, and successful tonal modulation to a more somber voice when life goes awry for the McTeagues in chapter 13, a modern reader unaware of all that transpired when Norris was working for *The Wave* might naturally assume that this was a labor of love to which he dutifully gave all of his available time since the winter of 1895 and, according to Denison Hailey Clift, even two years earlier. Clift referred to the fall of 1893, when, as reported in the San Francisco press, Sarah Collins had an experience like the one given to Trina. The janitress of the Felix Adler Free Kindergarten, she was murdered by her alcoholic husband Pat when she refused to give him money. Stabbing her repeatedly, he left his knife buried to the hilt in her neck.[1] Clift went on to relate his understanding of how Norris composed the novel, specifying a total of eighty-nine days as the time it took to conclude it:

> The novel was conceived while Norris was yet in college at the State University. The middle parts of the book were written while the novelist was taking a graduate course at Harvard University, and the conclusion, with its realistic, grim descriptions of the untamed mining country, was done up in the wilds of Placer County. Perhaps you remember how McTeague left San Francisco immediately after the murder of Trina, and made straight for the Big Dipper Mine, where he had spent his youth as a car-boy. When the dentist reached the mine he entered the office, looking for the foreman. There is a description here of the men in that office, and one man is described as "a tall, lean young man, with a thick head of hair surprisingly gray, who was playing with a half-grown Great Dane puppy." Norris meant this to be a picture of himself, for in this very room the closing chapters of *McTeague* were written.[2]

As has been seen, though, Norris had not written *McTeague* through its "middle parts" when he left Harvard. As Norris reminded Lewis E. Gates, it was still in "embryonic" form then. As to where the project stood as of the late summer of 1897, several of his *Wave* writings indicate that he had not forgotten it, but these were not necessarily spinoffs from a larger, relatively finished manuscript. Pieces such as "Judy's Service of Gold Plate," anticipating Maria's and Zerkow's debuts in the novel, were just as likely discrete trials of *McTeague*-related conceptions. Moreover, while Norris testified in his 9 April 1900 letter to Charles F. Lummis that he *began* the novel in 1895, he made two other important points. The first supports Clift's assertion that he left *The Wave* to "finish" *McTeague* in the "fall of '97," and the second clarifies what Norris meant by "finish" the novel: he told Lummis that he "wrote it" not in eighty-nine but one hundred days that fall.[3]

Norris and his contemporaries declared again and again that he did indeed then pull together what he had on hand and completed ("wrote") the novel in the form that, in many of its leaves, can be seen in the manuscript collections of research libraries across the United States. Where he processed the sketches and drafts of passages into the manuscript Doubleday and McClure used as the typesetting copy in December 1898 he and others besides Clift uniformly reported. Fiji William Allen Wood's eulogy in the *Phi Gamma Delta Quarterly,* for example, characterized the visit to the Big Dipper Mine thus: Norris was living "the hearty miner's life . . . cutting a trail between the Big Dipper and Iowa Hill mines." Wood had also heard of the eighty-nine to one hundred days: "The story contains 125,000 words and was written in a little less than three months, though he was collecting the material for it over a period of two years."[4] In 1902 Wood was echoing John D. Barry who, when reviewing *McTeague* on 18 March 1899, also sounded the "solitude" note: "Two years ago, [Norris] decided to make a book" of his Harvard sketches, "and he joined a friend who was working at a mine in the mountains, where he could write in solitude." By 1900, this story Norris repeatedly communicated appears to have been incorporated in press releases, for a prepublication notice of *The Octopus* in the *Washington Times* described him as "a rapid and methodical writer, counting 3,000 words of copy a fair day's task, but he comes to his work after careful preparation and with a full mind, and prunes and revises with infinite care. Though 'McTeague' was written in one hundred days, its author had been two years collecting the material for it, and the same careful and honest workmanship has marked the making of all his books."[5]

Three decades later, when interviewed by Walker, that friend at the Big Dipper Mine, Seymour Waterhouse, confirmed and qualified the scenario given by Norris in conversation and correspondence. Walker's summary of what Waterhouse said reads in its entirety:

> Late in 1897 he came up to write *McTeague;* two or possibly three months. Before the snow came, but it was getting cool; note collars in picture. He [Waterhouse] met him at Colfax and they rode on horses on the trail. He [Norris] was always making notes; he wrote most of *McTeague* there—had part in ms.—but left with some undone as he read a later part of it to him at another time. He [Waterhouse] didn't think much of it as a story as it was lugubrious. Tried to advise him to revise his work a little more carefully but Frank maintained that that tended to kill the freshness of it. He is quite sure that Frank was not working on any novel at the University; they were rooming together.

Whether eighty-nine or a hundred days, Norris had left behind him in San Francisco the clutch of articles and short stories to appear in *The Wave* during his absence, and he was free to devote his attention wholly to the manuscript with which he returned to San Francisco by 9 December 1897 when he wrote to Eleanor M. Davenport on the stationery of the Bohemian Club.[6] As to Waterhouse's recollection that some of the manuscript was as yet "undone" and that Norris read "a later part of it" to him at another time, Norris may have revised portions at a later date.

In sum, then, *McTeague* was at last on paper by early December 1897.

On 11 December 1897, in "Happiness by Conquest," Norris was in very good spirits and announced to readers of *The Wave* that, for him, happiness consisted in overcoming obstacles to the achievement of one's goals. The major obstacles behind him were considerable. He had, he fondly thought, finally succeeded in fashioning a collection of tales that, when it soon appeared in the bookstores, promised to elevate him to peer status with the man he viewed as the greatest short-story writer of his time, Rudyard Kipling. But the more formidable obstacle he had overcome and the more potent cause for renewed self-confidence was *how* he had since developed the novel that was in "embryonic" form in 1895. It was the same work Lewis E. Gates read in the rough, and yet it was not.

The surviving evidence indicates that, at Harvard, all that Norris had was a brutal drunk who physically abused his kindergarten-teacher wife (who had not won five thousand dollars in a lottery), beat her to death, fled to the Arizona desert, killed the sheriff who pursued him, and then found himself handcuffed to that lawman's corpse. This was certainly not enough for a full-blown novel, nor was it any more than the makings of a cautionary tale illustrating more forcefully than many others of the same stripe the lamentable consequences of alcoholism. It was Zolaesque only in its unsqueamish presentation of gruesome detail; it lacked the deterministic themes that are requisite in the work of a thoroughgoing Zolaist. If *McTeague* was to become a naturalistic novel of degeneration like the one treating characters higher up the socioeconomic scale, *Vandover and the Brute,* he had to flesh out the noisome temperance tale of 1895. He had to reconstitute it in the way that he did by December 1897.

He could not introduce the hero and the heroine as already degenerate, as they were in the Harvard themes, since it was essential to demonstrate and account for their descents to such a condition. Once Norris turned back the clock so that the drunk of 1895 was only an occasional drinker of beer and thus suitable for courtship, the question was, How might a man of such limited intelligence and with the hulking appearance of a Neanderthal attract the pretty little German-Swiss maid, Trina? Here was a formidable problem. Norris solved it by means of one of the resistless forces of nature to which he referred in "The Puppets and the Puppy." As in *Vandover*—the late 1897 status of which remains anyone's guess—human sexuality is the force that moves forward the plot. It drives Mac and Trina into marriage, just as it motivates Vandover to the fateful seduction of Ida Wade that formally initiates his decline. The next challenge was to fabricate a credible explanation for Mac's plunge into alcoholism and Trina's into obsessional miserliness.

A chance event like the fall from a swing that occasions Trina's visit to McTeague's dental parlors for treatment, or her winning five thousand dollars in a lottery, not only limns the antiteleological, naturalistic theme of life's unpredictability. Ironically, the happier development also proves a major cause of Trina's decline, traceable in retrospect to the fact that the winning of the lottery produces a consequence exactly opposite of what one might expect: While it initially enhances her feelings of well-being, the prize proves deleterious in its effects over time since it triggers and then exacerbates the immigrants' daughter's sense of insecurity. That is, she now has five thousand dollars that she might *lose,* thus beginning her obsessive concern with preserving and adding to that "nest egg."

The ostensible stroke of good fortune contributes to the demise of Dr. and Mrs. McTeague in another way. Her winning the lottery enrages the man who is no longer the brother-in-law of McTeague seen at Harvard. Now the cousin who gave up Trina to his best friend, Marcus is soon governed by an *idée fixe*. The five thousand dollars would have been his, he quirkily reasons, had he married her; and Marcus becomes convinced that the McTeagues have cheated him of at least a portion of the fortune. His rage intensifies when McTeague breaks his arm during a wrestling match at a picnic, and he wreaks his vengeance upon the couple by causing Mac to lose his practice—after Mac and Trina have experienced since their engagement a dramatic rise in their standard of living and social status. Surrendering the finer things of life to which they have become accustomed is traumatic.

And so, the rise of the McTeagues having been halted, Norris has positioned his hero and heroine to demonstrate the Darwinian consequences of being thrown into a lower socioeconomic environment to which they do not successfully adapt. Their stressful loss of income initiates their long slide in a work that now begins to manifest blatantly the "novel of degeneration" structure typed in Zola's *L'Assommoir*. Trina's "Swiss" hoarding instinct, a genetic inheritance explained for the reader earlier in the novel, comes to dominate her personality as she sinks to the level of the demented Maria and then to that of the lunatic Zerkow. Depressed because of his loss of not only income but also his identity as a professional, the Irishman (or "Teague") finds his comfort in whisky. True to the genetic predisposition inherited from his binge-drinking father, he too proves when under its influence "an irresponsible animal, a beast, a brute."[7] And thus a sadomasochistic relationship develops between the two erstwhile lovers. They spiral downward, as out of control as Zola's Gervaise and Coupeau and destined to meet their fates as victims of irresistible forces at work in their lives.

But that is not all that Norris did with his draft of *McTeague* in embryonic form. Along the way, he added two subplots not even hinted at in Cambridge. One features a happy and the other a grisly denouement: Old Grannis and Miss Baker at last come to know the bounty of love and enjoy idyllic bliss; Zerkow kills his common-law wife Maria and then drowns before the authorities can apprehend him.

Heredity manifesting its control of the individual, the shaping influence of environment demonstrating its power, and chance events taking one's life experience in unanticipated directions—the thematic essentials of naturalistic fiction are all here in full, as they are not in the Harvard "themes," nor in any one of Norris's *Wave* short stories, nor in any prior novel by another American author.

Again, that Norris was able to integrate all of this in the fall of 1897 is a marvel. Put one way, the complex structure Norris achieved as he put together the pieces of the novel that he had drafted since 1895 was an engineering feat. Put another way, Edgar Allan Poe's explanation in "The Philosophy of Composition" of how he completely planned "The Raven" *before* crafting it may come to mind, as may the above-quoted observation in the *Washington Times* that Norris "comes to his work after careful preparation and with a full mind," ready to implement the plan he has developed. In eighty-nine to a hundred days, Norris had overcome all of the obstacles the composition of *McTeague* presented, and he was presumably experiencing, to use his own phrase, "happiness by conquest."

Resuming his duties as book reviewer, translator of French fiction, essayist, and editor in December 1897, Norris gave no attention to short stories. Rather, he had in mind the commencement of a long one that Cosgrave could serialize and that would, in succeeding decades, puzzle students of his canon, or cause them to feel embarrassment for Norris, or both. How could the author of the "Ways That Are Dark" short stories, the daring and avant-garde *McTeague,* and—at whatever its stage of completion at this point—*Vandover and the Brute* do what Norris did next? How could he so masterfully transcend the limitations of popular American literature of the time with such works and then stoop to pander to the marketplace by embracing so old-fashioned a genre as the adventure-romance? Why did he fall back on shopworn properties such as shanghaiing, piracy, battle, murder, and sudden death—not to mention the eternal fictional staple, "love interest"—to spin a yarn, when his obvious sophistication made possible so much better choices?

One answer, though not a flattering one, was that for all of its modernity in 1897, it would be—and was—difficult for Norris to place *McTeague* with a respectable American firm willing to risk its reputation by publishing it, as was also the case with the collection of "Ways That Are Dark" short stories that never did appear in bookstores. Indeed, it was only after he had established his credentials as a novelist by publishing with Doubleday and McClure the adventure-romance in question that that firm decided to throw caution to the wind and bring out *McTeague.* Norris, one might say, stooped in late 1897 with *Moran of the Lady Letty: A Story of Adventure off the California Coast* to conquer in early 1899 with *McTeague.* That, however, is not the whole of the story. From another point of view—Norris's own on this nautical romance project—stooping was not even a part of the enterprise.

No matter how much some readers may today enjoy the fantastic adventures of Ross Wilbur and Moran Sternersen in *Moran,* no one is likely to break from critical tradition by claiming that its low ranking as a literary achievement is an affront to good taste or common sense. *Moran* is not *McTeague,* nor *Vandover.* Still, that does not mean that one should dismiss it as a mere "potboiler." Rather than a radical departure from what is typical in the Norris canon, *Moran* is remarkably congruent—surprisingly so, perhaps, if one takes into account how Norris's aesthetic principles had developed since 1894–95 when he was exposed to Lewis E. Gates's program for reviving romanticism with an infusion of realism. Building upon that theoretical foundation in his book reviews and literary essays for *The Wave,* Norris was positioned by late 1897 to conceive of the more obviously Kipling- and Stevenson-inspired *Moran* as a Zolaesque fusion of romanticism and realism.

How these terms—realism, romanticism, and naturalism—were either employed with precision or indiscriminately bandied about at the turn of the century may now seem inconsequential. But, again, Norris's own conceptions of what the three terms signified are pertinent to why and how he fashioned *Moran of the Lady Letty* as he did.

One may recall that, in his 1895 essay "Our Unpopular Novelists," Norris advised readers not to higgle over terms: a good read is a good read, whether it be written by the realist Howells, the romantic Scott, or the naturalist Zola. Since then, as a critic, he had had to take more seriously such terms in the lingua franca of the literary world. Along the way, he sharpened the definitions to which his studies at Berkeley introduced him and with which he again had to deal at Harvard; and by the time he was completing *McTeague* and commencing *Moran,* Norris had rather fully revealed what he admired in all three schools. .

As to realism, on 2 May 1896 Norris celebrated the American avatar of that aesthetic in his review of *A Parting and a Meeting,* admiring without qualification Howells's minimization of his authorial presence and maximization of the illusion of real life in "a real story, of real people and of real places." The hero and heroine "are flesh and blood characters from first to last"; and Norris the horse-lover delighted in how "even the old chaise horse becomes a character, 'making snatches at the foliage and from time to time chomping thoughtfully on his bit as if he fancied he might have caught a leaf in his mouth.'"[8] Eight months later, on 17 January 1897 in the *San Francisco*

Examiner, he was even more enthusiastic. Addressing the question, "What Is Our Greatest Piece of Fiction?" Norris proposed two works, one of which was Howells's *A Modern Instance.* Manifesting realism's crowning virtue, fidelity to life as we know it, this novel was "great" because "it is true, relentlessly and remorselessly true to American life." Norris proclaimed that Howells treated the "serious problems of American life" with "a consistency and a plausibleness that are convincingly beyond any possibility of doubt, and with a thorough technical knowledge of the novelist's trade that . . . places the book among the masterpieces of fiction."[9]

Norris was hardly a sworn foe to realism, and reviewers were correct in observing its influence in *McTeague.*[10] As two major historical investigations have revealed, the novel's setting is almost photographically true to the San Francisco Norris knew: even the like of the enormous gilded molar Mac uses as an advertisement once hung outside the second-story bay windows of dental parlors at the northwest corner of Kearny and Geary Streets.[11] *McTeague's* dialogue, like *Moran's,* is appropriate for its minimally educated and unsophisticated cast of characters, and their behaviors make sense in light of their characterizations, if one grants the existence of types of persons not seen in Howells's and Jane Austen's novels but very much present in the realist George Eliot's *The Mill on the Floss.* There can be no question that Norris was intent upon developing personages who "are flesh and blood characters from first to last"—no matter how unlike the typical Howells character or how grotesque they become during the courses of their experiences. Norris's are no mere stick figures on which he hung attributes.

But he did have a problem with realism in one respect—or, more accurately, with one variety of realism. He bridled when it moved past technical considerations such as dialogue and character construction to postulate limits on what kinds of subject matter or story situations could be termed true-to-life and thus admissible in a work of art. Unacceptable for Norris was "life" being narrowly defined to exclude what would be termed the more romantic aspects of reality as he knew them from his own experience on three continents, across California, and especially in idiosyncratic San Francisco. When, for example, he identifies in "An Opening for Novelists" subjects for short stories begging for the attention of a San Francisco Kipling, he is quite serious when complaining about fiction that excludes any event that might possibly be considered out of the ordinary. In the midst of his attack on Les Jeunes, he provides several examples of what he has in mind with regard to unlikely incidents that do, indeed, occur in San Francisco: "While you are rounding a phrase a sailor has been shanghaied down there along the water front; while you are sustaining a metaphor, another See Yup [a member of a Chinese tong] has been hatcheted yonder in Gambler's Alley; a man has time to be stabbed while you are composing a villanelle; the crisis of a life has come and gone while you have been niggling with your couplet."[12] Crises describable as melodramatic do not constitute the whole of life, argues Norris, but they certainly form a part. Tong wars in Chinatown, reported in the newspapers, are actualities as much as social receptions on New Year's Day. Sarah Collins's brutelike husband did cruelly murder her, and shanghaiing was not an unknown phenomenon on San Francisco's Barbary Coast waterfront.

Why not have Ross Wilbur drink a drugged Manhattan cocktail and Captain Kitchell's men shanghai him from a waterfront dive in the first chapter of *Moran*? Why be a slave to ordinary experience when San Francisco abounds in extraordinary events? How can one term unrealistic the representation of what *does* happen? And to cite another real-life example, was it unrealistic that Norris arrived in South Africa at just the right moment to experience the Jameson Raid and its aftermath? Need one hide under a bushel such a melodramatic development, the stuff from which true-to-life romances can be made, because it does not conform to normal expectations of quotidian life?

Thus, despite his admiration for William Dean Howells in 1896 and 1897, and for his *The Rise of Silas Lapham* articulated years later by Curtis Jadwin in *The Pit*, Norris identified his limitations as a novelist and spokesman for realism in "Zola as a Romantic Writer" in June 1896. This kind of realism by which Norris is unwilling to be confined, he explains, features "characters [who] live across the street from us. . . . We know all about them, about their affairs, the story of their lives. One can go even further. We ourselves are Mr. Howells's characters, so long as we are well behaved and ordinary and *bourgeois*, so long as we are not adventurous or not rich or not unconventional. . . . He will have none of us if we are out of the usual." Howells, the artful documentarian of average middle-class American life, is thus accurately characterized. Norris acknowledges him as interesting and even charming in his stories of "commonplace people," but he also chides him for modeling an unwillingness to go beyond "the smaller details of every-day life, things that are likely to happen between lunch and supper, small passions, restricted emotions, dramas of the reception-room, tragedies of an afternoon call, crises involving cups of tea." There is no place for the eye-popping events of *McTeague*—and real life—in such a microcosm, nor is there for what one encounters in chapter 3 of *Moran*, where one finds its shanghaied hero now glad to have been kidnapped, enjoying his new, more manly life at sea and delighted to have escaped from the "dramas of the reception-room" pictured in chapter 1.

In short, another kind of realism, like the romantic-realism or realism-infused romanticism promoted by Lewis E. Gates, was possible. Rudyard Kipling had shown the way to such a broader view of life in 1890 with *The Light That Failed;* and, three weeks before "Zola as a Romantic Writer" appeared, Norris had observed an expansive variety of realism in *Rome.* Zola's extensive, finely detailed descriptions of Rome as it actually is and his analytic portrayals of the inner workings of the Vatican bureaucracy bespoke an exhaustive fidelity to things-as-they are in the realm of Pope Leo XIII. In this same book review, Norris went on to complete his depiction of Zola as the paradigmatic author worthy of imitation by anticipating the main point that he would develop in "Zola as a Romantic Writer." He would not recant his interpretation of Zola as a realist. He would only offer an inarguable observation of the obvious: Zola was not, thank God, a *Howellsian* realist limited to treating ordinary experience had by commonplace characters.

In "Zola as a Romantic Writer," Norris had two motives. His primary interest was not in demeaning Howells (though this has been taken as the unfortunate effect) but in identifying and celebrating Zola as a literary romantic who exercised his license as such to treat the *extra*ordinary. Having erased the distinction between Zola's naturalism and a more broadly defined, non-Howellsian realism in "Zola's *Rome,*" he now did the same with naturalism and romanticism:

> The naturalist takes no note of common people, common insofar as [like Howells's characters] their interests, their lives, and the things that occur in them are common, ordinary. Terrible things must happen to the characters of a naturalistic tale. They must be twisted from the ordinary, wrenched out from the quiet uneventful round of every-day life, and flung into the throes of a vast and terrible drama that works itself out in unleashed passions, in blood, and in sudden death.
>
> Everything is extraordinary, imaginative, grotesque even, with a vague note of terror quivering throughout like the vibration of an ominous and low-pitched diapason. It is all romantic, at times unmistakably so, as in *Le Rêve* or *Rome,* closely resembling the work of the greatest of all modern romanticists, Hugo. We have the same huge dramas, the same enormous scenic effects, the same love of the extraordinary, the vast, the monstrous, and the tragic.

Thus does Norris move toward his conclusion, in which he offers an admiring definition of literary naturalism that marks his break from Lewis E.

Gates—who did not identify Zola as his ideal for the renovation of western literary culture. Norris finds in Zola's fiction the ideal fusion of what is best in the two schools: "This is not Romanticism. . . . It is not realism." Rather, rising from the realism-romanticism dialectic imaged here is the Zolaesque synthesis of opposing values. Rooted in but transcending both, Zola's "is a school by itself, unique, somber, powerful beyond words. It is naturalism."[13] And Norris did not later change his mind: he argued—or recycled—exactly the same point in a 1901 essay.[14]

Thus, when Norris is describing what is naturalistic, or romantic-realistic, in Zola's works, he is aptly characterizing as well what one encounters in *McTeague* and *Vandover.* In addition, as strange as the notion may at first seem to those who have already formed a low opinion of *Moran* as a canonical anomaly, that work too presents a hero who finds himself "twisted from the ordinary, wrenched out from the quiet uneventful round of every-day life, and flung into the throes of a vast and terrible drama that works itself out in unleashed passions, in blood, and in sudden death." Indeed, *Moran* meets the bill in all of these particulars.

Oddly enough, given his prejudices, William Dean Howells was more than pleased when he reviewed *Moran.* As though against his better judgment, he confessed that he read this "romanticistic" story with "breathlessness." He even acknowledged the successful infusions of realism: the reader "will find a good deal of reality in the society man himself, as well as the pirate-souled skipper, and the several Chinese cooks who manage the crew"; and the "story gains a certain effectiveness from being so boldly circumstanced in the light of common day, and in a time and place of our own."[15]

That Norris intended *Moran* to deal from the start in "unleashed passions, in blood, and in sudden death" was clear in the first of its thirteen installments, which began: "This is to be a story of battle, at least one murder, and several sudden deaths."[16] About what else would happen, however, Norris could not be more exact as the first chapter appeared in *The Wave* on 8 January 1898, for he had not thought through this work the way he had *McTeague.* He wrote the installments against weekly press deadlines, unsure where the tale would take him. In a 12 March 1898 letter to Eleanor M. Davenport's mother Elizabeth, for example, he expressed uncertainty with regard to what he should have his hero and heroine do in the next installments.[17] By that point, he had developed Ross Wilbur from an effeminate suitor of the delicate Miss Josie Herrick in San Francisco, to a reluctant but then enthusiastic freebooter becoming expert in the piratical arts off the coast of Baja California, and next to a he-man who has killed for the first time in a scuffle with Chinese competitors. Along the way he wins the admiration and love of the hypermasculine Moran Sternersen, the female pirate of the tale, who looked down upon him as a pantywaist upon first acquaintance. The adventure-romance does not end happily, however. Norris decided to take his characters back to San Francisco. There Hoang, the insidious leader of the Chinese pirates, stabs Moran to death before disappearing into Chinatown with the fortune in ambergris Ross and she obtained during their adventures in Mexico's Magdalena Bay.

The novel is infused with naturalistic themes. Ross's "rise" to muscle-rippling masculinity actually involves a descent to a more primitive condition of mankind required for adaptation to a survival-of-the-fittest environment in which brutal, dog-eat-dog values prevail. Here the consequences of degeneration to a lower, more animalistic state are the opposite of those seen in *McTeague* and *Vandover.* In the logic of this novel, this is a "fortunate fall." Ross becomes a veritable barracuda like Alvinza Kitchell, the shanghaiing captain of the *Bertha Millner.* When Kitchell dies, shortly after Ross discovers on the sinking *Lady Letty* the unconscious daughter of its dead captain, she—Moran Sternersen—assumes control of the *Millner;* and this beefy Norse descendent of Viking stock is just as rapaciously greedy and amoral as Kitchell was. Her motto is, "Might makes right." For example, to get what she wants from Hoang, she inserts a file in his mouth, binds his head so that the teeth are clenched, and works the file in and out until he is ready to lisp the information she demands.

When Ross initially feels the attraction of this woman so unlike the Josie Herricks of San Francisco, Norris has good reason to add a Zolaesque essential to the mix. Ross is definitely aroused when he registers her scent: "[H]er hair, her neck, her entire personality exhaled a fine, sweet, natural redolence." And later, one night as she slept on the beach at Magdalena Bay, a voyeuristic Ross finds himself motivated to lean "toward her, so close that he could catch the savor of her breath and the smell of her neck, warm with sleep . . . and it seemed to him as if her bare arm, flung out at full length, had some sweet aroma of its own."[18] All that is necessary to make a successful courtship possible is that he experience an atavistic lapse to a precivilized condition like hers. Ross achieves apotheosis when he breaks completely from the world of candied almonds and party favors during the battle with the Chinese pirates: the "brute within" has emerged to look down with satisfaction upon the man at his feet whom he has just slain. Ross's experience is that of the hero of 1893's "Lauth": "The knowledge that he could kill filled him with a sense of power that was veritably royal." In 1898, though, Norris sees a larger signifi-cance in the lapse to the condition of Zola's *bête humaine:* "It was the joy of battle, the horrid exhilaration of killing, the animal of the race, the human brute suddenly aroused and dominating . . . centuries of civilization."

In the same battle, Moran too undergoes such an experience, having become a berserker as she "lapsed back to the Vikings and sea-rovers of the tenth century . . . deaf to all reason."[19] She is so out of control that, in her savage fury, she turns on Ross with her dirk!

This initiates the grand "love scene" of *Moran,* and it is so bizarre that perforce one recalls that—beyond considerations of realism, romanticism, and naturalism—there is another dimension of Norris's art that cannot, or should not, be overlooked. As in *McTeague, Vandover,* and many of his *Wave* and pre-1896 writings, Norris was an author possessed of a sense of humor. Or, more precisely, his was a bright, perky, affirmative sense of humor at times; and, at other times, it was a dark, perverse, or at least unsettling one. For example, an inebriated Captain Kitchell notes that the deceased Cap-tain Sternersen's false teeth have fallen out. Kitchell puts them back into the mouth of Moran's father. He then notes that they are upside down, howls with laughter, commits the unfortunate to burial at sea, and then cracks jokes when the sharks arrive to dispose of the corpse. A similarly peculiar sense of humor is displayed when Moran attacks Ross.

Ross tries not to hurt her as she rushes upon him. Yet, she is indeed ber-serk, and they are soon punching each other, trading blow for blow—"though he never once forgot that this last enemy was the girl he loved." Moran's fists twice bring Ross to his knees, and then he sees his chance to end the scuffle. He "planted his knuckles squarely between her eyes"—but to no discernible effect. Finally, Ross catches her around her neck, pivots, swings her off her feet, and slams her onto the beach. To keep her down on her back, he drops his knee on her chest and leans forward to pin down both hands. Immobi-lized, she soon recovers her wits, smiles, and expresses her admiration of him: "'What a two-fisted, brawny dray-horse it is!'" Looking up into his eyes, the space above her nose beginning to swell from the punch Ross landed there, she acknowledges his conquest of not only her body but her soul: "'[M]ate, do you know, I love you for it.'"[20]

Norris's fellow contributor to *The Wave,* Juliet Wilbor Tompkins, sug-gested and—who knows for sure?—perhaps fully clarified in 1928 what one

should make of the scene. She related that *Moran* "grew out of Frank's desire
to stage a physical fight between a man and a woman." Tompkins undoubtedly knew, to some degree, whereof she spoke since they stayed in touch
after both had moved to New York City and the *Wave* serial became a book.
According to her, Norris declared that he "loved that fight."[21] As pertinent
is Norris's declaration in a 13 March 1898 letter to Harry M. Wright, after
he had forwarded the installment in question to *The Wave:* "I've had more
fun writing the yarn than anything I've got hold of yet." That the novel was
both a serious effort and in some respects a lark was Norris's own opinion of
it when, on 31 December 1899, he told William Dean Howells, "I was flying
kites,—trying to see how high I could get without breaking the string, showing off a little I'm afraid."[22]

In the yet-to-be-written *Blix,* the journalist Condy Rivers sends a collection
of his short stories to a New York City publisher. It is declined, but the letter
of rejection encourages him to write a book-length tale of action and adventure. He does so, and the same firm also declines his manuscript, entitled
"In Defiance of Authority." With the second rejection, however, comes an
even greater encouragement, an invitation to work for the magazine that the
company publishes.

This sequence of events squares with what was going on behind the
scenes in Norris's life in late 1897 and early 1898. Like Condy's collection of
short stories, Norris's "Ways That Are Dark" was stillborn. Like Condy, he
had decided to write an action and adventure tale. It was appearing serially in
The Wave, and—as with his short stories—Norris was sending tearsheets of
the chapters eastward when, like Condy, he received his formal offer of employment from an eastern publisher. This occurred in February 1898 when,
unlike Condy, Norris had not yet completed the composition of his novel of
action and adventure. *The Wave* had published only six of its thirteen chapters,
and at least six awaited Norris's attention. Especially noteworthy is the time
at which the job offer arrived: Norris had not yet composed *Moran's* grand
love scene; the pressure in respect to *Moran's* being his means of advertising
his talent in New York City was suddenly off; and this likely explains why he
decided it safe to indulge in, or risk, such a comic romp.

Given the nod by S. S. McClure's right-hand man, John S. Phillips, Norris at last followed Gelett Burgess to the East Coast, to complete the writing
of *Moran* and to find a taker for the *McTeague* manuscript.

15

NEW YORK CITY AT LAST

When Frank Norris wrote on 9 December 1897 to his former University of California classmate Eleanor M. Davenport, he reflected that she would probably cut his acquaintance upon hearing that work for *The Wave* prevented his acceptance of her invitation to a "Dutch treat party." He complained that there "is no night that I can call my own now until after the Christmas edition is on the streets."[1] That 18 December issue included no fewer than five pieces from his hand: three articles, a "Little Drama of the Curbstone" sketch, and his "Perverted Tales" parodies of Rudyard Kipling, Stephen Crane, Bret Harte, Ambrose Bierce, and Anthony Hope. This was followed on 25 December by two articles, a translation from the French of a short story by Ferdinand Bloch, and a book-review column that he coauthored with John O'Hara Cosgrave. On 1 January 1898, Norris made his last appearance as the multitasking journalist and associate editor of *The Wave*, reviewing several new books and seeing the *Vandover*-related sketch, "At Home from Eight to Twelve," into print.

He could not know it then, but as his serialization of *Moran of the Lady Letty* began its run on 8 January he was only a few weeks away from ending his association with the West Coast weekly. And it was not many days thereafter that, once again, Norris was away from the editorial offices on Montgomery Street, writing installments of *Moran* on the fly and doing what was needful to effect his escape to New York City.

Norris's next surviving letter, also addressed to Davenport, found him more than halfway across the continent on 12 February 1898. At the Planters Hotel in St. Louis he was answering a note he had received from her two days earlier, forwarded from New Orleans. Less than twenty-three hours away from St. Louis via the Illinois Central Railroad, Norris had come north from New Orleans to visit the woman he would marry in 1900, nineteen-year-old Jeannette Black.

As Jeannette told Franklin Walker, she met Frank—seven and a half years her senior—at a dance in the fall of 1896, a "sub-debutante affair." They carried on "a mild flirtation" through the summer of 1897, when she left San Francisco and became a student at the Monticello Female Seminary near St. Louis, in Godfrey, Illinois. After the February 1898 visit, recalled Jeannette, Norris was to return to New Orleans and write up the Mardi Gras festivities for *The Wave*. But the five-day carnival, commencing on 18 February, began without him. He never observed the fête, nor did he write anything about the preparations for it, because of another letter that had reached him in the meanwhile.

There was a third destination in his itinerary for late January through early February, to which he alluded obliquely when replying to Davenport on 12 February: "[B]y the way I have some rather good news from the McClure syndicate."[2] He had also visited New York City before then, and the good news was a pending job offer from the McClure's editorial offices there. Two days later he received John S. Phillips's formal proposition, dated 11 February 1898. Norris replied immediately: "I shall most certainly take advantage of your offer to write for your syndicate and for the magazine at the salary we spoke of (fifty dollars per month)." He assured Phillips that he would make himself "sufficiently useful . . . to justify an increase of the amount after a short time," and he looked forward to receiving the check for train fare Phillips had offered. "I shall leave St. Louis then in about a week from today, if I receive the transportation within that time."[3]

Despite the far-from-munificent monthly salary, March 1898 found Norris in an upscale neighborhood in Manhattan, at 10 West Thirty-third Street. The stylish five-story brownstone (no longer extant) was less than half a block from Fifth Avenue. On the other side of the street now stands the Empire State Building.[4] In 1898, however, Norris saw another grand edifice across Thirty-third Street when he headed downtown in the mornings to the McClure offices in the Lexington building at 142 East Twenty-fifth Street. It was one of the preferred destinations of wealthy visitors to New York, the Waldorf-Astoria Hotel.

No longer living cost-free with his mother at the Hotel Pleasanton and not seeing his salary grow by leaps and bounds as winter became spring, Norris did not avail himself of his family's considerable wealth. Striking out on his own at last as he began his twenty-ninth year, he came to experience for the first time a financial pinch when he arrived in the city the week after he had heard from Phillips. A fellow Fiji from Norris's chapter who in 1894 began the study of law at Columbia University, Edward A. Selfridge, informed Walker that he found Frank "in a cheap small back bedroom somewhere in the 30s on the East side"—from which, if Selfridge was correct, Frank had moved to West Thirty-third Street by mid-March. Recalled Selfridge, Norris "had very difficult sledding when he was in New York [and] he was very hard up financially." He was so strapped that Selfridge "not only gladly loaned him some money at various times but often took him out to dinner [and] gave him a square meal, all of which was a great pleasure to me on account of our unbroken friendship." Another Berkeley graduate and Fiji, Frederick A. Juilliard, and Selfridge "were about the only intimates he had" at this time.

Jeannette and Frank corresponded regularly, and she too testified that he "was very hard up in the East." She took him seriously when he wrote that he "had enough for board, room, and seven stamps a week."

In the two surviving letters written while he lived on West Thirty-third Street, Norris did not complain about his financial status, and it is likely that it was not so severe as Selfridge and Jeannette remembered over thirty years later. Norris focused in his letters on the work he was doing for McClure. To Eleanor Davenport's mother, he apologized on 12 March for not being able to send her the manuscript she had requested for a fund-raising publication to be entitled *Mariposa*. Elizabeth Davenport was editing a collection of local authors' writings for the Ladies' Relief Society of Oakland, to be sold at fifty cents for the benefit of the Old Ladies' Home.[5] Norris pleaded his expanded workload since 19 February as his reason for disappointing her, saying nothing about his financial state.

> You can have no idea of the difficulty of keeping up even with the hammer and tongs work of a New York publication such as the McClure magazine and syndicate.
>
> I am writing for both and being naturally anxious to create a favorable impression at the outset have asked for all the assignments and details they can give me. I have been so busy that I have had time to write even to my mother only once since my arrival here three weeks ago. Keeping up my serial in the *Wave* at the same time does not tend to lessen the number of working hours per day.

Would you tell Miss Davenport that I have started up another Leander-Justin Sturgis dialogue on "The Little Miseries of Life." This is for the syndicate however and don't appear in the magazine. How do you like *Moran?* I am in two minds about [the heroine's] end and do not now know whether she should be killed or go to Cuba with Wilbur.

Referring in his last sentence to what was on everyone's mind then—the sinking of the battleship *Maine* in the harbor of Havana, Cuba, on 15 February 1898, which he had written into his *Wave* serial—he informed her of a professional opportunity on the horizon because of the likelihood of war with Spain: "I myself have a half promise in the matter of war correspondence for the syndicate in case of 'unpleasantness.'"[6]

The next day he wrote to Harry M. Wright, thanking him for his complimentary comments about *Moran.* Norris proudly informed him that the story "seems to catch on everywhere. I've already had an offer for it from the McClure people." He meant not the syndicate nor the magazine but the book-publishing firm Doubleday and McClure Company, housed in the same offices on East Twenty-fifth Street. "I've been told that the editor [Frank N. Doubleday] was enthusiastic over it and that his wife is reading regularly and asking for more. . . . The first scheme was to syndicate the yarn, but now they're talking of making a book out of it."

Norris did refer in very general terms to his income in this letter. He was hardly singing the blues, though, when announcing that "Burgess is coining money [here], and Ernest Peixotto is already almost famous, Juliet Wilbor Tompkins draws down $135.00 a month, and I hope to be right up with the procession by next summer." Indeed, he was delighted with his situation, which he described to Wright in terms quite different from Selfridge's.

You see I've moved up a peg and am with McClure's writing on a salary, and I declare the salary is more in evidence than the writing. New York is *all right,* I've got a nifty little room in a mighty nifty place just opposite the Waldorf hotel—hot potatoes—and Eddie Selfridge and I absorb nourishment together at a fairish joint on Madison Avenue. I think I am going to "get on" now, my stuff seems to take pretty damn well, much better than I expected, and lots of people—big people in a way—have patted me on the head and chucked me under the chin. I may have a volume of short stories out before long, but that's in the air just now. Also Stone and Kimball have written me to ask if I could do some Chinese yarns for them, had heard I was eminently fitted.[7]

To Elizabeth Davenport and Wright he was pleased to announce that he had met the author of *Chimmie Fadden,* Edward Townsend. The icing on the cake was an evening spent at the home of William Dean Howells on 7 March. Norris confided to Elizabeth Davenport that he "had a most charming visit. I find him one of the most delightful men imaginable and, as you told me, especially fond of a good joke."[8]

Norris did not say more about what joking took place, but Gelett Burgess told Walker of one prank perpetrated by Norris and possibly enjoyed by Howells that same evening.

> After the *Lark* had ended publication, I went to New York, and found, when I arrived, a card of William Dean Howells. . . . Frank came for me. I was dressing. We were to call in evening dress. Frank watched me dress with that ironic, devilish smile of his on his lips the while. It was not until we had been in Mr. Howells' drawing room for almost an hour that I discovered to my horror, that instead of having put on my tail coat, I had, by inadvertence put on my "cutaway" coat with my evening vest and trousers. Frank had known it all the time, and had said nothing to me, letting me make a fool of myself, and enjoying my embarrassment and mortification to the full.

It seemed that Norris's dream was coming true. Hardly the stereotypical starving, lonely artist whose dedication to his muse kept him chained to his desk in a garret, he was having a jolly time—in formal evening wear and otherwise—in spite of his low salary. Professionally, he was, according to his own testimony in mid-March, seeing nothing but bright developments on the near horizon.

When the *Wave* serialization of *Moran* completed its run on 9 April 1898, McClure syndicated it, and it appeared in installments from 4 to 19 May in the *New York Evening Sun*. At least one other newspaper, the *Chicago Inter Ocean*, followed suit in late August and early September. Maximum cash value was extracted from the novel, that is, before the book publication discussed in March occurred in late September. But as April passed, little else changed with regard to Norris's comment to Wright that his salary was more in evidence than his writing.

As for the manuscript Norris had promised Mrs. Davenport, he instead sent her a previously published short story, "Outward and Visible Signs: III," which had appeared in the *Overland Monthly* in 1894. Its subtitle became its sole title, "After Strange Gods," when Davenport printed it in *Mariposa* in April 1898. Along with the *Moran* serializations, these two works comprised the whole of his publication activity that spring; both were mere reprintings. The newspapers took no syndicated short stories nor fictions of any kind. *McClure's Magazine* identified in its pages nothing from his hand. A month after he had written his letters to Wright and Elizabeth Davenport, Norris had good reason to feel discouraged.

The U.S. Congress made possible a revival of self-confidence and an opportunity to display his talents on 25 April 1898 when it declared war on Spain. The "half promise in the matter of war correspondence" became the whole. Norris was to represent *McClure's Magazine,* and the leap upward from a regional weekly to a prestigious monthly magazine with a healthy national circulation was now a fait accompli. In addition, the gratification was personal in another respect, for this impassioned patriot very much wanted to be on the scene when the United States punished Spain for its infamous act in Havana Harbor.

Along with the rest of the nation, Norris learned shortly after the destruction of the armored cruiser *Maine* that 230 sailors, twenty-eight marines, and two officers had perished or were missing and presumed dead. Eight more would later die from injuries. Along with virtually everyone else, Norris was convinced by a naval board of inquiry and *Cuba Libre* journalists such as the *New York World's* Sylvester Scovel that a torpedo was the external cause of the initial explosion. The alternative explanation was internal combustion in a forward coal bunker located next to an ammunition magazine, and this had to come to mind since safe storage of coal compressed by its own weight was a common problem at the time. When the *Oregon* left the West Coast for Cuba on 19 March, for example, it experienced a coal-bunker fire as it neared Peru. Captain Sigsbee, reassigned from the *Maine* to the *St. Paul* as the war got under way, also had to deal with one. But no one blamed Sigsbee for negligence in the weeks following the loss of the *Maine.* Spain was the *bête noire* to be crushed for its inhumane treatment of Cubans, reported sensationally in the press for years, and its cowardly act of sabotage.

For Norris, the war was personal in another respect, as is evident in the way in which he worked the sinking of the *Maine* into the plot of *Moran of the Lady Letty.* Not seen in the version published as a book but present in the *Wave* serialization was his projection of his response to the event onto his hero. How a character in a literary work feels does not necessarily reveal the emotional condition of his creator, of course. But that the spanking-new *Maine* made its maiden voyage up New York Bay on its way to Newport, Rhode Island, when Norris was in Manhattan on 5 November 1895 does square with Ross Wilbur's keening for the loss of that cruiser.

When chapter 12 of *Moran* appeared in the 2 April issue of *The Wave*, Ross returns from the Hotel del Coronado to his ship anchored offshore, and he confirms what Moran and he had heard from a fisherman.

> "It *was* true about the *Maine*. Let's get up here in the quarter-deck—I've something to propose to you."
> Moran laid her arm across his shoulder and the two walked aft.
> He told her of the affair which had roused the nation as nothing since Sumter had done, told it between his teeth, his voice shaking with excitement.
> "Why," he added as he finished, "why, she was ours, she was *mine*, she belonged to every one of us. I saw her once in New York harbor, and I was so proud of her," tears started to his eyes. "Such a queen she was, and white, why she fairly dazzled you—and her big grim peace-makers putting their snouts out of her turrets. She came up the harbor there, slow, you know, as though she was making a royal progress, and every little tug, and ship and ferry-boat dipped their colors and saluted her. Why, you just *loved* her, as though she was something alive, and now—and now——No," he broke off, "you can't understand, Moran, how can you? It's no affair of yours—you're not an American."[9]

Ross proposes that they become filibusters, using their ship to transport war materiel to the Cuban insurgents who had, since 1895, been trying to overthrow the Spanish government.

Maudlin now, after the passage of a century, the bereaved Ross Wilbur's sincerity squares with Norris's own tone in all of the articles he wrote about the war and the interviews he gave after its conclusion. Like the other American journalists who went to Cuba, Norris carried a gun, put himself into the thick of the action, and was just as intent as the generals on seeing the Spanish vanquished.

Ernest Peixotto, married in January 1897 to his former art student, Mary "Molly" Hutchinson, was living at the Judson boarding house on Washington Square South when Norris came to New York. His diary records Norris's first visit to their apartment on 25 February. On 3 March they were again together to celebrate the birthday of their fellow student at the Académie Julian, Guy Rose. Then journalist and short-story writer Edward Townsend, his wife, and Norris were Peixotto's supper guests on 6 March. Following a 16 March visit, the last entry for 1898 citing Norris was dated 29 April: "Frank Norris leaves for Key West."[10]

Before he departed, Norris had already begun to gather "impressions" that might someday make good copy for *McClure's Magazine.* Thanks to Edward A. Selfridge, he was able to get behind the scenes to observe preparations for the war effort, since his old friend was a lieutenant in New York's Seventy-first Volunteer Regiment. It was to assemble at Camp Black at Hempstead, Long Island, and Norris paid him a visit there. This occurred either before 29 April, when Selfridge was involved in making arrangements for the encampment, or, if Peixotto's diary was in error, circa 2 May, when the Seventy-first marched from its armory on Park Avenue between Thirty-fourth and Thirty-fifth streets to the East River, rode ferries to Long Island City, and boarded the train that carried it to Hempstead.

Selfridge badly mangled what transpired at Camp Black when he gave his account to Walker. Norris may indeed have arrived before 29 April, for Selfridge thought that Norris had not yet been assigned to cover the war but only "hoped to get [to Cuba] as a correspondent." Then again, over thirty years later, Selfridge appears to have misremembered the sequence of events, since he also dated Norris's visit to the camp to "just before we left for Cuba." In fact, the Seventy-first remained at Hempstead long after Norris's departure for Florida, inconvenienced by a shortage of potable water and demoralized by not only its standstill condition but bad weather that turned Hempstead Plains into a sea of mud fifteen miles long and three miles wide. Selfridge did not leave Camp Black until 14 May 1898, when steamers transported the Seventy-first to Jersey City and thence by train to Lakeland, Florida, a small town thirty miles to the north of Tampa, where Selfridge detrained on 16 May. Norris had been in Key West for well over a week before Selfridge escaped from misery on Long Island.

Time and the vagaries of memory appear to have conflated two encounters with Norris prior to their seeing each other again in Cuba, the first on Long Island and the second in or near Tampa. The latter meeting did occur, literally, "just before we left [Florida] for Cuba." On 29 May, the Seventy-first was ordered from Lakeland to Tampa as final preparations for the invasion of Cuba were under way. By 8 June Norris and Selfridge were nine miles to the southwest of the city on troop transports docked at Port Tampa. During the previous few days, before Selfridge boarded the *Vigilancia* and Norris the *Segurança,* they likely groused together, as virtually everyone involved in the war effort did by then, about the seemingly endless delays and countless frustrations that characterized the first months of the war. Journalists in Key

West and Tampa had found little to write about; soldiers had marked time wondering when the fighting would start.

Returned to Manhattan from Camp Black, the veteran journalist who had covered the Jameson Raid in the Transvaal and then northern California for almost two years doffed the cap of the prose-fiction writer and again donned that of the impressionistic essayist. He was more than ready to produce full-scale articles for *McClure's Magazine,* as distinguished from dispatches of the sort newspaper reporters such as Scovel hastily wired to their editors. And this was a "real" war. His experience during the South African debacle was one thing. What was commencing now would constitute the greatest adventure of his short life.

16

THE ROCKING-CHAIR WAR

On the road once more, destination Key West, Norris had a choice of routes. Henry M. Flagler's East Coast Railroad line had reached Miami by 1896. Since no roadway connected the string of small islands that ran from the mainland to Key West, the last leg of the journey was on regularly scheduled Mallory Line and Peninsular and Occidental steamships. This was the itinerary of Charles Sanford Diehl of the Associated Press.[1] As with Miami, so with Tampa. It was possible to get there from Manhattan in as little as thirty-four hours.[2] Entraining on 5 May 1898 a few hours to the south from New York in Washington, D.C., George Kennan of *The Outlook* arrived in Tampa the next day. He sailed the following evening for Key West, debarking early in the morning of 8 May.[3]

Norris never disclosed in print which of the two routes he took. He did, however, make a noteworthy slip in the manuscript of the first article he is known to have drafted, "News Gathering at Key West."[4] He wrote and then cancelled "Tampa" when he meant Key West, strongly suggesting that he had recently been there. No "news gathering" was going on at Miami, and Norris never referred to that city in any of his writings.

Norris, like Kennan, had the opportunity to visit the military and journalistic center of activity in the city, the spectacular Tampa Bay Hotel (now Plant Hall of the University of Tampa). Built at the cost of three million dollars by the railway and shipping magnate Henry B. Plant between 1888 and 1891, this grand hotel of five stories and 511 rooms sported Victorian gingerbread and was topped by Moorish minarets, domes, and cupolas. It dwarfed all other buildings in the city, giving whimsical oriental expression to the Gilded Age taste for the extravagant. Rare was the journalist from the Northeast and Midwest who was not startled by its appearance and did not comment upon its peculiarity. It had closed at the end of the winter tourist season but, with the declaration of war, it reopened to receive U.S. military leaders and foreign attachés who would observe the conduct of the war from the American side. Its wide veranda was repeatedly photographed by the daily press as, from late April through early June, officers and journalists waited for "something to happen" during what came to be known as the "rocking chair" phase of the war.

Kennan wrote about his first sight of this architectural extravaganza in a manner startlingly like that of Norris when rendering his impressions of things sensational for *The Wave:*

> A nearly full moon was just rising over the trees on the eastern side of the hotel park, touching with silver the drifts of white blossoms on dark masses of oleander-trees in the foreground, and flooding with soft yellow light the domes, Moorish arches, and long facade. . . . Two regimental bands were playing waltzes and patriotic airs under a long row of incandescent lights on the broad veranda . . . [and] the impression made upon a newcomer, as he alighted from the train, was that of a brilliant military ball at a fashionable seaside summer resort. Of the serious and tragic side of war there was hardly a suggestion.[5]

In his observation of how lighthearted the wartime scene was, Kennan registered exactly the same sense of the inappropriate atmosphere of levity that Norris did in "News Gathering" after he had spent a few days at Key West.

How long Norris remained in Tampa is as uncertain as when he left Manhattan. Available now are none of the letters he wrote to Jeannette Black during the war, which she told Walker she shared with fellow members of a literary society at the Monticello Female Seminary. In light of subsequent events, it is clear that he had boarded one of the Plant Line steamers, the *Mascotte* or the *Olivette*, by 6 May at the latest for the overnight cruise down the coast.

To have a porter carry one's bags from the docks near the Custom House at the western end of the island to the dollar-per-night Key West Hotel on Duval Street did not take long. In 1898 all points between which Norris moved when in the southernmost city of the United States involved only a short walk—or, for five cents, a ride on the mule-drawn street car that ran on six miles of track through the city. Although a thriving commercial center, the locus of Fort Taylor, and the port from which the U.S. navy's North Atlantic fleet conducted its winter exercises for years, Key West was then what it is now—an out-of-the-way, raffish town redolent with a distinctive, Cuban- and Bahamian-influenced character. In its own way at the other end of the continent, it smacked as much of a "frontier town" as Iowa Hill and the other remote communities in California that Norris described for *The Wave.*

Now long practiced at overturning his readers' conventional expectations in his fiction and nonfiction, Norris began writing in characteristic, eye-catching fashion in "News Gathering at Key West."

> For him who smelleth the battle not very far off, Key West in war time is a great disappointment. . . . You want to see excitement, turmoil, activity, the marching and countermarching of troops, the excited going and coming of couriers a-horseback, the glint of epaulets and brass at street corners. You ask to hear the harsh snarl of drums, the scrape of the gunlock against the cartridge belt, the tramp of soldiery, and perhaps the sullen roll of a passing battery on an adjacent street. You want to see officers in earnest conversation on the curbstone, and, ah, you want to see the war correspondent in all his glory, leaping from the dispatch boat before she is even made fast to the dock, dashing ashore in all the panoply of pith helmet, norfolk jacket and field glasses, a bundle of dispatches in one hand, racing his fellows to the telegraph office, "getting in his stuff," beating his rivals, making a scoop.

Norris instead found himself in an environment disturbingly like that of the Hotel del Monte and the Hotel del Coronado: "[Y]ou could easily imagine yourself in a sea port summer resort at a time when a visiting cruiser or monitor was [anchored] off the hotel." Out of sight to the south, the U.S. navy was in a decidedly passive posture, maintaining a blockade rather than spearheading the conquest of Cuba.

There were journalists aboard Admiral William Sampson's flagship *New York* who were able to wire to their editors firsthand accounts of the action. Richard Harding Davis, for example, witnessed the shelling of Matanzas to the east of Havana on 27 April. Two days later, on the deck of the same ship when it was to the west of Mariel, Stephen Crane saw the exchange of fire at Cabañas. But such moments had been rare, and neither encounter with the enemy had amounted to much. Most of the visible activity had to do with the mooring of commercial vessels that had tried to approach Cuba, were stopped, and then impounded at Key West. To the north, the army bureaucracy seemed to be taking forever to organize its divisions. In the face of such stasis, there was little for a journalist to do.

> The Key West hotel is the head quarters for the correspondents as well as for the navy officers on shore leave and the army men from the camp outside the town. At this hotel then you would certainly count upon an activity equal at least to that of a political headquarters during a convention. But I shall carry away from the Key West Hotel only a picture of a row of men in white ducks and yachting caps sitting on the veranda, smoking and tranquilly chatting together or tossing nickels into the street for the little nigger bootblacks to "scrabble" for. They are doing nothing, these war correspondents, waiting merely; waiting for something to turn up.

Worse, some of the military men and journalists were blithely engaging in social amenities at a time when they should have been "remembering the *Maine*" and the sufferings of the long-tormented Cubans awaiting deliverance. "I have even seen a group of officers and correspondents in a devoted circle around one of the three or four smartly dressed women—officers' wives who are at the hotel—as if famine and fighting were not within six hours easy steaming, as if the *Maine* still rode the ocean under the eye of heaven, and as if the Spanish-American War of 1898 had not been declared." Here is the edgy voice of *Moran's* Ross Wilbur when denouncing his friends for entertaining themselves at the Hotel del Coronado while the news of the sinking of the *Maine* was still fresh. Norris's abruptly revealed purpose is the exposure of decadence in Key West at a time when he felt that singleminded dedication to a holy cause was a moral imperative.

The grievous problem for most of the journalists was that, unlike Davis and Crane, they had seen nothing worth reporting whatsoever, neither on shore nor off the Cuban coast. Only a blessed few were aboard the blockading warships or on the boats following them that their newspapers had put at their disposal. Norris estimates that there are "four hundred and fifty or five hundred correspondents now at work gathering news of the war"; and, as his exposé continues, he speculates that the "vast majority of these men will return to their homes after the signing of the peace articles with not nearly so clear an idea of real war as they would gain from a fourth of July sham battle at a National Guard summer encampment."

Norris ends the first section of his manuscript by observing that, out of the nearly five hundred journalists who made possible what had thus far appeared in newspapers and magazines, only ten or so had actually "seen a shotted gun fired." In fact, only two press boats were in the right place at the right time, to see what Davis and Crane had witnessed. One was present at Matanzas "by what was considered a miracle of good luck." The other "happened to be on the spot" during the shelling of Cabañas. Confides Norris, "as far as I can learn, no other news has been collected at first hand and by eye witnesses [on] any of the newspaper boats upon this station."

By 7 May 1898, Norris had introduced himself to Stephen Crane's colleague and immediate superior in the chain of command at the *New York World*, Sylvester Scovel, "the chief correspondent of the New York paper to whom I had letters." Early the next morning, at half-past four, Scovel pounded on Norris's door, shouting from the hallway, "We're going right out," and, "You've got twenty minutes." Norris was aboard the *World* press boat in fifteen. By five o'clock Scovel, Crane, and he were preparing to take breakfast as the *Three Friends* was cutting through the aquamarine sea, trailing black coal smoke. A channel free of mines led them southward from Key West through a reef toward Sand Key. As the seagoing tug capable of eighteen knots finally entered open water, it accelerated forcefully and maintained speed for the six hours it took to sight Cuba.

In this second part of "News Gathering at Key West," Norris again plays popular illusions against observed realities while recounting his experiences at sea. As the *Three Friends* was "thrashing and screwing her way through transverse furrows of water" on 8 May, he registers the fact that, despite the distance of only ninety miles, the conditions off Cuba are unlike those one enjoys at the comparatively placid Key West. All daydreams about the sensuous delights afforded by the balmy, tropical splendor of an island fronting the Caribbean Sea are dashed. The currents off Cuba's north shore are powerful; and, as spring advances toward the rainy season, the trade winds grow stronger, often reaching twenty knots in the afternoon. Relates Norris, the two forces "run counter to one another, whipping up a sea that would not be out of place off Hatteras or Cape Race." So much for Edenic, postcard-perfect conceptions of the dulcet charms of the "Pearl of the Antilles."

As in the first part of the article, the magnitude of what is at stake in the war against Spain is abruptly recalled. Norris, without warning, waxes patriotic, and his animus against Spain resurfaces as they approach the coast. The somber subject of the war must not be forgotten in the absence of scenes of conflict and the face of new sensations. The iron note of high seriousness is sounded when he sights Cuba on the horizon as "a blur, a smudge, a faint blue haze." But this time he declaims in a pathetic voice, rather than the wrathful one he used when chiding those in Key West for frivolity in wartime. A more meditative Norris gazes into the distance and reflects upon "the object of so much spilled blood, the cause of so much misery, for which so many millions of money have been spent, the rock which is to wreck a nation, to disintegrate a dynasty, to free a people, Cuba, the queen of the Antilles, stretching out there between the indigo of the Southern Atlantic and the pale faint blue of the half tropic sky." Coming closer to shore, he maintains this mood, though—ironically—there is no feature of the landscape that suggests that Cuba is a cause either for lugubrious sentiment or for hope of a more humane and egalitarian future for its long-suffering natives. Ashore, "nothing was in view but trees—palm trees and green grass. There was nothing to indicate a country racked and harried from end to end, war-ridden, famine-stricken." Nor was there a sign of its being "a place of horrors," warranting for Norris the *ne plus ultra* description of profanation familiar to readers of the New Testament: Spanish Cuba is "an abomination of desolation."

Terminating his conscientious reflection with a biblical superlative he believes appropriate for the ultimate sink of iniquity in his time, Norris returns to the narrative of his first experience on a press boat as he recalls the rapid approach of an American warship familiar to a man with a long-term fascination with the "Great White Fleet" now sporting battleship gray. The *Helena* "was an old friend of mine," reports Norris, "and I should have known her anywhere."

The captain of the *Three Friends* immediately stopped its engines upon sighting the *Helena,* for good reason. The protocol on the blockade was the firing of a shot across an unidentified ship's bow if it seemed to be fleeing or merely looked suspicious. Delay was not advisable. In such rough water, aim was difficult, and a shell might easily hit a press boat. Even a "blank" (one without an explosive charge) might cause mortal injury to crew members and journalists if it missed its intended mark. Throughout the war, numerous correspondents reported that navy ships abruptly halted them without warning, with a shell passing precariously close to the rigging, smokestack, or hull.

Norris relates that, as the two vessels drew near to each other, a voice came from the *Helena* through a megaphone: "'What news have you of Dewey?'" That was the pressing question of the hour and of several days previous; and Norris thus documents the point in his nation's history at which it was possible for Americans to take pride in the emergence of the United States as a proven naval power in the same class with England and Germany.

All of America knew, shortly after the declaration of war, that Commodore George Dewey was on his way to the Philippines with the intent of destroying the Spanish fleet harbored there. Suspense ran high. A positive outcome was uncertain because, before and well into the war, Washington consistently overestimated Spain's naval power. When Dewey's fleet engaged the Spanish ships at Manila Bay on 1 May 1898, the battle proved a veritable cakewalk. But from Washington to Key West anxiety was keen as Dewey approached his foes, and apprehension mounted as the days passed because, before the battle commenced, Dewey had ordered the severing of the cable to render the Spanish incommunicado, thereby cutting himself off as well. The lack of hard information about the battle until 7 May did not, of course, prevent William Randolph Hearst's *New York Journal* and similarly irresponsible newspapers from printing sensational headlines and patent fictions about an American victory, many days before it was actually possible to celebrate Dewey's triumph. But it was not until six days after the 1 May victory that Sampson finally wired confirmation from Hong Kong. And thus the question posed to the *Three Friends* on 8 May 1898: Have more authoritative sources than Hearst and his kind confirmed the victory?

Sylvester Scovel—to whom Norris assigns the sobriquet "The Press"— could now speak with confidence through a megaphone about the fact of the matter established the day before. "'Nothing new, Sir. The previous dispatches have been confirmed. He seems to have about destroyed the entire Spanish fleet.'"

Norris illustrates that such is the typical experience of journalists and navy men, lusting for not only the sight of combat but information as to what, exactly, was going on in the Pacific and in their immediate vicinity. The warships and the press boats were, Norris explains, "meeting constantly" to obtain the latest news and, that failing, to gossip. "Not a blockading ship did the *Three Friends* sight, that did not bear down upon her at once. One time we even saw the *Dolphin* fire a blank shot across the bows of the *New York Herald* boat. Primarily no doubt the blockader comes down upon the dispatch [boat] to know what her business may be. But even when assured of her character the war ship generally heaves to for a little talk. Heaven knows they are lonesome enough on their stations, these blockaders. But blockaders and dispatch boats alike are eager for news." And this is how reporters obtained the majority of news stories about the Cuban blockade, second- and thirdhand.

The exposé of how newspaper men such as Scovel and Crane gather news continues. Scovel does not witness a single reportable event; he merely asks the officer aboard the *Helena* if "anything has been happening along here." It is a better-than-average news day for Crane and him, since the officer replies in the affirmative. Yesterday, "the forts to the East and West of Morro [at the mouth of Havana's harbor] opened fire on the *Vicksburg* and *Osceola*. . . . Cut away some of the *Vicksburg's* rigging, otherwise did no damage." They snatch at a second datum when the officer relates that there was "an exchange of shots between the torpedo boat *Dupont* and the shore batteries of Cardenas."

Another development discussed through megaphones as the two vessels rolled near each other was the beginning of the first truly major action of the North Atlantic fleet during the war. Scovel asked about the disappearance from the scene of the larger ships, cruisers such as the *Indiana* and *Iowa*, as well as the *New York*. "Gone to Porto Rico, we think," came the reply. The officer's surmise was correct: the bombardment of San Juan would occur shortly, on 12 May 1898. The principal vessels in the fleet, along with numerous press boats, were that very day wending their way eastward toward Puerto Rico. This, too, seemed to be good news. In another sense, though, it was bad, since Norris and his two colleagues had missed the opportunity to be present at Puerto Rico for one of the most significant stories of the month. In going to the Cuban coast rather than following Admiral Sampson, they had unwittingly settled for secondhand reports of recent actions nearby when they might have observed firsthand the grand bombardment spectacle that numerous other journalists enjoyed at San Juan.

"While we screwed and floundered our way back to Key West" on 9 May, Norris reported, Scovel and Crane were writing up the two stories they had obtained. One was the firefight of 7 May between the Spanish at Havana and the Americans aboard the *Vicksburg* and *Morrill* (not the *Osceola*, as they had been told and as Norris stated in his manuscript). The other bit of information was also inaccurate; the exchange of fire between the shore batteries and the *Dupont* and *Hornet* did not occur at Cardenas but at Matanzas on 6 and 7 May. When they landed at Key West, however, the two representatives of the *New York World* actually had little to show for their efforts. Newspapers across the United States had already reported both developments. The third datum, Sampson's departure for Puerto Rico, was not only dated but useless. The military censors would allow no one to reveal that movement of the fleet.

Norris does not tell the reader what he was doing as Scovel and Crane were preparing copy to be wired to New York City. But on the return trip to Key West he was certainly not worrying about the possibility of being "scooped" by reporters or censored. As is apparent in his manuscript, Norris *could* use the two reports of action on the Cuban coast—not for their news value but for illustration of how reporters gather news. He could also treat Sampson's advance upon San Juan, again not as news but as an occasion for relating an amusing anecdote concerning one clever fellow who found a way to trick the army's news censor, Captain R. E. Thomson:

> Only one correspondent so far as [is] known, has been able to fool the censor. When the main body of the fleet went to Porto Rico, every newspaper man in Key West knew of it within ten hours, but every one of them despaired of getting the news by the censor. One man alone, succeeded. At four in the afternoon he wired his paper, "Newspaper fleet have gone to Porto Rico." Then a few hours afterward at a time when the censor had forgotten the text of his telegram because of the multitude of others that had followed after it, he wired "Omit first word of my last dispatch."

Norris could write about anything he liked for a simple reason: Unlike Scovel, whose obligation was to provide timely copy and, if possible, beat his competition, Norris knew that everything that might appear in *McClure's Magazine* would be, literally, history when it saw print. As with Crane and Richard Harding Davis when they were writing for monthlies rather than dailies, Norris's assignment was to provide *McClure's* with retrospectives, pieces on recent history rather than immediate developments. At the very earliest, nothing he wrote could appear in print for three or four weeks.

Thus, he indulges in two ruminations that he judged might engage the interest of *McClure's* subscribers, also at their leisure, perhaps at home on a Sunday evening after they had cleared the table, put the children put to bed, and read the newspaper.

One is a flamboyant exercise of his imagination, with which Norris concludes the second half of "News Gathering" in the big bow-wow manner. He returns to the scene that provoked him in Key West, focusing again on the display of social amenities before the hotel veranda. The war correspondent in a straw hat and the "smartly dressed summer girl," lulled into complacency by the quiet before the outbreak of large-scale hostilities, do not "appreciate the dramatic possibilities of their situation." But Norris, despite the "quiet and calm" on the blockade and the nondescript appearance of Cuba viewed from a distance, discerns what is transpiring beneath the placid surface of quotidian life in Key West. With his mind's eye, he can perceive the tremendous, history-shaping forces at work about him. Resorting to a Zolaesque conceit after donning the cap of the geopolitical seer, he melodramatically asserts that

> the quiet is deceptive and the calm makes one forget the possibility of storm. Force is here, a vast, resistless, terrible Force, that a moment's warning may unleash in a wild red riot of fire and blood. And in the end, back of all this, back of the petty scheming of correspondents, back of all this small world of ships and men, back of the gold lace of the officers, and the gray flanks of the war ships, one comes to remember far up there in Washington the calm, strong man with the smooth shaven face and quiet, resolute lips, who holds this force in leash.

Next shifting his attention from the ever-pale, somber visage of President William McKinley to the American people, Norris mimics the saber rattling of those like William Randolph Hearst, who had called for a strike against Cuba long before the sinking of the *Maine*. He even appropriates dialogue and imagery from Exodus as he compares the impending liberation of the Cubans to the freeing of Israel from slavery in Egypt. Not a coda but a crescendo serves as his finale: "[O]ne feels the vague, vast uplift of the Nation, the calm, slow, terrible movement of an entire people united and aroused, conscious of its magnificent power, the Nation who has said to Spain 'Let my people go.'" Moses and Aaron spoke for God before Pharaoh; to Norris's mind, America's manifest destiny is to do the same before Spain's queen.

The other prolonged reflective moment, though not another nationalistic homily, would have been equally out of place in a typical press dispatch. It has to do with the presence of Stephen Crane on the *Three Friends*.

Nothing else in Norris's Spanish-American War writings has drawn as much attention as the passage in question. Crane's biographers have again and again quoted or paraphrased it. Historians portraying the early phases of the Spanish-American War have proven almost as enamored of it when attempting to re-create the context in which the war correspondents labored. Because of this sketch, both kinds of scholars have concluded that Norris—as yet an unknown on the national stage—was jealous of the younger man who had achieved international visibility three years earlier with *The Red Badge of Courage*. Norris's widow suggested that he was at least mean-spirited when producing it. She related to Walker that later—when Crane and he were in Cuba—her husband found him unlikable. Jeannette said that Crane "drank too much and made a fool of himself." And yet it is not inappropriate to come to a different conclusion regarding Norris's attitude toward Crane in "News Gathering at Key West": that Crane, the international celebrity, simply offered too promising an opportunity for the production of amusing copy to pass up, given the degree to which his appearance when aboard the *Three Friends* was startlingly different from what Norris or anyone else familiar with Crane's fine writing and his public persona might have expected. That is, the droll portrait was not maliciously personal; Norris simply could not waste good "material" at a time at which there was little else to write up. Moreover, would Crane, whose flair for lampooning was as well exercised as Norris's, have declined the opportunity were the table turned?

A contemporaneous context for Norris's representation of Crane is required. In the popular imagination at the turn of the century, there were two referents for "the literary artist." One was the image of the velvet-jacketed man of letters at his leisure, perhaps tugging on his pipe while leaning against a mantle or, alternately, sitting at his escritoire with pen in hand and manuscript before him. The second was that of the bohemian dressed down sufficiently to violate the more traditional image of the gentleman author. Norris posed for photographers in both modes, as did Crane. But on the *Three Friends,* Norris observed a world-renowned novelist *en déshabillé* to such a degree that a chimney sweep would type sartorial elegance in comparison. Further, Crane-baiting had since 1895 become a major sport among the wittier book reviewers and literary essayists, who vied with each other for the honor of having fashioned the cleverest parody of his style or the most telling satirical portrait of this young man whose eccentricities begged for sendup treatment. Their main targets were Crane's linguistic idiosyncrasies and his unconventional uses of color in his imagery. Norris had already made a contribution to this literature in "The Green Stone of Unrest" section of his 1897 collection of parodies, "Perverted Tales."

Now he had the opportunity to focus on style in a different way, and so he proceeded to tweak Crane, whom he dubbed the "Young Personage":

> Table there was none and the plunging of the boat made it out of the question to write while sitting in a chair. The correspondents took themselves off to the cabin and wrote while sitting in their bunks. The Young Personage was wearing a pair of duck trousers grimed and fouled with all manner of pitch and grease and oil. His shirt was guiltless of collar or scarf and was unbuttoned at the throat. His hair hung in ragged fringes over his eyes. His dress-suit case

was across his lap and answered him for a desk. Between his heels he held a bottle of beer against the rolling of the boat, and when he drank was royally independent of a glass. While he was composing his descriptive dispatches which some ten thousand people would read in the morning from the bulletins in New York I wondered what the fifty thousand who have read his war novel and have held him, no doubt rightly, to be a great genius, would have said and thought could they have seen him at the moment.

Many years later, R. W. Stallman rushed to Crane's defense, yelping that "Crane could not have cared less" about what the *McClure's Magazine* readership would have thought about the figure he cut that day. Although there is no known photograph of Norris aboard the *Three Friends,* Stallman then turns upon him and whacks him for not looking like Crane but instead like a mincing patrician with "his hair parted carefully down the middle and a scarf tied around his neck."[6] It is a paradoxical moment in Stallman's biography, since it contains photographic portraits in which Crane himself sports neatly parted hair and radiates gentility in jacket and cravat.

There are other reasons for concluding that Norris was not "out to get" Crane. For example, he merely mentioned that Crane was drinking a beer— he did not refer to the behavior of an alcoholic. Another journalist and old friend of Norris's who, according to Charles Norris, courted Ida Carleton in the late 1880s or early 1890s, James F. J. Archibald, was not so kind. Like Norris's widow, he told Walker that Crane "drank a good deal" during the war; and, Archibald quipped, Crane's posthumous collection of war-related pieces, *Wounds in the Rain,* might more appropriately have borne the title *Shots in the Rain*—shots of whisky. That Norris was a man without a chip on his shoulder in Key West is suggested even more strongly in other ways. He did not cut his acquaintance with Crane when they returned from the Cuban coast on 9 May 1898. This Norris made clear when, earlier in the second half of the Key West article, he relates that there was at least one other interaction between the two men. "I do not know how many papers and magazines [Crane] represented but he has since told me that to fulfil his contracts the war must last something over five years." The same conversation or an additional one appears to have informed another description suggestive not of envy but merely Norris's recognition of the high status in Key West of the author of *The Red Badge* and the journalist who had in 1897 reported the Greco-Turkish War. "The Personage was a big enough man to be independent of even the chief correspondent [for the *New York World*] at Key West and went directly to the cable office with his stuff as soon as we got in . . . the smaller men turn in most of their dispatches to their chief who edits them in a way and compares them with the other information already in hand." If Crane's success did rankle, here was an opportunity for Norris to display his fangs, since he himself was undeniably one of the "smaller men." Though Norris was a credentialed correspondent, the "big man" *McClure's* had dispatched to Key West was one of the journalistic stars of the day, Stephen Bonsal.

Finally, one other bit of information offered by Gregory Mason in 1939 as he attempted to describe what it was like to be a journalist in the early days of the war should be taken into account. Mason gave neither date nor location, and the snippet he provides in his *Remember the Maine* concludes all too abruptly, but the moment depicted suggests amity rather than enmity between the two men:

> In a Florida bar Stephen Crane and Frank Norris were discussing women's fashions. In an old copy of *Leslie's Weekly,* Crane had just read:
>
> > B. Altman & Co. are introducing the Princess Corset-Skirt, a recent Paris novelty, consisting of a regular Corset and Skirt combined in one piece of material in such a manner as to form a single garment, and designed by the Paris Modistes in connection with the coming fashion in Princess Gowns. And in addition are also exhibiting the Corset-Chemise.[7]

One only wishes that Mason—not present at that Florida bar because, in 1898, he was only nine years old—had disclosed more of what his unnamed source saw and overheard that day. It should come as no surprise, however, to readers of Crane and Norris that their similarly sardonic senses of humor resulted in their shared amusement over the more freakish developments in the world of high fashion.

One would also like to know how many more times Norris put to sea with Crane, Scovel, and other journalists through May, as he again and again had good reason to repeat the complaints about military inaction with which he had peppered "News Gathering at Key West." How he spent the rest of the month is a matter for speculation and not of record.

Opéra comique was the term bandied about as the Spanish-American War refused to act like a real war and as the correspondents themselves contributed to the cause for merriment. Not long after the declaration of war, American newspapers began announcing that the U.S. army's invasion of Cuba would begin at any moment, only to have to trumpet the same news again and again through May and well into June. The troop transports would not depart from Port Tampa until 14 June 1898; but on 5 May J. M. Maxwell was proclaiming in a headline for the *Chicago Daily Tribune* that "Troops May Go to Cuba Today." The next day in the same newspaper, W. J. Rouse sounded the alarm as though for the first time, "Invasion Is Imminent."[8] These and other premature declarations contradicted for a while the similarly vigorous pronouncements that Puerto Rico was to be invaded. One hardly knew what to think as Norris maintained his post at Key West.

Encouraging low seriousness of the kind that had upset Norris in "News Gathering at Key West" were other developments, for example, the earnestness with which some of those anxious for a "big" story magnified what they saw or had heard about second- and thirdhand. On 1 May, the Civil War veteran Ambrose Bierce, writing a war-commentary column for the *San Francisco Examiner,* could not keep a straight face before the bombastic language used by reporters to describe Admiral Sampson's 27 April bombardment of Matanzas. Indeed, his own newspaper, in true Hearst style, had run these preposterously sensational headlines on 28 April: "American Guns Boom Liberty to Cuban Ears / Shot and Shell Thrown into the Fortresses of Matanzas / Spanish Forts Fall before Us / . . . Not a Shell Struck the American Ships, / but Many Spaniards Are Thought to Have Been Killed."[9] Bierce roared over proclamations such as "Demolished Matanzas in Eighteen Minutes" after having determined the simple fact of the matter: Sampson "suffered no damage and probably inflicted none." Cuba's Governor-General Blanco confirmed the latter point, cabling to Madrid that the U.S. bombardment had resulted in only one fatality—and the victim was a mule. Bierce took special delight in reminding his readers of this journalistic humbug of late April when criticizing how in mid-May the press had again magnified the importance of an engagement at the southern port city of Cienfuegos: "It was a trivial affair, hardly superior in dignity to our glorious victory at Matanzas, where several of our big cruisers and a monitor pot-shotted a Spanish mule."[10] The artist Frederic Remington was less amused by what was, and was not, taking place in Key West and off the Cuban coast. Bored to tears by the tedium of the blockade and the absurdity of not being able to find anything worthy of a drawing, he wired Hearst, asking to be released from his *New York Journal* contract. Norris was as ludicrously situated at the expense of *McClure's,* having to resort to imagination to picture what was invisibly transpiring beneath the "quiet and calm."

As Norris returned from his first trip to the Cuban coast on 9 May, and as Admiral Sampson's ships steamed toward Puerto Rico for their 12 May bombardment of San Juan, however, events were beginning to take a more serious turn.

On 11 May 1898, the Spanish shore batteries at Cardenas opened fire on the torpedo boat *Winslow* and the cruiser *Wilmington*. The consequences disclosed over the succeeding days were far from droll. On the immediately disabled torpedo boat, five men—following the lead of Ensign Worth Bagley—gallantly exposed themselves to enemy fire as they secured a tow line from the *Hudson*. They died while doing so, and at Key West the medical officer W. R. Hall and the good sisters at the Convent of Mary Immaculate treated the wounded. On 12 May, the Reverend Gilbert Higgs conducted the funeral service for four of the *Winslow's* dead at St. Paul's Episcopal church on Duval Street. Over two hundred followed the hearse to the city cemetery for their burial. The next day there was a separate service for Bagley, a handsome, popular twenty-five-year-old who had been a football hero at the U.S. Naval Academy. Fourteen survivors from the *Winslow* and fifty other sailors and marines accompanied the coffin to the *Mascotte,* which carried it to Jacksonville, Florida, where Bagley's brother was waiting to accompany the corpse to Raleigh, North Carolina, for interment. This was a sobering story of the good dying young, and it was read in newspapers across the country. He was thus mourned nationally as the first hero of the war. What Norris and his colleagues at Key West knew, but which the vast majority of them did not report, was the gruesome manner in which he died. The *Chicago Times-Herald* was one paper that did not demur: "[S]truck by an exploding shell," Bagley fell on the splintered deck of the *Winslow* with his "face blown off."[11]

Not until 14 May did the nation know the fate of another who was, in fact, the first soldier slain. While Bierce would make light of what occurred at Cienfuegos on 11 May, Seaman John Reagan died from fire from the shore while cutting a cable connecting Havana and Santiago de Cuba.

Reported a day earlier, on 13 May, was news of a less melancholic but as serious action. The "Gussie Expedition" was an event about which Norris afterwards learned every detail from his fellow San Franciscan and traveling companion throughout the Cuban campaign, James F. J. Archibald. Archibald wrote and drew for the *San Francisco Evening Post,* publishing his war articles as well in *Scribner's Magazine* and *Leslie's Weekly.* He was a key figure in Norris's life through early August, when they returned together to New York City from Cuba, for he opened a good many doors because of the influence he wielded within the army. He was an aide-de-camp of Colonel Evan Miles as well as a reporter; and the California-based First Infantry for which Miles was the senior officer as the war began was formerly under the command of the man now directing the American army being assembled in Florida, General William Shafter. In Tampa, Colonel Miles assumed even higher status as he was put in command of two additional regiments, the Sixteenth and Twenty-fourth infantries. Archibald was, in short, as well connected as possible within the Fifth Army Corps that went to Cuba.

Departing the night of 20 April 1898 with the "First Foot" from the Presidio in San Francisco, Archibald had reached Port Tampa by ship from New Orleans on the thirtieth. Shortly thereafter he had a filibusterlike experience of the kind about which Norris's hero had fantasized in *Moran of the Lady Letty.* On 9 May, an antiquated Mallory Line sidewheeler that brought a smile to many a newspaper man's face left Port Tampa loaded with ammunition and supplies to be delivered to the Cuban insurgents. Under the command of Captain Joseph H. Dorst of the Fourth Cavalry, the *Gussie*—a name that also amused—sailed with Archibald and companies E and K of the First Infantry, stopping at Key West the next morning, and then proceeding toward Havana after being towed out to sea by a pressboat under Sylvester Scovel's command, the *Triton.* They turned westward toward Mariel, searching for a locale at which it appeared safest to attempt an anchorage and deciding upon Arbolitos Point near Cabañas. Facing rifle fire from the woods before them, the soldiers, supported by the guns of the naval vessels accompanying the *Gussie*, rowed ashore and landed for the first of the U.S. army's encounters with the Spanish; and they accomplished their mission. Archibald earned a special place in history that day: shot in his left arm, he was the first American wounded in combat on Cuban soil. He was in his glory, and in several *San Francisco Evening Post* articles he did not neglect opportunities to remind his readers of his command of one of the boats that went ashore and to relate how the healing of his arm was proceeding.

On 10 May, when Norris might have enjoyed Archibald's influence to find a place among the soldiers from his home state as the *Gussie* stopped at Key West, it was not he but *McClure's* other correspondent, Stephen Bonsal, who went aboard and thence to Cuba. Bonsal's "The First Shot on Cuban Soil" appeared in the July 1898 issue of *McClure's*—which contained nothing signed by Norris.

As the blockade continued, preparations for the invasion were proceeding at Tampa. Before Norris departed Key West, he may have participated in one of the grand *opéra comique* events of late May, given the press boat arrangement McClure had made with the *New York World*. There were "ten or more correspondents" aboard the *Sommers N. Smith* when it steamed eastward on 24 May, according to the photographer Jimmy Hare. Hare named only five: George Lynch, Charles M. Pepper, Walter Scott Meriwether, and the *World* reporter with whom Norris had sailed on the *Three Friends*, Sylvester Scovel. Stephen Crane joined the group at sea, leaping from the *Three Friends* onto the *Smith's* deck off the northern coast of Cuba.[12] Only one historian, who does not cite his information source, has placed Norris aboard the *Smith*.[13]

The newsmen were searching for what had come to be known as "The Phantom Fleet," Spanish warships on their way across the Atlantic to Cuba, or perhaps Puerto Rico, or perhaps even the East Coast of the United States, where they might bombard major port cities. The invasion of Cuba could not begin until the status of this threat was determined; and the *Smith's* journalists circumnavigated Cuba with the hope of sighting the squadron. They returned to Key West without success on 2 June, to learn when they debarked that the only press boat that sailed all the way around Cuba during the war had passed the "Phantom Fleet" shortly before the U.S. navy sighted it hiding in the harbor of Santiago.

With them or not when they returned to Key West, Norris by then had no reason to remain on the island. With the Spanish armada trapped at Santiago, the troop ships could sail from Port Tampa. There need be no more delays.

Before he left, he enjoyed a special treat. An "old friend" like the *Helena* had just arrived to join the noble crusade against Spain. The battleship *Oregon* built at San Francisco's Union Iron Works, about which he had written a dithyramb for *The Wave*, had completed its sixteen-thousand-mile voyage from San Francisco to Key West after taking on coal at Jupiter, Florida.

Again in Tampa after a voyage northward of approximately twelve hours, Norris once more had reason to hold forth about great disappointments. He found a situation in which the Lord of Misrule reigned. A good deal of suffering had already occurred, long before the American soldiers experienced the devastating effects of the Spanish Mauser rifles. For weeks most of the soldiers had marked time there, outfitted with uniforms inappropriate for Florida in late spring. The government-issued shirts, for example, were flannel. Lieutenant Edward A. Selfridge and his New York Seventy-first Volunteer Regiment had escaped from the cold and wet Camp Black at Hempstead, Long Island, only to suffer from high temperatures and a degree of humidity to which most Americans who lived at considerable distance from the Gulf of Mexico were wholly unaccustomed. What Selfridge and James F. J. Archibald did not tell Norris he could easily see for himself in a short while. Potable water that was not brackish was in short supply. As in Key West, where enteritis was a malady that everyone knew as well as malaria and yellow fever, shallow wells were responsible for considerable abdominal distress and potentially fatal illnesses. Supplies of various kinds, including food, were difficult to access in freight cars because they had been packed in unsystematic ways; and, because of poor record keeping, it was difficult to determine which boxcars contained what. Rail access to Port Tampa from Tampa was wholly inadequate to the traffic as the date of embarkation neared: two rail lines came into Tampa, but—hard to believe—only one ran from the city to the port, where only nine ships could be docked and loaded at one time.

It was one thing to witness what Jeannette recalled from one of Norris's letters, the preparations for the shipping of caskets to Cuba. However gloomy a cause for reflection, they were a necessity. Not so understandable was the U.S. army's being so obviously unprepared for the task assigned it by the Congress.

Things were little better once the flotilla had sailed. Richard Harding Davis, for example, noted that the "water on board the ship was so bad that it could not be used for purposes of shaving. It smelled like a frog-pond or a stable-yard, and it tasted as it smelt." But while the gentlemanly Dick Davis would not even splash his face with it and "drank appollinaris water or tea," the soldiers "had to drink the water furnished them, except those who were able to pay five cents a glass to the ship's porter, who had a private supply of good water which he made into lemonade." That this bon vivant's name had since the early 1890s brought to mind among literate Americans the sophisticated and expensive cuisine of Delmonico's Restaurant in New York City does not mean that he was exaggerating when he focused on the low quality of the food available aboard: "villainous" was the word for it.[14] The canned meat consumed in Cuba came to be known as embalmed beef.

Unfortunately, what was true of Port Tampa and the transports would be true of Cuba, too, where the war effort was plagued by poor transportation capabilities, disorganization in supplies distribution, and—worst of all—inadequate medical support for those brought down by the Spaniards' terribly efficient riflemen. Reading the various contemporaneous descriptions of this war and historical studies published since is an eye-opening experience, so patently incompetent were those involved in planning the Cuban campaign and so great were the sufferings of their trusting victims in uniform. At war's end, Theodore Roosevelt and other high-profile figures in Santiago had to bypass the military bureaucrats and appeal directly to President McKinley and the public to bring home immediately the malnourished and fever-ridden Americans before they all died, not from bullets and shrapnel but from disease.

When one turned away from the confusion about them in Tampa, little relief was offered by the spectacle of sand, palmettos, pines, and scrub oaks; and, today, most will strain to imagine just what it was like in June, in a world without air conditioning anywhere. Selfridge and Norris—and James F. J. Archibald, who had been there for over a month—had to find it a heartening development that their departure would take place so soon as 8 June. Selfridge and the others in Company K of the New York Seventy-first boarded the *Vigilancia* after suffering a humiliation engineered by the former police commissioner of the city from which they hailed. Originally scheduled to depart on the *Yucatán*, the Seventy-first arrived at the dock to find that Theodore Roosevelt had decided on the spot to make their assigned transport the Rough Riders'; and, since this celebrity group had already boarded, the rule of possession being nine-tenths of the law applied. It was, of course, no mere stroke of luck that Captain Roosevelt, just stepped down from the position of assistant secretary of the navy, had his way. Selfridge and his fellows had to stand at ease in the sweltering heat until their reassignment to another transport was accomplished.

Norris fared much better. The majority of the journalists sailed on the coastal steamer *Olivette*. Thanks to Archibald's influence, Norris instead went to General Shafter's flagship *Segurança* to join a few other privileged correspondents. Archibald, aboard by 6:00 P.M. on 7 June, gloated in print over being so happily situated: "There are six correspondents on board the flagship, and we have been the cause of various objections raised by the other ninety-and-nine on the *Olivette*. They do not relish the idea of being on another ship while a few are so near [army] headquarters [aboard the *Segurança*]." The other five—Frederic Remington, Casper Whitney, Richard Harding Davis, Frank Norris, and Stephen Bonsal—"and myself constitute the literary end of the party on the flagship."[15] Norris thus enjoyed access to the commander of the First Division's Second Brigade, Colonel Evan D. Miles. Moreover, in the midst of General Shafter's staff, he was literally at the center of military intelligence and thus had the opportunity to record something of the inside story on refinements of the invasion plans. Perhaps the most delightful development, though, was Norris's meeting and getting to know one of the American artists he admired most, Remington—the inestimable master of equine portraiture whom Norris had praised without qualification in *The Wave* in 1897, dubbing him "Frederic the Great."[16] Archibald related to Walker that the two men enjoyed each other's company during the voyage to Cuba; and later, standing on a hilltop next to an artillery battery, Norris and Remington would observe together one of the major actions of the war at El Caney.

Conditions on Shafter's flagship were otherwise only a slight improvement over those in Tampa. Davis, who continued to whine over matters great and small, felt neglected, never suspecting that his domineering personality and penchant for carping might have had something to do with how others responded to him. He complained that

> life on board the head-quarters ship was uneventful for those who were not in command. For [the military leaders and their staffs], tables and desks were spread in the "social hall," and all day long they worked busily and mysteriously on maps and lists and orders, and six typewriters banged on their machines until late at night. The ship was greatly overcrowded; it held all of General Shafter's staff, all of General Breckinridge's staff, the Cuban generals, the officers and five hundred men of the First Regiment, all the foreign *attachés*, and an army of stenographers, secretaries, clerks, servants, couriers, valets, and colored waiters.[17]

Jammed together thus on 8 June as the loading of the transports was completed, the multitude waited for their departure from the bay. The fleet did not sail that day. Would nothing go right in this war?

There was a report of the presence of Spanish war vessels along the route it was to take, through the Old Bahama Channel and around the eastern end of Cuba to the vicinity of Santiago. Archibald understood on 12 June, when the flotilla had still not left Tampa Bay, that "several Spanish warships, cruisers and torpedo boats, were sighted outside Edgemont Key."[18] And so new problems developed. Soldiers found that the temperatures below deck in the uninsulated ships were ovenlike. Horses and mules were perishing in the holds, and offloading of their corpses along with the animals still alive commenced. Before long the ships had to be resupplied as the hiatus continued.

Morale, already a problem, did not improve with this anticlimax of nearly a week's duration.

The report of Spain's second "Phantom Fleet" then proved unfounded. By the morning of 14 June the reloading of the transports was completed, and the water supplies of all were replenished. At last, at 9:00 A.M., both the ships that had been at anchor and those tied to the dock began to move toward the mouth of Tampa Bay. They carried 819 officers, 15,058 enlisted men, thirty civilian clerks, eighty-nine correspondents, 272 teamsters and packers, and 2,295 horses and mules.[19] Aboard as well were regimental bands. As Shafter's flagship joined the fleet, Norris and Archibald had the peculiar experience of hearing "Hail to the Chief" played, out of sync, by fifteen different bands on as many ships.

What could be more appropriate than cacophony? Yet, four months after the sinking of the *Maine* and almost two since the war formally began, there was reason to take heart. The yankees, or gringos, were at last on their way.

WITH NORRIS AT EL CANEY

Once in the Gulf of Mexico, the thirty-one transports formed three columns and proceeded south toward Key West with the protection of the U.S. navy. Ten hours later, the *Olivette,* refitted as a hospital ship and carrying the other correspondents, followed in the flotilla's wake. Thus began on the *Segurança* what Stephen Bonsal termed the six "days of almost unbearable monotony." There was "not an incident to divert the mind" as, day after day, the jettisoned horses and mules, dead from heat prostration, bobbed in the ship's wake, "floating about in the opalescent seas." The "wigwagging from the other ships with their sad stories of want of water and the spread of typhoid fever" was constant.[1] For 580 nautical miles, all coped as best they could as they learned firsthand what Norris had learned in early May about winds, currents, and rough seas off the Cuban coast. Seasickness was rampant.

Turning west on 20 June 1898 at Punta de Maisí on the southeast coast of Cuba, the fleet anchored off Guantanamo after a day of choppy seas and more seasickness than usual. The *Segurança* went ahead to meet the *New York,* which had arrived off Santiago on 30 May. Admiral Sampson left the *New York,* sailing west past Santiago with General Shafter on the *Segurança* to Aserraderos. There, at an encampment in the hills, the two met with the Cuban general Calixto García and other officers in the insurrectionist army to discuss the part that the revolutionaries would play in the taking of the primary target of the Americans, Santiago. They were accompanied ashore by Richard Harding Davis, Frederic Remington, Casper Whitney, Stephen Bonsal, and—Archibald informed Walker—Archibald and Norris. High seriousness was, of course, in the air. The spectacle of General Shafter waddling from the beach and making his way up a mountain path to García's camp, however, had to have tickled Norris. Photographs of him on horseback now naturally elicit laughter—and sympathy for the dumb brute that had to bear such a burden in 1898. Political cartoonists were merciless when caricaturing the rotund figure topped with a pith helmet. Shafter weighed well over three hundred pounds, or, as the joke went among journalists, one-sixth of a ton. He spent much of the war not only to the rear of the front lines but either seated or supine in his tent, unable to deal with the heat and depending upon his senior officers in the field to modify appropriately his strategic decisions.

The Cubans at Aserraderos suggested that Shafter land his troops at Daiquirí, a village sixteen miles to the east of Santiago. It was estimated that fewer Spanish soldiers were there than at Siboney, seven miles down the coast to the west. Siboney did offer much better anchorage for the offloading of troops and supplies, but it would be used only after the army had secured it by land from Daiquirí.

Because of bad weather, the next day came and went without a landing of troops. According to Lieutenant Charles D. Rhodes, who was aboard the same ship as Norris, tedium was broken only at midday with the spectacle of a waterspout one-half mile in height, toward the foot of which one of the warships fired. Cheers rose from all of the transports as something even more spectacular was seen, a direct hit that eliminated this threat to the fleet.[2] It was not until 22 June, after the bombardment of Daiquirí concluded, that Shafter sent in the first wave of soldiers, forbidding journalists to accompany them. Only a few managed to sneak ashore that day, and Norris was not among them. Archibald, as an aide-de-camp rather than a journalist, did not have to engage in subterfuge. He received permission to land with the First Infantry and see it plant the American flag on Cuban soil; with Brigadier General William Lawton leading this and another regiment in the Second Division, he also participated in the taking of Siboney.

On 23 June Norris landed at Daiquirí. As he relates in his article "With Lawton at El Caney," he delayed there only long enough to readjust his pack and then push on westward.[3] Down the road to Siboney, his path would cross Stephen Crane's once more, and he would catch up with Archibald and the First Infantry. Selfridge and the New York Seventy-first—in the First Division—began debarking from the *Vigilancia* at Siboney as Norris was trudging there; and, while it appears that the two old friends did not meet then, Norris soon received news concerning action seen by Selfridge's regiment. Fighting had commenced in earnest four miles along the inland trail toward Sevilla.

Wrote Norris about the next day, "One morning we heard sounds of firing off in the hills, and ten hours later knew that Guasimas had been fought." That is, on 24 June, according to the memoir of George R. Van Dewater of the Seventy-first, Selfridge's regiment was dispatched to Las Guásimas, immediately to the north, where reinforcements were desperately needed by the Second Cavalry Brigade—the First, Tenth, and First Volunteer (Rough Riders) Cavalry.[4] A woefully inexperienced Captain Theodore Roosevelt, Colonel Leonard Wood (formerly President McKinley's private physician), Crane, Davis, and other correspondents had walked into an ambush on two narrow trails running through dense foliage. There they took their first painful measure of the firepower of Spanish marksmen hidden from sight, who knew the terrain well and how best to conduct war on their home ground. One officer and fifteen men were killed; six officers and forty-six men suffered wounds. Hit in the spine, Edward Marshall of the *New York Journal* saw the end of his tour of duty.

Over the next few days, according to "With Lawton," the rhythm to which Norris had become accustomed at Key West and Tampa resumed: "[N]othing extraordinary happened. We marched and countermarched, broke camp and pitched it." Norris depended upon Archibald to mitigate the very "basic" conditions in which they lived. Archibald's great contribution to their mutual cause was his invention of a hammock in which they slept. Norris also enjoyed the benefit of a guide made available by Colonel Miles to his aide-de-camp Archibald. Norris christened this fellow drawn from the ranks of the Cuban rebels Bonito—that is, "Handsome"—because he was so remarkably ugly. He proved "a great help," remembered Archibald when interviewed by Walker. Bonito also proved a case in point, as Archibald—like many another American journalist and soldier—gradually developed a lower and lower estimate of the character of the Cuban freedom fighters. Explained Archibald to Walker, Bonito had served the Cuban cause for three years; yet, what he was most proud of was not his dedication but the immaculate condition of his rifle. Archibald noted that even the interior of the barrel was shiny, and he later learned the secret of Bonito's success. He had never fired the gun.

Lawton's division did not remain long in the vicinity of Siboney but began its move northward. Norris was pleased when it "moved forward by easy

marches to a point on the Santiago road about three miles south of El Pozo."
He was now much closer to what would become the scene of the major battles
of 1 July. But no fighting was in evidence, and the routine of standing still
recommenced. For "three days we lay there, trying to keep dry," he lamented
in "With Lawton." Cuba's rainy season had commenced that year in mid-May.
Another problem was the inadequate and poor food—beans, bacon, hardtack—even at this early stage of the invasion. A varied diet, observed Norris,
meant "devising new methods of frying mangoes in bacon grease." Not only
in "With Lawton" did Norris register such conditions. In a late August 1898
Oakland Enquirer interview, he returned to this theme when describing the
trials endured between 23 and 30 June:

> Think of marching all day up trails with seventy pounds on your back; for
> lunch, hardtack with a little sugar and water, getting drenched to the bone
> in the afternoon, eating half-raw bacon because the wood was so wet the fire
> wouldn't burn, coffee that was yellow water, and soaked hardtack, and then
> turning in to sleep in wet clothes and under wet blankets. We had this sort
> of continuous performance for seven eternal days . . . but our hardships were
> trivial when you think of what the men, the regulars, went through with, or
> were killed or died trying to go through with, as the case might be.[5]

Yet another trying situation developed as time passed. Norris soon found
himself in the rear rather than the vanguard of the Fifth Army Corps as
brigades passed the regiment to which he was attached, heading northward
toward El Caney and westward to the San Juan Heights.

It was, apparently, at about this time—between 28 and 30 June—that
Norris met Lieutenant Selfridge. Selfridge told Walker,

> I was not surprised to see [Norris] turn up one day shortly before the battle
> of San Juan. Jim Archibald was with him [and] they were a sorry looking
> couple—I know Norris never knew how to rough it [and] if Jim Archibald did,
> his appearance was decidedly against him—neither had any kind of equip-
> ment [and] apparently they had not been near soap [and] water or a razor for
> some time. They had no rations [and] were ravenously hungry, so I not only
> invited them to share my next meal with me, but gave them hardtack, bacon
> [and] coffee to take with them.

It was also at this time that the hammock mates, in the company of the artist
and illustrator Howard Chandler Christy, visited a knoll to the northwest of
El Pozo where on 1 July the Americans would position an artillery battery as
the assault on the San Juan Heights began.

On 30 June 1898, ten thousand Americans were ready to confront slightly more than a thousand Spaniards who enjoyed the advantage of high ground at the town of El Caney and at the San Juan Heights. Word circulated that action would commence the next day, and then the move toward the two fronts began. The First Volunteer Cavalry broke camp at noon, waited and waited, and then—in the midafternoon—followed the First and Tenth Cavalry. Theodore Roosevelt succinctly characterized the ordeal in *The Rough Riders:* "The heat was intense as we passed through the still, close jungle, which formed a wall on either hand. . . . Once or twice we had to wade streams. Darkness came on, but we still continued to march. It was about eight o'clock when we turned to the left and climbed El Poso hill."[6] As did Selfridge's regiment, the Rough Riders assembled there for the attack on the Heights that, to their west, defended Santiago.

Experiencing similar delays, Norris and Archibald, accompanied by Bonito, went another way. They passed to the east of El Pozo and continued north toward El Caney. Late that afternoon the artillery battery commanded by one of the tragic figures of the war, Captain Allyn Capron, rumbled by. Norris does not acknowledge this when mentioning him by name in "With Lawton," but Capron's son—also a captain—had been shot to death during the first significant engagement with the enemy, at Las Guásimas. At 5:00 P.M., Norris departed from his encampment with General William Ludlow's and Colonel Evan Miles's brigades. They positioned their regiments approximately one mile away from El Caney, Ludlow's to the southwest of the front and Miles's (including San Francisco's First Infantry) to the south, serving as a rear guard should the Spanish attempt to flank Ludlow from the west. General Adna R. Chaffee's brigade at the southeast would bring the total number of American soldiers in place to 5,400 (versus the 520 Spanish in El Caney under the command of General Joaquin Vara del Rey). Like Roosevelt, Norris found the march hard going. He had purchased a horse from a Cuban in Siboney, Archibald told Walker, and having to lead it through the muck of the foot trail was no easy matter:

> The column, consisting of Lawton's division, went forward through the night by fits and starts, now doubling when the word was passed back to close up, now halting in mud up to its legging tops, . . . now moving forward at a snail's pace, and now breaking up completely, when the tired men eased belt and blanket-roll and dropped into the drenched grass by the roadside for a moment's rest. The march had not been long, but it had been wearisome; for

on Cuban trails the men must march in single file, and the column is always elongating or contracting.

° ° °

Then there was the monotonous squash of many boots churning up the mud of the road, the click of swinging cups against bayonet scabbards, the indefinable murmur of a moving army that recalls the noise of the sea or of forests.

° ° °

We went into camp toward ten o'clock, under orders to light no fires, nor even pipes, and to talk no louder than a whisper. One wondered at this until, some half hour later, when we were eating our supper of hardtack, cold bacon, and water, we heard . . . the enemy's pickets, not a quarter mile away.

Again, Norris did not comment on Captain Capron's son, and his single direct reference to Las Guásimas in "With Lawton at El Caney" was distinctly uninformative. In his description of the march to El Caney, however, Norris did register his understanding of the hard lesson learned at Las Guásimas: "There was no talking in the ranks." On 24 June, many of those ambushed by the Spanish had been ambling along, chattering as though on their way to picnic when the firing upon them commenced.

Overnight Capron had hauled his artillery up a hilltop over a mile to the southeast of El Caney. Norris was there by 5:00 A.M. with other journalists, gulping down breakfast as the battery made final adjustments. Across a field covered with tall grass and bushes and dotted by groups of palms, El Caney "was plainly visible—red roofs, a white wall or two, the twin towers of the church." Before the town "on a sugar-loaf knoll" stood a stone fort, "a blockhouse of unusual size." On its "one salient tower" was "a flame-colored tongue of bunting, the flag of Spain." Not noted by Norris were five smaller, wooden fortifications about the town, surrounded by trenches and barbed wire the way the blockhouse was. Suddenly, to the left, Ludlow's brigade began firing, and Norris had the warrant for displaying one of his signature traits as a writer who specialized in aural effects. How does a modern battle *sound*?

The firing of rifles on the battlefield is not loud; it is not even sharp when heard at a distance. The rifles sputter, as hot grease sputters, the shots leaping after one another in straggling sequence, sometimes in one-two-three order, like the ticking of a clock, sometimes rushing confusedly together, and sometimes dropping squarely in the midst of an interval of silence, always threatening to stop, yet never quite stopping; or again coming off in isolated rolls when volley firing is the order. But little by little the sputtering on our left gathered strength and settled down at length to steady hammer-and-tongs work.

Norris then surrendered to the temptation to use another well-exercised routine in his repertoire.

As in "News Gathering at Key West," Norris is surprised to find that things-as-they-really-are do not measure up to his expectations. Sighting a Spanish cavalry troop leaving El Caney, riding westward down the road to Santiago, Captain Capron decides to shell that column. Norris criticizes the artillerymen in the way that he used to berate unaccomplished football players when he served as a sports commentator for *The Wave*. "I confess to a certain amount of surprise and a little disappointment. I had imagined the handling of a battery in actual battle would be a little more businesslike, that the orders would be given with more precision. The captain was on foot, his coat and waistcoat were off, and at every movement he hitched his suspenders over his shoulders. The men did not hurry in serving the guns. They went to the caissons, groped among the ammunition, and talked excitedly while they were cutting the fuses." No wonder that the patently undisciplined battery failed at its attempt.

Norris does not so directly criticize Capron for another matter. But, perhaps engaging in self-censorship, he recorded a faux pas that, at the end of the day, would have been a subject of discussion for those evaluating the performance of Lawton's division. Ludlow was moving forward at the left toward the stone fort fronting the city; General Chaffee's brigade had at dawn advanced to a ridge to the east of El Caney. Lawton's men were coming within range of the stone fort and the wooden blockhouses, and Capron did not seem to be taking this into account while indulging in pot shots at the fleeing Spanish horsemen. There was every reason to make haste in destroying the blockhouse; further, Capron needed to make every shot count, since he was working at a disadvantage from the start. The mere four guns at his disposal were small ones. Light artillery only was available to Capron and to Captain George Grimes, who shelled the San Juan Heights that same day. Thanks to the mismanagement of the army's administration, no heavy artillery was to be had.

What actually happened when the Spanish cavalry appeared, though, is called into question by Archibald's *San Francisco Evening Post* article on the morning's activities. Archibald exculpated Capron and directed his criticism instead at the men who were manning the cannons; he went on to celebrate what he saw as a successful outcome, crediting Frederic Remington *and himself* for saving the day. Modesty is not one of the distinguishing traits of Archibald's war articles. He reported that when the artillerymen

> had sighted their pieces [on El Caney] and charged them and were about to fire . . . Frederic Remington and myself discovered, through our glasses,

a column of horsemen leaving Caney, going toward Santiago. I immediately reported the fact to General Lawton . . . and he ordered the guns to be trained on them, but none of the artillerymen could make them out. We endeavored to show them, but at the range, about a mile and a half, they could not find them, so Remington took one gun and I the other and trained and sighted them. They fired shrapnel into the column with great effect, scattering them like chaff before a gale.[7]

How Norris's account can be reconciled with Archibald's is not clear—certainly not as clear as the latter's penchant for grandstanding before his readership.

Norris's criticism of Capron's battery, however, is of brief duration in the full context of "With Lawton at El Caney." He briskly moves on to sound a more positive note, expressing his admiration of Capron's accuracy when his guns fired on the stone fort. "Such gunnery as we witnessed that morning I never again expect to see equalled. It could not be surpassed for it was well nigh perfect." With a succession of shots and adjustments for range, Capron found his hilltop target, and Norris reveled in the spectacle of each explosion, as "great fountains of brown earth sprouted from the location of the trenches and rifle pits, and pinwheels of smoke, mortar dust, brick, and stone whirled off the surface of the fort as the great projectiles struck. . . . And now the flag was down."

Norris was not the only journalist to report the most impressive—or luckiest—shot of the day, which took down the Spanish flag. He was, though, the man uniquely qualified to render what occurred next. It was the stuff of adventure romances surcharged with positively pornographic representations of violence. Norris treated the scene as though he were fashioning a short story, and thus he was truly in his element at last as he described what happened after the flag pole was shattered.

> "Look out, now!" cried the battery captain. "There'll probably be a man come out to set it up again; get him with shrapnel, if you can."
> A man did come out; we could see him dodge from an embrasure around an angle of the fort.
> "He'll be on top in a minute; get him now with shrapnel. Who's ready there? Whichever gun is ready, fire!"
> Number four fired. The shell was still screaming when we caught sight of the man scrambling upon the ledge . . . near the broken staff. Then, right over the fort, right over the staff, and over the Spanish soldier's head, the little ball of white cotton leaped into view. "Got him!" shouted the entire battery, as the bursting shrapnel wiped the man from the wall . . . as a sponge would wipe a slate.

The journalists, too, cheered wildly.

The bombardment of El Caney went on for much longer than anyone in the Fifth Army expected would be necessary. The advance of the soldiers up the hill also took hours more than Shafter and Lawton anticipated. At one point General Shafter, who badly needed additional support at the San Juan Heights, directed the Second Division to withdraw—an order that General Lawton ignored. And Norris wondered at how the Spanish at the fort could continue their resistance, given that five out of every six shells fired by Capron struck the trenches they occupied. Recognition of the enemy's fortitude was mandatory, and Norris tipped his hat to them. "We shall remember these Spanish soldiers of El Caney for not until late in the afternoon . . . did they finally consent to leave—what was left of them." His was not the only American testimony to the mettle displayed by the enemy. The Cuban response was different. The Cubans beheaded forty Spanish soldiers who were turned over to them after the cessation of hostilities.[8]

It was a curious war. Support for it in the United States had much to do with inflammatory descriptions of Spanish cruelty in the press; but the Americans in Cuba soon discovered that the revolutionaries, when they had the upper hand, were indistinguishable in their behavior from, and just as inhumane as, their oppressors. There were other, less gruesome developments that are just as puzzling today. At noon on 1 July, for example, the siege and the defense of El Caney simply stopped. The Spaniards and Americans took a lunch break of more than two hours. It was not until three o'clock that Norris could first clearly see the Americans reanimated, as they moved up the hill before the fort and the town, "a dozen tiny specks scattered out in an irregular line in a grain field. . . . Then, far to the left, more specks . . . running about like excited ants, advancing always. . . . The battery held its fire now; our men were too close to the enemy. The end was beginning" as the soldiers converged upon the stone fort. The observers with Norris were "all beside themselves in the tension of the moment." And now the article reaches its climax: "Then suddenly the charge began, full in view now, far off at the base of the sugar-loaf hill with its battered, shrapnel-shattered blockhouse. There they were, our soldiers, our men, crowding upward, the moving specks converging into a mass, a great wedge-shaped mass that pushed up and up and up the slope of the hill. We could hear them cheering, so at least we thought, and we ourselves cheered—no, it was not cheering." Here Norris, the literary naturalist and evolutionary theorist, takes the opportunity to interpret human nature in terms of how stressful situations may reveal the primitive, animalistic heritage of modern man, the "brute within" that unexpectedly asserts itself to dominate the civilized, rational self. An atavistic lapse occurs. The group of which Norris is a member does not do anything so refined as cheer the American victors but responds in the manner presumably typical among cave men: "[N]o, it was not cheering; we yelled inarticulately, just a primitive bellow of exultation, an echo of the stone age!"

Having recovered his composure, Norris left Capron's battery, riding down the knoll with Bonito and leaving his mount with him in a grove of palms. He wanted to experience vicariously the charge up El Caney hill; and, "following in the wake of the charge," he climbed the sugar-loaf hill and gained the blockhouse and its lines of trenches.

Norris's state of exhilaration soon dissipated. As the firefight continued behind the blockhouse, at the northwest corner of El Caney, Norris had his first close look at the consequences of the rifle and pistol fire and, worse, the shrapnel that "smashes its man, flings him down, and drives and dints him into the dirt." The interior of the fort was "a horror, the trenches beyond description." The dead Spanish soldiers were to be seen elsewhere, too: in "grisly postures halfway down the slope" and lying in an adjacent pineapple field. The "strange, acrid, salty smell of blood" was in the air.

Across a stream from the stone fort was the town itself, from which civilians in various stages of distress were soon beginning to emerge. As Archibald and he approached it, they passed women on the verge of hysteria who permitted "themselves to be herded like sheep." One whose husband had been killed during the shelling was sobbing and "biting her hands in an excess of grief." A matron of sixty-five was carrying on her back another "surely more than ninety." He had seen nothing so extreme during his South African adventure.

Entering El Caney, Norris was enlisted to aid a corporal in a search for Spanish soldiers, reflecting later that Archibald and he were "foolhardy in going along." Archibald once more offered a different version of events in which he, one may not be surprised to learn, played a more prominent role. According to him, not a corporal but he himself was in charge: "I finally obtained permission to go into the town, and, with Frank Norris and a corporal and three men, we went through El Caney."[9] Whatever the exact circumstances, it was the single known instance in his life in which Norris actually pointed a gun at anyone. "We cocked our revolvers. . . . It was uncanny work to let one's self into these houses." They took into custody forty wounded men in one of the larger buildings fronting the plaza. And then, when Norris was on his own, "Two Spanish soldiers in a blockhouse, and unhurt, gave themselves up to me, thinking perhaps that I was some sort of officer. I had them walk in front of me, and allowed myself a full breath only when I was once more under the cover of our own rifles." Unlike the Cubans, the Americans treated their captives with considerable civility, which—according to Archibald—surprised the Spanish, since they fully expected execution on the spot. When he returned to Siboney, Norris saw one of his prisoners in the stockade there. "We recognized each other simultaneously, and shook hands as old friends, across the barbed wire, genuinely glad to meet again."

Before they left El Caney that evening, Archibald and Norris shared a shocking, truly unforgettable experience. Both of them would include it in their accounts of the day. Norris was succinct: "In the mayor's house I came suddenly upon the body of a plain-looking girl, lying on the floor, her hair across her face like a drift of seaweed. She had not been shot; she had been stabbed!" Archibald was more expansive when writing for *Leslie's Weekly:*

> In one old house, that looked as though it might belong to a wealthy family, was a most tragic scene. On the floor was a beautiful young girl, dressed richly in a loose gown of light material, and sticking into an ugly wound in her breast was a knife, while the blood had formed a black pool on the tiled floor. A few feet away a Spanish officer sat with his head on the table, drunk. Through the barred window one could see the little old church, and at the opposite side the open door led into a beautiful court-yard. No amount of shaking could arouse the man, and he slept on, heedless of the evidence of a terrible crime. I had him carried away, and never saw him again. I pulled the knife from the body and drew a sheet over it, and wondered if there was no limit to the horror of war.[10]

In his illustration for the first of Archibald's nine "What I Saw in the War" articles for *Leslie's Weekly,* Howard Chandler Christy topped Archibald as he further idealized the "plain-looking girl" Norris found. He also rendered the scene yet more melodramatically, adding a narrative touch involving an American soldier arriving alone and too late to prevent the foul deed committed by an unidentified assailant. Most noteworthy in these three portrayals of the scene, though, is the omission of an important datum by all three gentlemen, which Norris later confided in a letter to Ernest Peixotto.[11] Neither Norris nor Christy nor Archibald publicly disclosed the fact that the young woman had been raped.

The conclusion of "With Lawton at El Caney" records a transition from the jubilation over victory earlier on 1 July to Norris's somber emotional state by that evening. He began the day by wanting to see all, and he had seen too much by the time Archibald and he joined the march of Lawton's division away from El Caney. Psychologically and physically, they were all exhausted. "Our army had won a victory, had fought from dawn to dark and had defeated the enemy. It was the time for triumph, for exultation. Instead of that, a feeling of depression lay upon us, and upon the soldiers with whom we were marching. There was no great talk. It was a sorrowful army marching through the twilight after victory." The next day would take him to another scene at which the fighting continued.

18

FROM EL CANEY TO SAN JUAN
HEIGHTS TO SANTIAGO

All was not as he made it seem when Norris fashioned the dramatic conclusion of "With Lawton at El Caney." The finale featured the striking picture of the wearied but resolute Second Division pressing on to the San Juan Heights, to support the Americans in their drive toward Santiago. "It was ten o'clock at night when we again set our faces toward Santiago," wrote Norris. He made no mention of the nearly disastrous event that occurred down the road in the early hours of 2 July 1898.

With El Caney in American hands, General Lawton's next step was to lead his men toward the Heights, but for the second time within twenty-four hours a major miscalculation occurred. The first had to do with General Shafter's strategic plan for 1 July. Shafter, who spent the day in his tent coping with heat prostration, assumed that Lawton would have taken El Caney by 10:00 A.M.—by noon at the latest. He was then to march toward the Heights. Not until 4:00 P.M., however, did he quell Spanish resistance, and—as Norris noted—it was dark before the victors could begin their trek to the second front. According to Archibald, Lawton misjudged the capabilities of his Cuban guides, who took his division directly toward Santiago and thus into harm's way, rather than to the south and then westward to the Heights. "We supposed," wrote Archibald, "we were on the way to El Pozo, but the guides . . . lost their way, and after marching the whole division until late that night it was discovered that we were on the wrong road."[1]

When Norris and he caught up with the First Infantry—"three miles down the Santiago road" was Norris's estimate of the distance in "With Lawton"—they found that it had become the advance guard. They settled down for a much-needed rest among the bivouacked soldiers along the sides of the road, and then they heard the order to extinguish all campfires. The First Infantry pickets had detected Spanish soldiers ahead. Not wanting to involve his fatigued division in a night fight in unfamiliar territory with a force of undeterminable strength, the general ordered a silent march to the rear at 3:30 A.M. Recalled Archibald, "we marched all that night through utter darkness" back toward El Caney and thence down the road to El Pozo. "The morning came on so gradually and we were so tired that no one seemed to notice it, and what brought it to our notice was the commencement of firing over on San Juan Hill."

Along the way on the muddy road to El Pozo, they took turns riding Norris's horse and had another extraordinary experience. They met the celebrity who liked to think that the Spanish-American War was more properly the *New York Journal's* war. Mounted on one of the horses he had purchased in Jamaica immediately before his arrival at Siboney was William Randolph Hearst. He had come to Cuba on his yacht *Sylvia* to see the campaign for himself and to report how the American army was wielding its terrible swift sword to free a people whose interests were his own. He too had spent the greater part of 1 July at El Caney and especially enjoyed learning of his correspondent James Creelman's fearlessness when leading the Americans to victory at the stone fort. Norris, Archibald, and he chatted at length. Hearst, apparently no worse for wear after the rigors of the day and much of the night, dismounted to allow Archibald to ride his jet-black steed. They parted near El Pozo, Hearst going on to Siboney to arrange for the cabling of the El Caney story he had written. "A good fellow," Archibald remarked to Franklin Walker.

When Archibald also told Walker that Norris "was under fire during the entire campaign," he meant that, from 1 to 3 July especially, and then during the intervals alternating with truces that followed, they both visited the front lines repeatedly as the army devoted itself to two tasks: advancing westward toward Santiago in the face of Spanish resistance, and extending the American lines to the north and then west. The plan was to encircle Santiago and cut it off from reinforcements said to be on their way from Manzanillo. "From the earliest dawn until late at night the fighting went on," wrote Archibald about 2 July at the San Juan Heights, "as our forces slowly fought their way nearer to the Spanish lines" with virtually no artillery support. Behind the skirmish line, snipers concealed in royal palms also "did deadly work" with their Mausers, the smokeless powder used by the Spanish making detection of their perches very difficult.[2] Lieutenant Charles D. Rhodes succinctly characterized their experience that day in a diary he later published. Ensconced in the Spanish trenches taken by the Americans the day before, Rhodes and those immediately about him enjoyed their secure position as "a continuous stream of bullets passed over our heads, cutting the leaves from the trees." Even in the trenches, though, one could not feel wholly safe. "As I started to write these notes," continued Rhodes, "a piece of six- or eight-inch projectile fell at my feet not six paces away. It was yet hot to the touch when I picked it up."[3]

When interviewed after the war, Norris described what it was like at the San Juan Heights:

> At San Juan I saw a whole regiment lying for two days under the Cuban sun, and I never knew what heat could be until I got under that sun—for two days under the sun, lying flat, just under the crest of a hill without food and without water, with not a hand's breadth of shade, every man weighted down with his blanket roll, haversack, canteen, ammunition belt and rifle and hanging on there like bulldogs, never a whine, and doing that rather than abandon the position they had taken by assault, and go back 250 yards, where there was plenty of shade, water and protection from the Mausers. When the rain came they would be drenched to the skin, when the sun was out they would be almost literally roasted, when it was intensely cold (towards three in the morning), they would be chilled to the marrow. For two days those men neither ate nor drank, nor slept, nor even had the satisfaction of walking to stretch their legs. The moment a man raised up he would get a Mauser [bullet] in the head or neck. Some of them went delirious from the sun and lack of food and water and rest, and got down on their knees and cried like little children and it would have been easy and perfectly safe to retreat. I don't believe the idea of falling back even entered their heads. We would go off for hours on our own business and come back and find them still there. We would cook our lunch, eat it, go up the hill and they would still be there, we would turn in and sleep the night through, wake up in the morning, train our glasses on them, the position, and there the regiment would be, just the same as ever, wet and starving and thirsty, harassed by sharp shooters, but hanging on like the thousand bulldogs they were. You can't whip such men, you know. You can kill them, you can starve them in Andersonville or you can blow them up in Havana harbor but you can't whip them. That's how and why we won this war, the American soldier did it, not the officers.[4]

This is not to say that Norris and Archibald were constantly at the front. "Several days" after the victory at El Caney, wrote Archibald, they followed

Hearst to the coast where they exchanged greetings with the Spaniards in the Siboney stockade whom they had taken prisoner in El Caney. Like another Second Division aide-de-camp, Lieutenant Rhodes, it was Archibald's duty to travel about, serving as the eyes and ears of the Second Brigade's Colonel Miles. Thus, after spending the day at the Heights on 2 July, Archibald slept at El Pozo that night, until the sounds of a heavy bombardment woke him. The guns of the "Phantom Fleet" commanded by Admiral Pascual Cervera y Topete had "commenced throwing shells into our lines" just before the Spanish soldiers in the trenches subjected the Americans to withering rifle fire.[5] This action continued until noon on 3 July, when Shafter sent Captain Joseph H. Dorst, who had led the First Infantry during the *Gussie* expedition in May, to parlay with Spain's General José Toral. Under a flag of truce he delivered a demand for unconditional surrender.

General Shafter did not overplay his hand when sending such a message. The U.S. navy could bombard the harbor and city at any time; American soldiers were encircling Santiago from the east; and Shafter then thought, incorrectly, that Spanish reinforcements from Manzanillo had not reached Santiago. But the decisive event of 3 July was the destruction of the Spanish fleet as it tried to reach open sea from Santiago Harbor. That day, Archibald and Norris left the Heights and visited the wounded at the field hospital. What they found was alarming.

On 1 July, 205 Americans died, and the Spanish wounded 1,180.[6] By 3 July many more had been shot or hit by shrapnel. At the hospital, Archibald reported in *Leslie's Weekly,* they found men who had been without water, food, sleep, shelter, or medical attention for forty-eight hours.[7] Norris described the same scene in a late August 1898 letter to Ernest Peixotto,[8] also recording the pathetic evidence of the lack of foresight of those military planners whose display of incompetence in Tampa in June was merely a prelude to their performance in Cuba.

George Kennan's unsettling description of this field hospital in *Campaigning in Cuba* more than confirms Norris's negative assessment. It turns out that Norris unintentionally made the situation appear better than it was when he referred to a "Division hospital" in his letter to Peixotto. At this time a single facility established three miles east of Santiago on 29 June served the wounded of all three divisions. At Tampa, Shafter had at his command over fifty ambulances; yet he brought only three to Cuba, and Kennan never saw more than two. By the evening of 1 July ten surgeons and approximately forty attendants staffed the hospital; they were overwhelmed by the hundreds needing attention through 3 July. Kennan found men suffering their wounds on the ground, waiting for attention in the open air for hours. The "hospital" comprised only three tents. Things were little better for the wounded once they had been treated. Explained Kennan,

> Of course the wounded who had been operated upon, or the great part of them, had to lie out all night on the water-soaked ground; and in order to appreciate the suffering they endured the reader must try to imagine the conditions and the environment. It rained in torrents there almost every afternoon for a period of from ten minutes to half an hour, and the ground, therefore, was usually water-soaked and soft. All the time that it did not rain the sun shone with a fierceness of heat that I have seldom seen equaled, and yet at night it grew cool and damp so rapidly as to necessitate the putting on of thicker clothing or a light overcoat.

To make matters worse, the medical personnel had removed the shirts of many of the wounded at the bandaging stations immediately behind the front lines. They arrived at the field hospital "half naked and without either rubber or woolen blankets; . . . . there was nothing to clothe or cover them with."[9]

On 5 July, Archibald and Norris returned to El Caney. As he told the readers of his article "*Comida:* An Experience in Famine," Norris was now riding a "broncho pony from Southern California."[10] Where and how he found his new mount he does not explain; presumably it came from San Francisco with the First Infantry. The ride into El Caney late that afternoon was, related Archibald, a stomach-turning experience: "[T]he half-buried bodies of the Spanish soldiers . . . produced a horrible odor." Moreover, it seemed "impossible to conceive that human beings could live in such filthy surroundings as there were at Caney while the refugees occupied the town."[11]

These refugees from Santiago had fled what they thought was the unleashed wrath of General Shafter. When demanding the surrender of Santiago, he had threatened to bombard the city. Around midnight on 4 July, not Shafter but the American fleet shelled the fortifications at the harbor's mouth, triggering panic among the populace, who assumed the city at large was the target. A mass exodus of civilians began early on 5 July. El Caney was the destination of most of them. George Kennan estimated the number of those who had fled Santiago at fifteen thousand;[12] Norris put the figure at thirty thousand. Whatever the exact number, the noncombatants jammed the town, arriving without food and with few belongings other than the clothes on their backs. Hunger and sickness were already apparent everywhere, since food had been in short supply in Santiago. Disorder in El Caney was rampant among thousands occupying space appropriate for a few hundred. Archibald registered a second time in the same article the noisome conditions he found: "There was no attempt at any sanitary arrangement, and the mango-peelings, refuse of all fruits, and filth indescribable made an unbearable stench that bred disease on all sides. The water supply . . . came from a little brook that flowed through one side of the village. Children were bathing in it, women washing their clothes, and this same water supplied the drinking-water of the place."

How filthy and malodorous were the surroundings in which Norris spent two days? Archibald's disgust requires contextualization to be appreciated. He did not complain in this manner about Siboney months later when he wrote his memoirs for *Leslie's Weekly;* and that locale too was, to say the least, sordid.

George Kennan, like Norris and Archibald, had spent a significant amount of time in and out of Siboney since 24 June, and he was aghast at what he found upon each return. When the debarkation of the troops began there, the surgeons attached to the U.S. navy recommended the incineration of all of the houses to eliminate obvious sources of infection. Instead, these hovel-like structures were occupied, and the order to disinfect them was given. "Chloride of lime," however, "was not used anywhere, and the foul privies immediately in back of and adjoining the houses were permitted to stand in the condition in which they were found, so that the daily rains washed the excrement from them down under the floors to saturate further the already contaminated soil." When Kennan returned from a trip to the front on 9 July, conditions had become worse.

> No attempt, apparently, had been made to clean or disinfect it; no sanitary precautions had been taken or health regulations enforced; hundreds of in-credibly dirty and ragged Cubans—some of them employed in discharging the government transports and some of them merely loafers, camp-followers, and thieves—thronged the beach, evacuating their bowels in the bushes and throwing the remnants of food about on the ground to rot in the hot sunshine; there was a dead and decomposing mule in one of the stagnant pools behind the village, and the whole place stank.[13]

Again, Archibald did not comment on this noisome environment. But El Caney, at which he encountered no visual nor olfactory evidence of "sanitary arrangements," demanded attention in print.

Norris, ironically on two counts, did not comment. The first irony is that Norris remains today the most olfactorily oriented novelist in American cultural history. But, as with the victim of rape he discovered in El Caney, he chose in *"Comida"* to write in the genteel manner preferred by most editors of respectable magazines. The second is that, with the publication of *McTeague* in early 1899, Norris would become notorious in American literary history for his unsqueamish descriptions of "unmentionables" in 1890s high- and middle-class culture. Yet, it was Archibald who wrote about the fetid in the frank but "tasteless" manner then thought of as naturalistic.

The two men's articles on their experiences in El Caney over the next two days differ—as do many accounts of the war—in minor factual details. More worthy of note, though, is Norris's restraint when depicting a large mass of people on the verge of starvation. Here in El Caney was the "human animal" under stress, its veneer of civilization worn away by the "struggle for existence" already well advanced. In chapter 9 of *Vandover and the Brute,* Norris pictures a situation in which the law of self-preservation sanctions the killing of a man when not doing so means one's own death or the death of one's child. But in *"Comida"* he chooses not to use his recollections of El Caney as the means of fabricating a Zolaesque description of an atavistic lapse. Instead, Archibald assumed the persona of the literary naturalist in a second way, as he described the devolved creatures before him in precivilized, amoral, and blatantly animalistic terms.

Captain Stewart Brice of General Shafter's staff arrived at El Caney on 6 July to deliver two wagonloads of *"comida"* (food). Norris did not even briefly note the event. Archibald, however, described "such a scene as might be expected of a pack of hungry wolves, but not of human beings. . . . They fought, scratched, and bit each other like dogs. Well-dressed women fought with paupers, women struck each other, and children were trampled in the fight for food." Later in the same article, Archibald related that he witnessed a similar scene on 5 July, a few hours after Norris and he had arrived and prepared corn mush for distribution to the refugees:

> [H]undreds of hungry people were clamoring—yes, more than that, they were fighting—for a chance to get at a portion of the food. They all had a dish of some sort . . . and they used these dishes as weapons. They struck each other over the head in their wild attempt to get to the front. Women and children, weak from hunger, fainted and were trampled in the mad rush. I could think of nothing like it so much as the dropping of a piece of meat to a pack of hungry wolves. They were not human, they lost all semblance of human beings in their actions; they were actually animals, nothing more.[14]

While Archibald here played the role of the "American Zola," a decidedly more humane Norris displayed in "*Comida*" only compassion in the face of misery, striving more conventionally to elevate what he saw in El Caney to the level of tragedy:

> It was yet light enough to see—to see about three thousand children, half of them naked, the other half ragged beyond words. What a mass! Close to the gate the jam was terrific; they were packed as sand is packed, so that they moved, not as individuals, but as groups, and masses, swaying forward and back, and from side to side, without knowing why. I could see but a pavement of faces, crushed together cheek to cheek, upturned, pinched and agonized, shrill-voiced with the little rat that nipped and gnawed at their poor starved stomachs. Farther on, where the press was not so great, the children reached toward me empty cans, pots, pails, tin cups, vessels of all sizes and descriptions, and they put their hands (not fingers) to their mouths with always the same cry of unutterable distress, "*Comida! Comida!*"

Note that no one strikes another with cans, pots, pails, and tin cups. There is no pitiless competition for food. It was essential, Norris apparently concluded, to preserve the dignity of his subjects if the pathos of their condition was to stand forth.

The Red Cross staff worker on the scene in El Caney was an elderly man from Brooklyn whom Norris had met previously, perhaps on several occasions since the arrival of Clara Barton's Red Cross team at Key West on 29 April. Both men were there and at Tampa at the same times, and their paths crossed again at the field hospital near El Pozo and at Siboney. Archibald made clear why Norris, when composing "*Comida*" after his return to the United States, interrupted his story of suffering humanity to execute a portrait in homage of C. C. Bangs. Wrote Archibald, "The noble man gave his life for this work, for he contracted fever from this foul place and died."[15] His resistance compromised by the sixteen-to-eighteen-hour work days he put in while at El Caney, he did not survive a bout with calenture.[16] Norris's eulogy of Bangs—whom he mistook for a physician—reads:

> Let us pause to make a note of Dr. Bangs, for he was at last the right man in the right place. He was a stout man, with a very red face and a voice like the exhaust of a locomotive. He wore an absurd pith helmet battered out of all shape, and his beard was a fortnight old. But there was the right stuff in Dr. Bangs. Early and late, hot or cold, rain or shine, the doctor toiled and

toiled and toiled; feeding the thousands, building fires, sending this man for wood and that man for water, perspiring, gesticulating, bellowing, but in the end "getting the thing into shape," directing and dividing the stream of supplies till the last refugee was fed.

The feeding of the multitude at El Caney by Norris and Archibald, under the direction of Bangs, took place across the main plaza of the town at the walled terrace of a church then serving as a kitchen. Norris and Archibald labored from 5 to 7 July, cooking batch after batch of mush, creating a soup from two cows that Generals Lawton and Ludlow made available, and waiting for the delivery of cases of condensed milk.

The milk never arrived, and Norris and Archibald noted the consequence: the death of an infant. Norris opted for succinctness when announcing this, trusting in the power of understatement: "I know of one little baby who died in its mother's arms for lack of it." Archibald was more expansive and, in his narrative, he once more appears more Norrisean than the novelist who would three years later, in *The Octopus,* similarly situate a starving Mrs. Hooven on the streets of San Francisco begging for food for her little daughter. Archibald pictured the frantic mother thus:

> "Will you not give me some milk for my baby?" she begged, with tears streaming down her face. "He is only a few weeks old, and yet has had nothing to-day . . . he will die." She fondled the tiny child in her arms, and the anguish pictured on her face was really terrible.
>
> "There is no milk here," I answered, "but some may turn up soon." And yet I knew only too well that there was none nearer than Siboney, over ten miles away, and with no possible way of getting it.
>
> "But my baby will die," the poor mother wailed. "I do not care for myself; I am starving, but I don't care. It is for my baby."
>
> Yet there was no food for that little one, and I heard of the half-demented mother, the next morning, carrying the little lifeless body about, crying and moaning and refusing to put it down. It had starved in her very arms while she was helpless. Yet this was only one case in many.[17]

Archibald does not inform his reader why he told the woman it was possible that milk might arrive soon. Norris does, making clear why, by 7 July at the latest, he was rapidly developing the negative attitude toward the Cuban allies already commonplace among correspondents.

> We stayed at Caney nearly all the next day, helping the doctor, who but for us was entirely alone. As for the relief committees composed of Cubans, the less said of them the better. They were supposed to cooperate with the

doctor, and might have been of immense service during those terrible three days of famine. They were there, these committees, for we saw them as they came to offer congratulations and to be presented. But beyond this their activity did not go. They did absolutely nothing—lighted never a fire, gathered never a stick of wood, drew never a quart of water.

"I don't want your congratulations!" the harassed, overworked doctor bellowed: "I don't want your presentations! I want wood, I want *water*, and oh, I want those fifty cases of *condensed milk!*"

The loss of this condensed milk was a grievance which the doctor could not forget. To the Cubans had been entrusted the duty of transporting fifty cases from Siboney to Caney. The milk never arrived.

In his article about "The Surrender at Santiago," Norris would only imply what he makes explicit here concerning the Cuban revolutionaries and the inevitable bureaucrats: Generally speaking, they were worthless as allies, choosing to depend upon the Americans to do what was necessary not only to defeat the Spanish but to care for the civilians affected by the war.

Since Norris's racism and imperialistic orientation have, over the past several decades, received much attention from race-focused commentators reluctant to be associated in any way with European and American imperialism, his unflattering imaging of the Cuban rebels may be dismissed as a predictable gesture. But Norris, in his Spanish-American War writings, casts them in a negative light only twice. In fact he took the high road and chose not to document in greater detail the behavior of the rebels—unlike many another American journalist. For example, the photographer Burr McIntosh, throughout *The Little I Saw of Cuba*, dismisses them all as thieves and cowards whose principal motivation throughout the Cuban campaign was to exploit the largesse of the Americans; his memoir is an angry exposé in which he constantly comments upon their contemptible, self-serving behavior. As to their courage, or lack thereof, it was common knowledge after 1 July that a large rebel force—a "couple of thousand," reported Archibald—had been held in reserve to the northwest of El Caney the day that town was taken. In fact, they had been ordered by Shafter not to participate in the assault on El Caney.[18] But Archibald was incensed because, after the cessation of hostilities, when the Cubans might have aided the American effort by stopping some Spaniards who were fleeing to Santiago, they did nothing. "Later in the afternoon," wrote Archibald, "the Cubans came down from . . . the hills where they had been watching the Americans mowed down for their benefit. There they sat, eating their rations—American rations—while the good Americans were sacrificing their lives for them, and not offering to go into the fight." When some proceeded to strip the dead Americans of their valuables, Archibald was not at all displeased by what he saw in

> a part of the field where a colored regiment had been fighting, and [where] some of their men were searching for the bodies of their comrades. A little way off a couple of Cubans were going through the pockets of a dead colored soldier, when a big sergeant caught sight of them. He did not hurry, nor did he call to them to desist, but walked calmly up to where they were carrying on their dastardly work. I wondered at his calmness, but my wonderment was soon satisfied, for as he came up they merely looked up and started to work again, when, quick as a flash, he drew his six-shooter and shot them both dead, and calmly returned his pistol and knelt beside the body of his comrade to make it ready to be carried to where the burying squad was at work. Three or four officers saw the act, but not one of them even reprimanded him.[19]

Elsewhere, Archibald again does what he never did for the Cubans. It is difficult to dismiss his attitude toward the Cuban insurrectionists as merely a manifestation of racism, given the appreciative treatment he once more gives African American soldiers—"four big, husky, colored troopers of the Tenth Cavalry"—who admirably maintained order in the town.[20]

Norris exaggerated when he declared in "The Surrender at Santiago" that it was the Americans alone who won the war. Even Archibald admitted that *some* Cubans fought. Still, it is unlikely that the American soldiers of various racial and ethnic backgrounds would have clamored for a retraction.

It was at the church where they cooked and distributed corn mush and soup to the hungry that Norris and Archibald spent their two nights at El Caney and Norris took notes on his immediate surroundings. Ever sensitive to the incongruous, he pictured in *"Comida"* the bizarre transformation that a house of God had undergone in wartime. Holes had been knocked in the walls so that the Spanish could fire their Mausers from within. Cartridges, bayonet scabbards, and haversacks were strewn across the floor and even littered the altar. The church had also served as a hospital during the siege. The evidence of surgery conducted therein was palpable; Norris and Archibald discovered an amputated arm half-buried in the soil on the terrace. The Episcopalian Norris was chagrined to confess that he too contributed to the "extremely and intensely profaned" environment. He had to tether his pony in the church, since the locals would carry off anything that could be sold, and he used the communion rail as a rack for his saddle. A breeze then stirred the soiled altar cloth, spooking the pony, who "for a moment had that whole place by the ears." Perhaps motivated by the desire to save something of high aesthetic value not yet ruined, Norris removed a painting from its frame above the altar and rolled it up; and aide-de-camp Archibald, Walker was informed, was hard-pressed to prevent Norris's arrest for looting when military authorities discovered what he had done.

Capping the shocking sights, the heart-rending cries of the starving refugees, and the foul odors was yet another unanticipated experience at El Caney. When one encounters the bizarre in Norris's prose fiction and is inclined to dismiss it as a mere invention intended to startle the reader, it is helpful to recall that, in Norris's experience, life was capable of developments more outrageous than might be imagined by Rudyard Kipling, Robert Louis Stevenson, or even Emile Zola. Bangs demonstrated this as he came up behind Archibald and Norris as they warmed themselves before a fire before turning in for the night. He caught them by surprise when they turned at his approach and heard him exclaim suddenly "in that thunderous trumpet voice" of his: "'Well, fellows, here's something I do every night that you can't do at all!' and with the words he took out his left eye and polished it on a leg of his trousers. I was faint in an instant, the thing was so unexpected, so positively ghastly. Not even the sight of the division hospital, a week before, had so upset me." And the eerie, gothic experiences continued the next morn when they awoke after passing the night on the terrace. They had protected themselves from rain with boards they found in the church; daylight revealed that one, "coated thick with a glaze of dull red," had obviously been used as a platform for surgery. Then they saw the amputated arm sticking out of the dirt between them. Worse, Archibald told Walker that Norris discovered upon waking that, through the night, his head had rested on a Spanish amputee's leg.

After noon on 7 July they departed, leaving the Red Cross to continue its work. "We stayed and worked as long as we could," Norris explained, and then they turned from the sensational scenes of mass suffering to a prosaic annoyance that had become a constant for them: muddy trails and roads. As their "steaming horses toiled through mud, fetlock deep," on the road to the south, they thought again of what they had experienced at El Caney. The "vague murmur of the crowd in the plaza came back to us," Norris wrote in his conclusion, "prolonged, lamentable, pitiful beyond expression—the cry of people dying for lack of food."

Over the next several days, the series of truces initiated on 3 July came and went as Generals Toral and Shafter exchanged messages concerning the conditions of a surrender. On 11 July at 2:00 P.M. the firing ceased and was not renewed. Then, on 13 July, the two generals met personally for the first time under an old ceiba tree, afterwards known as the Surrender Tree, where they at last made real progress toward an honorable resolution. Still, Toral could not seal the agreement on his own. General Ramón Blanco in Havana—and Madrid—had to approve the terms of the surrender of Santiago. Finally, on 16 July, word of Spain's approval circulated among the Americans.

Following their return from El Caney on 7 July, Norris and Archibald divided their time between the front at San Juan Heights, the nearby division headquarters at the Hacienda Santa Cruz, and Siboney.[21] In mid-July the two men were visiting another hacienda that became the headquarters of the Second Division's Second Brigade on 12 July. Viewed from a distance, it dominated the landscape. Lieutenant Rhodes noted in his diary that it was conspicuous for many miles because it was overhung by a tall, strikingly beautiful flamboyant, or poinciana, tree.[22] Presiding within was not Colonel Evan Miles, who had fallen ill and sought treatment at Siboney on 10 July. The man to whom Archibald was now aide-de-camp, formerly a lieutenant colonel in the First Division, was Brigadier General Chambers McKibben. In "The Surrender at Santiago," Norris relates that Archibald and he arrived at the Hacienda San Pablo on 14 July.[23] Lieutenant Rhodes noted the same in his diary: "War correspondents, Frank Norris and Jim Archibald are our guests today"; they arrived as Stephen Bonsal departed.[24] Two days later, and with two good nights' rest behind them, Archibald and Norris were still euphoric over the positive change that had been wrought in their lives—"blissfully contented," wrote Norris in "The Surrender," "because at last we had a real wooden and tiled roof over our heads." He recalled that "even the tarantulas—Archibald shook two of them from his blanket in one night—had no terrors for us."

On 16 July, Norris and members of McKibben's staff were seated with their feet on the railing of the veranda. Norris ruminated over the San Juan Heights in the distance to the west—a "crest of hills, in a mighty crescent that reached almost to the sea," where the American army was entrenched, its Maxim and Hotchkiss guns and its Krag-Jorgensen and Springfield rifles ready for action. Norris imagined the soldiers at the Heights "alert, watchful, straining at the leash, waiting for the expiration of the last truce that had now been on for twenty-four hours." Doing so did not tax his imagination, though, since he had visited the front on 12 July, and he returned again for a compelling reason. San Francisco's First Infantry had moved forward to an advanced position as skirmishers.

Norris and his comrades began to sing. Inside the hacienda a supine General McKibben smoked his pipe and applauded their efforts. The war seemed very distant to Norris: "The night was fine and very still. Cuban fire-flies, that are like little electric lights gone somehow adrift, glowed and faded in the mango and bamboo trees, and after a while a whippoorwill began his lamentable little plaint somewhere in the branches of the gorgeous vermilion Flamboyant that overhung the hacienda." Even the dense, humid air, redolent with the smell of "vegetation that reeks and smokes and sweats," provided a pleasurable sensation, bringing to mind the "thick and stupefying," incense-suffused atmosphere of "the interior of a cathedral after high mass."

Here we encounter the sole record of idyllic experience in all of Norris's known war writings. He savored the moment in part because it offered such a pleasant contrast to what he had seen earlier that day. In his diary, Lieutenant Rhodes jotted down how Norris had dismounted at the hacienda that day to report on "the great distress seen along the Caney road—old women, bed-ridden and sick, hobbling along in the endeavor to return to Santiago" from El Caney.[25]

Norris's revery abruptly ends with the arrival of an orderly carrying a dispatch for the general. It is the great moment long awaited, the end of the Santiago campaign. After a three days' wait, General Toral informed General Shafter that Madrid had approved the surrender terms on the sixteenth.

The news was not wholly unexpected. Lieutenant Rhodes had already noted in his diary that General McKibben "left us early this morning to visit corps and division headquarters." He returned "to tell us that General Shafter has signed the articles of capitulation."[26] There is no jubilation in Rhodes's voice, though, for a simple reason. The surrender had been the subject of discussion since the fourth, and Shafter had already accepted Toral's modifications of his terms. But, though Shafter had signed the agreement, he had not yet issued a formal declaration that Toral had done the same. In short, it was not until the later arrival of the messenger on horseback with the official announcement of peace that there was finally a cause for celebration. Norris's reader, then, may expect something on the order of a grand tableau commemorating the historic event, or at least a vignette picturing the euphoria of the victors at Hacienda San Pablo.

But the reader of Norris's treatments of previous events will not be surprised by his decision to introduce a variation upon a familiar theme. This time, the "great disappointment" has to do with the notion that the "orderly that brought the dispatch should have dashed up at a gallop, clicked his spurs, [and] saluted." Instead, "he dragged a very tired horse up the trail, knee deep in mud, brought to, standing with a gasp of relief, and . . . pushed his hat back from his forehead." The novel reader and playgoer expects him to say with a crisp tone in the King's English, "'The commanding general's compliments, sir.'" Instead, he drawls, "'Say, is here where Gen. McKibben is?'"

The reader of "The Surrender of Santiago" may be surprised by the less obviously manipulated moment that follows, ringing true to human nature and, in consequence, proving more interesting than Norris's well-rehearsed skill at deflating conventional expectations.

General McKibben's reaction to the message? "'Hum,' muttered the general reflectively between his teeth. 'Hum. They've caved in.'" That's it, save for an afterthought concerning the First Infantry, which was then dug in at the front. The laconic general turns to Lieutenant Dennis E. Nolan of the "First Foot" and observes nonchalantly, "'Well, you won't have to make that little reconnaissance of yours . . . after all, Mr. Nolan.'" And what of Norris and the others? They have no idea how to respond to the good news. Rather than leap for joy, they stare together at a "little green parrot who lives in the premises" who then "trundled gravely across the brick floor." Norris relates that "for an instant we all watched her with the intensest attention." Neither words nor thoughts appear appropriate for the occasion. It is, psychologically, a true condition realistically depicted, and a master touch on Norris's part. "The Surrender," however, is not wholly the product of a literary realist. Norris was not at a loss for words, or hyperbole, when recalling what transpired the next day.

By the morning of 17 July, when Shafter made arrangements for the Spanish surrender in an open field outside Santiago, the general had had enough of the press. He gave orders to exclude journalists and Cuban soldiers from the proceedings. The correspondents could watch the surrender from a distance, through binoculars, if they chose. Crestfallen, Norris and Archibald nonetheless saddled up in case there might be last-minute exceptions, and luck was with them. They successfully appealed to one of Shafter's staff, his son-in-law Captain McKittrick, who told them to fall in at the rear of any one of the generals' staffs.

They were not the only ones who found a way to circumvent Shafter's orders. Later in the day, following the formal surrender ceremony when the

Americans occupied Santiago, many more journalists produced accounts of the raising of the American flag over the governor's palace in the city.

At the surrender itself, following trumpet marches and fanfares announcing his arrival, silence descended as General Toral rode forward from the city to meet Shafter, and the Americans received him with a show of great respect. They returned the sword of the slain commander of the Spanish fortifications at El Caney, whose extraordinary dedication to duty had elicited admiration from all who had observed his remarkable display of courage in the face of disaster. In the shade of a distant tree, the photographer James Hare, along with the majority of correspondents, bided his time during the ceremony, per Shafter's orders. He recalled for his biographer, "Everyone had at least a small box camera and had expected . . . to take a lot of snaps; but the universal retreat to the shade did not make for the taking of good pictures."[27] How they felt when they saw Archibald and Norris with a camera in hand on horseback only a few yards away from Shafter and Toral is easily imagined. The privileged view from Norris's saddle was thus doubly splendid:

> I cast a quick glance around the scene: at the Spaniards in their light blue uniforms, the red and lacquer of the *guarda civile*, the ordered Mausers, the trumpeters resting their trumpets on their hips, at our own array, McKibben in his black shirt, Ludlow in his white leggins, and the rank and file of the escort, the bronzed, blue-trousered troopers, erect and motionless, upon their mounts. It was war and it was magnificent, seen there under the flash of a tropic sun with all that welter of green to set it off, and there was a bigness about it so that to be there seeing it at all and in a way part of it made you feel that for that moment you were living larger and stronger than ever before.

At which point, a crescendo advanced in its development, the patriotic Norris—again astride his "little white bronco" that morning, as he later wrote in "The Surrender of Santiago"—took the leap to alt-C at his writing desk. Transcending time and space in his excitement, he proclaimed, "It was Appomattox again, and Mexico and Yorktown." He was certain that he was not alone in his perception of a world-historical event, no matter how silent were the soldiers looking on. "Back along the Spanish and American trenches thousands of men stood in line and watched, Santiago watched, and Washington, and Spain, and the United States, the two hemispheres, the old world and the new, paused on that moment, watching."

This was not his last peak experience. With the surrender concluded, it was time to enter Santiago. "Shall I ever forget that ride? We rode three abreast" toward the city, "always at a rapid trot and sometimes even at a canter, the general himself always setting the pace." Then, "after so many days of sailing, of marching, of countermarching, and of fighting," they had assumed possession of the long-sought prize, at which point Norris again moves beyond personal perceptions to interpret and express those of his fellow Americans. He becomes the omniscient author articulating for the cast of characters assembled about him a point of view that he is certain they share. In addition, he historicizes the moment in racial terms now largely archaic but quite familiar to his own generation:

> Here we were in the city at last, riding in, hoofs clattering, sabres rattling, saddles creaking, and suddenly a great wave of exultation came over us all. I know the general felt it. I know the last trooper of the escort felt it. There was no thought of humanitarian principles then. The war was not a "crusade," we were not fighting for the Cubans just then, it was not for disinterested motives that we were there, sabred and revolvered and carbined. Santiago was ours—was ours, ours, by the sword we had acquired, we, Americans, with no one to help—and that the Anglo-Saxon blood of us, the blood of the race that has fought its way out of a swamp in Friesland, conquering and conquering and conquering, on to the westward, the race whose blood instinct is the acquiring of land, went galloping through our veins to the beat of our horses' hoofs.

As if this omission of the role played by the African Americans and those soldiers of Mediterranean extraction were not enough to periodize his perspective and provoke amazement in today's readers, this ecstatic Anglo-American dashed yet further into the realm of the politically incorrect: "Every trooper looked down from his saddle upon Cuban and Spanish soldiers as from a throne. Even though [I was] not a soldier, it was impossible not to know their feeling, glorying, arrogant, the fine brutal arrogance of the Anglo-Saxon, and we rode on there at a gallop through the crowded streets of the fallen city, heads high, sabres clattering, a thousand iron hoofs beating out a long roll, triumphant, arrogant, conquerors."

One is not surprised to learn from Walker's interviews with Norris's widow that Frank very much liked another author of the time who thought and wrote similarly—Theodore Roosevelt, whom he met a week or so later and with whom Archibald and he dined in Santiago on several occasions.

There remained one other climactic experience that day. At noon, sharp, after General Shafter and some of his officers had dined as guests of Santiago's governor, the Americans assembled before the governor's palace. A band played "The Star-Spangled Banner" as the American flag ascended the flagpole mounted on the roof, which Norris recalled as "perhaps the most intense" moment of the campaign. "I have heard the *Miserere* in the Sistine Chapel, and in comparison with the raising of the flag over the city of Santiago it was *opéra comique*." Again Norris builds a crescendo, ending "The Surrender of Santiago" with quasireligious imagery and nationalistic *éclat*:

> For perhaps a full minute we stood with bared heads reverently watching the great flag as it strained in the breeze that, curiously enough, was now steady and strong, watching it as it strained and stiffened and grew out broader and broader over the conquered city till you believed in the glory of it and the splendour and radiance of it must go flashing off there over those leagues of tumbling water till it blazed like a comet over Madrid itself.
>
> And the great names came to mind again: Lexington, Trenton, Yorktown, 1812, Chapultepec, Mexico, Shiloh, Gettysburg, the Wilderness, Appomattox, and now—Guasimas, San Juan, El Caney, Santiago.

John Philip Sousa's march "Stars and Stripes Forever" followed the national anthem. Heard next was the popular air the Americans had constantly sung, hummed, and whistled through the campaign, "There'll Be a Hot Time in the Old Town To-night."

That evening, Archibald and Norris had good reason to wonder, What next? They would not join the relatively few correspondents who went on to Puerto Rico for the brief campaign conducted there.

Archibald remained attached to the staff of General McKibben, who served as the military governor of Santiago. Like Lieutenant Rhodes, with whom Norris and he shared some meals at the Café La Venus across the square, Archibald had access to lodging at the palace over which Old Glory now flew. They stayed for one week, during which time Norris endured pronounced symptoms of malaria. He may also have contracted any number of collateral diseases, given the unsanitary conditions in Santiago and virtually every other locale he had visited since 23 June.

Norris recovered sufficiently to warrant their move to more spacious quarters across the square. "After the first week at the palace," wrote Archibald, "I occupied the ground floor of a fashionable restaurant as a sleeping-apartment by swinging my hammock from a heavy sideboard to the grill-work in the door." When the proprietor of Café La Venus showed up a few days later, Archibald persuaded him to accept the arrangement and to do the cooking, "although we had nothing but plain army rations to cook."[28] In free hours, Norris and Archibald played poker, their wagers consisting of military decorations they had begun collecting. Their souvenirs of the surrender of Santiago included a Mauser rifle and a portion of the Spanish flag that once flew over the palace; the latter was still in Norris's possession when he was interviewed in San Francisco in late August.[29]

On 20 July, General McKibben was relieved of the onerous task of imposing and maintaining order upon Santiago as the refugees continued to return, businesses reopened, and normalcy was more or less restored. He withdrew with Rhodes to the hacienda San Pablo, where he resumed his regular duties. Replacing him was the commanding officer of the Rough Riders, Leonard Wood, M.D., who had risen from colonel to major general since late June. A prime consideration leading to his installation as governor was the pressing need to clean up the pest house that Santiago was and to lower the incidence of new medical cases among the American soldiers. (He did not succeed.)

Archibald's arrangement with his restaurateur-landlord blossomed. The owner was not only gifted in the preparation of sauces that transformed rations into "some very excellent Spanish dishes" but, when Archibald appropriated some flour, he displayed noteworthy bread-making talent. Archibald invited Wood and Theodore Roosevelt, now a colonel, to visit. In part because the proprietor also had an "excellent stock of wines," they and a good many other officers began joining Norris and Archibald for meals. It "was not long before the commissary department got in quantities of food from the ships, and through General Wood's orders I arranged for the restaurant-keeper to purchase government supplies, and he soon opened his establishment to the public at reasonable prices."[30]

The improved diet and medical care did not, however, reverse the effects of Norris's maladies. A few other transports took veterans of the campaign back to the United States before theirs departed. Still, the *Iroquois,* a Clyde Line passenger ship converted to take the Fifth Army to Cuba from Tampa on 14 June, was one of the earliest to leave Santiago. Newspaper accounts differ with regard to when the *Iroquois* departed, citing 31 July and 1 August.[31] But Norris was back in New York City thirteen days before Edward A. Selfridge, now a captain of the New York Seventy-first Volunteer Regiment, debarked at Camp Wikoff at Montauk Point, Long Island.

The weather was fair, and it was an uneventful voyage. Archibald told Walker that the ship was bound for Puerto Rico and changed course for New York upon the proclamation of peace between the United States and Spain, but his memory had failed by 1930. The signing of the peace protocol took place seven days after Norris and he debarked at Manhattan. Moreover, if there was such a change of orders, it occurred before the *Iroquois* departed Santiago with a mere twenty-one passengers and an empty cargo hold, for its assignment was to sail directly to and take on supplies at New York City and then transport them to Puerto Rico. In transit to Puerto Rico, it was also to onload soldiers at a port in the South.[32]

The *Iroquois* arrived at New York at 7:00 A.M. on 5 August 1898. Before Captain E. Kemble took his ship to its dock, the passengers went onto the quarantine boat *James W. Wadsworth,* where health officers disinfected their clothing and other effects; there Norris and Archibald bathed as well. That afternoon the city's health officer examined the men aboard, ordering the quarantine of none. At 3:00 P.M., Norris and the others boarded the tug *C. R. Stone* and landed at Pier 3 at the foot of Moore Street on the East River.[33]

It must have seemed much longer, but it had been only three months since Norris crossed the East River to visit Lieutenant Selfridge at Camp Black.

19

A QUICKENING PACE

When Norris came back to New York City from Cuba, he was not quarantined by the medical authorities. But, in fact, he was in a debilitated condition as he made his way to his apartment on West Thirty-third Street. All that is known of what he was able to do professionally before going to San Francisco to recuperate is that, on 12 August 1898, he signed the contract for the Doubleday and McClure publication of *Moran*.[1] He did, however, take the time in a letter sent on 11 August to tell Ernest Peixotto of his immediate plans. Declining an invitation to visit Peixotto in Chadds Ford, Pennsylvania, he recalled the hardships at El Caney, the discovery of the raped and murdered young woman, and the suffering he witnessed at the field hospital near El Pozo. "I want to get these things out of my mind and the fever out of my blood and so if my luck holds I am going back to the old places for three weeks and for the biggest part of the time I hope to wallow and grovel in the longest grass I can find in the Presidio Reservation on the cliffs overlooking the ocean and absorb ozone and smell smells that *don't* come from rotting and scorched vegetation, dead horses and bad water."[2]

According to his widow, recurring fever was nothing new to Norris, thanks to either dengue or an initial malarial infection—the "African fever"—contracted in the Transvaal. But he ran high temperatures every afternoon after he reached his mother's rooms at the Hotel Pleasanton, and he was almost as sick as James F. J. Archibald, who required hospitalization.[3] As of 27 August

1898, when Norris's return was first written up in *The Wave*, he was up and about in San Francisco, giving interviews. The *Oakland Enquirer* treated him as a celebrity exciting "much interest not only because of his experiences at the front during the Cuban campaign but also his success as a California author. . . . singled out for especial privileges" as a journalist, "along with Stephen Crane, Richard Harding Davis, and Frederic Remington." The interviewer announced the forthcoming publication of *Moran* and touted Norris's skill as a fiction writer whose "virility and intensity of purpose reminds one of Victor Hugo." He brought with him from Cuba not only a piece of the American flag that flew above the governor's palace in Santiago but "another souvenir of his experiences in the shape of the Cuban malaria, which has told severely on his otherwise robust frame. Were it not for the change of his appearance his friends would hardly realize through what ordeals he had passed, for he quite ignores personal suffering in his enthusiasm over the American soldier." The interviewer looked forward to the publication in *McClure's Magazine* of his war articles, which "will not appear until the holidays."[4]

The *San Francisco Chronicle* interview was of the same cloth, save that Norris used the occasion to exonerate so far as he could the New York Seventy-first Volunteer Regiment. On 16 July the *New York World*, in an article by Sylvester Scovel, had charged the regiment with cowardice during the 1 July attack on the San Juan Heights.[5] Its rival, the *New York Journal*, began slamming the *World* for maligning the regiment, thus precipitating an outpouring of articles and testy editorials on the facts of the case. Declaring "I happen to know something of this matter," Norris—who was not at the Heights but El Caney when the alleged show of spinelessness occurred—sympathetically pleaded the regiment's case: "They were in a tight place, and were mercilessly hammered with shrapnel" on the heavily wooded, muddy path that came to be known as "Bloody Bend." Still, he observed that they did halt when they "should have marched on further to a more protected position"; and the men did become "panicstricken" as sharpshooters "were picking off their officers." Norris acknowledged a lack of discipline among the men and a want of confidence in the officers. But, he declared, "Captain E. A. Selfridge, who hails from California, and Major Koech, were two of the very few officers who kept their heads. They got about a battalion together and got them forward under heavy fire."[6] In short, Norris hedged. He admitted the legitimacy of Scovel's point of view, which was shared by Theodore Roosevelt.[7] At the same time, he kindly cleared the name, locally, of his fellow Fiji Selfridge.

Norris also drew attention from John O'Hara Cosgrave. Three months earlier *The Wave's* editor related that he had received from Norris a letter sent after one of his pressboat trips to the Cuban coast.[8] Welcoming the war correspondent home, Cosgrave was of a like mind with the *Oakland Enquirer* interviewer: "His descriptions of the fighting, which ought to be first rate, will appear in due course in [*McClure's Magazine*], illustrated by snap shot photographs. Mr. Norris tells me that he caught the only view of the surrender of General Toral, he being the one correspondent present armed with a camera."[9]

Confident that the Cuban adventure had proven a fine investment of his time and talent, Norris was misjudging his fickle New York employer, whose unpredictability was legendary. It would be months, however, before he discovered how professionally unproductive was the mission on which S. S. McClure sent him at the risk of life and limb. *McClure's Magazine* would not acknowledge his role as a correspondent in any meaningful respect. Nothing that he wrote about the Cuban campaign appeared in its pages. Even worse

General Toral's surrender to General Shafter. *McClure's* illustration, from a photograph taken by Norris.

Americans and Cubans at the surrender ceremony. *McClure's* illustration, from a photograph taken by Norris.

was a slight not imagined by Cosgrave when he noted that Norris was the only one to photograph the surrender of General Toral. *McClure's* did use two of the photos—for illustrations of Stephen Bonsal's article on "The Fight for Santiago" in the October 1898 issue.[10] While the other photos taken by Bonsal were duly credited to him, Norris's were attributed only to an unnamed correspondent of *McClure's*. Yet worse, the two photos were keyed to Norris's "The Surrender at Santiago"—which, like "News Gathering at Key West," did not see publication at all during his life. Since Bonsal's article did not deal with the surrender ceremony, Norris's photographs related to nothing described by Bonsal.

Norris remained in San Francisco through mid-October, contributing to *The Wave* a mildly gothic romance featuring an old salt who is dotty on two points: He is convinced that victims of drowning at sea do not actually die until someone brings them to the surface and that they do not age if they remain submerged. Already possessed of these beliefs as a boy, this deep-sea rescue diver decided not to bring up a pretty young woman who went down with a ship off of Los Angeles, near Santa Catalina. She became the secret romantic attachment he maintained through subsequent decades; and, at the tale's end, he descends to the wreck to share her company for eternity in the submarine realm of "The Drowned Who Do Not Die." Summary makes the short story published on 24 September 1898 appear at its worst; in fact it is a rather successful blending of realistic detail and the fabulous in the long-established literary tradition in which it stands. Be that as it may, the tall tale is of inarguable value biographically in that it is one of the confirmations of the autobiographical dimensions of the novel *Blix* and, on at least one point, the accuracy of the account that Norris's widow gave Franklin Walker of his courtship. It was during one of their outings that Jeannette Black and Frank met the source of the fanciful short story he put into print in *The Wave:* Captain Joseph Hodgson of the U.S. Life Saving Service and its San Francisco Bay station. He also had provided Norris with the information he needed for the 18 September 1897 *Wave* article "Life-Line and Surf-Boat." He was also the source of the technical language and nautical detail in the novel that Norris dedicated to him, *Moran of the Lady Letty.*

As to the courtship pictured in *Blix*, Jeannette remembered meeting Frank in the autumn of 1896. By that time, and well before she turned eighteen, she was already an oft noted participant in a social group devoted to dancing, the Saturday Fortnightly. She too was a member of San Francisco's upper crust whose doings were regularly reported in *The Wave*. Not quite so well off as the Norrises, who still owned the elegant home on Sacramento Street, she lived on a less fashionable block, at 1324 Octavia. Her semi-invalid father Robert McGee Black, then in his sixties, was the son of a protestant clergyman and had emigrated from Rathmullan, County Donegal, Ireland. One of the forty-niners, he made enough money in following years in Virginia City, Nevada, to retire comfortably. Indeed, Jeannette's wardrobe was very much up to snuff and positively commented upon repeatedly in *The Wave's* social columns. She made her first of thirteen appearances therein on 1 February 1896 as "'a striking-looking girl, with deep, brown eyes, blue-black hair, and clear, olive complexion.'"[11] Her run of fourteen months in *The Wave* ended on 8 May 1897, with her last reported appearance in society.

As Jeannette told Walker, Frank and she had carried on a "mild flirtation until the summer of 1897, when the events of [*Blix*] took place." A key event

Jeannette Black (at left) at ten years of age. (Courtesy of the Bancroft Library, University of California at Berkeley.)

in that novel directly relates to Jeannette's disappearance from the social columns: its heroine, Travis Bessemer, decides not to "come out" as a debutante; and its hero, Condy Rivers, applauds her decision to forswear all forms of high-society "foolishness." "No more foolishness" is their motto. Instead of maintaining a relationship of the kind dictated by social convention, Condy and she become chums who together do what interests them. This includes accompanying Condy on his journalistic assignments, and thus in *Blix* they pay a visit to a whaleback steamer, where they hear from an elderly seaman the same yarn spun by Captain Joseph Hodgson that provided the plot essentials for "The Drowned Who Do Not Die." The nonfictional consequence on 12 June 1897 was Norris's *Wave* article "A Strange Relief-Ship," dealing with the same grain-transport vessel *City of Everett*.

As in *Blix*, Frank and Jeannette pulled off what she termed the "Luna Restaurant stunt," that is, they succeeded in their attempt at matchmaking at that Mexican restaurant at the corner of Vallejo and Dupont Streets.[12] They fished together at San Andreas Lake and took long hikes in the Bay Area. They had fun without frequenting the cotillions and pink teas so abhorrent to *Moran's* Ross Wilbur. As with Travis Bessemer, so with Jeannette Black: although her mother, née Carolina Virginia Williamson, was a voice instructor, Jeannette could not could not carry a tune. As with Condy, so with Frank:

He did not suffer from an addiction to gambling, but Frank too lived with his mother, worked for a weekly publication, was excited about fishing, read to Jeannette at length from his beloved Kipling, and was anxious to become a novelist. Like Condy, Frank did fall in love with his female pal.

When Jeannette, in July 1897, left San Francisco for a two-week stay across the bay in Mill Valley, Frank followed her to anticipate Condy by telling his chum that friendship was no longer enough. And how accurate Jeannette could *sometimes* be after three decades will be seen in Frank's article on a group of houses built in the Japanese style on the hillsides at Mill Valley. "Japan Transplanted" was published on 31 July 1897, after his return from the visit to Jeannette.

As may be seen in the idealized portrait of Travis Bessemer as the epitome of the "California girl" in her most natural and morally admirable manifestation, Norris was infatuated. There was the visit to St. Louis in February 1898, when Jeannette was following in her mother's footsteps at the Monticello Female Seminary in Godfrey, Illinois; the flow of letters from Key West, Tampa, and Cuba to Godfrey during the war; and now the recuperative period in which she was his constant companion for nearly two months.

It was not long before Norris resumed his work, initiating the composition of *Blix* and preparing for the expansion of 1897's tale of a failed Arctic exploration venture, "The End of the Beginning," into the novel *A Man's Woman*.[13] The latter project resulted in yet more conversations with Captain Hodgson. He shared with Jeannette and Frank his recollections of the Arctic as a member of a party sent to rescue the survivors of an ill-fated attempt to reach the North Pole. (Oddly enough, the doomed exploration vessel that departed from San Francisco in July 1879 was the *U.S.S. Jeannette*.) Since the heroine of *A Man's Woman* was to be a nurse, Norris also conferred about medical matters with his fraternity brother Albert J. Houston, M.D., to whom that novel would be dedicated.

On 11 October Norris wrote to Elizabeth H. Davenport from the Hotel Pleasanton, informing her that he was "very well pleased" with the physical appearance of the recently published *Moran* and announcing his impending return to New York City.[14] By 22 October he was settled once more at 10 West Thirty-third Street, and by then he knew that *McClure's* would take neither "With Lawton at El Caney" (then entitled "From Dawn to Dark—Fighting") nor "The Surrender of Santiago." He had placed both essays with a literary

agent, Paul Revere Reynolds, who sold them to a more prestigious monthly, *Century,* for two hundred dollars.[15]

What was taking place that autumn with Jeannette Black is less certain. She did not return to the Monticello Female Seminary, due, she told Walker more than once, to a mastoid infection. Given that antibiotics were not available in 1898, mastoiditis was a serious medical problem that might result in the spread of the infection from the area of the skull immediately behind the ear to the muscles of the neck. Possible were meningitis (infection of the tissues covering the brain and spinal cord) and the development of an abscess within the brain. Jeannette related that it was soon after Norris had gone back to New York that she visited some friends, came down with the illness, and returned to San Francisco. Afraid that she would lose her hearing, she wrote Frank "that he had better break off the engagement." Before the end of October, he replied, declaring that "he would come out [west] if she continued to make a fool of herself," that is, if she again suggested that they end their informal engagement.

What she did not explain to Walker was how the medical problem that manifested itself in late October prevented her return to the seminary for the start of the school year on 26 September 1898—nor when and how the infection she described was successfully treated.

Gertrude Norris's friend, Bertha Rickoff, offered Walker a different scenario. Rickoff's version makes one especially wary of what she had to say to Walker because of the mean-spirited nature of most of her comments. Here was a woman with some axes to grind. For example, Rickoff claimed that, after Frank returned from South Africa, Gertrude was grooming her as a daughter-in-law. That was not to be, however. Bertha would not have him: Frank struck her as "a man of the world, quite fast," and she "decided that he was not for her. He was only interested in a woman in order to live with her. . . . [H]e used to go over [the bay] and stay with one married woman in Sausalito." Further, he would never engage in small talk with Bertha. He had no manners. "Once he picked up a macaroon from the floor at a fine dinner at her house and ate it." Contrary to what Jeannette had said, Rickoff pictured Frank as a compulsive gambler. And to top it all, this bluestocking claimed that she had taught Frank how to write.[16]

Bertha declared that Jeannette "was terribly common." After Frank and she married, they "had a dinner for Howells and . . . Jeannette looked pretty but couldn't say a word, she was so dumb." Rickoff recalled once seeing a picture of Jeannette in Frank's room and hearing Gertrude speak of her as "that hussy."

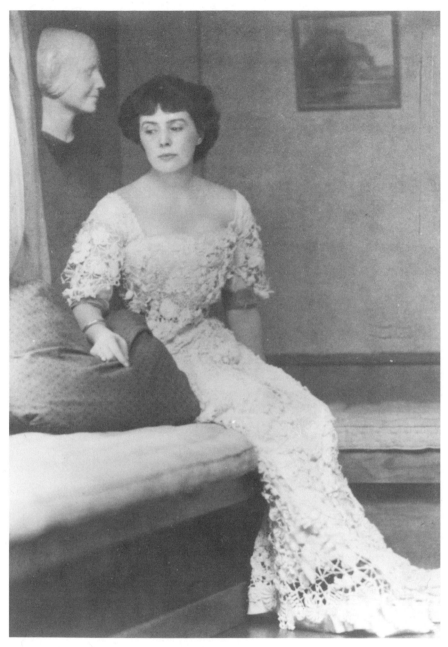

Jeannette Black Norris, 1902. (Courtesy of the Bancroft Library, University of California at Berkeley.)

However catty, Rickoff was in fact Gertrude's confidante—possibly her only one, given Gertrude's *grande dame* demeanor: "Mrs. Norris had high social aspirations but was never quite successful because she was too brilliant. . . . She was by all odds the most brilliant woman in San Francisco." Rickoff could speak with unquestionable authority on some matters. She was, for example, correct when she explained that Norris's English publisher, Grant Richards, was responsible for the bowdlerization of *McTeague,* demanding that Norris rewrite the scene in which Auguste Sieppe wets his pants. Walker dismissed her testimony, along with virtually everything else she said. He did not even mention in his biography the English publisher's alleged censorship. But empirical verification of Rickoff's claim surfaced in 1989, proving that she knew whereof she spoke in 1930.[17] Not only Gertrude and Rickoff had a low opinion of Jeannette. So close a friend as Harry M. Wright opined to Walker that Frank "had had his affairs and always rather liked flashy women—his wife was rather inclined to be flashy." When Frank first met "Nettie" in San Francisco, Wright "was not much impressed" and "did not think she came from a good family." Wright, like Rickoff, "never did like her very much."

After Walker completed his four interviews with Jeannette, he turned to this woman after whom—according to Jeannette—Norris used to name horses that he rode. Walker met with Rickoff only once, on 29 May 1930, and it is obvious from her response that he had asked her about Jeannette's mastoid infection. Bertha began her reply with, "Frank had to marry her." In his notes, Walker later typed and then struck out the observation that it was a shotgun affair. Frank, Rickoff continued, "was very decent about it after he got her into trouble. The affair with the mastoid was merely a screen; Rosenstirn took care of it. . . . Next morning, [Gertrude] said [to Jeannette] she would tear her hair out if she said anything about it"—that is, about the abortion.

What was "off," chronologically, in Rickoff's testimony was the sequence of events implied. Frank and Jeannette were not even formally engaged until the greater part of a year later. *The Wave* reported the "just announced" engagement on 5 August 1899, and their 1900 marriage took place almost six months later. Moreover, the date for the ceremony was not set that summer of 1899: the *Chronicle* and *Examiner* informed their readers, "it is understood that it will not be in the near future" and that the "wedding will not take place for some time yet."[18] The union was hardly a shotgun affair. But Dr. Julius Rosenstirn was indeed the Norris family physician. Vis-à-vis his possible performance of an abortion in 1898, the city directory makes a noteworthy contribution. Previously listed as a "surgeon and physician," he changed his description in 1899 to "surgeon and gynecologist."

Still, there is no indication that Norris married in 1900 for any other reason than love, and all of the evidence concerning the quality of the marriage—save one brief testimony—spells a particularly happy union. His brother Charles reflected in 1930 that he always thought Frank loved her much more than she loved him.

Back in New York and developing the manuscript of *Blix*, which would be dedicated to the mother who thought her son's lover was a "hussy," Norris was projecting in the novel an image of Jeannette that appeared a corrective designed to give Gertrude reason for second and more positive thoughts about the woman who would become her daughter-in-law.

True, Travis Bessemer is characterized in ways that might have further alienated Gertrude from Jeannette. She is quite different from the elocutionist and bluestocking who became known as San Francisco's most "brilliant" interpreter of Robert Browning's poetry. And Norris did appear to take one mild swipe at his mother in *Blix*. Travis is the New Woman of the 1890s who believes that women should have "some occupation," and she hopes to study medicine. Gertrude comes to mind when one hears Travis rejecting exactly the lifestyle that Gertrude, like Annie Derrick in *The Octopus*, had long since embraced: "'[I]sn't studying medicine, Condy, better than piano playing, or French courses, or literary classes and Browning circles? Oh, I've no patience with that sort of girl!'"[19]

But the main thrust of *Blix* was much more positive. Travis, nicknamed "Blix" by Condy (like Jeannette, whom Norris nicknamed "Buck"), attractively transcends all such generational and cultural distinctions as she makes her first appearance in the novel as a demigoddess worthy of a portrait by William Bouguereau.

> She was young, but tall as most men, and solidly, almost heavily built. Her shoulders were broad, her chest was deep, her neck round and firm. She radiated health; there were exuberance and vitality in the very touch of her foot upon the carpet, and there was that cleanliness about her, that freshness, that suggested a recent plunge in the surf and a "constitutional" along the beach.
>
> She impressed one as being a very normal girl: nothing morbid about her, nothing nervous or false or overwrought. You did not expect to find her

introspective. You felt sure that her mental life was not at all the result of thoughts and reflections germinating from within, but rather of impressions and sensations that came to her from without. . . . She was just a good, sweet, natural, healthy-minded, healthy-bodied girl, honest, strong, self-reliant, and good tempered.[20]

What more could Frank's mother want? *Blix* also answers that question.

To "sell" a future daughter-in-law in a Victorian moral frame of reference, the clinching argument was the satisfaction of a criterion enunciated by John Ruskin in his 1865 collection of essays *Sesame and Lilies.* The ideal wife, the queen to her king, is an inspiration to her husband, and her benign influence enables him to realize his full potential as a male. The ideal fiancée would also, of course, exercise such an uplifting, transformative influence, perhaps bringing to mind David Copperfield's "ministering angel," Agnes. Thus, later in *Blix*, Condy falls under the refining spell of such a maiden as they together look out the bay window of her home, gazing upon the star-studded sky above San Francisco Bay. Condy turns toward Blix, observing her profile in the darkened room.

> The line of the chin and throat and sweet round curve of the shoulder had in it something indescribable—something that related to music, and that eluded speech. . . . The sloe-brown of her little eyes and flush of her cheek were mere inferences,—like the faintest stars that are never visible when looked at directly; and it seemed to him that there was disengaged from her something for which there was no name; something that appealed to a mysterious sixth sense—a sense that only stirred at such quiet moments as this. . . . It seemed to him as if her sweet, clean purity and womanliness took a form of its own which his accustomed senses were too gross to perceive. Only a certain vague tenderness in him went out to meet and receive this impalpable presence; a tenderness not for her only, but for all the good things of the world. . . . Her sweetness, her goodness, appealed to what he guessed must be the noblest in him. And she was only nineteen. Suddenly his heart swelled, the ache came to his throat and the smart to his eyes.
>
> "Blixy," he said, just above a whisper; "Blixy, wish I was a better sort of chap."
>
> "That's the beginning of being better, isn't it, Condy?" she answered, turning toward him, her chin on her hand.

What mother would not want for her son such an influence, prompting him, as Condy says, "'to do the right, straight thing, and be clean and fine'"?[21]

One still must wonder whether the argument succeeded with Gertrude Norris. The novel certainly did succeed with Juliet Wilbor Tompkins, editor of the *Puritan* monthly magazine, however. Available for distribution in late February 1899 was the March issue containing the first installment of the novel's serialization. By December 1898 Norris had completed the project—save for the final polishing he would give the work prior to its book publication by Doubleday and McClure in September 1899.[22]

⁓

Through the end of 1898, only one other short story by Norris appeared in a periodical, and at last it was *McClure's*—his first publication in that magazine. This was "Miracle Joyeux," but not the work of the same title that appeared in *The Wave* on 9 October 1897. Then, it will be recalled, Norris was on a tear, writing a series of sensationally unconventional stories that might have appeared in a collection aptly titled "Ways That Are Dark." The 1897 "Miracle Joyeux" was, in its own way, just as provocative as "A Case for Lombroso" and "A Reversion to Type"; but it was disqualified from inclusion in the planned book featuring studies of the bizarre, perverse, and degenerate in *modern* life. In this short story Norris had drifted back nineteen centuries for his setting and cast of characters to craft a scenario featuring none other than Jesus of Nazareth.

The *Wave* tale raised the question, How human was the "God in man made manifest" described in the refrain of song number sixty-seven in the 1892 Episcopalian hymnal that Norris knew? Given a free rein by Cosgrave in 1897, he emphatically answered the question by fashioning a miracle-working hero who grants a single wish to two miscreants who despise each other and whose avarice would turn anyone's stomach. There is, though, a condition that riles both of these embodiments of selfishness: the first to ask, Jesus tells them, will receive half as much as the second. This results in a violent altercation between the misers, neither of whom can countenance anyone having more than he. Which will go first and receive less? Finally, one strikes the other in the face, prompting the latter's angry request of blindness in *one* eye—which, of course, means total loss of sight for the man who struck him. And so it was for the two men in Norris's parable, which sensationally illustrates the deleterious effects of greed and more soberly prompts reflection upon the personality of the deity pictured in the New Testament.

This was not the kind of theologically probing short story *McClure's* published in its pages.

After returning from San Francisco in October 1898, Norris kept the original narrative frame for this story within a story. But, eliminating the misers, he transformed the piece into a more sentimentally powerful but intellectually soft one for *McClure's*. In the December 1898 version, the Prince of Peace uses his supernatural powers not to mete out justice and a well-deserved punishment but to bring joy into an innocent little girl's life. The adaptation was perfect for the Christmas issue. Indeed, in 1906 Doubleday, Page, and Company published it as *The Joyous Miracle* for the Christmas giftbook market.

In December Norris also sent to *Century's* associate editor Robert Underwood Johnson a new opening for "With Lawton at El Caney," written along the lines that Johnson had suggested.[23] (No subsequent mention of the other essay *Century* took but never published, "The Surrender of Santiago," appears in Norris's correspondence.) He thanked Isaac F. Marcosson of the *Louisville Times* for his appreciative review of *Moran*.[24] Then, on 31 December 1898, he closed the year by expressing his appreciation to William Dean Howells for so positively evaluating *Moran* in the 26 November issue of the *Literary World*, announcing that "Mr. Doubleday has now in the presses a novel of mine, to appear in the spring, of an entirely different style from *Moran*." At this late date, one may be surprised to note, it was still not entitled *McTeague: A Story of San Francisco*. Norris thought that it would instead appear as *The People of Polk Street*. "It is," he continued, "as naturalistic as *Moran* was romantic and in writing it I have taken myself [and] the work very seriously. I earnestly hope that if you ever have occasion to review it I will be more deserving of your encouragement than I am afraid I was in the case of *Moran*."[25]

Meanwhile, by 15 December 1898, when he wrote to Robert Underwood Johnson, Norris had moved from midtown to downtown Manhattan, to 61 Washington Square South—the widow Catherine Branchard's boarding house next-door to the Anglesea, where Ernest Peixotto and his wife Mary now had an apartment. Down the street at number 53 was the Judson, at which the Peixottos first resided in 1897 and again in 1899, and where Norris took meals and later resided for a short while on several occasions. Living on the square as well was another San Franciscan, Juliet Wilbor Tompkins, the editor of *Puritan*.[26] It was from Branchard's establishment that he wrote Harry M. Wright, recalling this old friend's recent visit to New York and announcing on 5 January the impending triumph that had been years in the making: "It's been pretty lonesome since you left but I have been making up for lost time [and] working pretty steady. Also proofs of my next novel have begun to come back from the printers and I'm kept fairly busy correcting 'em. I think Peixotto will do the cover design."[27] *McTeague* was at last nearing publication. Bound copies were available to Norris by 22 February 1899, when he inscribed the one he sent to Lewis E. Gates.[28] In March, *McClure's Magazine* presented its readers with a second work from his hand, reprinting from the 17 July 1897 issue of *The Wave* "'This Animal of a Buldy Jones.'" *Century* also published that month his article on the feeding of the Cuban refugees at El Caney, "*Comida:* An Experience in Famine."

Things were looking up now. But the winter of 1898–99 was not a happy one for Norris. For one thing, the San Franciscan used to a more temperate climate found himself in the midst of one of most severe winters on record: the "Blizzard of '99" swept the East Coast in mid-February. Visitors to the Statue of Liberty could walk to Bedloe's Island across the ice from the Battery. This, in part, accounted for the psychological condition to which he referred in a letter written a few months later, during a visit to San Francisco. On 7 May 1899, he wrote to New York, bidding Ernest and Mary Peixotto a bon voyage for their trip to Europe commencing on 10 May. He wondered when they all would be together again and told them that he would never forget "how much you both helped to make this hard winter of '98–99 easy for me. What I should have done without you I honestly don't know, because there were times when the whole thing was something of a grind, and it didn't seem worth while to go on at all. Well, somehow one does pull through with such help as yours . . . and believe me when I tell you I owe you both more than I can ever express."[29]

The bleak weather conditions were one thing. Much more stressful were two other developments to which Norris referred. First, the writing of *A Man's Woman* that winter was not going well. The seminal short story "The End of the Beginning" reflected clearly in 1897 Norris's "enthusiasm for Arctic exploration" to which Jeannette testified; but, she also told Walker, one of the reasons that "the book was not so good was that he had lost his enthusiasm" for writing it. "The ideas rather cramped the characters." This was always a problem for Frank, she said, but with this novel the difficulty was almost insurmountable.

Readers of Norris's now least-popular novel will be inclined to agree that it "was not so good." The main theme was indeed constricting. The explorer Ward Bennett—named after Bennett Island, which was discovered during the voyage of the *U.S.S. Jeannette*—types the egotist unswervingly intent upon having his own way; the professional nurse Lloyd Searight is as self-absorbed and determined to make her will and ideal conception of herself prevail. He loves her, and she loves him; but the relationship of these prickly titans becomes a battle of galvanic wills resulting in their mutual alienation. A grand melodrama rages on until depression and physical illness wear down the sharp edges of Ward's personality. He emerges at length from the sick room a new man sensitive to the fact that Lloyd has suffered as much as he. She too has been weaned away from self-centeredness in the hours spent at his bedside. This New Woman of the 1890s with a profession decides to embrace a more traditional feminine identity, placing Ward's interests above hers. Despite his objections, she turns away from nursing to be his helpmate, the "man's woman" who makes it possible for him to return to Arctic exploration. The psychodrama ends on as positive a note as Norris could manage, but the greater part of the plot features in high relief two decidedly unpleasant, humorless, and—following their alienation—neurotic characters whose bouts with melancholy described at great length are not compensated for by their simultaneous leaps to better mental health as the novel ends. Even Norris did not enjoy being in their company, as he made clear almost a year later, on 22 November 1899, in a letter to Isaac F. Marcosson. By then the work had completed its July-October serialization in the *San Francisco Chronicle* and another of September-October in the *New York Evening Sun,* and Norris's chagrin was apparent: "It's a kind of theatrical sort [of story] with a lot of niggling analysis to try to justify the violent action of the first few chapters. It is very slovenly put together." He even distanced it from his naturalistic writings, in spite of the psychological determinisms that govern Ward and Lloyd and the inclusion of *McTeague*-like, gruesome detail, which prompted the *New York Times* reviewer to declare that a novel should be neither "a chamber of horrors nor a surgical journal."[30] While working on *The Octopus* in November 1899, he told Marcosson that *A Man's Woman* is "different from my other books, but it's the last one that will be, if you understand what I mean. I am going back *definitely* now to the style of [*McTeague*] and [will] stay with it right along."[31]

The trouble he was having with its composition in 1898–99 was also reflected in an earlier, very different letter that he sent to Marcosson in March 1899. *Blix*, already accepted by Frank N. Doubleday for book publication, was everything that *A Man's Woman* was not proving to be: *Blix*, Norris wrote, is "essentially . . . a love story. But what I have tried to do was to turn out a love story that would not slop over. No sentimentality—everything healthy and clean and natural. [It] does not belong to any 'school' so far as I can see. It's not naturalism and it's not romanticism; it's just a story. Nothing very violent happens. There are no disagreeable people in it and it finishes—to my notion—happily."[32] That is, the jubilant *Blix* was everything that the morbidly analytical *A Man's Woman* was not, and so was the pleasant experience of fictionally treating his own happy experiences with Jeannette Black, who did not suffer the psychological irregularities assigned to Lloyd Searight.

Also complicating the situation, and perhaps dictating the main characters' descents into misery, was a recurrence of malarial symptoms. Jeannette understated the seriousness of his condition when relating only that Frank "was not well that winter." Bruce Porter, who had returned from Europe and was also living on Washington Square by March 1899, did not downplay the severity of Norris's bout with ill health when he gave Walker a rather alarming portrait of Norris in April 1899 as he departed New York for San Francisco:

> Well, he left New York too ill to do more than sit gaunt [and] shaken in the hansom that carried us to the [train] station. Established in his section [of the passenger car], he revived to a grin: "Bruce, see that?"—as he waved a little swagger stick between his hand—"I'm going to walk down Sutter St[reet], swinging that!—And they'll say *'That's Frank Norris!'*"
> I never liked him better than at that moment, pitiable in his weakness, going "home" to his boyish reward, for the struggle and the travail—but with his goal attained.

Not all of his goals had been attained, however. Only a few weeks before, Norris had defined a new one, or—viewed in another way—no less than three.

Up the street from Norris's apartment—the "cheap room" with a double bed recalled by Harry M. Wright—was 80 Washington Square East. Like the Judson on the south side of the square (now a New York University dormitory), the Benedick still stands (as Paulette Goddard Hall on the same campus). It is the same apartment building Edith Wharton featured in her 1905 novel *The House of Mirth*. Gelett Burgess was a resident in 1899, and it was a virtual artists' colony housing, at different times, still prominent painters such as John H. Twachtman, Emil Carlsen, and J. Alden Weir. Bruce Porter also had rooms at the Benedick; and it was there, Porter told Walker, that Norris announced the project that took him back to San Francisco in April.

[H]e dropped in upon me at odd hours: mostly neighbouring midnight, when he saw my light turned on.

He, apparently, had no life outside his work and refused every social contact.

He had won a first place with the triumph of *McTeague* and there was eagerness on all sides—waiting to see him and hail him. But ill, intense, he had promptly dedicated himself to a bigger work—He was brooding the complete Trilogy of "Wheat"—and was getting the warp of *The Octopus* onto the loom. He was bothered, tangled in loose threads.

He burst into my room one morning before five o'clock—flung himself at the foot of my bed, exhausted and satisfied. He had made his leap an hour before,—had cleared his entanglements and had his story [and] his form, and couldn't contain himself at daylight.

This was in mid- to late March, given that Norris first refers to the three novels "in my head" in a 22 March 1899 letter to Elizabeth Davenport.[33] Not until a few days later did he spell out his plan in a letter to William Dean Howells:

I think there is a chance for somebody to do some great work with the West and California as a background, and which will at the same time be thoroughly American. My Idea is to write three novels around the one subject of *Wheat*. First, a story of California (the producer), second, a story of Chicago (the distributor), third, a story of Europe (the consumer) and in each to keep to the idea of this huge Niagara of wheat rolling from West to East.

I think a big Epic Trilogy *could* be made out of such a subject, that at the same time would be modern and distinctly American.

The idea is so big that it frightens me at times but I have about made up my mind to have a try at it.[34]

Norris pitched the concept to S. S. McClure and Frank N. Doubleday. As the editorial staff member Henry Lanier told Walker, the trilogy caught their imaginations, and "we left [Norris] free to work it out in his own way, not requiring any reading or office reports till he was ready." By 5 April Norris's plan had been approved by his superiors. Then he informed Harry M. Wright, "I am leaving for California Monday next, to be gone, very likely, until fall."[35] *The Octopus* required historical research and *in situ* observation of life amidst California agriculturalists and the railroad monopoly against which they had been pitted for decades. Thus the ride in the hansom with Bruce Porter to the train station on 10 April 1899.

Norris was moving forward at a dramatically quickened pace, after so many changes of course, long delays, and disappointments. Since his previous trip to the West Coast eight months before, he had seen the publication of *Moran* and *McTeague*. *Blix* was written, its serialization begun, and its forthcoming book publication assured. He had begun work on *A Man's Woman*, to be syndicated by S. S. McClure, and he would refer to the manuscript as "just finished" on 13 June 1899.[36] Now he was free of editorial duties at the McClure establishment and continuing to draw salary as he initiated the research necessary for the composition of *The Octopus*.[37] It was all coming together, at last.

20

"THE WHEAT STUFF IS PILING UP B.I.G."

Bailey Millard was a literary columnist for the *San Francisco Examiner* and an occasional contributor to *The Wave*. Norris and he had been friends since at least 1896. It was in response to Millard's question—what is the Great American Novel?—that Norris replied in the *Examiner* in January 1897. He cited not one work but two: William Dean Howells's *A Modern Instance* as the finest study of American life; and Lew Wallace's *Ben-Hur, A Tale of the Christ* as the finest work written by an American author. The distinction was a meaningful one for him. It was also an odd but telling combination, in that the first was a touchstone work of realism and the latter an exemplar of literary romanticism. The former, Norris explained, is great because it is "true, relentlessly and remorselessly true." The latter was the "best" when judged by a different standard that he had applied in 1896 when celebrating Emile Zola's *Rome*. "It is the tremendous drama" of *Ben-Hur* that has made it so famous, Norris wrote. Unequalled were "the gorgeous scenes of life and movement and color—the vast scenic background against which vivid and significant action, hurried and intense, is wrought out."[1] Arrived in California to create as dynamic a romance, one that was as factual and "relentlessly" true as he could make it, Norris was formally greeted by Millard in the most exuberant manner on 28 May 1899.

It was not the first eulogium that Millard delivered with breathlessness. A little over two months earlier, having read *Moran* and *McTeague* and been informed that *Blix* was being serialized in *Puritan,* he had proclaimed Norris's progress in New York City a "dazzling record" of achievement. He also understood that *A Man's Woman*—then entitled "The Heroine"—was ready for the press. "All this within six months!"[2] What most impressed him now, though, was the way a New York publishing firm rewarded such talent and deemed Norris's new project worthy of substantial investment:

> If you were to step up to any person of your acquaintance and quietly inform him that Bokhara rugs were coming into fashion as spring wraps for apoplectic infant alumni, because the queen of nanny goats had solemnly decreed it, the statement would appear no more sane and credible than a certain absolute fact that I am about to record. . . . The strange and wonderful fact is this: A great publishing firm has sent across the continent in palace sleeping cars at its own expense a writer whom ten months ago it had never heard of, and is paying him a high salary to write a series of novels about California, for which it will give him magnificent royalties. Think of that, ye obscure and neglected novelists of this pleasant Western land; think of it and hold up your head in hope!

Yet again he referred to Norris as a "high-salaried" author sent in "a palace car . . . to California to study us and make us live in literature"; and Millard gave full credit for such a wise decision to Frank N. Doubleday. He did not mention McClure, from whom Norris would separate along with Doubleday by the end of the year. What Millard thus suggested was proving the fact of the matter: Norris had become one of Doubleday's pet authors.

Millard's article was based upon old and new conversations with Norris and, though he does not acknowledge it, correspondence extending for well over the previous year. How far back in time Millard could go is seen in his recollection that Norris began writing *Moran* on Edward Townsend's old desk at the Bohemian Club and continued its composition in Omaha, St. Louis, and New York, as well as three locales at which Norris is not otherwise known to have stopped between January and March in 1898: Chicago, Philadelphia, and Manunka Chunk, New Jersey. More recently, Millard had learned of the charge given to Norris in New York, and Norris's epistolary style is obvious in Millard's quotation of Doubleday's exhortation: "Go back to California. Do for that country what Kipling [also a Doubleday and McClure author] did for India. Plot out a series of novels about the people there. Put in plenty of blood and bowels. Keep 'em up to the *McTeague* standard, and write, write, write." Norris appears to have informed Millard of his plans for his trilogy before he entrained for California.

One wonders, therefore, exactly what Norris actually *said* in person to Millard in San Francisco, especially when Millard quotes a declaration immediately reminiscent of 1896's "The 'English Courses' of the University of California" and 1897's "An Opening for Novelists." It was far from likely that a fellow literary essayist and years-long friend was learning for the first time that Norris "has supreme contempt for the kind of writing done by the men of the academic school," or that Norris struck a wholly new note for Millard when he said "that a literary course in college is the worst kind of training for a writer." Norris's "An Opening" is echoed again, along with the first paragraph of *Moran:* "'While your college man is polishing his sentences,' [Norris] remarked to me the other day, 'battle, murder and sudden death are being done in the next block and he cares not to record them.'" Also a vintage opinion of Norris was another statement Millard attributed to him: "'I don't believe in style. . . . "Write of things as you see 'em" is my motto; pare down, and give the readers the story and not a mass of fluff and froth. When I want to write about anything I go to headquarters and study it up. It is knowledge of things that gives you the real touch. I like the vivid thing, and that's what the reader likes and is willing to pay for.'"[3]

If these quotations are more or less accurate accounts of what Norris had to say that spring, he had definitely recovered from the recurrence of malarial symptoms Bruce Porter observed on 10 April in New York. Reinvigorated and rehearsing before Millard the anti-aestheticist literary principles he recently assigned to Condy Rivers in *Blix,* Norris was posed to conceptualize one of the main characters of *The Octopus* as a writer with the same sentiments who turned to the California wheat fields to find an epical subject to which he could give "the real touch." That character, the poet Presley, would finally prove inept in this respect, and others. Norris, however, was determined not to fail, despite the difficulties with effecting a "real touch" that he experienced with the manuscript of *A Man's Woman.*

When Norris got on his high horse and began pontificating on literary matters, it is noteworthy that he did not alienate those who knew him. He had publicly chastised Les Jeunes like Ernest Peixotto for the artificiality of their productions and lambasted Gelett Burgess for spending his talents in the service of the silly. Yet he had no better friends in New York than these two men. In his article, Millard disagreed with Norris regarding the importance of "style," but he protested in the mildest way. While he appears the martinet in print, Norris remained as congenial as ever for those who knew him well.

As of 28 May, Norris had good reason for being sanguine besides the confidence of Doubleday. His English publisher Grant Richards had brought *Moran* into print as *Shanghaied* on 15 March 1899, and Richards had recently informed him of the opinion on the romance given by a writer Norris greatly admired, the creator of Sherlock Holmes.[4] Millard reported that Arthur Conan Doyle had judged *Shanghaied* the best book of its kind since Robert Louis Stevenson's *Ebb Tide*.

Even better news arrived three days after Millard's article appeared. On 31 May Norris again heard from Richards when, at the Hotel Pleasanton, he received from him Doyle's verdict on *McTeague*. "What I think," wrote Doyle, "is that you have got the great American Novelist and I am not sure that you have not got the great American novel. It is tremendously good— splendid—and if it does not sell at once must have a steady demand. Such a book cannot go under. I would not alter a word."[5] Richards declined to take Doyle's advice regarding alterations; Norris did, as Richards demanded through Doubleday and McClure's London offices, rewrite the pants-wetting scene before Doyle's letter was forwarded to him.[6] But that was no great matter, given his transatlantic success and, shortly afterwards, the burgeoning fame in San Francisco that attended the quotation of Doyle's letter in the 24 June issue of *The Wave*.[7]

As when Norris recuperated from his Cuban adventure in the late summer and early autumn of 1898, he again enjoyed in late April 1899 the company of Jeannette Black. Writing to Ernest Peixotto on 7 May, he described a scene that might have been pulled from *Blix,* Norris at the beginning of his letter playing the part of the sometimes scatterbrained Condy Rivers: "I wanted to write you . . . to say bon voyage but of course I have forgotten [your ship's] name, though you told me often enough. It's a wonder I don't forget my own name these days, I'm having such a bully good time. Feel just as if I was out of doors playing after being in school for years." It was life imitating art: "Jeannette and I spent the whole afternoon on the waterfront yesterday among the ships (*on* and all over *one* of them), came back and had tea and pickled ginger on the balcony of our own particular Chinese restaurant over the Plaza and wound up dining at Luna's Mexican restaurant 'over in the Quarter.'" (Like Luna's, the Chinese restaurant near Portsmouth Square was the same seen in *Blix* and, on 28 August 1897 in *The Wave*, "The Third Circle.") As did Travis and Condy, Jeannette and he went to the Presidio military reservation, where they "sat down and wallowed in the grass . . . and I'm just having the best time that ever was—voila tout." At his leisure in his mother's rooms in the Pleasanton, he also found time to try to square away a matter that had been settled in 1894, formally requesting "honorable dismissal" from the University of California. The petition form he completed was returned to him with the notation that the formality was now doubly a fait accompli.[8]

As to the work for which he was on salary, Norris announced to Peixotto in the same 7 May letter, "The Wheat stuff is piling up B.I.G." Save for a final revision of *A Man's Woman* for book publication, that project was now in the past; and it appears that he was so confident because of the progress he was making with his research that he thought he might complete composition of *The Octopus* during his planned visit to the ranch of Dulce Bolado Ashe to the east of Monterey and south of Gilroy, near Tres Pinos: "I may be [in California] longer than I first expected. Mebbe till late in the fall, and I donno why I should not write my immortial worruk at a wheat ranch any way. I think it will come to that."

It did not, in fact, come to that, since the investigative project to which he had committed himself was truly a formidable one for a man whose history included pronounced dislike of writing research papers for his professors at the University of California and who, until the winter of 1899, had shown no sign of interest in or familiarity with the relationship between California agriculturalists and the Southern Pacific Railroad. He underestimated how much work would be involved in gathering and putting into perspective the information he needed to accomplish the tasks he identified to Harry M. Wright on 5 April: "I mean to study the whole question as faithfully as I can and then write a hair lifting story. . . . I mean to do it thoroughly.—Get at it from every point of view, the social, agricultural, [and] political.—Just say the last word [on] the R.R. question in California."[9]

A Man's Woman, based mainly on conversations with Captain Joseph Hodgson, appears to have required no more additional research than consultation of two records of attempts to reach the North Pole, the titles of which Jeannette remembered: George W. DeLong's *The Voyage of the Jeannette* and Fridtjof Nansen's *Farthest North.*[10] It was a very different situation with *The Octopus.* Norris rose to the occasion, but it would not be until a year and a half later, the winter of 1900–1901, that his manuscript went to the typesetters.

That spring Norris had not only a topic with which to work but, according to Millard's article published in May, a thesis he intended to advance in *The Octopus*. Millard, whose enthusiasm for *Moran* knew no bounds, advised the young "annalist and analyst" not to abandon the adventure-romance genre and "write only books with purposes"—which, in the parlance of turn-of-the-century literary critics, meant fictions designed to develop an argument and prove a point. The point in question was suggested several paragraphs earlier when Millard related that the "first novel of his new series is to . . . tell of the battle of the people with the railroad." Since the *San Francisco Examiner* had a history of hostility to the Southern Pacific, the polemical phrasing may have been Millard's rather than Norris's. However, on 16 October 1899, after he had returned to New York, Norris informed a Mrs. Lilla Lewis Parks that she would be disappointed in her hope that he would be a celebrant or defender of corporations like the Southern Pacific. She had suggested in a letter that he use the powers displayed in *McTeague* and *Blix* "to handle the subject of 'Trusts' in a way to convince the public that the Trust is a modern innovation—a business evolution that has come to stay, if rightly handled and honorably dealt with." Norris flatly declared that he was "enlisted upon the other side," though he assured her that he was "very anxious to hear [her] arguments . . . in favor of the trust."[11] Although the term had not yet been popularized by Theodore Roosevelt, it seems that when he came to San Francisco Norris was intent upon writing a "muckraking" book like Zola's *Germinal* that singlemindedly championed the cause of "the people" oppressed by a ruthless corporation.

But before proceeding, he needed the facts of the case. Norris approached the matter in a variety of ways. First, there was straightforward desk work focused on relatively recent events in California. According to his widow, he spent many hours at the Mechanics' Institute Library in the city. There were also the files of the newspaper with which Norris had long had a healthy relationship, the *San Francisco Chronicle*. Another major resource was the daily that employed Millard. The *Examiner's* files comprised an unequaled compendium of the sins of the California railroads and of the surviving member of the group of four that had governed the Central Pacific, Collis P. Huntington, who now headed the Southern Pacific. In the winter and spring of 1896, William Randolph Hearst, the owner of the *Examiner* and the *New York Journal,* had turned Ambrose Bierce loose upon Huntington to monitor and sensationally expose his unsuccessful attempt at persuading Congress to provide a near-indefinite extension of the Southern Pacific's debt repayment to the federal government. Bierce was far from sympathetic. Whatever degree of animus Norris held against the Southern Pacific when he came to California, the *Examiner* did not lessen it.

How energetic Norris was in this kind of research may be gleaned in a doctoral dissertation by Robert D. Lundy. He was the first to examine in the Frank Norris Collection at the Bancroft Library the remains of a single notebook, one of at least three kept by Norris when researching *The Octopus*. In them Norris assembled clippings from 1899 periodicals—articles that dealt with the railroad's operations, Huntington's problem with federal debt, complaints about freight rates, legal actions, and the machinations of the state's railroad commission, which had the power to effect fair shipping-rate adjustments. His reading ranged from Henry George's *Progress and Poverty* to a catalogue describing combines, harvesting machines that cut, thresh, and clean wheat for bagging. It also included a newspaper clipping describing a woman who starved to death on the streets of New York City, which would give rise in *The Octopus* to Mrs. Hooven's fate in San Francisco thanks to the ruthless predations of the railroad. Possibly present in one of the now-lost notebooks were transcriptions or clippings of two poems by Edwin Markham that championed the oppressed in the way that the one written by Presley would. These were Markham's fabulously popular, Jean François Millet–inspired "The Man with the Hoe" and "The Toilers." Then again, Norris may have known both poems nearly by heart. The 1899 collection containing them was quite familiar to Norris. Markham, too, was a Doubleday and McClure author.[12]

Turning from the *Examiner* and other sources of invective directed at the Southern Pacific, Norris consulted not only the *Wave's* less hostile takes on the trust but its opinion on other subjects incorporated into *The Octopus*. For example, an 18 March 1899 article by John T. Flynn, "The Silent Forge," made its way into the surviving notebook and became the base text for a monologue delivered by one of the novel's minor characters, the industrialist Cedarquist.[13] Flynn criticized a proposal for the funding of a million-dollar exposition, a Pacific Ocean Fair like Chicago's world's fair of 1893 and San Francisco's Midwinter International Exposition of 1894. He thought so frivolous a use of public and private capital preposterous in light of the inability of the Pacific Rolling Mills to find investors who, instead of dallying with fairs, might have made it possible for the firm to remain in business and continue providing employment for fifteen hundred men. He lamented that at present the "only sign of life manifested within [the mill's] walls is in the sale of its remnant materials. Most of this consists of scrap steel." Why bring tourists and potential investors to the Bay Area only to see such a sign of economic debility? In *The Octopus,* Cedarquist is even more outraged over a similarly proposed fair. He finds it ludicrous that a "million dollars [would be] spent to attract the Eastern investor [to San Francisco], in order to show him an abandoned rolling mill wherein the only activity is the sale of remnant material and scrap steel."[14]

Norris's second research strategy was to go beyond print to individuals in the know for information. The Norrises had long been well connected socially in San Francisco, and Jeannette thought that Seymour Waterhouse arranged luncheons with officers of the Southern Pacific for Frank. But John O'Hara Cosgrave was even more fully networked, and he was a great admirer of Collis P. Huntington. Huntington, who lived in New York City, had just begun his semiannual visit to San Francisco in late April. None of Norris's contemporaries indicated when, to conduct an interview, he was ushered into the office of the titan cast as Shelgrim in the novel. Harry M. Wright remembered only that Norris did enjoy a visit with him.[15] But a 1 May 1899 letter on *Wave* stationery to S. S. McClure indicates that Norris planned to see Huntington well before his return to New York City, on 14 May or shortly thereafter: "The Wheat affair is building up *Big* and I am getting the stuff pretty well in hand and hope to have an interview with C. P. Huntington before the end of the week. I want to pull off this interview as soon as I can and before I go down upon a wheat ranch. Huntington will not be here for long and nothing is doing on the ranches just now."[16]

Cosgrave pulled strings not only in this instance. His role in assisting research "from every point of view" is documented in a request for an interview with John P. Irish. Norris's undated letter to Irish employs Cosgrave's name as the abracadabra ensuring a friendly reception.[17]

In 1899 the naval customs officer of the port of San Francisco, Irish was a onetime teacher who had read law and become an attorney in Iowa. He turned to journalism as the editor of the *Iowa State Press* and served three terms in the legislature of this dominantly agricultural state. He moved to California in 1880 to edit both the *Oakland Times* and San Francisco's *Alta California.* A "Gold Bug" Democrat well versed in economic and political matters, he was indeed conservative but conformed to no present-day cartoons of ideologues at odds with liberals intent upon social amelioration. He was, for example, a champion of Japanese immigrants and for a quarter-century the director of the California Blind Directory Home. He wrote "Some

Live Topics," a column for *The Wave*, until 1894, when Cosgrave moved him to the editorial page, and that year he sparred with the populist Arthur McEwen of the *Examiner*, whom Norris certainly should have interviewed as well. If anyone could expose the Southern Pacific down to each and every peccadillo, it was the volcanic McEwen. Whether Norris did meet with him, however, is anyone's guess.

McEwen had energetically supported Eugene V. Debs and the unionists who participated in the violence-suffused Pullman Strike, which was suppressed by President Grover Cleveland's attorney general, Richard Olney. He also sanctioned the felonious blocking of the U.S. mails on the Southern Pacific lines during the strike, demanded a 25 percent reduction of shipping rates, led a movement to nationalize the Southern Pacific, and—to boot—accused *The Wave* and other California periodicals of being in Huntington's pocket. In his "Reply to McEwen," Irish denied this "mendacious indictment" of *The Wave;* and, as may be seen in his editorial, he sided with Cleveland, the railroads across the nation, and the "respectable press" in opposition to the anarchy and plainly undemocratic expedients for change promoted by McEwen.[18] Here and elsewhere in *The Wave,* Irish demonstrated his full grasp of the particulars that bore upon the railroad question, local and national—which is why Cosgrave referred Norris to him as an information source. When *The Octopus* appeared in print, his influence and that of like-minded defenders of the status quo told.

Norris remained sympathetic to the people battling the Southern Pacific, the sins of which were fully utilized in *The Octopus.* But it is as clear that at some point—if not during his research, then later as he composed—he realized the complexity of the situation would require a balanced perspective if he was to fashion a credible indictment of the railroad. Thus he made his portrait of the antirailroad anarchist Caraher and his portrayal of Presley as a bomb thrower intent upon killing the railroad's local agent, S. Behrman, as unattractive as Zola's of the revolutionist Rasseneur and the nihilistic anarchist Souvarine in his similar tale of conflict between the people and a mining company, *Germinal.* As he distanced himself from radicals, Norris also imaged himself as the fair-minded author by deciding not to demonize Huntington when picturing him as the character Shelgrim. Displaying considerably more authorial detachment than he had in *McTeague,* Norris let Shelgrim have his say in defense of his corporation's business practices and allowed the reader to decide what to make of the apologia. Norris may even, in the judgment of some, have leaned too far in this direction when prefacing this scene by having

Presley observe how humane the head of "the octopus" is in his treatment of an alcoholic employee with three children, whom he does not fire but gives a chance at rehabilitation. This is not the "ogre" Presley expected to meet, and not the Collis P. Huntington pictured by McEwen and Bierce.

When respectfully interviewed by Presley, Shelgrim explains why his railroad operates the way it does and must, citing the economic laws that govern for-profit enterprises and ensure bankruptcy when ignored. They boil down to this: consumer demand for wheat and other crops such as the hops the character Dyke harvests results in the supply generated by growers seeking to profit from their production; and the consumer and producer create a demand for transportation satisfied by a railroad with a raison d'être no more philanthropic than the motives of the profit-seeking growers and bargain-hunting consumers. The wheat grower seeks the highest per-bushel price possible, not hesitating to gouge the consumer; the railroad likewise seeks the highest shipping rate it can get, gouging the producer and consumer. Such are the conditions in place in a capitalistic system; and, declares Shelgrim, if responsibility for unfortunate consequences is to be identified, it is not individuals but the system itself to which one must turn. "'Blame conditions, not men,'" is the advice he offers Presley—which Presley accepts without protest.[19]

There was, of course, another reason for Norris to have Shelgrim hold forth thus. Citing deterministic forces governing the economic realm regardless of the individual, Shelgrim fully contributes to the Zolaesque character of *The Octopus*—as does Presley, who comes away from the interview with the conviction that Shelgrim is correct in claiming that the individual counts as little in how the economy works as in the inexorable operations of nature at large. "Forces, conditions, laws of supply and demand," Presley thinks to himself, are the colossal and irresistible determinants governing each and every "human atom."[20] These are not the only naturalistic notes Norris sounds in the novel. Two other recurring themes concerning human nature in Norris's earlier writings surface, the first having to do with the vice with which he was most preoccupied in his canon: greed. But those characters associated with the all-grasping "octopus" are not wholly different from the far-from-saintly ranchers in this respect. The ranchers, and especially their leader, Magnus Derrick, are also thralls to the acquisitive instinct. Second, the railroad certainly bullies the ranchers. But, hiring and firing at will and used to absolute control of everyone and everything on their own large domains, the wheat barons' own appetite for dominance is powerful, and they do not suppress it.

Looming large in the ranchers is the instinct for maintaining top-dog status in the territory they have marked as theirs. Macrocosmically and microcosmically, Norris infuses *The Octopus* with the deterministic themes one expects from an "American Zola."

And yet, despite the naturalism of *The Octopus*, the scene in Shelgrim's office is designed to gall the thoughtful reader not inclined to assume that free will and conscience are chimeras. When Presley remains silent as Shelgrim declares that conditions, not individuals, are responsible for what occurs in the San Joaquin Valley and elsewhere, readers who have given a modicum of thought to ethics may wonder why Presley does not speak up. The response to Shelgrim that begs for utterance is: Insentient forces, conditions, and natural laws are at work in the economy, but this does not obviate the fact that Shelgrim and the equally sentient individuals in his employ *choose* to do what they think conditions demand—if they are to maintain a stranglehold on the ranchers. They are not "human atoms"; like the ranchers, they make choices, and they can choose not to act upon "demands" made by external conditions or by the greedy and domineering "brute within." Even the sexually aroused McTeague exercises choice when restraining himself as Trina lies unconscious in his dental operating chair; and none of the willful, equally assertive railroaders and ranchers is as dimwitted as he.

Presley may be mum on the question of individual moral responsibility because he is typically ineffectual as a thinker and an artist—"a bungler at the world's workbench," Norris terms him at one point.[21] As Norris maintains his balanced perspective on the two groups competing in the economic arena, however, another reason for Presley not to raise ethical considerations is that he—like the reader—is fully informed on how the ranchers have done the same as the railroad, losing the moral high ground by deciding to fight the railroad's bribery of public officials and the press with bribery. Both sides in the conflict display feet of clay.

At the same time and even with the lambs led to the slaughter showing fleece that is far from white, Shelgrim's corporation—or the Southern Pacific—takes the hit for a far more serious offense than is committed by Norris's ranchers. And thus the third kind of research Norris did. Much of the information Norris gathered had to do with what was happening in the 1890s, but the main plot of *The Octopus* is based upon a crisis that the Southern Pacific precipitated in the late 1870s, when Charles Crocker was the president and Gertrude Norris's son was a schoolboy in Chicago.

❧

The crisis that leads to the climax in the main plot of *The Octopus* Norris pulled forward twenty years to be anachronistically integrated with the data he extracted from the 1890s, and the shameful triumph of the railroad in the novel is directly related to what transpired in May 1880 in the southern San Joaquin countryside near a stream running from the Kings River to now-dry Tulare Lake through two counties, Fresno and a portion of Tulare that is now in Kings County. The stream's name was Mussel Slough, and the sensational particulars of the Mussel Slough Tragedy, or Mussel Slough Massacre, first described in the local newspaper, the *Visalia Weekly Delta,* make it immediately apparent why the story was reprinted in newspapers far and wide, as well as why Norris seized upon the incident for its powerful fictional potential. He was not the first. The situation was one of the inspirations for Josiah Royce's 1887 novel *The Feud of Oakfield Creek* and the focus of W. C. Morrow's more comprehensive fictional treatment in 1882's *Blood Money.* Norris refers to neither novelist nor these publications in any of his writings, nor did he ever mention Mussel Slough by name. He refers only to an irrigation ditch in *The Octopus.* Thus, it is possible that he did not discover the event until he began his research in California—whereupon a work intended to deal with the contemporary scene abruptly became much more historical in character.

The situation in Tulare and Fresno Counties dated back to the 1860s and the arrangement between the federal government and the Central Pacific's and Union Pacific's joint construction of the transcontinental rail line completed in 1869. The federal government gave every other section of its land on both sides of the rails to these companies; those sections alternating with the railroads' were retained for distribution to settlers. This was also the case as the Southern Pacific lines extended down the San Joaquin Valley from northern California.

Settlers quickly arrived to claim the government sections in the Valley. Southern Pacific circulars enticed them to settle on its own sections as well, even before it had lain the rails necessary for the railroad to claim ownership. The Southern Pacific's advance prices were attractive. As quoted in a resolution of a Grand Settlers' League representing hundreds of Tulare and Fresno landholders, they were advertised as ranging from $2.50 per acre upward, land with tall timber at $5.00 and that with pine at $10.00. Most were available at $2.50 to $5.00, and the pamphlet assured settlers that improvements of the land would not affect price when, at some time in the future, the rail lines were in place and they would be able to purchase their sections.

In 1878, the railroad's land agent Jerome Madden was busily sending out letters later printed for public examination in the *Visalia Weekly Delta*. They made the surprising announcement that the prices of individual homesteads were not as previously advertised but in the range of twenty to thirty dollars per acre and were for sale *to anyone* who might want to purchase them immediately. A meeting was called at Hanford, then in Tulare County and six miles to the south of Mussel Slough. The participants formed the league to represent its interests before the Southern Pacific, the federal circuit court, the U.S. Supreme Court, the California legislature, and the U.S. Congress. In February 1880 Charles Crocker denied what the league had claimed, asserting that the circular said only $2.50 upward and ignoring the promise not to base evaluations upon improvements the settlers made. As of then, the settlers had met with no success in their legal actions and petitions to legislators.

Researching the situation was not a demanding task. From one issue of the *Visalia Weekly Delta* published on 7 May 1880, or either in a reprinting or a summary of its lengthy "Appeal to the People" in another periodical, Norris and anyone else might get up to speed regarding the historical background for the "tragedy" reported in the next week's issue. And it is noteworthy that Norris's quotation of the original terms under which the railroad's sections were offered for sale is identical—save for italicizations—with that given by the *Delta*.[22]

Norris thus had more than was necessary to fashion the main plot through book 1 of *The Octopus*. He need only add to this cause for complaint on the part of his ranchers another, comparatively minor one voiced by the character Magnus Derrick and his son Harran before the announcement of the elevated land-purchase prices: the short-haul rate the Southern Pacific charged. Farm machinery from the east was transported at the long-haul rate to northern California. The Southern Pacific then applied a different, intrastate rate, one that was disproportionately higher given the shorter distance to a local delivery point such as Hollister or Tres Pinos.

Book 2 deals with the actions of the Grand Settlers' League and what followed the Southern Pacific's refusal to honor its original terms, its decision to dispossess the settlers who would not or could not purchase the land on which they had "squatted," and the implementation of its plan to sell the properties to anyone willing to accept the elevated prices. As the *Visalia*

Weekly Delta reported in full with eyewitness accounts on 14 and 21 May, the railroad's property assessor, William H. Clark, and U.S. Marshall Alonzo W. Poole arrived in Hanford on 10 May 1880. Fearing the worst, settlers began assembling. The next morning, Clark and Poole rode out of town with two local men in league with the railroad, Mills D. Hartt and Walter J. Crow. They went directly to the residence of William B. Braden; and, as in *The Octopus* with the home of the rancher Annixter, they placed all of his household goods in the road.[23] Marshall Poole put Hartt into legal possession of the property. The four then proceeded to the acreage of Henry D. Brewer and John Storer to put Crow in possession. A small group of League members intercepted them, and a gunfight erupted. Seven men were instantly killed or later died from their wounds.

Eyewitness accounts of how and why the first shot was fired vary. No one opined that it was premeditated. Hartt related that the settler James Harris precipitated an exchange with Crow, but it was not clear why. Clark gave a different account, claiming that he was talking to Harris when he was suddenly shot. What is clear is that, within a few seconds, all hell broke loose. The most active participant was Crow, an expert marksman armed with a breechloading shotgun and a variety of other guns in his wagon. When the firing ceased, the settlers James Harris, John E. Henderson, and Iver Kneutson were dead. Wounded and brought with the dead to the house on the Brewer and Storer ranch were Hartt and the settlers Dan Kelley, Edwin Haymaker, and Arch McGregor, whose land was next on the list for possession. Only Haymaker survived his wounds. Crow fled. A never-identified settler tracked him down and executed him.[24]

In making use of the gunfight, Norris illustrated more fully than in any other scene of *The Octopus* what he meant in 1896 when declaring that the characters in a naturalistic work are "flung into the throes of a vast and terrible drama that works itself out in unleashed passions, in blood, and in sudden death."[25] Seemingly made-to-order were the particulars of 1880, especially the fact that the firing appeared to have been accidentally initiated.[26] In his novel, Norris was again faithful to historical fact: as with the house on Brewer's and Storer's ranch, in *The Octopus* wives, children, and parents go to Hooven's nearby home to mourn the dead and the dying.[27] Yet again, Norris balanced his presentation. It is clear that the ranchers are not blameless. Magnus Derrick's son Harran is one of the fatalities; "'God help me and forgive me'" is Magnus's prayer.[28] But Norris places squarely on the railroad the much weightier onus for valuing profit, property, and power more highly than the lives of loved ones. With regard to choosing sides, he situated himself in 1901 where he said he would when writing to Lilla L. Parks in October 1899.

Norris also drew on his past experiences in the California countryside, recorded in his earlier writings, and those had "on the ground" as he visited the wheat-growing areas in the state. As he told Harry M. Wright on 5 April 1899, it was essential to get to California while the wheat was young so that he could observe and later describe the crop as the first pale green shoots emerged from the brown soil—and thus two memorable scenes of the kind that he would fashion with exuberant lyricism.[29] Two weeks later, *The Wave* made it clear that he was intent not only on spot checks but an extended stay "on one of the big wheat ranches of the interior valleys."[30] How otherwise to write an epic of the wheat in which the life span of the grass itself is prominent to the point at which it is a veritable player in the drama depicted?

As of 1 May, when he wrote to S. S. McClure about his progress, Norris had judged that nothing of great import was yet happening on the wheat ranches. But by 27 June, when he posted a letter from a hotel in Stockton in the northern San Joaquin Valley, he was observing the progress of the crop.[31] Whether he went so far south as Hanford to see both the land under cultivation and the scene of the 1880 gunfight is not a matter of record. What is, though, is his lengthy visit to the Santa Anita ranch south of Hollister near Tres Pinos in San Benito County. There he was the guest of Gaston Ashe and his wife Dulce, and Gaston remembered Frank's stay fondly when he responded to Franklin Walker's request for information in 1930. *The Octopus,* he recalled, "was written from day to day on the impressions and stories [Norris] gathered in conversation and observations" during his residence there. "He was a most delightful comrade and full of personality and magnetism." Dulce was more expansive when she wrote to Walker about Norris's month-long visit and, in a subsequent personal meeting with Walker, extended Norris's stay to "about six weeks." Although Gaston and Frank had Bohemian Club membership in common, and all three were attending the same social gatherings in San Francisco as early as 1889, she informed Walker that Ernest and Mary Peixotto had "sent him" to her with a letter of introduction, explaining that Norris wished to witness the harvest. In mid-August when the harvest took place, Norris had been in residence for several weeks.[32] An especially obliging hostess, Dulce made daily trips to Tres Pinos to pick up his mail. He

was anxious to receive letters from Jeannette Black, who became his fiancée
that summer. Dulce too thought that he wrote most of *The Octopus* there.

Such was not, in fact, the case, but Norris was indeed producing drafts
of material he would use, and Dulce was the source of much of the Span-
ish-California information that Norris recorded. "He was always looking for
'stories' from everyone with whom he talked," explained Dulce. She noted
with some pride that she contributed to the first chapter of book 1 the romantic tale Presley hears at Solotari's restaurant, concerning Señor De La
Cuesta's disappointment on first seeing the woman he had married by proxy.
The true story told by Dulce to Norris was that of her great-uncle, Governor
Juan Bautista Alvarado.

A barn dance held on the ranch also made its way into the concluding
scenes of book 1. So did a prominent setting for one of the subplots, the
Mission San Juan Bautista to the north of the ranch. And so did the D. M.
Morse seed farm, visible east of the mission, in the vicinity of which Angéle
Varian's daughter lives. What Dulce did not mention to Walker was of primary
importance for Norris. The Southern Pacific having extended its line to Tres
Pinos in the mid-1870s, the town was then what it is not now: a busy storage and shipping center for livestock and the wheat and hay that Norris saw
harvested. And it was a locus in which he could obtain firsthand information
about the railroad's policies and practices.[33]

Dulce's most important personal contribution to Norris's project, however,
was her behavior as—by Norris's standards—an aesthete. She vividly remembered his holding forth in characteristic fashion as an enemy to "style." Like
Bailey Millard when recalling Norris's preference for "blood and bowels" in a
work of art, she too recalled his article of faith, that "if a book had entrails," it
did "not have to have style." Unlike Millard, Dulce protested against this with
passionate conviction: "I violently disagreed, being a great lover of [Walter]
Pater and [Robert] Browning." And she went on to explain to Walker that
"later [Norris's] brilliant Mother, who was one of the first promoters of the
Browning Society of San Francisco, invited me to become a member." Dulce
became the model for Annie Derrick, Presley's hostess at the Derrick ranch
who is infatuated with Pater, Charles Lamb, John Ruskin, and poets whose
works appeared in *Lark*-like literary magazines. While Norris would distance
himself from the character as he developed his manuscript, he himself was
the model for Presley when ranting against literariness early in the novel.
Poor Mrs. Derrick in *The Octopus* has the same experiences as Dulce: "That
[Presley]—outside of his few chosen deities—should care little for literature

[as she defines it], shocked her beyond words." For Mrs. Derrick, Presley's "indifference to 'style,' to elegant English was a positive affront. His savage abuse and open ridicule of the neatly phrased rondeaux and sestinas and chan-sonnettes of the little magazines was to her mind a wanton and uncalled-for cruelty."[34] As with the cameo portrait of himself at the Big Dipper Mine in chapter 20 of *McTeague,* Norris thus stepped directly from the Santa Anita Ranch into *The Octopus.* So too did the Tres Pinos setting in which Dulce and her guest congenially agreed to disagree. Intent upon treating the San Joaquin Valley's wheat fields, Norris relocated the locale he had come to know best that summer. From the area northeast of Salinas and southeast of Santa Cruz, he carted it from the valley on the east of the Gabilan mountains over the Diablo range and into the San Joaquin.

Further employing poetic license, he invented the gothic, "Ligeia"-like subplot of *The Octopus* that has almost nothing to do with the conflict between the ranchers and the railroad but, instead, incorporates the theosophist Elena Blavatsky's and her disciple Annie Besant's theory of the transmigration of souls, which he had treated satirically in 1897's "The Puppets and the Puppy." As Zola did in *Rome* when he had his heroine's heart literally burst because of an excess of passion as she held her dying lover in her arms, Norris threw off all restraints when treating the story of the character Vanamee's inability to accept the death of his lover Angéle when giving birth to the daughter of the never-discovered man who raped her. Indeed, he out-Zolaed Zola, whose heroine in *Rome* does not come back from the dead two decades later to—as Vanamee believes—occupy her daughter's body and resume her relationship with him. Norris wrote to Isaac F. Marcosson in September 1900, when he was nearing completion of *The Octopus,* that the Vanamee-Angéle subplot "is the most romantic thing I've yet done." He termed it "pure romance—oh, even mysticism, if you like, a sort of allegory—I call it the allegorical side of the wheat subject."[35] The credible allegory he appears to have had in mind then was the conventional one: that, as new plants spring from seemingly dead, dry seed, so life perennially emerges from death in the natural order. Angéle died, but her daughter was born. Life goes on, renewing itself. Less credible than that allegory but certainly more imaginatively engaging was what Norris superimposed upon it, the "pure romance" that ends with the emotionally unstable and rationally unhinged Vanamee's declaring to Presley that Angéle herself "has returned to me." As when he is with Shelgrim, Presley is once again mum, as Norris prompts the reader to recognize a specious assertion.[36] And so this subplot finally does reveal a single thematic linkage with, or ironic counterpoint to, the main one. Given that none of the slain wheat ranchers does or is likely to return from the dead, what is real—their deaths at the hands of the railroad's representatives—is doubly underscored by Vanamee's lunatic denial of mortality. So too are Mrs. Hooven's death from starvation and the miscarriage suffered by Annixter's widow.

Not so inventive or distant from the main plot is the secondary one involving the discharged railroad employee, Dyke, who plants a crop of hops because of elevated demand and thus market price. Astounded to learn that the railroad has noted the same increase in the per-bushel price and, to his ruin, raised its shipping rate proportionally, his rage eventuates in his becoming a train robber and subsequently fleeing into the mountains to escape the posse that pursues him. And it is here that we see Norris mining his own earlier writings, recycling information for a grander purpose than meeting *Wave* press deadlines. Published in June 1896, "Man-Hunting: The Coast Range as a Refuge for Bandits" opened with a reflection on San Francisco as the center of modern civilized life on the West Coast. Yet, Norris noted, only three hours to the south, in the coastal mountain ranges, "you will find yourself in the heart of a country that has been, and that is even now, a very paradise for outlaws, bandits, and fugitive criminals."[37] In the backcountry of this region, the legendary bandits Jesus Tejada, Tiburcio Vàsquez, and Juan Soto easily eluded the law. That was decades earlier, he confessed. But more recently, in 1889–92, John Sontag and Chris Evans—the former a onetime train brakeman, the latter a farmer, and both embittered against the Southern Pacific—dynamited and held up trains and, like their Mexican predecessors, evaded capture in the same mountains. A posse finally shot Sontag to death in Tulare County, and Evans served a long prison term.[38] What was true of the coastal mountains was also true of the Sierra Nevadas running south through eastern Fresno and Tulare Counties into Kern County, which are the setting for Dyke's flight and capture.

Norris drew on two other previous experiences in the same region that he recorded in *The Wave*. The Mission San Juan Bautista at which he set key scenes featuring Vanamee was not a discovery made when Norris was the Ashes' guest. Two years earlier, in July 1897, he attended the hundredth-anniversary celebration held there. "Birthday of an Old Mission" included an appreciation of the parade, the Mexican food served, the ethnic costumes of the servers, and a bishop's sermon delivered during high mass. Also, in a September 1900 letter to Isaac F. Marcosson, Norris gives the impression that in 1899 he had crossed the Diablo range to the great valley to the east and had his first experience of harvesting machinery: "I helped run and work a harvester in the San Joaquin—that is I helped on the sacking-platform—but of course you don't know where that is."[39] But this was not a wholly new situation for Norris. At harvest time in 1897 he described the output of the San Joaquin Valley and, with some enthusiasm, "the largest harvester ever built, . . . propelled by steam, and [cutting] a swath of the tremendous width of fifty-four feet." He opined that it is "quite worth the trip to Stockton to see this enormous engine at its work, rolling through the grain knee deep, as it were, like a feeding mammoth, its teeth clicking and clashing before it, its locomotive rumbling behind. . . . Before its passage the wheat is mere standing grain, yellowy and nodding in the summer sun; after it has passed the wheat is grain in sacks ready for shipment." Norris was hardly the naïf concerning wheat harvesting when he left New York in April 1899. And in the same article he focused on another *Octopus*-related bit of information concerning a famine-relief shipload of grain carried to India by a steamer that had already played a role in the composition of *Blix:* the *City of Everett.*[40] Two months earlier, in an 1897 *Wave* article, Norris gave full attention to this philanthropic gesture by San Francisco's Committee of the Indian Famine Relief Fund and contributors living in Kansas, Iowa, Nebraska, and elsewhere across the United States.[41] Two thousand six hundred tons of grain and legumes went on their way to India—as a like amount of wheat does at the conclusion of *The Octopus,* in the ship on the deck of which a mentally and emotionally debilitated Presley is ruminating on the significance of the deaths and losses of property to the railroad that he has witnessed in the San Joaquin Valley. He is not aboard the *City of Everett* but another vessel, the *Swanhilda.* Yet here again Norris's experience as a *Wave* journalist is pertinent: that is the name of a ship bound for San Francisco from Australia with a hold full of coal that he focused upon in a January 1897 article, "Hunting Human Game." In this respect, Norris's term of duty with *The Wave* was an apprenticeship for writing portions of *The Octopus.*

One other journalistic experience merits mention: South Africa in 1895–96. Prior to the Jameson Raid, John Hays Hammond had prepared for the uprising of the Uitlanders against the Boers, storing rifles in the Johannesburg office building where he worked. The rancher Annixter does the same in his house, in the event that the ranchers' league may have to resort to the use of arms to prevent the railroad's seizure of his and others' property. A more significant echo of the South African experience in 1896, though, will perhaps be recalled. Norris had complained that one of the reasons that the

Uitlanders' scheme for taking control of Boer Johannesburg failed was that the long-planned uprising in the city that Jameson was supposed to trigger did not occur: the hundreds pledged to support him balked. Further, the hundreds who might have at least rushed out of the city and, only twelve miles away, rescued Jameson from capture by the Boers did nothing of the sort. A similar complaint is heard in *The Octopus* when, at the irrigation ditch, the hundreds of league members who swore to oppose evictions with deadly force do not materialize to support the few ranchers who are there. Betrayal by one's own in the Transvaal became betrayal by one's own near Hanford. Norris never got over his attachment to the Uitlander cause: after the outbreak of the Boer War in October 1899, he would once more trash the Boers and exalt the English in an article published in the *San Francisco Examiner.*[42]

Returning to New York in late August 1899, Norris combined what he had extracted from his various sources of information: the writings of others, interviews with informed observers and participants in the "battle of the people with the railroad," his experiences in the vicinity of Tres Pinos and in the San Joaquin Valley, and his own earlier writings. But the successful outcome of his courtship of Jeannette Black, to whom he was now engaged, and his preparation for the writing of *The Octopus* were not the only consequences of his April-August visit to California. In May he had written a short story that appeared in the *San Francisco Examiner* in early June, a mordant variation on the flowering-of-true-love tale of *Blix:* "'As Long as Ye Both Shall Live'" pictured two former lovers who refuse to admit they are no longer in love and persist in their obstinacy through a marriage ceremony. That month he also dropped his *Octopus* work to reply at length in an *Examiner* article, "A Miraculous Critic," to J. F. Rose-Soley, who had chided him for "nautical" errors of fact in *Moran of the Lady Letty.* Cosgrave, of course, was less critical upon the appearance of "With Lawton at El Caney" in the June *Century.* He ranked Norris's prose superior to that of more famous war correspondents such as Richard Harding Davis and Caspar Whitney because of his "extraordinary keenness of perception and rare ability at rending the sights and sounds of battle."[43] As to his forthcoming books, Norris had corrected the proof for *Blix*, in press in August and September at Doubleday and McClure. And it is likely that he initiated his revision for later book publication of the syndicated version of *A Man's Woman*, which began appearing in the *San Francisco Chronicle* on 23 July 1899.

On his way back to New York City, he may have recalled telling Bruce Porter in April that he would walk down Sutter Street and people would know him for a literary celebrity. Such was certainly the case. How could it have been otherwise by the end of the summer, with *Moran* and *McTeague* published by American, English, and Canadian firms, and both known by San Franciscans to have been praised by Arthur Conan Doyle? In addition to reports on his doings by Bailey Millard and Cosgrave, *A Man's Woman* was running in the *Chronicle*. Two shorter pieces had seen print in the *Examiner*, another in *Century*, and he had been puffed as an author in announcements of his engagement to Jeannette.

After he had left town, the greatest admirer of *Moran* the world will ever know—Bailey Millard—could even assume with impunity that his *Examiner* readers would find of cardinal interest anything touching upon his favorite book. At the beginning of September, an illustrated article on the extraction of ambergris from a dead whale by those aboard the bark *Morgan* appeared in the *Examiner's* Sunday supplement. Norris had featured the same event in *Moran*, and life was now imitating art. What more reason was required for Millard to elevate an event of inarguably low significance to prominence via a rather full summary of how Norris depicted its fictional analogue?[44]

The hometown boy had made good, and he would do even better now that he had the wherewithal to write *The Octopus*.

21

PROFESSIONAL ADVANCES AND
PERSONAL COMMITMENTS

In late August 1899, Norris was again residing on Washington Square and taking his meals at the Judson Hotel.[1] According to Jeannette, he then interviewed Collis P. Huntington—for the second time—and they "grew to be good friends." Indeed, before Huntington's death in August 1900, Frank and she dined at his palatial home on Fifth Avenue at Fifty-seventh Street. Farther up Fifth Avenue at the mansion now housing the National Academy of Design, they were once the house guests of the sculptress Anna Hyatt Huntington, the wife of Collis's stepson Archer. Jeannette saw nothing ironic in this. But such coziness with the Huntingtons is at least remarkable since Norris returned from California still a champion of "the people." This he once again made clear in a 9 November 1899 letter, his second written to Lilla Lewis Parks.

After Parks received his mid-October declaration that he was opposed to the Southern Pacific, she had made another effort to exercise a trust-friendly influence on *The Octopus.* Her letter is not available, but Norris's reply indicates that she suggested an easy solution to the railroad-monopoly problem in California: the presence of a second octopus might immediately erase the ill effects produced by one.

That competition *could* make a difference was true. Such was the case when, between 1895 and 1898, a new railroad company, the Valley Road, laid its rails from Stockton down the San Joaquin Valley to Bakersfield; then it began to build westward from Stockton toward the Pacific coast. The Southern Pacific adjusted its San Joaquin rates downward, and the Valley Road came to be popularly known as "the People's Road." What Parks had in mind in late 1899, though, was a much grander corporation coming into competition with the Southern Pacific: the Atchison, Topeka, and Santa Fe. It ran through the southwest to Los Angeles and San Diego and would, after it formally absorbed the Valley Road in July 1899, extend its lines through the San Joaquin and beyond to reach Point Richmond on San Francisco Bay by 1900. That year it not only ended the Southern Pacific's monopoly on oceanic shipping from the Bay Area but was providing regular transcontinental service from San Francisco to New York via Chicago.[2] Such developments, in fact, marked the beginning of the end for the Southern Pacific's stranglehold on California. Parks thus proved to be far from dotty in her speculations.

In his reply, Norris was not, of course, prescient of such developments to come. Nor was a *San Francisco Chronicle* journalist who on 25 May 1899 saw burgeoning amity in the relationship between the two large corporations. He described their cooperative arrangement, opining that it "certainly does not indicate a big fight between the two giants."[3] Norris had observed signs of the same and politely informed Parks on 9 November 1899 that the panacea she envisioned was the stuff of dreams. He explained that the Southern Pacific, the Atchison, Topeka, and Santa Fe, and the smaller affiliated lines that the two leviathans had not yet devoured were enjoying a mutually agreeable price-fixing arrangement, pooling their interests to maintain high rates.[4] And no matter how well he got along with Huntington personally, or to what degree he was sympathetic in his portrait of Huntington as Shelgrim, Norris's attitude toward the Southern Pacific as the invincible menace seen twenty years earlier at Mussel Slough did not change. In *The Octopus* it may appear a necessary evil, given the role it and other lines played in making the United States a breadbasket for the world. But because of its inhumane operations, it was an evil nonetheless.

As time passed, Norris found that there were aspects of the situation with which he had not fully dealt when in California, and his research was ongoing. On 22 November 1899 he wrote to his friend at the *Louisville Times* who had recently given *Blix* a rave review, Issac F. Marcosson, about a matter that one would think he had already investigated to some degree but about which he was not confident. "The situation in my story is this: There is a certain group of farmers who, despairing of ever getting fair freight rates from the Railroad or of electing a board of Railroad Commissioners by fair means themselves, set about gaining their ends by any means available. . . . They are prepared to spend a very large amount of money to accomplish this." Norris had by then, it appears, gone no farther in his draft of *The Octopus* than chapter 3 of book 1—approximately a hundred pages in the first edition—where the ranchers meet to discuss the means of achieving lower shipping rates and they first use the word "bribery." Moreover, at this stage of the composition he was even uncertain as to how many of his wheat growers would be involved in the conspiracy: "I think they form a kind of ring of six or eight men." Norris asked Marcosson if he could tell him how the ranchers "would go about to get their men in? Do you think it *could* be done at all? What I am anxious to get hold of are the *details* of this kind of game, the lingo, and the technique, etc., but at the same time, want to understand it very clearly."[5] As he continued to forge forward with the manuscript that would result in a volume of 652 pages, there was yet more research to do. Telling Marcosson almost ten months later, on 13 September 1900, that "[t]he Squid is nearing conclusion," he related that he had been "in correspondence with all kinds of people during its composition, from the Traffic Manager of a western railroad to the sub-deputy-assistant of the Secretary of Agriculture at Washington."[6]

As would be the case with *The Pit*, Norris dated *The Octopus's* prefatory note on this volume's relationship to the others in his trilogy when he finally completed his manuscript. And so it was not until 15 December 1900 that he ended the long trek begun in the winter of 1898–99.

Much else had happened after he left California. *Blix* required only the correction of proof before its publication in mid-September 1899. More time, however, was needed for the completion of his revision and then the proofing of *A Man's Woman*, given its book publication at the beginning of February 1900. The version distributed to newspapers by S. S. McClure the previous summer was rife with infelicities indicating that Norris, in ill health during the composition and shifting his interest to the wheat-trilogy project, was not inclined to give it his full attention. Numerous stylistic improvements at the sentence and paragraph levels were now necessary if the book was to make a respectable showing. Even the characterizations were initially botched in particular respects. For example, readers of the *San Francisco Chronicle* encountered in the first chapter a secondary character, Adler, who is a lowly cook. In the next he is instead a sailing master, a sophisticated professional who later demonstrates a full command of technical literature on Arctic exploration. The hero, Ward Bennett, is markedly religious in the first chapter. Not particularly noteworthy are his carrying his copy of the *Book of Common Prayer* to the Arctic or his reading aloud from its "Order for the Burial of the Dead" when interring a fallen comrade. But the hubristic Ward goes well beyond Episcopalianism in the *Chronicle* when declaring that God is with him and thus he cannot fail. Yet, despite such an ardent show of belief in his divinely ordained destiny, he demonstrates no signs of such fervent religiosity in later chapters, not even when he falls into a fit of depression because he feels responsible for the death from typhus of his best friend, Richard Ferris, nor even when he loses the love of the nurse Lloyd Searight—and plunges her into depression—by preventing her from doing her duty in Richard's sickroom where she would have been exposed to infection. Norris made the appropriate corrections, elevating Adler to his rightful status and stripping Ward of a special role in providential history.

The most remarkable gaffe in the McClure syndicate's version of *A Man's Woman,* however, was Norris's radical alteration of the hero's and heroine's personalities in the final chapters. On his own or perhaps at the suggestion of a McClure editor, Norris had decided to leaven the gloomy, sturm-und-drang plot, going so far as to attempt a heartwarming, happy, and even frolicsome ending. Certainly Norris's readers would appreciate *some* uplift after the conflict-ridden hero's and heroine's prolonged descents into self-questioning introspection and self-pity, not to mention Ward's own delirious bout with typhus. Norris went too far in this direction, though. In the serial version he transformed the personalities of the heretofore mirthless, narrowly focused, and ploddingly dutiful Ward and Lloyd into those of the joshing Condy Rivers and perky Travis Bessemer of *Blix.*

Ward, the apotheosis of single-minded determination to have his own way, and the frantic Lloyd became jolly, even effervescent spirits, cleverly engaging in glittering repartee and deftly making tongue-in-cheek literary allusions to Anthony Hope's *The Prisoner of Zenda,* which the original personalities they so abruptly replaced could not have hoped to understand, much less articulate. Their capacity for joie de vivre is wholly unanticipated in the previous chapters, and in revision Norris wisely toned down the scene by excising some of their banter.[7] That done, he was finished with the most miserable composition experience he is known to have had. He was free to return to *The Octopus,* in which he would take considerable pride and pleasure.

Shortly afterwards, when writing to Ernest Peixotto on 16 February 1900, he delighted in an unprecedented development. Booksellers had taken all of the 3,500 copies of the first printing of *A Man's Woman*—before its formal publication on 3 February.[8] The novel might prove an embarrassment among the literati, but Norris very much needed the royalties it promised to produce. And to this end, he later in 1900 responded to negative reviews complaining about the shudder-inducing aspects of the novel by rewriting the graphic description of a surgical procedure.[9] Although Bailey Millard had made much of him as a "high-salaried" author when he came to California in April, Norris was not that—and thus the long delay before his formal engagement in July 1899 and, over six months later, his marriage to Jeannette Black.

As 1900 and the wedding in February approached, so did a promising new professional opportunity that made the marriage financially possible. As early as September 1899, Norris knew of the likelihood that a new publishing company would be formed in New York and that he might enjoy a better position with it. Jeannette recalled that it was then that she received a letter from him telling her that she should put on "hold" their Blixian plan for her to pursue a career in medicine. Becoming a physician was out of the question. Dropping out of the Monticello Female Seminary in 1898, Jeannette had not completed her secondary education, and unlike Frank she never attended a college or university. Thus, like the heroine of *A Man's Woman*, she was instead to begin studying nursing in October at the Training School for Nurses on California Street at Maple in San Francisco. But now, if things worked out for Frank as he hoped they would in the months ahead, she could take the more traditional route from single blessedness to connubial bliss. Although she was the inspiration for his glowing portrait of a self-sufficient New Woman in *Blix,* Jeannette jumped at the chance to make a less demanding transition from dependency on her parents to being cared for by her breadwinner in New York.

Norris was indebted to S. S. McClure for giving him his entré into the New York publishing world in early 1898. One of McClure's other employees and Norris's superior, the poet Sidney Lanier's son Henry, wrote to Walker that Frank came east "in a blaze of excited hopefulness over the career which he felt had been suddenly offered him." Once within the McClure establishment, however, things did not go as well as Norris thought they would. And thus Lanier observed that Norris became at length "quite disturbed over the uncertain outlook" for him at the firm.

As evidenced by the serializations of *Moran* and *A Man's Woman,* he did enjoy the opportunity to see his novels appear in newspapers. As of December 1899, though, only once did the prolific *Wave* short-story writer achieve syndicated publication—the reprinting of 1896's "A Salvation Boom in Matabeleland" in four newspapers.[10] Something was wrong at *McClure's Magazine,* too. His short stories had appeared therein only twice; moreover, the Cuban campaign correspondent for *McClure's* had to turn to a literary agent to see his war articles published elsewhere. The third arm of the Mc-Clure establishment, Doubleday and McClure Company, had on the whole treated him much better. There were setbacks even there, of course. The publication of *McTeague* occurred almost a year later than it might have because, as John S. Phillips told Walker, Doubleday was understandably uneasy about its "realistic contents." And, when Norris submitted the manuscript of *Vandover and the Brute* at some time before November 1899, Doubleday and McClure declined it, as did two English publishers, William Heinemann and Grant Richards.[11] Still, *Moran, McTeague,* and *Blix* were in the bookstores. Frank N. Doubleday was proving a much better friend than McClure.

Norris's position with McClure was a curious one. It is clear that he handled conventional correspondence with authors and their representatives.[12] He also engaged in editing, proofreading, and evaluation of manuscripts submitted to not only the syndicate but the magazine and Doubleday and McClure. He certainly was writing new short stories, even though the syndicate is not known to have placed them with newspapers. The fact of the matter, though, is that no one has ever been able to establish Norris's job description, for good reason: There was none. What he once termed his "hammer and tongs" work was whatever was needed at particular moments. Norris's experience in this respect was not unique. When he wrote to Phillips on 9 January 1900 to explain why he had decided to jump ship, he was only one of many talented individuals who finally had to go elsewhere because of McClure's managerial foibles. For example, the muckraking journalistic luminaries Ida Tarbell, Lincoln Steffens, and Ray Stannard Baker—and even Phillips—abandoned McClure in 1906 to found their own magazine, *The American.* McClure was long on ambition and "vision," attempting in 1899 to incorporate the bankrupt Harper and Brothers into his empire and bringing aboard the former editor of the *Atlantic Monthly,* Walter Hines Page, to play a role in that unsuccessful venture. Running a tight ship was another matter and the burden of the more practical-minded John S. Phillips.

Norris's main complaint was that he was thoroughly misunderstood by his boss. Why, he wondered when writing to Phillips, did McClure offer him the position of subeditor for *McClure's Magazine?* Of what real use could he be in the management of either the magazine or the syndicate? McClure should have been able to see "what I was fitted for and how out of place I should have been in his business." What galled him most was that McClure somehow could not register the fact that Norris's sole ambition and talents were literary—not managerial, editorial, or clerical. It was as though McClure had little time for authors in his own house, especially in 1899, when he was preoccupied with swinging the Harper and Brothers deal, and that spelled insecurity for Norris. "It's not that I distrust Mr. McClure in the slightest degree.—You know that." But, Norris confided to Phillips, McClure had proven so unfocused and imperceptive that, no matter what promises he made, "I am afraid that he would forget all about me in one week's time" as new possibilities for expansion commanded his attention.[13] Norris chose to secure a safer berth and more promising passage with two others who had decided to bid farewell to McClure: Doubleday and his focused and dependable new partner, Page. Doubleday, Page, and Company, founded in December 1899, would not make the same mistakes with him that McClure had.

Doubleday also brought Henry Lanier with him downtown, from East Twenty-fifth Street to Union Square, and on 30 December 1899 Lanier defined the position that Norris would have with the new firm. It would enjoy exclusive rights for serializations and book publications of his works. Norris would receive thirty dollars per week, eighteen of which was an advance payment made against royalties, that is, deducted from his semiannual earnings for his publications. The additional twelve dollars would be straight salary for five half-days' office work, with the remainders of those days "free for your writing."[14]

The time Norris spent at the Doubleday, Page offices on the third floor of 34 Union Square was in part like that formerly given to various duties ten blocks away at McClure's. The difference was, however, remarkable. Rather than parceling out his time to the syndicate, a monthly magazine, *and* a book-publishing concern, his office work focused on book publications only. His half-days were given to the task of evaluating submissions. Thus, Norris's tour of duty as a "go-fer" was over, and the next plateau to reach was a degree of success that would enable him to move beyond all such work-for-hire by making the wheat-trilogy novels best-sellers.

The financial arrangement and, before that, the invitation to join Doubleday and Page in their new enterprise was congruent not only with the professional promise Doubleday saw in Norris but—as is sometimes the case—with other, more personal affinities between the two men. Like William Dean Howells, with whom Norris dined on many occasions, according to Jeannette, and like Hamlin Garland, who met Norris in early 1900 and testified in his 1901–2 diaries to his extraordinary personal charm, and like the recently widowed Mrs. James A. Herne, who would entertain Jeannette and Frank repeatedly in 1901–2,[15] Doubleday did not hesitate to socialize with the employee only eight years his junior. Jeannette told Franklin Walker of visiting Doubleday's home, where they were dinner guests along with Howells and Mark Twain. But there was another reason that the two men hit it off so well.

The Reverend E. P. Gould presided over Norris's wedding ceremony at St. George's Episcopal church on 12 February 1900, after Gertrude had accompanied to New York the young Californienne she at least once referred to as "that hussy" in Bertha Rickoff's presence. Having reconciled herself to the inevitable, Frank's mother was one of the two witnesses. The other was the man who had become a close friend. He was not one of the artists who had fled San Francisco to Manhattan, nor was he a Fiji. Doubleday, a member of St. George's since the fall of 1897, was Norris's fellow communicant there (Norris had formalized his relationship with the parish in January 1899).[16]

How birds of a feather flock together—professionally, socially, and even religiously—may be seen yet again among the senior members of the firm who, unlike Norris at this time, could afford to live in the upscale neighborhood in the vicinity of St. George's. East Sixteenth Street runs east from Union Square for three blocks to the church facing Stuyvesant Square; Henry Lanier lived one block away from St. George's on this street, at 103, and Doubleday lived at at 116. Walter Hines Page lived just to the north near Gramercy Park, at 105 East Nineteenth; and by December 1900 he, too, had joined St. George's.

The two locales bear a special significance in an account of Norris's life. The offices on Union Square immediately relate to Norris's public identity as a professional novelist. St. George's is significant in a very different way, disclosing a dimension of his personality not immediately apparent in his writings nor prominent in the recollections of the majority of his friends and acquaintances.

Given his reputation, then and now, as a literary naturalist and an admirer of the emphatically atheistic Emile Zola, Norris was this church's most unlikely member. Even if one were not aware of his enthusiasm for Zola, his four areligious novels published through early 1900 and the one still in manuscript, *Vandover and the Brute,* would suggest that Norris was not himself religious. *McTeague,* for example, depicts a world bereft of supernatural or spiritual significance. *Vandover* may even seem antireligious to fundamentalists who expect divine intervention in the affairs of men and women. Twice do characters in that novel directly appeal to God for resolutions of the crises they face, and both times they experience disappointment. Thus Norris's seemingly peculiar relationship with Doubleday and Page as a fellow Episcopalian—a relationship not dealt with by Franklin Walker in his biography but one that raises questions that provide access to Norris's private convictions and limn the religious orientation that would at last manifest itself in *The Octopus.*

What may strike some as a paradoxical or insincere affiliation was not necessarily the result of a desire to cultivate a self-serving relationship with Doubleday, though Norris's 1898–99 patron at Doubleday and McClure may indeed have had something to do with his selecting St. George's in 1899. Aside from the fact that none of his contemporaries ever suggested that Norris was hypocritical or sycophantic, other factors warrant a less cynical conclusion about his motivation. True, only two short stories published in 1897 and 1898 with the same title, "Miracle Joyeux," suggest positive religious reflections on his part. (These were the two pieces featuring Jesus as hero: one version of "Miracle" images his compassion; the other pictures him meting out justice, as in Matthew 25:31–46.) Otherwise, his canon as it had thus far developed had given little reason to conclude that he was Christian in any meaningful respect. All that can be inferred from his many quotations and paraphrases of the Bible and the *Book of Common Prayer* is an Episcopalian background. But, as will be seen, in the book on which he was working in 1900 Norris no longer played his cards so close to his vest. Like his membership at St. George's, *The Octopus* prompts one to consider the possibility that Norris, influenced by Zola and having much in common with a- and antireligious contemporaries such as Ambrose Bierce, Stephen Crane, and Theodore Dreiser, differed from them by privately maintaining his faith in the typically reserved manner for which Episcopalians have long been chided by members of more demonstrative denominations.

The first pertinent consideration regarding this literary naturalist's private beliefs is that Norris would not have been the first person to make a

Kierkegaardian leap into faith—either despite the cautions given by reason, or on account of the perceived limitations of that faculty. His fellow Fiji Albert J. Houston, M.D., did not think that such was the case. Houston told Walker that he himself, a former Sunday-school teacher, lost his religion at the University of California: "[M]y religion had evaporated." His opinion was that Norris was little different from him: while Gertrude was a "staunch formalist" who read the Bible aloud twice a day and conducted family prayer at bedtime, Frank "did not have a deeply religious nature" and was "not really religious at all." Rather, thought Houston, whatever the degree of attraction Episcopalianism may have had, it was only its "aesthetic qualities" that appealed to the artist in Norris. He thus disagreed with Fiji Harry M. Wright. Wright knew a different Norris who was "a good orthodox Episcopalian." For Norris, he declared, it was the "one thing one did not question." Giving Houston's testimony a different twist, he cited Norris's mother's influence as a positive factor in this regard.

Jeannette agreed with Wright. To the possible surprise of readers of *Moran, McTeague, A Man's Woman,* and even the pleasant but not at all religious *Blix,* she declared to Walker that her husband was "very spiritual." But she complicated matters when it came to a finer definition of how that spirituality manifested itself. She put herself at odds with Wright on one point, offering the qualification that Frank was "decidedly not orthodox." She also ran at cross-purposes with Houston when explaining to Walker that Frank "disliked particularly the high church" tradition within Episcopalianism—the more elaborate or "aesthetic" liturgical practices, the splendiferous costuming of the ministers, the use of incense, and other irritants for those Episcopalians like her husband with a "low-church," Protestant preference for the plain and simple. To wit, she recalled a trial of a service in Roselle, New Jersey: "[H]igh church—no good." They did not repeat the visit to St. Luke's.

Jeannette, however, was reared as a Presbyterian; and, although she too became a member of St. George's in March 1900, it does not appear that she ever became acculturated to the degree that she knew what her husband meant by "high church." For example, after describing Norris's distaste for Romish pomp, she unwittingly contradicted herself by saying that Frank "loved to go to the Catholic Church for the beauty of its services." High-church services in the Episcopal church are very much like those in the Roman Catholic; the main difference then was that the former were conducted in English and the latter in Latin. Moreover, when opining that Frank was not orthodox, she appears to have thought that "high-church" is synonymous with "orthodox." In fact, one may be truly orthodox and "low-church" at the same time—and that is a good reason for Frank's having signed on at St. George's and, when his daughter was born in 1902, having her baptized at a similar church while the Norrises were the house guests of friends at Southampton, Long Island.

St. George's was as "low" as one might go, as is first suggested when one views its front from Stuyvesant Square across Rutherford Place, or it would immediately be apparent to those familiar with the architectural consequences of post-1820s, Oxford Movement–generated controversies with the Anglican-Episcopalian community. Completed in 1848, the structure's German Romanesque style dictated by its evangelical rector, the Reverend Dr. Stephen Tyng, was a statement against the too–Roman Catholic, or high-church, forms of Episcoplianism represented downtown by the Gothic Revival Trinity church at Broadway and Wall Street. Within St. George's, one sees another statement: The interior is that of a meeting hall in which sermons are preached and heard. As in other kinds of frankly Protestant environments, the "word"—the exegesis and practical application of scripture—is central, and the church is constructed accordingly. To the same end, St. George's does *not* have an articulated chancel designed in the Roman manner and bespeaking a greater emphasis on the sacrament of Communion than is common in more Protestant churches.[17] Anything smacking of high-church or papistic influence would have been out of place during Tyng's tenure from 1845 to 1878, or later in the nineteenth century, when St. George's most prominent member and senior warden, the evangelical J. Pierpont Morgan, handpicked the rector Norris knew, the Reverend William S. Rainsford.

Rainsford was the Irish-born son of a low-church, evangelical Anglican clergyman who, like Morgan (a descendant of Jonathan Edwards), emphasized the importance of faith vis-à-vis salvation and downplayed the emphasis on "good works" associated with the Roman tradition. The son was like the pietistic father, until his experience with the working class in London and Toronto prompted his embrace of the Social Gospel movement. Low-church in style and ardent in his religious convictions, Rainsford embodied during his ministry at St. George's the most memorable theme in the Epistle of James, that faith without good works is dead. Impressed by Rainsford's energy, sophistication, and dedication to good causes, Morgan provided him with ten thousand dollars per year (beyond his salary) to support the social-outreach projects he outlined in late 1883.[18] Thus did Rainsford begin in 1884 to remake the image of St. George's as one of the city's older churches that had been newly revived and transformed into a place where great things were being done for the poor and especially the children of newly arrived immigrants. Educational and vocational-training programs proliferated as he targeted lower Manhattan and children like the heroine of Stephen Crane's *Maggie,* Richard Harding Davis's Rags Raegen, and the "little micks" to whom Norris would refer in *The Pit.* The charismatic minister captured not only Norris's attention but a goodly portion of his time and energy.

How well Norris came to know Rainsford is suggested in surviving pages of the record he kept of manuscripts he read for Doubleday, Page in 1902.[19] On 5 February 1902, he received Rainsford's manuscript for *The Reasonableness of Faith.* According to this record, which lists over three hundred titles, it was the only one that Norris returned "by hand," three days after its receipt. Doubleday, Page published this collection of sermons in May of that year, and Jeannette told Franklin Walker that her husband was personally responsible for seeing it through the press. She also told him that Norris found the collection "trite" after it had appeared in "cold print." In any case, the volume makes clear what appealed to him in Rainsford's Christianity. Like the more famous Phillips Brooks of Boston, Rainsford cared little for the niceties of dogma and creedal specifics. He emphasized instead the social ethic articulated by Jesus and promoted concern for one's neighbor as the means of emulating this "God in man made manifest." An evolutionist, he invoked Darwin as well as Herbert Spencer when calling for personal improvement and social amelioration; and, very likely reassuring the literary naturalist in his congregation, Rainsford rooted the religious impulse not in tradition nor in one's mother's influence but in an *instinct* that had not become vestigal over the course of human evolution. The minister even echoed the author of *McTeague* and *The Octopus* by writing about the "dormant brute within,"[20] those antisocial, selfish impulses that require suppression if one is to elevate his or her own condition and enhance those of others. Rainsford's concern over the negative effects produced by the well-heeled and powerful who formed trusts militating against the welfare of the working class is also noteworthy. The only identifiably "trite" element in Rainsford's thought was his occasional display in his sermons of a teleological view of evolution—though he is never so extreme in this respect as the more visionary idealist Joseph LeConte.

How well Rainsford knew his parishioner is only suggested in the single extant page of a letter he wrote to Jeannette, expressing his sympathy upon Norris's death and detailing his fond recollections of his personality. They were on a first-name basis, and the text on this page ends thus: "It only seems to me the other day since he came to me at the church door, and said he would like. . . ."[21] What Norris then wanted is now, of course, undiscoverable. Though Rainsford may thus have begun referring to Norris's desire to be married at St. George's, he may also have been recalling his having volunteered to participate in the church's social-outreach program. Happily, Rainsford eulogized Norris publicly, making more specific his reasons for admiration in the monthly magazine that Walter Hines Page edited and that Doubleday, Page published, *The World's Work*:

> We need today men who can see, who, seeing things and men as they are, can still firmly believe—believe in the general soundness of life, the "worth-doing" of it all. And still more, we need men who can put down accurately what they see sanely. Such a student, believer, artist was Frank Norris.
>
> He has left us in the very morning of his life. He has gone before he struck the stride of midday marching. The best he has given had promise of still better work. But he lived enough, and put enough life into his [writings], to give notice to all that he is of those who, even in youth, are content with nothing less than to see life sanely, and to see it whole.
>
> The honesty, the bravery, the faith of the man, all live in his work. The pity of it [is] that time was given to him only to make a beginning. Frank Norris's work rings true—always true. There is not one unmanly or unhealthy note struck. He takes it for granted that ordinary people, if we could only really see them, are interesting enough to write about, yet he never knows a trace of the sordid.
>
> It was my privilege to be counted among his friends for years. I seldom have met so lovable a man. He had unquestionably great dramatic power. He believed with all his soul in the future of democracy, and ever and always he tried to serve his fellow man.[22]

Most pertinent, in light of Jeannette's comments on her husband's relationship with him, are Rainsford's emphases upon Norris's interest in "ordinary people" and demonstration of a desire "to serve his fellow man." This impulse he chose to act upon when Rainsford provided him the opportunity to work with underprivileged youths through a Boys' Club he had created in 1884.

The kind of volunteerism to which Norris gave himself was noted by Walker during two interviews with Jeannette and described in fine detail by Rainsford in his *Story of a Varied Life: An Autobiography*. Far from reticent in 1922 when recounting his accomplishments at St. George's, where he increased membership from two hundred to over four thousand by 1899, Rainsford touted as another great success this Boys' Club that metamorphosed from a simple means of providing local youths "a good time" into an educational enterprise with a library of its own and a vocational program featuring instruction in typesetting, stenography, drawing and modeling, and carpentry. By 1891, the program included "over five hundred youths, between fourteen and twenty, owning some sort of connection with the church" and learning a trade. The instructors—"gentlemen visitors," he termed them—were assigned to "groups of from twelve to twenty," and it was their responsibility "to be present on certain nights at the school." Among them was Frank Norris, eminently qualified to deal with drawing and modeling and the rudiments of prose composition.[23]

In October 1899 Norris began drawing a triquet—a traditional symbol for the Trinity—beneath his signature in his letters,[24] another, understated confirmation of his commitment to what Rainsford stood for. No, he did not in 1899 become a religious zealot of the sort he pictured in 1902 when he developed the characterization of the fundamentalist, Dwight L. Moody–inspired Curtis Jadwin in *The Pit*. Nor was Rainsford of that stripe, though his interest in reaching out to the underprivileged does anticipate Jadwin's formation of a Sunday school in Chicago for the children of mainly Irish immigrants. Also noteworthy in that novel is Norris's negative characterization of his heroine as a self-proclaimed Episcopalian "'of the straightest sect of the Pharisees.'" Laura, unlike Rainsford and Norris, defines her Episcopalianism as primarily formalist and doctrinaire. That is, she is high-church like the Gertrude Norris described by Jeannette; telling of Norris's opinion of the type, Laura declines to do what Rainsford and Norris did in lower Manhattan when Jadwin invites her to serve as a teacher of his "little micks" in Chicago.[25]

Following his marriage at St. George's, Norris twice displayed in print either the change in his perspective that had been wrought in New York City or the point of view that he had not previously chosen to articulate. In the later instance, a "Simplicity in Art" essay published in January 1902, his primary focus was literary as he held forth on the inferiority of too-gorgeously wrought, baroque styles of writing. But his decision to express in high-church terms his disdain of unnecessary complexity and ornamentation in literary art—using for an analogy worship that was "an affair of gold embroidered vestments and costly choirs, of marbles, of jeweled windows and of incense"—is revealing. More striking, though, because wholly unprecedented, is his choice of terms when offering as a positive artistic paradigm the unadorned, elaboration-free

Nativity story in the Gospel of St. Luke. To his mind it is superior to anything from the hand of Shakespeare or Milton, and it prompted him not only to echo Isaiah and Handel but to disclose what Harry M. Wright had termed "the one thing one did not question." Unmistakable is the expression of faith folded into his declaration that "all our art—the art of the better-minded of us—is only a striving to get back to the unblurred, direct simplicity of those writers who could see that the Wonderful, the Counsellor, the mighty God, the Prince of Peace, could be laid in a manger and yet be the Savior of the world."[26] In this reference to a savior one finds the single instance in which Norris made such an overt disclosure, in his own voice, of his allegiance to what is traditionally termed the "vertical" dimension of religious experience: the relationship between man and the deity.

As to the "horizontal" dimension of Christianity seen in caring for one's neighbor—for example, at Rainsford's Boys' Club meetings—Norris appropriated an essential of the St. George's ethos when, in 1900, he developed the two most positive male characterizations of *The Octopus.* As in *McTeague,* altruism and even decency are at a discount in this novel in which the main characters are motivated by financial gain and the San Joaquin Valley becomes the competitive arena in which dog-eat-dog values prevail and might makes right among those driven by the acquisitive instinct. The Roman Catholic priest, Father Sarria, is exceptional: He ministers to those of Native American and Iberian descent who are living at the lowest levels of the agrarian society in the San Joaquin Valley. Without an irreverent wink to the reader, Norris fashions a figure in harmony with the Beatitudes celebrated by Jesus in the Sermon on the Mount. Lest this be viewed as an interpretive stretch, Norris also develops the character of the rancher Buck Annixter in such a way as to make clear that he is not ironic nor sardonically critical when picturing Father Sarria as a good shepherd to his flock of "half-breeds" and "greasers." After experiencing a radical change in his personality, Annixter begins to act in ways like the priest's and even delivers a veritable Sermon on the Mount of his own.

Introduced as an irascible, antisocial, and domineering loner given to disagreeing with and bullying his fellow ranchers and his field workers, this combative misanthrope manifests additional self-centeredness in his relationship with the daughter of one of his employees. Hilma Tree finds Annixter attractive and is delighted when it appears that he feels affection for her, whereupon she learns that he sees her only as a source of sexual recreation. Rebuffed by her, Annixter at length discovers that he has unwittingly fallen in love. That is, for the first time in his life he cares about someone else, and he is willing to care for her in a traditional marriage. In short, having the experience of loving another requires a self-transformation, the results of which further transform, or elevate, him.

The theme was not a wholly new one for Norris. Travis Bessemer had a similarly benign effect on Condy Rivers in *Blix*. More closely related, though, is the story of Lloyd Searight and Ward Bennett in *A Man's Woman:* Norris somewhat clumsily had them experience a radical personality change brought about by their discoveries that there was good reason to look beyond their own personal problems and care instead for each other. *The Pit* too would focus upon the rewarding experience of transcending self-centeredness and forming a relationship of mutual concern. What is unique in *The Octopus* is that Norris has his hero, who becomes so different from the rapacious railroaders and the other ranchers who are equally hellbent upon serving their own interests only, spell out in full the "religion" he declares he has embraced, thanks to his marriage to Hilma. His only male friend, Presley, is amazed to see the change wrought in this erstwhile Darwinian bulldog, and thus Annixter's explanation:

> "Pres," he exclaimed, "she's made a man of me. I was a machine before, and if another man, or woman, or child got in my way, I rode 'em down, and I never *dreamed* of anybody else but myself. But as soon as I woke up to the fact that I really loved her, why it was glory hallelujah all in a minute, and, in a way, I kind of loved everybody then, and wanted to be everybody's friend. And I began to see that a fellow can't live *for* himself any more than he can live *by* himself. He's got to think of others. If he's got brains, he's got to think of the poor ducks that haven't 'em, and not give 'em a boot in the backsides because they happen to be stupid; and if he's got money, he's got to help those that are busted, and if he's got a house, he's got to think of those that ain't got anywhere to go. I've got a whole lot of ideas since I began to love Hilma, and just as soon as I can, I'm going to get in and *help* people, and I'm going to keep to that idea the rest of my natural life. That ain't much of a religion, but it's the best I've got, and Henry Ward Beecher couldn't do any more than that. And it's all come about because of Hilma, and because we cared for each other."[27]

Reverend Rainsford might easily have used this speech as a text for a sermon. Indeed, *The Reasonableness of Faith* develops the same concept, acknowledging the importance of tending to self-interest and the value of self-reliant individualism while chastising those who choose not to look beyond self and demonstrate concern for the welfare of others: "Amazed at our own temporary success, drunken with the prospects of growing fortune, we forget that a people and a society where each man works for himself alone cannot be made to hold together. Egotism is the sin of the hour—self-seeking the infidelity of to-day."[28] And in the event that the reader has not registered how Annixter represents an ideal, Norris reprises his theme a chapter later, exalting Annixter as becoming more and more "tolerant and generous, kind and forgiving"—his progress tragically cut short when he dies during the gunfight at the irrigation ditch.[29]

As he was composing *The Octopus,* Norris had another opportunity, away from St. George's, to "get in and help people." In mid-May 1900, shortly after he saw the publication in *Collier's Weekly* of his spirited memoir describing "Student Life in Paris," there arrived a manuscript by an unknown, neophyte novelist. Harper and Brothers had rejected it earlier that month. As he related to its author in a 28 May letter, Norris recommended it to his superiors as the "best novel" in manuscript that he had read since he cast his lot with Doubleday. Lanier was then reading it, after which Page would as well, Norris told the author; then the three would "have a pow-wow on it and come to a decision."[30] This was Theodore Dreiser's *Sister Carrie,* and according to Jeannette, her husband was smitten. She remembered him bringing home the manuscript one afternoon, passing the night with it, and finishing it in the morning.

Page spoke for the firm at the time, since Doubleday was abroad until July. Dreiser learned from him on Saturday, 9 June, that Doubleday, Page, and Company was "'very much pleased'" with his novel and extended its congratulations "'on so good a piece of work.'" He asked Dreiser to call at his offices on Monday. At the end of the meeting, there was an oral agreement to publish it.[31]

Norris's involvement in what later came to be known as "L'affaire Doubleday"—after the scandalous Dreyfus Affair in France—was purely a matter of business in one sense: He found a veritable masterpiece in Dreiser's sympathetic tale of a "fallen woman" whose lapses in virtue do not preclude her rise from the working class to the upper reaches of American society. If the lurid *McTeague* merited publication, so should this much less explicit naturalistic novel depicting the determinisms that carry Carrie Meeber to fame and fortune while others ensure the ruination of her paramour, George Hurstwood. But Norris's developing relationship with Dreiser was more than a matter of business. As had John O'Hara Cosgrave, William Dean Howells, and Double-day with him, Norris befriended Dreiser. He invited him to his apartment in the Anglesea on Washington Square, where Jeannette and he were now living, to meet with him the night before Page's 9 June letter arrived. He likely was the first to give Dreiser the word that some changes in the manuscript were necessary: that he would have to strip out the names of actual persons, periodicals, and businesses and revise some suggestive wording.

In early July, after Dreiser had left town to vacation in Missouri, Norris had a similar conversation with Dreiser's close friend Arthur Henry, the author of the romance *A Princess of Arcady* published by Doubleday, Page later in the year. Henry was informed that Lanier insisted on such revisions. Jeannette, who had also read the manuscript and saw no reason for changes, was present as well. Frank's counsel was that Dreiser should not make a stand against the revisions, "if the matter were made a serious issue." It *was* a serious issue, as it turned out. Henry met with Lanier. He then wrote to Dreiser, telling him that Lanier "intimated to me that he would be opposed to publishing the book unless the changes were made."[32]

This, however, did not precipitate the crisis in the making. That eventuated when Doubleday returned to New York and the firm rendered a new verdict. Page wrote to Dreiser on 19 July 1900: "'To be frank, we prefer not to publish the book, and we should like to be released from the agreement with you.'"[33] Meanwhile, behind the scenes, Dreiser's sole in-house advocate at this point, Frank Norris, had again met with Arthur Henry to inform him of what was afoot. And the next day, 18 July, he wrote to Henry before Page could see his own letter to Dreiser typed:

> I have just had a talk with Mr. Page about Dreiser, and it seems that he—Page—has written a long *personal* letter to Dreiser, in which there is much more than a "turning-down" of *Sister Carrie*.
> He thinks—and so do I—that it should go to Dreiser at once so I would not hold it up as we talked of doing last night.
> Page—and all of us—Mr. Doubleday too—are immensely interested in Dreiser and have every faith that he will go far. Page said today that even if we waited till T.D. got back [from Missouri] it would yet be time for Macmillan or some other firm to get out *Sister Carrie* as a fall book.
> Mr. Page has some suggestions to make to T.D. and is very anxious to have a talk with him as soon as he gets back.

Sensing that he was possibly violating the trust of his employers for Dreiser's sake, Norris added a postscript, *"Keep this letter."* He asked Henry to inform

Dreiser immediately of what was transpiring but not, under any circumstances, to circulate his letter.[34]

Dreiser was not interested in Page's suggestions for finding another publisher. Returned to New York, he held Page's and Doubleday's feet to the fire, insisting that an oral agreement was as good as a written one among gentlemen. Since they were indeed gentlemen, they executed a formal contract on 20 August 1900, and Norris signed it as witness. *Sister Carrie* was published on 8 November 1900, and it was a commercial and critical failure. Doubleday, Page, and Company did nothing to promote sales beyond permitting Norris to persist in his support of Dreiser by sending out no less than 127 review copies. One went to William Heinemann, who would publish an abridged edition of the novel in England the next year.[35] Norris championed *Sister Carrie* in person as well, telling the novelist Morgan Robertson that "it is a wonder"[36] and urging his own English publisher, Grant Richards, to woo Dreiser as a promising author.

Richards, in his autobiography, proves one of the least reliable witnesses of Norris's life, in this instance confusing what was transpiring at Doubleday, Page in the summer of 1900 with what Norris told him about events the following spring during a luncheon at the Waldorf-Astoria. Still, one can trust the general impression Norris made upon Richards. He recalled Norris's declaration that Dreiser is "'worth two of me.'" As to *Sister Carrie:* "'Magnificent stuff. I'd give everything I have to be able to observe and write like that'"; "'[I]t's a wonderful book.'" According to Richards, Norris was not party to the suggestion that Dreiser find another publisher, instead advising him "to sit tight—that is, to hold [Doubleday, Page] to their [oral] agreement to publish." As to why Doubleday, Page did not promote *Sister Carrie,* he alleged that Norris blamed Mrs. Doubleday, "the Old Man's wife," who obtained "a set of proofs . . . and then—well, she kicked like hell. . . . Every Puritan, old-fashioned instinct she had was outraged." This *may* have been Norris's opinion of what happened, though it is unlikely that he referred to his friend Doubleday as "the Old Man." Doubleday declared in his autobiography that his wife had absolutely nothing to do with the matter, and he repeated the same in a letter to Walker, adding that the rumor that she effected the elimination of the pants-wetting scene in *McTeague* was also false.

In the spring of 1901, when Richards was in New York, Norris promised to send him a copy of the already difficult-to-find *Sister Carrie.* It reached him a few days before he sailed back to England. "What I remembered most vividly," wrote Richards, "is Frank Norris's generous enthusiasm for the book of his protégé, his insistence on its merit. Praise from the man who was to write *The Octopus* was praise indeed."[37]

That, however, was not all there was to tell about Norris's persistence in boosting Dreiser through the spring of 1901. In May 1901, Norris went beyond conversation to print in a *Chicago American* article, complaining about how publishers promote particular books that become successes, while they neglect others that consequently fail. Two cases in point were the unsuccessful recent books by Dreiser and Arthur Henry:

> And speaking of good things in American fiction it may not be inappropriate nor premature to call attention to the work of two very young men, whose work (each has published one book) has appeared unheralded, unadvertised and unfortunately unheeded, except by one or two critics who know good work and have the interests of the American novel at heart. These men are Theodore Dreiser and Arthur Henry. To my mind Dreiser's *Sister Carrie* is the best thing in our output of realistic fiction since *A Modern Instance.*
>
> Both the young authors, appearing in the very heyday of romantic fiction, are grim, uncompromising realists. This fact is the real significance of their work. They are young men, they are ambitious to succeed, they are, like so many young writers, susceptible to influence, and yet deliberately they choose to enter what is at the moment the most unpopular field in all the realm of novel writing—realism. The ill success—from a popular point of view—of *Carrie* and [*A Princess in Arcady*] has no whit deterred or discouraged either of the respective authors.
>
> Hardly has the ink dried on the initial—and only—editions of their first novels when they are hard at second books—Dreiser I believe is on his third. Remember these two names, Theodore Dreiser and Arthur Henry; for beyond all question, if the pair "stick it out" and hold to their ideals and enthusiasms and keep the pace with which they have started out, they will be important writers in ten years or so from now, when the blessed reaction sets in and the G[eneral]. P[ublic]. turns to what is worthwhile rather than to what is advertised.[38]

Arthur Henry was certainly a closer friend of Dreiser. But Norris's display of ardor in first enabling and then promoting Dreiser as a novelist—personally gaining nothing by doing so and even risking displeasure at Doubleday, Page—was as extraordinary as it was kind.

Meanwhile, to turn back to February 1900, Frank and Jeannette Norris enjoyed a honeymoon unlike the one his brother Charles knew years later. Frank was not unkind to his mother. But, rather than become his house guest for the next two weeks, she was on the train to San Francisco in short order, and the newlyweds were left to themselves in their apartment on Washington Square. Jeannette said little about their first days as husband and wife, save that they were in one respect like the halcyon ones that they spent together in San Francisco, commemorated in *Blix*. Like Condy with his "Blix," Frank played his decade-old banjo—a five-string manufactured by the A. C. Fairbanks Company in the early 1890s.[39] Jeannette sang—badly. Frank told her that he would permit her to do so only as often as he wed.

Once they were married, related Jeannette, they kept to themselves. She spoke of a "closed corporation." But, such judgments being relative, this suggests only how active Jeannette had been socially in San Francisco. Arthur Goodrich, a fellow employee at Doubleday, Page, lived "only a stone's throw away," and one also finds in Walker's interviews and correspondence that over the following months old friends and new comprised a social network of which Gertrude Norris might have been envious. San Franciscans on the square, such as Juliet Wilbor Tompkins, were welcome at their home. Burgess, residing next door for a while at 61 Washington Square South, saw them occasionally and registered the fact that the worshipful Frank was "absorbed in Jeannette." The Fiji George Gibbs related that in 1900 he lived six weeks at the Judson Hotel near the Norris's apartment. In their orbit was the Stevenson clan. According to Isobel Field, Robert Louis Stevenson's stepdaughter, Norris had made her acquaintance in New York in 1898. He then visited her to discuss an article by Cleveland Moffett on volcanos, "When Mountains Blow Their Heads Off," that would appear in the September issue of *McClure's Magazine*. When Frank "brought his bride to see us as soon as they came back from the honeymoon," Isobel was a member of the newlyweds' circle, along with her artist son Austin Strong, her novelist brother Lloyd Osbourne, and her mother Fanny Osbourne Stevenson.

Jeannette also recalled Hubert Henry Davies, "a young Englishman with some money, who used to be at the house frequently." He liked to while away his time by reading the manuscripts Norris brought home. John Harrold, employed by Tiffany's, would drop in; he lived down the street at the Benedick. Even Isaac F. Marcosson stopped by for dinner that summer, his appearance surprising Frank, who had not previously met him and thought him a much older man.[40] Jeannette too was surprised, she told Walker without a trace of compunction, since they had no idea that he was a "little Jew, but very likeable." Then, of course, there were those whom Frank and Jeannette had met at St. George's. This roster suggests only the tip of an iceberg, though.

By the end of the summer of 1900 the Norrises were preparing to flee too-gregarious New York City. Frank, after all, had a large novel to complete and an unending stream of book manuscripts to evaluate for Doubleday, Page, and Company.

Earlier that summer they had vacationed for two weeks at Greenwood Lake in northern New Jersey, Jeannette recalled. The choice of that lake was the consequence of a weekend in Connecticut spent with the Laniers and other house guests connected with New York publishing firms during which, according to Lanier, Norris developed a passion for bass fishing. Returned to Manhattan, related Jeannette, "they decided to get out into the country" and boarded a train with the intent "to live wherever they landed." In that whimsical way "was the spot chosen" across the Hudson River in suburban New Jersey.

In 1931 Theodore Dreiser's secretary, Evelyn Light, replied to Franklin Walker's request for information about the Dreiser-Norris relationship. Dreiser, she informed him, could remember only three times that he was with Norris, fogetting the occasion in August 1900 when the two signed the contract for *Sister Carrie*. The first occurred in early June, when he was received by Jeannette and Frank at the Anglesea on Washington Square. Another took place at an unspecified time when Frank "was living at Doubleday's house" (May 1901). The last meeting in 1900 occurred in Roselle, New Jersey—where the Norrises had moved by early September.

22

THE *ENFANT TERRIBLE* NO MORE

On 15 October 1899 the *Washington Times* book reviewer looked back over his past year's reading experiences. These included an adventure story "dealing with types absolutely new in fiction" in a medium "realistic to the last degree." From the author of *Moran* a few months later had come *McTeague,* a "half-disgusting, but perfectly accurate analysis of a semi-barbarous modern man, done with the realism of Zola and the idealism of Balzac." From these studies of "wild turmoil" and then the "grewsome," Norris had turned, surprisingly, to produce a "humorous love-idyl." *Blix,* declared the reviewer, "will be a revelation to those who have not read between the lines of the author's earlier works. It is fresh and simple and wholesome, full of idealism and high thought, without being sentimental or metaphysical, and the vein of drollery that runs through it gives life, vivacity and a certain careless strength and abandon to the whole." As sensitive to the comical in Norris's sensibility as many twentieth-century critics would prove oblivious, the reviewer offered this speculation: "Perhaps Mr. Norris's next undertaking will be to give us something purely humorous."[1]

The next undertaking, the same reviewer found almost four months later, was not that. Striking the naturalistic note again with its portrait of "the civilized man in whom civilization is only a veneer," *A Man's Woman* also brought forward a modern heroine who is a "worshiper of force."[2] Norris's sense of humor *was* displayed. But, before he unexpectedly transformed Ward Bennett and Lloyd Searight into figures worthy of a comedy of manners toward the end of the novel, the only moments fashioned as risible were of the "black humor" variety: How could the hero and the heroine forget that their intimate friend Richard Ferriss is a double amputee? Ward, anxious to express his gratitude for some good news Ferriss delivers, asks to shake hands with him; Lloyd is irritated when Richard does not help her descend from her carriage and is as chagrined as Ward when she recalls "with the suddenness of a blow . . . that Ferriss had no hands."[3] A Man's Woman is not McTeague, but in it Norris had reprised the enfant-terrible behaviors typical of his more sensational, taboo-violating short stories for 1897 issues of The Wave.

A Man's Woman, though, was the last of Norris's self-conscious attempts to shock, if not stun, the American reading public by such means as had earned Zola notoriety many years earlier. By the time that this novel appeared in book form, he had evidently set a new course for himself as a writer intent upon attaining wider fame by different and more palatable means.

When writing The Octopus, he did not make a clean break from his French mentor. Norris remained the Zolaist, signing himself "The Boy-Zola" in a 9 June 1901 letter to Isaac F. Marcosson.[4] This made immediate sense to Marcosson. Reviews of The Octopus repeatedly gave Norris warrant to refer lightheartedly to himself thus. Later that year, this would be reinforced by references such as Howells's to his "epic of Zolaesque largeness" and William L. Alden's to Norris's assured position in the literary world as a writer in "the family of Zola."[5] Still, the new novel was different from McTeague and A Man's Woman, as a largely negative Bookman review noted in May 1901. The reviewer lamented Norris's having mirrored in his own writing a similar change in Zola's: "Nowhere has [Zola's] influence been so marked as in The Octopus, and nowhere has it been so little to [Norris's] advantage. And this is because it is the influence of Zola the symbolist, the author of Paris and Fécondité, rather than the old-time Zola of Nana and L'Assommoir." Or, as the Washington Times reviewer put it more positively, "There is something like Zola about Mr. Norris, as many of his critics have remarked; but it is Zola with all the Gallicism taken out of him, purified, strengthened, set in the clean, fresh air of the West."[6] Shortly after Norris's death, Henry Morse Stephens observed the same turn away from the "coarse" and "hideous" in his early 1903 eulogy.[7] Norris was no longer fascinated with the untouchables and unmentionables he treated in high relief in so many of his earlier embraces of Zolaism. He was no longer inclined to make his readers' flesh creep.

On the threshold of middle age, married in the church at which he was an active communicant, looking forward to parenthood, confident of steady income and of one day becoming self-sufficient as a professional novelist living solely upon royalties, Norris was beginning to adventure upon life in a much more conventional way. Thus another reason for Jeannette's and his relocation from bohemian Washington Square to the staid suburbs of Manhattan across the Hudson River, and from an apartment to a house that they could call home.

Norris's six-month contract with Doubleday, Page, and Company expired at the end of June 1900, and the firm drafted another that he signed in mid-August. The terms were unchanged, until Doubleday amended them on 6 September 1900: To accomodate his move to Roselle, Norris would now "give the first three days of the week to office work instead of coming half of every day."[8] Ferries operated by railroad corporations such as the New York Central, the Pennsylvania, and the Erie crossed the Hudson River to their terminals. By water and rail Norris would have to commute to the city. But, with the new arrangement, he would have whole days to himself at home, and during the next three months he completed the *Octopus* manuscript. Visitors were relatively few. The Franklin Walker papers at the Bancroft Library identify only three San Franciscans who made the trip: Juliet Wilbor Tompkins, Dr. Albert J. Houston, and Seymour Waterhouse. Waterhouse, married in April 1899, brought his wife, the fiancée Frank and Jeannette had met in St. Louis in 1898. The Englishman Hubert Henry Davies continued to pay visits. He was, Jeannette recalled, working on the play that would become a hit in 1903, *Cousin Kate,* and he read to them from another manuscript entitled "Aida of Wyoming." The only major distraction for Frank that Jeannette could recall was the house they had chosen in summer weather. It proved poorly insulated as autumn advanced, and Frank labored mightily to coax an antiquated furnace into service adequate to preclude the donning of winter wear indoors.

Norris was brimming with confidence and announced on 13 September 1900 to Isaac F. Marcosson that he had nearly completed his draft: "Hooray! I can see the end." Getting to this point, he declared, was "the hardest work I ever have done in my life, a solid year of writing and 4 months preparation—bar two months."

How much new work actually remained to be done is suggested in his description in this letter of how he had designed the reading experience: "The movement of the whole business is very slow at first—don't really get under weigh [*sic*] till after the first 15,000 words (it's about 200,000 words long), then, with the first pivotal incident it quickens a bit, and from there on I've tried to accelerate it steadily till at last you are—I hope—just whirling and galloping and tearing along till you come *bang!* all of a sudden to a great big crushing END, something that will slam you right between your eyes and knock you off your feet—all this I *hope* for. Sabe?"[9] That Norris was not yet near the end of *The Octopus* in its final form, though, will be seen in the fact that the novel does not conclude with a "great big crushing END." The climax of the main plot that is describable thus—the killing of Buck Annixter and the others at the irrigation ditch—occurs on page 522 of the 652 in the first American edition. If he meant a later event, such as the railroad agent S. Behrman's being buried alive in the hold of a wheat-transport ship, the novel still concludes without another big bang, given that it satirically terminates with the shepherd Vanamee's and then the poet Presley's orphic reflections on how good inevitably emerges from all apparent evil. Less than overwhelming are the accounts of how they "cope" with traumatic losses—of a lover and of a close friend, respectively—by means of denial. Their pathetic but finally loony erasures of the significance of Angéle Varian's and Buck Annixter's cruel deaths hardly promised to knock readers off their feet, save from disbelief that anyone could take seriously such transcendental moonshine.

Thus, Norris labored on past the irrigation-ditch gunfight scene until mid-December, Jeannette noting that his three days' service at the Doubleday, Page offices had become two per week. Adding new text and pruning what he had already wrought, Norris informed Marcosson that he cut no less than fifty thousand words before he was finished.[10]

When Isobel Field and her son Austin appeared after Christmas to help Frank and Jeannette ring in the new year, they were able to read the manuscript. Jeannette's first recollection of 1901 was the argument that broke out among them concerning what she termed the "melodramatic portion" of the novel. She did not specify *which* melodramatic portion she had in mind. Possibly she meant the alternating sections of book 2, chapter 8—the counterpointing passages describing the fabulously elaborate dinner at the Gerard mansion attended by Presley and depicting the homeless Mrs. Hooven's death by starvation. But there are quite a few such flights into the extravagant.

Norris's correspondence of the fall and early winter of 1900 finds him at the Doubleday, Page offices having the opportunity to do another good deed like the ones he did for Dreiser. His indulgent overseer of the *Wave* days,

John O'Hara Cosgrave, was ready to make his break to the East Coast. In November, with Norris's help, he joined the firm, replacing Chauncey M. McGovern as the editor of one of its periodicals, *Everybody's Magazine.*[11] Norris's correspondence also finds him at home in Roselle maintaining old ties in another way when, on 20 November 1900, he wrote a long epistle in verse to his fraternity brothers in San Francisco. The occasion was a Fiji reunion at the Poodle Dog restaurant the night before the annual Stanford-Berkeley football game. As in *McTeague* with the dialogue of Trina's parents and in *The Octopus* with that of "Bismarck" Hooven and his wife, Norris displayed his mastery of the broken English spoken by German immigrants. The comical address of forty-six lines begins:

To The Committee: **An Exile's Toast.**

Gesundheit! *Ach mein lieber vriendts. Dot note she gome today.*
You're dining beit der Poodle in der same ol' jolly vey;
While me, ach Gott, du Lieber Gott, I've sit me down undt wept
Dot your kindt invitationing I cannot yet accept.
De Poodle! Doand I know der blace, say blind mein eye opp tighdt
Undt standt me bei der Plaza on, I findt der haus alle righdt.
Der gless-ware I've ge-broken dere, der sboons I hef ge-stole!
Der vhiskey Chimmie Vhite hef drunk from aub der sugar-bowl!
Ach dose were days. . . .[12]

Less pleasant was Norris's letter in early December 1900 to his English publisher, Grant Richards, about his not having received sales statements for his four novels, the royalty payments for three of which were nearly a year overdue. Having no reply to "some half dozen" earlier queries of the kind, he threatened to find another transatlantic publisher.[13]

At the same time, Norris also involved himself personally in the design of the binding of *The Octopus,* having been struck by the appearance of Henry James's 1897 novel *What Maisie Knew* and giving a copy to the designer so that he "may follow it *exactly.*"[14] The ornamental gilt stampings that had caught his eye reappeared almost exactly on the casing of *The Octopus* and, later, *The Pit.* Displaying a marketing sense not seen earlier in his career, and determined to extract the maximum cash value from the novel that he felt would put him over the top as a major American author, B. F.'s son had also begun to try to sell *The Octopus* as a serial—on his own and not through Doubleday, Page. Meeting with no success, he once more turned to the literary agent Paul Revere Reynolds, on 17 December 1900, reporting that he had failed with three magazines: *Munsey's, Collier's,* and the *Saturday Evening Post.* He asked Reynolds to take it to S. S. McClure for him, assuring Reynolds that "the damn thing is far and away my best."[15] Reynolds fared no better, however; and by 2 January 1901 Norris advised him to give up on trying to place the exceptionally lengthy manuscript. In the same letter, he turned to another matter related to income: the imperative need to find a more trustworthy English publisher than Grant Richards, one who would pay Norris the royalties his books earned. Reynolds's new assignment was to approach an English competitor, William Heinemann, and ask for either an advance royalty on the first thousand copies of, or a lump sum purchase of the English book rights for, *The Octopus.* As Norris closed this letter, his sense of outrage again flared up, and he added a postscript: Offer it to anyone in England, save Richards.[16]

Reynolds succeeded in interesting another British firm, Constable and Company. But in mid-January, Norris learned that Doubleday had already reached an agreement for the English publication of *The Octopus*—with Richards![17] Norris would never escape from Richards's clutches.

That same month, John O'Hara Cosgrave had two opportunities to show his gratitude to Norris for helping him find a berth at Doubleday, Page. As editor of *Everybody's Magazine,* he responded positively to Norris's reworking of *Yvernelle* into a short story set in California: "The Riding of Felipe" would appear in the March 1901 issue. Cosgrave also took up the formidable task of serving as an in-house reader and thus as one of the editors of the book manuscript that Norris felt he had to see in print before mid-March.[18]

Between books while awaiting the proof for *The Octopus* and long before its royalties would supplement his Doubleday, Page salary, Norris experienced another twist of fate like that binding him to Grant Richards. In late January 1901 he received a query from an editor of *The Youth's Companion:* Might he have a novel on hand that was suitable for its readership?

Had Norris received the invitation in time, he might have been able to turn *The Octopus* into a version appropriate for American youths by cutting the Vanamee-Angéle subplot, minimizing the many passages giving symbolic treatment to the wheat, and condensing elsewhere to render a western adventure tale dealing with the "war" between the ranchers and the railroad. (In 1902, he would similarly tailor the manuscript of *The Pit* for serialization in the *Saturday Evening Post.*) But the best Norris could do on 1 February

1901 was offer a short story: "I shall write it between now and the middle of next week and forward it as soon as it is ready." He was as good as his word, but whatever he submitted was not good enough to command the $150 for which he asked when he enquired about the disposition of the piece on 15 February. The manuscript was returned to him, but not to the address from which he had previously written the editor. "My address in the future," Norris informed him, "will be as per this letter head," that is, Doubleday, Page at 34 Union Square.[19] Otherwise it would not reach him, since Jeannette and he were then vacating their icebox of a house in Roselle, New Jersey, never to return.

Their destination was Chicago.

In 1897 Norris had declared with absolute confidence that there "are certain cities in the world which are adaptable to the uses of a writer of fiction," for example, Paris, London, Rome, and, of course, San Francisco. But, he continued, "there are others which are not." The same story laid in Berlin, Vienna, and Hamburg would be "ridiculous." So too Chicago: "[N]o romancer has yet had the hardihood to attempt to write of Chicago or Buffalo." Taking it for granted that it was a preposterous notion, he exclaimed sarcastically, "Imagine a novel of Chicago." Anyone with "an instinct for fiction" would know that it is "not suitable as a background for a novel, a short story or drama."[20]

So much for certainties amidst the ever unpredictable flow of events pictured in *McTeague* and *The Octopus.* For, according to his plan for the trilogy developed in the winter of 1898–99, it was now time to turn from the production of wheat to its distribution to the nation and abroad. That spelled Chicago and the Board of Trade Building in which the speculators and their agents bought, sold, and sent wheat on its way to the consumer. "All the traffic will bear" was the measure by which the railroad adjusted its shipping rates in California, its analysts meticulously determining how much of a grower's profit could be extracted without putting him or her out of business. Norris assumed that Chicago would offer a similar manifestation of what some may term business acumen and others the rapacious greed prevalent in and encouraged by a laissez-faire capitalist economic system. Not across a state or region but within one building in the grain pits one might witness the "bear" struggling with the "bull," the former gambling on profits made when per-bushel prices fall, and the latter profiting on the yield obtained when prices rise. Actually, what transpired in the Board of Trade was more complicated than this, as Norris discovered. Not since he was a student of mathematics at Berkeley did he find himself so intellectually challenged as he was when trying to comprehend the complex machinations of speculation in commodities like wheat.

Arriving at the Hotel Newberry in late February, Norris immediately visited his colleagues in the publishing industry, and Jeannette and he began making the rounds in Chicago's literary and artistic circles. Wallace Rice, previously associated with other local periodicals and currently a book reviewer for the *Chicago American,* expected them at a gathering at his home the evening of 2 March 1901. The recent press of work related to *The Octopus,* however, caused Norris to extend his apologies: "Mr. Doubleday has been throwing proof into me in two hundred page lots and today culminated the business with the balance of the page proof of the book accompanied by an imperative demand for haste."[21] The schedule for correction of proof, then the standing type, to be followed by the production of plates, printing, and binding was tight. That same day *Publishers' Weekly* announced that *The Octopus* would appear shortly, and a week later it included an advertisement of its forthcoming publication on 23 March 1901.[22] Norris thus heeded Doubleday's imperative. As of the first week of March, what actual research for *The Pit* Norris had performed amidst his socializing and grunt work on the *Octopus* proof is not known.

The next week another matter having nothing to do with *The Pit* drew his attention. Writing to Rice on 16 March 1901, he offered his apologies for missing another social gathering the previous evening. He had had to meet with an attorney "retained in a most unhappy cause."[23]

B. F. Norris, at sixty-four, had passed away in Chicago at the Lexington Hotel. The chief and determining cause was acute enteritis (inflammation of the small intestine). Contributing to his demise over the twenty days that Dr. Arthur R. Elliott treated him were kidney stones (pyelitis chromis calculous, "suppression of urine" and inflammation of one kidney or both), and stomatitis (inflammation of the mucous tissue in the mouth).[24] B. F.'s immune system had collapsed in the face of bacterial, and possibly viral, infection.

His son was not in mourning; nor did he attend the funeral service at the hotel and interment in Graceland Cemetery. The death had occurred over four months earlier, on 26 October 1900, and the burial five days after that. The "unhappy cause" requiring the services of Thomas B. Marston, Esq., was instead a challenge to B. F.'s will.

His brother Charles and Jeannette emphasized the fact that Frank had since 1894 been adamant about the impossibility of a reconciliation with his father and the acceptance of any money that B. F. sent him. The checks he received after the divorce he immediately destroyed. The distribution of the estate was another matter, though, given the thirty-dollar-per-week arrangement Frank had with Doubleday, Page, and the fact that the share of the estate that might have been his would have exceeded his minimal earnings at 34 Union Square for three years. The reason for legal action was that, unfortunately for Frank and Jeannette, B. F. had put his estate under the sole control of his third wife Belle. In his will, he requested that she, "in case it shall be convenient for her to do so," give five thousand dollars to Frank. Her doing so, however, "shall not be obligatory."

The executrix did not find the surrender of this sum "convenient." Rather, despite the renewed efforts of Frank's attorney in early 1901, she would decide by June that one hundred dollars was enough for each of the surviving sons; Frank, in fact, never received even that.[25]

And so was the father-son relationship wholly terminated in 1901, almost as unhappily as Gertrude's and B. F.'s marriage had been in 1894 when she had to take him to court to ensure a fair settlement.

Not long after the meeting with their Chicago attorney, the Norrises decided to disappear from sight because, as Jeannette explained to Walker, Frank was having the devil of a time getting any work done in Chicago. His 16 March 1901 letter to Rice makes clear what the problem was. He excused himself for having missed the gathering of well-heeled Chicagoans with cultural interests—writers, artists, and musicians—who met each Friday in the Fine Arts Building on Michigan Avenue near the Art Institute.[26] Among the better-known authors associated with this retreat for the aesthetically inclined were Hamlin Garland, Henry Blake Fuller, and John T. McCutcheon. The novelist, playwright, and travel writer Hobart Chatfield-Taylor was, with his wife, the "center of the circle," said Jeannette. On 15 March Norris was to have been one of the two honored guests, the other a French painter and illustrator for *Century* and *McClure's* magazines, André Castaigne, who had studied in Paris under Gérôme and, six years before Norris, in Bouguereau's atelier at the Académie Julian. The meeting room for the group, "The Little Room," was named after a popular short story of the same title by Madelene Yale Wynne, published in August 1895 in *Harper's Monthly*. Like Rudyard Kipling's "The Phantom Rickshaw," this mystery tale focuses on a seemingly spectral entity, a "little room" the existence of which eludes empirical confirmation and may, indeed, occupy the realm of the imaginary as a space set apart from the everyday walks of life. That is, in Chicago the actual Little Room provided a temporary escape from the coarse world of money getting and vulgar displays of wealth.

Thus there was another incentive for the Norrises' withdrawal from an environment so similar to the bohemian one on Washington Square and that of Les Jeunes in San Francisco. In *The Pit,* Norris would celebrate Chicago rather than denigrate it as vulgar. He would wax rhapsodic, as positively as Carl Sandburg later did, about this center of industry and trade as the visible, palpitating "Heart of the Nation." For example, he would proclaim that,

> Here, of all of her cities, throbbed the true life—the true power and spirit of America; gigantic, crude with the crudity of youth, disdaining rivalry; sane and healthy and vigorous; brutal in its ambition, arrogant in the new-found knowledge of its giant strength, prodigal of its wealth, infinite in its desires. In its capacity boundless, in its courage indomitable; subduing the wilderness in a single generation, defying calamity, and through the flame and débris of a commonwealth in ashes, rising suddenly renewed, formidable, and Titanic.[27]

And so the Norrises bid goodbye to the Chatfield-Taylors, Mr. and Mrs. Rice, and another new acquaintance, the novelist George Horton. They bid adieu as well to an old friend outside that coterie of *littérateurs,* the Fiji George Gibbs, who informed Walker that he was "constantly" with Frank in Chicago. The Norrises announced that they were on their way to California—and instead moved to another hotel in Chicago. Now they were able to spend the time they needed in the public library to obtain the information necessary for turning fact about recent developments at the Board of Trade into fiction. When they accidentally ran into friends, Jeannette remembered with some glee, they would tell them that they were just passing through on their way back to New York.

Just before Jeannette and he went "underground," Frank thanked Wallace Rice "for the letter to Mr. Leiter." It was just what he wanted, and he was confident that "it will produce the desired result."[28] Whether he enjoyed a meeting with him none of his contemporaries recalled. This included Charles, who emphasized his father's resemblance to *The Pit's* hero rather than Leiter's. But Norris's primary model for the character Curtis Jadwin was indeed Jo-

seph Leiter, an 1891 graduate of Harvard and the recipient of a graduation
gift from his father Levi of an even one million dollars. Considerably more
generous with his son than B. F. had been with Frank, Levi Leiter, too, was
a self-made Chicagoan with a summer home at Lake Geneva, Wisconsin. He
had struck it rich in dry goods. With Potter Palmer and then Marshall Field
he developed the nationally famous department store—bearing only Field's
name after 1881—that filled a whole block bordered by Wabash Avenue and
Randolph, State, and Washington Streets. He derived further revenue from
two Leiter Buildings, one of which, built in 1891, housed Sears, Roebuck
and is now acknowledged as a landmark in architectural history. Levi also
speculated in grain, as would his well-heeled son in the late 1890s. This latter
use of Joseph's wealth accounts for Norris's desire to interview him.

Joseph Leiter was the main reason for the hours spent in the public
library's newspaper files. As *The Octopus* became an exposé dealing with the
Southern Pacific, *The Pit* was to rake another kind of muck discoverable in
the gothic pile that was the old Board of Trade Building at the end of LaSalle
Street. (The present building on the same site dates from 1928.) Once again,
Norris cast the limelight upon a relatively small number of individuals who
controlled the flow of wheat to the consumer for their own benefit, giving
little thought to the consequences of their self-aggrandizing behavior. In
1901 Leiter, thanks to his much-publicized attempt in 1897–98 to corner as
much American wheat as he could and dictate its per-bushel price, was still a
familiar figure to newspaper readers. As with newspaper coverage of attempts
to reach the North Pole in the case of *A Man's Woman,* articles concerning
the murder of Sarah Collins in San Francisco in *McTeague,* and, with regard
to *The Octopus,* a seemingly endless stream of journalistic attacks upon the
Southern Pacific, Norris was again taking his prompt from the press. And
his research on Leiter dealt with the events that were reported daily as Norris completed his tenure with *The Wave,* worked for S. S. McClure in New
York, and sailed from Port Tampa for Cuba.

This real-life Napoleon of LaSalle Street provided the script to which
Norris stuck rather closely in *The Pit.* Leiter was no stranger to the wheat
pit prior to June 1897. But it was then, when wheat sold at sixty-five to sev-
enty cents per bushel, that he began to pour his wealth into purchasing op-
tions—agreeing to a future delivery of wheat, waiting until the price advanced
sharply, and then selling the contracts at a profit. When actually involved
in selling wheat itself, he tended to avoid "short" contracts obliging him to
deliver wheat that he did not have on hand when he made the deals. Most

of his transactions were "long"—he purchased millions of bushels on the assumption that the price would rise. And rise it did, repeatedly. Thanks to the Spanish-American War, Leiter was reaping grand profits by meeting foreign demand at prices ranging from $1.60 to $1.85. Like Curtis Jadwin, he had effectively cornered the market and routed competitors such as Phillip D. Armour. Then, as in *The Pit,* Leiter made a fatal mistake by assuming that he could maintain his corner by buying more and more wheat at elevated prices in the face of an expected new bumper crop promising a supply that would exceed demand. Wrote a contemporary observer of the debacle, "Leiter's failure was due to his apparent belief that he could set aside the law of supply and demand. He failed to recognize the difference between a fictitious price of his own creating, at which but little wheat could be sold, and the natural price, dependent on legitimate conditions." When—as Norris later put it in his novel—a veritable Niagara of grain descended upon him in June 1898, even Leiter's father withdrew his support and the son had to sell out, offering contracts on the September delivery of eight million bushels at the market price—then seventy-one cents, much lower than what he had been paying in his attempt to keep the price up.[29]

By the time that Norris finished his research in Chicago, he had recovered from periodicals the outline of Leiter's rise and fall, and he had perhaps discussed the experience with the man who lived it. He had also conferred repeatedly with George Gibbs, who coached him on how to portray Jadwin as a savvy speculator and on the technical details concerning wheat trading that he would need to weave into the plot. Gibbs was confident that Norris had obtained from him all that he needed to know about the operations of the market by the time he left Chicago, telling Walker that they met frequently for tutoring sessions and that it was "many weeks" before Norris "could understand the short side of the market and how anybody could sell a thousand or a million bushels of wheat when he did not possess them."

By the end of March, Norris was already losing his grasp of the matter as Jeannette and he left Chicago for California. According to Jeannette and Charles, Frank would have to be tutored once again upon his return to New York City if *The Pit* was to make technical sense. And thus the acknowledgment to a journalist employed by the *New York Sun* that appeared in the book: "The author's most sincere thanks for assistance rendered in the preparation of the following novel are due to Mr. G. D. Moulson of New York, whose unwearied patience and untiring kindness helped him to better understand the technical difficulties of a very complicated subject."[30]

Why Norris stopped work on *The Pit,* and on 31 March 1901 was a west-bound passenger on the "Overland Limited,"[31] may have had something to do with the October 1900 death of B. F. and the disposition of his estate. Also, Jeannette's father, Robert McGee Black, had passed away on 2 December 1900. Jeannette is not known to have returned to San Francisco then, and perhaps she now took the opportunity to travel farther west to spend time with her mother and siblings Francis and Edna. But the primary motivation may likely be heard in Frank's confident prediction to Bruce Porter when leaving New York for California in April 1899: "I'm going to walk down Sutter St. . . . And they'll say *'That's Frank Norris!'*" Frank had made good on his boast then, thanks to the attention given him in local periodicals. Now he was sure to fare even better as a celebrity, for he would be in his home town when copies of *The Octopus* first reached the bookstores and when on 7 April 1901—Easter Sunday—the *San Francisco Chronicle* declared beneath a photographic portrait of him that "Frank Norris is a San Francisco man, who, in a few years, has reached a place among the ablest of American novelists." *The Octopus,* it proclaimed, "is his best. It surpasses in fidelity to life and in power of narrative the work of any other Western novelist, with the single exception of Hamlin Garland."[32]

One is not surprised to learn from Seymour Waterhouse that Gertrude rose to the occasion. She arranged for a reception at which Jeannette and her fair-haired boy were the guests of honor. "Very grand" was Waterhouse's opinion of the fête. Norris was again the center of attention when, on 18 April 1901, fifty Fijis regaled him at a dinner held in the Merchants' Club at the Mutual Life Building. He modestly responded to a toast by recalling that the Phi Gamma Delta could boast of two other accomplished authors, the abolitionist James C. Redpath and General Lew Wallace of *Ben-Hur* fame.[33]

By the end of April, the Norrises had left San Francisco, and in early May they were residing at the Judson Hotel on Washington Square. But, related Jeannette, they also stayed for a week at Frank N. Doubleday's home—where, as Evelyn Light informed Walker, Theodore Dreiser paid Norris a visit. Dreiser may have dropped by to discuss his interest in buying the plates for and unbound sheets of *Sister Carrie,* in which he hoped to interest a more supportive publisher than Doubleday, Page had been. More likely the primary reason for the call was that the copy of the novel Norris sent to William Heinemann had been received positively; the British publisher was to include a condensed version of it in his Dollar Library series. The Norrises then departed the city for a vacation in the country, bypassing Roselle and locating in northern New Jersey's Passaic County for two months. This was at Greenwood Lake where, according to Jeannette, Frank did *not* spend time on *The Pit* but—like that novel's hero when on his honeymoon—instead indulged his passion for bass fishing. He did have some work to do, though. Wallace Rice had arranged for him to contribute a column to the *Chicago American*, and the mainly chatty series of thirteen articles on literary matters that appeared in its weekly *American Art and Literary Review* began on 25 May 1901. As for his half-days' commitment to Doubleday, Page, he would periodically commute on the Erie Railroad to Jersey City, and thence to Manhattan, to pick up batches of manuscripts for evaluation.

Meanwhile, *The Octopus* was realizing the investment Doubleday, Page had made in its author's research trip to California two years earlier. Four days after it was published, a second printing was necessary.[34] By July 1901, when the Norrises returned from their "vacation," the novel published by 1 April was in its fourth—possibly fifth—American printing, and the Canadian firm George N. Morang had issued it as well. By September, the first British printing was available for sale in England and its colonies.[35] Walker cites no-longer-extant Doubleday records indicating that, by the end of 1902, it had sold 33,420 copies in the United States. Though not a "best-seller" like *The Pit,* if the benchmark for such status is approximately one hundred thousand copies,[36] it was that spring proving *Norris's* best seller to date, and by summer's end he enjoyed greater visibility than he had ever known before. Demand for other work from his hand manifested itself that fall in a second series of articles, this one for the *Boston Evening Transcript*. Through the winter of 1901–2 pieces on literature and culture appeared in the *The World's Work* and the *Brooklyn Daily Eagle*. In April he commenced a series of seven essays for *The Critic*. An accomplished novelist, a theorist dealing with heady issues such as the relationship between the "real" and the "fictional" in art, and an "insider" willing to disclose what takes place behind the scenes in the publishing world, he was at last achieving the status of a national celebrity whose short stories were easy to place. Not only on San Francisco's Sutter Street but Chicago's Michigan and New York's Fifth Avenues, one had reason to say "that's Frank Norris" as he labored over the manuscript of *The Pit*.

23

"WHOSO DIGGETH A PIT
SHALL FALL THEREIN"

In July 1901, after two months at Greenwood Lake, the Norrises returned to Manhattan and their temporary abode on Washington Square, the Judson. In the fall of 1901, as was noted in the record of parishioners at St. George's church,[1] they moved far uptown to an apartment building on the west side of the city. Their new home on the edge of Hamilton Heights was the Riverview apartment building at the corner of Broadway and 148th Street, where—as in Roselle—they were far enough removed from the city's center to be able to pick and choose the occasions on which they would interact with friends. Jeannette remembered only one instance in which they entertained at home. Frank's companion in Cuba, the journalist James F. J. Archibald, supped with them, and they argued over the Boer War. Norris recorded in a 17 December letter to Gelett Burgess (then in San Francisco) an impending dinner at which Lloyd Osbourne, Juliet Wilbor Tompkins, Hamlin Garland, and his wife Zulime would be present.[2] But an earlier visit by Katherine Herne—the wife of the recently deceased pioneer-realist playwright James A. Herne, whom Norris had interviewed for *The Wave* in 1897—and her actress daughter Julie was much more noteworthy.[3] Having failed to place *The Octopus* at a magazine in the spring, Norris leaped at their proposition to adapt the novel for the stage, inviting them to call on 19 November to "talk it all over."[4]

His social life still under control, Norris began one of the most productive phases of his career, completing work on the discrete versions of *The Pit* published as a *Saturday Evening Post* serial and then in book form and turning out articles and short stories at a clip that brings to mind the frenetic pace he maintained when on the staff of *The Wave*. It was as though he was no longer a manuscript reader for Doubleday, Page. But being a self-supporting novelist was still a goal rather than an achievement, and so he continued to visit Union Square, picking up and returning the submissions he reviewed at home and putting in office time as well.

The workload did not tell, according to Arthur Goodrich, who was then employed in the Doubleday, Page editorial department and on the staff of *The World's Work*. Writing to Walker, he happily remembered an unflappable colleague who always had time to be gracious in the most upbeat way: "Whenever [Frank] stopped at my desk for a chat, it always gave a new lift to my day. There was a sort of tonic quality about him, quiet and simple though he was, that stirred and warmed you." In a postscript Goodrich returned to this same theme with renewed appreciation: "I can see him now, as he would come blowing in, with his boyish face and gray hair and his long confident stride and an air of quiet good cheer which never failed. And what a grand sense of humor he had!"

At home when dealing with *The Pit* through early June 1902, however, Norris was not quite the same fellow. In fact, Jeannette's characterization of the situation in which he found himself is quite similar to that which she gave of the frustrated author wrestling with *A Man's Woman* during the winter of 1898–99. Walker's interview notes summarize her comments concerning the composition of *The Pit:* "It did not give him scope for his abilities. Used to groan over it a good deal. Was glad to get it done. Would often tear portions up." And there was good reason for discontent: the situation was one of déja vu in another sense.

Despite the obvious plot differences between the two novels and the greater richness of the characterizations in *The Pit*, the new work was remarkably like *A Man's Woman*. Norris was once more developing a central theme having to do with the perils of self-absorption, as the two-dimensional Ward Bennett and Lloyd Searight became the much more engaging three-dimensional Curtis Jadwin and Laura Dearborn Jadwin. In regard to basic types of characterizations, the literary naturalist was again fashioning a pair of egotists governed by appetites for dominance manifested in their compulsive need to have their own way. As in *A Man's Woman*, he focused on a hero and heroine determined in their behavior by superegos demanding realization of their ideal conceptions of themselves. Thus, he also returned to the task of making literary use of what he had observed in his parents' disastrous relationship—employing more directly his histrionic mother as the model for Laura and, as his brother Charles opined to Walker, drawing "to the life" his self-centered father in the personality of Curtis Jadwin. This time he would not make the same mistakes as he treated Laura and Curtis's courtship, marriage, and alienation from each other. And yet, as he rose to the occasion, the task he had reassigned to himself was burdensome. He had been "here" before.

There were yet other pressures that he felt as he attempted to build upon the success of the first volume of his trilogy of the epic of the wheat. He called upon George D. Moulson, who lived nearby in Washington Heights, to help him with the difficult-to-grasp details concerning market speculation. But he also had to rely on Edwin Lefevre, the 1901 author of *Wall Street Stories,* for additional assistance.[5] He was concerned about income as well, resulting in an outpouring of saleable short stories and articles. He was the sole provider. The dramatic adaptation of *The Octopus* did not materialize, and Jeannette had become pregnant at the time that *The Octopus* was published, at the very end of their stay in Chicago, on the "Overland Limited," or at the beginning of their visit to California. Jeannette Williamson Norris, nicknamed "Billy," would be born in Manhattan on 9 January 1902.

The Pit had to be a grand success ensuring financial security for his family.

The title of *The Pit,* of course, literally refers to the wheat-trading area, or pit, in the Board of Trade Building. It is also symbolic. Laura, obsessed with the romantic concept of how her amorous experience *should* be, is drawn to the verge of a pit when her husband becomes immersed in speculation in wheat and neglects her; she almost leaps into it, in the manner of Gustave Flaubert's Emma Bovary and Kate Chopin's Edna Pontellier, when an adulterous relationship with the artiste Sheldon Corthell appears to promise satisfaction of her need for ideal romantic love. Curtis, truly fixated on cornering and maintaining his control of American wheat by outwitting his competitors, dramatically demonstrates the truth of the biblical proverb concerning the individual who unwittingly creates the means of his own destruction: He is the wise man who digs a pit to trap the less wise and then proves the fool who falls into it.[6] Biographically, being in a "pit" also proves a relevant trope for the man who was at his writing desk at 3605 Broadway, attempting to illustrate how a lust for success as either a romantic lover or a Napoleon of LaSalle Street can effect the undoing of typical naturalistic characters who are thralls to such compulsions.

The pit, or trap, in which Norris found himself may be seen in the constraints that he had fashioned for himself in 1898–99 by electing to write a series of three novels, each of which had to feature American wheat in high relief. Thus, in November 1901, when writing to Isaac F. Marcosson, he related that the "wheat motive is continued the same as in *The Octopus*—a great and resistless force moving from west to east, from producer to consumer." There was no escaping that. The wheat was the one "character" that did not disappear as Norris turned from the large cast of the first volume of the trilogy to the much smaller group of brand-new personages in the second. And, indeed, for fictional purposes, the wheat had to be treated as a character, so prominent was its role. Exercising poetic license in his letter to Marcosson, Norris personified this insentient commodity and economic force as "benevolent and beneficent as long as it is unhampered, but destroying all things and all individuals who attempt to check or divert it."[7] Thus the ruination of Curtis Jadwin, whose overconfidence-become-megalomania prevents him from acknowledging a fact about the supply-demand dynamic that his more levelheaded broker Sam Gretry has no trouble seeing: Demand, expressed by the price levels to which Curtis has boosted wheat, brings forth a superabundance of the stuff that agriculturalists have rushed into cultivation. When he tries to "check or divert" the new bumper crop by purchasing all he can to maintain the high per-bushel price for which he is responsible, the glut of wheat breaks the price to end his "corner" and empties his coffers. He is overwhelmed by the deluge of grain that—figuratively speaking—floods the Board of Trade in *The Pit's* penultimate chapter and carries him into a physical and mental breakdown.

Telling this story, however, was not the main reason that Norris groaned over his manuscript and tore up portions—though, again, getting the technical details right was certainly a trial. Had Norris elected to tell *only* a muckraking tale set in Chicago's Board of Trade, his task would have been much simpler, especially when compared with what he labored mightily to accomplish in the multidimensional *Octopus*. Indeed, he did write such a piece, the short story "A Deal in Wheat," which appeared in *Everybody's Magazine* in August 1902. However, in his novel he wanted to do more than expose the self-aggrandizing manipulators whom Curtis represented. Accordingly, he decided to integrate another plot that had nothing to do, necessarily, with speculation in wheat and that soon rendered the novel's composition much more a trial of his skill.

As of November 1901, by which time he had drafted the first two chapters, he was treating Laura, rather than Curtis, as the principal character. In the same letter to Marcosson he made clear this cross-purpose that would complicate the composition of this volume of the trilogy: "The story is told through Laura Dearborn. *She occupies the center of the stage all of the time,* and I shall try to interest the reader more in the problems of her character and career than in any other human element in the book." As with Petrarch, a Laura figure was his infatuation. As if to underline this, in chapter 4 Norris assigns her the part of a character named Beatrice in an amateur theatrical—bringing to mind Dante's preoccupation with a female figure in *Divina Commedia* and *Vita Nuova.*

To tell this prima donna's psychologically focused tale Norris needed only two elements: the heroine's courtship by and ill-considered marriage to a man with whom she actually shares few interests, one as incompatible as B. F. Norris was with Gertrude; and a Romeo of a husband who loses his amorous appetite for her—as did B. F. for Gertrude. Norris initially thought he could eat his cake and have it too: picturing in the foreground the loneliness endured by the "scorned woman" who waxes neurotic as the months pass and considers having her needs met by another man; and, in the background, using the neglectful husband's experiences at the Board of Trade to demonstrate for *The Pit's* readers how the wheat "moves from west to east" benevolently for some while wreaking havoc for others. Yet doing so was not easy. Eventually, the plan proved impossible to realize since it meant diminution of his treatment of the raison d'être for this installment of the wheat trilogy—which, he found, required keeping Curtis at center stage.

It is undeterminable now how far Norris went beyond the Laura-focused first two chapters before he realized the problem created by a heroine with no personal interest in wheat speculation, who never develops even a minimal understanding of the activity that captivates Curtis. He perhaps advanced to the present chapter 4, wherein Laura is as much at center stage. But the third chapter, whether written before or after the fourth, clearly signals Norris's post-November 1901 recognition of the need for a change in plan: The wheat had to be brought to the fore, and Laura had to surrender the stage to Curtis. Thus, she appears not at all in the third chapter, as Norris describes at length a day's trading at the board, during which Curtis's first large-scale "deal in wheat" fatefully whets his appetite for speculation. She would thenceforth have to wait in the wings from time to time as Curtis took his turn as the center of attention. After chapter 5, as Mr. and Mrs. Jadwin come to lead separate lives—he midtown at his broker's offices near the Board of Trade, and she uptown in their mansion near Lincoln Park—so great is their alienation that Norris had to split subsequent chapters into discrete, alternating Laura and Curtis sections. Norris's challenge was to give equal attention in counterpoint manner to two principal characters whose stories are minimally connected until the last pages, when Curtis fails, Laura chooses to stay with him rather than run off with Corthell, and the "divorced" story lines finally become one as husband and wife attempt to form a more perfect union.

Norris was attempting two kinds of novel in one. Thus the groaning and tearing of manuscript leaves recalled by Jeannette as her husband coordinated two main plot lines plus a subplot involving Laura's younger sister and her beau. The wonder is that Norris was able to achieve the coherence he did. In fact, the sprawling, character- and subplot-crowded *Octopus* appears unruly when compared to its compact, tightly structured successor.

Norris dealt with yet another problem, the solution of which effected a more remarkable difference between *The Octopus* and *The Pit*.

As the reviews of *The Octopus* continued to appear through 1901 and even well into 1902, Norris enjoyed some that rose almost to the level of admiration that B. O. Flower, the editor of *Arena*, lavished upon him. He declared the novel nothing less than "a work of genius."[8] That in a prepublication notice and two reviews Isaac F. Marcosson was once again effusive in his praise of Norris's art is not surprising.[9] But it is remarkable that on 7 April 1901 George Hamlin Fitch of the *San Francisco Chronicle*, whose earlier reviews of Norris's books were hardly uncritical celebrations of a fellow San Franciscan, found *The Octopus* decidedly impressive. He had mixed feelings about Norris's Zolaesque habits of reiterating the defining traits of his characters and of "working up a hundred petty details that have no other value [than] to give realism to his story." Still, he concluded that "the book is the strongest that Norris has yet written. It is full of the vitality of real life. It is written with a pen of iron, in the virile style that made Kipling famous. It lays hold upon the reader, and no one who takes it up will ever be able to efface it from the memory."[10] Jack London was as laudatory as Marcosson, his only qualification resulting from his irritation with Norris's realism. While some twenty-first-century readers may dub *The Octopus* too romantic for postmodernist tastes, it was, ironically, the close attention to real-world detail for which the great Kipling himself was chided that galled the otherwise enthusiastic London. Minute accuracy of the kind valued by realists was not London's cup of tea: "One feels disposed to quarrel with Norris for his inordinate realism. What does the world care whether Hooven's meat safe be square or oblong; whether it be lined with wire screen or mosquito netting; whether it be hung to the branches of the oak tree or to the ridge-pole of the barn; whether, in fact, Hooven has a meat safe or not?"[11] Such quibbles were predictable. Then and now they distinguish a "puff" from an authoritatively "objective," positive evaluation of a work of art; and complaints of this sort—familiar from treatments of his previous novels—did not influence Norris's writing of *The Pit*. Nor did other reviews that, after sounding positive notes, regretted the melodramatic moments of book 2: the blameless Mrs. Hooven's starvation and the suffocation by wheat of the villainous S. Behrman.[12]

What did make a difference was criticism of Norris for having fashioned certain characters in *The Octopus* to serve as his spokespersons in, as it was then pejoratively termed, "a novel with a purpose": one in which an author, in his or her own voice or via his personages, obviously advances a moralistic or didactic thesis. For example, Shelgrim's apologia for the amoral operations of his railroad being dictated by the iron law of supply and demand was seen by some reviewers as Norris's means of exculpating him for what appeared in hundreds of earlier pages the immoral consequences of his conscienceless behavior as corporate head. That Presley is dumbfounded upon hearing this monologue of the sort treasured by Social Darwinists of the period, and that he even accepts Shelgrim's pronouncement as irrefutable, enraged one of the earliest reviewers. He assumed that Presley is Norris's primary spokesperson—and therefore that Norris, too, accepted as valid in all respects Shelgrim's self-characterization.

To Norris's undoubted surprise, this reviewer was none other than his Chicago friend and companion at Little Room gatherings who arranged for him to write the series of weekly articles for the *Chicago American*. Wallace Rice did not mince words. Referring to Shelgrim's "Blame conditions, not men" speech, he termed the novel's "philosophy" a "hideous" one: "[I]t is the doctrine of personal irresponsibility. . . . Most unfortunately it is the plea which Mr. Norris represents as wholly converting the most intelligent character in his book, the character with which he asserts the greatest degree of personal intimacy and for which he makes the greatest appeal for the reader's sympathy."[13] Presley is an artist intent upon writing a poetical epic about the American West; Norris is an artist who had just written a prose epic set in the American West. Therefore, to Rice's mind, Presley *is* Norris, and thus the novel sanctions Shelgrim's Social Darwinism.

Norris did not chide Rice for his misreading. Nor did he point out that the novel, as it progressed, repeatedly gives its readers reason to be less and less sympathetic toward Presley and to quash the notion that he served as the author's alter ego. True, early in the novel Presley does articulate a "manly" aesthetic and pronounced distaste for "feminine" and too artificially "literary" values. He echoes not only Condy Rivers in *Blix* but Norris himself in his literary essays. Thereafter, however, Presley is the singular effete figure among a cast of decidedly manly males who, unlike Norris with *The Octopus*, proves utterly incapable of fashioning an epical treatment of life in the West. Further, while Norris conceived of himself as writing from real life in *The Octopus*, Presley's *only* literary accomplishment is a poem he derives not from life itself but secondhand, from another work of art picturing the economically oppressed. As Shelgrim correctly points out when Presley visits his office, his verses enjoying success in the national press merely repeat what Jean François Millet had already "said" in his world-famous painting, *The Man with the Hoe*; in this sense the poem is at worst a plagiarism and at best a paraphrase.[14]

Instead of offering clarifications, Norris chose to smooth over the situation after he recovered from Rice's blistering criticisms: "*I understood the situation perfectly* in the matter of the Review," he wrote to Rice, "and respect you for your convictions which our personal friendship did not deter you from expressing."[15]

Writing for the *Boston Evening Transcript* in a much more positive vein but also focusing on Shelgrim's troubling monologue, George H. Sargent did not view either Presley or Shelgrim as Norris's stand-ins. Yet, like Rice, he expected novelists to use their works as bully pulpits. He was disappointed that *The Octopus* "offers nothing in the way of amending the situation" faced by a nation being abused by trusts. Sargent was more indulgent than Rice, though. He counseled patience with a still-young author: "[W]e must remember that he is not as yet the seer or theorist, but that he is presenting us, in this first work [of the trilogy], the conditions only of the mighty problem. He does not pretend to be the leader sent to guide this people in their dealings with that mighty modern force, the trust."[16]

To Sargent, Norris was more forthcoming than he had been with Rice.

On 9 June 1901 he thanked him for his generous treatment of the novel. Then he politely challenged Sargent's assumption about what a novelist can, or should, be expected to accomplish in such a way as to indicate that none of his characters—much less he himself as narrator—was qualified to serve as a seer with a pat solution for all of the problems inherent in the contemporary socioeconomic sphere: "You ask if I shall attempt any solution of the [trust] problem. I hardly think so. The novelist—by nature—can hardly be a political economist; and it is to the latter rather than to the former that one must look for a way out of the 'present discontents.'"[17] The most Norris could do in *The Octopus* was to picture the historical and present situations in California as he understood them and from the varying points of view of his many characters. Even the relevance of Annixter's social ethic, echoing the essentials of the Sermon on the Mount and suggesting the value of concern for others as a means of mollifying an inhumane economic order, reflects only one point of view expressed by a character, about which the reader may draw his or her own conclusion. (Oddly enough, no reviewer looked past Shelgrim and Presley to consider Annixter as Norris's means of making a positive contribution to the discussion of how corporations and trusts might develop a more benign rationale for their operations.)

Presley's point of view in the Shelgrim speech scene was not the only one deemed disturbing. At the close of the novel, when Presley's symptoms of clinical depression are fully evident, Norris relates the poet's Panglossian thoughts about the relative unimportance of the mayhem wreaked in the San Joaquin Valley. Influenced at this point not only by Shelgrim but by Vanamee's more recent preachment on the ultimate meaninglessness of evil and the unreality of death, Presley struggles to cope with the debacle he has witnessed in the San Joaquin Valley and especially the cruel death of his friend Annixter. Coming to the consoling conclusion that good always and necessarily emerges from evil, and that in the larger view only the good in the end remains, Presley is thus Norris's means of committing another great sin, according to Rice. Again assuming that Presley's thoughts were Norris's own, Rice termed the poet's ruminations *the author's* "babyish plea" for the preposterous notion that real, palpable evil originated by individuals may be explained away by reference to destiny and elemental forces at work. A second review appearing in the *Boston Evening Transcript*—not written by Sargent but by another, less-restrained critic—thundered the same criticism. This unsigned piece rightly gibbets Presley for his too-optimistic idealism and erasure of true evil. Yet it concludes that this desperate vision-ary is actually Norris assigning Presley his own Pollyanna-like denial of the significance of events such as Annixter's death, his widow's miscarriage, An-nie Derrick's loss of her son Harran, and Mrs. Hooven's starvation. In part a positive estimate acknowledging the "indisputable proof of the author's power," the review registers double disappointment when noting how such talent has been misused:

> [A]las! the author is not content to tell the story. He must preach, moralize, attempt to deal with the mystery of evil. He is not content to let the conscience of his readers draw the inevitable moral. . . . Presley the poet—not unlike Edwin Markham in some respects of his career—is permitted to reappear and moralize, and come to the lame conclusion that despite all the satanic procedure by which the wheat farmers have been despoiled of their own, it is atoned for by the fact that the wheat grown on their ranches saved the lives of starving Indians or hungry Americans and Europeans. The implica-tion of the last chapter of the book is that all the corporation did in spoil-ing the individuals was inevitable, the necessary method of conducting the transportation business.[18]

This is not to say that the majority of reviewers collapsed the distinction between author and character or felt that Norris was unwilling to allow his readers to make up their own minds about the events he depicts and his char-acters' thoughts and statements. In the *Overland Monthly,* for example, the unsigned author erred when terming Presley "the medium of observation" for the reader. The novel is not restricted to his point of view. Still, when discuss-ing the ending and how one may not agree with Presley, this reviewer—like Sargent before him—did not mistake the neurasthenic poet for Norris.[19]

One upshot of the drubbings administered to *The Octopus* is immediately apparent in *The Pit:* no character in that work is interpretable as Norris's spokesperson, even when he or she, like Presley in the early pages of *The Octopus,* expresses an opinion that Norris had publicly held. He was dou-bly careful to maintain authorial distance and to ensure that Curtis, Laura, Corthell, Charles Cressler, Landry Court, and Page Dearborn would not be confused with him any more than McTeague and Trina could be.

Another consequence is the article that appeared in *The World's Work* in May 1902, as his *Pit* labors were nearing an end. "The Novel with a 'Purpose'" brought forward a notion with which he had first dealt in print in 1896 when he reviewed Mrs. Jarboe's novel *Robert Atterbury* along with Howells's *A Parting and a Meeting*. He then preferred the way in which the realist refrained from intruding into his tale to declare his own point of view; and he as energetically detested the way in which Jarboe never let the reader forget the author for a moment as she preached as much as she narrated the story of her hero and heroine. Both were writers with a "purpose" in that each had a point of view. But Howells wisely accomplished his ends by credibly fashioning his characters and the plot in such a way that they suggested for the reader's consideration a concept that the characters themselves never directly address as such—one that Jarboe rails against: that marriage and sexual relationships between males and females who care for each other need not, and perhaps should not, be avoided by those seeking spiritual improvement in their lives. In short, Howells let the incidents recorded in his story give rise to the point over which the reader was invited to ruminate.

Five years later Norris remained of a like mind. He noted in "The Novel with a 'Purpose'" that the best kind of fiction embodies three intents: to tell something; to show something; and to prove something about life as it actually is. All great novelists, such as Hugo and Zola at their best, demonstrate this, Norris argued; and he acknowledged that proving something ultimately involves "preaching" of a sort. But the great novel "preaches by telling things and showing things" from which the reader may infer a truth or truths. Its author selects "from the great storehouse of actual life the things to be told and shown. . . . The preaching, the moralizing, is the result not of a direct appeal by the writer, but is made—should be made—to the reader by the very incidents of the story."[20]

In *The Octopus,* such incidents dealing with the conflict between the growers and the railroad provide in the aggregate the solution to the problem addressed by Rice and other critics: they cause Shelgrim's apologia to collapse upon itself without any direct comment from Norris or rebuttal by Presley being necessary. Likewise, Presley's worldview at the conclusion reveals its absurdity, as the reader recalls the numerous incidents in the novel that contradict it. It would appear that Norris had trusted his contemporaries to see this on their own, only to find that some could not. Norris does not refer to *The Octopus* in this essay, but the carping reviews of it were the thorn in his side that, months after the novel's publication, prompted this reflection upon how authors worth their salt *show* rather than *tell* when it comes to generating their themes.

❧

Norris did not always refrain from expressing his own opinions in his prose fictions. In *McTeague,* for example, he offers interpretive, evaluative, and even wryly comical commentary at particular moments, just as his beau ideal in regard to authorial self-effacement, William Dean Howells, occasionally offers an opinion in *The Rise of Silas Lapham.* But such moments occur less frequently than one might think. For example, in chapter 2 of *McTeague,* when McTeague becomes sexually aroused and types a classic Victorian moral reaction to the promptings of the vile instinct that clamors for satisfaction, Norris is not disclosing his own priggish, nearly hysterical prudishness when posing the question of why McTeague could not love Trina "purely, cleanly" in an asexual way. Rather, it is the reaction of the puzzled McTeague, who "could not understand this thing," that Norris expresses in terms familiar to a genteel and morally scrupulous readership of the 1890s.[21] In this instance, as at the end of *The Octopus* and in early scenes as well, Norris employs a narrative technique familiar to many readers of Flaubert and Zola—but obviously not to Rice and his ilk. Anticipating stream-of-consciousness writing in the twentieth century, this *style indirect libre,* or free indirect discourse, functions similarly as the author assumes that the reader will discern the junctures at which narrative point of view changes radically from that of the author to that of the character whose perspective is being articulated. The narrative voice remains in the third-person singular but, unannounced, the sentences begin to serve a new function, expressing McTeague's or Presley's state of mind rather than Norris's own until, again without announcing the shift, Norris terminates the free indirect discourse with a return to the conventional third-person description. Or, as seen in the visionary conclusion of Zola's *Germinal,* as well as that of *The Octopus,* a chapter may end without a return to the author's point of view.[22]

Given that this technique has received markedly less attention than stream-of-consciousness narration and, alas, that Norris never discussed it in his literary essays, a succinct example is in order. This may be seen in a short story that appeared after Norris's death as "The Wife of Chino," in the January 1903 issue of *Century.* Once aptly entitled "The Wife of Uriah" in manuscript,[23] this reworking of the David-Bathsheba story in II Samuel deals with the attempt by Chino Zavalla's randy wife to seduce his boss, and it takes the Anglo-Saxon hero named Lockwood to the point at which she—a Mexican-American like her husband—almost succeeds. At the last moment, the hero recoils from Felice. Italics indicate Norris's use of free indirect discourse to give expression to Lockwood's repulsion:

> She would have taken his hand, but Lockwood . . . was on his feet. It was as though a curtain that for months had hung between him and the blessed light of clear understanding had suddenly been rent in twain by her words. *The woman stood revealed. All the baseness of her tribe, all the degraded savagery of a degenerate race, all the capabilities for wrong, for sordid treachery, that lay dormant in her, leaped to life at this unguarded moment, and in that new light, that now at last she herself let in, stood pitilessly revealed, a loathsome thing, hateful as malevolence itself.*
> "What," shouted Lockwood, "you think—that I—that I . . . oh-h, it's monstrous. . . ." He could find no words to voice his loathing.

In light of Norris's reputation as a racist and the stereotypical representations of "hot-blooded" Latins in *The Octopus*,[24] one may be prone to overlook in the third sentence the sudden change to Lockwood's point of view on the "loathsome" Latina. One will thus also miss the return to Norris's point of view in the fifth sentence. But to read the passage thus is to replicate the experience of those who fail to recognize the way in which Presley's final thoughts in *The Octopus* are at odds with the conclusions already drawn by the reader from Norris's portrayal of the conflict between the growers and the railroad. Were Norris, rather than Lockwood, interpreting the manifestations of Felice's "degenerate" race and ethnicity, he would be contradicting himself elsewhere in the work. For Chino Zavalla is descended from the same "degenerate" gene pool as his wife. Yet Norris fashions him as a model employee as measured by the Protestant work ethic or other Anglo-Saxon standards. As with the Mexican-American hero of "The Riding of Felipe," published in *Everybody's Magazine* while Norris was researching *The Pit* in Chicago, there is nothing of the "sordid" or "loathsome," latent or active, in Chino Zavalla's personality or "race." In short, Lockwood is the racist whose thoughts are thus vented in the same way that Presley's optimistic evolutionary idealism is. Norris is only, so to speak, the messenger reporting in the third-person singular his characters' ways of seeing things.[25]

Norris did forthrightly preach his own mind in 1901–2 in many of the forty-nine articles that appeared in the *Chicago American, Boston Evening Transcript, Brooklyn Daily Eagle,* and two magazines, *The World's Work* and *The Critic.* These he wrote in hours taken away from work on *The Pit* and the seventeen short stories that saw publication after he completed *The Octopus*, and the majority dealt with his personal point of view on literary matters as well as on conditions in the turn-of-the-century publishing industry.

The twenty-eight of these articles posthumously gathered by Charles, Jeannette, and her closest friend Isobel Field in *The Responsibilities of the Novelist and Other Literary Essays* vary widely in quality and, unfortunately, reveal neither the three editors' command of the whole of Norris's nonfiction writings nor their ability to separate wheat from chaff. It is unimaginable that Norris would have authorized the inclusion of gossipy, income-producing "filler" for newspaper columns. Absent in the 1903 collection were truly important *Wave* period articles such as "Fiction Is Selection" and the appreciations of William Dean Howells. Astonishingly, neither "Zola as a Romantic Writer," "Zola's *Rome*," nor "A Summer in Arcady" was present to define the theoretical foundation of 1896 upon which Norris's identity as the "American Zola" rested. Charles, Jeannette, and Isobel likewise omitted his fourth important statement of the naturalistic aesthetic that had more recently been printed as "Frank Norris's Weekly Letter" in the 3 August 1901 issue of the *Chicago American*. They chose only the least-significant piece touching upon Zola's practice as a writer, "A Plea for Romantic Fiction"; it emphasizes very briefly only the romantic dimensions of Zola's art. Reading the volume today, one would have no reason to suspect that Norris was a literary naturalist or even a significant figure in the history of literary theory.

Norris's estate was not large, and their interest in late 1902 and 1903 was in providing for his survivors by capitalizing on the popularity of *The Pit* with a posthumous collection of his essays and an equally hastily assembled book of short stories also published in 1903, *A Deal in Wheat and Other Stories of the New and Old West*. It too included only recently published works, many of which—Jeannette informed Walker—were frankly potboilers dashed off for supplemental income. Having inarguably "arrived" as a novelist, Norris enjoyed in 1901–2 the boon that had been the late Stephen Crane's, was Richard Harding Davis's from the early 1890s on, and would be Jack London's: Periodicals would take anything from his hand, including rather broad tall tales that were essentially expanded anecdotes, for example, "The Passing of Cock-Eye Blacklock," in which the hero fishes with dynamite and "passes" when his dog retrieves a stick with its fuse still burning. By July 1902, when this slight entertainment appeared in *Century*, he no longer needed to be concerned about caviling critics lamenting what might appear a falling off in the quality of his work. As Jeannette informed Walker, by then Norris already enjoyed the ultimate acknowledgment of his achievement and assurance of continuing success as a novelist: competitors of Doubleday, Page, and Company had attempted to lure him into their stables of writers with offers for *The Pit*—before he had finished writing it.

It is most unlikely, then, that Norris viewed his 11 December 1901 article "The 'Volunteer' Manuscript," describing the treatment of unsolicited manuscripts by firms such as Doubleday, Page, as anything other than a possibly interesting but ultimately ephemeral bit of work-for-hire. The same is true of other peek-behind-the-scenes pieces dealing with the publishing industry at large, such as "The Unknown Author and the Publisher," "Fiction Writing as a Business," and "What Frank Norris Has to Say about the Unknown Writer's Chances." "Frank Norris on the Ways of Critics," reprinted as "Newspaper Criticisms and American Fiction" in *Responsibilities,* offers a far-from-startling exposé of book reviewers: they don't often read the books they evaluate. The enfant terrible of the *Wave* years reappeared briefly in November 1901 to provoke bluestocking subscribers of the *Boston Evening Transcript* with "Why Women Should Write the Best Novels—and Why They Don't." This waggish reflection on why women of Norris's class *should* (leisure time, typical ladies-seminary education emphasizing the arts, and the natural feminine "gift" of writing ability), and why they *don't* (more restricted life experience than males, "nerves," and perfectionist tendencies that work against them), is of some lasting value, however. For it contrarily accentuates his admiration of Ellen Glasgow's achievement in a 1900 novel published by Doubleday, Page, *The Voice of the People.* She, at least, had risen above the ill effects of nineteenth-century constructions of gender.[26] Also, this essay provides an explanatory gloss on the female characters—with and without literary ambitions—in the Norris canon who are negatively imaged because of their "nerves" (Lloyd Searight in *A Man's Woman*) and the effects of living in sheltered environments like that from which the "nerves"-free Travis Bessemer turns away to become a New Woman in *Blix* (Annie Derrick in *The Octopus*).

In fact, most of what is of enduring value in Norris's 1901–2 essays is similarly self-referential, echoing the most salient points he made in his *Wave* articles of 1896–97 and resonating with the recently completed *Octopus.* For example, as "The Novel with a 'Purpose'" directly relates to narrative technique in *The Octopus* and *The Pit*, "The Mechanics of Fiction" focuses on Norris's plot-development methodology in both. On 4 December 1901 in the *Evening Transcript,* this essay on effective plotting offered little that could be termed new in 1901, since it deals in terms familiar to anyone who passed through a "literary" course of study at schools such as the University of California: characters are introduced as a setting is established; an event triggers a sequence of incidents in the plot; the consequences constitute "rising action," leading to a crisis point at which the eventual outcome of the story will be seen to have been determined by an event or decision; the denouement, or falling action, resulting from the crisis follows, leading to the conclusion. The climax, or emotive high point, may occur at the time of the crisis or closely proximate; or, as in *The Octopus* and *The Pit*, it may occur toward the end of the denouement. On 13 September 1900, Norris had laid out just such a plan for *The Octopus* in the letter he sent to Isaac F. Marcosson.[27] In "The Mechanics," though, he gave an even more exact description of what he had already done in *The Octopus*, suggesting that each chapter of a novel should mimic the whole by replicating as fully as possible the narrative structure just described. He did not note that chapters abounding in secondary crises and climaxes invite the description of "melodramatic," which of course does apply to this novel and *The Pit* but was not an epithet—or pejorative—that Norris wanted the public to apply to his work or himself.

"A Neglected Epic" and "The Frontier Gone at Last" were similarly self-referential articles. They have drawn considerable attention because they exalt the Anglo-Saxon and focus upon the resistless "westering" of the all-conquering race. Both echo the character Cedarquist in *The Octopus*, who sees the transpacific nations as the new frontier into which the American businessman will extend the "great march" that began in the swamps of Friesland, lo, so many centuries ago. Norris's tone in "A Neglected Epic," however, is one of lamentation in that no American had yet produced the kind of national epic in which other countries rightfully take pride; no one had produced one treating the period of roughly forty years in which Americans subdued the wilderness beyond the Mississippi River and imposed law and order upon the "Wild West." He complains that Bowie, Travis, and Crockett at the Alamo have not received the treatment afforded Old World heroes such as Achilles, Roland, and Grettir. At the same time, though, Norris surely knew that he was encouraging thus a complimentary response to his criticism of American literature. *The Octopus*, his "Story of California," as the subtitle reads, went well beyond being an epic of the wheat only, as it touched upon the period in which California was, until 1848, under Spanish control; focused on forty-niners such as Magnus Derrick, who turned from prospecting to cultivation of the soil; recalled the Mussel Slough Tragedy of

1880; and treated conditions in the onetime frontier state that brought the reader down to the end of the nineteenth century.

"The Frontier Gone at Last" echoes Frederick Jackson Turner's 1893 thesis concerning the national significance of the closing of the American frontier. Yet it reflects Norris's state of mind more than it facilitates a clearer perception of the Anglo-Saxon's role in the history of conquest and civilization. Written at roughly the same time as "A Neglected Epic" for *The World's Work,* but appearing ten months earlier in the February 1902 issue, this essay is of much greater autobiographical importance. It marks a change in perspective on the matter of racial superiorities and inferiorities as, toward its end, the nearly thirty-one-year-old author poses this question: "[B]ut is it not possible that we can find in this great destiny of [the Anglo-Saxon] something a little better than mere battle and conquest, something a little more generous than mere trading and underbidding [one's business competitors]?" Like Annixter after he experiences something "better" thanks to the change in his personality wrought by Hilma Tree, Norris appears to have risen above demeaning racial categorizations when suggesting that it may be best to "take the larger view, ignoring the Frieslanders, the Anglo-Saxons, the Americans. Let us look at the peoples as people and observe how inevitably as they answer the great Westward impulse [that] the true patriotism develops. . . . Not our present day selfish conception of the word, but a new patriotism, whose meaning is now the secret of the coming centuries." It does not remain a secret for many paragraphs. Given the increasing interactions—commercial and otherwise—among nations, boundaries are widening; and "patriotism widens with the expansion, and our countrymen are those of different race, even different nations." Norris implies the welcome outcome of all this in the rhetorical question with which the essay ends: "Will it not go on, this epic of civilization, this destiny of all races, until . . . we who now arrogantly boast ourselves as Americans . . . may realize that the true patriotism is the brotherhood of man and know that the whole world is our nation and simple humanity our countrymen?"[28] The point of view is not that of 1897's "A South-Sea Expedition," in which the imperialistic *Wave* author celebrated the colonization of Bougainville by the "big-boned, blonde, long-haired type—the true Anglo-Saxon type."[29] Nor is the voice that of Norris in 1898 when he savored the triumph of the Anglo-Saxon over the Latin in "The Surrender at Santiago." Perhaps continuing to display the influence of the Reverend William S. Rainsford, and the sharper edges of his personality having been ground down by accumulated experience as he matured, Norris penned the happiest essay of the lot when rising to a perception of the brotherhood of mankind.

Norris "preached" even more strenuously and revealed just how seriously he took the writing of *The Octopus* and *The Pit* in the several essays in which he sounded the theme given its fullest expression in "The Responsibilities of the Novelist" and echoed resoundingly in "The True Reward of the Novelist" and "The Need of a Literary Conscience."

As their titles suggest, these are veritable secular sermons in which the Reverend Rainsford and William Dean Howells could delight. The "dean" of American letters had blazed the trail down which Norris went as an essayist, motivated to moralize about the profession of authorship because of the extraordinary popularity of the novel as an art form at the turn of the century. A novelist may reach ten, twenty, or a hundred thousand readers and thus wield an influence greater than that of any speaker in a church pulpit. With such power to mold public opinion, explained Norris, one must not forbear to wear the mantle of social responsibility. Whether romantic, realist, or naturalist, the novelist must not play the *saltambanque* or the charlatan. An unwavering dedication to truth telling and commitment to sincerity are the moral requisites for his or her high office as novelist. Or as Norris put it in one of his seven "Salt and Sincerity" articles for *The Critic,* aptly characterizing his own recent work as a short-story writer, if an author intent upon doing good "is one of the 'best men,' working for a 'permanent place' [in the literary world], he will turn his attention and time, his best efforts, to the writing of novels, reverting to the short story only when necessary for the sake of boiling the Pot and chasing the Wolf."[30] The novelist's reward for acting in accordance with so high a standard? The "True Reward of the Novelist" is the ability to say in all honesty, "I never truckled; I never took off the hat to Fashion and held it out for pennies. I told them the truth. They liked it or they didn't like it. What had that to do with me? I told them the truth; I knew it for the truth then, and I know it for the truth now."[31]

Shortly before his death, Norris's seventh and last "Salt and Sincerity" article was printed in the late September 1902 issue of *The Critic.* In it he echoed William Dean Howells's concern for the impressionable young reader whose outlook on life and rapidly forming personality would be affected, for good or ill, by the quality of the literature to which he or she was exposed. Like Mark Twain, who demonstrated as serious a conviction in *Adventures of Huckleberry Finn* when emphasizing the deleterious effects of Tom Sawyer's reading of blood-and-thunder adventure romances, Norris worried over certain kinds of books being put into the wrong hands and a possible dearth of the right kind being available to American youths. By then the father of an eight-month-old daughter, he risked the charge of cloying sentimentality by fretting over the quality of prose fiction reaching the "Very Young Girl." It was his opinion that "the young girl takes a book to heart infinitely more than a boy," and thus it profoundly influences her, negatively or positively, for life.

> The boy—*his* story once read—votes it "bully," takes down his cap, and there's an end. But the average Very Young Girl does not read her story: she lives it, lingers over it, weeps over it, lies awake nights over it. So long as she lives she will never quite forget the books she read when she was sixteen. It is not too much to say that the "favorite" books of a girl at this age become a part of her life. They influence her character more than any of us, I imagine, would suspect or admit. All the more reason, then, that there should not only be good books for girls, but plenty of good books.[32]

One sees the concern of a doting father of thirty-two years but also finds him again writing self-referential prose in yet another way: The novel then in press featured a heroine whose reading experience is a primary determinant of her personality, which, Norris makes abundantly clear in his most allusive novel, is an aggregate of roles played and concepts illustrated by the characters to which she has been exposed. To a large degree, the heroine of *The Pit* is what she has read; further, Laura's identity is as mightily determined by aesthetic experience extending well beyond novels by writers such as Thackeray, Charlotte Brontë, George Meredith, and—at two extremes—Ouida and William Dean Howells. These influences extend into nonfiction such as John Ruskin's reflections on ideal womanhood and manhood in *Sesame and Lilies;* poetry such as Tennyson's *Idyls of the King;* plays by Shakespeare, Racine, and Sardou; operas such as *Faust* and *Carmen;* and even compositions by Mendelssohn, Beethoven, Liszt, and Stainer that suggest modes of behavior attractive to a young woman with a vivid imagination who is especially susceptible to musical stimuli. She is considerably more sophisticated than Madame Bovary, whose early reading of romances torridly featuring romantic love results in preposterously high expectations for her own experience of love, her neurotic behavior when reality never measures up to her ideal conception of it, and ultimately her suicide. The course of Laura's experience runs along the same lines until Norris proves kinder to his heroine than Flaubert was.

By 4 June 1902, when he completed *The Pit,* Norris had given Laura and her husband a second chance at happiness and the opportunity to rise above the past to fashion a new life away from Chicago—in the West, to which Norris himself was then preparing to return, never again to see New York City nor to work for any publisher as a manuscript reader. Thanks to American and transatlantic royalties from five novels, payments for his articles and short stories, an advance from the *Saturday Evening Post* for a serial version of *The Pit,* and more generous terms for the new novel than Doubleday, Page had given for his previous books,[33] Norris was finally accumulating the where-withal to enter a new phase of his career: that of a self-supporting novelist who might live and work anywhere he chose.

He chose to return to San Francisco.

24

FAREWELL TO GOTHAM

Before he left New York City, Norris discharged two duties ensuring that his departure from Doubleday, Page, and Company was a friendly one. As may be seen in the record he kept,[1] he filed his evaluation of manuscript number 1,738 on 20 June 1902—the last of 291 assigned to him since the beginning of the year. The other was an errand on which the firm sent him. For the first time since his return from Cuba he was to serve as a journalist. By remarkable coincidence, he did so for the editor of *Everybody's Magazine* whom he had persuaded Frank N. Doubleday to hire. As he neared the acme of his career as an author, circumstances provided him with the opportunity to measure how far he had come. He was reporting once again to the man who had given him his start as a professional writer, John O'Hara Cosgrave, his former boss at *The Wave*.

The occasion at the end of June for Norris's train ride to Wilkes-Barre, Pennsylvania, and visits to nearby towns was the Anthracite Coal Strike that the United Mine Workers of America called for in March 1902 and that began in May. The novelist would now demonstrate as a journalist the truth of his assertion concerning *The Octopus* in his 9 June 1901 letter to George H. Sargent: Norris was not a political economist, and that is glaringly obvious in "Life in the Mining Region." As in his *Wave* years, he would only offer the impressions of an observer; and, as in his Spanish-American War articles, he exercised one of his favorite ploys.

He was surprised—really very much surprised—to find that his expectations of simmering unrest and sporadic outbreaks of violence, prompted by newspaper and magazine articles, were wide of the mark. All he could report was what he saw, which was rather tame; and nothing resembled the horrendous living conditions of the workers and the class warfare pictured at the Voreux mine in Zola's *Germinal.* The corporation was not brutalizing anyone within sight. The strikers did not appear particularly pinched. He could understand the miners' demands for higher wages, shorter hours, and improved working conditions; he could understand, too, that businesses are not run as charities and that the maximizing of profit motivates capitalists. But his main concern in this article, which would appear in the September 1902 issue of *Everybody's,* was the approach of autumn and winter, when homes would require heating, industry would continue to need coal, and workers would face unemployment should factories shut down. That it was time for reasonable individuals on both sides to come together and work out a solution—as finally occurred, when President Roosevelt intervened and a commission arbitrated an agreement in March 1903—is the distinctly unremarkable, "soft" theme with which Norris concluded this fair-and-balanced, or fence-straddling, article. The piece was just right for *Everybody's Magazine,* a middle-of-the-road monthly designed to provide entertainment for a wide-spectrum readership rather than stimulate controversy and risk alienating subscribers.

It was very much like the *Saturday Evening Post,* which also did not care to serve up matter that was radical—either politically or literarily. This presented a problem for the American Zola that summer. *The Pit* was not *McTeague.* It features no sadomasochistic interactions between husband and wife. It was also not *A Man's Woman.* There are only two dollops of violence: Curtis Jadwin strikes his broker in the face when the latter informs him that the game is up; and the financially ruined Charles Cressler commits suicide, offstage. But adultery, whether actual or strongly suggested as a possibility for Curtis Jadwin's wife, was out of the question for the *Saturday Evening Post.* Norris revised accordingly, delivering a version of the novel in which Laura does not seriously consider becoming Sheldon Corthell's paramour. He also eliminated or downplayed the more neurotic moments in Laura's history. Compared with the heroine the readers of the unbowdlerized book would know in early 1903, the Laura of the *Post* is a veritable model of mental health. In short, Norris sanitized the novel, and an editor or editors at the *Post* further condensed it to fit the weekly's format.[2]

When all of this occurred before the serialization began on 20 September 1902 cannot be determined, save that the copy given editorial treatment at the *Post* had to have been in hand at its offices by mid-August. Norris may have revised a carbon copy shortly after he submitted the original typescript to Doubleday, Page in early June. If there was no typescript, a holograph manuscript was given to Doubleday, Page, and Norris had to wait for receipt of two sets of galley proof, one of which he used for the *Post* revision. Happily, we do know that by July 1902 proof was in his hands, thanks to Julie Herne. She said so in 1952 as she recalled for James D. Hart the relationship that had developed between the Norrises and her family since late 1901: "The dramatization [of *The Octopus*] never materialized, but our meeting led to a memorable friendship. Frank and Jeannette lived within a few blocks of our home, and during that winter [1901–2] we saw them frequently. They spent nearly all the following summer with us and my mother was godmother to their little girl, Billy. Frank was writing *The Pit* when we met, and that summer I read galleys aloud to him and Jeannette."[3]

Where the Norrises stayed for some weeks with Julie, and where Jeannette bid Frank goodbye when he went to Wilkes-Barre, was the summer home of the late James A. Herne in the township of Southampton, Long Island. Situated on ninety acres, it was a spacious, two-and-a-half-story Queen Anne structure up to par with other "cottages" of the very well-to-do in the vicinity. On the grounds surrounding Fresh Pond were drives and well-maintained gardens. The property's waterfront on Little Peconic Bay was a half-mile in length and sported bath houses; there was a long dock at which one might secure a yacht. While they were at "Herne Oaks"—*Hearts of Oak* was one of Herne's successful plays—Billy was baptized across the South Fork of Long Island, at St. Andrew's Dune Church on the Atlantic shore. As Julie noted, her mother Katherine Corcoran Herne was one of the two sponsors at the Episcopalian ceremony conducted on 13 July 1902. George DeWitt Moulson, who had contributed so much to the technical accuracy of *The Pit*, then became Billy's godfather.[4]

On 18 July 1902, the now footloose novelist wrote to the editor of *Century*, Richard Watson Gilder, who had just published "The Passing of Cock-Eye Blacklock." Norris announced that—of all things—he "may go around the world in the course of the next few months," stopping at "some dozen far Eastern and Mediterranean ports." He wanted to know if Gilder wished to

commission a series of travel articles and thus help defray the cost of the long voyage. Were he interested, he might write Norris at the St. Dunstan's Hotel, at the corner of Sutter Street and Van Ness Avenue in San Francisco.[5]

The Norris family was leaving New York in four days, and Jeannette was sure that Frank secured a contract for the writing of travel pieces, though she did not mention what firm issued it.

A new adventure in Frank Norris's life was taking shape. It would not, most likely, be on a par with his jaunt to South Africa and participation in the Cuban campaign. Still, it was the best one possible, since his wife would accompany him across the Pacific to India and on to Europe, where he would study settings for the third volume of his wheat trilogy. *The Wolf* would depict the consequences in countries such as Italy of how the profit-hungry parties pictured in *The Octopus* and *The Pit* manipulated the supply of American wheat.[6]

Billy was to remain in San Francisco. Jeannette told Walker that the two grandmothers would care for her during the months that she and Frank would be circumnavigating the globe.

Given Norris's experiences as the child of feckless parents, one's attention is naturally drawn to evidence of how Jeannette and he behaved when their turn came. Charles did not provide a clue when speaking with Walker. Jeannette did characterize Frank as paterfamilias—very briefly. The only cameo available is, unfortunately, a negative one in Walker's transcription of what Jeannette rather unkindly said concerning an event that took place in San Francisco: "Up to this time Frank had taken the baby as a joke and somewhat of an encumbrance. One day they took one of their old walks through the Presidio; one of the old steam trolleys whistled while Frank was carrying the child, whereupon it jumped in his arms, cuddling up next to his shoulder." Frank then quipped, "By Jove, the child has brains!" She might have mentioned that her husband's affection for Billy manifested itself when he prepared the manuscript leaves detailing for the typesetter of *The Pit* the forematter including the title page, dedication, and list of characters to appear in the novel. That Billy was neither a joke nor an encumbrance he strongly suggested in the holograph dedication of the volume to Jeannette Williamson Norris.[7] Jeannette Black Norris said nothing of the kind, however.

As to Billy's mother in 1902, she revealed nothing about herself as a parent when talking with Walker in 1930, save that it was difficult for her to find a nurse for her daughter when they arrived in San Francisco. (In New York, she had not wanted for one; Frank immediately employed a nurse for the child.)[8] After Frank's death, as may be seen in the letters of Charles and Kathleen Norris, the "encumbrance" was felt by Jeannette. Unlike her husband in 1902 and well before, she delighted in the freedom essential to the upscale "bohemian" lifestyle that marriage to a novelist afforded her.

One of the reasons Norris longed to leave New York City was the same that motivated him to attack Gelett Burgess and Les Jeunes in 1897's "An Opening for Novelists": He detested the hothouse, "arty" scene and its corrupting influence on genuine talent. He again made this clear in the autobiographical short story "Dying Fires," published in the July 1902 issue of *Smart Set*. It was his parting shot at New York and other habitats of the dilettantish beau monde. To Jeannette he had denounced bohemianism as "anathema"; its smug pretensions to unconventionality were little more than a matter of "drinking beer out of tea-cups." His widow, however, would continue to flourish in such a milieu. She became the protégée of Mrs. Robert Louis Stevenson. Then she lived for years, rent-free, with Fanny Stevenson's daughter Isobel Field—in the company of her brother Lloyd Osbourne and her son Austin Strong—before she remarried into mainstream American life with Frank Preston, and did the same again with her third husband, Charles Black. As Richard Allan Davison has observed, Norris family correspondence after Frank's death pictures Jeannette alternating between "indulgence and neglect in her care of her young daughter."[9] To Davison, it is also apparent that Charles and his wife Kathleen served to a remarkable degree as Billy's surrogate parents.[10] Had Frank lived longer it cannot be said that the outcome would have been different. What can be proposed more surely is that Jeannette Black Norris differed in important respects from the endearing portrayal of her as Travis Bessemer in *Blix*. Dulce Bolado Ashe, Frank's hostess at the Santa Anita ranch in 1899 and later Gertrude's close friend, phrased the fact of the matter succinctly for Walker: Jeannette could not be termed a good mother.

To the end, though, Frank was infatuated with the woman with whom he detrained at the Oakland mole and then boarded the ferry that took them to San Francisco at the end of July 1902.

At a time when even working members of his class indulged in vacations that today appear exorbitantly protracted, Norris once again was initiating a months-long hiatus from labor other than the sending out of short stories already in hand. Given his productivity in 1901–2 as an essayist, short-story writer, novelist, and manuscript reader for Doubleday, Page, he certainly had earned some time off. But when he reached San Francisco, he postponed for several days his immersion in leisure, instead hitting the ground running because of a great injustice about which he had read on his way west.

Jeannette could not forget her husband's livid reaction when he was apprised of a ruthless attack launched against an old acquaintance, Dr. William M. Lawlor. The previous August, Lawlor had, thanks to the support of Governor Henry T. Gage, enjoyed the latest of several political appointments. He replaced Dr. A. E. Osborne as the superintendent of the California Home for the Care and Training of Feeble-Minded Children, located north of San Francisco in the Sonoma Valley at the town of Glen Ellen. (This was the same institution in which Jack London would situate his 1914 short story "Told in the Drooling Ward.") The sensational reports on Lawlor's heinous behavior in the months that followed had begun in the 5 July 1902 issue of the *San Francisco Chronicle* under the front-page headline, "Cruelty to Helpless and Imbecile Inmates Charged against Home for Feeble-Minded." The *Examiner* followed suit: "Dr. W. M. Lawlor Confesses Brutality beyond Worst in History of California." Yet more damaging for Lawlor was the announcement in the 8 July issue: "Governor Orders Investigation of Charges against Dr. Lawlor."[11] Even the governor pictured by San Francisco reporters as having given so undeserving a man so lucrative a position appeared to have turned against him—though charges of cronyism persisted in the newspapers, since Lawlor was successfully resisting immediate removal from the home.

Lawlor submitted his resignation on 12 July,[12] while the Norrises were still enjoying the hospitality of Julie Herne. Yet he was not going gently into the good night, for he worded the resignation as effective upon appointment of his successor. The newspapers seized upon this, convinced that he was trying to extend his and his wife's salary arrangements as long as possible, as well as their residence on the home's grounds. As late as 29 July, Lawlor was still on the premises, and the *Chronicle* was declaring with some exasperation, "Gage's Friend Lawlor Must Go."[13]

The press was so merciless through mid-October, when the Lawlors finally departed and the debacle at last ceased to be newsworthy, because of the undeniably sensational nature of the accusations leveled against him.

He is accused of shutting children up in a dungeon and allowing them to remain there for days at a time, and to subsist, meanwhile upon bread and water; he is charged with lacing helpless children into an invention known as the "Camisole," an improvement as a means of torture over the straitjacket and tying them to the floor of a darkened room to remain for two or three days without care or attendance; he is said to have inaugurated an atmosphere of fear in the government of the children, thereby lessening the possibility of their improvement or recovery.[14]

This was, however, merely a summary provided by the *Examiner.* Many another article catalogued his alleged cruelties in the horrific detail provided by his former employees. And Lawlor made himself appear even more monstrous by playing down the significance of the accusations. He confessed in his letter of resignation only to an "error in judgment in adopting a means of preserving discipline among that portion of the inmates of the home that are inclined to be unruly and troublesome." What appeared lurid crimes to the journalists he saw as merely regrettable faux pas.

There was yet one other factor known to the public that contributed to the negative image Lawlor projected. He had previously served as the chief physician at an institution Norris repeatedly visited in 1897 when working for *The Wave.* Norris had culled two articles from such experiences: "New Year's at San Quentin" and "A Lag's Release." The doctor who went to extremes in disciplining his charges at the home appeared to have been applying the same methods he used with the more troublesome inmates at San Quentin Prison.

There was, in short, little hope for Lawlor's recovering his good name or being asked to withdraw his resignation. Yet, related Jeannette, Frank "went out immediately" to Glen Ellen to offer his assistance and, on 2 August 1902, to accompany Lawlor and one of his three sons to a meeting of the home's trustees at which Dr. William J. G. Dawson would be elected Lawlor's successor. What followed was an adventure the like of which Norris's planned round-the-world cruise would be hard-pressed to equal.

During the meeting, Colonel J. F. Harrington, Lawlor's explosively outspoken nemesis since early July, rose to denounce once again the man he had repeatedly berated in the press. As he concluded, Lawlor's son said something insulting to him, and Harrington pushed him, calling him a "'damn young whelp.'" Order restored, Lawlor rose to complain that he "'had been vilified from one end of this State to the other,'" protesting that the journalists had misrepresented him and that "'no one is so foolish as to place any reliance'" on their libelous articles. The last straw, he declared, was the report that he had "'billeted [his] three sons on the State'" at the home. That was a lie, he went on, and if "'Colonel Harrington made that statement he lied, and he knows he lied.'" The volatile Civil War veteran and attorney then leaped to his feet and shouted back at Lawlor, "'You are lying! You can take that any way you please, and I'll meet the whole Lawlor family, one at a time, anywhere. I can whip the whole lot of you.'" Whereupon Harrington pulled a pistol from his hip pocket.[15]

The report in the *San Francisco Chronicle* was even more sensational than that in the *Examiner*. The *Chronicle's* version rivals Norris's more melodramatic moments in *The Octopus*. The scene was set thus: "When Dr. Lawlor entered Parlor 1 [of the Grand Hotel in San Francisco], he carried a dress-suit case full of books and papers, and was accompanied by Frank Norris, the young novelist, and Theodore M. Lawlor, a broad-shouldered son, who has just come of age." Dr. Lawlor then withdrew to the hallway, where he engaged in a heated argument with one of the home's trustees, Thomas F. Rooney. Returned to the meeting room, a still-agitated Lawlor contained himself as best he could while the election of Dr. Dawson took place. Then the grand confrontation with Harrington began. The "rising action" of the emotionally stormy "plot" peaked thus:

> Harrington was on his feet again, this time his right hand passing to his rear hip as he arose. The hand came into view on the instant and it clasped a revolver, the shining barrel of which glistened in the clear sunlight. He started toward Lawlor, bringing his arm up, but Frank Norris, who had slowly approached the Colonel while Lawlor was speaking, clasped him from the side, pinioning Harrington's arm as in a vice. He turned the maddened man half way round, the young novelist's strength equaling that of half a dozen such slender frames as he held captive.
>
> "Drop that gun!" panted Norris.[16]

And so it was that Frank Norris saved the day, as though the hero of a dime novel—truth trumping fiction in this instance.

But that was not the end of the matter. Lawlor's complaint—or one of them—was that the press had not allowed him to present his case to the public. "If I could have a hearing, if my side could be told, the people would be aghast" at the degree to which the journalists had demonized him.[17] Norris, having personally investigated conditions at the home and reviewed reports made by medical professionals who preceded him, was as outraged as Lawlor. Thus, on 6 August 1902, he presented the case against the *Examiner*, *Call*, *Chronicle*, and *Bulletin:* "[D]uring all the course of the crusade against Dr. Lawlor, not one single newspaper has allowed him to speak in his own defence."

Norris chose to give Lawlor's side of the story in an article that Jeannette saw repeatedly declined by the San Francisco newspapers to which her husband offered it for publication. It was finally published on 11 August by a weekly, *The Argonaut,* as a letter to the editor. At face value, Norris's testimony was compelling, for he observed that in "the reports of physicians sent to examine . . . the conditions of the home, in the testimony of witnesses examined before committees, sworn evidence absolutely and unequivocally refuting the charges has been brought forward again and again. The reports and the testimony have been read or pronounced in the presence and hearing of reporters . . . and by them deliberately ignored." Moreover, he declared, not "one feeble-minded or imbecile child has ever been punished since Dr. Lawlor took charge."

> One of the misapprehensions on the part of the public is that the inmates of this home are all children, and are all feeble-minded. Nothing could be further from the truth. Out of three hundred and twenty-two male inmates, one hundred and sixty-seven shave. Of the female inmates, more than half are mature women, while a very large number of young men have been sent to the home whose proper place is in the insane asylum or reformatory. Among this number are six who are, in particular, unruly, intractable, and vicious. Their ages are thirty, thirty-two, twenty-seven, eighteen, and sixteen, respectively. They are insane only in their criminality; fear of punishment is all that keeps them in submission. Not ten days ago one of them attempted to stab one of the attendants. Another has frequently tried to set fire to the dormitory. The half-dozen were a constant source of trouble under the [previous] administration of [Dr. Osborne].[18]

And so Norris proceeded, point by point, noting that Dr. Osborne too had dealt firmly with problem cases and that the former employees testifying against Lawlor had been discharged because *they* had dealt too harshly with the children and the adults at the home.

Norris's letter to the editor was to little avail. The no-longer-slight, memorably unmuscular Berkeley student recalled by his classmates might prevail over an armed man during an administrative hearing. But no one could resist the inertial force of the "yellow" press once set on its course by the sensational revelations of early July. Moreover, had his letter resulted in a fairer public hearing for Lawlor, the optimal outcome could have been only a mitigation of the charges against him.

In fact, male youths did not spend time in a "dungeon" or "black hole," but Dr. Lawlor did confine some for days in a weakly illuminated room. He did restrain females in a straightjacket-like "camisole" tied to rings in the floor in another, "better lighted and ventilated" room. The investigators whom Norris cited put into more rational perspective the actual situation at the home than the San Francisco reporters had; but Drs. Hatch and Young did report that bread and water was the fare in both rooms, and they criticized Lawlor for a "grave error of judgment based probably on mistaken ideas of the class of people he was caring for."[19] Contrary to what Norris had averred, one could not dismiss as fiction the charge that a "mute idiot," a ten-year-old, and a "low-grade patient" who "talks in signs and mumblings" were among twelve named residents Lawlor sent to the "dark cell."[20] Norris was clearly convinced that he was on the side of the angels when defending Dr. Lawlor. The "forlorn hope" to which he gave himself was, however, doomed from the very start.

Norris received some good news that fall, though. On 14 October 1902, the disgraced but ever persistent doctor attended a meeting of the Board of Trustees of the home, by virtue of the fact that he was the ex-officio secretary of the board until the appointment of another. The San Francisco Chronicle termed a resolution that was passed during the meeting a "thin whitewash coat" for Lawlor. But Norris could take some pleasure in noting that one of his main points of defense for Lawlor was acknowledged: The resolution admitted that "some of the criticisms of the public press are exaggerated and as a reflection on his personal character are unwarranted." The board reaffirmed the verdict that Lawlor had made "errors of judgment" but exonerated him "from the charge of cruelty and from having committed any crime of moral wrong."

Norris's thoughts on what followed next during this meeting must remain a matter for speculation, given that it will strike some as outrageous: Having been ousted from the superintendency, with his successor already appointed and the board wanting to deal next with the posting of the successor's bond and then his formal installation as superintendent, Dr. Lawlor asked for permission to withdraw his letter of resignation! He actually believed that he could regain his position and that his wife would not have to resign that day as the matron of the home.[21] Permission was denied.

After seeing his defense published, Norris turned his mind to less vexing matters, once again becoming with Jeannette and Billy the guest of a wealthy devotee of the arts and her family. This was the matron of the group Jeannette found so compatible in New York and with whom Frank and she had rung in the new year in 1901: the Stevenson clan.

In late 1899, Fanny Stevenson had discovered Gilroy, California, when awaiting completion of the construction of her mansion at the corner of Lombard and Hyde Streets in San Francisco. Accessible by rail to the south was this Santa Clara County town that now bills itself as the garlic capital of the United States. Six miles to the northwest on a heavily wooded hillside, she had found the perfect spot for a country home with wide verandas on two sides, which she dubbed Vanumanutagi (Vale of the Singing Birds) in happy memory of her residence with her late husband at Vailima in Samoa. It was to this retreat that the Norrises came to stay with Fanny, her children Lloyd Osbourne and Isobel Field, and her grandson Austin Strong. Frank and Jeannette, too, fell in love with this redwood-shaded locale in the coastal mountain range to the north of San Benito County, where he had visited Gaston and Dulce Ashe in 1899. As Fanny's biographer, Nellie Van de Grift Sanchez, relates, "Mrs. Stevenson became very much attached to [Norris], and he in turn was so charmed with the place . . . that he determined to buy a ranch in the neighbourhood," which he would name after the more expansive one of Annixter in *The Octopus:* Quien Sabe.[22] From the manager-owner of the nearby Redwood Retreat Hotel, Douglas Sanders, he purchased for five hundred dollars—the figure cited by Charles—ten acres adjoining the Stevenson property, on which stood a one-room log cabin.[23]

Returned to San Francisco, Norris was honored across the bay in Berkeley on 12 September 1902. By invitation he shared the stage at the Harmon Gymnasium with the professor of Semitic languages Jacob Voorsanger. Rabbi Voorsanger spoke on "The University as a Democracy," and Norris's contribution to the proceedings was a reading of his broadly humorous short story to appear in *Ainslee's* in January 1903, "Two Hearts That Beat as One."[24] The next day his attention was on Gilroy when he wrote to Sanders about an arrangement they had discussed for upgrading Quien Sabe. The "additions and improvements" would cost $550, more than the property itself. Norris was, in short, enjoying the splurge that the three thousand dollars or more advance from the *Saturday Evening Post* made possible. He was even in the market for a horse, asking in his letter to Sanders if he would keep his eyes peeled for one appropriate for riding and pulling a carriage.[25]

At the same time Norris also wrote to Fanny Stevenson, requesting that Lloyd Osbourne, too, be on the lookout for a horse and telling her that he would be making his initial payment of $250 for Quien Sabe by the first of

October. He also announced that "our famous round-the-world trip has been curtailed to a modest little excursion Samoa-wards and back." Or perhaps they would "get as far as Sydney." They would not go to France, nor to any other European country, and they expected to "come to Quien Sabe in February."[26] No explanation for the change in plan is extant, nor do we know how the decision not to visit Europe would affect the composition of, and particularly the continental setting for, *The Wolf*. Possibly illuminated by this recent development, though, is an otherwise cryptic entry in his list of things to do, referred to by Jeannette: Frank was to see Doubleday and "eat crow." For he would not be able to honor his arrangement to write round-the-world travel articles for one of Doubleday, Page's magazines or, by agreement with the firm, for another periodical or newspaper syndicate.

The most likely motivations for the abbreviated voyage were, first, his determination to settle in San Francisco among his old friends and in the house on Broderick Street his mother was able to give him—thanks to the divorce settlement she had obtained in 1894.[27] Second, the pull of Gilroy was strong. Norris bragged about the delights of his ranch to one of his professional associates in New York, "I can shoot deer from my front windows. The quails are a pest. There's a trout stream just around the corner. We have the Stevensons for near neighbors. This beats a New York apartment."[28]

These were Norris's halcyon days, save for one unfortunate development first referred to in his mid-September letter to Douglas Sanders. Jeannette had fallen ill while they were with Fanny Stevenson, and he assured Sanders that she was now feeling much better. Her illness in Gilroy, however, was but a prelude to the critical condition that Dr. Julius Rosenstirn diagnosed upon their return to San Francisco: acute appendicitis. Rosenstirn, it will be remembered, was the gynecologist who, Bertha Rickoff confided to Walker, performed an abortion for Jeannette in 1898. Since 1897 he had been the chief of staff at Mount Zion Hospital, and there Jeannette successfully underwent an appendectomy. Frank visited her regularly in the hospital during her recuperation, of course—but she remembered only a single detail about his visitations. One of her avocations was basket making, and Frank brought her the raffia she needed, only to be told by her doctor that it must be taken away immediately since it was a possible source of bacterial infection. Never a matter to be taken lightly, surgery was infinitely more risky in 1902 than now. Should infection occur before, during, or after a procedure, antibiotics could not provide a remedy. They did not exist in 1902, nor would they for more than two decades.

This trial was over by mid-October 1902, and the Norrises stored their furniture and arranged for Billy's care during their absence. They would soon embark on their voyage. Jeannette remembered the auspicious day on which Frank purchased their fares for the excursion to Australia.

25

CREPUSCULE

Bruce Porter was one of the old friends from the *Wave* years with whom Norris was refreshing his relationship upon his return to San Francisco. Porter too had left New York City where, in the winter of 1898–99, Norris had burst into his studio on Washington Square to announce that he had worked out his plan for the trilogy of the epic of the wheat. During Jeannette's hospitalization, Norris paid him a visit concerning a much more momentous development. In his memoir of his friendship with Frank, Porter described the scene:

> He came into the studio in San Francisco, haggard and despairing.
> His wife was in the hospital: had been operated upon—was out of danger, he told me—and we lunched together and then walked to the hospital.
> Outside the door, we stood for a moment:
> "Bruce—I'm afraid!"
> I gave him the formal assurances: "His wife had come through—every thing was well."
> "Yes—but I'm *afraid!*"
> "Afraid of what, Frank?"
> "I'm afraid of *Death!*"
> He turned and the door closed behind him; and I never saw him again.[1]

In all of Norris's writings no self-disclosure of this tenor will be found. He came closest to acknowledging mortality in such anxious terms in what appears to have been an early work from his hand, the allegorical short story

"The Guest of Honor," not published until the summer of 1902. Therein, the middle-aged character Manning Verrill, after seeing his closest friends die one by one over recent years, confesses to his physician his fear for himself, *"By God, Henry, I'm afraid; I'm afraid of Death! It's horrible."*[2] Norris, however, was not writing in the first-person singular, and only Porter's memoir makes it clear that Jeannette's brush with death had affected him in ways that the passing of his father had not.

Recognition of his own mortality at age thirty-two may have been a factor in how he responded to an ailment that befell him as Jeannette came back to full health. Then again, given that there is no such testimony by an alienist of Norris's time, dread may have had relatively little to do with his seemingly casual response to the pickle in which he found himself over the weekend of 18–19 October 1902. One will never know exactly why Frank did not take more seriously the acute indigestion he was experiencing. But there was good reason on his part to assume that it would pass. He was no stranger to the consequences of having what may politely be termed a sensitive stomach.

Jeannette witnessed at least two such manifestations. That he took wine with dinner every night of their marriage need not recall St. Paul's advice to Timothy to "use a little wine for thy stomach's sake and thine often infirmities" (1 Timothy 5:23). But, in fact, Norris could drink only a little without getting sick. She also explained that in *Blix* her husband had pictured himself when Condy Rivers experienced gastrointestinal distress. A dish of creamed oysters results in Condy's enduring "a horrible night"—as happened to Frank during his courtship of Jeannette. It is more noteworthy, however, that once his symptoms lessen in their severity, Condy refuses to heed his doctor's diagnosis of ptomaine poisoning and prescription of two weeks' bed rest. About his doctor he protests, "'He's a flapdoodle.'" Condy is convinced that the diagnosis is off the mark; he dismisses his problem as "'nothing but a kind of a sort of a pain. It's all gone now. I'm fit as a fiddle.'"[3]

The Octopus is, of course, radically less autobiographical than *Blix*, but one aspect of the characterization of Annixter gives reason to remember that Frank was the son of a man whose chief cause of death was acute enteritis (inflammation of the small intestine). As in *Blix*, Frank may very well have taken a page from real life as he knew it when introducing Annixter to the readers of *The Octopus:*

> When Presley reached Annixter's ranch house, he found young Annixter himself stretched in his hammock behind the mosquito-bar of the front porch, reading *David Copperfield*, and gorging himself with dried prunes.

Annixter—after the two had exchanged greetings—complained of terrific colics all the preceding night. His stomach was out of whack, but you bet he knew how to take care of himself; the last spell, he had consulted a doctor at Bonneville, a gibbering busy-face who had filled him up to the neck with a dose of some hogwash stuff that had made him worse—a healthy lot the doctors knew, anyhow. *His* case was peculiar. *He* knew; prunes were what he needed, and by the pound.[4]

Whether Norris was wont to try the same remedy is not a matter of record; but his indigestion did not in fact go away, and he called upon Dr. Rosenstirn for a physical examination on Monday, 20 October.

Rosenstirn advised surgery—the same that Jeannette had undergone. Life imitating art, Norris responded to his physician as had both Condy and Annixter, even though—Porter Garnett told Walker—he knew better. When Jeanette was recuperating, he informed Garnett that "the reason death so often resulted from appendicitis was because the patient so frequently wished the operation deferred after the physician pronounced the case operable. 'If,' he said, 'the operation is performed immediately . . . there is almost no danger of a fatal result.'" But Norris, related the *San Francisco Chronicle*, "refused to believe his ailment of so serious a nature as to warrant . . . radical treatment." As in *Blix* with Condy, he felt much better the next day, and the *Chronicle* reported that he "seemed on the way to a speedy recovery." Instead, however, Norris was unwittingly giving a textbook demonstration of the sequence of events typically following the rupture of an inflamed appendix: the pain diminishes dramatically when it has burst, and the patient experiences a temporary feeling of restored well-being.

The bacteria-suffused contents of the appendix having emptied into the peritoneum (the membrane that lines the abdominal and pelvic cavities), Norris awoke at four o'clock Wednesday morning with "excruciating pains in the region of the abdomen." Rosenstirn found him at the hospital two hours later, administered an anesthetic, and opened his abdomen to find "an advanced state of general peritonitis, with gangrene and perforation of the appendix."[5] The newspapers did not report whether Rosenstirn attempted corrective surgery or did no more than was possible in 1902 by cleansing the abdominal cavity by means of irrigation and then inserting a drainage tube.

By Thursday evening Norris's temperature had dropped from 103° to 100°F. Although his patient's pulse had fallen, Rosenstirn did not give up hope. At 2:00 A.M. on Friday, a hospital spokesperson echoed Rosenstirn by reporting that Norris's condition was "encouraging"—"as promising as could be expected."[6] At his bedside while he dozed under the influence of an opiate, and while the toxins being generated did their deadly work, were Gertrude, Jeannette, and Charles.[7]

On Saturday morning, 25 October 1902, Frank's mother and wife were with him when he died at 9:15.[8]

At 11:00 A.M. on Monday his funeral service took place at St. Luke's Episcopal church. The interment the same day at Mountain View Cemetery in Oakland was for family members only.[9]

At the time of Norris's death, the sixth installment of *The Pit* had just appeared in the *Saturday Evening Post*. The serialization would conclude in the 31 January 1903 issue, and bound copies of the original, unbowdlerized version of novel were by mid-November in Doubleday, Page's hands. Anticipating the end of the *Post* serialization, the firm put the book on sale in early January. By mid-February it was available in Canada, Australia, and England. The English publisher, Grant Richards, also marketed in hardcover and paperback a "Colonial" edition. The demand in the United States for *The Pit* was so strong that *Publishers' Weekly* announced on 7 February that a fifth printing of twenty thousand copies was in process.[10] One of the best-sellers of 1903, *The Pit* prompted Doubleday, Page to capitalize on its success with a seven-volume, "Golden Gate" edition of the *Complete Works of Frank Norris* later that year. Before year's end it also rushed into print the collection of his short stories, *A Deal in Wheat and Other Stories of the New and Old West,* and that of his nonfiction writings, *The Responsibilities of the Novelist and Other Literary Essays.*

Frank N. Doubleday had not misplaced his faith in Norris as an author whose potential would someday be fully realized, though his contemporaries and he could never foresee the possibility that death would intervene before one word of *The Wolf* was put to paper.

The Pit received an unprecedented number of reviews.[11] None of his previous books drew anything like the attention showered upon it, in part because reviewers seized the opportunity to keen over the loss of one of the most promising and accomplished young American novelists. Indeed, many of these pieces embed laudatory characterizations of his personality and achievements that may serve as epitaphs. But none is so apropos as a statement of faith that Norris himself made in a book review that he wrote for *The Wave* in 1897, a few months before he received his big break and left San Francisco for New York City.

The volume was Horace Fletcher's psychological self-help tract, *Happiness as Found in Forethought Minus Fearthought*, and Norris's situation in December 1897 was that of a would-be novelist stuck in a dead-end job beyond which it was possible he would never move. Fletcher spoke directly to Norris's demoralization, advancing the alleviating notion that past failures cease to exist, except in memory, by virtue of the fact that they are in the past. To be immobilized by the recollection of them is to allow oneself to be trapped in a realm of experience that has nothing to do with the present and future unless one permits it. "Hopeful determination" in dealing with obstacles to contentment in the present and future, advised Fletcher, "will go far in the way of procuring Happiness." Norris saw value in this but offered what he believed was a more accurate specification of the source of contentment and even joy. To his mind happiness was not, as Fletcher suggested, a commodity to be procured for once and for all. Were such a state of satisfaction attained, Norris argued, in a way suggesting a Schopenhauerian insight into the nature of human desire, "we should be unhappy that we could attain nothing further." And thus his counterproposal regarding the *means* to happiness—the process of overcoming obstacles to success—being the *end* in itself: "One is inclined to believe that that is more nearly the right idea, that Happiness is *overcoming rather than attaining.* One can never attain and yet be happy, but there are plenty of chances of overcoming things"—each success bringing with it its quotient of happiness.

> Successful overcoming of obstacles—that's the real fun you can have for your money, nor will anyone admire you so much as for this. The feeblest of us feel a thrill for the successful hero. We like the vicious, wicked determination that suggests the thorough-bred bull dog, we cannot but applaud the fellow who sits down in his closet and thinks and plans a certain action or course of life, and who grips his teeth together and clenches his fist till the knuckles whiten and says, "By God, I'll put it through," and *does* put it through *just* as he had planned it. I say we cannot help but admire that fellow, whether he has planned a cotillion or a train robbery or a Congo expedition. But whether we condemn or applaud, whether we put him on a waxed dancing floor, or in the penitentiary, or on a lecture platform, it is all one with him. He has overcome his obstacles. He has known Happiness.[12]

As literary naturalist, Norris had illustrated the obstacles posed by heredity, the influence of an ever-changing environment, and the random developments for good or ill that go by the name of "chance." Characters such as McTeague and Vandover prove unequal to challenges before them. Ross Wilbur of *Moran,* Condy Rivers, and the heroes and heroines of *A Man's Woman* and *The Pit* fare better in the face of stressful circumstances. In *The Octopus,* Annixter overcomes the obstacles to physical and mental well-being inherent in his own personality, knowing joy by doing so—only to fall victim to circumstances beyond his control.

Frank Norris repeatedly experienced disappointment. The choice of painterly vocation did not pan out. He could not meet the requirements for graduation at the University of California. The South African adventure yielded little journalistically. The apprenticeship with *The Wave* dragged on with nary a taker for the collections of short stories he assembled. His affiliation with S. S. McClure in early 1898 marked a promising new development; but that too was a disappointment, particularly in regard to the meager consequences of his Spanish-American War experience. It was not until late 1898 that, at twenty-eight, he could seriously entertain the possibility that he would reach his goal of self-support as a professional novelist—which he had indeed achieved immediately before his death at the age of thirty-two.

"Successful overcoming of obstacles—that's the real fun you can have for your money." Norris had overcome his by dint of determination. "By God, I'll put it through," was his promise to himself, which he honored in full during the last four years of his brief life.

Notes

Since the documentary notes that follow are keyed neither to a "bibliography" nor a list of "works cited," those for each chapter provide full publication data upon the first citation of each book or article. Subsequent references to the same books and articles are to the author's name and, when we cite multiple works by the same author, to the title as well. The exception is works by Frank Norris, for which we give only the title and publication information, since it is clear in the chapters that he is the author of the work being cited.

Three symbols indicate the following information sources to which we make reference:

CL   *Frank Norris: Collected Letters,* ed. Jesse S. Crisler (San Francisco: Book Club of California, 1986).

FNC   The Frank Norris Collection, the Bancroft Library, University of California at Berkeley.

FWC   The Franklin Dickerson Walker papers, the Bancroft Library, University of California at Berkeley.

Among items of other kinds, *FWC* includes Franklin Walker's notes on his interviews of Norris's contemporaries in 1930–32 and the letters he received from them. The Bancroft Library has alphabetically arranged in individual folders, by the interviewees' or correspondents' last names, this relatively small but important collection from which we repeatedly—indeed, constantly—draw information. We have not documented in the notes each reference to or quotation of these records, choosing instead to identify in the chapters the contemporary of Norris who shared with Walker his or her recollections that may be easily accessed in the Bancroft's folders. When the same contemporaries' statements about Norris have appeared in print, however, we do cite the publications in these notes.

CHAPTER 1: FRANK NORRIS'S PLACE IN AMERICAN CULTURAL HISTORY

1. The majority of these memoirs and testimonials are collected in Joseph R. McElrath Jr., "Frank Norris: Early Posthumous Responses," *American Literary Realism* 12 (Spring 1979): 1–76.

2. Franklin Walker, *Frank Norris: A Biography* (Garden City, N.Y.: Doubleday, Doran, 1932).

3. Typical of reviews of the film was this speculation: "'If a contest were to be held to determine which has been the filthiest, vilest, most putrid picture in the history of the motion picture business, I am sure *Greed* would walk away with the prize'" (qtd. in Thomas K. Dean, "The Critical Reception of Erich von Stroheim's *Greed*," *Frank Norris Studies* 9 [Spring 1990]: 7–11).

4. Reviews of *McTeague* and Norris's other publications are collected in *Frank Norris: The Critical Reception*, ed. Joseph R. McElrath Jr. and Katherine Knight (New York: Burt Franklin, 1981).

5. See Joseph R. McElrath Jr. and Jesse S. Crisler, "The Bowdlerization of *McTeague*," *American Literature* 61 (March 1989): 97–101.

6. "Theory and Reality," *The Wave* 15 (2 May 1896): 8. Jarboe's pseudonym was Thomas H. Brainerd.

7. Norris appreciatively reviewed Allen's novel in "A Summer in Arcady," *The Wave* 15 (25 July 1896): 9.

8. "A Plea for Romantic Fiction," *Boston Evening Transcript*, 18 December 1901, 14.

9. *FNC*.

10. See Richard Allan Davison, "The Marriage, Divorce, and Demise of a Father of Novelists: B. F. Norris," *Frank Norris Studies* 8 (Autumn 1989): 2–5.

11. After declaring that supply and demand determine how his railroad functions and that men "'have only little to do in the whole business,'" Shelgrim expostulates: "'Control the road! Can I stop it? I can go into bankruptcy. . . . But otherwise if I run my road, as a business proposition, I can do nothing. I can *not* control it. It is a force born out of certain conditions, and I—no man—can stop it or control it'" (*The Octopus* [New York: Doubleday, Page, 1901], 576).

12. "'I corner the wheat!'" exclaims Jadwin. "'Great heavens, it is the wheat that has cornered me! The corner made itself. I happened to stand between two sets of circumstances, and they made me do what I've done'" (*The Pit* [New York: Doubleday, Page, 1903], 284).

13. "A Deal in Wheat," *Everybody's Magazine* 7 (August 1902): 173–80.

14. "Life in the Mining Region," *Everybody's Magazine* 7 (September 1902): 241–48.

15. *CL*, 157–59.

16. See Alvin Toffler, *Future Shock* (New York: Random House, 1970).

17. "Salt and Sincerity: [5]," *The Critic* 41 (August 1902): 178–82. Norris's seven articles with this title have been misnumbered in posthumous collections of his writings. For clarification regarding these and other mis- or renamed works, see the index to Joseph R. McElrath Jr., *Frank Norris: A Descriptive Bibliography* (Pittsburgh: University of Pittsburgh Press, 1992).

18. The most influential and thus representative interpretation of Norris as antagonistic to the intrusion of the technological-industrial order into the American landscape is Leo Marx, "Two Kingdoms of Force," *Massachusetts Review* 1 (October 1959): 62–95. The substance of his argument was later incorporated in Leo Marx,

The Machine in the Garden (New York: Oxford University Press, 1964), 16, 343–44, despite Donald Pizer's 1963 rejoinder pointing out that the *misuse* of "the machine" is instead the negative theme developed in *The Octopus.* See Donald Pizer, "Synthetic Criticism and Frank Norris," *American Literature* 34 (January 1963): 532–41.

19. "On a Battleship," *The Wave* 15 (17 October 1896): 7; "A Strange Relief-Ship," *The Wave* 16 (12 June 1897): 7; "From Field to Storehouse," *The Wave* 16 (7 August 1897): 6–7; and "Sanitary Reduction," *The Wave* 16 (25 December 1897): 8–9. These represent only a small sampling of Norris's short works of the kind.

20. William B. Dillingham, *Frank Norris: Instinct and Art* (Lincoln: University of Nebraska Press, 1969), 113; June Howard, *Form and History in American Literary Naturalism* (Chapel Hill: University of North Carolina Press, 1985), 88–103, 116–27.

21. "Frank Norris—Student, Author, and Man," *University of California Magazine* 8 (November 1902): 349–56 (expanded from "The Farewell Tribute of a Friend to the Late Frank Norris," *Oakland Enquirer,* 27 October 1902, 5).

22. Richard Allan Davison, "*Of Mice and Men* and *McTeague,*" *Studies in American Fiction* 17 (Autumn 1989): 219–26.

23. Donald Pizer, *Twentieth-Century American Literary Naturalism* (Carbondale: Southern Illinois University, 1982); and *The Theory and Practice of American Literary Naturalism* (Carbondale: Southern Illinois University Press, 1993).

24. Emile Zola, "The Experimental Novel," in *The Experimental Novel and Other Essays,* trans. Belle M. Sherman (New York: Cassell, 1893), 1–54.

25. See Joseph R. McElrath Jr., "'One Thing One Did Not Question': The Christian Perspective of Novelist Frank Norris," *Literature and Belief* 21.1–2 (Winter 2001): 1–25.

26. "Frank Norris Writes Cleverly about Child Fiction for Old Readers," *Brooklyn Daily Eagle,* 8 February 1902, 10.

27. "Plea for Romantic Fiction," 14.

28. *The Pit,* 346.

29. "A California Artist," *The Wave* 16 (6 February 1897): 9.

30. *McTeague* (New York: Doubleday and McClure, 1899), 89.

31. Jean Strouse, *Morgan: American Financier* (New York: Random House, 1999); Alyn Brodsky, *Grover Cleveland: A Study in Character* (New York: St. Martin's, 2000).

CHAPTER 2: ANTECEDENTS

1. *CL,* 108, 57.

2. "The Frontier Gone at Last," *The World's Work* 3 (February 1902): 1728–31. In 1898, Norris had sounded a similar note when celebrating the American victory over the Spanish in Cuba: "Santiago [de Cuba] was ours—ours, ours, ours, by the sword we had acquired, we, Americans, with no one to help—and the Anglo-Saxon blood of us, the blood of the race that has fought its way out of a swamp in Friesland, conquering and conquering, on to the westward, the race whose blood instinct is the acquiring of land, went galloping through our veins to the beat of our horses' hoofs"

("Untold Thrilling Account of Santiago's Surrender," *New York Sun,* 13 July 1913, sec. 7, 2).

3. "Outward and Visible Signs: V, Thoroughbred," *Overland Monthly* 25 (February 1895): 196–201; "A Defense of the Flag," *Argonaut* 32 (28 October 1895): 4.

4. Information on Gertrude's ancestry is derived from Samuel Bradlee Doggett, *A History of the Doggett-Daggett Family* (Boston: Rockwell and Churchill, 1894); Church of Jesus Christ of Latter-day Saints, <www.familysearch.com>; Lawrence Fobes, *The Fobes Family in America* (Atlantic Highlands, N.J.: N.p., 1976); and <sml.simplenet.com/smlawson/wales.htm>.

5. Charles H. Brigham, *Biographical Sketch of Rev. Simeon Doggett* (Boston: Crosby, Michaels, 1852), 6.

6. One could argue, of course, that Reverend Forbes, as a mere transplant to Holland from his native Scotland, hardly qualifies as a Frisian ancestor of Norris. But while Norris's Separatist progenitors, the Fullers, temporarily resided in Leiden, one of them, Samuel Fuller, married Bridget Mary Lee three years before the Pilgrims departed from Holland. She was the daughter of Joos Lee, a Dutch native.

7. Lawrence K. Hall, *Doggett of Springfield* (Springfield, Mass.: Springfield College, 1964), 10.

8. See *Bailey & Edwards' Chicago Directory* (Chicago: Edwards and Co., 1868), 246; *Edwards' Official Directory for 1869* (Chicago: Richard Edwards, 1869), 242; *Edwards' Thirteenth Annual Directory . . . of the City of Chicago* (Chicago: Richard Edwards, 1870), 224; *Edwards' Fourteenth Annual Directory . . . of the City of Chicago* (Chicago: Richard Edwards, 1871), 265; 1870 Illinois Census for Cook County; and 1880 Nebraska Census for Lancaster County.

9. *D. B. Cooke & Co.'s Directory of Chicago for the Year 1858* (Chicago: D. B. Cooke, 1858), 73. Charles G. Norris stated that his uncle "Thee (Theophalus) [*sic*]" started a private school "somewhere near the city" and that Gertrude was "an assistant teacher" there. When the school "broke up," Theophilus enlisted in the army on the Union side, and his sister Gertrude "went to Chicago and found a position in the public schools" (Charles G. Norris to Charles Caldwell Dobie, 20 June 1927, Charles Caldwell Dobie papers, the Bancroft Library). There is no evidence that such was the case, and it is unlikely that a young Chicago attorney had time to devote to such a venture. As will be seen below, Gertrude did teach—for her brother Simeon. She left his school in Iowa to find employment in Chicago.

10. In the same letter to Dobie (ibid.), Charles Norris noted the conditions under which Gertrude's two siblings died. Jane B. Hewitt cites Theodore's military affiliation in *The Roster of Union Soldiers (1861–1865)*, vol. 24, ed. Jane B. Hewitt (Wilmington, N.C.: Broadfoot Publishing, 1998), 38, and Lawrence's in vol. 2 (1997), 327.

11. "Untold Thrilling Account of Santiago's Surrender"; "A California Author," *Oakland Enquirer,* 29 August 1898, 4.

12. See the 1870 and 1880 Massachusetts censuses for Worcester County.

13. See the 1870 Illinois Census for Cook County. Note that Gertrude's parents were then living with B. F. and her. The census taker, assuming that Samuel Doggett was the head of the household, listed the Norrises as Doggetts.

14. John Milton Colton, *A Genealogical Record of the Descendants of Quartermaster George Colton* (Philadelphia: Wickersham Printing, 1912), provides information on B. F.'s mother's ancestry.

15. Their marriage is recorded in Fred Q. Bowman, *10,000 Vital Records of Western New York, 1809–1850* (Baltimore: Genealogical Publishing, 1985), 163.

16. Josiah's farm of eighty acres, or one-eighth section, was located in Plainfield Township, Kent County; see *Illustrated Historical Atlas of the County of Kent, Michigan* (Chicago: H. Belden, 1876), 31.

17. The 1840 Michigan Census Index, vol. 5, 125, suggests that there may also have been an older sister, name unknown, who would have been at least ten years old at the time of the census but not more than fifteen. If "female 10–15" does refer to a daughter rather than a hired girl living with the family, she had either married or died before the 1850 census was taken. Richard A. Reinhardt of Carmel, California, supplied much of the information given here on the family of Josiah Norris, Reinhardt's great-great-grandfather through Josiah's second son, James Henry Norris. See also the 1840–80 Michigan censuses for Washtenaw, Kent, and Ottawa Counties, as well as the 1870 and 1880 Illinois Censuses for Cook County.

18. "Night Watchman Hurt by Explosion in Vapor Stove Works," *Grand Rapids Herald,* 14 September 1900, 1; "Died from His Burns," *Grand Rapids Herald,* 6 October 1900, 3.

19. Curtis Jadwin shares with his friend Sam Gretry his memories of his "little sister" Sadie, who died from "galloping consumption" when she was "about eighteen" (*The Pit* [New York: Doubleday, Page, 1903], 200). B. F.'s sister Sarah—the diminutive for which is Sadie—was instead his big sister by more than two years. But that she died at "about eighteen," or around 1851, squares with the censuses of 1850 and 1860, with Norris's use of his father as one of the models for Curtis Jadwin, and with his brother's testimony to Walker. Charles ranked Jadwin as "the best portrait my brother ever drew. He is my father to the life."

20. *Edwards' Annual Directory* (Chicago: Edwards' New Directory Office, 1866), 704; this is the first directory containing Josiah's name. His military affiliation is cited in *The Roster of Union Soldiers (1861–65),* vol. 30, ed. Janet B. Hewitt (Wilmington, N.C.: Broadfoot Publishing, 1998), 298. His pension papers are in the U.S. Army Archives, Washington, D.C. Josiah is buried in Graceland Cemetery, Chicago, alongside his two wives and daughter.

21. B. F. lived in Kent County with his parents until after the 1850 census was taken, thereby eliminating the jeweler Wright L. Coffinberry—who had closed his store by then—as his employer in Grand Rapids. Vernon Shaw, who had only arrived in 1848, probably had not developed enough business to take on an apprentice, and certainly William Preusser, arriving in 1850, had not. The later arrival of two other jewelers, N. T. Butler and Henry Brinsmaid, precludes their candidacy as B. F.'s patron. Thus, Dikeman logically seems the most likely possibility. See "The Jewelers of Grand Rapids," *Jewelers' Weekly* 4 (31 August 1887), 1612, 1615–16, and 1619–20; and *Grand Rapids and Kent County, Michigan,* vol. 2, ed. Ernest B. Fisher (Chicago: Robert O. Law, 1918), 96, 206, and 808.

22. *FNC;* see Jesse S. Crisler, "Norris's Library," *Frank Norris Studies* 5 (Spring 1988): 1–11.

23. B. F.'s Lockport household is described in the 1860 Illinois Census for Will County. His first marriage is recorded in "Illinois Statewide Marriage Index, 1763–1900" (an ongoing project of the Illinois State Archives and Illinois State Genealogical Society), <http://www.cyberdriveillinois.com/departments/archives/marriage.html>.

24. Chicago city directories from 1865–68 record the addresses of B. F. Norris and Co., his own residences, those of Gertrude's and his relations, and those of his business associates. They include *J. C. W. Bailey & Co.'s Chicago City Directory, for the Year 1865–66* (Chicago: John C. W. Bailey, 1865); *Halpin's Eighth Annual Edition Chicago City Directory 1865–66* (Chicago: T. M. Halpin, 1865); *Edwards' Annual Directory* (Chicago: Edwards, 1866); *John C. W. Bailey's Chicago City Directory* (Chicago: John C. W. Bailey, 1866); *Edwards' New Chicago Directory* (Chicago: Edwards, 1867); and *John C. W. Bailey's Chicago City Directory, 1867–68* (Chicago: John C. W. Bailey, 1867).

25. The only known copy of this catalogue, located by Donna Danielewski in 1997, is now preserved in the local business literature collection at the Chicago Historical Society. Fortunately, it was published at a strategic moment—after the great Chicago fire—and reprinted in its pages were several laudatory notices of B. F.'s firm published in various New York and Illinois periodicals. Although undated, these notices, used by B. F. for promotional purposes, shed light on his progress as a businessman prior to 1872.

26. Chicago city directories track the succession of B. F.'s partners as well as changes in the firm's official name. Alister's marriage in Cook County is recorded in "Illinois Statewide Marriage Index, 1763–1900."

27. See the 1860 Illinois Census for Will County and the 1870 and 1880 Illinois Censuses for Cook County.

28. James B. Stronks, "B. F. Norris (Senior) in Probate Court, with New Light on Frank Norris as Son," *Frank Norris Studies* 12 (Autumn 1991): 3–5.

29. Hall, 10.

30. *Halpin and Bailey's Chicago City Directory for the Year 1861–62* (Chicago: Halpin and Bailey, 1861), 100.

31. Statistics on Gertrude's teaching career appear in the tenth through twelfth annual reports of Chicago's public schools covering 1 January 1863 through 1 October 1866: Department of Public Instruction, City of Chicago, *Tenth Annual Report of the Board of Education for the Year Ending December 31, 1863* (Chicago: Chicago Times Book and Job Printing House, 1864), 60; *Eleventh Annual Report of the Board of Education from January 1, 1864, to August 31, 1865* (Chicago: Jameson and Morse, 1865), 56 and 88; *Twelfth Annual Report of the Board of Education, from September 1, 1865, to August 31, 1866* (Chicago: Rounds and James, 1866), 118 and 145.

32. Laurence Locke Doggett, *Man and a School* (New York: Association Press, 1943), 2.

33. "Amusements," *Chicago Republican,* 24 December 1866, 3.

34. Cowell, a native of Scotland, had climbed dizzying theatrical heights in New York City, playing roles such as Rosalind in *As You Like It,* before coming to Chicago where she became a member of the McVicker's troupe in 1865. See Richard Allan Davison, "Gertrude Doggett Norris: Professional Actress, Dramatic Reader, and Mother of Novelists," *Book Club of California Quarterly News-Letter* 56 (Winter 1990): 5.

35. "Amusements," *Chicago Republican,* 25 December 1866, 2.

36. "Amusements," *Chicago Evening Journal,* 24 December 1866, 4; "Amusements," *Chicago Tribune,* 25 December 1866, 4. The *Chicago Times* agreed, terming her debut "'a flattering success.'" How thoroughly Gertrude was being groomed for success by Cowell and the management of McVicker's will be seen in the *Times* and *Tribune's* having begun giving her debut attention as early as 16 December (qtd. in Davison, 10).

37. Only one newspaper reviewed *Faint Heart* ("Amusements," *Chicago Times,* 1 January 1867, 4). But other Chicago papers duly advertised this second appearance on stage, noting the favorable impression she had made in *Pizarro.* See the "Amusements" columns in the *Chicago Evening Journal,* 31 December 1866, 4; *Chicago Republican,* 31 December 1866, 3, 3 January 1867, 7, and 8 January 1867, 8; and *Chicago Tribune,* 30 and 31 December 1866, 4. Several reviews also treated positively her performance in *Othello.* See the "Amusements" columns in the *Chicago Evening Journal,* 31 December 1866, 4; *Chicago Republican,* 31 December 1866, 3, and 7 January 1867, 3; and *Chicago Tribune,* 30 and 31 December 1866, 4.

38. Accepting Charles G. Norris at his word, Franklin Walker assigned Gertrude roles in Tom Taylor's *Ticket-of-Leave-Man* and Edward Bulwer-Lytton's *The Lady of Lyons* (*Frank Norris: A Biography* [Garden City, N.Y.: Doubleday, Doran, 1932], 7). In her memoir, Charles's wife Kathleen added J. R. Planché's *Diplomacy,* Charles L. Young's *Jim the Penman,* and an English adaptation of Alexandre-Louis de Villeterque's *Enquermond, Sire de Rosemont,* asserting that in all four she played opposite Lester Wallack, after whom she named her third son—actually Albert Lester Norris— "Lester W. Norris" ("Family Gathering" manuscript, 39, Norris Family papers, the Bancroft Library). In an interview, Kathleen also recalled James Sheridan Knowles's *The Hunchback* (Roland E. Duncan, "An Interview with Kathleen Norris," typescript of interview conducted in 1956–57 [Berkeley, Calif.: Regional Oral History Office, the Bancroft Library, 1959], 87). Donna Danielewski augmented the list with H. T. Craven's *Miriam's Crimes* ("A Biography of Frank Norris," Ph.D. dissertation, Florida State University, 1997, 8). With the exception of *Jim the Penman,* which most likely was not staged anywhere until 1887, Gertrude may have performed in all or some of these plays in the five months after she made her debut and before her career was terminated by marriage. Confirmation that she was a player in any of them, however, is not available.

39. "Married," *Chicago Tribune,* 29 May 1867, 4. The "Illinois Statewide Marriage Index, 1763–1900," also records this marriage, as does the *Chicago Republican,* in a remarkable manner: "Harris-Daggett—May 27, at 295 Chicago Avenue, by Rev. Robert Collyer, Mr. Benjamin F. Harris to Miss Gertrude S. Daggett, both of this

city" ("Married," *Chicago Republican,* 29 May 1867, 8). At the time of his marriage, B. F. was situated in spartan quarters at 25 Washington Avenue; Charles told Walker that his parents lived in a single room above a photography shop when they were first married. But they soon moved to a more appropriate residence for a man of his financial standing, 789 Wabash Avenue, where they lived for two years. *John C. W. Bailey's Chicago City Directory, 1867–1868* (Chicago: John C. W. Bailey, 1867), 724; *Bailey & Edwards' Chicago Directory* (Chicago: Edwards and Co., 1868), 666.

40. *Historical Sketch of Unity Church, Chicago* (Chicago: Ingersoll Bros., 1880), 1–3; and *Robert Collyer: A Memorial* (Chicago: N.p., 1912), 7.

41. Stronks.

CHAPTER 3: THE CHICAGO YEARS, 1870–85

1. *Charles & Kathleen Norris: The Courtship Year,* ed. Richard Allan Davison (San Francisco: Book Club of California, 1993), collects Charles's and Kathleen Thompson's 1908–9 exchange of letters in which Gertrude's, as well as Charles's, recollections of Frank are recorded.

2. Charles Caldwell Dobie, "Introduction: Frank Norris, or Up from Culture," *The Responsibilities of the Novelist: The Joyous Miracle,* vol. 6 in *The Argonaut Manuscript Limited Edition of Frank Norris's Works* (Garden City, N.Y.: Doubleday, Doran, 1928), v–xxxii; reprinted in *The Complete Edition of Frank Norris,* vol. 6 (Garden City, N.Y.: Doubleday, Doran, [1929]), v–xxxii.

3. Dobie, xiii and xv.

4. Roland E. Duncan, "An Interview with Kathleen Norris," typescript of interview conducted in 1956–57 (Berkeley, Calif.: Regional Oral History Office, the Bancroft Library, 1959), 83.

5. See *Charles & Kathleen Norris;* Richard Allan Davison, *Charles G. Norris* (Boston: Twayne, 1983), 8–9; and Kathleen Norris, *Family Gathering* (Garden City, N.Y.: Doubleday, 1959), 83. Regarding her recognized ability for giving dramatic readings, see Richard Allan Davison, "Gertrude Doggett Norris: Professional Actress, Dramatic Reader, and Mother of Novelists," *Book Club of California Quarterly News-Letter* 56 (Winter 1990): 8–19.

6. *The Pit* (New York: Doubleday, Page, 1903), 225.

7. Only a few sentences in an 1896 cablegram from South Africa, quoted in a newspaper article and explaining succinctly the reasons why Norris had not earlier contacted his mother, have been discovered. See Jesse S. Crisler, "Norris in South Africa," *Frank Norris Studies* 7 (Spring 1987): 4–7.

8. "To My Ma: and not to [be] loaned to anybody" is the 4 May 1899 inscription in the copy of *McTeague* that he gave to Gertrude; "To my Ma" in *The Octopus* is dated "April 1901" (*CL,* 215 and 222). Both volumes are at the Bancroft Library.

9. Dobie, viii–ix.

10. In the larger city's society columns tracking the activities of economic titans such as George D. Pullman and prominent professionals such as the physician after whom she named Charles, Dr. Charles Gilman Smith, Gertrude made only occasional appearances. For example, it was reported that Mrs. B. F. Norris was assisted

by her niece Ella, Mrs. William M. Alister, when she received callers on New Year's Day ("New Year's Calls," *Chicago Tribune*, 31 December 1879, 6). That "Miss Jennie Forsyth is visiting Mrs. B. F. Norris at Geneva Lake" was reported in "Our Society," *Chicago Tribune*, 25 July 1880, 10.

11. "Wants Big Alimony," *San Francisco Chronicle*, 4 January 1894, 7.

12. Charles Caldwell Dobie, "Frank Norris; or, Up from Culture," *American Mercury* 13 (April 1928): 412–24. Publication of the *Argonaut* edition of Norris's works was announced five months later.

13. Dobie, xvi–xvii.

14. James B. Stronks describes the house and the upscale neighborhood near Lake Michigan—"one of the most fashionable enclaves in the city"—in "Frank Norris and the Eighth Grade," *Frank Norris Studies* 7 (Spring 1989): 2–4.

15. The renumbering of 722 Michigan Avenue was noted in "Birthplace of a Novelist," *Chicago Tribune*, 4 December 1939, 4. For announcements of the Norrises' sojourns at Lake Geneva, see "Our Society," *Chicago Tribune*, 6 June 1880, 2, and 19 September 1880, 12. By 1881 B. F. owned two contiguous lots fronting the north side of the lake on Main Street at the eastern corner of Warren Street (Tax Rolls for Walworth County, Area Research Center, Anderson Library, University of Wisconsin at Whitewater). Gertrude referred only to their "Summer House at Lake Geneva" when she inscribed a Christmas present to Frank in 1883: James Baldwin's *Story of Roland* (New York Scribner's, 1883). See Jesse S. Crisler, "Norris's 'Library,'" *Frank Norris Studies* 5 (Spring 1988): 1–11.

16. In 1914, when Charles was managing the publication and marketing of *Vandover*, he too saw it as a moralistic tract. So suggests the text he authored for the dust jackets of advance copies of the novel sent to book reviewers: "We are sending this advance copy to you, first, because of the interest that attaches to the author's unrevised [that is, never polished] draft, and second, because this tremendous piece of realism conveys a moral lesson that no one who reads it can forget. If, like Arthur of old, you are engaged as minister or layman in making the sway of the Brute grow less and less in the land, then this story has a message for you—as it has for every human being who fights the eternal fight between good and evil in his own soul" (Joseph R. McElrath Jr., *Frank Norris: A Descriptive Bibliography* [Pittsburgh: University of Pittsburgh Press, 1992], 154).

17. Information concerning the Norrises' membership in and participation at several churches was derived from the archives of the following: First Presbyterian church and Westminster Presbyterian church in Grand Rapids, Michigan (microfilmed records at the Grand Rapids Public Library); Trinity Episcopal church in Chicago (some of the records of which are housed at St. James's Cathedral, Chicago); the Second Presbyterian church in Chicago; St. Luke's Episcopal church in San Francisco; the First Presbyterian (Old First) church in San Francisco; and Plymouth Congregational church in Chicago (housed at the Chicago Historical Society).

18. "In Society," *The Wave* 16 (13 February 1897): 10.

19. Mrs. Otto Kralovec Jr., *Four Score Years: The Story of the Central Church of Chicago* (Chicago: N.p., [1955]), 1.

20. "Funeral of B. F. Norris," *Chicago Evening Post,* 29 October 1900, 5.

21. Guest Register, Hotel del Coronado Collection, 1887–1977, Special Collections, San Diego State University Library.

22. Duncan, 87.

23. The incomplete runs of the annual catalogues of the Allen Academy (Allen's in the 1877 catalogue) and those of the school Norris subsequently attended in Chicago, the Harvard School for Boys, are available at the Chicago Historical Society and the Illinois State Historical Society in Springfield. These describe their educational programs, and each volume lists the students enrolled during the immediately past academic year.

24. "Five Steamships Leave This Port," *New York Times,* 6 June 1878, 8; "Marine Intelligence," *New York Tribune,* 11 September 1878, 8. Incorrectly giving Frank's age as "7 years," B. F. applied for a U.S. passport on 2 May 1878 (Passport Applications [9 April–9 May 1878], no. 6514, M-1372, National Archives, Washington, D.C.).

25. See n.23 above.

26. *Brief History of Greece with Readings from Prominent Greek Historians* (New York: A. S. Barnes, 1883). See Crisler, "Norris's 'Library.'"

27. The required text for a History of France course was Elizabeth S. Kirkland, *A Short History of France for Young People* (Chicago: Jansen, McClurg, 1879). With Norris's signature appeared his academic affiliation, "Harvard School." But it was also inscribed to "B. Frank Norris" as an 1878 Christmas present from "Cousin Ella"—Ida Carleton's older sister—and her husband "W. Allister." See Crisler, "Norris's 'Library.'"

28. *Vandover and the Brute* (Garden City, N.Y.: Doubleday, Page, 1914), 11–12.

29. "Western Types: An Art Student," *The Wave* 15 (16 May 1896): 10.

30. "Story-Tellers vs. Novelists," *The World's Work* 3 (March 1902): 1894–97.

31. This boarding school and its academic program are described in a promotional pamphlet at the Bancroft Library, *Belmont School, 1886–87.* It lists the students of 1885–86 and 1886–87; Charles is listed in the catalogues for 1891–92 and 1892–93.

32. "A Lincoln Man Tells of Norris," *The Star* (Lincoln, Neb.), 22 November 1902, 16.

33. Duncan, 83.

34. Davison, *Charles & Kathleen Norris,* 21.

CHAPTER 4: THE CITY BY THE BAY

1. *FNC.*

2. *San Francisco Chronicle,* 2 June 1884, 4; "Real Estate Transactions," *San Francisco Chronicle,* 19 October 1884, 2; "The Social World," *San Francisco Chronicle,* 21 October 1884, 2. As was noted in chapter 3, Charles understood that he had spent the winter months of 1884–85 in the Palace Hotel. This suggests either that Charles was in error or that Gertrude's plan to reside on Sacramento Street was not realized, perhaps because of remodeling and interior-decoration work being done in the house B. F. purchased.

3. "The Social World," *San Francisco Chronicle*, 9 June 1885, 2, 16 June 1885, 2, and 4 August 1885, 2.

4. M. C. Sloss to James D. Hart, 3 December 1952, James D. Hart papers, the Bancroft Library.

5. When applying for admission to Harvard College in 1894, Norris stated that he had been a student at the Boys' High School for one year (Harvard University Archives). He may have been a student there for some time. But, through much of the twentieth century, members of its especially vital alumni association who wished to confirm his attendance failed to find evidence of it.

6. "Funeral of Virgil Williams," *San Francisco Examiner*, 21 December 1886, 3.

7. "The Hopkins Institute," *The Wave* 16 (25 September 1897): 9.

8. "Western Types: An Art Student," *The Wave* 15 (16 May 1896): 10.

9. "New Advertisements," *San Francisco Chronicle*, 5 February 1885, 2.

10. "Romanticist under the Skin," *Saturday Review of Literature* 9 (27 May 1933): 613–15. An example of Norris's work was reproduced in this article, a drawing of a pointer that exemplifies his "fairly good pen and ink technique."

11. "The Art Exhibit," *San Francisco Chronicle*, 23 April 1887, 6; Minutes of the San Francisco Art Association, 1887, Archives of the San Francisco Art Institute; "Easel and Brush," *San Francisco Chronicle*, 12 June 1887, 14.

12. "The Social World," *San Francisco Chronicle*, 2 February 1886, 6, 9 February 1886, 6, 16 February 1886, 6, and 9 March 1886, 6.

13. "The Social World," *San Francisco Chronicle*, 16 March 1886, 6, 6 April 1886, 6, and 8 June 1886, 6.

14. *FNC*.

15. "The Social World," *San Francisco Chronicle*, 14 September 1886, 6, and 22 December 1889, 15; "The Social World," *San Francisco Examiner*, 29 December 1889, 17.

16. The Ashes' copy of *The Octopus* is in the Barrett Collection, Alderman Library, University of Virginia; see *CL*, 225.

17. "Easel and Brush," *San Francisco Chronicle*, 12 June 1887, 14.

18. "How It Strikes an Observer," *The Wave* 15 (12 December 1896): 7. While his tone was bantering, he was quite serious when declaring that "to my thinking there are three things that are preeminently beautiful, that are perfect of their kind, a ship under full sail, a pretty, well dressed woman and a well groomed thoroughbred horse."

19. "Holiday Literature," *The Wave* 16 (11 December 1897): 8.

20. "The Social World," *San Francisco Chronicle*, 13 June 1887, 6, and 20 June 1887, 6.

CHAPTER 5: FROM OUT OF THE BLUE

1. "Deaths," *San Francisco Chronicle*, 21 June 1887, 6.

2. "The Week in Chicago," *Jewelers' Weekly* 4 (6 July 1887): 832.

3. "Diphtheria," *San Francisco Examiner*, 17 June 1887, 8.

4. "The Social World," *San Francisco Chronicle*, 27 June 1887, 6. A similar an-

nouncement appeared the following week in the same column, 11 July 1887, 7. It referred to their departure "last week," but this was merely a recycling of the 27 June announcement. Repetitions of the kind were commonplace in this and the *San Francisco Examiner's* social columns.

5. "The Week in Chicago," 832.

6. "The City," *Chicago Tribune*, 9 July 1887, 8; "Marine Intelligence," *New York Times*, 10 July 1887, 3; "Shipping News," *New York Tribune*, 17 July 1887, 14.

7. "French Notes," *San Francisco Chronicle*, 24 July 1887, 6 (dateline 23 July); "The Social World," *San Francisco Chronicle*, 15 August 1887, 6.

8. *FNC*.

9. "The Social World," *San Francisco Chronicle*, 29 August 1887, 7.

10. *The Pit* (New York: Doubleday, Page, 1903), 209.

11. "The Social World," *San Francisco Chronicle*, 24 October 1887, 6.

12. "A California Vintage," *The Wave* 14 (12 October 1895): 7; "A Steamship Voyage with Cecil Rhodes," *San Francisco Chronicle*, 19 April 1896, 15; "Latin Quarter Christmas" and "Among Cliff-Dwellers," *The Wave* 16 (2 January 1897): 7, and (15 May 1897): 6; "Untold Thrilling Account of Santiago's Surrender," *New York Sun*, 13 July 1913, sec. 7, 1–2.

13. "New York Passenger Lists, 1851–1891: April 1888," <www.ancestry.com>; "The Social World," *San Francisco Chronicle*, 4 June 1888, 6.

14. "Marine Intelligence," *New York Times*, 19 August 1888, 6; "Verdendal's Chat," *San Francisco Chronicle*, 26 August 1888, 14.

15. "The Lester Norris Memorial Kindergarten," *Ninth Annual Report of the Golden Gate Kindergarten Association* (San Francisco: George Spaulding, 1889), 21–25; "Lester Norris, Produce Exchange, and Pacific Kindergartens," *Fourteenth Annual Report of the Golden Gate Kindergarten Association* (San Francisco: George Spaulding, 1894), 106–31.

CHAPTER 6: THE ACADÉMIE JULIAN

1. "The Palette," *San Francisco Chronicle*, 1 May 1887, 1; "Art in Britain," *San Francisco Examiner*, 30 May 1887, 7.

2. "The Country Club at Del Monte," *The Wave* 14 (31 August 1895): 7.

3. "Our Unpopular Novelists," *The Wave* 14 (5 October 1895): 7.

4. *The Pit* (New York: Doubleday, Page, 1903), 248–49.

5. Ibid., 199.

6. "Western Types: An Art Student," *The Wave* 15 (16 May 1896): 10.

7. "A California Artist," *The Wave* 16 (6 February 1897): 9.

8. "Personal," *New York Tribune*, 25 April 1888, 4.

9. "Student Life in Paris," *Collier's Weekly* 25 (12 May 1900): 33.

10. "'This Animal of a Buldy Jones,'" *The Wave* 16 (17 July 1897): 5.

11. "Buldy Jones, *Chef de Claque*," *Everybody's Magazine* 4 (May 1901): 449–59.

12. The students at the Julian who enjoyed careers as professional artists are listed by name alphabetically and the particulars of their courses of study are given by

Catherine Fehrer, *The Julian Academy: Paris, 1868–1939* (New York: Shepherd Gallery, 1989). Norris is not listed, but Fehrer informed James D. Hart that Norris studied in Bouguereau's atelier in 1887–89; that his address was given as 35 Boulevard Haussmann; and that his city of origin was recorded as New York rather than San Francisco (Fehrer to Hart, 12 April 1989, James D. Hart papers, the Bancroft Library).

13. *Vandover and the Brute* (Garden City: Doubleday, Page, 1914), 220–29; David Teague, "Frank Norris: The Novelist as Visual Artist," Ph.D. dissertation, Florida State University, 1994, 226–29.

14. *Vandover and the Brute*, 66–67.

15. "Fiction Is Selection," *The Wave* 16 (11 September 1897): 3.

16. William Dean Howells, "Novel-Writing and Novel Reading," *Selected Literary Criticism of William Dean Howells: Volume III, 1898–1920*, ed. Ronald Gottesman, vol. 30 of *A Selected Edition of W. D. Howells* (Bloomington: Indiana University Press, 1993), 217.

17. *The Pit*, 199–200.

18. "A Problem in Fiction," *Boston Evening Transcript*, 6 November 1901, 20.

19. "The Sketch Club Exhibit," *The Wave* 15 (28 November 1896): 9.

20. Ernest Peixotto, "Romanticist under the Skin," *Saturday Review of Literature* 9 (27 May 1933): 613–15.

21. *FNC.*

22. Peixotto, 614. According to the passport application tendered to the American Legation in Paris, dated 24 June 1889 and witnessed by his uncle William M. McAlister, Norris intended to return to the Unites States "in about two months." In the meantime, the "artist" would use the passport for the purpose of "travelling in Europe" (Emergency Passport Applications, Passports Issued Abroad [1877–1907], no. 83, M-1834, National Archives, Washington, D.C.).

23. *Vandover and the Brute*, 15.

24. "Shipping News," *New York Daily Tribune*, 2 September 1889, 8; "New York Passenger Lists, 1851–1891: 2 September 1889," <www.ancestry.com>; "Verdenal's Chat," *San Francisco Chronicle*, 18 August 1889, 13, 25 August 1889, 15, and 1 September 1889, 15.

25. "Clothes of Steel," *San Francisco Chronicle*, 31 March 1889, 6.

CHAPTER 7: STARTING OVER

1. William B. Dillingham, *Frank Norris: Instinct and Art* (Lincoln: University of Nebraska Press, 1969), 25.

2. "The 'English Courses' of the University of California," *The Wave* 15 (28 November 1896): 2–3. Norris addresses the same problem in "Why Women Should Write the Best Novels," *Boston Evening Transcript*, 13 November 1901, 20; "Novelists of the Future," *Boston Evening Transcript*, 27 November 1901, 14; "Frank Norris on Novelists to Order While You Wait," *Brooklyn Daily Eagle*, 22 February 1902, 8; and "Salt and Sincerity: [2]," *The Critic* 40 (May 1902): 447–50, wherein he proposes training for writers along the lines enjoyed by artists at the Académie Julian.

Yet again complaining that literary courses like those at the University of California do not qualify one for a profession as a "literary man," Norris predicted that "the so-called general 'literary' or 'classical' courses will be relegated to the limbo of Things No Longer Useful" by the end of the twentieth century ("Salt and Sincerity: [3]," *The Critic* 40 [June 1902]: 550–55).

3. "To the President and Faculty of the College of Letters," dated "Nov. 1891," *CL*, 24.

4. H. M. Wright, "In Memoriam—Frank Norris: 1870–1902," *University of California Chronicle* 5 (October 1902): 240–45.

5. Charles G. Norris, *Frank Norris* (Garden City, N.Y.: Doubleday, Page, [1914]), 6.

6. "To the President and Faculty of the College of Letters," 25.

7. The title page of the *Vandover and the Brute* manuscript *(FNC)* was originally dated 1889. Norris later crossed out the first "8" and added a "5" to the right of the "9," thus revising the date to 1895.

8. William Dallam Armes, "Concerning the Work of the Late Frank Norris," *Sunset* 10 (December 1902): 165–67.

9. *The Pit* (New York: Doubleday, Page, 1903), 105–6.

10. Norris, *Frank Norris,* 14.

11. Norris's University of California transcript (handwritten and including a memo-randum on his "conditions," satisfactions thereof, and circumstances resulting in failing grades), *FNC;* a second "Transcript of Record" and memorandum listing the courses Norris took each academic year (both typed), obtained by Walker in 1930 *(FWC).*

12. "To the President and Faculty of the College of Letters," 24.

13. "The Social World," *San Francisco Examiner,* 29 December 1889, 17.

14. "Social World," *San Francisco Chronicle,* 30 June 1890, 8, and 7 July 1890, 8. The listing of "Mrs. B. F. Morris Jr." in both issues indicates garbled transmissions of the information received by the society columnist. Gertrude was married to B. F. Norris Sr. The "Jr." can indicate only that B. F. Norris Jr., or Frank Norris, was the fourth member of the party.

15. *McTeague* (New York: Doubleday and McClure, 1899), 284.

16. Wallace W. Everett relates that Norris prepared for his entrance examinations at the Urban Academy, where Senger taught, in "Frank Norris in His Chapter," *Phi Gamma Delta Quarterly* 52 (April 1930): 560–66. City directory listings reveal that Norris's French-literature professor, Félicien V. Paget, was also employed by the Urban Academy at this time.

17. The withdrawal and dismissal were recorded and dated on Norris's transcript *(FNC).*

18. Everett, 560–66.

19. "Students at the Fair," *San Francisco Chronicle,* 7 May 1893, 11.

20. Frank M. Todd, "Frank Norris—Student, Author, and Man," *University of California Magazine* 8 (November 1902): 349–56.

21. Norris's contributions to these publications are described in Jesse S. Crisler,

"Norris and the *Blue and Gold:* The Novelist as College Man," *Analytical and Enumerative Bibliography* 4.2–3 (1990): 110–28, and "Frank Norris, College Man," *Resources for American Literary Study* 28 (2003): 111–20.

22. "Berkeley," *San Francisco Chronicle*, 30 November 1892, 5, and 5 December 1892, 8. Todd identifies Norris as a founder of the Skull and Keys organization. See Todd, "Frank Norris," 352.

23. The Witness, "Splashes," *The Wave* 11 (11 November 1893): 2; a program identifies Norris as the author of words and music *(FNC)*.

24. The Witness, "Splashes," *The Wave* 12 (31 March 1894): 4.

25. Benjamin Weed, "The Genesis of the Greek Theater," *California Play and Pageant* ([Berkeley]: English Club of the University of California, 1913).

26. "Society," *San Francisco Examiner*, 21 December 1891, 5; "Amateur Theatricals," *San Francisco Chronicle*, 21 December 1891, 5.

27. The play was mistitled *One Bat* by The Witness, "Splashes," *The Wave* 10 (13 May 1893): 3, and in "Berkeley," *San Francisco Chronicle*, 10 May 1893, 4. Clarification is offered in Ernest Peixotto's 1893 diary (Ernest Clifford Peixotto papers, the Bancroft Library), where the Skull and Keys' performance of *Our Boys* on 12 May, followed by dinner at Mrs. Norris's, was noted. The following week, Norris's performance was praised in "Festivities at Berkeley," *The Wave* 10 (20 May 1893): "Frank Norris acted his part of the brainless English swell to perfection and everyone applauded him to the echo. He said he was nervous, but he didn't show it at all, and his mother was awfully proud of him" (10).

28. Norris was deemed "a tremendous success and blushingly responded to innumerable recalls" (The Witness, "Splashes," *The Wave*, 12 [19 May 1894]: 3).

29. The first known submission was to Houghton, Mifflin, and Co., where the manuscript was declined on 30 December 1890. See Joseph R. McElrath Jr., "Frank Norris as Aspiring Writer," *Frank Norris Studies* 23 (Spring 1997): 7–8, and "Houghton, Mifflin's Rejection of *Yvernelle*," *Frank Norris Studies* 25 (Spring 1998): 2.

30. Reprinted in *Frank Norris: The Critical Reception*, ed. Joseph R. McElrath Jr. and Katherine Knight (New York: Burt Franklin, 1981), 1–8.

31. The Witness, "Splashes," *The Wave* 9 (1 October 1892): 6–7.

32. *Charles & Kathleen Norris: The Courtship Year*, ed. Richard Allan Davison (San Francisco: Book Club of California, 1993), 102.

33. "Art and Literature," *San Francisco Chronicle*, 6 March 1893), 10; the copy displayed in Chicago is in *FNC*.

34. "Bourdon Buried," *San Francisco Chronicle*, 6 June 1891, 8.

35. *The Octopus* (New York: Doubleday, Page, 1901), 102–3, 120–22.

36. "Berkeley," *San Francisco Chronicle*, 19 April 1893, 10.

37. Norris types Kipling and Stevenson as "masculine" in "An Opening for Novelists," *The Wave* 16 (22 May 1897): 7. He awards Zola the "iron-pen" sobriquet in his review of "Zola's Rome," *The Wave* 15 (6 June 1896): 8.

38. See, for example, Charles Child Walcutt, *American Literary Naturalism* (Minneapolis: University of Minnesota Press, 1956), and Warren French, *Frank Norris* (New York: Twayne, 1962).

39. Franklin Walker, *Frank Norris: A Biography* (Garden City, N.Y.: Doubleday, Doran, 1932), 58 and 75. The principal scholars who developed the concept of Norris as a LeContean evolutionary idealist are Robert D. Lundy, "The Making of *McTeague* and *The Octopus*," Ph.D. dissertation, University of California at Berkeley, 1956; Gilbert Schloss, "Frank Norris: Form and Development," Ph.D. dissertation, University of Wisconsin, 1963; and Donald Pizer, *The Novels of Frank Norris* (Bloomington: Indiana University Press, 1966). Subsequent interpreters who have not accepted their hypothesis have circumvented the issue; McElrath, however, has advanced the argument that Norris embraced neither LeConte's idealism nor the ardent religious perspective that colored it. See Joseph R. McElrath Jr., "Frank Norris's 'The Puppets and the Puppy': LeContean Idealism or Naturalistic Skepticism?" *American Literary Realism* 26 (Fall 1993): 50–59, and "'One Thing One Did Not Question': The Christian Perspective of Novelist Frank Norris," *Literature and Belief* 21.1 and 2 (Winter 2001): 1–25.

40. Crisler, "Norris and the *Blue and Gold*," 119.

41. "Frank Norris Writes Cleverly about Child Fiction for Old Readers," *Brooklyn Daily Eagle*, 8 February 1902, 10.

42. Though he lived until 1901, LeConte never referred to Norris. See Joseph LeConte, *The Autobiography of Joseph LeConte*, ed. William Dallam Armes (New York: D. Appleton, 1903).

43. The Witness, "Things and People," *The Wave* 15 (30 May 1896): 8. Such testimony to LeConte's lecturing ability and popularity among Berkeley's undergraduates is heard again and again in Lester D. Stephens, *Joseph LeConte: Gentle Prophet of Evolution* (Baton Rouge: Louisiana State University Press, 1982), 253–57, 290–91, and 296.

44. Joseph LeConte, *Evolution: Its Nature, Its Evidences, and Its Relation to Religious Thought* (New York: D. Appleton, 1891), 300–301. The proposition that matter and developments in the material world occur within the mind of God, or that physical reality is now continuously thought into existence by God, are given close attention by LeConte in *The Conception of God: A Philosophical Discussion Concerning the Nature of the Divine Idea as a Demonstrable Reality, by Josiah Royce, Joseph LeConte, G. H. Howison, and Sidney Edward Mezes* (New York and London: Macmillan, 1897).

45. LeConte, *Evolution*, 367, 369.

46. *The Octopus*, 652, 636; *The Pit*, 246.

47. Guest Register, Hotel del Coronado Collection, 1887–1977, Special Collections, San Diego State University Library.

48. "The Social World," *San Francisco Chronicle*, 3 August 1891, 5, 17 August 1891, 5, 28 September 1891, 5, 11 January 1892, 5, and 25 January 1892, 5.

49. Guest Register, Hotel del Coronado Collection.

50. "The Social World," *San Francisco Chronicle*, 1 February 1892, 5.

51. Guest Register, Hotel del Coronado Collection; "The Social World," *San Francisco Chronicle*, 22 February 1892, 5; "Society," *San Francisco Examiner*, 26 September 1892, 5; "Society News," *San Francisco Chronicle*, 15 October 1892, 10.

52. "Society News," *San Francisco Chronicle,* 19 January 1893, 10; Guest Register, Hotel del Coronado Collection; "The Social World," *San Francisco Chronicle,* 5 June 1893, 8; "Students at the Fair," *San Francisco Chronicle,* 7 May 1893, 11.

53. The Witness, "Splashes," *The Wave* 9 (24 September 1892): 2.

54. *Charles & Kathleen Norris: The Courtship Year,* 104.

55. "Wants Her Share," *San Francisco Morning Call,* 4 January 1894, 3; James Stronks, "B. F. Norris (Senior) in Probate Court, with New Light on Frank Norris as Son," *Frank Norris Studies* 12 (Autumn 1991): 3–5. No reference to Belle appears on his passport application dated 19 August 1892, but by then B. F.—residing at the Victoria Hotel in Chicago—was planning a trip abroad and a return to the United States "within one year" (Passport Applications [1 August–30 September 1892], no. 43877, M-1372, National Archives, Washington, D.C.).

56. "Mrs. Norris Petitions for Alimony," *Chicago Tribune,* 4 January 1894, 2.

57. "Wants Big Alimony," *San Francisco Chronicle,* 4 January 1894, 7.

58. "Wants Her Share," *San Francisco Morning Call,* 4 January 1894, 3.

59. "Offered His Wife $100,000," *Chicago Daily News,* 4 January 1894, 1.

60. Stronks, 3.

61. "San Jose," *San Francisco Examiner,* 22 July 1894, 17.

62. Norris's application forms and the letters from Henry Senger and James Sutton are in his Undergraduate Student Folder, Harvard University Archives. His application discloses the Norrises' brief residence at the Brunswick Hotel.

CHAPTER 8: THE SHORT-STORY WRITER IN THE MAKING AT BERKELEY

1. *Grand Production of Trilby . . . Presented by A. M. Palmer's Unrivalled Company,* clippings from a Boston Theatre program, week of 13 May 1895, Rauner Library, Dartmouth College.

2. Forty-four of the sketches or "themes" submitted by Norris to Professor Lewis E. Gates and his associates in 1894–95 *(FNC)* appear in *A Novelist in the Making,* ed. James D. Hart (Cambridge, Mass.: Belknap Press of Harvard University Press, 1970), 57–102. Another theme (Special Collections, Stanford University Libraries) was published separately as a keepsake, *A Student Theme by Frank Norris* (Berkeley, Calif.: The Frank Norris Society, 1987).

3. "At Damietta," *Occident* 19 (31 October 1890): 74–75.

4. "Brunhilde," *Occident* 19 (21 November 1890): 110.

5. "Les Enervés de Jumièges," *Occident* 19 (12 December 1890): 135.

6. James D. Hart, "The Freshman Themes of Frank Norris," *Frank Norris Studies* 2 (Autumn 1986): 1–2.

7. "The Jongleur of Taillebois," *The Wave* 7 (Christmas issue; [19 December 1891]): 6–9.

8. "The Finding of Lieutenant Outhwaite," *Occident* 20 (13 March 1891): 49–51.

9. Norris's astounding command of the Kipling canon is demonstrated in Joseph R. McElrath Jr., "'The 'Ricksha That Happened': Norris's Parody of Rudyard Kipling," *Frank Norris Studies* 15 (Spring 1993): 1–4.

10. "Outward and Visible Signs: IV, After Strange Gods," *Overland Monthly* 24 (October 1894): 375–79.

11. Like Norris's parody of Kipling, that of Davis was collected, along with others of Anthony Hope, Bret Harte, and Stephen Crane, in "Perverted Tales," *The Wave* 16 (Christmas issue [18 December 1897]): 5–7. Unlike Kipling's and Davis's, the influences of Hope, Harte, and Crane are not discernible in Norris's Berkeley writings.

12. "The Coverfield Sweepstakes," *Occident* 19 (19 December 1890): 145–47.

13. "Outward and Visible Signs: [II], The Most Noble Conquest of Man," *Overland Monthly* 23 (May 1894): 502–6.

14. "The Son of the Sheik," *Argonaut* 28 (1 June 1891): 6.

15. Donald Pizer, *The Novels of Frank Norris* (Bloomington: Indiana University Press, 1966), 15–16.

16. "Lauth," *Overland Monthly* 21 (March 1893): 241–60.

17. John S. Partridge, "The Pineal Eye: A Record of Atavism," *The Wave* 13 (Christmas issue [22 December 1894]): 19–21.

18. Franklin Walker, *Frank Norris: A Biography* (Garden City, N.Y.: Doubleday, Doran, 1932), 81–82; Pizer, 25–26. The most recent attempt to determine when Norris began reading Zola's novels has again demonstrated that it is not possible to establish a specific date. See Christine Harvey, "Dating Frank Norris' Reading of Zola," *Resources for American Literary Study* 24 (Fall 1998): 187–206.

CHAPTER 9: THE NASCENT ZOLAIST AT HARVARD COLLEGE

1. *CL,* 64–65. The volume is in the Barrett Collection of the Alderman Library at the University of Virginia. A copy of Norris's Harvard grade transcript is in the *FNC.*

2. John Schroeder takes a partial measure of Norris's familiarity with Shakespeare in "The Shakespearean Plots of *McTeague*," *American Literary Realism* 14 (1981): 289–96. He finds evidence of Norris's use of *Two Gentlemen of Verona, A Midsummer's Night's Dream, The Merchant of Venice,* and *Othello. The Pit* is similarly allusive, keyed at different points to *Twelfth Night, Macbeth, Hamlet, Romeo and Juliet,* and *Julius Caesar.*

3. James D. Hart relates that Norris received a C+ in his Shakespeare course. "Introduction," *A Novelist in the Making* (Cambridge, Mass.: Belknap Press of Harvard University Press, 1970), 13. But both the Harvard transcript itself and a 1930 report on the same in *FWC* contradict this.

4. "The 'English Courses' of the University of California," *The Wave* 15 (28 November 1896): 2–3.

5. Gates's personality and intellectual orientation are discussed by John S. Coolidge, "Lewis E. Gates: The Permutations of Romanticism in America," *New England Quarterly* 30 (March 1957): 23–38; and "Lewis E. Gates," *Dictionary of Literary Biography* vol. 71, ed. John W. Rathbun and Monica M. Grecu (Detroit: Gale, 1988), 82–86. See also Donald Pizer, *The Novels of Frank Norris* (Bloomington: Indiana University Press, 1966), 27–31; and Robert D. Lundy, "The Making of *McTeague* and *The Octopus*," Ph.D. dissertation, University of California at Berkeley, 1956, 41–53.

6. Quoted are the surviving original English 22 submissions *(FNC)*, dated 22, 24, 27 November and 8 December 1894, then 20, 23, 30 November and 18 December 1894.

7. These comments appeared on the themes dated 11 January, 19 February, and 8 March 1895.

8. Lewis E. Gates, *Studies and Appreciations* (New York: Macmillan, 1900), 2–5.

9. William Dean Howells, *Criticism and Fiction* (New York: Harper and Brothers, 1891), 6–17.

10. William Dean Howells, *The Rise of Silas Lapham* (New York: Penguin, 1986), 202.

11. Gates, *Studies and Appreciations*, 2–5, 28, 41, and 145.

12. Ibid., 75 and 59.

13. Ibid., 7, 28, 57; *The Pit* (New York: Doubleday, Page, 1903), 404.

14. Hart, *Novelist in the Making*, 18–27. His annotations of the individual themes are mainly devoted to establishing the relationships between the themes and chapters of *Vandover, McTeague,* and *Blix* (57–102).

15. *CL,* 108.

16. *Vandover and the Brute* (Garden City, N.Y.: Doubleday, Page, 1914), 60–61.

17. Ibid., 70–71; *Blix* (New York: Doubleday and McClure, 1899), 25–26.

18. Charles G. Norris, *Frank Norris* (Garden City, N.Y.: Doubleday, Page, [1914]), 7–8.

19. *FNC.*

20. *Vandover,* 209–12; *The Pit,* 27–33.

21. *Vandover,* 146, 127, 161–62, 114, 49–50, and 43–44.

22. Norris deals with *Lourdes, Rome, Nana, Germinal, L'Oeuvre, La Bête Humaine, La Débâcle,* and *Le Rêve*—in that order—in "Zola as Romantic Writer," *The Wave* 15 (27 June 1896): 3. His review of Zola's *Rome* appeared three weeks earlier in *The Wave* 15 (6 June 1896): 8.

23. *CL,* 65, n.2.

24. Joseph R. McElrath Jr., "Frank Norris as Aspiring Writer," *Frank Norris Studies* 23 (Spring 1997): 7–8.

25. Norris, *Frank Norris,* 6.

26. Announced by The Witness in "Personalities and Politics," *The Wave* 14 (2 November 1895): 6.

CHAPTER 10: ADVENTURING UPON LIFE

1. "The Country Club at Del Monte," *The Wave* 14 (7 September 1895): 7.

2. Qtd. in Richard Allan Davison, "Zelda Fitzgerald, Vladimir Nabokov and James A. Michener: Three Opinions on Frank Norris's *McTeague,*" *Frank Norris Studies* 9 (Spring 1990): 11–12.

3. "The Country Club at Del Monte," *The Wave* 14 (31 August 1895): 7.

4. Louis J. Budd, "Objectivity and Low Seriousness in American Naturalism," *Prospects* 1 (1975): 41–61; Joseph R. McElrath Jr., "The Comedy of Frank Norris's *McTeague,*" *Studies in American Humor* 2 (October 1975): 88–95.

5. "Our Unpopular Novelists," *The Wave* 14 (5 October 1895): 7.

6. *Vandover and the Brute* (Garden City, N.Y.: Doubleday, Page, 1914), 230–31.

7. Quoted are the original Harvard themes, dated as indicated *(FNC)*.

8. *The Octopus* (New York: Doubleday, Page, 1901), 51.

9. Emile Zola, *The Debacle,* trans. Leonard Tancock (New York: Penguin, 1972), 198; *La Bête Humaine,* trans. Leonard Tancock (New York: Penguin, 1977), 45.

10. "Zola's *Rome,*" *The Wave* 15 (6 June 1896): 8.

11. "A California Vintage," *The Wave* 14 (12 October 1895): 7.

12. Emile Zola, *Germinal,* trans. Stanley and Eleanor Hochman (New York: New American Library, 1970), 7.

13. The Witness, "Personalities and Politics," *The Wave* 14 (12 October 1895): 6.

14. Jesse S. Crisler, "Norris's Departure for Johannesburg," *Frank Norris Studies* 3 (Spring 1987): 4–5.

15. The Witness, "Personalities and Politics," *The Wave* 14 (2 November 1895): 6.

16. The Gossip, "Splashes," *The Wave* 13 (2 November 1895): 10. Hammond and his wife went to South Africa in 1893, where he served several mining companies as a consultant ("The Social World," *San Francisco Chronicle,* 21 September 1893, 9). His lucrative employment by Cecil Rhodes and the success of several other Americans working for the English are the subjects of "A Yankee in South Africa," *San Francisco Examiner,* 29 July 1894, 14.

17. John Bonner, "Causerie," *The Wave* 15 (15 February 1896): 5.

18. Charles G. Norris, *Frank Norris* (Garden City, N.Y.: Doubleday, Page, [1914]), 8.

19. "Mail & Shipping Intelligence," *The Times,* 8 November 1895, 10; John E. Weems, *The Fate of the "Maine"* (College Station: Texas A&M University Press, 1992), 197; "The Maine in Service," *New York Times,* 18 September 1895, 9.

20. "Mail & Shipping Intelligence," *The Times,* 18 November 1895, 6, 22 November 1895, 10, and 6 December 1895, 6.

21. Norris, *Frank Norris,* 8–9.

22. "A Californian in the City of Cape Town," *San Francisco Chronicle,* 19 January 1896, 19.

23. Jesse S. Crisler documents San Francisco press coverage of Gertrude Norris's attempts to locate her son in "Norris in South Africa," *Frank Norris Studies* 7 (Spring 1989): 4–7. The articles quoted below are reprinted therein.

24. "Topics in California," *New-York Daily Tribune,* 29 December 1895, 20.

25. Joseph R. McElrath Jr., *Frank Norris: A Descriptive Bibliography* (Pittsburgh: University of Pittsburgh Press, 1992), 19.

26. "From Cape Town to Kimberley Mine," *San Francisco Chronicle,* 26 January 1896, 1. Norris also provided a brief, comical description of his trip to Kimberley in a University of California student magazine: "A South African Railway Experience," *Occident* 30 (23 January 1896): 22–23.

27. "In the Compound of a Diamond Mine," *San Francisco Chronicle,* 2 February 1896, 10.

28. "In the Veldt of the Transvaal," *San Francisco Chronicle*, 9 February 1896, 1.

CHAPTER 11: THE JAMESON RAID

1. Charles G. Norris, *Pig Iron* (New York: Dutton, 1926), 348.
2. "In the Veldt of the Transvaal," *San Francisco Chronicle*, 9 February 1896, 1.
3. "The Uprising in the Transvaal," *San Francisco Chronicle*, 9 February 1896, 17.
4. Thomas Pakenham, *The Boer War* (New York: Random House, 1979), xxv.
5. Howard Hensman, *History of Rhodesia* (Edinburgh: Blackwood, 1900), 85–90.
6. Ibid., 89–90.
7. See "A Christmas in the Transvaal," *Sunday Examiner Magazine* (*San Francisco Examiner*), 17 December 1899, 6.
8. "The Frantic Rush from Johannesburg," *San Francisco Chronicle*, 1 March 1896, 8.
9. "Mail & Shipping Intelligence," *The Times*, 17 January 1896, 10, 1 February 1896, 10, and 5 February 1896, 5; "Arrival of Mr. Rhodes," *The Times*, 5 February 1896, 5.
10. "Rhodes and the Reporters," *The Wave* 15 (11 April 1896): 5.
11. "Tales of the Day," *The Wave* 15 (18 April 1896): 16.
12. "A Steamship Voyage with Cecil Rhodes," *San Francisco Chronicle*, 19 April 1896, 15.
13. "Mail & Shipping Intelligence," *The Times*, 10 February 1896, 6; "Overdue Ships Here," *New York Tribune*, 17 February 1896, 10.
14. "Folk Found in the Lobbies," *San Francisco Examiner*, 17 February 1896, 6.
15. (Harry) Hull McClaughry to A. Edward Newton, 12 May 1931, Special Collections, Boston Public Library.
16. John W. Lovell was a cheap-reprint publisher despised within the industry because of his pirating practices prior to the passage of the International Copyright Law in 1891 and his aggressive attempts, beginning in the 1870s, to corner the reprint market. Lovell, Coryell, and Company was one of the several subsidiaries of his United States Book Company. Founded with Vincent M. Coryell in 1892, Lovell, Coryell's future was already in doubt when it accepted Norris's manuscript; in 1894, the parent company went bankrupt. The bank that held it in receivership renamed it the American Publishers Corporation, and in 1896 Lovell, Coryell was no longer in business.

CHAPTER 12: THE *WAVE* JOURNALIST

1. Guest Register, Hotel del Coronado Collection, 1887–1977, Special Collections, San Diego State University Library.
2. "An Impression of Collis P. Huntington," *The Wave* 22 (18 August 1900): 12; and "Collis P. Huntington in a Character Study," *The Wave* 22 (25 August 1900): 2.
3. "Library Notes," *The Wave* 15 (25 January 1896): 9.

4. "In the Library," *The Wave* 15 (7 March 1896): 8.

5. Untitled caption for a photograph of Norris, *The Wave* 15 (Christmas issue [19 December 1896]), 6; Boswell Jr., "Things and People," *The Wave* 18 (27 August 1898): 3.

6. *CL*, 108–9.

7. *American Labor and Its Foreign Leaders: Editorials from the San Francisco Wave* [San Francisco: The Wave, 1895.]

8. Will Irwin, Introduction to *The Third Circle* (New York: John Lane, 1909), 8–9.

9. Ibid., 9.

10. "A Steamship Voyage with Cecil Rhodes," *San Francisco Chronicle,* 19 April 1896, 15.

11. "The Santa Cruz Venetian Carnival," *The Wave* 15 (27 June 1896): 8; "Guests Crowd the Town," *San Francisco Examiner,* 21 June 1896, 11; "Society Here and Elsewhere," *San Francisco Chronicle,* 22 June 1896, 10.

12. *McTeague* (New York: Doubleday and McClure, 1899), 379–80.

13. "Zola's *Rome,*" *The Wave* 15 (6 June 1896): 8.

14. "Moving a Fifty-Ton Gun," *The Wave* 15 (7 November 1896): 5.

15. "With the Peacemakers," *The Wave* 15 (13 June 1896): 4.

16. "On a Battleship," *The Wave* 15 (17 October 1896): 7.

17. "Sanitary Reduction," *The Wave* 16 (25 December 1897): 8–9.

18. *McTeague,* 380.

19. *The Pit* (New York: Doubleday, Page, 1903), 421.

20. "Western City Types: The 'Fast' Girl," *The Wave* 15 (9 May 1896): 5.

21. "Man-Hunting," *The Wave* 15 (13 June 1896): 8; "A Strange Relief-Ship," *The Wave* 16 (12 June 1897): 7; "From Field to Storehouse," *The Wave* 16 (7 August 1897): 6–7; "Birthday of an Old Mission," *The Wave* 16 (3 July 1897): 9.

CHAPTER 13: WRITING PROSE FICTION FOR *THE WAVE*

1. Boswell Jr., "Things and People," *The Wave* 17 (5 March 1898): 7.

2. C., "November Magazines," *The Wave* 16 (6 November 1897): 12.

3. Norris was at the Sierra Nevadas before 9 September 1896, where he executed two drawings of female figures on the stationery of the Big Dipper Mine. He inscribed and dated one to Seymour Waterhouse and the other to George D. Blood *(FNC).*

4. "A Salvation Boom in Matabeleland," *The Wave* 15 (25 April 1896): 5.

5. Charles Dickens, *The Posthumous Papers of the Pickwick Club* (Oxford: Oxford University Press, 1948), 102.

6. "'Man Proposes,'" *The Wave* 15 (23 May 1896): 6.

7. "'Man Proposes': No. 2," *The Wave* 15 (30 May 1896): 7.

8. "Suggestions," *The Wave* 16 (13 March 1897): 7.

9. "Among Cliff-Dwellers," *The Wave* 16 (15 May 1897): 6.

10. Don Graham, "Frank Norris, Actor," *Book Club of California Quarterly News-Letter* 41 (Spring 1976): 38–40.

11. "The Theatres," *The Wave* 16 (6 March 1897): 11.

12. Miss Cricket, "A Debutante's Diary," *The Wave* 16 (13 March 1897): 10.

13. The Witness, "Things and People," *The Wave* 15 (9 May 1896): 7.

14. Gelett Burgess, *The Purple Cow!* (San Francisco: William Doxey, 1895), n.p. (single printed folio of four pages).

15. See Gelett Burgess, *Vivette; or the Memoirs of the Romance Association* (Boston: Copeland and Day, 1897). The Goops appeared in numerous periodical publications and, before his death in 1951, Burgess had published eight "Goop books" for children.

16. "An Opening for Novelists," *The Wave* 16 (22 May 1897): 7.

17. Ernest Clifford Peixotto papers, the Bancroft Library.

18. Charles L. Crow, "Bruce Porter's Memoir of Frank Norris," *Frank Norris Studies* 3 (Spring 1987): 1–2. The dates of Burgess's employment by *The Wave* are given by Joseph M. Backus, *Gelett Burgess: Behind the Scenes* (San Francisco: Book Club of California, 1968), 9, 121, and 128. All of the *Wave* articles Burgess is known to have written are reprinted therein.

19. "Metropolitan Noises," *The Wave* 16 (22 May 1897): 9.

20. "The Puppets and the Puppy," *The Wave* 16 (22 May 1897): 5.

21. "Little Dramas of the Curbstone," *The Wave* 16 (26 June 1897): 9.

22. "Sailing of the 'Excelsior,'" *The Wave* 16 (31 July 1897): 7.

23. Eleanor M. Davenport, "Some Younger California Writers," *University of California Magazine* 3 (November 1897): 80–82.

24. *FNC.*

25. Davenport, "Some Younger California Writers," 81.

CHAPTER 14: THE NOVELIST AT LAST AT WORK

1. "Twenty-nine Fatal Wounds," *San Francisco Examiner,* 10 October 1893, 12.

2. Denison Hailey Clift, "The Artist in Frank Norris," *Pacific Monthly* 17 (March 1907): 313–22.

3. *CL,* 108–9.

4. Grant Allen Wood, "A Golden Bowl Broken," *Phi Gamma Delta Quarterly* 25 (December 1902): 157–63.

5. John D. Barry, "New York Letter," *Literary World* 30 (18 March 1899): 88–89; "Literary Notes," *Washington Times* 11 November 1900, pt. 2, 8.

6. *CL,* 42–43.

7. *McTeague* (New York: Doubleday and McClure, 1899), 2.

8. "Theory and Reality," *The Wave* 15 (2 May 1896): 8.

9. "What Is Our Greatest Piece of Fiction?" *San Francisco Examiner,* 17 January 1897, 30. The influence of this novel by Howells has never been measured, but anyone familiar with Norris's canon will see again and again that it was as important a model for his non-Zolaesque writings as Kipling's short stories were.

10. A remarkable number of reviewers saw *McTeague* as a realist novel rather than a naturalistic or a romantic work. See "A Story of San Francisco," *New York Times* (Saturday Review of Books and Art), 11 March 1899, 150; "A Western Realist," *Washington Times,* 23 April 1899, 20; Jeanette Gilder, "The Lounger," *The Critic* 34

(May 1899): 398; Nancy Huston Banks, "Two Recent Revivals in Realism," *Bookman* (American), 9 June 1899, 356–57; and "A Rough Novel," *Boston Evening Transcript,* 22 March 1899, 10.

11. A photograph (ca. 1878) of the building and the molar suspended from a sign reading "Dentist" is reproduced in "San Francisco, 1865–1900," at the "American Hurrah!" website, <http://americahurrah.com>. For identifications of *McTeague's* real-world referents in San Francisco and elsewhere, see Robert D. Lundy, "The Making of *McTeague* and *The Octopus,*" Ph.D. dissertation, University of California at Berkeley, 1956, 145–53; and Jesse S. Crisler, "A Critical and Textual Study of Frank Norris's *McTeague,*" Ph.D. dissertation, University of South Carolina, 1973, 39–62.

12. "An Opening for Novelists," *The Wave* 16 (22 May 1897): 7.

13. "Zola as a Romantic Writer," *The Wave* 15 (27 June 1896): 3.

14. "Frank Norris' Weekly Letter: [9]," *American Art and Literary Review* (*Chicago American*), 3 August 1901, 5.

15. William Dean Howells, "American Letter," *Literature* 3 (17 December 1898): 577–78.

16. *Moran of the Lady Letty: A Story of Adventure off the California Coast* (New York: Doubleday and McClure, 1898), 1.

17. *CL,* 47.

18. *Moran,* 104–5, 175.

19. Ibid., 215–16.

20. Ibid., 217–21.

21. Juliet Wilbor Tompkins, Introduction to *The Argonaut Manuscript Limited Edition of Frank Norris' Works* (Garden City, N.Y.: Doubleday, Doran, 1928), vol. 9, ix.

22. *CL,* 49–50, 60.

CHAPTER 15: NEW YORK CITY AT LAST

1. *CL,* 42.

2. *CL,* 45.

3. Joseph R. McElrath Jr. and Sal Noto, "An Important Letter in the Career of Frank Norris," *Book Club of California Quarterly News-Letter* 55 (Summer 1990): 59–61.

4. A photograph of the house may be seen in the pictorial files, arranged by street addresses, of the New-York Historical Society.

5. "A Charity Magazine," *San Francisco Chronicle,* 8 May 1898, 21; "The Mariposa Magazine," *San Francisco Chronicle,* 15 May 1898, 4.

6. *CL,* 47.

7. *CL,* 49–50.

8. *CL,* 48.

9. "Moran of the Lady Letty," *The Wave* 17 (2 April 1898): 5–6.

10. Ernest Clifford Peixotto papers, the Bancroft Library.

CHAPTER 16: THE ROCKING-CHAIR WAR

1. Charles Sanford Diehl, *The Staff Correspondent* (San Antonio: Clegg, 1931), 262.

2. "Starting for the South," *New York Tribune,* 15 May 1898, 4.

3. George Kennan, *Campaigning in Cuba* (New York: Century, 1899), 2.

4. "News Gathering at Key West" was first published as "On the Cuban Blockade," *New York Evening Post,* 11 April 1914, pt. 3, 6; quoted below is the manuscript *(FNC).*

5. Kennan, 2.

6. R. W. Stallman, *Stephen Crane: A Biography* (New York: George Braziller, 1968), 354–55.

7. Gregory Mason, *Remember the Maine* (New York: Henry Holt, 1939), 130–31.

8. J. M. Maxwell, "Troops May Go to Cuba Today," *Chicago Daily Tribune,* 5 May 1898, 2; W. J. Rouse, "Invasion Is Imminent," *Chicago Daily Tribune,* 6 May 1898, 3.

9. "American Guns Boom Liberty to Cuban Ears," *San Francisco Examiner,* 28 April 1898, 1.

10. Ambrose Bierce, "War Topics," *San Francisco Examiner,* 1 May 1898, 18, and 29 May 1898, 13.

11. "Five Slain by Spanish Shell," *Chicago Times-Herald,* 13 May 1898, 1.

12. Cecil Carnes, *Jimmy Hare: News Photographer* (New York: Macmillan, 1940), 53.

13. Joseph Pais, "Spanish-American War Log," unpublished database (Key West: Key West Art and Historical Society, 1998), entry for 24 June 1898.

14. Richard Harding Davis, *The Cuban and Porto Rican Campaigns* (New York: Scribner's, 1898), 94–95.

15. James F. J. Archibald, "With Transport Fleet off Tampa," *San Francisco Evening Post,* 21 June 1898, 1–2.

16. "Holiday Literature," *The Wave* 16 (11 December 1897): 8.

17. Davis, 92.

18. Archibald, 1.

19. G. J. A. O'Toole, *The Spanish War* (New York: Norton, 1984), 254.

CHAPTER 17: WITH NORRIS AT EL CANEY

1. Stephen Bonsal, *The Fight for Santiago* (New York: Doubleday and McClure, 1899), 71.

2. C. D. Rhodes, "Diary of a Lieutenant," in *The Santiago Campaign* (Richmond, Va.: Williams Printing, 1927), 345.

3. "With Lawton at El Caney," *Century* 58 (June 1899): 304–9. In a holograph draft of the beginning of this article, but not in the published version, Norris briefly described the monotony of the voyage, his sighting of the U.S. warships blockading the Santiago Harbor, the meeting with the Cubans at Asseraderos, and preparations for the landing of the troops at Daiquirí. See Joseph R. McElrath Jr., "Scenes from the Spanish-American War: Frank Norris's Holograph Draft of an Introduction to 'With Lawton at El Caney,'" *Frank Norris Studies* 3 (2003): 7–8.

4. George R. Van Dewater, "The Seventy-first Regiment, New York Volunteers at Santiago de Cuba," in *The Santiago Campaign* (Richmond, Va.: Williams Printing, 1927), 127–46.

5. "A California Author," *Oakland Enquirer,* 29 August 1898, 4.

6. Theodore Roosevelt, *The Rough Riders* (New York: Scribner's, 1899), 113–14.

7. James F.J. Archibald, "Before and After Santiago's Fall," *San Francisco Evening Post,* 22 July 1898, 1–2.

8. William Randolph Hearst, "Laine's Valor on Santiago's Field," *San Francisco Examiner,* 5 July 1898, 5.

9. Archibald, "Before and After Santiago's Fall," 1–2.

10. James F. J. Archibald, "What I Saw in the War: No. 1," *Leslie's Weekly* 87 (20 October 1898): 314.

11. *CL,* 52–53.

CHAPTER 18: FROM EL CANEY TO SAN JUAN HEIGHTS
TO SANTIAGO

1. James F. J. Archibald, "What I Saw in the War: No. 2," *Leslie's Weekly* 87 (8 November 1898): 350. Norris, without blaming the Cuban guides, described the same development in an interview, "Witnessed the Fall of Caney," *San Francisco Chronicle,* 28 August 1898, 8.

2. James F. J. Archibald, "What I Saw in the War: No. 3," *Leslie's Weekly,* 87 (17 November 1898): 390.

3. C. D. Rhodes, "Diary of a Lieutenant," in *The Santiago Campaign* (Richmond, Va.: Williams Printing, 1927), 360.

4. "A California Author," *Oakland Enquirer,* 29 August 1898, 4.

5. Archibald, "What I Saw in the War: No. 2."

6. G. J. A. O'Toole, *The Spanish War* (New York: Norton, 1984), 322.

7. James F. J. Archibald, "What I Saw in the War: No. 6," *Leslie's Weekly* 87 (29 December 1898): 522.

8. *CL,* 52–53.

9. George Kennan, *Campaigning in Cuba* (New York: Century, 1899), 130–49.

10. "*Comida:* An Experience in Famine," *Atlantic Monthly* 83 (March 1899): 343–48.

11. James F. J. Archibald, "What I Saw in the War: No. 4," *Leslie's Weekly* 87 (1 December 1898): 430.

12. Kennan, 157.

13. Ibid., 159–60.

14. Archibald, "What I Saw in the War: No. 4."

15. Ibid.

16. Clara Barton, *The Red Cross in Peace and War* (Washington, D.C.: American Historical Press, 1899), 620 and 650.

17. Archibald, "What I Saw in the War: No. 4."

18. O'Toole, 343.

19. Archibald, "What I Saw in the War: No. 2."

20. Archibald, "What I Saw in the War: No. 4."

21. James F. J. Archibald, "What I Saw in the War: No. 7," *Leslie's Weekly* 88 (5 January 1899): 6; and "What I Saw in the War: No. 8," *Leslie's Weekly* 88 (19 January 1899): 46.

22. Rhodes, 374 and 377.

23. "The Surrender of Santiago" was first published as "Untold Thrilling Account of Santiago's Surrender," *New York Sun,* 13 July 1913, sec. 7, 6.

24. Rhodes, 378.

25. Ibid., 379.

26. Ibid.

27. Cecil Carnes, *Jimmy Hare: News Photographer* (New York: Macmillan, 1940), 91.

28. James F. J. Archibald, "What I Saw in the War: No. 9," *Leslie's Weekly* 88 (2 February 1899): 86–87.

29. "A California Author," 4.

30. Archibald, "What I Saw in the War: No. 9."

31. "Dead and Sick in Cuba," *New York Times,* 2 August 1898, 3; "Port of New York," *New York Herald,* 6 August 1898, 12.

32. "No Cots for Sick Soldiers," *Chicago Daily Tribune,* 6 August 1898, 2; "Col. Brogan Reaches New York," *Boston Globe,* 6 August 1898, 5.

33. "Big Transport Iroquois Arrives Here," *New York World,* 5 August 1898, 3.

CHAPTER 19: A QUICKENING PACE

1. *FNC.*

2. *CL,* 52–53. The recently discovered envelope containing this letter *(FNC)* was postmarked in New York on 11 August 1898 and 12 August in Chadds Ford.

3. Boswell Jr., "Things and People," *The Wave* 18 (27 August 1898): 3.

4. "A California Author," *Oakland Enquirer,* 29 August 1898, 4.

5. [Sylvester Scovel], "Conduct of the 71st New York at Charge of San Juan," *New York World,* 16 July 1898, 1.

6. "Witnessed the Fall of Caney," *San Francisco Chronicle,* 28 August 1898, 8.

7. Stanley Wertheim and Paul Sorrentino, *The Crane Log* (New York: G. K. Hall, 1994), 329.

8. Boswell Jr., "Things and People," *The Wave* 17 (21 May 1898): 3.

9. Boswell Jr., "Things and People," *The Wave* 18 (27 August 1898): 3.

10. Stephen Bonsal, "The Fight for Santiago," *McClure's Magazine* 11 (October 1898): 499–518 (see 513 and 515).

11. Quoted in Joseph R. McElrath Jr., "Frank Norris's *Blix:* Jeannette Black as Travis," *Frank Norris Studies* 11 (Spring 1991): 9.

12. Denison Hailey Clift locates Luna's in "The Artist in Frank Norris," *Pacific Monthly* 17 (March 1907): 313–22. Included are photographs of Luna's and, three blocks to the southwest, the Chinese restaurant overlooking Portsmouth Square, also described in *Blix.* In the 1890s Dupont Street ran south from the bay between Stockton and Kearny, like the present Grant Street.

13. When interviewed, Jeannette was inconsistent with regard to when Norris wrote *Blix.* Twice she said that it was written during the winter of 1898–99. But she also stated that it "must have been practically finished" when Norris returned to New York City from San Francisco in October 1898.

14. *CL,* 54.

15. *CL,* 55.

16. Amy Johnson describes Rickoff's minor achievements as a local literary critic in "'A Talent for the Inappropriate': Bertha Monroe Rickoff as a Foil to Frank Norris," *Frank Norris Studies* 16 (Autumn 1993): 1–6.

17. Joseph R. McElrath Jr. and Jesse S. Crisler, "The Bowdlerization of *McTeague*," *American Literature* 61 (March 1989): 97–101.

18. [Untitled paragraph], *The Wave* 20 (5 August 1899): 19; "Social Records of Interest," *San Francisco Chronicle,* 4 August 1899, 9; "She Will Be an Author's Bride," *San Francisco Examiner,* 6 August 1899, 13.

19. *Blix* (New York: Doubleday and McClure, 1899), 199.

20. Ibid., 6–8.

21. Ibid., 107–8.

22. See Debra D. Munn, "The Revision of Frank Norris's *Blix*," *Resources for American Literary Study* 10 (Spring 1980): 47–55.

23. *CL,* 59. See Joseph R. McElrath Jr., "Scenes from the Spanish-American War: Frank Norris's Holograph Draft of an Introduction to 'With Lawton at El Caney,'" *Frank Norris Studies* 3 (2003): 7–8.

24. *CL,* 57–58.

25. *CL,* 60.

26. James E. Knott to James D. Hart, 18 May 1954; Juliet Wilbor Tompkins Pottle to James D. Hart, 4 September 1952 (James D. Hart papers, the Bancroft Library).

27. *CL,* 61.

28. *CL,* 64–65.

29. *CL,* 79.

30. "Mr. Norris's Ultra Realism," *New York Times* (Saturday Review of Books and Art), 10 February 1900, 82.

31. *CL,* 93.

32. *CL,* 67.

33. *CL,* 69.

34. *CL,* 73.

35. *CL,* 75.

36. *CL,* 84 and 87.

37. *CL,* 75.

CHAPTER 20: "THE WHEAT STUFF IS PILING UP B.I.G."

1. Bailey Millard, "What Is Our Greatest Piece of Fiction?" *San Francisco Examiner,* 17 January 1897, 30. Norris's letter to Millard (*CL,* 39–40) appears under the subtitle, "He Thinks Its [*sic*] 'Ben-Hur.'"

2. Bailey Millard, "Frank Norris Makes a Stir," *Sunday Examiner Magazine* (*San Francisco Examiner*), 12 March 1899, 30.

3. Bailey Millard, "How California Is to Be Put into Novels by Frank Norris, Who Writes the 'Vivid Thing,'" *Sunday Examiner Magazine* (*San Francisco Examiner*), 28 May 1899, 30.

4. Norris's appreciation of Arthur Conan Doyle's Sherlock Holmes stories will be

seen in "Fiction in Review," *The Wave* 15 (18 July 1896): 12, and "A Steamship Voyage with Cecil Rhodes," *San Francisco Chronicle,* 19 April 1896, 15.

5. *CL,* 82–83.

6. See Joseph R. McElrath Jr., *Frank Norris: A Descriptive Bibliography* (Pittsburgh: University of Pittsburgh Press, 1992), 30. For the original and revised scene at the Orpheum Theater, see 323–28.

7. Boswell Jr., "Things and People," *The Wave* 19 (24 June 1899): 7.

8. *CL,* 77, 79, and 81. Peixotto, on assignment from *Scribner's Magazine,* was en route to Paris to produce architectural drawings. Prior to their departure the Peixottos were the guests of honor at a musicale performed in the New York studio of one of Norris's other friends who lived on Washington Square, John Harrold ("Here and There in the Artist World," *San Francisco Chronicle,* 14 May 1899, 19).

9. *CL,* 75.

10. George W. DeLong, *The Voyage of the Jeannette,* ed. Emma DeLong (Boston: Houghton, Mifflin, 1883); Fridtjof Nansen, *Farthest Norris,* 2 vols. (New York: Harper and Brothers, 1897).

11. *CL,* 89. Norris drafted his reply on the second page of Parks's letter of 16 October 1899 *(FNC).*

12. Edwin Markham, *The Man with the Hoe and Other Poems* (New York: Doubleday and McClure, 1899). See Joseph R. McElrath Jr., "Edwin Markham in Frank Norris's *The Octopus,*" *Frank Norris Studies* 13 (Spring 1992): 10–11.

13. Robert D. Lundy, "The Making of *McTeague* and *The Octopus,*" Ph.D. dissertation, University of California at Berkeley, 1956, 214–15.

14. John T. Flynn, "The Silent Forge," *The Wave* 11 (18 March 1899): 15; *The Octopus* (New York: Doubleday, Page, 1901), 302–3.

15. Harry M. Wright, "In Memoriam—Frank Norris: 1870–1902," *University of California Chronicle* 5 (October 1902): 240–45.

16. Jesse S. Crisler, "Four New Frank Norris Letters: Part One," *Book Club of California Quarterly News-Letter* 56 (Summer 1991): 67–75. Huntington's arrival and impending departure were noted in "Plans for Huntington's Big Banquet," *San Francisco Call,* 27 April 1899, 9; and "Mr. Huntington's Banquet," *San Francisco Call,* 13 May 1899, 4.

17. *CL,* 80.

18. "A Reply to McEwen," *The Wave* 13 (22 September 1894): 3–4.

19. *The Octopus,* 571–76.

20. Ibid., 577.

21. Ibid., 468.

22. "An Appeal to the People," *Visalia Weekly Delta,* 7 May 1880, 2; *The Octopus,* 117–18.

23. *The Octopus,* 506.

24. "The Mussel Slough Tragedy," *Visalia Weekly Delta,* 14 May 1880, 3; "The Mussel Slough Massacre—Further Accounts by Eye-Witnesses," *Visalia Weekly Delta,* 21 May 1880, 3. See also J. L. Brown, *The Mussel Slough Tragedy* (n.p: 1958); Richard Maxwell Brown, *No Duty to Retreat* (New York: Oxford University Press,

1991); and Charles L. Crow, "Frank Norris's San Joaquin," *The Californians* 6 (July-August 1988): 54–56.

25. "Zola as a Romantic Writer," *The Wave* 15 (27 June 1896): 3.

26. *The Octopus*, 516–22.

27. Ibid., 516–37.

28. Ibid., 535.

29. Ibid., 368–69, 392–93.

30. Boswell Jr., "Things and People," *The Wave* 19 (22 April 1899): 6.

31. *CL*, 85.

32. To the east of Tres Pinos in Madera and Fresno Counties the harvest began in the second week of August, as was related by Carroll Carrington, "They're Harvesting the Wheat Now in the Largest Wheat Field in the World," *Sunday Examiner Magazine* (*San Francisco Examiner*), 13 August 1899, 24.

33. See Marjorie Pierce, *East of the Gabilans* (Santa Cruz, Calif.: Western Tanager Press, 1987).

34. *The Octopus*, 61.

35. *CL*, 123.

36. *The Octopus*, 636.

37. "Man-Hunting: The Coast Range as a Refuge for Bandits," *The Wave* 15 (13 June 1896): 8.

38. James D. Hart, "Sontag, John," in *A Companion to California* (Berkeley: University of California Press, 1987), 486–87.

39. "Birthday of an Old Mission," *The Wave* 16 (3 July 1897): 9; *CL*, 123.

40. "From Field to Storehouse," *The Wave* 16 (7 August 1897): 6–7.

41. "A Strange Relief-Ship," *The Wave* 16 (12 June 1897): 7.

42. "A Christmas in the Transvaal," *Sunday Examiner Magazine* (*San Francisco Examiner*), 17 December 1899, 6.

43. "In Bookdom," *The Wave* 19 (10 June 1899): 11.

44. Bailey Millard, "A Novelist's Fancy," *Sunday Examiner Magazine* (*San Francisco Examiner*), 3 September 1899, 26.

CHAPTER 21: PROFESSIONAL ADVANCES AND PERSONAL COMMITMENTS

1. Jeannette recalled this for Franklin Walker but not Frank's address. It is likely, however, that he had moved into the apartment previously occupied by the Peixottos, at the Anglesea, 60 Washington Square South. It was to this address that he brought his bride several months later.

2. Oscar Lewis, *The Big Four* (New York: Alfred A. Knopf, 1959), 371, 405–12.

3. "Policy of the Santa Fe Road Outlined," *San Francisco Chronicle*, 25 May 1899, 1.

4. *CL*, 90.

5. *CL*, 93.

6. *CL*, 123.

7. *A Man's Woman* (New York: Doubleday and McClure, 1900), 234–35. See Linda

A. Dover, "Frank Norris' *A Man's Woman:* The Textual Changes," *Resources for American Literary Study* 13 (Autumn 1983): 165–83; and Joseph R. McElrath Jr., *Frank Norris Revisited* (New York: Twayne, 1992), 87–88.

8. *CL,* 104. The size of the first printing was stated by Russell Doubleday in a 26 February 1932 letter to Franklin Walker *(FWC).*

9. See Joseph R. McElrath Jr., *Frank Norris: A Descriptive Bibliography* (Pittsburgh: University of Pittsburgh Press, 1992), 330–31.

10. Charles Johanningsmeier, "'Rediscovering' Frank Norris's 'A Salvation Boom in Matabeleland,'" *Frank Norris Studies* 22 (Autumn 1996): 1–6.

11. Phillips did not mention to Walker the submission of the *Vandover* manuscript to Grant Richards, documented in Norris's 27 November 1899 letter to Richards (*CL,* 94). Contrary to what Charles Norris told Walker, there is no reason to conclude that Frank had not completed the manuscript by 1898 or, at the latest, some time in early to mid-1899. This squares with Jeannette's claim that after their marriage in early 1900 Frank never worked on the manuscript, which was then in the state in which Richards saw it. It was in the same state when Charles Norris later edited it for 1914 publication, cutting a whole chapter that disgusted him, he told Walker.

12. See *CL,* 68 and 97.

13. *CL,* 101–2.

14. *CL,* 99–100.

15. *CL,* 172, 185–86. Garland recorded his meeting Norris in New York "about New Years 1900" in a copy of *Blix* at the J. Pierpont Morgan Library, New York.

16. *Register of Marriages* and *Family Record,* 1896–1902, St. George's Episcopal church. Included in the latter are the other records of membership cited below.

17. Francis Morrone, *The Architectural Guidebook to New York City* (Layton, Utah: Gibb Smith, 1998), 127–29.

18. Jean Strouse, *Morgan* (New York: Random House, 1999), 218–22.

19. *FNC.*

20. W. S. Rainsford, *The Reasonableness of Faith and Other Addresses* (New York: Doubleday, Page, 1902), 53–54.

21. *FNC.*

22. W. S. Rainsford, "Frank Norris," *The World's Work* 5 (April 1903): 3276.

23. W. S. Rainsford, *The Story of a Varied Life: An Autobiography* (New York: Doubleday, Page, 1922), 249–51, 294, 307–8.

24. *CL,* 89. In November 1899 the same symbol also begins to appear regularly in inscriptions in his books that he gave to his friends. See, for example, *CL,* 217.

25. *The Pit* (New York: Doubleday, Page, 1903), 122–26.

26. "Simplicity in Art," *Boston Evening Transcript,* 15 January 1902, 17.

27. *The Octopus* (New York: Doubleday, Page, 1901), 467–68. See also Hamlin Garland, "Under the Lion's Paw," in *Main-Travelled Roads* (Boston: Arena Publishing, 1891), 217–40. In this story, a similar "religion" not related to any particular church body is professed by the character Stephen Council.

28. Rainsford, *Reasonableness of Faith,* 255–56.

29. *The Octopus,* 498.

30. *CL,* 113.

31. Quoted in James L. W. West III, *A Sister Carrie Portfolio* (Charlottesville: University Press of Virginia, 1985), 55.

32. Ibid., 75.

33. Quoted in *CL,* 119.

34. *CL,* 118–20.

35. West, 61 and 74; Richard L. Lingeman, *Theodore Dreiser: At the Gates of the City* (New York: Putnam, 1986), 310.

36. W. A. Swanberg, *Theodore Dreiser* (New York: Scribner's, 1965), 86.

37. Grant Richards, *Author Hunting by an Old Literary Sportsman* (New York: Coward-McCann, 1934), 169–74; *CL,* 150–51 and 181; Joseph R. McElrath Jr., "Grant Richards's Letters to Frank Norris," *Resources for American Literary Study* 19.1 (1993): 53–56.

38. "Literature in the East," *American Art and Literary Review* (*Chicago American*), 25 May 1901, 8.

39. Thomas Blues, "A Note on Frank Norris's Banjo," *Frank Norris Studies* 12 (Autumn 1991): 7–10.

40. Isaac F. Marcosson, *Adventures in Interviewing* (New York: John Lane, 1919), 240. Marcosson misdated the July visit at the Anglesea as occurring in 1901 rather than 1900.

CHAPTER 22: THE *ENFANT TERRIBLE* NO MORE

1. "A California Novelist," *Washington Times,* 15 October 1899, pt. 2, 8.

2. "The New American Novelist," *Washington Times,* 18 February 1900, pt. 2, 8.

3. *A Man's Woman* (New York: Doubleday and McClure, 1900), 43 and 79. Norris made similar use of Trina's loss of two fingers and her thumb in *McTeague* (New York: Doubleday and McClure, 1899), 352. See Zola's similarly dark-comic exploitation of Gervaise Coupeau's congential limp in chapter 3 of *L'Assommoir.*

4. *CL,* 160.

5. [William Dean Howells], "Editor's Easy Chair," *Harper's Monthly* 103 (October 1901): 824–25; William L. Alden, "London Letter," *New York Times* (Saturday Review of Books and Art), 5 October 1901, 722.

6. "The Trilogy of Wheat," *Bookman* (American) 13 (May 1901): 212–13; "The Novel of the West," *Washington Times,* 2 June 1901, pt. 2, 8.

7. Henry Morse Stephens, "The Work of Frank Norris: An Appreciation," *University of California Chronicle* 5 (January 1903): 324–31.

8. *CL,* 120–21.

9. *CL,* 123.

10. Isaac F. Marcosson, "Some Recollections of Frank Norris," *Louisville Times,* 27 October 1902, 4.

11. *CL,* 126–28.

12. *CL,* 129.

13. *CL,* 133.

14. *CL,* 135.

15. *CL,* 134–35.

16. *CL,* 140.

17. *CL,* 141.

18. *CL,* 142.

19. *CL,* 145–46.

20. "An Opening for Novelists," *The Wave* 16 (22 May 1897): 7.

21. *CL,* 147.

22. Joseph R. McElrath Jr., *Frank Norris: A Descriptive Bibliography* (Pittsburgh: University of Pittsburgh Press, 1992), 73.

23. *CL,* 149.

24. "Physician's Certificate of Cause of Death," record 20843, Department of Health, City of Chicago, Bureau of Vital Statistics, Clerk's Office, County of Cook, Illinois.

25. James B. Stronks, "B. F. Norris (Senior) in Probate Court with New Light on Frank Norris as Son," *Frank Norris Studies* 12 (Autumn 1991): 3–5.

26. *CL,* 149.

27. *The Pit* (New York: Doubleday, Page, 1903), 62–63.

28. *CL,* 149.

29. The unnamed observer's detailed account of Leiter's rise and fall, "The Story of the World's Greatest Corner," appeared in *The Ticker and Investment Digest* 8 (August 1911): 155–60. See Joseph R. McElrath Jr. and Douglas K. Burgess, "Joseph Leiter: Frank Norris's Model for Curtis Jadwin in *The Pit*," *Frank Norris Studies* 2 (2002): 20–24.

30. *The Pit,* [viii].

31. *CL,* 152–53.

32. Charles L. Crow, "Bruce Porter's Memoir of Frank Norris," *Frank Norris Studies* 3 (Spring 1987): 1–2; "Frank Norris, Author of 'The Octopus,'" *San Francisco Chronicle,* 7 April 1901, 28.

33. "Banquet to Frank Norris," *San Francisco Chronicle,* 18 April 1901, 12.

34. "The Book and the Public," *Town Talk* 9 (18 May 1901): 24–25.

35. See McElrath, *Frank Norris: A Descriptive Bibliography,* 71–79.

36. Franklin Walker, *Frank Norris: A Biography* (Garden City, N.Y.: Doubleday, Doran, 1932), 286. By 1932, according to Walker, Doubleday had sold 59,985 copies of *The Octopus* and 189,751 of *The Pit.* Not counted, of course, were foreign sales and "cheap reprintings" produced by other publishers.

CHAPTER 23: "WHOSO DIGGETH A PIT SHALL FALL THEREIN"

1. *Family Record,* 1896–1902, St. George's Episcopal church, New York City.

2. *CL,* 177.

3. "Herne, the Unconventional," *The Wave* 16 (27 February 1897): 9. Julie identified the unsigned interviewer as Norris in a 1952 letter to James D. Hart ("Letters Regarding Janet Black," James D. Hart papers, the Bancroft Library). Unaware of this letter in 1992, McElrath did not attribute the interview to Norris in *Frank Norris: A Descriptive Bibliography* (Pittsburgh: University of Pittsburgh Press, 1992).

4. *CL,* 170–72.

5. "Frank Norris and Edwin Lefevre," *Bookman* (American) 16 (January 1903): 441–42.

6. Proverbs 26:27.

7. *CL,* 173.

8. B. O. Flower, "The Trust in Fiction: A Remarkable Social Novel," *Arena* 27 (May 1902): 547–54.

9. Isaac F. Marcosson, "Some Observations on Books and People," *Louisville Times,* 16 March 1901, 10; "Frank Norris, Realist," *Louisville Times,* 6 April 1901, 13; and "The Epic of the Wheat," *Louisville Times,* 13 April 1901, 13.

10. George Hamlin Fitch, "Books for Spring," *San Francisco Chronicle,* 7 April 1901, 28.

11. Jack London, "The Octopus," *Impressions Quarterly* 2 (June 1901): 45–47.

12. "The Octopus: A Story of California," *Outlook* 67 (20 April 1901): 923–24; [William Dean Howells], "Editor's Easy Chair," *Harper's Monthly* 103 (October 1901): 824–25.

13. Wallace Rice, "Norris's 'The Octopus,'" *American Literary and Art Review* (*Chicago American*), 6 April 1901, 5–6.

14. The same criticism, perhaps offered by Collis P. Huntington when Norris interviewed him, applies to Edwin Markham, whose poem "The Man with the Hoe" was a nationwide success in 1899. Less well known was another proletarian poem by Markham, the title of which is exactly that of Presley's: "The Toilers." See Joseph R. McElrath Jr., "Edwin Markham in Frank Norris's *The Octopus,*" *Frank Norris Studies* 13 (Spring 1992): 10–11. The other poet given rough treatment in *The Octopus* is Joaquin Miller; see Benjamin S. Lawson, "The Presence of Joaquin Miller in *The Octopus,*" *Frank Norris Studies* 6 (Autumn 1988): 1–3.

15. *CL,* 154. Despite Norris's attempt to mend his friendship with Rice, it had ended by 10 September 1901. See Norris to Isaac F. Marcosson, *CL,* 164.

16. George H. Sargent, "The Epic of the Wheat," *Boston Evening Transcript,* 22 May 1901, 18.

17. *CL,* 157 and 159.

18. "The Octopus," *Boston Evening Transcript,* 31 July 1901, 12.

19. "Books to Read or Not to Read: An Epic of Wheat," *Overland Monthly* 37 (May 1901): 1050–51.

20. "The Novel with a 'Purpose,'" *The World's Work* 4 (May 1902): 2117–19.

21. *McTeague* (New York: Doubleday and McClure, 1899), 32. For a representative contrary reading of the narrative technique employed in this passage and similar moments in *Vandover and the Brute,* see Stanley Cooperman, "Frank Norris and the Werewolf of Guilt," *Modern Language Quarterly* 20 (September 1959): 252–58. As Charles Dobie and Franklin Walker did decades earlier, he concludes that Norris was a puritanical Victorian troubled by human sexuality rather than a literary naturalist capable of an amoral acceptance of it as natural.

22. See, for example, the conclusion of chapter 4 of book 2, which, beginning with "Ah—yes—the Wheat," closes with Presley's reflections (only) on the insignificance

of the "human insect" dwarfed by the "great, majestic, silent ocean of the Wheat" (*The Octopus* [New York: Doubleday, Page, 1901], 448).

23. "The Wife of Chino," *Century* 65 (January 1903): 369–78. The manuscript is in the California Collection of the California State Library at Sacramento.

24. See Reinaldo Silva, "The Corrosive Glance from Above: Social Darwinism, Racial Hierarchy, and the Portuguese in *The Octopus,*" *Frank Norris Studies* 1 (2001): 2–8.

25. For a discussion of the use of free indirect discourse in *Vandover and the Brute* and two exemplary passages in *The Pit*—one in the book version and another that is unique to the *Saturday Evening Post* serial—see Joseph R. McElrath Jr., *Frank Norris Revisited* (New York: Twayne, 1992), 57–58 and 115. See also Barbara Hochman, *Frank Norris, Storyteller* (Columbia: University of Missouri Press, 1988), 2–3.

26. At the back of his copy of this novel *(FNC)*, Norris wrote, "This is a good story." He was admiring a fellow author displaying a naturalistic sensibility. For example, the sentence he marked describes the heroine in terms of heredity: "She was happy because happiness is ours in the cradle or not at all—because it is of the blood and not of the environment" (*The Voice of the People* [New York: Doubleday, Page, 1900], 382).

27. *CL*, 123–24.

28. "The Frontier Gone at Last," *The World's Work* 3 (February 1902): 1728–31.

29. "A South-Sea Expedition," *The Wave* 16 (20 February 1897): 8.

30. "Salt and Sincerity: [2]," *The Critic* 40 (May 1902): 447–50 (erroneously entitled "Salt and Sincerity: I" in *The Responsibilities of the Novelist and Other Literary Essays* [New York: Doubleday, Page, 1903], 251–62).

31. "The True Reward of the Novelist," *The World's Work* 2 (October 1901): 1337–39.

32. "Salt and Sincerity: [7]," *The Critic* 41 (October 1902): 363–67.

33. The contracts for Norris's books *(FNC)* specify a royalty of 10 percent on the retail price, except in the case of *The Pit.* His publisher's confidence in this novel's becoming a runaway best-seller resulted in these terms: 10 percent of retail price on the first five thousand copies; 12.5 percent on the second five thousand; and 15 percent on all copies sold thereafter. As to the placement of the novel with the *Saturday Evening Post,* this did not occur until some time after early to mid-spring, when Norris wrote to Hamlin Garland, "I *may* sell the serials of *The Pit* for $3,500 to a Skindicate" (*CL*, 193). That is, he had not yet placed it with the weekly magazine for, as Charles recalled, three thousand dollars..

CHAPTER 24: FAREWELL TO GOTHAM

1. *FNC.*

2. For the same conclusion regarding the significance of the textual variants in the two versions of the novel, see Gwendolyn Jones, "Frank Norris's *The Pit:* 'A Romance of Chicago' and 'A Story of Chicago,'" *Frank Norris Studies* 21 (Spring 1996): 1–8; and Douglas K. Burgess, "Frank Norris's *The Pit: A Romance of Chicago:* A Critical

Edition," Ph.D. dissertation, Florida State University, 1997. Burgess presents the most telling substantive revisions in "Appendix II: Selected Substantive Variants" (437–501).

3. "Letters Regarding Janet Black," James D. Hart papers, the Bancroft Library.

4. We are indebted to the Reverend Peter M. Larsen of St. John's Episcopal church in Southampton for checking the *Record of Baptisms* of St. Andrew's (held by St. John's). Larsen derived additional information, such as Billy's birth date and Moulson's sponsorship at the baptism, and made it possible to locate the long-since subdivided Herne estate.

5. *CL,* 200.

6. *The Pit* (New York: Doubleday, Page, 1903), viii.

7. Tipped into a copy of *The Pit* are Norris's manuscript leaves indicating how the preliminary pages should be typeset: the dedication reads "Dedicated / to / My Daughter / Jeannette Williamson Norris" *(FNC).* However, when published by Doubleday, Page, and Company, *The Pit* displayed an uncharacteristically wordy dedication to Charles G. Norris, which led Bruce Nicholson to speculate that Charles intervened to effect a dedication to himself. See Bruce Nicholson, "Frank Norris's 'Dedication' in *The Pit," Frank Norris Studies* 25 (Spring 1998): 1–2.

8. *CL,* 183.

9. Davison continues, speculating on one lamentable outcome of Jeannette's relationship with her daughter: "In the hands of this single parent, Billie [*sic*] appears as a pretty, well-dressed and somewhat pampered little girl, but already showing [in references to her in Charles and Kathleen Thompson Norris's 1908–9 correspondence] hints of the troubled qualities that undoubtedly contributed to her suicide in 1942 at forty-one" (Richard Allan Davison, *Charles & Kathleen Norris: The Courtship Year* [San Francisco: Book Club of California, 1993], 22).

10. Richard Allan Davison to Joseph R. McElrath Jr., 25 May 1996.

11. "Cruelty to Helpless and Imbecile Charged against Home for Feeble-Minded," *San Francisco Chronicle,* 5 July 1902, 1; "Dr. W. M. Lawlor Confesses Brutality beyond Worst in History of California," *San Francisco Examiner,* 7 July 1902, 3; "Governor Orders Investigation of Charges against Dr. Lawlor," *San Francisco Examiner,* 8 July 1902, 3.

12. The letter appears in "Dr. Lawlor Yields to the Inevitable," *San Francisco Examiner,* 13 July 1902, 9.

13. "Gage's Friend Lawlor Must Go," *San Francisco Chronicle,* 29 July 1902, 5. See also "How to Throw Out Lawlor Is the Problem," *San Francisco Examiner,* 17 September 1902, 9; "Why Is Lawlor Still at Glen Ellen Home?" *San Francisco Chronicle,* 24 August 1902, [13]; and "Awaiting Curtain in Lawlor Drama," *San Francisco Examiner,* 4 October 1902, 5.

14. "Stories Are Told of Cruelty and Abuse at Glen Ellen Home for Feeble-Minded," *San Francisco Examiner,* 6 July 1902, 9.

15. "Lie Passed and a Pistol Drawn when Dr. Lawlor Assailed Colonel Harrington," *San Francisco Examiner,* 3 August 1902, [1].

16. "Disgraceful Scene Marks the Dismissal of Dr. Lawlor from Home of Feeble-Minded," *San Francisco Chronicle,* 3 August 1902, 13.

17. "Dr. Lawlor's Version," *San Francisco Chronicle*, 3 August 1902, 13.

18. "Frank Norris Defends Dr. Lawlor," *Argonaut* 51 (11 August 1902): 87.

19. "Lawlor to Be Dismissed when the Board Meets," *San Francisco Examiner*, 11 July 1902, 3.

20. "Governor's Representative Hears Horrifying Tale of Lawlor's Acts," *San Francisco Examiner*, 9 July 1902, 3.

21. "Lawlor Goes Out at Last," *San Francisco Chronicle*, 15 October 1902, 14.

22. Nellie Van de Grift Sanchez, *The Life of Mrs. Robert Louis Stevenson* (New York: Scribner's, 1920), 271–78.

23. Tracy Gifford, "Frank Norris in California's Central Coast," *Frank Norris Studies* 30 (Autumn 2000): 2–6. The privately owned cabin, designated a national historic landmark by the U.S. federal government, is located on a gravel road running to the west from Redwood Retreat Road.

24. "U.C. Meeting," *Oakland Enquirer*, 12 September 1902, 2.

25. The letter to Sanders at the Gilroy Historical Museum—discovered by Tracy Gifford (see "Frank Norris in California's Central Coast")—is transcribed, without title, in *Frank Norris Studies* 30 (Autumn 2000): 1.

26. *CL*, 201.

27. Jeannette refers to the house on Broderick Street, and Norris's declaration of his decision "to settle down in California" is quoted in "Notes about Authors," *American Author* 1 (October 1902): 338.

28. *CL*, 202.

CHAPTER 25: CREPUSCULE

1. Charles L. Crow, "Bruce Porter's Memoir of Frank Norris," *Frank Norris Studies* 3 (Spring 1987): 1–2.

2. "The Guest of Honor," *Puritan* 5 (July 1902): 8, 22; (August 1902): 32–33.

3. *Blix* (New York: Doubleday and McClure, 1899), 124–25.

4. *The Octopus* (New York: Doubleday, Page, 1901), 24.

5. "Young Novelist Is Critically Ill," *San Francisco Chronicle*, 23 October 1902, 8.

6. "Frank Norris May Live," *San Francisco Chronicle*, 24 October 1902, 9.

7. "Life of Norris Hangs by Thread," *San Francisco Chronicle*, 25 October 1902, 2.

8. "Frank Norris, Novelist, Is Dead," *Oakland Enquirer*, 25 October 1902, 1.

9. "Deaths," *San Francisco Chronicle*, 26 October 1902, 22.

10. Joseph R. McElrath Jr., *Frank Norris: A Descriptive Bibliography* (Pittsburgh: University of Pittsburgh Press, 1992), 104.

11. One-third of all of the known reviews of eleven books by Norris published through 1914, when *Vandover and the Brute* finally saw print, are about *The Pit*. See Joseph R. McElrath Jr. and Katherine Knight, *Frank Norris: The Critical Reception* (New York: Burt Franklin, 1981), 183–297.

12. "Happiness by Conquest," *The Wave* 16 (11 December 1897): 2.

Index

JOSEPH R. MCELRATH JR. is the William Hudson Rogers Professor of English at Florida State University and Associate Dean for Academic Affairs in its College of Arts and Sciences. His publications include *Frank Norris Revisited, Frank Norris: A Descriptive Bibliography,* and fifty articles on Norris. For his research on Norris and other American literary figures, he has received the John Frederick Lewis Award of the American Philosophical Society, the Lyman H. Butterfield Award of the Association for Documentary Editing, and the Sylvia Lyons Render Award of the Charles Waddell Chesnutt Association.

JESSE S. CRISLER, professor of English and associate chair of the Department of English at Brigham Young University, is the director of its Center for the Study of Christian Values in Literature and serves as editor of its journal *Literature and Belief.* Author of over twenty articles on Frank Norris, his books include *Frank Norris: Collected Letters* and *Frank Norris: A Reference Guide.* He is the coeditor of *John Steinbeck: The Contemporary Reviews, Charles W. Chesnutt: Essays and Speeches,* and *An Exemplary Citizen: Letters of Charles W. Chesnutt, 1906–1932.*

The University of Illinois Press
is a founding member of the
Association of American University Presses.

Composed in 10.5/13.5 New Caledonia
with Copperplate and Univers display
by Jim Proefrock
at the University of Illinois Press
Designed by Paula Newcomb
Manufactured by Thomson-Shore, Inc.

University of Illinois Press
1325 South Oak Street
Champaign, IL 61820-6903
www.press.uillinois.edu